D0906229

COMPANIES AND MEN

Business Enterprise in America

This is a volume in the Arno Press collection

COMPANIES AND MEN
Business Enterprise in America

Advisory Editors
STUART BRUCHEY
VINCENT P. CAROSSO

*See last pages of this volume
for a complete list of titles*

Northwestern Mutual Life

A CENTURY OF TRUSTEESHIP

Harold F. Williamson

and

Orange A. Smalley

ARNO PRESS
A New York Times Company
1976

Editorial Supervision: ANDREA HICKS

———◆———

Reprint Edition 1976 by Arno Press Inc.

Copyright © 1957, by Northwestern
 University Press
Reprinted by permission of Northwestern
 University Press

Reprinted from a copy in The State Historical
 Society of Wisconsin Library

COMPANIES AND MEN: Business Enterprise in America
ISBN for complete set: 0-405-08062-X
See last pages of this volume for titles.

Manufactured in the United States of America

Publisher's note: All illustrations have been
reproduced in black and white in this edition.

———◆———

Library of Congress Cataloging in Publication Data

Williamson, Harold F
    Northwestern Mutual Life : a century of trusteeship.

    (Companies and men)
    Reprint of the ed. published by Northwestern Univer-
sity Press, Evanston, Ill., which was issued as v. 4
of Northwestern University studies in business history.
    Bibliography: p.
    1. Northwestern Mutual Life Insurance Company,
Milwaukee. I. Smalley, Orange A., joint author.
II. Title. III. Series. IV. Series: Northwestern
University studies in business history ; v. 4.
[HG8963.N97W5 1976] 368.3'006'577595 75-41787
ISBN 0-405-08102-2

Northwestern Mutual Life

A CENTURY OF TRUSTEESHIP

NORTHWESTERN UNIVERSITY
STUDIES IN BUSINESS HISTORY

Northwestern

Mutual Life

A CENTURY OF TRUSTEESHIP

by

Harold F. Williamson

and

Orange A. Smalley

ILLUSTRATED BY JOHN FARAGASSO

NORTHWESTERN UNIVERSITY PRESS   EVANSTON, ILLINOIS
1957

DESIGNED AND PRODUCED BY STAHLEY THOMPSON ASSOCIATES
NEW YORK

Library of Congress Catalog Card No. 57-12317
Printed in the United States of America

To
Arline
and
Rose

Preface

THIS volume, the fourth in the Northwestern University Studies in Business History, was prepared under the auspices of the Northwestern University Committee on Business History. This committee considers the merits of proposed business history projects, advises in the planning and staffing of acceptable projects, and acts as a board of critics. Under an arrangement between The Northwestern Mutual Life Insurance Company and the Northwestern University Committee on Business History, the Company made a grant that was distributed through the University to meet the expenses of preparing the manuscript. It was agreed that the authors should be given full access to the Company's records and should have complete freedom in conducting their research and preparing the manuscript for publication. The terms of this agreement were fully met; indeed the objectivity and unstinted cooperation of the management have made the authors' task exceptionally rewarding.

The authors welcomed the opportunity to prepare the history of The Northwestern Mutual Life Insurance Company and to add it to the list of historical accounts of leading American business institutions sponsored by the Northwestern University Committee on Business History. We conceived our task essentially as a study of entrepreneurship in action; a description and analysis of the major managerial decisions that have primarily affected the evolution of the Northwestern Mutual over the space of a century.

As is true of any business institution, many of these decisions were influenced and conditioned by changes in the economic and social framework within which the Company operated and over which its management could exercise little control. The response to external forces largely explains the features that Northwestern Mutual has shared in common with other business concerns—especially other life insurance companies. It was the decisions of management within the range where discretion could be exercised that largely account for the unusual features of the organization over time. The principal characteristic that distinguished the Company was an overriding sense of trusteeship and personal responsibility—a philosophy that successive generations of Northwestern Mutual management have carefully preserved and consistently applied.

It is impossible to measure our indebtedness to the many individuals throughout the Northwestern Mutual organization who aided us in our work. Their contributions covered the spectrum from insights on the background and significance of broad policy decisions to answers to questions that only those skilled in actuarial science can answer. We are further obligated to our colleagues and associates for their helpful suggestions at various stages in the preparation of the manuscript. We are particularly indebted to Lloyd G. Allen and Herbert D. Werner for research assistance, and for the editorial contributions of Clarence L. Ver Steeg and Rose M. Smalley. Finally, we deeply appreciate the encouragement and patience of our families during the six-year span that covered the preparation of this book.

Evanston,
Illinois
July 1957

HAROLD F. WILLIAMSON
ORANGE A. SMALLEY

Contents

Tables

APPENDICES

Charts

Northwestern Mutual Life

A CENTURY OF TRUSTEESHIP

INTRODUCTION

A Century of Trusteeship

EVEN the most sanguine member of the Wisconsin Legislature that approved the charter of the organization which was to become the Northwestern Mutual Life Insurance Company could hardly have envisioned the future growth of that institution. As of January 1957, within two months of the centennial anniversary of the granting of the charter, the Company had truly assumed gigantic proportions. Its assets were valued at over $3.57 billion and income during the year amounted to $489 million. The Company's insurance in force was approximately $8.4 billion, covering over one million policyholders. Measured in terms of assets, Northwestern stood fourteenth among the billion-dollar companies of the United States; and of firms located west of the Alleghenies, it was outranked only by General Motors, United States Steel, and the Bank of America. Measured by the same yardstick, Northwestern was sixth in size among all American life insurance companies and first among those located west of the Atlantic seaboard.

Northwestern's position at the beginning of 1957 was a far cry from the organization that one hundred years earlier was scarcely more than a dream in the mind of its original promoter. Its evolution over the intervening years spanned a period in American social and economic history during which the country changed from an agrarian to an industrial economy, from a rural to a predominantly urban pattern of living. The Company shared with other business enterprises the periodic booms and depressions; the long-term secular increase in population, physical production and consumption, income, and capital formation. Its members served in five wars and many were buried on battlefields as widely separated as Gettysburg and Missionary Ridge, Belleau Wood and the Argonne, New Guinea and Bastogne, Seoul and Pusan.

Northwestern also had much in common with other American life companies over these years. It faced the problem of convincing people of the need for insurance protection, of devising policy contracts to fit changing human needs, of building up effective selling methods, of developing new investment outlets in response to changed technical and economic circumstance. It shared with other life companies in the vast increase in personal, private security in the United States which grew from an average of $25 of insurance in force per family in 1860 to over $8,000 in 1956.

In the process of providing insurance protection for individuals and their families, the Company and its fellow insurers contributed much to the nation's economic development by bringing together the scattered personal savings of policyholders and making them available for investment. The more than eleven hundred life companies operating in 1956 had become an integral part of the financial fabric of the United States. As security back of their total assets of $85.8 billion at the end of that year, the members of the industry held 4 per cent of the total federal debt, 44 percent of the long-term obligations of business and industry, and 25 per cent of the aggregate private mortgages of the country.

Although Northwestern shared the experience and had much in common with other life companies that operated over the past century, the organization also developed certain characteristics that were unusual, if not unique, among members of the industry. Among large insurance institutions Northwestern has been distinguished by the consistent simplicity of its operations. The Company has never offered more than a limited number of policy contract types. It has studiously avoided entering certain fields of insurance or methods of distribution such as industrial, accident and health, and group insurance. The nature of the risks to be accepted for insurance has been rigorously limited; with the single exception of the semi-tontine policy that occurred in the 1880's, Northwestern has been a most conservative merchandiser. It has welcomed competition on the basis of low net cost, while remaining fully capable of meeting any rival on more than even terms in the area of services to policyholders.

Back of Northwestern's primary objective of providing those who could meet its standards of risk selection with maximum protection at low cost was a management philosophy that was, and has remained, conservative in character. Back of this conservatism is a dedication to the principle of trusteeship, a sense of responsibility which became firmly imbedded in the tradition and structure of the organization at an early date; as the Company grew it was not deflected from this high objective, as was true of many other fiduciary institutions. Northwestern's trustees have been active in the Company's affairs: willing to attend regularly the meetings of the board, to contribute to policy decisions, and to serve faithfully on permanent and special committees.

It was, in fact, the original formation, born of necessity, of an executive committee of trustees to represent the whole board between regularly scheduled meetings that not only helped strengthen the sense of trustee responsibility, but set a pattern for the use of the committee system that continued to be a distinctive feature of the Northwestern management. In addition to providing safeguards against the dom-ination of the Company by one man, the success of the Executive Committee through the formative years of the organization prompted both its continuation and the appointment of additional committees to handle other management functions as the need arose. Northwestern was not the first business enterprise to make use of the committee system in its management, but it has been one of the few companies in which the method has been used successfully without becoming subordinated, at least on occasion, to the will of a strong executive.

How these characteristics evolved and the circumstances surrounding the decisions that provided a "built-in" sense of conservatism and trustee responsibility in the organization forms one of the most significant aspects of Northwestern's history. But they are only part of the story of an institution that, far removed from the financial and insurance centers along the Atlantic seaboard, took full advantage of its location to become and remain one of the leading life insurance companies in the industry.

As a fiduciary, financial institution the operations of a life insurance company fall logically into two broad categories: one having to do with underwriting and marketing activities, the other with the investment of funds entrusted to the company by policyholders. In relating the history of Northwestern the major objectives have been to recreate as nearly as possible the circumstances under which these major functions were carried out by the Company, to indicate how their evolution over time affected and were in turn influenced by decisions of the management, and to evaluate the performance of the organization.

For purposes of description and analysis the century of men and events which bridged the gap between the multi-billion dollar giant of 1957 and the vision of its promoter has been divided into five major time periods: 1857–1873; 1874–1907; 1908–1932; 1933–1946 and 1947–1956. It so happens that these time periods coincide with the administration of one or more of the chief executives of the Company. Of much greater importance in selecting these chronological divisions, especially as Northwestern never became a "one-man" organization, was the fact that each covers an important and distinguishable phase in the Company's evolution.

CHAPTER ONE

Founding of the Company

A T the halfway point in the nineteenth century, life insurance was an institution of
long standing. Yet the prototype of organizations devoted to bringing this device aggressively
to the attention of those who needed it was scarcely
fifteen years old in America when the man who
founded The Northwestern Mutual Life Insurance
Company began promoting the concept of a domestic mutual company among his friends and neigh-
bors in Janesville, Wisconsin. The panic year of
1857 was hardly the most propitious time for launch-
ing a new enterprise, nor did the near-frontier condition of the new state seem to offer an ideal location for a life insurance venture. But fresh from a
successful selling career with one of the most prominent eastern life insurance companies, the promoter
had no reservations that an organization modeled
upon that enterprise could be successfully established in the environment of the upper Middle West.

Creating a Setting for a Life
Insurance Company

It is doubtful if a company devoted exclusively
to life insurance would have been successful in Wisconsin prior to the late 1850's. It was during this
decade that the state, and indeed much of the Middle West, was being transformed from a frontier
community to a more mature settled society. Before
that decade transportation facilities were practically
nonexistent; the rewards of farming rarely exceeded
subsistence; and, quite understandably, the flow of
wealth into the area was as yet limited. On the political as well as the economic side, the state was an in-
fant, having become a territory in 1836 and admitted
as a state as late as 1848. Scholars have described
the period before 1850 as "the pre-railroad era,
when goods and services moved slowly and labo-
riously. Prosperity was more prospective than actual, [although] the promise was based on solid substance and a population of varied resources."[1] Wisconsin was still a land of pioneers.

Pioneers live not only in the realities of the present but in the promise of the future, and it was this
dream which attracted thousands of people into the
state, some of whom played essential roles in the
founding of the new life insurance company. By
1850 a transportation revolution was under way that
would in time enable the region to achieve national
recognition. Although Lake Michigan had served
importantly as a transportation link for the port
communities, now railroads began to push into the
interior, so that by 1857 the lines of the Milwaukee
and Mississippi and the LaCrosse and Mississippi
reached the western boundary of the state.[2] This
stimulus to the economy can be measured by the
startling increase in population which more than
doubled during the decade from approximately
300,000 to over 770,000. By 1860 the population of

Milwaukee alone reached 45,000, which placed it twentieth among the cities of the United States where it had only ranked as thirty-sixth in 1850.

What this vigorous economic growth meant for the possibilities of life insurance is evident. Although an area that is just emerging from a pioneer status does not offer a good market for life insurance, a relatively well-developed economy does. Although insurance companies had been incorporated in Wisconsin before 1857, they were devoted almost exclusively to fire and marine insurance. When companies did offer life insurance—only two are recorded as late as 1859—it was only carried as a minor part of their full insurance line.[3] With the great economic change that had taken place during the 1850's, the way was open to startling new developments. This essential fact was grasped by one of the most colorful figures in the history of American life insurance who, through an unusual coincidence, had recently migrated to Wisconsin.

General John C. Johnston

The gentleman with the idea—the catalyst, so to speak—was John C. Johnston, one-time Brigadier General of the 37th Brigade of the New York State Militia. Although the identification of his date and place of birth is uncertain, Johnston was probably born in 1783 at or near Catskill, New York. It is clear that he spent the greater part of his life at Catskill where, in addition to his military duties, he taught in the Catskill Village School, operated a planing mill and sash and door factory, and even tried his hand at making and selling invalid chairs. In 1850, at about age 67, Johnston left Catskill to seek a new career in New York City.

Although it is not certain whether or not Johnston intended this new career to be in life insurance, he was soon working for the Mutual Life Insurance Company of New York, along with two of his students from the Catskill School, Henry Hazen Hyde, and his son, Henry Baldwin Hyde. The impression these three men made on life insurance developments in the United States was extraordinary. The elder Hyde went into sales and later became general agent in Boston for Mutual Life. The son, Henry Baldwin, stayed with the New York office until 1859, when he left the company to form the Equitable Life Assurance Society of America, soon a formidable competitor of Mutual Life.

Johnston's own career with Mutual Life was brief but spectacular. He showed unusual abilities as a life insurance solicitor and in the short period of three years had the most successful agency in New York.[4] Between 1850–53 he and his son, who was associated with him, sold 1,382 policies out of the total of 8,043 which were on the books of Mutual Life of New York at the end of 1853.[5] Moreover, Johnston "got proxies as well as new insurance," becoming so powerful that he played a significant role in making Frederick S. Winston president, after forcing out Joseph Baldwin.[6]

Soon after this election Johnston decided to give up his agency and move to the Middle West, suitably encouraged by the Mutual Life officers who apparently were uneasy at having so powerful an individual among their agents. The Company gave him a lump sum of $30,000, representing the commuted value of his renewal commissions, and a paid-up policy on his life for $5,000. In return Johnston agreed that neither he nor his son would ever directly or indirectly enter into the "service of any other life insurance company whatever or interfere directly or indirectly with the election of trustees [of the Mutual Life] except by voting as members of the Company." This pledge was supported by a $10,000 bond to be forfeited if the agreement was broken.[7]

It is evident that General Johnston made this pledge in good faith. At least seventy years old at the time, he no doubt looked forward to living out his life as a gentleman farmer. In 1854 he purchased a farm of some 3,000 acres in Rock County near Janesville, Wisconsin, where he settled down to raise prize farm animals. According to an account published in 1856, Johnston was practicing a type of commercial farming quite out of the ordinary.

> [He had] . . . 840 acres under improvement; 600 to crops, and 240 into timothy meadow. General Johnston, the past year, raised 360 tons of timothy hay, 5,000 bushels wheat, 10,000 bushels corn, 1,500 bushels oats, 800 bushels rye, 500 bushels potatoes. He has six horses, 2 mules, and 260 head of cattle, of which 125 are cows, and 11 yoke of

General John C. Johnston

oxen; and employs from 15 to 30 men. He cuts all of his grain and hay by machinery or reapers and mowers. He has one of the largest and most commodious brick farm houses, with convenient barns and outbuildings which, together with land of superior quality, renders his situation one of the most desirable, not to say the largest farming establishments in the State.[8]

Farmer Johnston Introduces an Idea

At this point the idea became fused with the setting, for soon after arriving in Wisconsin Johnston's restless, resourceful mind was already considering the establishment of a life insurance company modeled after Mutual of New York. In introducing this idea Johnston recognized first the significance of the economic transformation of the 1850's, and then that a company organized on a mutual basis was particularly suited to the region.

Mutual life insurance companies were still relatively new in the United States. Until about 1842 life insurance had been typically sold by large trust companies, with paid-in capital, in which life insurance was subordinated to the business of writing marine or fire insurance; but beginning that year a number of mutual companies were formed that revolutionized the life insurance business.[1] Devoted exclusively to life underwriting, they began operations with no investments or operating capital, the necessary funds for operations being the premium payments made by the insureds.* Unlike the trust companies, the mutual companies emphasized selling because for them premium income made the difference between success and failure. By 1857 the practicability of the new type of life insurance company had been demonstrated by such companies as Mutual Life of New York, New England Mutual, New York Life, Mutual Benefit, State Mutual, Connecticut Mutual, and Penn Mutual.

The Formation of the Mutual Life Insurance Company of Wisconsin

Despite the demonstrated vigor of mutual life companies, the optimistic outlook of the future, and unbounded confidence in the soundness of life

---

* In some instances the sponsors of the early mutuals did provide "guarantee funds" made up of personal notes. All such funds were retired as soon as it seemed expedient to do so. Cf. Stalson, 111–112.

insurance, it still took courage and determination to start an insurance company in Wisconsin in 1857. To sell the idea and principles of life insurance to prospective members was in itself a formidable task, but it is a tribute to General Johnston's powers that he was able to persuade thirty-six leading citizens of the state to sponsor a petition to the legislature for the granting of a charter. Drawn principally from the area near Janesville, the group included many prominent figures in the social and economic life of the state,* a large percentage of whom were interested in politics. Indeed at least two were members of the state legislature when the charter was granted.

The bill to incorporate the Mutual Life Insurance Company of Wisconsin was introduced in the legislature early in 1857 by David Noggle, one of the charter members of the Company. It was passed as Chapter 129 of the Private and Local Laws of 1857 and approved March 2, 1857.

Except for the amount of insurance which had to be sold before operations could begin and modifications necessary to make it a part of Wisconsin law, the charter of the new company was identical to the charter of Johnston's former company, the Mutual Life Insurance Company of New York.† The principal provisions included the power to insure the lives of its respective members and to grant annuities. It was a purely mutual organization and anyone insuring with the Company automatically became a member as long as his insurance remained in force. Except for real property to be used as a place of business, investments were limited to mortgages on unencumbered Wisconsin real estate, and government, state, and municipal bonds. Every five years an accounting of profits was to be made and an equitable division credited to members. There were to be thirty-six trustees, all residents of the State of Wisconsin. The headquarters of the Company were to be at Janesville, and $200,000 worth of insurance had to be subscribed before the Company could officially start operations.

To sell this amount of insurance was no easy task, and without the drive and enthusiasm of General Johnston it is doubtful if it could have been accomplished. Johnston enlisted E. L. Dimock of Janesville, Milton Rowley of Whitewater, and H. G. Wilson of Milwaukee to help him solicit. Even with this assistance and with the provision that only half the premium payments had to be paid in cash and the rest by personal note, almost two years elapsed be-

---

*See Appendix A.
†See Appendix B.

Janesville, 1857

fore the required amount was pledged.* Finally on November 25, 1858, the Company began to issue the necessary policy contracts, the first policy for $5,000 appropriately going to General Johnston.

Meanwhile progress had been made toward a formal organization of the Company. At a meeting of the trustees on August 18, 1858, the following officers, all of Janesville, were selected: Joseph A. Sleeper, president; Alexander Graham, vice president; and Henry W. Collins, secretary. Some four months later, on December 31, 1858, Josiah Flint Willard was made treasurer. In view of Johnston's background it is interesting that all four original officers were native New Yorkers. Sleeper, a lawyer by profession, had moved to Wisconsin in 1848, where, after a short stay in Milwaukee, he settled in Janesville. Graham had come to Wisconsin about 1857. He subsequently served as a representative from the Janesville area in the state legislature for several terms. Collins had been in Wisconsin since 1853 and was engaged in manufacturing. Willard, after early success as a merchant in New York, had moved to Janesville for his health a few years before. One of his daughters, Frances Willard, became well known as a temperance leader.

Except for replacing one of the original trustees who resigned in February 1858, General Johnston, possibly because of his agreement with Mutual Life, was not elected to office. But as the leading personality associated with the organization, he undoubtedly approved, if he did not pick, the newly elected officers.

Although he was not an officer, Johnston did not intend to let his entrepreneurial efforts on behalf of the new company go unrewarded. The precise nature of his request was brought out at a meeting of the trustees held on October 18, 1858.* At that time he proposed that he be given a contract as general agent at an annual salary of $2,000. He was to be assisted in his work by his grandson, John H. Johnston (or a substitute), who was to be paid whatever the officers thought he was worth. In addition, the General proposed that following his death his grandson or his substitute should receive 5 per cent of the future cash premiums on all policies issued up to that time. These payments were to continue as long as the policies remained in force and the grandson or his substitute remained in the employ of the Company. The Company was not to be obligated after Johnston's death to pay his survivor more than the income from premiums as a salary. But neither could the latter be fired except for "malfeasance, nonfeasance, or misfeasance." Finally in recognition of the fact that

> the said John C. Johnston has got up this company at his own risk and charge and he has obtained for it a large subscription, now know ye all whom it may concern, that on the 1st day when this company shall issue its first policy they shall issue to John C. Johnston a paidup policy of $5000.

This was a most interesting and unusual proposal, especially the part which called for giving the grandson or his substitute a vested interest in all policies sold up to the time of the General's death, and the

---

* Of the total, General Johnston personally solicited $113,500, Rowley $50,400, Wilson $28,000, and Dimock $12,000.

* The proposed contract is reproduced in full in Appendix B.

Joseph A. Sleeper

ton for his part in organizing the Company and they approved the issuance of a paid-up policy of $5,000 to him. They were also willing for Johnston to continue as general agent. Beyond this they were unwilling to go, and all portions of the contract pertaining to the vesting of the renewal interest in John Henry Johnston or his substitute were stricken from the document, which was then approved.

While disappointed at his failure to secure an attractive legacy for his grandson, or substitute member of the family, General Johnston did not lessen his efforts to complete the sale of the $200,000 worth of insurance necessary before the Company could start operations. A contemporary who saw him going up and down the streets of Janesville, Whitewater, and Madison, where his chief work was done, suggested that, "With his long white hair, his tall form, thin visage, extended coattails, he needed only the scythe and the hour glass to be a striking image of 'Old Father Time' himself, and so a fitting representative of his own work, to persuade people to protect their loved ones against loss that was sure to come at the grim reaper's hand."[10]

Moving the Company to Milwaukee

Despite the setback on his proposed contract, Johnston probably hoped to keep the Company at Janesville where he could maintain a strong influence in its management, but it was a losing fight.

provision that his grandson or his substitute should continue in the service of the Company. It is not difficult to envision some of the results which would have followed if this contract had been adopted. Cash premium income on the policies sold during Johnston's service to the Company would have been reduced 5 per cent which, figured at compound interest for the life of the policies involved, could have meant an appreciable financial drain on the organization. Moreover, the provision that Johnston's grandson or his substitute should remain an employee of the Company except for "malfeasance, nonfeasance, or misfeasance" could have tied the hands of the management in working out its sales organization, even though there was no compulsion to pay him any salary beyond the renewal commissions.

What considerations actually influenced the trustees who were asked to accept this contract are not known. The record reveals only that they were willing to acknowledge an obligation to General Johns-

First of all, Johnston was having trouble keeping the original sponsors interested in the organization. On November 8, 1858, Joseph Sleeper, the president of the Company, resigned. He was replaced by Henry W. Collins, whose job as secretary went to E. L. Dimock of Janesville. The following month Alexander Graham, the vice president, resigned, to be replaced by A. H. Scoville of Whitewater. A second and more serious development from Johnston's point of view was the fact that a group of Milwaukee businessmen were attracted to the prospect of moving a going insurance company to their own city. By the end of November 1858 about one-third of the original thirty-six trustees had resigned and their replacements had brought a number of Milwaukee representatives on the Board, a trend that continued the following year.

The first step in setting the stage for the transfer

First Home Office—1857
Exchange Block, Janesville

of the Company to Milwaukee came when the state legislature, in February 1859, struck out the section in the charter calling for the location of the Company in Janesville. The question was raised officially on March 7, 1859, at a meeting of the trustees held in Janesville. According to the minutes, the time of the meeting was originally set for 4:00 p. m., but was adjourned to "await the expected arrivals from Milwaukee."[11] S. S. Daggett, H. L. Palmer, Dr. E. B. Wolcott, M. S. Scott, and C. D. Nash of that city arrived about seven o'clock. They took their places with Collins, the president; Dimock, the secretary; Agent Johnston; and S. C. Spaulding, M. C. Smith, James H. Knowlton and Benjamin F. Pixley, all trustees from Janesville.

After a report on business for the preceding quarter and the acceptance of the resignation of two trustees who were not present, the following resolution was offered:

> RESOLVED, that from and after the close of this meeting, the office of the Company be located in the City of Milwaukee, and the operations and business of this Company shall be carried on in said City of Milwaukee, so far as the same can be done at a principal office, and that the President and Secretary be authorized to remove the books and papers and property to Milwaukee, and to do whatever may be necessary to carry into effect this resolution.

The minutes further recorded that in the vote which

Henry W. Collins

Home Office—1858
Lappin Block, Janesville

followed, there were eleven votes in favor of the resolution, with Johnston casting the only dissenting vote. It is interesting that the trustees from Janesville, who, if united, could have defeated the resolution, subscribed to the change in location.[12]

Johnston's defeat became a rout. Immediately following the passage of this resolution, provision was made for the next election of trustees to be held in Milwaukee, whereupon President Collins and Vice President Scoville, after offering their resignations, were replaced by S. S. Daggett and Dr. E. B. Wolcott respectively. The next morning the new officers left Janesville for Milwaukee, carrying all of the assets and records of the Mutual Life Insurance Company of Wisconsin in a small black leather-covered trunk.

For General Johnston the move to Milwaukee marked the end of his association with the organization and of his hopes of ·etaining an important voice in the management. Within a few days, on March 12, 1859, he relinquished his contract as general agent (including the original $5,000 life policy) in return for a cash settlement of $700 and a new paid-up policy of $5,000, naming his wife as beneficiary. Soon thereafter he moved to Madison, where, about one year later, he died.

General Johnston left an enviable record. He brought the idea of a mutual life insurance company to Wisconsin. He aroused sufficient enthusiasm among leading Wisconsin citizens to get the necessary backing to secure a charter from the state. He was personally responsible for most of the insurance that needed to be sold before the Company could begin operations. Whether Johnston's reward was commensurate with his contributions is impossible to prove, and the fact that his immediate realizations fell far short of his aspirations is of passing interest. What is important, however, is that Johnston's creative business personality conceived an institution whose growth, achievements, and reputation stand as a living monument to his idea.

CHAPTER TWO

The First Decade of Operations: Management and Sales

THERE is a real question as to why the Milwaukee group was so interested in taking over control of an organization that was barely organized and with few, if any, tangible assets. Unlike a corporation or trust company, a mutual company offered no prospective profits from the ownership or sale of securities. On the other hand, a mutual life insurance company involved no capital investment on the part of the promoters. As J. Owen Stalson, an authority on life insurance, declares when commenting on the formation of the early eastern mutuals, the entrepreneurs "rightfully foresaw in the prospective success of a mutual of their own founding a personal gain in position, security, and income which was not lightly to be set aside."[1]

Aside from personal benefits, the newly organized mutual offered an additional attraction. This was the prospect of building up capital funds that could do much to stimulate economic growth in a region where capital was scarce.

That both types of motives prompted the Milwaukee group is confirmed by the observation made some years later by Peter von Vechten, one-time trustee of the Company (1874–1878) and deputy collector of internal revenue at Milwaukee, who was an acquaintance of General Johnston in Catskill. Writing in the *Catskill Examiner* (April 5, 1907), he told how Johnston met a number of prominent citizens including "S. S. Daggett, W. J. Whalley, Josiah Noonan, Dr. L. W. Weeks, and several other fire insurance men." While this group accepted the General's enthusiasm about the prospect of a life insurance venture with some reservations, "some of them were conversant with the results of Mutual Life of New York, which had accumulated from February, 1843 to January 1, 1858, assets to the amount of $5,374,933, and saw there was something in it for themselves and those who were to come after them."

The Management Group

In view of the Company's potential, it is noteworthy that by the end of April, 1859, four of the five trustees who had carried the "little black trunk" from Janesville had been elected officers. Samuel Slater Daggett was president, Dr. E. B. Wolcott was vice president, C. D. Nash was treasurer. Henry L. Palmer was appointed legal counsel, and Hiram Wilson was named to take over General Johnston's duties in charge of sales. The newcomer to the official family was A. W. Kellogg.

On the whole the new management group brought both talent and prestige to the fledgling concern. In President Daggett, the Company was fortunate in having an experienced executive. Born

Samuel S. Daggett

in Attleboro, Massachusetts, in 1812, Daggett had come to Milwaukee in 1844, where he and his partner, Enoch Richardson, set up a variety, or department, store. In 1848 the business was sold, and the following year Daggett became president of the Milwaukee Mutual Fire Insurance Company. He resigned his presidency with the fire insurance company in 1858, although he continued as a director for some years afterward.

By all accounts Daggett was a well known and influential citizen of Milwaukee, and his election as head of the new life insurance company undoubtedly lent prestige to the organization. He was respected for his business judgment and common sense and played an important role in the evolution of management policies during his administration.

Dr. E. B. Wolcott was also well known, both in Milwaukee and in the state. A native of New York, he had served as an army surgeon before moving to Milwaukee in 1839, where he entered private practice and took an active interest in civil and business affairs. He also became associated with the Wisconsin state militia and became surgeon general of the group during the Civil War. It was this latter service that prompted him to resign as vice president in

1863, although he continued as consulting physician until 1864, and as trustee until his death in 1880.

C. D. Nash, the treasurer, brought an important financial connection to the new concern. Born in Vermont, he had come to Milwaukee in 1843 where he engaged in banking. He had been associated with Daggett in the Milwaukee Mutual Fire Insurance Company and was president of the Milwaukee Bank at the time of his election as treasurer. He held this position for some thirty-three years, in addition to serving on the Executive and Finance Committees of the Company for various terms and as trustee until his death in 1897.

A. W. Kellogg, the secretary, had moved from Connecticut to Milwaukee with his parents in 1836 when he was seven years of age. After finishing school, he was in business for a brief period, when he decided to attend college. He entered Wesleyan College in Connecticut in 1855, graduating Phi Beta Kappa in 1858. Kellogg was looking for a job when the opportunity came to become secretary of the Mutual Life Insurance Company of Wisconsin at an annual salary of $600.*

For over a year after his election in April 1859 Kellogg was the only full-time employee in the Home Office, with the result that he functioned more or less as comptroller, actuary, assistant agency director, stenographer, and office boy. He recalled that "when he went to the bank, and even did a little soliciting for life insurance the office was closed."

Under the circumstances, Kellogg was responsible to an unusual degree for working out the detailed procedure for the business and for building an effective working organization in the Home Office. That he was held in high esteem within the Company is shown by the increases in his salary, by his continued re-election to the office—usually with no opposing candidates—and by his election, upon nomination by the Executive Committee, as a trustee in January 1866. He withdrew as a candidate when a resolution was passed by the Board, apparently on a matter of principle and not of personality, that "it was not deemed proper that the Secretary be a trustee." [2]

According to the charter, the final responsibility for the management of the Company rested with the

---

* According to Kellogg, two other candidates for the job were brothers of trustees. "A member of the Board, and a friend of . . . [Kellogg's] suggested that the salary had been fixed so low with the expectation that 'you would not accept and then one of the others would be elected, but you disappointed them and it [the salary] will be made all right.'" Kellogg MS. 45.

Policy No. 1

trustees. It was clearly impractical for all thirty-six trustees, who met regularly only four times annually, to do more than lay down broad policies and act as a review body. For effective operation some one person, or a small group, had to be given authority to act on their behalf to develop operational procedures and to recommend changes to the full board.

If either the president or the vice president, both trustees, had been full-time officers at the outset, this authority might have been delegated to either or both of them. But the business did not warrant the full time of either Daggett or Wolcott, and it is unlikely that either was prepared, even if it had been offered, to accept this responsibility along with his other activities. Whatever the precise reasons, on June 28, 1859, by unanimous action the trustees established an executive committee of five trustees, including the president and vice president as *ex officio* members, "possessing all of the powers and authority of the board of trustees when [the full board was] not in session." Elected to the committee were Henry L. Palmer; James Bonnell, a merchant; Charles F. Ilsley, a Milwaukee banker; and, of course, S. S. Daggett and Dr. Wolcott, *ex officio* members.

This far-reaching decision put the effective control of management policies in the hands of a working committee which met at frequent intervals. Had the officers of the Company reported only to the full board, their power as officeholders to influence major policies would have been considerable. Under this arrangement, the president and the vice president functioned as executive officers, but their influence was exercised as individual members of the Executive Committee and subject to the majority will of the group. This step, which began as a measure of expediency, marked the germination of the committee system which was expanded and became a prominent feature of the management organization of the Company.

Prospects and Problems Facing the New Management

The embryonic character of the organization in early 1859 was recalled many years later by Secretary Kellogg.

There was an office about sixteen by twenty with four walls, plenty of light, and little else, except a table, a few chairs, and

an incoming safe. There was a small set of books with no entries for nearly a month and no posting for three months with no one to explain the entries except the City Agent Wilson, and he was not an accountant and only knew of Milwaukee matters. There were a few blank policies and some applications and some pamphlet copies of the Charter, with an unpaid bill of $63.25 for printing them. . . .

There were practically no agents' supplies except a small pamphlet and a few tables of rates, and in fact few agents to supply; there were no instructions to agents or medical examiners, there was no literature and no one but Wilson to help in its creation.[3]

From Kellogg's account it is clear that the new management faced a formidable task. The Company was barely organized, with limited assets and few precedents established for the practical operation of a life insurance business. To be sure, the organization was not starting *de novo*. Two of its officers, Daggett and Nash, had had practical experience with a mutual fire insurance company. Thanks to General Johnston, the framework of its operations, drawn from the Mutual Life of New York, had been written into the charter, and the experience of a decade or more of other Eastern mutuals was available.

Actually the fundamental principles that distinguish the operation of a life insurance company had been developed from experience that had its beginnings in Western Europe and antedated the Eastern mutuals by several hundred years. These principles still apply to life insurance operations.

In simplified terms, an insurance company under its policy contracts agrees, in return for income received from policyholders (premiums), to pay specific sums to beneficiaries at the time of the death of the policyholders. If the company is to meet its contractual obligations and remain solvent, therefore, it is especially important that premium rates be determined in such a way that funds will be available when needed.*

Three major factors—the expected mortality rate of policyholders, earnings on investments, and the cost of running the business—are taken into account in the calculation of premium rates. Provided

---

* It should be noted that the same basic principles apply to other conventional types of policies, including endowments, which provide for payment of the amount of the policy either at a specified maturity date or at death if that occurs before the maturity date.

Back cover of first advertising pamphlet

the insured are not atypical, it is possible, by reference to mortality tables based on actual mortality experience, to estimate how many individuals in various age groups will die during a particular year. If everyone took out insurance on a year-to-year basis (i.e. one-year term insurance) premium rates would simply be set in such a way that the income during any year would be sufficient to meet the claim payments for that year, in addition to the expenses of operating the business.

As people grow older, however, their expected mortality rate rises and premium rates for one-year term policies would have to increase with age. For this reason most insurance is sold under the level premium system which calls for fixed level premium payments, either for a term of years or for the life of the insureds.

The level premium plan introduces the element of investment into the operations of a life insurance company; it also makes the calculation of premium rates a more complicated process. The bulk of the claims against a company will come due during the later years the policies are in force. To provide for these future payments the amount collected during the early years must be in excess of current needs.

This "excess" income is set aside as a reserve behind the policies and invested as a guarantee that funds will be available when needed. How much has to be collected in advance to provide adequate reserves depends in part on the interest that can be earned on the investment of the reserves. If the prospective interest rate is high, the amount needed to be collected can be lower; if the prospective rate is low, the amount of the reserves must be correspondingly higher. Thus in calculating reserves both the expected mortality rates and an assumed earning rate on investments are taken into account. Actual premium rates are based upon interest and mortality assumptions which will produce safe and adequate reserves, and also upon an allowance to cover the costs of operations and a provision for unforeseen contingencies (expense loading). It should be added that in setting premium rates, life insurance companies generally allow an extra margin of safety in all their calculations.

To the extent that actual mortality experience is lower than "expected" on the basis of the actuarial tables used, that interest income is above the estimated rate, or that expenses are below the amounts provided in premium rates, a life company will accumulate more funds than are needed and specifically earmarked for policy reserves. These go into a surplus account and in a mutual company are used to pay dividends to policyholders. These dividends are in effect refunds of unused or unneeded portions of the premium. Thus to the holder of a policy with a mutual company, the gross premium rates do not measure the true cost of the insurance which must take into account the dividends received.

Because of the unusual and unique features of life insurance, the function of calculating premiums and the mortality tables upon which such calculations are based has long since been assumed by actuaries specially trained for the task. For the better part of a decade, however, Mutual Life of Wisconsin followed the practices of the established companies, especially Mutual Life of New York, in setting its own premium rates, contract terms, and standards for the selection of risks.* The number of qualified actuaries in the United States at the time was too small and the expense of hiring their services too large for a newly organized concern. Mutual Life of New York, for example, did not employ its first full-time actuary, Charles Gill, until 1849, some six years after the company had started operations.[4] Metropolitan's first actuary was hired in 1879, ten years after the company was reorganized under its present name.[5] All of the prominent actuaries of the time, including Charles Gill, Sheppard Homans, Elizur Wright, and Joseph P. Bradley, appear to have been self-trained individuals with a flair for mathematics and an interest in insurance matters.

Although there was some danger that the new Wisconsin company would in this manner inherit the mistakes of other companies, this hazard should not be exaggerated. Most companies of the day were quite conservative in their insurance practices. Moreover, the Company did on occasion employ the services of an expert on a consulting basis. While eventually it would be desirable to employ a full-time actuary who could develop insurance procedure adapted to Company requirements and circumstances, this decision was postponed until 1870.

Marketing Development

By far the most pressing problem facing the newly formed Mutual Life Insurance Company of Wisconsin was to increase its sales of life insurance. As matters stood, the Company ran two risks: that the income would be inadequate to continue operations; and that the policyholders would be so limited in number that the risk probabilities, as calculated for the more general experience or the mortality tables, would not apply. At this time survival was dependent upon the expansion of sales.

The precarious position of the Company with respect to both these hazards was dramatized on November 21, 1859, when news of a railroad accident reached Milwaukee. An excursion train bearing a number of prominent Wisconsin citizens to the opening of the Chicago and Northwestern Railroad from Janesville to Fond du Lac had been derailed after striking a cow, and fourteen passengers lost their lives.* Fortunately only two persons insured by the Company were involved: one an immediate victim of the accident, the other dying a few weeks later as a result of injuries. The two policies amounted to $3,500.

Even $3,500 exceeded the amount the Company had on hand by $1,500. President Daggett, however, insisted that the losses be paid immediately without taking advantage of a sixty-day grace period in the policy contracts. With the approval of the Executive Committee, arrangements were made to borrow the necessary funds, backed by a note which Daggett personally endorsed. This prompt payment of claims undoubtedly did much for the reputation of the Company, and Daggett did not overlook the opportunity to call the attention of the public to the advantages of life insurance. A leaflet, shown in Exhibit 1, was prepared on the subject and was widely distributed in Wisconsin and Minnesota.

When moving to increase its sales, the Company quickly recognized, as had its Eastern predecessors, that few if any services are more dependent on personal solicitation for successful sales than life insurance. Even if convinced of the merits of life insurance, it is a rare individual who will assume the initiative in taking out a policy. A large number of

---

* In May 1860 the Company sent Kellogg east to attend the Life Underwriter's Convention in New York and to consult with officials of the principal insurance companies in Boston, Hartford, and New York. Among the prominent insurance executives he met were F. S. Winston and Sheppard Homans of Mutual Life of New York, Morris Troublin of New York Life, Henry Baldwin Hyde of the Equitable, Walter S. Griffith of Home Life, W. A. Brewer of Washington Life, Guy R. Phelps of Connecticut Mutual, Rodney Davis of Traveler's, and Ben F. Stevens of the New England Mutual. He also met and was greatly impressed by Elizur Wright of Boston, already famous as an actuary. (Kellogg MS. 63).

* Kellogg recalled that "there was naturally quite a consternation at the office of the Company on receipt of the news, as the excursion was chiefly made up of passengers from Watertown, Fond du Lac and Oshkosh, en route to Janesville to aid in the celebration; and all along the line there were policy holders, so that the names of the killed and injured were eagerly scanned as they slowly dribbled in, to ascertain how hard the Company had been hit, and whether or not it had been altogether overwhelmed with disastrous losses so near the beginning." Kellogg MS, 57.

prospects, and this was especially true of the mid-Nineteenth Century and later, have to be educated in the basic principles of insurance and their attention must be directed to the specific benefits available to themselves or their beneficiaries. To accomplish this, a vigorous sales policy and sales force were imperative.

Marketing procedures throughout the industry were far from stabilized or standardized by 1859. Among the unsettled questions were these: how and how much to pay agents, how best to recruit and train a sales force, and what kinds of policy contracts would best appeal to customers. Moreover, the year 1859 marked the beginning of a new phase of competition within the industry which, over the succeeding decade and beyond, included a sharp increase in the number of insurance companies, an enlargement of the sales territory of individual concerns, a proliferation of the types of policy contracts, increasing commission rates, and extensive raiding of competitors' sales forces—all of which contributed to keep the marketing relationships in the industry in a state of flux. It was against this general background that Mutual Life of Wisconsin launched its marketing program.

The immediate responsibility for building and supervising a sales organization during Daggett's administration was delegated to an elected official called the "general agent," whose functions would be more accurately described in modern terminol-ogy as those of "director of agencies." Hiram G. Wilson, who had succeeded General Johnston to this position in 1859, served until 1864 when he was succeeded by John G. McKindley, who had been a local agent of the Company since 1862. A former school principal in Kenosha, McKindley held the job until 1867, when he resigned and was replaced by Heber Smith, an especially dynamic person. A one-time county sheriff and a member of the Wisconsin Legislature, he was so active on behalf of the Company that it came to be known during his term in office as "Smith's Company." [6] He held the office of general agent until 1874, having in the meantime been elected a trustee and vice president in 1869.

Indicative of the importance attached to the job was the fact that until 1868 the general agent was paid a larger salary than either the president or the secretary, although it should be recalled that the president did not serve full time. Wilson started out at a salary of $1,200 per annum plus a commission of 10 per cent of the first-year premium on any insurance he personally solicited. His base salary was successively raised over the following four years so that when he resigned in 1864 he was receiving $2,500. McKindley, throughout his term of office, was paid an annual salary of $3,200, and when Heber Smith took office in 1867, he received the same amount; the following year the figure was raised to $5,000, and subsequently to $6,000.

Train wreck in 1859 that caused the Company's first death claims

TO THE CITIZENS OF WISCONSIN.

WHILE reflecting upon the recent terrible disaster upon the Chicago and North-western Railway, which has unexpectedly thrown so many families into sorrow and mourning, the undersigned would avail himself of the opportunity of more fully impressing upon the attention of the public, the consideration of the important subject of LIFE INSURANCE.

This mournful calamity has already resulted in the sudden and untimely death of twelve of our citizens, most of them leaving companions and orphan children without their natural protectors, and some of them without the means of competent support. Three of these twelve, perhaps more, had wisely set apart from their earnings and vested a small annual sum in a Life Insurance Policy for their friends, which in their present hour of sorrow and darkness, will secure for them the present means of a home and competence, until the brighter skies of the future shall dawn upon them. How easy and how exceedingly wise it would have been, had all of them left such a boon to their bereaved and afflicted survivors. It would not, indeed, have restored their loss, but it might have mitigated and softened their afflictions, by relieving them from the fear of want and destitution.

I allude to these sad scenes to illustrate the importance of *timely Life Insurance.* A small amount invested annually, while in life and health, and which can be done without inconvenience by almost any man, will, upon his death, leave to some dear friend, say a brother, sister, mother, or a companion, a present competence, and a most grateful heart.

Have you, reader, a family of dear ones who may at any time be thrown lonely and destitute upon the charities of a cold world, and will you not make this slight sacrifice for their protection from destitution when you are gone? Are you without a family? Have you not a sister, or a brother, or a mother, or some kind friend, on whom you would delight to confer such provision for earthly comfort, to be enjoyed by them in each an hour of sadness and adversity? Then make this small sacrifice from your ordinary yearly earnings or luxuries.

THE MUTUAL LIFE INSURANCE COMPANY OF THE STATE OF WISCONSIN, whose office is at Milwaukee offers you these advantages on favorable terms. It is a Home Company, and its officers and managers are known to you as men of integrity and prudence. Its entire profits are to be divided among the insured, and owing to the lower rate of mortality and the higher rate of interest in our State, these profits must be greater than those of Eastern Companies. Its Agents can be found in all the principal towns in the State.

Do not wait for an Agent to call upon you, but go at once and attend to this matter of vital importance to yourself and family.

S. S. DAGGETT, President.

H. G. KELLOGG, Traveling Agent,
Will be at the PLANTERS' HOUSE, Watertown, for a few days, to receive applications, &c.

EXHIBIT 1—leaflet distributed after the train wreck to call attention to the advantages of life insurance

Types of Insurance and Contract Provisions

From 1858–1860, the Company sold only ordinary life policies, under which the insured paid level premiums until death, when his beneficiary received the face value of the policy. The Company insured no one over the age of fifty-six years, and the total amount at risk for any one person was limited to $5,000. Such policies might, however, be taken out under a joint life form which insured both husband and wife for the benefit of the survivor; or single policies for husbands and wives, each naming the other as beneficiary. No policies were issued on the lives of unmarried women, but a widow might insure her life for the exclusive benefit of her children, and a few policies of this description were issued.

But this limited offering soon proved inadequate. Throughout the 1860's Mutual of Wisconsin was meeting increasing competition from other companies. Not only had the Eastern companies expanded their sales in the West but Mutual in turn entered the Eastern and Southern markets. Moreover, there was a sharp increase in the number of life insurance companies in the United States, rising from 38 in 1859 to 113 in 1868. The Company's agents, like those of other companies, continued to apply pressure on the management to modify existing contracts or to offer new and more attractive policies.

The management, of course, was interested in maintaining and increasing sales and keeping an alert and productive sales force. At the same time, it was the particular responsibility of the Company's officers and trustees to weigh all proposals and contract modifications and new policies in light of the long-run effect on the well-being of the organization. There was a real danger to the financial stability of the Company if it sold policies which would not return sufficient funds to meet future obligations. As long as the Company was without the full-time services of a trained actuary, it was in no position to lead in devising new policy contracts.

The Company's response to competitive pressure, therefore, was restricted to two new contracts introduced in late 1860 or early 1861. The first of these was a limited payment life policy under which the insured could secure a paid-up policy at the end of a designated number of years.* This type of contract was designed especially to appeal to persons who wished to provide for insurance protection during the years when their earning capacity was high. The most popular of these policies was the ten-year limited payment life contract which the Company featured.

The second new policy form introduced at this time was the endowment plan of insurance. As explained by one of the Company's sales brochures for 1868: "Insurance on this plan secures a provision for one's family in the event of early death and also a sure support for his old age, thus providing

---

* Apparently the Company followed very quickly the example of New York Life, which first introduced this type of policy in the late 1850's.

against the two life contingencies, viz.; dying early and living long." To give this double protection the policies were made payable to the insured upon his attaining a given age, which he could select between ages thirty and seventy, or to his beneficiary if he died before then.

The popularity of these new policies was demonstrated by the figures on the types of insurance sold by the Company for 1865 and 1867. According to the annual statement for 1865, a total of 4,297 new policies had been issued during that year, of which "2,320 were life policies with premiums all payable in ten years, and 427 Endowment Assurance policies, at various ages." In the statement for 1867, the total number of new policies issued was reported at 9,866, of which 3,099 were ten-year limited payment life policies; 514 endowment policies other than ten-year; and 1,244 ten-year endowment policies. The statement went on to say, "The large proportionate increase in these classes of policies gives gratifying evidence that the special advantages offered by this Company thereon are becoming more and more appreciated, and the true interests of the public in insurance better understood."

As a matter of fact, the management encouraged the sale of the limited payment policies by giving its agents approximately the same commission rates on premiums on the ten-year payment policies as were paid on the premiums from ordinary life policies. There was good reason for this practice. For a new and small company, limited payment life insurance enabled it to build up its reserves in a relatively short period. The only embarrassment would come if attractive investment outlets were not available, a contingency that did not arise.

Specific Contract Provisions

According to the early policy contracts issued by the Company, if the insured "died by his own hand or by the hand of justice or in consequence of a duel, or in violation of any law, or if any of the statements in the application should be found in any respect untrue, or in failure to pay premiums when due, in every such case the policy shall become null and void and of no effect and all previous payments thereon shall be forfeited to the Company." Although these provisions were typical of the contracts offered by most life companies, two of these conditions may strike the modern observer as being unduly harsh. One was the provision that the contract would be canceled and the previous premium payments forfeited if any statement in the applica-

A sample of the policy form used from January 1, 1860 to March 1863

tion should prove untrue. While this provision was designed to protect the Company against fraud, it allowed cancellation even if the statement involved had no relevance to the insurability of the applicant. Secondly, this same penalty could be invoked if premium payments were not paid on time. This lat-

ter provision protected the Company against paying out death claims on policies which had not been fully paid for, but it made no provision for compensating the policyholder for the premium reserves that had been credited to his policy. It should be noted, however, that Mutual of Wisconsin, together

with the other better companies, did not act on trifling technicalities but only when the policyholder intended to defraud.

By 1860 the Company had also adopted an informal procedure of allowing its members to reinstate a lapsed policy provided they could still pass the necessary medical examination and provided that they paid the back premiums with interest. After two annual payments, the Company also offered any of its members who wished to discontinue their insurance an option of receiving an "equitable cash value" for their policies, or a new paid-up contract which would insure to the beneficiary of the holder at his death "a reversionary sum equal to the present value of the policy surrendered."

Meanwhile, pressure was being brought to bear upon the industry as a whole to make some contractual provision for compensating policyholders who had failed to keep up their premium payments. This movement was spearheaded by Elizur Wright, the most famous actuary of the day, who had been ap-

pointed insurance commissioner for Massachusetts in 1858. Wright had become increasingly concerned about the inequities arising out of lapsed policies, and in 1861 a bill he sponsored was passed by the Massachusetts Legislature. Under this legislation all life companies doing business in the Commonwealth were required to provide single premium term insurance in case policies were allowed to lapse.*

Even before the Massachusetts law was passed—possibly in anticipation of its enactment—a few of the life companies began to initiate changes in their policy contracts providing for nonforfeiture. Mutual of Wisconsin followed the lead of New York Life, authorizing the inclusion of nonforfeiture provisions

---

* See Stalson, 309–310. More specifically, "four-fifths of the net value of the policy as shown by the Combined or Actuary's Table of Mortality, less debts, was to be used to buy a single premium term policy for the face amount of the policy as of the age on payment."

in its ten-year limited payment life contracts.* The formula adopted was quite simple. On a policy with a face value of $1,000, after two premiums had been paid, the insured was entitled to $200 worth of paid-up insurance; after three payments, $300; and after four payments, $400; and so forth.

Over the following few years the Company extended the nonforfeiture provision. In 1863 the privilege was allowed the holders of ten-year limited payment life policies after payment of one premium. In 1867 the ten-year endowment and the ordinary life policy contracts became nonforfeiting after two annual premiums had been received.

Selection of Risks and Mortality Experience

The mortality calculations under which the Company operated were based upon certain assumptions regarding the life expectancy of its potential insureds. If management was to provide the minimum margin of safety for its operations, some procedure had to be applied which would permit effective screening of applicants for insurance protection. Even where the results of variance from such standards could be calculated accurately, problems of nonequitable treatment of applicants existed and had to be taken into account. Manifestly, selling insurance at standard rates to those who, because of occupation, individual health, or place of residence represented substandard risks, would have discriminated unfairly against some of the policyholders.

The selection of risks was made on at least three levels. First, certain conditions respecting such things as travel, occupation, and place of residence were written into the policy contracts, and, if violated, rendered the contract nonenforceable. Secondly, by refusing applicants because of their possible susceptibility to particular diseases, or because of hazards arising from occupations or geographical residence, the Company narrowed its range of risk. And finally, in contrast to these more general restrictions, each applicant for insurance was required to pass a medical examination.

The first policies of Mutual of Wisconsin, like those of other companies at the time, contained numerous restrictions.[7] They were rendered null and void, for example, if the insured without consent shall

---

* Under the New York Life plan the "value" of the policy was used as a single premium to buy paid-up insurance for such an amount as this value would purchase at the date of the lapse and at the then age of the policyholder. See Stalson, 318.

pass beyond the settled limits of the United States (excepting into the settled limits of the British provinces of the two Canadas, Nova Scotia or New Brunswick) or shall visit those parts of the United States which lie west of the 100° of west longitude, or between the 1st of July and the 1st of November those parts which lie south of the southern boundaries of the states of Virginia and Kentucky or shall be or reside within ten miles of the Mississippi or Missouri Rivers between the parallels of 36° 30 min. and 40° of north latitude (except while journeying), or shall enter upon a voyage on the high seas.

The same provisions for cancellation applied if the insured were to become employed in any capacity in service on any "sea, sound, inlet, river, lake, or railroad," or engage in any military or naval service (the militia not in actual combat excepted).

In the "Instructions to Agents" (published in 1859) attention was called to the fact that the Company did not insure anyone "when either of the parents of the party whose life is to be assured, has died with consumption, and the disease has appeared among the said party's brothers or sisters." Exceptions were made if the applicant "should be remarkably robust and vigorous, and over thirty-five years of age." These instructions appear to have been taken bodily from Mutual Life's literature on the subject. The Company was not selling outside Wisconsin at this time; yet its "southern agents" were cautioned about determining whether their applicants were "fully acclimated." The tests were "by birth and continued residence in the place where insurance is sought, by long continued summer residence, and during seasons when endemic and epidemic seasons prevail, by having had the disease incident to the climate or locality." Acclimation to yellow fever was not considered complete unless the applicant had had the disease and continued to live in the places where it was endemic.

The instructions to medical examiners were explicit and detailed. In addition to the age, weight, and health of the applicant, the doctors were to inquire about the age and health of parents and other relatives, if alive, and causes of death if not. They were also asked to determine whether the party resided in a locality which was subject to endemic or epidemic disease, and if so, whether or not he had been acclimated. The Company wanted to know whether the applicant was temperate in his habits of life and whether he had always been so. Doctors were urged "not to recommend any party to the

In 1865 the astonishing restriction was put into the contract that rendered it null and void if the insured "shall enter upon an aerial voyage." At the same time the voyages on the high seas were forbidden, "or working or managing a steam engine in any capacity or engaging in aiding or abetting any insurrection against the government of the United States."

For an extra premium, the Company would at times waive the restrictions written into the policy contracts. For example, an insured could reside within ten miles of the Mississippi or Missouri Rivers between the latitude of 36° 30 min. and 40° north by paying one-fourth of 1 per cent extra premium. A voyage around the world involved the payment of a 2 per cent premium, while crossing either the Isthmus of Panama, Nicaragua or Tehuantepec cost an extra 1 per cent. Restricted occupations were also insurable by the payment of additional premiums. Locomotive engineers and freight train conductors, for instance, were insurable at an extra rate of 1 per cent.

The outbreak of the Civil War raised a question as to the status of those who were engaged in military service. In April 1861 the Executive Committee passed a resolution that the Company "adopt the action of the convention of the eastern com-

Company who there is reason to suspect of having only temporarily reformed." In all doubtful applications the examiner was asked to pay particular attention to the weak points of the case and in his certificate of examination to express "in an especial manner his views upon those points."

During the earlier years of the operation of the Company the chief reliance for the accuracy of the medical examination was placed largely on the local medical examiners. Kellogg recalled that for some years he personally "examined and passed upon all applications unless there was some special reason for referring them to . . . Dr. E. B. Wolcott, who came in two or three times a week to look over the special applications."[8] The Company tightened up on its medical examinations in 1864 when Dr. Lewis McKnight was appointed medical director on a part-time basis, with a salary of $1,000 a year. From this time on there was a routine medical examination of all applications at the Home Office.

From 1859 through 1865 some further restrictions were inserted into the policy contracts. Beginning in 1862 the policy was not enforceable if the insured should die of "any injury received when in a state of intoxication." The following year the contract was subject to cancellation "if the insured shall become so far intemperate as to impair his health or induce delerium tremens." In the same year the contract was declared null and void "if the insured should engage in the manufacture of gunpowder or fireworks or other highly inflammable or explosive substance, or in submarine operation, blasting, or mining."

panies with regard to war risks upon existing policies, viz., to grant war risks on those insured remaining north of the 34th parallel of north latitude for 5 per cent extra annual premium to be paid in advance, and to those going south of said 34th parallel, for 5 per cent additional extra premium."

On August 7, 1862, a resolution was passed to the effect that the Company would grant war permits to any of its members who should volunteer or be drafted into the military service of the United States upon the same terms as those outlined in 1861. This privilege, however, was not to be extended to policies issued after that date. This position was modified somewhat the following year when on March 9, 1863, it was resolved that "whenever a person insured in this Company shall be drafted into the military service . . . the Company will give a war permit when desired to the amount of a thousand dollars upon the usual terms." The following November the privilege of obtaining a war permit was extended to drafted men and volunteers then having policies with the Company. The final resolution affecting war risks during this period was passed on February 13, 1865, when the extra premium was set at a flat 5 per cent per annum to cover service in any part of the United States.

Back of these various regulations regarding war permits lay a desire to be fair and equitable to the Company's existing policyholders. The reluctance to grant the permits to new policyholders was based on the sound premise that if this were done the Company's risks would be atypical of its ordinary risks. In other words, individuals would take out insurance in anticipation of war service. A large number of such risks could have given the Company an unusually high mortality rate.

How many of the Company's insureds actually served in the armed forces during the Civil War is not known. Out of deaths incurred in combat only seven claims, amounting to a total of $8,500, were presented to the Company.

Following the end of the Civil War the Company moved to modify its restrictions on travel and residence. Beginning in 1867 travel to or from California and travel or residence in any part of America or Europe north of the Tropic of Cancer was permitted without the payment of extra premiums. For travel or residence outside of these limits, prospective policyholders were urged to inquire from the Company about extra premiums. In 1865 the clause in the contract applying to inebriates was changed. Instead of leading to a cancellation of the contract without recourse, it was provided at this time that "if such a person whose life is hereby assured shall become in any sense an inebriate the policy will be canceled upon payment to the insured of the surrender value as determined by the Company's table."

It will be noted from Table II-1 that the Company's actual mortality experience for the period 1858–1868 ran between 67.75 per cent and 81.60 per cent of "expected losses." This record shows that the methods of selecting risks had given better results than the experience indicated in the mortality tables upon which premium rates had been based. How well the Company was doing compared to other insurance institutions is not possible to determine. In the annual statement of January 1867, covering the business of 1866, it was pointed out that

> although so many new risks have been taken, the risk selection of the past has been fully maintained and we are therefore confident the quality of the risks will compare favorably with those of any other company, and, since the great bulk of them are in the smaller towns, villages and farming districts of the west, it is evident that they will be less exposed to cholera should it ever again appear than those of most other companies.

TABLE II-1

Northwestern Mutual:
Mortality Experience, 1858–1868

Year of Issue	Expected Losses	Actual Losses	Percent of Actual to Expected Losses
1858	$ 37,907	$ 27,000	71.23
1859	212,241	146,200	68.88
1860	278,840	201,900	72.41
1861	201,658	153,100	75.92
1862	344,165	270,200	78.51
1863	714,813	484,280	67.75
1864	1,552,695	1,110,199	71.50
1865	1,912,763	1,350,029	70.58
1866	2,022,857	1,621,243	80.15
1867	2,928,430	2,389,599	81.60
1868	3,137,944	2,435,382	77.61

Source: Henry F. Tyrrell, *Semi-centennial History*, 324.

Two years later in reporting on the business for the year 1868 it was stated,

> the mortality record has again been favorable, for while the death losses have been one-hundred sixty-seven, amounting to

$326,413, thus making an average loss of over $1,000 per working day, the percentage of loss has been about the same as last year. This shows only three-fourths of the average percentage of those companies reporting last year to Massachusetts and a still less proportion of the expectation of loss by the tables.

Premiums: Methods of Payment and Rates

From the beginning the Company permitted premiums to be paid annually, semi-annually, or quarterly, but the question as to whether personal notes should be accepted as partial payment on premiums was never entirely resolved. Personal notes up to 50 per cent of the premium were accepted until December 1860, when the Executive Committee passed a motion to the effect that on and after February 1, 1861, all premium payments must be made in cash. This was an interesting decision. From a marketing point of view the advantage of allowing the insured to pay a part of the premium in the form of notes was obvious. This was particularly true because of the tendency of agents of mutual companies to stress the argument that dividends would be sufficient to cover the amount of the note obligations. Perhaps the Executive Committee believed that too high a proportion of the premium payments was being made in this form, perhaps it was merely imitation of the practice of Mutual Life of New York which since 1846 had required cash payment of all premiums.[9]

Evidently the provisions regarding cash premium payments put the Company into a poor competitive position, and early in 1863 the matter was reconsidered. The Company had earlier accepted premium

notes, although there was no specific provision in the charter covering this method of payment. Legal sanction was sought when the Wisconsin Legislature was petitioned for a change in the charter provisions which would allow the Company to accept notes as part payment of premiums. Under legislation approved March 23, 1863, Section 11 of the Company's charter was amended to read as follows: "The Company may loan to policyholders in said Company from time to time sums not exceeding one-half (½) of the annual premiums on their policies upon notes to be secured by the policy of the person to whom the loans may be made."[10]

Before putting the premium note system back into operation, the management consulted with Elizur Wright. Upon his recommendations the loan plan was reinstated in 1864 in modified form. In a pamphlet explaining the cash and note system of the Company, the following statement was made:

> Five years of experience and observation had convinced the managers of this Company that a loan may be made to the policyholder of such a portion of the premium as shall be equal to the value of the policy at the end of the year without detracting in any degree from the safety or stability of the Company, for it is certainly safe to loan to each policy so much as is secured by the policy itself, and these loans are made without expense as well as without danger of loss.

The relative merits of the cash and note system over the cash system were vigorously debated all during this period. In their advertisements the various companies made much of the fact that they either did or did not accept this type of payment for premiums. Mutual Life of New York, for example, in a broadside issued July 20, 1867, by its general agent for the Northwestern states, stressed the fact that it and three other companies, Equitable of New York, Germania of New York, and Washington of New York, were all cash companies. The others it designated in somewhat scornful terms as "note" companies, and went on at some length to indicate what advantages were to be obtained from insisting upon cash premiums.

A comparison of the gross premium rates of the leading companies for the year 1867 (shown in Table II-2) indicates the almost perfect identity between the rates of Mutual of Wisconsin and those of Mutual Life of New York. It will also be noted how close the various companies were in their premium rates on ordinary life policies, although a greater difference existed in the premium rates on limited pay life and endowment policies. Undoubtedly these differentials were used as a part of a sales argument, but most companies emphasized the net cost, which took into account their respective dividend policies. Because dividend policies generally were in a state of uncertainty at this time, objective comparison between the various companies on this basis is not possible.

Dividends

Among the stronger selling points of a mutual life insurance company was the fact that the members shared in the distribution of accumulated funds which were in excess of death claims paid, expenses of operation, and allocations to policy reserves. One of the very first sales brochures published by the Company in 1858 said, "In the experience of life companies, up to this time in America, with moderate expenses, each company has made over fifty per cent on the premiums paid." Emphasis on the size of dividends was one of the fundamental arguments used by management in pointing up the superiority of Mutual's policies.

According to the charter of the Company, at the end of five years from the time its first policy was issued, it "shall cause a balance to be struck of the affairs of the Company and shall credit each member with an equitable share of the profits of said Company." As the first policy had been issued in November 1858, management, during the middle of 1863, began the preparations for payment of its first dividend. Establishment of the dividend scale required careful actuarial computations. Lacking a professional actuary, management employed Elizur Wright as a special consultant.* During September 1863, at the invitation of the Company, Wright came to Milwaukee and met with the members of the Executive Committee.

On this occasion Wright made two important recommendations. The first was that the Company set aside a reserve of 10 per cent above the net valuation of mortality at 4 per cent interest; the second was a proposal to divide the surplus in such a manner that each member would share in it according to the ratio of his contributions. Wright's first recommendation as commissioner was ultraconservative. The reserves of the Company had been calculated on a basis that the investments would earn 4 per cent. Actually, the company was re-

---

* For a short biography of Elizur Wright, probably the most famous name in life insurance, see Stalson, 231–236.

ceiving considerably more than this rate of interest on its assets. Therefore, the Executive Committee decided, after receiving Wright's estimates of the amount payable in dividends to each group of policyholders, to add a 40 per cent addition to those amounts, which practically eliminated the 10 per cent reserve called for in the original recommendation.

Wright's second recommendation, however, was adopted intact and involved a departure from the two alternative methods then followed by other companies in the industry in distributing surplus. One of these was to base dividends on the face value of the policy in force; the other, to allocate on a basis of the amount of premiums. Both methods were inequitable insofar as the treatment of policyholders was concerned.

In a letter to A. W. Kellogg dated April 6, 1864, which was printed and distributed by the Company to its policyholders, Wright explained the methods he used to compute the surplus. To ascertain the amount of surplus which was to be distributed, the policies were valued by the Actuaries' Table of Mortality, the rate of interest being assumed at 4 per cent. Surplus was the difference between the valuation of the policies made in this fashion and the assets of the Company. Further, it was assumed that each policy had contributed surplus in two ways: first, by the excess of the premium over the net cost of the insurance on the supposition of the aforesaid mortality and interest, with no expenses; and second, by interest on the minimum net value of the policy in excess of the assumed rate up to the time of distribution. "As the whole amount of contributions to surplus thus obtained is to the whole sum to be divided, so is each policy's particular contribution to its own cash dividend." This was an eminently fair method of calculating surplus as a basis for dividends.

The Executive Committee hoped to declare the

TABLE II-2

Selected Life Companies: Comparative Premium Rates Per $1000, 1867

	Ordinary Life Ages			10-Year Life Ages			Endowment Age 30, Payable at Ages		
Name and Location	25	40	55	25	40	55	40	50	60
Connecticut Mutual, Hartford, Connecticut	$19.87	$32.00	$59.75	$45.82	$63.90	$96.05	$126.36	$55.64	$35.23
Equitable Life Assurance Society, New York City	20.17	31.73	58.98	43.28	59.46	88.82	95.27	44.29	29.65
John Hancock, Boston, Massachusetts	19.80	31.50	59.40	44.78	61.68	92.24	106.25	48.33	31.33
Mutual Life, New York City	19.89	31.73	57.58	41.95	57.44	81.83	95.26	44.61	30.04
Mutual Benefit, Newark, New Jersey	20.40	32.00	57.80	46.90	64.78	93.10	115.06	52.57	33.90
New England Mutual, Boston, Massachusetts	19.80	31.50	59.40	44.78	61.68	92.24	106.25	48.33	31.33
New York Life, New York City	20.40	32.00	60.00	45.84	63.35	93.90	97.00	44.03	30.94
Northwestern Mutual Life Milwaukee, Wisconsin	19.89	31.73	57.58	41.95	57.45	81.84	95.26	44.61	30.04

SOURCE: Table Compiled by D. P. Fackler, Consulting Actuary, *The Insurance Monitor and Wall Street Review*, Vol. XV, No. 8 (August 1867), 482, New York.

dividend in January 1864 as a "New Year's present." It took Wright somewhat longer to make the necessary calculations than had been originally anticipated, however, and the official declaration was not made until February 29 when notices were sent to the policyholders. The dividends averaged about 40 per cent of the premium payments made by the insured up to that time. The dividend was not payable in cash but could be taken in one of three ways: first, when the policyholders had given notes in part payment for their premiums, the dividend was used to pay off the balance due on such notes; second, when the premiums had been paid in cash, the dividend could be used against subsequent premium payments; or third, it could be applied to the purchase of additional insurance by those policyholders who were still insurable.

The first dividend declaration by the Company raised the question in the minds of policyholders and agents as to the future policy respecting dividend payments. A change in the Company's charter, made in 1863, gave the management the option of declaring dividends annually, every two years, every three years, or to continue on the five-year basis. The Executive Committee in March 1864 took steps to put the Company on an annual dividend basis by providing that the next dividend should be made two years following the first and thereafter that declarations would be made annually. Actually the Company did not follow this schedule, for the second dividend came in March 1867, at which time policyholders were credited with amounts which ranged from 40 per cent on certain types of policies to 53 per cent on others.[11] No further action on dividends was taken by the Executive Committee until January 1869, when it was decided to make the dividends on the business of 1867 and 1868 payable during 1870. Meanwhile, beginning in March 1867, the Company wrote into the policy contracts a provision that the policyholder would be entitled to share in the distribution of dividends only after the policy had been in force for three years. This provision gave policyholders an additional incentive to keep their insurance in force in order to share in the accumulated dividend.

Widening the Market

In the earlier years, the Company confined its sales activities to Wisconsin, but a decade later its market was national in scope. The first solicitation of business outside the state was made in 1859 when

Wilson, general agent, visited the St. Paul-Minneapolis area, although formal entry into Minnesota was delayed until 1861, when J. H. McKenney of Rochester was appointed the first local agent in the area. From that time forward expansion was rapid. In 1860 a license was obtained to sell insurance in Iowa and in 1862 a similar arrangement was made in Massachusetts. During 1864, under McKindley, agencies were started in Illinois, Indiana, Michigan, and Nebraska. In 1865 Kansas, Ohio, and Pennsylvania were added. In 1866 the Company moved into the *post bellum* South by starting agencies in Alabama, Kentucky, Tennessee, in addition to Missouri, Colorado, and Idaho. Heber Smith carried on this expansion beginning in 1867 when California, Georgia, Mississippi, Oregon, Washington, and West Virginia were added to the fold. During 1868 sales representatives began work for the Company in Arkansas, Maine, Maryland, New Hampshire, Vermont, and New York.

This expansion of the Company's sales territory was a part of, and to some extent in response to, the expansion of the sales territories of the Eastern companies. At the outbreak of the Civil War those companies that had been doing a Southern business sought new markets in the area between the Appalachians and the Mississippi. Thus Mutual of Wisconsin, which was just beginning to extend its own sales representation, was confronted almost from the outset by this initial intensive "invasion" of Eastern companies into the areas it itself was seeking to expand. At the conclusion of the war the Eastern companies began to push their sales in the trans-

Mississippi region even more vigorously. The Wisconsin company took an active part in this movement in addition to establishing its own sales representatives in the South and in the Eastern markets.

By the end of 1868 the market of Mutual Life of Wisconsin had become national in scope. Even earlier its sales territory had expanded beyond the boundaries of the state, and the trustees and officers were conscious of the sales advantages of removing any implications that the Company was merely a local or state institution. One move in this direction came in March 1863, when the legislature provided that twelve of the thirty-six trustees could be residents of states other than Wisconsin. It was now possible to elect to the Board prominent individuals outside the state.

Building a Sales Organization

There were several specific problems shared by the rest of the industry that had to be answered before Mutual Life of Wisconsin could recruit and maintain a satisfactory sales organization: how much to pay agents to secure their services; how to link their income with successful sales effort; how to enlist the loyalty of good agents toward the Company; and finally, how best to organize the agents so that they could be most effectively supervised by the Home Office.

The management met these problems through the adoption of a "general agency" system, a solution similar to that used by the majority of the American life companies. Under this plan responsibility for recruiting, training, and maintaining agents in the field was delegated to general agents, directly under contract with the Company.* It was likely that General Johnston, drawing on his experience with Mutual of New York, had this system in mind for Mutual of Wisconsin when he took the title "General Agent." But it took almost a decade of experimentation before the Wisconsin company came to accept the system, which, when it was finally adopted, became a permanent policy.

It was clearly impractical to have an elaborate sales organization as long as the number of agents was small and the sales territory was limited. When the Company first began, and for some time thereafter, its insurance was sold through local agents. It was the principal function of the general agent to appoint the local representatives and to stimulate them by occasional visits.

---

* For a general description of the evolution of this system see Stalson, Chapter XVI.

Ordinarily the local agents were assigned definite sales territories: a city, a county, or two or three counties, depending on the potential amount of business. For example, in July 1862 O. Curtis of St. Paul, Minnesota, agreed "to use all due diligence and exertion to promote the interests of the . . . Company" in the St. Paul area and "not to act as the agent of any other Life insurance Company" during the life of the contract. Joseph C. Green, on January 6, 1864, was given a local agent's contract covering the Minnesota counties of St. Paul, Ramsey, St. Anthony, Minneapolis, and Hennepin. Willard Merrill, later prominent in the Company's history, entered into a contract on February 18, 1865, under which he was to "solicit applications and collect premiums for insurance in the city and town of Janesville in Rock County, Wisconsin."

It is quite likely that the very first agency contracts provided the same terms believed to have been accepted by General Johnston, i.e., 10 per cent of the first-year premiums and 5 per cent on renewal premiums. At least one of the first contracts on record, dated August 29, 1861, offered R. O. Kellogg, brother of the Company's secretary, a commission of $8.00 per policy with a face value of $1,000 or more or the alternative (which he chose), a commission of 10 per cent on first-year premiums, plus traveling expenses of $1.50 per day when away from home.

There was a definite tendency to increase commission rates after 1861, however, and in some instances to add allowances. In the contract given to Curtis in 1862, for example, the rate was 15 per cent on first-year premiums and 5 per cent on renewals. In addition, he was allowed $100 per year office rent and $50 for advertising. Joseph C. Green was given 20 per cent and 5 per cent commissions. A year later the Company added a $500 per year allowance for office and other expenses. Willard Merrill's contract of February 1865 called for a 20 per cent commission on first-year premiums and 5 per cent on renewals, although if he did not sell fifty-five or more acceptable policies of $1,000 or more during the year, the first-year commission rate was to be 10 per cent, the renewal rate remaining the same.

The granting of renewal commissions to agents as long as they remained with the Company recognized the important effect this method would have in tying the agents to the Company by financial interest. As the number of policies sold by a particular agent increased and remained in force, his incentive to seek employment elsewhere diminished. The case of R. O. Kellogg, mentioned above, who was not given any

Company advertisement in August, 1868 issue of
HARPER'S NEW MONTHLY MAGAZINE

renewal interest, brought home to the management the weakness of his type of contract. After making an excellent record with Mutual of Wisconsin, he left to join the Home Life Company of New York as their general agent "for the Northwest" with an office in Chicago.[12]

Although the Company continued to contract directly with local agents, the commission rates in such contracts during 1867 and 1868 were reduced in some instances to 15 per cent and 5 per cent, and in others to 10 per cent and 5 per cent on first-year premiums and renewals. Salary and other allowances were no longer included. The reliance, however, on local agents alone did not work out satisfactorily. Most of the local agents worked only part-time and had other interests which kept average production down. The appointment of more local representatives did not by itself offer a satisfactory solution. In fact, the increase in their number by 1863 had made the job of supervision and stimulating sales effort by the Home Office increasingly difficult.

To meet this problem the Company began to employ traveling agents who might either be sent into any area where sales were lagging or allowed to operate in any territory that seemed promising. They were to work with the local agents, usually by request, and commonly split first-year commissions with the local agent on policies that were sold by joint effort. One of the first of these contracts, and a representative one, was signed on January 25, 1862, with Heber Smith, who was soon to become general agent (superintendent of agencies) at Milwaukee.

This contract reads in part that Smith agrees and binds himself to devote his whole time and energies to the service of the [Company] in soliciting applications for life insurance, collecting premiums, and in every other way advance the interest of the said Company that may be in his power to so do and be governed by or act in consultation with the President and the management of the Company during the time of service. Smith's contract was signed by President Daggett.

There was some uncertainty as to how the traveling agents should be paid, and the problem was never satisfactorily resolved. In 1863, for example, the Company paid Heber Smith $1,200 per year and "reasonable" traveling expenses. For the same kind of work, a year later, Hiram Lowell was allowed $1,700 but no traveling expenses. Eugene H. Merry, beginning in June 1865, was paid 9½ per cent on first-year premiums on policies which he sold in northern Illinois, but was allowed no renewal com-

missions. In September of the same year, Thomas J. Yorks was given a contract to travel wherever he wished and under which his full compensation was 15 per cent of the first-year premiums.

Even on other than compensation grounds the employment of traveling agents did not prove thoroughly satisfactory. As the Company's sales territory grew, the problem of recruiting and supervising local agents became more difficult. In order to secure active and full-time workers who would be bound to the Company by mutual interest in the future, and to provide a more convenient and permanent method of supervising local agents, the system of district or state agencies—subsequently called the "general agency system"—emerged.*

The Company's first district agency contracts indicate how the general agency was established. Heber Smith, for example, was assigned a district agency for Illinois in January 1865. In return for a salary of $3,500 per annum and traveling expenses, his duties under the contract were to "devote his entire time, energy, and ability to the work of procuring applications, collecting premiums, appointing agents and physicians with the consent and approval of the Company in the said state." This contract also contained the following clause:

> It is further agreed that if the said Heber Smith, at the end of the time, wishes to make other arrangements, he hereby agrees that he will give this Company the first opportunity to retain his services before making a contract with any other party or company, and that he will not work for any other party or company, and that he will not work for any other insurance company during these years.

The inclusion of this last clause gave some protection against losing a good general agent, but it did not put the Company in a very strong bargaining position. Early recognition of the desirability of giving the district or general agents greater financial incentive for remaining with the Company is shown in the agreement made with S. T. Lockwood who succeeded Heber Smith in Illinois in 1866.†

Under a five-year contract, signed May 1 of that year, Lockwood was assigned the state agency for

---

* By 1868 it had become customary to refer to the state and certain district agencies as "General Agencies," although this term was not written into the contract forms until later.

†Smith was employed by the Home Office to assist McKindley, the general agent.

Illinois "to have the supervision of such work in the said state, the appointment of agents and physicians, subject to the approval of the Company." During the first year he was to receive $2,000 and "reasonable traveling" expenses, and an allowance for office rent in Chicago. During the last four years of the contract he was to receive 20 per cent commission of the first-year premiums on all policies sold in the state. For the entire five years he was allowed a 7½ per cent renewal commission on all policies in force at the time he took over as well as on any policies that should be sold during the time he held the contract. These were gross commissions, for out of the renewal commissions from the start, and from the first-year commissions after the first year, Lockwood was required "to carry out the contracts of the Company with agents now employed in said state and by securing and paying new agents [and] with their combined work make a thorough and efficient canvass of the state." The Company put a ceiling on the rates, 20 per cent on first-year premiums and 5 per cent on renewals, which Lockwood could in turn grant local agents out of his own commissions. As an additional incentive, it was further provided that

> during said first year the said Lockwood shall have the privilege of spending the Sabbath at his home in Janesville (the Company paying his fares) whenever he may be on Saturday in northern Illinois and can do so without detriment to the Company.

This contract shows how far the Company was willing to go after 1865 to maintain and develop a good agency organization in a promising territory.

A salary, plus allowances, during the first year gave the agent financial security when he first started. Assuming that he paid the full 20 per cent to his local agent for first-year commissions, he had a strong incentive from his 2½ per cent of renewal commissions to build up a strong, productive agency force.* By the end of 1867 the form of district or general agency contracts had become more simplified and standardized.

A sampling of local agents' contracts, who by this time were almost all under direct contract with general agents, indicates that the most common schedule was 15 per cent and 2½ per cent respectively on first-year premiums and renewals. These rates, it should be noted, were not necessarily uniform among local agents for they were subject to bargaining between the local agents and the district or general agents. The latter group, however, was vitally interested in building and retaining a productive local agency force, and the principle of giving renewal commissions contingent upon continued employment with the district or general agent and the Company was well established.

With the extension of the general agency contract, the Company finally developed an agency organization which, except for one important lapse, has been maintained down to the present time. As Kellogg observed,

> The agency work became a complete and easily supervised system, the Home officers

---

* In this case even this kind of a contract did not prevent Lockwood from resigning. In 1867 he joined with McKindley, the Company's general agent, in taking a general agency covering the Northwest for the Globe Mutual Life Insurance Company of New York.

Heading used on policy forms from March 1863 to March 1865

CENTRAL AGENCY
MUTUAL LIFE INSURANCE CO., OF WISCONSIN,

Madison, 16th Jan — 1864

Dear Friend

I have yours of yesterday evening report as desired. Sprague had not been [illegible] but he felt [illegible] and was [illegible] over treatment [illegible] for which he had written. had promised and [illegible] supposed [illegible] action of Committee [illegible] You will refer to his last letter or [illegible] he [illegible] he will make [illegible] immediately — he felt aggrieved and decided to quit [illegible] But I thought we could not afford to lose him. have succeeded in inducing him to go to work again — but this time upon the bonus & commission plan — Same terms as to [illegible] Please make a note of that on Rem. book — and send me a copy of the same he commenced work yesterday 15th on said terms — and will make up and settle up [illegible] business to that date. I hope to have much satisfaction [illegible] the change of terms — and also that the Co. will realise even more in future than in past. The next thing is to [illegible] Pickard — will keep him if I can make terms in which I can feel justifiable. — Am getting up new circular will send copy soon as got. [illegible] for gen. and free circulation — hope to get the inside track again ere very soon —

Truly yours,
Wilson

Kellogg Sec.

A letter from General Agent H. G. Wilson to A. W. Kellogg, secretary of the company and the [Home Office] general agent putting the pressure upon the state and district agent and he in turn upon his smaller district and local agents; and thus a large business was secured.[13]

Agent Training and Sales Promotion

In the 1860's the formal training of agents, both for Mutual Life of Wisconsin and the industry in general, understandably lay many years in the future. Such training and advice as the agents received came largely from the Company's district or traveling agents who worked with a novice agent and showed him by example how sales could be made. It has already been noted that certain of the traveling agents were required, as a part of their contract, to sign up local agents and work with them during their early breaking-in period. The contracts of the district and state agents always read that they should enlist an agency force and insure that it was operating effectively.

In its pamphlet entitled *Instructions for the Government of the Agents and Positions* and issued in 1859, the Company did lay down some general principles regarding success in selling life insurance. After noting that an inquiry was often made by agents, especially newly-appointed ones, as to what course they should pursue to become successful, the following rules based on "observation and experience" were suggested:

1. The Agent should have a Policy on his own life (if an insurable one) in the Company he represents. If you apply to another to take a Policy, and he asks you, 'Are you assured?' and you say, 'No'—what becomes of your argument in its favor? Example will be stronger than precept.

2. The Agent should make himself intelligently and fully acquainted with the fundamental principles and the general usages of the Company he represents, and satisfy himself that they are sound and just, and will realize the advantages promised, and then he should study to acquire readiness and skill in presenting and applying them.

3. The Agent should first apply to his personal friends and connections, and get them to obtain Assurance; and then to the most intelligent and influential persons in the community, as they will most readily appreciate the claims and advantages of Assurance, while their names and example will be a passport and recommendation to others. Every party Assured becomes an advocate and generally an active one, for Life Assurance.

4. Awaken interest by circulating pamphlets, reports, papers, and other documents and facts furnished you by the office for distribution, to be followed by personal appeal and argument. Active opposition is better for a good cause, like Life Assurance, than ignorance and apathy; as opposition awakens interest and inquiry, and the truth triumphs. Few, if any, are ever influenced by a mere newspaper advertisement to take a policy.

5. Persevering industry and unflinching determination to succeed by personal effort, will insure complete success—and nothing else will.

It is often stated as an apology for want of success, that 'there are so many Agents for Life Assurance in the place.' If your Company is manifestly the best represented, the 'many Agents' are a decided advantage. They help to excite inquiry and diffuse information, and the ground thus cultivated is but prepared for your harvest. Our most successful Agents are those who work where there is most competition.

There are not, probably, among the many millions of this country, more than 70,000 who have availed themselves of the advantages of Life Assurance.

In your own community a fractional portion only of the whole number are Assured, and your field is abundant.

In addition to this general advice agents were supplied with sales literature which pointed out the advantages of insurance in general, and the Company's policies in particular. These pamphlets and brochures, which were distributed among the prospective customers, outlined the principal sales arguments used by the Company's agents. Initially the emphasis in this literature was upon the advantages of insurance, "the need and value of protection for the loved ones of the family," and the differences between stock and mutual life insurance companies. In advancing the claims of the Company an appeal was made to local pride. A pamphlet issued in 1861 said, "It is worse than idle, it is simply ridiculous, to assert, as many are inclined to do, that we cannot have as good, safe and reliable companies in the West as anywhere else. There are as good men in the West and enough of them to compose the Company, and as honest and honorable men to manage it as anywhere in the world." Furthermore,

> thousands of dollars are annually sent out of the Northwest for life insurance to be invested at a low rate of interest in eastern cities or England which money, if kept at home and safely invested here as it ought to be, would tend much to relieve embarrassment in all branches of business and thus benefit the whole West. It becomes, therefore, both a duty and interest, not only of those desiring insurance but of all, to use their influence in building up this beneficial home institution.

Over the succeeding years, as the principles of life insurance became more widely understood, the emphasis was more and more placed upon the unique features offered the Company's policyholders. As Mutual Life of Wisconsin began competing in a wider area, and especially for the benefit of the Eastern market, great stress was placed upon the ad-

vantages of its geographical location. An advertisement in *Harper's New Monthly Magazine* for August 1868 is particularly revealing, for it stressed the growth of the West, its vigor, its security, and, not least of all, its more advantageous return on investments because of higher interest rates.

There was some danger that the development of the state and district agency system would result in a loss of contact between the Company and the agents, especially the local agents. The Company was early aware of the desirability of maintaining the good will and loyalty of its agency force. On the occasion of the annual meeting of the trustees in January 1867, the state agents and some of the district and local agents were invited to Milwaukee to confer with the trustees and the officers. This experience was so fruitful that a year later "the leading agents of the Company, state, district and local, who were in the city by the invitation of the officers were, for the first time, formally invited by the trustees into conference with them to give information and voice the needs of their several agencies." This was

TABLE II-3

Northwestern Mutual: State and General Agents, 1868

NEW ENGLAND:
  H. G. Wilson & Co., Gen'l Agents, Mass., Maine, New Hamp. & Vt.,
    114 Washington St., Boston

MIDDLE ATLANTIC:
  Munsell & Smith, Gen'l Agents, Eastern Pennsylvania,
    428 Walnut St., Philadelphia

  George Dart, Gen'l Agent, Western Pennsylvania,
    Williamsport, Pennsylvania

EAST NORTH CENTRAL:
  Bates Bros., State Agents, Eastern Ohio and Western Virginia,
    Wooster, Ohio

  John Lokie, State Agent, Western Ohio
    Toledo, Ohio

  Martin & Hopkins, State Agents, Indiana and Kentucky,
    Journal Bldg., Indianapolis, Ind.

  Shugart & Dean, State Agents for Illinois,
    85 Washington St., Chicago

  Chas. Auringer, State Agent, Michigan
    111 Jefferson Avenue, Detroit

WEST NORTH CENTRAL:
  Martin & Perkins, State Agents, Iowa and Nebraska,
    49 Brady St., Davenport, Iowa

  Snow & Seely, State Agents, Missouri,
    316 Chestnut St., St. Louis

  F. E. Shandrew, State Agent, Minnesota,
    Winona

  Fisher & Adams, State Agents, Kansas,
    cor. 5th and Delaware Sts., Leavenworth

EAST SOUTH CENTRAL:
  J. S. Chapin, State Agent, Tennessee,
    34 Union St., Memphis

  J. A. Melcher, State Agent, Northern Alabama,
    Selma

SOUTH ATLANTIC:
  Davis & Seelye, Gen'l Agents, Northern Georgia and South Carolina,
    Atlanta, Ga.

PACIFIC COAST:
  Elmore & Rowe, Gen'l Agents, Pacific Coast,
    315 Montgomery St., San Francisco

SOURCE: Advertisement: *Harpers New Monthly Magazine*, August 1868.

the beginning of the custom of holding annual meetings of the agents in Milwaukee at which time they had the opportunity to meet and confer with the officers and staff of the Home Office.

Unfortunately there is no way of estimating the total number of agents under contract by the end of 1868. It is reported that the Company had some thirty-four agents in 1859.[14] Nine years later the figure must have been in the hundreds. In 1868 the Company did list some sixteen general and state agencies (see Table II-3). From this tabulation it may be concluded that the system was well established by that date.

Growth of Insurance and Selling Costs

The management had reason to be pleased with the expansion in the Company's sales over the ten-year period ending in 1868. As indicated in Chart II-1, with the exception of the slight drop between 1862 and 1863, the face amount of the policies issued increased each year, showing an especially rapid rate of growth after 1863. Compared with an amount of $555.2 thousand issued in 1859, the figure was just under $25.3 million in 1868. The Company's issues of new policies increased somewhat faster than the industry as a whole, and by the end of the period the Company's proportion of total sales was about 4.3 per cent compared to 1.87 per cent ten years earlier.

For a number of reasons the value of the policies issued by the industry and the Company did not add equivalent amounts to the insurance in force. In part this was because of a failure by applicants to accept policies that were issued. In part it was due to termination of contracts through death (or maturity) and lapses and surrenders.

The Company, which issued policies with face amounts of approximately $75.6 million during the period, expanded its insurance in force by some 66 per cent of this amount, or $49.6 million. This percentage addition was about the same as shown by the industry as a whole which added during the same period nearly $1.4 billion to insurance in force, or 67 per cent of new issues, totaling slightly over $2 billion.

Because of the stepped-up tempo of its sales, the Company, as indicated in Chart II-2, was able to add to its insurance in force at a faster rate than the industry as a whole. Measured by this standard, the Company, which had ranked twenty-fifth in the industry in 1860, moved up to fourteenth place in 1865 and was on its way to becoming the eighth

largest company, a goal that was reached by 1870.

Although data for a comparison with industry experience are not available, the Company was able to maintain its selling expenses at comparatively low levels. For the ten years 1859–1868, premium income aggregated some $6.05 million. Total selling and marketing costs (including such items as payments to agents, hotel and travel expenses, and license taxes) were slightly over $1 million, or approximately 16.6 per cent of premium income. This record is especially noteworthy in view of the increased competition after 1865.

Mutual Life of Wisconsin Becomes Northwestern Mutual

Throughout 1864 there was a growing feeling that something more spectacular should be done to call attention to the growing stature and future plans of the Company. This, it was felt, could be done by a change in the Company name. The subject was first considered informally by the Executive Committee on December 5, 1864. According to its minutes of December 14,

> After quite a discussion of the proposition to ask for a change of the Company [name] it was resolved to recommend to the Board of Trustees to ask the legislature for a change to one of the following: The Northwestern Life Insurance Company, the Northwestern Mutual Life Insurance Company, or the Mutual Life Insurance Company of the Northwest.

This recommendation was accepted by the Board and early in 1865 the legislature approved the change to The Northwestern Mutual Life Insurance Company.

An announcement sent out to the policyholders on February 5, 1865, said:

> The reasons for asking for such change were to take away any impression that the Company is merely a state institution, to identify it more thoroughly with its field of operation (now embracing Wisconsin, Michigan, Indiana, Illinois, Iowa, Minnesota, and soon to cover the whole Northwest) and to cause every citizen of the Northwest to feel a personal interest and pride in its prosperity.

Northwestern Mutual was on the threshold of a new stage in its history.

CHART II-1

Sales of Insurance :
Industry and Northwestern, 1859–1868

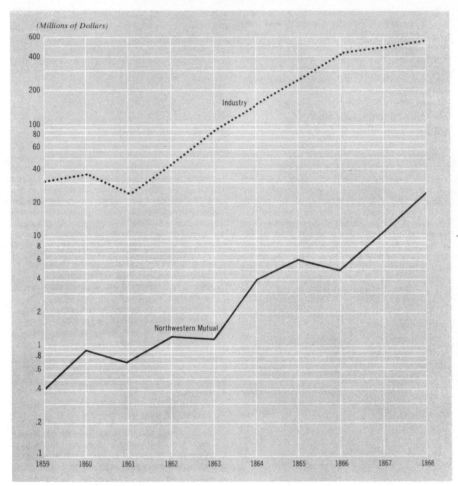

The semi-logarithmic or ratio scale is used to facilitate the comparison of two or more series of data of different magnitudes. The comparison is in terms of relative rather than absolute magnitudes. Equal vertical rises in the curves indicate corresponding percentages of increase. Equal drops indicate equivalent percentage decreases.

SOURCES: *The Year Book*, New York, Spectator Publishing Company, 1910, pp. 224-25. J. Owen Stalson, *Marketing Life Insurance*, Cambridge, Harvard University Press, 1942, p. 813.

CHART II-2

Insurance in Force: Industry and Northwestern, 1859–1868

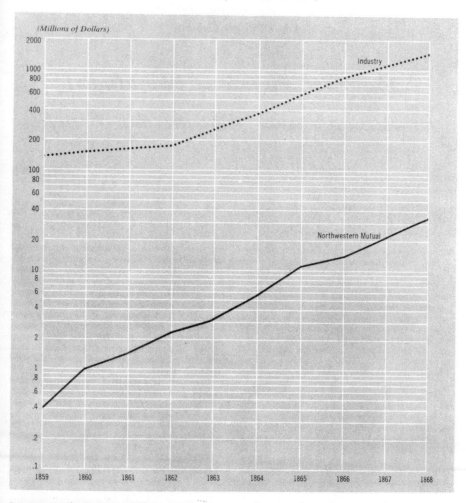

SOURCES: Appendix E; Stalson. *Marketing Life Insurance.*
p. 820-22.

CHAPTER THREE

The First Decade of Operations: Investments and Policyholder Benefits

IN addition to the growth in the amount of insurance in force, other measures of success of The Northwestern Mutual Life Insurance Company in its first decade can be seen in the sharp rise in the funds built up for investment, the expansion of the operations of the Home Office, and the benefits that were enjoyed by the policyholders. All three aspects required the attention of the management, but the problems that touched upon investments were, perhaps, the most exacting and novel. In fact, some of the decisions taken during these formative years became policies which have existed through a century of Company history.

The most noteworthy features of Northwestern's investment policies during the period ending with 1868 were first, the gradual expansion of the area within which loans were made, and second, the emphasis upon mortgage loans, especially upon loans on city property. The geographical expansion was attributable to an increasing amount of loanable funds and the development of a system of finding and inspecting attractive loan properties. The predominance of mortgage loans in the Company's investment portfolio was consistent with the objective of maximizing interest income without violating the principle of sound investment procedure. Although at times federal government securities and bonds issued by the state of Wisconsin during the Civil War sold at prices that made them attractive, the mortgage loan field was, on the whole, more appealing. In the purchase of government securities, and to a lesser extent Wisconsin state bonds, Northwestern was competing in a national market with other financial institutions, including other life insurance companies. In the mortgage loan field the competition was somewhat more restricted, especially so because New York companies at the time were prohibited by law from making mortgage loans outside the state. It was logical, therefore, for the Company to take full advantage of its geographical location and the demand for capital funds that existed in the Middle West.

As is shown in Table III-1, the Company's gross income grew from $13,000 for the first full year of operation to nearly $2.5 million in 1868. As would be expected during the first years of operations, the bulk of income came from premiums, and by the end of the decade interest earnings only amounted to about 3 per cent of the total.

An examination of Table III-1 shows, however, that the Company was adding substantially to the amounts available for investment even though as a percentage of gross income these amounts declined over the years. Several factors inherent in the early evolution of a life insurance organization were responsible for this decline. First, the Company paid no dividends to policyholders until 1863; afterward, when such dividends were paid, they consisted of insurance additions or premium reductions and did not involve a cash disbursement. The same was true of surrendered policies. Second, with the expansion of the business, marketing expenses increased perceptibly, rising at a rate somewhat faster than that enjoyed by gross income. Finally, payments of death claims increased, although at no time did these equal or exceed the expected mortality for the Company. The proportion of gross income made available for investment for the entire period ending December 31, 1868, was 68 per cent, falling from 71 per cent in 1859 to 65 per cent in 1868.

Thus during these years management succeeded in accumulating approximately $4.45 million over and beyond all expenditures and policyholder benefits. Of this amount some $3.77 million was invested in what can be termed "earning assets." The remaining amount, $680,000, included Home Office real estate and advances to agents, as well as accrued premiums and interest. Total admitted assets, however, amounted to $4.76 million at the close of 1868.

The earning assets of the Company during this period consisted of cash, mortgage loans, United States government bonds, state bonds, premium notes, and bills receivable. The cash item included funds in the hands of agents and funds available at the Company and in banks. Interest was received only on the bank deposits at a rate of around 4 to 4.5 per cent and probably did not at any time bring in any substantial income. The appearance of premium notes among the assets has already been discussed. This item grew rapidly from 1858 through 1860 when the Company decided to go on a cash premium basis. With the restoration of the premium note system in 1864 this account again expanded rapidly until the end of 1868 when premium notes totaled nearly $2 million.

Premium Notes as a Part of Investment Policy

Once the decision had been made to accept premium notes, and so long as this rule remained in force, there was no further discretion to be exercised by the management in controlling the amount of such notes. From an investment point of view there were certain advantages in this type of assets which were outlined at the time when the plan was reinstated. The expense involved was negligible and un-

TABLE III-1

Northwestern Mutual: Income, Expenditure, and Net Available for Investment, 1859–1868

	INCOME				EXPENDITURES				
		PREMIUM	INTER-	GROSS	PAYMENTS TO POLICY-	EXTERNAL	INTERNAL	TOTAL EXPENDI-	NET AVAIL- ABLE FOR
YEAR	CASH	NOTES	EST	INCOME	HOLDERS	EXPENSES	EXPENSES	TURES	INVESTMENT
				(In thousands of dollars)					
1859[a]	$8.2	$4.3	$0.5[e]	$13.0		$0.8	$2.9	$3.7	$9.3
1860[a]	15.0	11.0	0.3	26.3	$3.5	3.3	3.4	10.2	16.1
1861[a]	28.9	15.6	1.3	45.8	6.5	4.1	6.5	17.1	28.7
1862[a]	55.6	12.9	3.2	71.7	6.8	8.2	7.8	22.8	48.9
1863[a]	90.4	7.5	5.6	103.5	19.2		24.7[d]	43.9	59.6
1864[a]	170.6	29.6	11.4	211.6	25.5		50.4[d]	75.9	135.7
1865[b]	553.2	251.3	33.8	838.3	96.2	143.2	24.7	264.1	574.2
1866[c]	649.9	351.9	71.3	1,073.1	107.5	151.0	23.6	282.1	791.0
1867[c]	1,091.8	481.4	120.5	1,693.7	180.7	248.5	42.7	471.9	1,221.8
1868[c]	1,416.7	805.5	195.0	2,417.2	326.4	442.1	81.6	850.1	1,567.4
Totals	$4,080.3	$1,971.0	$442.9	$6,494.2	$772.3	$1,001.2	$268.3	$2,041.8	$4,452.4

[a] For year ending May 31.
[b] For nineteen months ending December 31, 1865.
[c] For year ending December 31.
[d] There was no separation of expenses during these years.
[e] "Other" income.

SOURCE: Appendix F, Tables 1-4: Comptroller's records of Northwestern Mutual Life Insurance Company.

der the rates worked out by Elizur Wright, the security was the borrower's policy reserve. Moreover, under the arrangements followed by Northwestern at the time, all dividends were applied first to a reduction of premium notes before being available for prepayment of premiums or the purchase of new insurance.

The Company's original premium notes bore interest at 7 per cent, a rate maintained throughout the period ending in 1868. As will be noted presently, this return was below the rate on other types of investment, but considering the security and the cost involved, premium notes represented an attractive form of investment.

The appearance of the item "Bills Receivable" among the Company's assets is unexpected. Unlike a manufacturing or mercantile establishment, there was nothing involved in the operations of an insurance company that would normally lead to the emergence of assets in this form. Actually the confusion arises from the accounting terminology used. In reality these bills receivable were additional premium notes accepted by special agreement from policyholders. The special character of this arrangement is shown by the fact that the interest rate on bills receivable was 10 per cent. This "penalty" rate

was a factor in keeping the total amount relatively low. The increases in this account during 1866 and 1867, which were due to business uncertainty following the end of the Civil War, suggest that policyholders resorted to this type of "borrowing" from the Company only when alternative sources of funds were not readily available.[1]

The Mortgage Portfolio

While the Company was able, between 1858 and 1860, to build up its earning assets by expanding premium notes and bills receivable, it was not until the middle of the latter year that funds were available for other types of investments. An entry in the Executive Committee minute book in August 1860 noted,

> During the last two months there have been two or three informal Committee meetings at which loans of $500 to G. J. Fowler on Lots #1 and #2 in Block 134, 4th Ward, one of $600 to Charles Horning on N-½ of Lot #4 in Block 88, 7th Ward, and $600 to J. H. Eldridge on E 80 ft. of Lot 6 Block 126, 1st Ward all in the City of Milwaukee have

been approved by the Committee and the papers and loans made accordingly — Also $500 additional was loaned Martin Butler.

These loans, totaling $2,200, were the modest beginning of Northwestern's mortgage portfolio. As shown by the entry in the minute book, these first loans were made upon urban real estate, and the interest rate charged was 10 per cent.

In making these original loans and in developing subsequent investment policies, the management of Northwestern Mutual operated under definite legal restrictions. The Company could, however, within limits, take steps to secure modification of these regulations. According to the original charter (Section 10),

> The whole of the premiums received for insurance by said corporation, except as provided for in the following Section, shall be invested in bonds, secured by mortgages on unincumbered real estate within this state. The real estate or other property to secure such investment of capital shall in every case be worth twice the amount loaned thereon.

The trustees (Section 11) also had the option of investing "a certain portion of the premium received, not to exceed one-half thereof, in public stocks of the United States or of the State, or of any incorporated city in the State." Apparently at the request of the Company the investment restrictions were relaxed in 1863 by removing the limitation that investments upon mortgages on unencumbered real estate could only be made on Wisconsin property.* This change gave the management a free hand in choosing the areas within which mortgage loans could be made.

The management was also operating, during this period, under general legislation affecting the rate of interest. An act approved March 10, 1851, by the Wisconsin Legislature limited the rate of interest which could be charged to 12 per cent per annum.[2] This act was amended in 1856 to read that the rate of interest should not be above $7 per $100 for one year, except that parties could contract for an interest rate not exceeding 12 per cent per annum by written agreement.[3] The next important legislation affecting the rate of interest came in 1866 when the maximum legal rate was set at 10 per cent per annum.[4]

---

* Wisconsin General Laws 1863, Chapter 323. The evidence that this action was a result of a request by the Company is inferential. The act applied only to the Company and it is most unlikely that the initiative for such action would have come from any other source.

The responsibility for making investments was carried out by the Executive Committee. Working within the charter provisions and the general legislation noted above, the main objective of the Committee was to invest the Company's funds so as to secure the maximum return consistent with preservation of principal. This objective may have been modified during the Civil War years by considerations of patriotism, and may also have been influenced to some extent by pressure to purchase State of Wisconsin bonds.

As is shown in Table III-2 next to premium notes mortgage loans constituted the most important investment outlet for the Company's funds during the period under consideration. This account grew steadily from the original $2,200, and by the end of 1868 was in excess of $1.5 million. There are no available data on the division of these loans as between urban and farm property, but the Executive Committee minutes covering the period indicate that the bulk of the mortgage loans, possibly in excess of 75 per cent, were made on the security of urban real estate.

The predominance of city loans can best be explained on grounds of convenience. Other considerations being equal, it was much easier to inspect and evaluate a given number of properties within a city or town than it would have been to examine the same number of properties in the country. Moreover, it was probably easier to negotiate with business and professional men who were more familiar with financial transactions than the average farmer.

After 1863, as already noted, the Company was permitted to make mortgage loans on property outside Wisconsin, but in fact very few loans were made outside the Milwaukee area. The reasons were twofold: good loan applications in this area were apparently sufficient to absorb the available funds; loans outside the area posed the problem of inspection of the property. On March 14, 1864, for example, action on a loan for $1,500 on 240 acres in Sauk County, Wisconsin, was postponed until "the secretary could correspond with our trustee at Portage, Mr. Adler, with regard to the value of the security." While this particular loan was not made, the Company did increase its lending activity outside the Milwaukee area in the next few years.

Until 1867, however, the Company confined its mortgage loan activity to Wisconsin. This policy was followed despite mounting loan applications from persons residing outside the state. Formal consideration of this policy came up before the Executive Committee on December 27, 1866, when Secretary Kellogg, in order to establish a basic policy de-

TABLE III-2

Northwestern Mutual: Distribution of Assets, 1859–1868

Year	Mortgage Loans	U. S. Gov't. Bonds	State & Muni- cipal Bonds	Premium Notes	Bills Receiv- able	Real Estate	Cash	Other	Total Admitted Assets
				(In thousands of dollars)					
1859[a]				$4.8			$3.6	$0.9	$9.3
				15.8	$1.4		7.8	0.5	25.5
1860[a]				15.8	1.4		7.8	0.5	25.5
1861[a]	$3.2			31.4	3.7		16.1	2.6	57.0
1862[a]	21.2	$4.2		44.2	11.1		22.2	3.9	106.8
1863[a]	49.5	9.2		51.8	19.8		27.6	4.4	162.3
1864[a]	95.6	25.0		81.4	31.6	$6.5	27.1	8.4	275.6
1865[b]	234.9	53.1	$31.5	332.7	62.2	14.9	62.2	114.9	906.4
1866[c]	504.6	97.7	37.0	684.5	102.5	45.0	107.1	170.4	1,748.8
1867[c]	942.2	97.7	32.0	1,165.9	168.1	45.0	194.0	481.3	3,126.2
1868[c]	1,584.4	123.7	1.0	1,971.5	17.4	128.9	70.5	858.0	4,755.4

[a] For year ending May 31.
[b] For nineteen months ending December 31, 1865.
[c] For year ending December 31.

SOURCE: Appendix F, Table 5 and Company records.

cision, brought before the Committee an application for a loan on property located in the interior of Minnesota. The Committee decided that "for the present . . . application for loans upon property outside the state" be declined, but a month later it reversed this decision. On January 28, 1867, two loans on property outside the state were approved: one for $5,000 in Indianapolis and a second for $3,000 on a block of stores in Dubuque, Iowa. While most loans continued to be made on property in Wisconsin, the Company gradually expanded its mortgage loan activity to other states, largely on urban property in such centers as Indianapolis, Dubuque, Chicago, and St. Paul.

With the geographic expansion of its loan business, the Company was forced to develop procedures for the inspection of property which could not conveniently be examined by the members of the Executive Committee.[5] This system, as it had evolved by the end of 1868, had the following characteristics. All applications for loans had to be made out on blank forms furnished by the Company giving the amount of the loan desired, the term of the loan, and the proposed rate of interest. A full legal description of the property offered as security was required. Appraisal of the value of the property by two or more responsible parties was necessary,

accompanied by testimonials as to the responsibility of the applicant and his credit rating. If a trustee of the Company lived in the vicinity, his approval of the loan was also required. Apparently, however, the Company began to depend more and more upon its insurance agents for suggestions and recommendations regarding loans. This reliance upon agents is understandable, for by this time the Company had salesmen located in the principal marketing areas throughout the United States.

The use of the Company's agents as finders or solicitors for loans is especially interesting because of a controversy which later arose within management over this practice. Obviously this role gave the agents an additional selling point in approaching prospective customers. It could easily lead to abuse if an agent were to make his recommendation for a loan contingent upon the applicant's purchase of an insurance policy. To be sure, the loan still had to pass the quite rigorous inspection of the Executive Committee, and there is no evidence to prove that the loans accepted through these channels were of poorer quality than those acquired by other means.

There was a danger, however, that sales of insurance policies would become more important in the recommendation of loans than the quality of the loan property itself. The management was not unaware of these dangers. As Kellogg pointed out, "Agents were not permitted to charge any commission upon the loan, and if it was suspected that anyone would get a commission, such suspicion would cause a declination of the loan." He went on to say: "Agents were carefully instructed to encourage and send in only such applications that if accepted and completed they would be proud to point to as the kind of loans made by the Company." [6]

Throughout 1861–1863 the interest charged on mortgage loans was generally maintained at the customary 10 per cent, although there were occasional exceptions when 8 per cent was charged. The terms of the loans ranged from two to five years, with the most common period being three years; interest was due, typically, on a semi-annual basis. Beginning in the second half of 1863 general interest rates began to decline, and during 1864 and 1865 most loans were made at 7 per cent. Apparently interest rates moved up during the first part of 1866, for at an Executive Committee meeting held on April 12, 1866, a motion was introduced to make all future mortgage loans at an interest rate of 8 per cent, payable semi-annually. Action was postponed on this motion until a week later, when on April 19 the motion was resubmitted. An amendment was suggested that the rate be made 9 per cent, but after some discussion the Committee voted 8 per cent as the minimum rate of interest, both for new loans and for renewals of old loans. This rate was maintained without exception to the end of 1868.

The Bond Portfolio

Because no record has been preserved of the bond portfolio during all of this period, it is difficult to establish any clear pattern of investment policy in respect to the Company's bond purchases for the years between 1862 and 1868. An examination of the available data gives the impression that the early purchases were made because of a desire to aid in the financing of the war. An entry in the minutes of the Executive Committee for February 21, 1862, notes that a resolution was passed to the effect that "further loans on real estate be suspended for the present until further action of the Committee for the purpose of accumulating a sum to invest in United States stocks or State bonds." By April 19, 1862, sufficient funds had been accumulated to authorize an investment of $4,000 in United States government "seven-thirty" stocks, so called because they bore an interest of 7.3 per cent. One year later the president was instructed to "invest all funds subject to loan in government 'five-twenties' until otherwise ordered."* Under this directive the government bond account was increased to slightly over $9,000 by June 1, 1863. With interest on mortgage loans

* The "five-twenties" were so named because they were subject to call in five years and redeemable at the end of twenty years. They bore an interest rate of 6 per cent. The first issue of "seven-thirties" ran only three years from the date of issue in 1861. See Davis R. Dewey, *Financial History of the United States*, 306.

TABLE III-3

Selected Life Companies: Gross Earning Rate on Total Assets, 1860–1868
Beginning Date of Operations Shown in ( )

Year	Northwestern Mutual (1859)	Rank	Mutual Life of N. Y. (1843)	Conn. Mutual (1846)	Equitable of N. Y. (1859)	Mass. Mutual (1851)	Mutual Benefit (1845)	National Life Vt. (1850)	New York Life (1845)
1860	—%	—	6.8%	6.9%	0.7%	2.1%	6.1%	5.6%	5.0%
1861	—	—	5.7	7.2	1.1	3.5	5.8	2.9	4.6
1862	5.1	(7)	7.7	7.0	9.2	4.1	6.5	8.6	8.2
1863	7.0	(8)	9.7	12.0	7.8	7.6	7.5	7.8	7.2
1864	8.1	(5)	10.7	11.9	6.7	5.1	7.1	9.2	8.7
1865	8.6	(1)	3.6	4.9	6.4	3.3	5.6	4.7	5.4
1866	6.7	(5)	8.0	8.0	6.3	9.4	7.0	9.1	5.6
1867	4.6	(8)	7.5	6.6	5.6	6.0	6.6	7.6	8.0
1868	5.5	(7)	3.4	7.0	6.6	6.8	6.7	8.6	8.0
Average rate (1862-68)	6.5	(7)	7.2	8.2	6.9	6.0	6.7	8.0	7.3

NOTE: Rates are calculated by dividing interest earnings, including net accrued interest, by the mean market values of assets for each year.

SOURCE: Lester W. Zartman, *The Investments of Life Insurance Companies:* (New York) Henry Holt and Co., 1906, 74-75.

still at 10 per cent, the purchase of these securities must have been made at some loss in interest earnings. It is doubtful if the "seven-thirties" or "five-twenties" sold below par during 1862 and 1863—indeed, as of July 1, 1863, the "five-twenties" were being quoted at 107¾.[7]

Between June 1, 1863, and December 31, 1865, the government bond account was expanded to $26,000. In view of the reduced rate on mortgage loans to about 7 per cent, government securities may have been attractive because of their yield during this period. It is quite possible, for example, that the management took advantage of an offer by the government, which ended about July 1, 1864, to purchase a new series of "five-twenty" bonds at par, which would have yielded 6 per cent.[8] This was less true, however, of later purchases: $5,000 of the new issue of "seven-thirties" in April 1865 (at a time when it was reported that these securities were in "heavy demand")[9] and $10,000 in "five-twenties" in September of the same year when these securities were being quoted between 107¼ to 108¼.[10] On December 15, 1865, the president was instructed to purchase $15,000 worth of 6 per cent United States government compound interest notes at a price which would "yield a 7 per cent return," i.e., at about 85.7.

The end of the war brought a management re-examination of investment policies. On January 15, 1866, the Executive Committee engaged in an "extended discussion" of the relative merits of mortgage loans compared with government securities. Unfortunately no statement of policy was recorded, but purchases were made sufficient to bring the bond account up to $97,700 by the end of 1866, where it remained until the end of 1867.

Interest in government bonds was renewed during 1868 in response to legislative action by various states where Northwestern was doing business. A number of these states passed laws which required life companies, selling insurance within their borders, to maintain a portion of their assets in the form of United States government bonds or other securities. As an accommodation the Wisconsin Legislature in 1866 set up an arrangement whereby Wisconsin-chartered life companies could deposit securities with the state treasurer, who would issue certificates of deposit to the officials of those states which required such deposits as a condition of doing business.[11]

Wisconsin state bonds occupied a relatively small part of the Company's total investments between 1864 and 1868. These bonds, bearing an interest rate of 7 per cent, had been issued in 1861 to raise money to pay and equip state troops for service in the Civil War. While it was understood that the federal government would reimburse the state for the expenditures involved, the bonds were sold in competition with other war issues, and some difficulty was experienced in their marketing.[12]

The Company's first purchase of Wisconsin bonds was made in February 1864 under instructions not to buy them at a price exceeding their par value. By June 1 of that year the total holding was $26,725. In February 1865 the president was instructed to make additional purchases at the best terms that could be secured "not to exceed 95." Two months later, on April 20, further purchases were authorized with the understanding that the securities could be purchased at prices ranging between 84¼ and 84½. At these prices the bonds were yielding a rate of interest which was quite attractive; nevertheless, as is shown in Table III-2 the account was reduced $5,000 during 1866 to $32,000 where it remained until the end of 1867. During 1868 the holding was further cut to $1,000.*

A comparison of Northwestern's earning record with those of a selected group of life companies for the period 1860–1868 is shown in Table III-3. While this record hardly substantiated the Company's advertising claims regarding the great investment advantages it enjoyed by virtue of its middle-western location, it nevertheless indicates a highly creditable performance. Northwestern's average rate of return of 6.5 per cent compares not unfavorably with the 6.9 per cent earned by Equitable of New York, which began operations in 1859.

Expanding the Home Office Operation

The Company's increasing amount of business was reflected in changes in the size and organization of the Home Office. Operations had begun in 1859 in a room rented from Hiram Wilson in a building located at the corner of Broadway and Wisconsin Avenue in Milwaukee. By 1862 these quarters had become inadequate, and arrangements were made to rent some rooms in the Iron Block located on Wisconsin Avenue. Within three years the opera-

_____

* In part this action may have been a wish to substitute United States government bonds for state bonds in the company's deposits at Madison. Wisconsin state bonds would not have the same acceptability for this purpose as the Federal securities.

tions had outgrown these quarters, and in 1865 the Company purchased a small building at 416 Broadway, formerly Main Street. During 1867 the problem of adequate space was again raised. After a considerable discussion on the part of the Executive Committee and the Board of Trustees, plans were made to construct a new building on the corner of Broadway and Wisconsin Avenue. It was hoped that the Company would be able to move into the new building some time toward the end of 1868 or early 1869. Complications with the architect and labor trouble encountered in the construction of the building delayed the move until early in 1870.

Meanwhile, there had been an expansion in the Home Office force. For the first year and a half of operations, Secretary Kellogg was the only full-time employee, and it was not until 1861 that he was given a helper. By 1867, the staff consisted of a cashier, bookkeeper, report clerk, policy clerk, six general clerks, and a full-time medical examiner. By 1867 the highly important office of actuary was also created, and Edward Ilsley, cashier since 1864 and father of Executive Committeeman C. F. Ilsley, was appointed to this post. Not trained as an actuary, his duties apparently were to work out dividends and other actuarial calculations under the

First Milwaukee office—1859 to 1862
S.W. corner, Main (now Broadway) and Wisconsin Streets

procedures established by Elizur Wright. The following year the office of assistant secretary was created and General Augustus Gaylord, Adjutant General of Wisconsin during the Civil War, was appointed to this position. Gaylord found so much work that he requested, and was granted, permission to appoint Major James M. Lynch, his former assistant in the Adjutant General's office, as his helper.

The expanding business and increasing responsibility of the officers was reflected in the salary scales over this period. Daggett, who had worked without pay for the first year and a half of the Company's operations in Milwaukee, received $500 in 1861. A bonus granted at the end of the year made his salary $1,000 for 1862. The following year he received $1,200, $2,000 during each of the succeeding two years, $2,500 in 1866, $3,500 in 1867, and $5,000 in 1868. Kellogg's salary had also been increased during this period. He had started out at $600 in 1859, and this amount was raised gradually until he too was receiving $5,000 in 1868. The total payroll for the year 1868 is shown in Table III-4. Aside from the opening few years, however, Home Office expenses in this period were consistently below 4 per cent of its total income.

TABLE III-4

Northwestern Mutual: Employees' Salaries, January, 1868

Samuel S. Daggett, President	$5,000
A. W. Kellogg, Secretary	5,000
Heber Smith, Agency Superintendent	5,000
Lewis McKnight, Medical Examiner	3,000
Dr. E. B. Wolcott, Consulting Physician	500
Edward Ilsley, Actuary	4,000
E. C. Jennings, Cashier	2,000
A. S. Willey, Bookkeeper	1,700
Clerks:	
L. Schunghardt	1,700
W. H. Farnham	1,700
George Austin	1,500
S. C. White	1,500
George H. Roundtree	1,500
J. P. Peck	1,200
George Young	1,000
C. D. Skinner	1,000
Pat Geraghty	600
	$37,900

SOURCE: Company records.

Benefits to the Policyholders

One yardstick that can be used to measure the performance of a life insurance management is to compare the total income received from policyholders with the benefits the company has been able to provide its insureds. Whether the ratio will be relatively high or low will depend essentially on how the organization handles its selection of risks, its costs of operation, and its investments.

As already indicated, the Northwestern management had reason to believe that its risk selection was not only better than the "expected" rate, but was superior to the general experience of the industry. As was also shown earlier, selling and promotional expenses and Home Office costs had been kept at moderate levels for an organization that was just getting under way, while the Company's investment record compared favorably with that achieved by other companies.

Success in handling these elements in the conduct of the business was reflected in Northwestern's ability to meet its obligations and add to its assets. In terms of being able to pay death claims, the Company had indeed progressed far from the point where claims of $3,500 had threatened its existence. As is shown in Table III-5, the total amount paid out during this period in satisfaction of death claims of its members was $772,300, equal to slightly under 12 per cent of its gross income. This amount, while testifying to the ability of the Company adequately to meet the basic requisite of the business, represented only a very modest outlay when measured against the total amount of Northwestern's insurance in force. As a percentage of the average amount of insurance in force, the amount of death claims paid at no time during the decade exceeded 1 per cent, and, except for the nineteen months ending on December 31, 1865, was never in excess of 0.76 per cent.

Although there had been some difficulty, as has been shown, in determining the amount of dividends to be paid policyholders, the Company's record in this respect was favorable. Dividends equal to $353,600 had been credited to the accounts of Company members, an amount equal to 5.4 per cent of total Company income for the period. Although dividends, both in gross magnitude and taken as a percentage of average insurance in force, were not, during the decade, on a level with those of later periods, they were nearly one-half the total amount paid to beneficiaries.

The entire life insurance industry during these years was notably illiberal in granting any reim-

TABLE III-5

**Northwestern Mutual: Total Income and Its Application to Policyholder Benefits,
1859–1868**

YEAR	GROSS INCOME (Thousands of dollars)	DEATH CLAIMS (Thousands of dollars)	(Percent of Gross Income)	DIVIDENDS (Thousands of dollars)	(Percent of Gross Income)	SURRENDERS (Thousands of dollars)	(Percent of Gross Income)	TOTAL (Thousands of dollars)	(Percent of Gross Income)
1859 [a]	$13.0	—	—	—	—	—	—	—	—
1860 [a]	26.3	$3.5	13.3	—	—	—	—	$3.5	13.3
1861 [a]	45.8	6.5	14.2	—	—	—	—	6.5	14.2
1862 [a]	71.7	6.8	9.5	—	—	$0.2	0.3	7.0	9.8
1863 [a]	103.5	19.2	18.6	—	—	4.6	4.4	23.8	23.0
1864 [a]	211.6	25.5	12.0	$17.4	8.2	5.8	2.7	48.7	23.0
1865 [a]	462.4	55.6	12.0	22.0	4.8	9.1	2.0	86.7	18.7
1865 [b]	375.9	40.6	10.8	0.2	0.1	5.1	1.4	45.9	12.2
1866 [c]	1,073.1	107.5	10.0	0.4	0.0*	20.8	2.1	128.7	12.0
1867 [c]	1,693.7	180.7	10.6	98.9	5.8	56.4	3.3	336.0	19.9
1868 [c]	2,417.2	326.4	13.5	214.7	8.9	88.6	3.8	629.7	26.0
	$6,494.2	$772.3	11.9	$353.6	5.4	$190.6	2.9	$1,316.5	20.2

NOTES: [a] For year ending June 1.
[b] For seven months, June 1, through Dec. 31, 1865.
[c] For year ending Dec. 31.

SOURCE: Appendix F, Table 2.
* For amounts equal to less than 0.05 per cent.

bursement to those members who were forced, for one reason or another, to lapse or surrender their policies. Northwestern Mutual, while sharing in this general characteristic, nevertheless did provide policies valued at $190,600 to policyholders who surrendered their contracts. The surrender rate, as is shown in Table III-5, never exceeded 4.4 per cent of total income; measured by average insurance in force the ratio ranged between 0.01 per cent and 0.2 per cent.

At the same time the Company was paying out or crediting benefits in various forms to policyholders, it added approximately $4.76 million to its total assets.

Interestingly enough, these policyholder benefits, both direct and indirect, totaled about $6.1 million, over 100 per cent of premiums received by the Company during the period.* This was a creditable record, especially during the formative years of a life company. Insofar as the standards of selection were preserved or improved, costs were kept within moderate bounds, and the rate of interest maintained on an expanding amount of investment funds, the man-

* For reasons that are given in Chapter Five, no attempt is made at this point to compare Northwestern's policyholder benefits with those of other life companies.

agement, judged by this yardstick, could expect to do even better in the future.

The Results of Ten Years of Operation

Whatever may have been the expectations of the group that brought the Mutual Life Insurance Company of Wisconsin to Milwaukee, the actual results after ten years of operations must have exceeded their most optimistic calculations. In the annual report to the policyholders covering the year 1868, the Executive Committee stated that General Johnston, during the time he was promoting the Company, "was constantly proclaiming that we might in a few years have a company in Wisconsin equal to the one he had left [Mutual Life of New York] for which people regarded him as an enthusiast or a monomaniac." The Committee went on to point with pride to the fact that "at the end of ten years we find the assets equal to the predictions of its founder and its membership nearly three times as great. And it has issued during the ten years more policies (and has a larger proportion of them in force we believe) than any other company in the

Home Office—1862 to 1865
S.E. corner, Water and Wisconsin Streets

country issued during the first twenty-three years of its existence ending with January, 1866." *

In terms of comparative rates of growth during the first decade of operations, the performance of Northwestern Mutual was even more impressive than the claims made by the management. Table

III-6 shows the growth of the Company compared with a selected group of life companies during the last seven of their first ten years of operations.* Of these companies, Northwestern showed the second highest rate of growth next to Equitable of New York (in the amount of insurance in force and the number of policies), and was first in the percentage increase in the value of assets. These results, however, are to some extent mis-

---

* At the end of 1868 Northwestern's assets were $4.25 million, and total policies outstanding numbered 27,887. At the end of 1857, the year that General Johnston first started to promote the new company, the assets of Mutual Life of New York were $4.48 million and it had 10,390 policies outstanding. See *Insurance Year Book,* 1910, 212–213.

---

* The third year was chosen as the base year to avoid using distorted, not to say astronomical, rates of growth.

TABLE III-6

Selected Life Companies: Indices of Comparative Rates of Growth Figures for Tenth Year of Operation as a Percentage of Figures for Third Year of Operation

COMPANY	BEGINNING DATE OF OPERATIONS	INSURANCE IN FORCE	NUMBER OF POLICIES	ASSETS
Mutual Life of New York	1843	360%	361%	955%
New England Mutual	1843	210	203	450
New York Life	1845	365	270	—
Connecticut Mutual	1846	—	250	1,225
Mutual Benefit	1845	129	122	446
Northwestern Mutual	1858	2,520	2,200	5,880
Equitable Assurance	1859	2,830	2,300	3,700
Metropolitan Life	1867	350	492	360

SOURCE: *Insurance Year Book*, New York: Spectator Publishing Co., 1910.

leading. It is no accident that the two companies that started operations in the late 1850's grew much more rapidly than those which began during the 1840's; life insurance grew slowly during the two decades ending 1860. In 1850 fourteen companies reported to the New York insurance authorities some $92 million insurance in force and assets of around $5 million. Ten years later seventeen companies reporting to the same authorities showed an aggregate amount of insurance in force of $163 million and assets of $24.2 million. At the end of 1870 seventy-one

companies reporting in New York listed an aggregate amount in insurance in force of around $2 billion and assets in excess of $269 million, a spectacular upsurge.

A somewhat clearer picture of Northwestern's comparative growth is shown in Table III-7, covering the period 1861–1868. In terms of percentage growth Northwestern was first among the companies compared in respect to the number of policies and amount of assets and second to Equitable in insurance in force. Even in terms of absolute

TABLE III-7

Selected Life Companies: Comparative Growth, 1861–1868

YEARS	NUMBER OF POLICIES (In thousands) 1861	1868	PERCENTAGE INCREASE	INSURANCE IN FORCE (In millions) 1861	1868	PERCENTAGE INCREASE	ASSETS (In millions) 1861	1868	PERCENTAGE INCREASE
Northwestern	1.25	27.89	2520%	$2.02	$50.04	2520%	$.085	$4.76	5600%
Equitable	1.19	27.67	2330	3.67	112.56	3050	.211	7.72	3650
Mutual Life	12.09	60.97	495	38.19	199.82	522	8.06	31.02	385
N. E. Mutual	4.88	21.29	435	15.42	66.06	430	2.06	7.21	350
New York Life	5.13	28.34	550	16.41	86.73	529	2.11	11.00	520
Conn. Mutual	10.46	50.47	482	—	—	—	3.89	18.15	465
Mutual Benefit	7.03	34.32	487	23.48	123.50	527	4.11	16.50	402
National Life	1.22	2.50	210	1.97	4.45	226	.29	.78	270

SOURCE: *Insurance Year Book*, 1910.

gains the Company showed up well in comparison with all but Mutual Life and Connecticut Mutual on the number of policies in force. As far as total insurance in force and assets were concerned, however, Northwestern Mutual was clearly outdistanced by the Eastern companies, with the exception of National Life of Vermont. While this situation was recognized by members of the Executive Committee, they were not disturbed. In the annual report for 1868 it was pointed out that "the Company's accumulations would have been still greater, no doubt, but from the very necessity of its location its business has not been sought among the accumulated wealth of the older commercial centers, but among the hardy bone and sinew of the nation. Thus though its policies are smaller, its basis is broader and its foundation and superstructure more stable and safe."

Credit for the accomplishment of the Company should go largely to the Executive Committee, for this Committee was responsible for the management policies developed during the decade ending 1868. To be sure, the Executive Committee was acting for the Board of Trustees and its actions were subject to review and reversal by the full Board, but so far as the records of the trustees' meetings indicate, no actions of the Executive Committee were rescinded, although there were some instances when the Committee's actions were subject to discussion and criticism. Indeed, the Executive Committee itself was careful to refer broad policy matters to the Board.

An examination of the minutes of the Executive Committee indicates that its actions were committee actions, and on most points the decisions were unanimous. In those cases where there was divided opinion, there seems to have been no regular division among the members. It is especially interesting that on such occasions Daggett was not infrequently in the minority. Thus while the president acted as executive head of the Company, and should be given credit for leadership, the implied purpose in setting up the Executive Committee, namely of not having the organization dominated by any one individual, seems to have been achieved.

The Executive Committee continued to be made up of representatives of business and financial leaders from Milwaukee, but their compensation was modest. Although initially they were paid $2.50 per meeting, this was finally raised to an annual salary of $500 in January 1868.

The close attention to expense of operation, the reluctance to use policyholders' funds in payment of high officer salaries, and the reluctance on the part of the Home Office to embark upon programs which did not conform to conservative practices were of great significance during these years. This minimization of incurred expenses (combined with low marketing costs, favorable investment earnings, and a careful selection of risks) was to provide a precedent that became characteristic of the Northwestern management in the years to come. Of even greater importance for its policyholders, this characteristic was to be instrumental in providing for life insurance at low net cost. It was this low net cost, in fact, which provided the impetus for the Company's remarkable record of growth and expansion over the following half-century.

President Daggett did not have an opportunity to share in this expansion for on May 22, 1868, after an illness of several months, he died at the age of fifty-six. In a sense, his death marked the end of a chapter in the history of Northwestern Mutual. He had taken office at a time when the Company was scarcely organized, and after ten years he left to his successor an organization which had successfully overcome the difficult problems of developing an effective marketing system and of establishing sound working principles of insurance and investment. Although Daggett cannot personally be credited for the entire success of the Company up to the conclusion of 1868, it would be incorrect to conclude that he was not a positive force in the development of Northwestern Mutual during those years. His re-election each year by the trustees was a tribute to his personal qualities, talents, and experience, and his continuous service on the Executive Committee from 1859 to 1868 meant that he was in a position to facilitate a continuity of management policies. General Johnston had provided the boldness, the imagination, and the idea to create Northwestern; President Daggett's consistency, determination, and reliable judgment carried the Company through its uncertain formative years when survival itself was at stake.

By 1868, however, Northwestern as an institution commanded the respect and attention of the entire life insurance industry. This was demonstrated most concisely in 1871, when the *Insurance Times* paid a signal tribute to Northwestern Mutual's progress.

The Northwestern Mutual Life Insurance Company of Milwaukee is indeed worthy of its foremost place and magnificent opportunities. It is a genuine product of the region in which it is planted. For the last thirteen years it has kept its marvellous pace with the march of the Northwest, strengthening with its strength, and augmenting with its progress. But it has never made one

Home Office—1865 to 1870
416 Main Street (now Broadway)

step in advance unwarranted by its own substantial increase. It has always had an ample basis of solid assets for all its undertakings, and having complied with the stringent laws of Massachusetts and New York, has at once broadened the area of its operations and confirmed its security by competing with the leading life corporations of the East on their own ground.

As to those infallible criteria of safety, vitality and vigor—surplus on hand and increase of policies in force—there is in one or the other, or both, of these respects, no company, young or old, with the exception of the Mutual Life of New York, that is not surpassed by the Northwestern Life of Milwaukee. . . .

It accordingly appears that the great Northwest possesses a life insurance institution that equals for system, safety, profit and excellent management any other in the world.

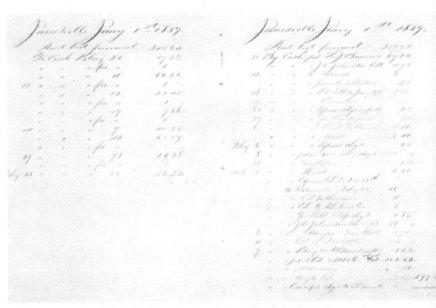

Pages from the Company's first Cash Book—lists income and expenses

CHAPTER FOUR

A Struggle for Control: 1869-1873

THE death of President Daggett was followed by a short chapter in the history of Northwestern Mutual which was marked by an internal struggle for control of the Company's management and policies. The agents, acting largely through their spokesman, Heber Smith, played an increasingly important role. Although the struggle appeared in many forms, it showed itself most vividly in the difference of opinion over investment policies. Despite the contention, however, the overriding impression of these years is the Company's continued vitality. This fact is the more remarkable when considered against the economic background. One of the severest depressions in American history was beginning—a depression that not only checked but temporarily reversed the rapid expansion of life insurance in the United States.

Management: A Contest for Control

As early as April 1868, when it was apparent that President Daggett was unlikely to survive his current illness, some of the trustees moved to challenge the position of Vice President Lester Sexton, the leading candidate to succeed Daggett. Although there was some preliminary maneuvering, the most obvious move was made at the regular quarterly meeting of the Board on April 8 when an interesting amendment to the Company's By-laws was introduced. It read: "In case of the absence or inability of the President to attend to his duties, a president *pro tempore* may be appointed by the Trustees who shall exercise all the powers and duties of the President." Quite obviously this was a maneuver to prevent Sexton from functioning as president during Daggett's illness, but it failed when a majority of the Board was unwilling to accept the amendment. A compromise amendment was passed, however, which provided: "A president *pro tempore* may be appointed by the Trustees who in the case of the absence or inability of the President and the Vice-president to attend their duties shall exercise all powers and duties of the President."

At this point C. F. Ilsley moved the election of James C. Spencer to fill the vacancy on the Board (to which he had been nominated the preceding day). After extensive debate the motion was finally passed. Ilsley then nominated Spencer as a candidate for the newly-created office of president *pro tempore*. Simeon Mills, president of the Bank of Madison, Wisconsin, who had been a trustee since 1857, nominated S. D. Hastings, State Treasurer, to the same office. In the voting which followed, Hastings was elected by the narrow margin of ten votes to nine, and as a result became a leading candidate for the presidency.

Following the death of Daggett, a special meeting of the Board was called for June 17, 1868, to elect his successor. Out of the twenty votes cast, Sexton received ten, Hastings nine, and A. W. Kellogg one. Since no candidate received a majority, it was decided to postpone the election until after the annual election of new trustees to be held the following January.

Sexton and Hastings were both among the group of nine trustees whose terms of office ended in January 1869. Over the preceding years it had become customary for the incumbent board to nominate the outgoing trustees as candidates for re-election. There was nothing to prevent the election of other candidates, but up to this time there had been virtually no opposition to the slate proposed by the Board. The pro-Sexton bloc saw in the situation an opportunity to insure the election of their candidate. With the cooperation of a group of the Company's agents, a drive was made to secure proxy votes from a sufficient number of policyholders to control the election. Under the rules of the Company the agents who attended the annual meetings were permitted to cast the proxy vote of policyholders.

This strategy worked. At the annual election held on January 13, 1869, a total of 7,684 votes were cast (compared with 271 in 1868 and 55 in 1867), and seven of the group nominated by the trustees, including Sexton, received the maximum amount of votes and were re-elected. The other two candidates proposed by the Board, Hastings and John Nazro, were badly defeated; Hastings received only ten votes. Their places on the board were filled by Heber Smith, the Company's superintendent of agencies, and S. S. Merrill of Milwaukee, general manager of the Chicago, Milwaukee, and St. Paul Railroad.

No longer a trustee, Hastings was ineligible as a candidate, and Sexton was chosen president at the meeting of the Board held immediately after the results of the trustees' election were reported. Even more interesting was the choice of Heber Smith as vice president, for this move, coupled with his election as a trustee, gave the agency group a strong representation in the Company's management.*

Lester Sexton was no stranger to the Northwestern Mutual, having been a trustee since 1858, a member of the Executive Committee since 1865, and vice president since 1866; but he had no opportunity to prove himself on his new job, for within two months after he took office, he was stricken with apoplexy and died on March 15, 1869.

---

* A number of trustees were apparently disturbed by the activities of the agents in influencing the election, for at this meeting a resolution was adopted to the effect that the officers of the Company were "not to pay the expenses or any part thereof of any persons attending the annual meetings of this Company, except such as are authorized by the Board of Trustees."

Again the C. F. Ilsley bloc tried to obtain control, this time by advocating the election of A. C. May.[1] At the trustees' meeting in April, those opposed to Ilsley were once again able to block his move, this time by persuading John H. Van Dyke to stand for election. On the first ballot Van Dyke received a majority of the votes, after which his election was made unanimous.

John H. Van Dyke assumed his responsibilities with considerable reluctance. Forty-one years of age, Northwestern's new president had already distinguished himself as a lawyer and business executive. Born in Mercersburg, Pennsylvania, he graduated from Marshall College in 1841. Following graduation, he read law in the Detroit firm of his older brother, Van Dyke and Emmons, where he specialized in maritime law. There he met the younger brother of the senior Emmons and in 1846 the two young men established the law firm of Emmons and Van Dyke in Milwaukee. The firm was highly successful. Through the firm's law practice Van Dyke established a number of business connections to which he devoted an increasing amount of his time.

His reluctance to accept the presidency of Northwestern Mutual seems to have been genuine, especially at the current salary of $5,000. At the meeting of the Board on January 12, 1870, the Salary Committee recommended that the figure be raised first to $6,000, and then to $7,500. Neither amount was sufficient to make it worthwhile for Van Dyke to devote the needed attention to the Company's affairs. When a small minority objected to a higher salary he offered his resignation, whereupon the amount was raised to $10,000 and a unanimous vote was passed to decline his resignation.

Marketing of Insurance

In Heber Smith Northwestern Mutual had a vigorous personality in charge of marketing. Superintendent of agencies, trustee, vice president, and member of the Executive Committee, Smith occupied a strategic position in the management hierarchy. As the officer immediately charged with responsibility of supervising the work of the agency force, however, Smith faced an increasingly formidable task as the market for insurance began to decline. He was understandably sensitive to any suggestions by his colleagues that would make his task more difficult.

In directing the Company's selling efforts Smith was content to operate within the agency structure as it had evolved by the end of 1868. Local agents,

John H. Van Dyke

There is no existing record of the number of agents representing Northwestern during these years. It is quite reasonable to suppose, however, that the agency force was increased, especially with the extension of sales into new areas. It is also possible that the onset of the depression might have caused more individuals to turn to insurance selling.

In any event, no attempt was made to recruit additional agents by changing the basic commission rates in effect in 1868. A move was made in 1872, however, to stimulate sales by introducing a bonus system, based on a sliding scale according to the amount of insurance sold in that year. For amounts over $50,000 but under $75,000, agents were paid an extra fifty cents per $1,000; for sales of $75,000 or more but less than $125,000, the rate was seventy-five cents. Successively larger sales were paid higher rates with the maximum of $2 per $1,000 being reached on amounts of $500,000 or more. Apparently this system was successful as it became an established policy for a number of years.

Aside from eliminating the requirement calling for extra premiums from insureds employed in several occupations, including railroad conductors, the management did little to attract policyholders through changes in policy contracts. Two new policies were introduced, one covering children and the other a non-participating whole life contract, but no special effort was made to push them and neither was popular.

Northwestern's sales literature during the period continued to emphasize the advantages of mutuality, the liberality of its policy contracts, the equitable treatment of its members, and the advantages of its location. With respect to this last point, the Company's sales pamphlet for 1873 stated that opportunities existed in the area for "constant investment of its funds with absolute safety at high rates of interest, as the demand for money is great, property is rapidly enhancing in value, and borrowers can readily afford to pay the high rates of interest demanded." A second advantage of the Company's location had to do with low mortality rates. It was pointed out that "the great bulk of its risks are scattered over the northwest where the climate is remarkably conducive to longevity and that most of its members being residents of smaller towns and villages and farms of the west are less subject to the sweeping destruction of cholera and other epidemics than the larger cities and more thickly populated portions of the country where some of the companies concentrate their business."

There is clear evidence that concern over the financial position of the Company affected the management's attitude toward pushing sales more vigor-

under contract with general agents, continued to make up the majority of the sales force, although the use of traveling agents employed directly by the Company was maintained.

There was a marked expansion of the Company's marketing area during the period. In 1869 Northwestern representatives began selling in North Carolina, Texas, and Utah; the District of Columbia, Florida, and New Jersey were added in 1870; and in 1871 a Canadian general agency was established at Brockville, Ontario. Agents were also appointed in South Dakota and New Mexico in 1873. These new areas added substantially to the Company's sales territory even though agents were withdrawn from Florida in 1871, Mississippi in 1872, and Arkansas in 1873.*

* Although the reasons for these withdrawals were not recorded, it is reasonably certain they occurred because it was believed that the mortality rates in these areas were below Company standards.

ously. Two decisions were especially important—decisions that were made in spite of the possibility they might dampen enthusiasm for Northwestern policies, at least over the short run. The first of these involved a change in the reserve ratio and the passing of dividend payments; the second was to return once more to an "all cash" basis of premium payments.

Change in Interest Assumption and Passing of Dividend

The series of events leading up to the passing of the dividend in 1870 began early in the year when Edward Ilsley, the incumbent actuary, presented his computations upon which the dividends for 1869 were to be based. It was discovered that in making his calculations Ilsley had failed to take into account a large item of prepaid premiums made during January 1869, and as result "had understated the reserves and overstated the surplus." [2] In the discussion which followed, the actuary contended that it was not necessary to consider these prepaid premiums in estimating dividends, an opinion that was seriously challenged by others.

To settle the controversy, President Van Dyke decided to call once more upon the services of Elizur Wright. Wright apparently paid little attention to the immediate issue but used the occasion to make a strong recommendation that the Company immediately change from calculating its reserves on the 4.5 per cent basis, required by New York, to a 4 per cent rate which he had recently been instrumental in introducing as a legal requirement for insurance companies doing business in Massachusetts.

Wright estimated that under the New York regulation the Company's surplus beyond the sum specifically set aside as policy reserves amounted to nearly $1.2 million. Under the application of the Massachusetts rule, it would be only about $700 thousand. He admitted that his suggestion might penalize somewhat those policyholders whose claims came due in a few years but that the great majority would benefit. In vigorous terms Wright urged the merits of his position. It was not enough, he declared, to have a "bare sufficiency" of reserves; the Company's reserve position should be "as impregnable as Gibraltar."

Against this eloquent argument there was the hard fact that to follow Wright's suggestion would reduce the Company's surplus to the point where dividends would have to be cut or postponed entirely for a year or so. Considering the importance

placed on the possibility of high dividends in the Company's promotion of sales, it was not easy for the management to decide to adopt the more conservative reserve ratio.

Yet this was the action taken by the Executive Committee on March 17, 1870, when the legal standard of Massachusetts was adopted, i. e., the Combined Experience or Actuaries' Table of Mortality, with interest at 4 per cent. In order to build up policy reserves quickly to the new standards, it was decided that no dividends would be distributed in 1870. A group of the leading agents of the Company was invited to Milwaukee, and the reasons for the actions were carefully explained. On April 8 policyholders were notified of these decisions.

Some of the competing insurance companies were quick in their attempts to capitalize on the situation. The agent of one rival brought out a circular stating that Northwestern Mutual's surplus had "gone where the woodbine twineth." The "practical results of the 'high interest theory' as regards profits in a western company" reminded him of the poem, "Dim faces of the dead and of the absent (dividend) come floating up before me—floating, fading, and disappearing." It was further alleged that Wright had been called in by the management to "sugarcoat the pill than whom no man in America can do it better." [3]

Agitation over this issue was of short duration. Within a year the Company's reserves had been brought up to required levels and in 1871 a dividend was declared covering both 1869 and 1870. It should also be noted that beginning with the distribution for 1870 all dividends were paid in cash. By 1872 Northwestern was again able to point out its favorable position relative to the industry in respect to dividends.

Emory McClintock Becomes Actuary

One important consequence of the discussion respecting reserve ratios and dividend policy was to bring to a head the growing dissatisfaction with the work of the incumbent actuary. On January 24, 1871, a committee of trustees was appointed to examine the work of the office and to make appropriate recommendations. Emphasizing that the integrity of the incumbent actuary had not been called into question, the committee reported that there was a lack of confidence "in the accuracy of the work of the actuary's department." It recommended the appointment of a trained actuary, a suggestion that was carried out with the appointment, on May 29, 1871, of Emory McClintock.

This appointment added a distinguished member to Northwestern's management. Born in Carlisle, Pennsylvania, in 1840, he had graduated from Columbia College in 1859. For two years after graduation he remained at Columbia as an instructor in mathematics, after which he went to Europe and studied chemistry at Göttingen University in Germany. From 1862 through 1866 McClintock served as Vice Consul of the United States in Bradford, England. While working for a private banking firm in Paris during 1866 and 1867, he became interested in actuarial work and studied the subject intensively. In 1868 he became actuary of the newly formed Asbury Life Insurance Company of New York, which he left to join the Northwestern Mutual staff three years later. For the following eighteen years McClintock served Northwestern with great skill and became recognized as one of the country's leading authorities in the field.

TABLE IV-1

Northwestern Mutual and Industry: Life Insurance in Force and New Business, 1869–1873

	Northwestern		*Industry*	
	New Business	In Force	New Business	In Force
		(In Millions)		
1869	$24.3	$50.0	$614.8	$1836.6
1870	22.4	59.6	587.9	2023.9
1871	16.6	65.2	488.6	2101.5
1872	12.7	62.4	489.9	2114.7
1873	13.2	64.2	465.6	2086.0

Source: Appendix E.

Return to a Cash Premium System

The second management decision that may have affected sales adversely, although it had the full endorsement of the agency force, came in 1872. In that year, after having accepted notes for some nine years as part payment for premiums, the Company reversed its position. More accurately, the decision to go on an "all cash" basis applied only during the first two years the policies were in force. After two full premiums had been paid, premium notes were accepted up to an amount not exceeding one annual premium. This action was a direct result of the passing of the dividends in 1870. Considerable misunderstanding resulted from that action, especially among policyholders who had counted on the dividend to pay off their note's held by the Company. Both management and the agents agreed that it was wise to avoid such misunderstanding in the future, even at the risk of a temporary loss in business.

Sales of Insurance and Insurance in Force

As Table IV-1 reveals, the momentum that had marked the Company's increase in sales of new insurance during the first decade of operations carried through 1869 into 1870. Thereafter sales began to lag, dropping to amounts in 1872 and 1873 that were approximately half the figure for 1869. While the total value of the new policies issued during the period was over $89 million, as a result of cancellations, deaths, lapses, and surrenders, the Company's insurance in force grew only by $5 million.

From Table IV-2 it is clear that selling costs as a percentage of premium income dropped somewhat from 1869 through 1873. This was primarily the result of reduced sales of new policies on which high first-year commissions were paid and which involved medical examinations. These items, combined with lower advertising outlays, more than offset the effect of the introduction and spread of premium taxes on the Company's total marketing costs.

How Northwestern compared with the industry in respect to new sales and insurance in force is also shown in Table IV-1. The comparison suggests that external forces rather than management decisions were the major factor in bringing about the difficulties encountered in maintaining sales. This conclusion is confirmed by the data in Table IV-3, which shows that Northwestern did about as well as the companies selected for comparison in maintaining insurance in force, although it did fall somewhat behind the industry as a whole.

While the Company's comparative record was thus reasonably favorable it did not satisfy a number of the agents and the agency director. They became increasingly impatient with the reluctance of the Executive Committee to stimulate sales by adopting the principle that the purchase of an insurance policy be required for obtaining a mortgage loan. By 1872 both the agents and their leader were in a stronger position to push their point of view as a result of the renewed struggle for management control that broke out again in 1871.

TABLE IV-2

Northwestern Mutual: Premium Income and External Expenses, 1869–1873

YEAR	AGENTS' COMPEN-SATION [a]	MEDICAL EXAMINA-TIONS	ADVER-TISING	TAXES [b]	TOTAL EXTERNAL EXPENSES	PREMIUM INCOME	EXPENSES AS A PERCENT OF PREMIUM INCOME
			(In thousands of dollars)				
1869	$379.0	$25.9	$17.3	$32.8	$455.0	$3,028.3	15.0%
1870	358.8	17.3	14.2	41.6	431.9	3,209.7	13.4
1871	320.4	18.6	18.3	37.2	394.5	3,113.5	12.6
1872	299.5	19.0	11.2	37.5	367.2	2,939.6	12.5
1873	269.4	17.9	8.0	40.9	336.2	2,952.5	11.4
	$1,627.1	$98.7	$69.0	$190.0	$1,984.8	$15,243.6	13.0%

[a] Includes salaries, travel and hotel expenses, and commissions.　SOURCE: Appendix F, Table 1, 3.
[b] Includes license fees, premium taxes, and real estate taxes.

TABLE IV-3

Life Insurance in Force: 1869–1873
(In millions)

YEAR	1869	1870	1871	1872	1873	1873 as a % of 1869
Total Industry	$1,837	$2,024	$2,101	$2,115	$2,086	114%
Mutual Life	216.9	242.0	228.8	264.6	289.5	134%
Connecticut Mutual	177.4	181.3	182.8	181.7	181.8	102%
Mutual Benefit	129.9	130.9	133.1	133.2	131.4	101%
New York Life	102.1	111.3	113.2	118.6	123.7	120%
Aetna	103.7	102.2	101.3	100.6	98.9	95%
New England Mutual	74.9	70.0	67.8	66.0	64.3	86%
Equitable	134.2	144.0	154.3	171.4	184.3	137%
Manhattan	45.6	43.5	42.1	42.3	42.0	92%
Massachusetts Mutual	28.2	32.5	33.3	32.6	32.6	115%
Average for nine Companies	—	—	—	—	—	109%
Northwestern Mutual	59.6	65.2	62.4	64.2	64.7	108%

SOURCE: Insurance Year Book, 1910.

Renewed Struggle for Management Control

The second attempt to take over control of the Northwestern management grew out of the indignation felt by the group of trustees headed by C. F. Ilsley over the defeat of Hastings for president in 1869. They were especially outraged at the part played by the agents in bringing about this defeat and disturbed by the election of Heber Smith as trustee. Their feelings were expressed in a sharply worded resolution proposed to the Board by J. A. Dutcher on January 12, 1870:

RESOLVED, that it is the opinion of the Board that no agent or employee of this Company has a right to use his position for the purpose of defeating any of the regular nominations made, and that any agent or employee using this position for that purpose shall be deemed unworthy of a position in the Company.

This resolution, interestingly enough, was passed without dissenting opinion, but it aroused considerable resentment on the part of the agents. A year later, at a meeting of the trustees held a day before the annual elections, the agents presented a resolution to the Board requesting that the previous resolution be "expunged from the record." In arguing their case the agents stated that they did not "understand it to be the peculiar privilege of the Board to create regular nominations or their duty [as agents] acting for and in behalf of the policyholders of the Company to support such regular nominations, unless in their judgment such support would be productive of the highest interest of said policyholders." It was the agents' opinion that the initial resolution was "conceived by a few members of the board designed to deprive nonresident policyholders of an unquestionable right thereby enabling them the more easily to accomplish their own selfish purposes." They termed the resolution "an insult . . . indicating a want of such confidence in the agents of the Company as they must enjoy on the part of those with whom they labor in order to succeed in their peculiar work."

A motion to adopt the recommendation of the agents to rescind the initial resolution passed twenty-five to five, John Plankinton, Ilsley, Dutcher, Spencer, and Simeon Mills voting in the negative. Moreover, the trustees, in an added effort to appease the agents, asked the latter to appoint a committee to meet with a similar committee from the trustees to nominate candidates for the annual election to be held the next day. But the agency group was not so easily placated; when the results of the election were announced four of the nine "official" candidates nominated for election—Ilsley, Dutcher, Nazro, and George B. Miner—had been defeated.

No longer able to operate within the Company as trustees, Ilsley and his associates decided to carry their case directly to the policyholders. An ill-advised attempt to have a Company clerk secretly compile a mailing list of policyholders was discovered and was influential in causing the Executive Committee to turn down a direct request for such a list. Nevertheless, a statement signed by Ilsley, Dutcher, and Nazro as a committee, and endorsed by Miner, James Bonnell, Hastings, and others, was circulated during December 1871. The main argument propounded was that over the preceding two or three years

> systematic and persistent efforts had been made by the agents-employees of the Company to obtain complete control of the Company's affairs by means of the proxies of absent members and by a meeting regularly organized and engineered by a few to decide who shall or shall not be elected to the board of trustees, and to dictate what measures shall or shall not be adopted by

the board, thus virtually taking the management out of the hands of those ostensibly chosen by yourselves and placing it in an irresponsible body whose personal interests are in a measure antagonistic to the general interests of the Company.

Proxies were enclosed with the circular, which policyholders were urged to sign and return to the committee, to be used at the next annual election.

The action of the Ilsley group started a general campaign that resulted in a considerable interchange of letters and other communications, all bearing on the subject of Company management and control. The controversy attracted the notice of the local press, incited published statements, inspired cartoons, and led to petitions.

At the election held January 31, 1872, however, the Ilsley forces were unable to muster more than a small minority of the votes cast.* As a gesture of protest, Spencer and May, members of the group who had not been up for re-election, handed in their resignations as trustees in identically worded letters stating that "the plan so generally adopted of allowing the agents and employees of the Company to control the elections and its business affairs is unwise and will, unless changed, be disastrous in its results."

On the whole, the election results were not only a triumph for the agency group, but they served to enhance the prestige and power of Heber Smith. His application for an increase in his $6,000 salary, which had been rejected in 1870, was granted in 1871, with a raise of $1,500. Van Dyke had been forced by circumstances to side with the agency group on the immediate issue, but in so doing had built up a strong rival for the top management position in the firm.

Investments and Investment Policies

Northwestern's annual gross incomes for the 1869–1873 period are shown in Chart IV-1. Of the total, amounting to almost $18.4 million, over $15.2 million was derived from premiums, including premium notes of about $1.6 million. The fact that some $3.2 million of the total income was made up of earnings on investments indicates the growing importance of the investment side of the business.

As is also shown, a little less than half the gross

---

* Less than one-third of the Company's policyholders, numbering over 35,000 at the end of 1871, were sufficiently interested to cast their ballots.

income went to pay policyholders and to meet expenses. Thus $9.3 million, or about 50 per cent of gross income, went to expand the Company's assets.

This amount of new funds to invest, in addition to the repayments of existing loans, put an increasing responsibility on the members of Northwestern's Executive Committee. How they moved to allocate these funds within the Company's investment portfolio is shown in Chart IV-2. The most significant change came in the mortgage loan account which made up more than two-thirds of the earning assets in 1873 compared to a proportion of about 50 per cent four years earlier. No breakdown is available for the division of the mortgage account between loans on urban and farm property, but an examination of the loan record indicates that the larger share continued to go into urban loans.

This increase in the proportion of mortgage loans

TABLE IV-4

Northwestern Mutual:
Total Amount at Loan by States, 1872

STATE	AMOUNT (In thousands)
Wisconsin	$2,572
Illinois	970
Indiana	929
Iowa	611
Minnesota	448
Kansas	273
Missouri	208
Kentucky	151
Michigan	111
Ohio	95
Georgia	60
Colorado	38
Nebraska	23
Total	$6,490

SOURCE: Company records.

CHART IV-1

Income, Expenditures, and Net Available for Investment: Northwestern, 1869–1873

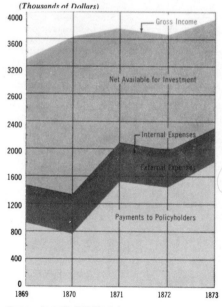

(Thousands of Dollars)

SOURCE: Appendix F, Tables 1-4.

came largely at the expense of premium notes. While the latter account (including a small amount of bills receivable) grew in absolute terms, the rate was noticeably slowed down after 1871 largely because of the decision to go on a "cash" basis in 1872. Still the second most important account, premium notes made up only about one-third of the total earning assets at the end of 1873.

The cash accounts were increased approximately four-fold chiefly because of unsettled economic conditions.* Bank deposits earned a small interest return amounting to around 3 per cent.†

Compared with the Civil War period the bond account was quite unimportant and, except for $1,000 of state bonds which were sold in 1869, was made up entirely of United States Government obligations. They were held, apparently, not because of the interest return but because they could be used

* The Company paid out the following amounts of cash for surrendered policies: 1870, $39,114; 1871, $89,072; 1872, $133,939; 1873, $170,360.
† Evidence of the interest rate on bank deposits is contained in the letter of May 31, 1873, from C. D. Nash, as president of the Milwaukee Bank, to Van Dyke offering to allow the Company interest of 3 per cent per annum on "such amount as your balance exceeds $10,000 receipting all exchange you might desire to deposit at par and furnishing without charge all you may need." He went on to state that this seemed to be about as well as he could presently propose to do "when you take into consideration that we cannot safely use this balance as we can deposits generally being liable to be drawn upon for very large amounts at any time which necessitates keeping the funds mostly in readiness for call."

TABLE IV-5

Selected Life Companies: Gross Earning Rate on Total Assets, 1869–1873

YEAR	NORTHWESTERN	RANK	MUTUAL of N.Y.	CONN. MUTUAL	EQUITABLE of N.Y.	MASS. MUTUAL	MUTUAL BENEFIT	NATIONAL LIFE VT.	NEW YORK LIFE
1869	6.4%	(6)	7.1%	7.3%	6.1%	7.8%	6.8%	9.7%	6.3%
1870	8.1	(1)	6.0	5.5	6.1	5.6	6.3	6.3	4.4
1871	7.8	(2)	6.2	7.0	6.1	7.1	6.8	8.2	7.2
1872	7.9	(1)	6.8	6.3	6.2	6.6	6.2	6.6	6.8
1873	8.3	(2)	6.7	6.8	6.6	6.1	6.9	8.5	6.9
Average	7.7	(2)	6.6	6.5	6.2	6.6	6.6	7.9	6.3

NOTE: Earnings include accrued interest.

SOURCE: Lester W. Zartman, *The Investments of Life Insurance Companies*, 74-75.

as a deposit which would enable the Company to do business in various states. In July 1871, for example, $100,000 worth of government bonds were withdrawn from Wisconsin (and mortgages substituted) and deposited in Canada in order to comply with the requirements for doing business in that country.

In expanding into mortgage loans the management took advantage of the relatively high rate of earnings this type of investment was returning. With the exception of 1869, when a number of loans were made at 8 and 9 per cent, the bulk of the Company's mortgage loans carried a 10 per cent interest rate during this period. There appeared to be no lack of acceptable loan applications at this rate of interest. In expanding its mortgage holdings, Northwestern began to lend in a much wider geographic area. How far this market had grown by 1872 is shown in Table IV-4.

As indicated in Table IV-5, the management was able to make good on the claim that the Company was located in an area where it could obtain a relatively high interest return on investments. Compared with seven leading companies, it moved in respect to interest earnings from sixth position in 1869 to first place in two of the succeeding four years and was second during each of the other two.

The Struggle over Investment Policy

Although the Company's insurance agents continued to solicit loan applications throughout this period, an increasing number of such requests were made directly to the Home Office. During the earlier part of the period the Committee considered

CHART IV-2

Distribution of Admitted Assets: Northwestern, 1869–1873

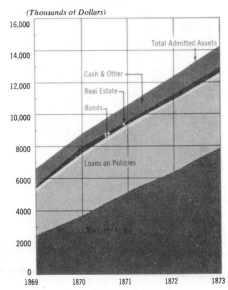

SOURCE: Appendix F, Table 5.

all such applications on a basis of merit, with little, if any, regard paid to whether or not loan applicants were policyholders in the Company.

Home Office—1870 to 1886
N.W. corner, Broadway and Wisconsin Streets

In view of the Company's investment record the majority of the members of the Committee were understandably reluctant to accept any restrictions on their lending operations. At the same time they were fully aware of the problem of stimulating sales, especially after 1870. For this reason they gave serious consideration to two proposals made by the agents early in 1871. The first was that loans be made in the various states in proportion to the sales of insurance in the states; the second, that more consideration be given to a linking of individual loans with the sale of Northwestern policies.

In general the policy followed was to link loans with the purchase of insurance as long as this procedure did not affect the quality of the loan or seriously reduce the interest rate. A number of such loans were made during the latter part of 1871.* The trustees must have been uneasy about this trend, however, for in January 1872 and January 1873 resolutions to tie sales even closer with investment policy were tabled.

This was the situation as of the middle of June 1873 when Heber Smith, who was the spokesman for the agents' position, wrote the trustees that there was a sharp difference of opinion between himself and the rest of the Executive Committee over loan policies. Smith's memorandum was presented at the July 9, 1873, meeting of the Executive Committee and, after a protracted discussion, a resolution favoring Smith's position was rejected. At a full meeting of the Board, held January 27, 1874, Smith again took up the question only to have the Board uphold the Executive Committee's decision.

The failure to obtain the cooperation of the incumbent board, although irritating, did not exhaust the alternatives available to Smith. Having been successful in meeting the earlier challenge of the Ilsley group, Smith and his supporters, armed with proxies, decided to take the issue into the annual election, a decision no doubt colored by Smith's own ambition to become president. At the election on January 28, 1874, of the 12,407 votes cast, John H. Van Dyke received only 194. Having failed of re-election as a trustee, Van Dyke was automatically disqualified to continue as president; Smith, on the other hand, was now in the strongest possible position, in relation to both management and policy decisions.

---

* One such example, which clearly by-passed the agents, was a four-year loan of $50,000 authorized in September for the Wisconsin Leather Company, bearing interest of 10 per cent but with the proviso that the rate would be reduced to 8 per cent if the partners would "furnish two dollars of life insurance for each dollar of the loan upon the all-cash annual plan and free from first commissions."

Summary of J. H. Van Dyke's Administration

During his administration President Van Dyke had attempted to reconcile the differences which rose within the organization without compromising the basically conservative management policies developed during the preceding ten years of the Company's history. This was no easy task, as he came into office at a time when the sales of life insurance were declining and when relations between the agents and a number of trustees were severely strained. He lent his support to moves designed to make the agents feel more strongly that they were an important part of the organization. He went along with the field force in their recommendation that a more experienced actuary be hired; he was a prime mover in the adoption of a more conservative interest rate assumption which strengthened the financial position of the Company, even at the risk of discouraging immediate sales. The same conservatism carried over to the investment side of the business when he stood with the majority of the Executive Committee (and trustees) against proposals which would link the sales of life insurance to investments.

Van Dyke could take pride in the performance of the Company during his short term of office. In terms of "benefits," both direct and accrued, Northwestern's policyholders fared noticeably better than they had during the first decade of operations. Death claims and matured endowments of $2.8 million, dividends of over $1.8 million, and surrender values of $1.9 million went directly to policyholders. These sums, added to an expansion in aggregate Company assets of some $9.3 million, brought the total benefits to approximately $15.9 million, an amount nearly 105 per cent of the $15.2 million received in premiums.

To be sure, a part of this favorable showing was to be expected of a life company that had been operating for fifteen rather than ten years. Yet it reflected the management's success in maximizing policyholder benefits by better risk selection, lowered operating costs, and a higher income from investments.

While Van Dyke left an organization that on the whole was financially stronger than when he had assumed office, his successors inherited some unfinished business. The depression of the 1870's was still to run its course, and the issue as to how closely investments were to be tied with insurance sales was not yet resolved.

CHAPTER FIVE

Management Policies in a Depression: 1874-1881

IN this period the struggle for control of management and Company policies was finally resolved in favor of the group which held that investment opportunities should be considered wholly on their individual merit and entirely separate from sales. It was fortunate that the conflict was over. The Company was entering the depth of the depression, and the problems raised in its wake were staggering. The management had to contend with the decline in over-all insurance holdings throughout the industry; it had to meet difficult sales and investment problems produced by the serious economic conditions; it had to implement its policy of divorcing investment from sales; and it had to strengthen its sales agencies at a time when competition was unusually severe. In a sense Northwestern Mutual was being critically tested during these years. That the Company emerged stronger than when it started was a genuine accomplishment.

Henry L. Palmer Is Elected President

Ironically enough, just when Heber Smith, vice president and superintendent of agencies, appeared to reach a pinnacle of influence over Company policy, he was in fact on the verge of defeat. When the trustees met to consider the election of a new president those opposed to Smith, either on the basis of personality or principle, moved to block his selection. These trustees rallied around the figure of Henry L. Palmer, much to Palmer's own surprise. "The position came to me entirely unsolicited and entirely unexpected," he wrote later. "I did not know [until] two hours before the election took place that it was contemplated at all."[1] To forestall any countermove by Smith, however, the supporters of Palmer did not place his name formally in nomination for the presidency, with the result that only two names, those of Smith and J. W. Cattel of Des Moines, Iowa, were submitted. When the votes were counted, Smith received ten, Cattel two, and Palmer eighteen.

There was, of course, much more at stake in the results of the election than the triumph of those who supported Palmer and the defeat of those who backed his principal rival. There was even more at stake than settling the question whether the Company was to be oriented primarily toward investment or marketing. Even though it may not have been entirely clear to the participants at the time, the basic issue involved the concept of trusteeship. More specifically would this concept be violated if, in investing funds entrusted by policyholders to the Company, considerations other than obtaining the highest returns consistent with safety were taken into account? The election results settled this question. The circumstances surrounding the election served to clarify this issue; the result was to settle it in favor of those who advocated the more conservative approach and to establish the principle as a permanent part of the management philosophy over the subsequent history of the organization.

Smith's defeat was complete. He failed to be re-elected vice president, losing out to O. E. Britt, seventeen votes to thirteen; neither was he renamed to the Executive Committee. Moreover, a special committee on lending policies recommended strongly that the Executive Committee be left free to exercise its judgment in making loans. On the specific issue at hand, the Committee was more cautious, but it did question whether a policy of tying mortgage loans to selling life insurance, however desirable from the agents' point of view, might not "lead to trouble in the future." The acceptance of this part of the report without further debate was virtually a mandate to the Executive Committee to continue its current lending practices. Smith was replaced as superintendent of agencies by Matthew Keenan, and on November 23, 1874, Smith resigned from the Board of Trustees. Interestingly enough, although Smith's association with Northwestern was severed, he maintained his policies with the Company.

John H. Van Dyke's official association with the Company was quickly re-established. At the trustees' meeting held on July 8, 1874, he was appointed to serve out the term of N. M. Jones, who had resigned. In October 1874 E. P. Allis resigned from the Executive Committee with the understanding that Van Dyke was to replace him. This request was honored and Van Dyke remained a member of the Executive Committee until January 1880 when he resigned, pleading the pressure of other work. He continued to serve as a trustee until July 1904.

Henry L. Palmer

In selecting Palmer as president, the trustees called upon one of the original group who had transferred the Company from Janesville to Milwaukee some sixteen years before. During the intervening years Palmer had been a trustee, served as the Company's legal counsel, and for a number of years was a member of the Executive Committee.

Henry L. Palmer was born on October 18, 1819, in Mount Pleasant, Pennsylvania, where he received a high school education.* In 1836 Palmer's family moved to Troy, New York, where he studied law and was admitted to the bar. In 1849 he migrated to Milwaukee and continued his legal practice. In ad-

Henry L. Palmer

dition to his professional work, Palmer was active in Wisconsin politics as an ardent Democrat. Although defeated as candidate for governor in 1863, he served as a member of the state assembly in 1853, 1860, 1862, and 1873, and as a member of the state senate in 1867 and 1868. He was elected a county judge of Milwaukee in 1873, holding this office until his election as president of Northwestern Mutual.

Fifty-four years of age at the time he took over his new position, "Judge" Palmer, as he was commonly addressed, brought some twenty-five years legal and legislative experience to his job as president. While not as experienced as his predecessors in financial and business affairs, his selection was clearly made with the view of continuing the Company's already established conservative investment policies. Palmer's abilities as an executive were yet to be tested, but he quickly established a reputation for his grasp of all aspects of the insurance business.

---

* Palmer had no middle name. He had adopted the "L" as a young man out of admiration for a friend whose first name and middle initial were Henry L.

President Palmer completely absorbed himself in his work and expected the same devotion from everyone connected with the Company. His stern and austere manner, especially during the early part of his administration, commanded more respect than affection, although this was tempered by his demonstrated fairness in his dealings with associates and employees.

Palmer was fortunate in having a group of experienced officers. With the exception of O. E. Britt, who was not an active executive, the officers had all either been appointed or had served during Van Dyke's term of office. Emory McClintock became actuary in 1871; Willard Merrill succeeded Augustus Gaylord as secretary in 1873; C. D. Nash's term as treasurer began in 1859. Even Matthew Keenan, the new superintendent of agencies, served with Palmer on Van Dyke's Executive Committee.

Nevertheless, Palmer was clearly stepping into a difficult managerial situation. Relations between the Company and the agents obviously had to be handled tactfully. Moreover, the Company faced extraordinarily difficult external conditions. The American economy was in the midst of a depression that was rivaled only by that of the 1930's in severity. The years 1874–1881 were marked by serious unemployment, falling price levels and interest rates, and a wave of business failures and heavy mortgage foreclosures. For the life insurance companies in the United States, it was a time of contracting sales, lower income, and shrinking investment opportunities. Total insurance in force fell by nearly 20 per cent between 1873 and 1881, and many life companies failed to survive, bringing losses to policyholders.

Marketing Development: Changes in Agency Organization

Matthew Keenan, a trustee since 1871 and a member of the Executive Committee since 1873, faced no easy task in directing the agency force in a declining market. There was no magic formula that could be applied to increase insurance sales during a major depression. Not only was the Company disturbed by economic conditions, but within the corporate structure itself there were divisions, arising out of Heber Smith's departure, that only time could heal. Moreover, in contrast to the Company's previous agency directors, Keenan was without experience as a life insurance agent. A native of Manlius, New York, he and his family moved to Milwaukee in 1837 when he was twelve years old.

As a young man he engaged in flour milling and by 1871 had established a sound reputation as a businessman. Because of the recent experiences with Heber Smith, Palmer and his associates apparently thought that it was important to have a strong personality to head the field force, preferably someone who had no previous connection with the Company's agency organization.

Statistics to indicate how far Northwestern had proceeded in establishing a general agency system prior to 1874 are unavailable. There is little question that Heber Smith had been working in this direction and that the principal responsibility for the operation of the field force was largely in the hands of the Company's state or general agents. On principle Keenan had no criticism of the general agency system, but he was dissatisfied with the performance of a number of the Company's general agents when he took over his new duties. However successful they may have been earlier, Keenan believed they had not responded adequately to the changed marketing conditions which brought more intensive competition. This developed as Northwestern expanded its sales into the eastern markets and eastern companies invaded the West after the Civil War.

Because contracts with general agents ran for periods ranging up to five or more years, it was not feasible to change the personnel overnight; Keenan therefore sought to supplement their work by the employment of more special agents. In reviewing his work in 1881, he observed, "We have succeeded in getting fields from under old state agency contracts and directly under the control of the Company, enabling the management to deal directly with soliciting agents and from these fields we have commenced to receive good results which we expect to see increased in the near future." [2]

Keenan had lost little time in modifying the Company's general agency structure. By 1876 the Company's sales territory was divided into some fifty-five specific areas, including twenty-one general or state agencies and four Canadian provincial agencies. The states of Michigan, Indiana, Ohio, Pennsylvania, New York, Massachusetts, and Virginia were further subdivided into twenty-two district and five local agencies. At the same time there was a sharp increase in the number of special and local agents who were assigned to existing state or district sales territories, but who were responsible directly to the Company. In January 1879 according to a report to the trustees, Northwestern had about six hundred agents in the field, of whom 460 reported directly to the Home Office. This meant that only about 140 local agents were under contract to general or district agents, a marked contrast to what would have been the case under a full-fledged general agency system.

These changes put a heavy responsibility for the operation of the agency organization on the Home Office. Keenan found it necessary, from time to time, to enlist the aid of George H. Roundtree and Thomas W. Buell, of the Home Office staff, in maintaining communications with the field. In 1874 J. S. Gaffney was appointed as "Superintendent of Agencies for the Eastern Department," with headquarters in New York City. Gaffney took care of contracts, personnel problems, and helped in recruiting agents in the Company's sales territory along the east coast. In other areas Keenan either called on certain of the Company's special agents to take care of such matters or handled them directly from Milwaukee.

As might be expected in view of the reorganization of the agency force, much of Keenan's effort was spent in securing and encouraging new men. He was particularly interested in individuals who had been successful with other insurance companies, but was cautious in awarding contracts. In nearly every instance he took the trouble to inquire into the reputation and character of applicants, even to the extent of writing to former employers. A promising candidate was frequently given his choice of territories which were open to local agents under direct contract with the Company, or offered a traveling or special agent's contract in a likely district. If the particular sales territory requested was already allocated, the prospect was referred to the general or district agent in charge. No formal training was given to these agents, but Keenan was of the opinion that every local agent needed the help of a "general or of some competent special [agent] to aid him out of a rut, to break new ground, to give him confidence and to increase his force, and to bring to a point business that had been deferred from month to month." [3] Results, asserted Keenan, would only come with personal solicitation and hard work.

Contracts with Agents

Northwestern, of course, was not alone in its efforts to augment its agency force. In face of the general decline in the demand for life insurance, virtually all of the companies were attempting to expand the number of their sales representatives. According to an editorial observation in 1869, companies were even then paying from 25 to nearly 100 per cent first-year commissions "as a matter of course," and

it was not at all unusual for new companies to pay 50 per cent first-year and no renewals, or 30 per cent first-year and 10 per cent renewals. [4] By 1874 the Connecticut Mutual was paying 30 per cent commissions on first-year premiums, plus four renewals of 10 per cent. New Jersey Mutual, in the same year, paid its New York general agent 65 per cent, which, with salary and expenses, brought the acquisition cost of new business up to 150 per cent of first-year premiums. Thus in spite of the general unemployment which accompanied the depression, there was no diminution in what Stalson has described as "the all but inevitable upward trend of commission schedules from 1868 to 1905." [5]

This trend was reflected in Northwestern's experience after 1874. While rapidly changing personnel and the large number of contracts negotiated directly with the Home Office resulted in minor variations, it is clear that commission rates and other payments to agents were much more liberal than they had been earlier. A general agent's contract signed in May 1875 with Contine, Ingram and Company, was fairly representative. The agency was to sell in New York City and three counties in northern Pennsylvania. The partners were to receive first-year commissions of 25 per cent and 7.5 per cent renewals. Out of these commissions the firm was to pay its own agents, but according to the agreement, "for the purpose of successfully developing and establishing the agency, and to cover the expenses of traveling, advertising, clerk hire, etc.," an additional commission of 15 per cent was allowed on new sales during the first year; 10 per cent during the second; and 5 per cent during the third. The Company also agreed to pay for office accommodations, provided the firm wrote $500,000 worth of new insurance annually.

Typically, contracts with traveling or special agents called for no renewal commissions, except on policies "sent to them for collection," for which they received from 1 per cent to 2.5 per cent of the premiums. These agents were also required to share equally their first-year commissions on any work done jointly with other agents in the territory. The commission rates varied, but there was some tendency both to increase the base rate and to give a bonus for a large volume of sales.

By contrast, contracts between the Home Office and local agents generally provided for commission rates of 20 or 25 per cent on first-year premiums and 5 per cent on renewals, with the proviso that the first-year commissions on any sales secured with the assistance of general or "special" agents should be divided equally. Such contracts ordinarily contained no bonus provisions, although it was not uncommon to insist upon a minimum amount of sales per year. Failure to meet the quota made the contract subject to cancellation on thirty days' notice by the Company.

From time to time, in order to attract the services of unusually promising candidates, the Company also entered into contracts which called for a straight salary. While he felt compelled to increase the number of this type of contract after 1874, Keenan had serious doubts about its effectiveness. As he wrote on one occasion, "The fact is with most agents a *salary* is more demoralizing than whisky, it seems to persuade them to put off until tomorrow what could be accomplished today." [6]

Agents received $1.54 million in commissions during these years, but while these were the most important source of income to the field force, Keenan's policy of encouraging new agents by supplementing commissions with rent and advertising allowances was apparent. Total salaries of $363,000 and expenses of $196,000 were paid by the Company between 1874 and 1882.

Relations with Agents

Northwestern did not rely on high commission rates alone to maintain effective and cordial relations with the agents. The custom of inviting the agents to gather in Milwaukee each January at the time of the annual meeting and election of trustees was continued, and the Company continued to pay the traveling expenses of agents who attended the meetings. Beginning January 1878, and continuing through January 1881, hotel bills as well as traveling expenses were paid. The practice of consulting with the agents on the slate of trustees to be submitted for election at the annual meetings was also maintained. This was done by appointing a committee of trustees to meet with a committee of agents on the selection of names. It is noteworthy that no contested elections took place during the seven-year period ending January 1882.

One important event affecting future Company-agency relations during these years came with the revival of a formal association of agents. In 1868 the agents had drawn up a constitution and by-laws and had elected officers, but for some unknown reason the organization was not continued and the group met only informally. In January 1877 a new constitution and by-laws were adopted and officers again selected. Edward J. Smith, the Company's general agent at Boston, was elected president and

Edwin S. Walker, Northwestern representative in Springfield, Illinois, was elected secretary and treasurer.

Once revived, the Association of Agents continued to operate throughout the Company's history and is unique in the annals of life insurance. From the onset it provided a forum for the discussion of questions of particular interest to the agents, served as the eyes and ears of the Home Office, and offered a facility where the officers of the Company could explain proposed innovations or procedures that might affect the agents and test their reactions. At the first meeting, for example, the association gave careful consideration to a new sales circular that the Company proposed, and suggested a number of modifications; they engaged in an extended discussion of "surrender values, lapsed policies, etc., . . . in which most of the members participated"; and a resolution was passed approving the Company's practice of declining to restore lapsed policies after one year. They also heard from Keenan, who talked "at some length upon the general interests of the Company and upon the work of the agents," as well as from "Mr. Dean, [who] spoke upon the subject of extra compensations to agents and favored the plan," and to "Mr. I. T. Martin, [who] spoke in opposition to extra compensation." [7]

Sales Promotion

The management discouraged agents from engaging in extensive advertising asserting that "men must be personally solicited . . . to secure success." [8] The sales literature which the Home Office provided its agents, however, reflected the changing American social scene. The traditional lengthy discussion of the advantages of taking out protection disappeared. As an 1877 brochure stated: "Life insurance is now so universal in this country, and has proved so beneficial in its results, that it is not necessary to enlarge upon its advantages." More emphasis was put upon the comparative merits of Northwestern. Among the advantages stressed was that it furnished insurance at exact cost; that its policy reserve basis of 4 per cent was the "highest reserve known to American experience"; that its location enabled the Company to invest its funds with absolute safety at high rates of interest; that its ratio of death losses to "mean amount of insurance has been lower than that of any other of the ten largest life companies"; and that its present average dividends "are equaled by those of no company in the country."

Agents were concerned with facilitating the purchase of insurance. Under the current policy contracts, the insured did not participate in dividends until the policy had been in force two years. Instead, the dividends for the first two years were credited to the policy and paid as an additional amount when the policy matured or the insured died. In 1880 a "large majority" of agents petitioned the trustees to reduce the first two premiums by 20 per cent in lieu of the declaration of the two post-mortem dividends.[9] This particular proposal was not approved, but the management did re-adopt a modified premium plan under which 25 per cent of the first two premiums could be paid in the form of a premium note bearing 7 per cent interest. Beginning the third year, however, premiums were payable entirely in cash.

Insurance Plans and Specific Contract Provisions

Although the late 1860's had been marked by the introduction of many novel policy contract plans by life insurance companies, Northwestern, which had restricted the number of its policy contracts prior to 1874, saw little reason to follow suit. As a result, through the year 1880 Northwestern added only one new plan to its line. This was an "additional life" (or decreasing life) policy introduced in January 1875. Under the proposal worked out by McClintock, in lieu of cash the contract provided dividends for an automatic extension of term insurance in addition to the face value of the basic policy. An amount of 50 per cent extra coverage was guaranteed for the first two years. It was assumed, but not guaranteed, that future dividends would pay for this additional protection. At any time the insured wished, he could without penalty convert his policy into an ordinary life contract.

The basic sales appeal of the new policy was pointed out in the Company's pamphlet for 1877:

> Those who are now in good circumstances and prefer the idea of a rapidly decreasing payment will be willing to pay the regular premium on one of the old style ordinary life policies. Those, however, who are improving in circumstances, but need at present all the money they can command, would prefer a policy on the 'addition plan.' The old plan costs more at first and less after a number of years than the new; some will prefer one plan and some the other.

Contrary to the expectations of the management, the new policy had only limited acceptance.

Despite urgent if sporadic requests by agents, the Company was also reluctant to make changes that would liberalize its policy contracts during this period. The sole exception involved the suicide clause. Prior to 1867 all contracts had provided that in case of the insured's suicide at any time during the life of the policy, the contract would be null and void. Abandoned from 1867 through 1871, the suicide clause was reinstated in 1872 with the provision that in case of suicide the Company would return only the premiums paid in on the policy.

This concern with suicide cases affected the entire industry, for when brought to court such cases invariably caused embarrassment to the companies.[10] Often definite proof was difficult to establish, and not infrequently, when the cases were decided in favor of the companies, the effect on public opinion

was likely to be unfavorable. Apparently the Northwestern agents prior to 1881 did not feel strongly that the Company's suicide provision was adversely affecting their competitive position. At the meeting of the Association of Agents held in January 1881, however, the group unanimously approved a resolution that the Company pay suicide claims in full or that the contract be so amended that the suicide forfeiture clause would not apply after the second year.[11] This resolution was accepted in principle by the Executive Committee to apply to all contracts issued after March 1881, but the time limit was fixed at three years rather than two.

Raising the Quality of Risks

Not only did the management refuse further to liberalize its policy contracts, it took steps to raise the quality of risks within the terms of existing policy agreements. One of the Company's strong selling points was its comparatively low mortality experience; in fact, Northwestern's ratio of actual losses to expected losses averaged approximately 83.2 per cent from 1869 through 1878. How well this figure compared with the record of other companies is difficult to measure, but there was a growing feeling within the Company that its experience could be improved.

On this premise, Actuary Emory McClintock recommended the withdrawal of the Company's sales representatives from certain southern areas; and a precise identification of risks that might be cancelled under the temperance clause in the policy contracts. By 1877 more than $100,000 of insurance had been cancelled as the result of McClintock's recommendations.

Dissatisfaction with the quality of the Company's risks continued, however, and in January 1877 the trustees' examining committee suggested that a more thorough check be made of local medical examiners and the Company's policyholders alike. Two special agents were assigned to this enormous task. Although no summary account of their work is available, in 1881 they reported 275 risks covered by $739,760 worth of insurance (about 1 per cent of the total in force) as impaired by ill health or intemperance. During that year sixty-one of these doubtful risks, representing $179,600 of insurance, were cancelled by lapse or surrender. Another four policies, representing $11,000, were cancelled by resolution of the Executive Committee, and three policy applications totaling $7,000 were declined as a result of adverse information received from special agents.[12]

Another example of the management's concern

with the quality of its risks came in May 1876 when an announcement was made to the agents that Northwestern would no longer insure women. The reason for this action was the Company's unsatisfactory mortality experience during the period 1858–1875, which for women averaged 96.5 per cent of the tabular (Actuary's Table) rates, compared with 77.9 per cent for men. This high rate was not so much a result of the differences in the general life expectancy of the two groups as it was a reflection of the high proportion of "self-selected" risks among women.[13] The percentage of the Company's total insurance that covered women at this time is not known, but it was probably quite low.

Sales Territory

Northwestern's conservatism applied with equal force to its sales territory. While Virginia, North Dakota, and Connecticut were added to the Company's marketing area, Canada, South Carolina, Tennessee, Rhode Island, and California were withdrawn. The decision to abandon the Canadian market in 1878 represented the most serious loss of business. The reason for withdrawal was the passage of a Canadian law which required that the reserves on policies held by Canadians with United States companies be invested in Canada. Rather than put such restriction on the Executive Committee's investment discretion, it was decided to give up the Canadian business entirely.

The net loss in sales territory between 1874 and 1881 undoubtedly had an effect on sales. "We have lost nearly 25 per cent of the volume of our annual business based upon the results of former years," observed Keenan. "Many of our competitors are prosecuting their business in the fields abandoned by Northwestern by reason of climatic, malaria, and other objections as well as oppressive legislation."[14]

Insurance Sales

At first glance the Company's sales record, shown in Table V-1, is not impressive, especially from 1874 through 1880. The amount of insurance sold fell sharply after 1875, and did not regain the 1875 level until 1881. Even this figure of approximately $15 million was markedly below the Company's previous high point in sales, $25 million, reached in 1869. Failure to maintain the previous volume of sales was reflected in the total amount of insurance in force which, as indicated, dipped to $61.4 million

TABLE V-1

Northwestern Mutual and Industry:
Life Insurance in Force and New Business,
1874–1881

	Northwestern		Industry	
	NEW BUSINESS (Millions)	IN FORCE (Millions)	NEW BUSINESS (Millions)	IN FORCE (Millions)
1874	$11.1	$64.7	$351.8	$1997.2
1875	11.1	65.3	299.3	1922.0
1876	12.7	67.1	233.4	1736.4
1877	11.4	67.5	179.2	1557.1
1878	7.8	64.4	158.3	1482.9
1879	6.6	61.4	178.3	1515.6
1880	7.6	61.9	243.7	1578.9
1881	8.7	65.0	283.2	1676.9

SOURCE: Appendix E.

in 1878 and by 1880 was just about equal to the amount reported seven years earlier.

Actually these data fail to show the highly creditable record of Northwestern in the face of its own conservative marketing policies and the difficulties which were being met by the life insurance industry generally. Total industry sales diminished after 1873; in 1878 they were less than half of the level four years earlier. Even by 1881 the amount reported was only 70 per cent of the 1874 volume. In contrast, the low point reached by Northwestern in 1878 was 68 per cent of the amount of new insurance it sold in 1874. By 1881 Company sales were almost 150 per cent of the 1874 base.

Marketing Costs

Northwestern's total "external" expenditures, 85 per cent of which were expended on the marketing of insurance for 1874–1881, amounted to $2.7 million. Annually these outlays declined from $433,000 in 1874 to $269,000 in 1879, then rose to $416,000 in 1881. Of the total, $2.1 million was paid to agents, $136,000 was spent for medical examinations, and $54,000 for advertising. Legal expenses were $143,000 and taxes amounted to $264,000, mostly for license fees and levies on premiums.

With respect to the cost of selling insurance. Keenan stated in 1881: "We are informed, and believe, some of the large companies have exceeded ours in terms of contracts or compensation to their agents

in both salaries and commissions." In particular, "Equitable and New York Life have been most liberal in commissions to agents, and yet we are forced to admit the cost of our new business has been excessive in some agencies." He thought that in respect to character, ability, and business reputation the Company's agents, as a class, "were superior to those of almost any other company." It had been hoped that "our work would not have cost 50 per cent of the premium, with usual exceptions. But the result is that the cost of many agencies has far exceeded such hope and estimate."[15]

In the absence of information on first-year premium income it is impossible to measure the effect of salaries, allowances, and more generous first-year commission rates on the cost of acquiring new business. As it was, the percentage of agents' compensation (and total expenditures) to premium income averaged only slightly above that for 1871–1873.

Reinsurance of the Minnesota Mutual Life Insurance Company

In 1875 Northwestern added over $1 million to its insurance in force by taking over the business of the Minnesota Mutual Life Insurance Company of St. Paul.* The Minnesota organization, under the presidency of General H. H. Sibley, had begun operation in 1870 with the initial backing of a group of prominent businessmen of the state. The purpose was to build up an institution that "would arrest in some measure the outflow of money [from the state] annually for life insurance and retain it for investments at home." Having no one with the ability of General Johnston to promote sales, "the enthusiasm of many of these gentlemen proved short-lived, so much so, that they did not aid even to the extent of taking out policies after organization."[16]

In an attempt to keep the organization going, General Sibley and a number of his associates pledged a sum of $100,000 as a guarantee fund against loss to policyholders. As policy reserves were built up this fund was reduced and amounted to only $8,000 in 1875. But the officers and directors, all of whom had other business interests, found operating the company an increasing burden, especially during 1873 and 1874. In 1875 it was decided to approach Northwestern Mutual with a proposal for reinsurance.

Nearly 1,100 policies were involved, aggregating $1,305,775 of insurance. After examining these poli-

---

* It should be noted that this company has no connection with the present day organization bearing the same name.

cies and the books of the company, McClintock and Northwestern's medical director, Dr. Louis Mc-Knight, recommended to the Executive Committee that the proposal be accepted. The policyholders were treated in every respect as members of Northwestern, except that a portion of their dividends was retained until policy reserves had been raised from the 6 per cent standard of the Minnesota company to the 4 per cent reserve requirement of Northwestern. As a part of the arrangements, General Sibley was elected a trustee.

This was the only instance of its kind in Northwestern's history. While the business acquired was on the whole satisfactory, the mortality experience on the risks was not up to Company standards; thereafter proposals of this type were rejected.

Investment Problems and Policies

The reduction in the rate of sales and insurance in force diminished both the Company's premium income and its total revenue. This decline was not matched by a reduction in expenditures, particularly payments to policyholders. As might be expected, the amount of insurance lapsed rose sharply, and values paid upon surrender of policies increased markedly during the depression. This increase (see Chart V-1), coupled with death claims, matured endowments and dividends paid, not only reduced the net amount available for new investment to about $5 million, as compared with approximately $9 million during the preceding five years, but in 1878 actually resulted in a "disinvestment" of $227,000, the only such experience in the Company's development. In addition to the absolute reduction in the quantity of investable funds available, the Company experienced some entirely new problems. Investment opportunities were seriously curtailed and interest rates, once panic conditions had passed, started to decline.

These problems demanded the utmost attention of President Palmer, Vice President Keenan, the Executive Committee and the Examining Committee. The latter committee was appointed under bylaws adopted by the Company in 1859. Composed of three trustees, not members of the Executive Committee, it had limited its functions to making a yearly audit of the Company's books up to this time. Under Palmer's administration the Examining Committee's role was broadened to include a review of management policies and administration. Its recommendations were most seriously considered by the Board and the Executive Committee. It remained active until 1908 when its functions were taken over by the present-day Policyholders Examining Committee.

The over-all effects of both external forces and internal management decisions on the Company's investment portfolio are shown in Chart V-2. Total admitted assets rose by $4.8 million, from $14.1 million in 1873 to $18.9 million at the end of 1881. While total earning assets remained relatively constant, especially from 1876 through 1879, there were several marked shifts in the various accounts relative to the total. The sharpest decline came in the proportion of premium notes and bills receivable from nearly 28 per cent in 1874 to 8.6 per cent in 1881. More significant in respect to the amounts involved was the drop in the relative importance of mortgage loans. These reductions were offset by a sharp expansion in the bond account, special real estate, and cash.

The investment managers, as already noted, had little influence over premium notes and bills receivable. The decline in premium notes was clearly a result of the 1872 decision to put premiums on a cash

CHART V-1

Income, Expenditures, and Net Available for Investment: Northwestern, 1874–1881

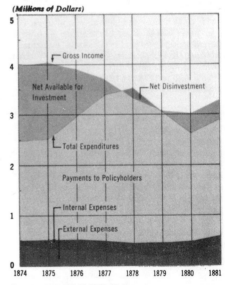

(*Millions of Dollars*)

SOURCE: Appendix F, Tables 1-4.

CHART V-2

Distribution of Admitted Assets:
Northwestern, 1874–1881

(Millions of Dollars)

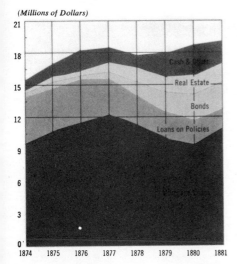

SOURCE: Appendix F, Table 5.

foreclosure. They were carried on the books at the cost of acquisition, plus such expenses as insurance and taxes incurred while they were held, minus income from rents and the sales of property.

Northwestern's first experience with distressed real estate occurred in 1872 when a small property in Leavenworth, Kansas, was foreclosed, involving a sum of $1,500. The account grew slowly to around $36,000 in 1874, but as the business depression ran its course, it became increasingly difficult for individuals to meet their financial obligations. Foreclosures became more frequent, and the Company's holdings of special real estate amounted to over $1.5 million by the end of 1880.

The acquisition of properties on such a scale raised a problem new in the experience of the management. While there was no question that the holdings should be liquidated, if for no other reason than that the Company's charter forbade the ownership of such real estate except on an emergency basis, there was the question of the timing of disposals. There is little doubt that all of the property acquired through foreclosure sale was bought at a price which just covered the amount of the mortgage, plus any accrued charges. (If anyone else had offered this amount or more at the foreclosure sale, the Company would not have bid on the property.) Considering the management's conservative policy of not lending more than 50 per cent of the valuation of a property, it might well be argued that with the revival of business all such acquisitions could easily be sold at prices above cost.

There were, however, pressures against a rigid application of this policy. The principal argument was the loss in earnings which might have been realized had the funds represented by this real estate been available for other purposes. Every effort was made, of course, to make these properties earn some income, chiefly rent. But during 1880, for example, income from rents and the sale of some holdings above cost amounted to $61,806; taxes, insurance costs, repairs, and other expenses, however, came to $72,200. In 1881 net operating income was only $1,-599, approximately 1 per cent of the total amount of the account.

There was apparently no great concern over the acquisition of special real estate through 1878, but in 1879 the trustees' Examining Committee gave the matter serious attention. In addition to the losses of income involved, the Committee advanced a further reason for hastening the liquidation of these properties. The examiners pointed out that the large holdings of such real estate by eastern companies had caused much unfavorable comment "in the public prints to the great prejudice and detriment of those

basis. The partial restoration of the premium note system in 1880 had little effect upon their downward trend. Bills receivable, already a negligible item in 1874, practically disappeared by 1881.

The remaining accounts, however, were clearly inter-related and came under the direct supervision of the investment group. Together, these mirrored the difficulties encountered in attempting to follow the Company's traditional policy of investing the bulk of its funds in mortgages. This connection is perhaps most dramatically revealed in the case of the special real estate account.

Special Real Estate

Special real estate consisted of those properties which formed the security for mortgage loans, and which were acquired through default of interest or principal, or as a result of the borrower's failure to pay taxes or maintain fire insurance in force. Most of these properties were purchased at foreclosure sale, although a few came into the Company's possession by voluntary surrender of the deed in lieu of corporations; and this Company cannot expect to enjoy immunity from criticism on that account, especially if, as the indications now are, that amount should be still further increased." [17] To prevent the account from rising to $2 million, the Committee further recommended that the tempo of sales of such property be speeded, but at the same time warned against cutting prices except for a few undesirable holdings.

The suggestions of the examiners were welcomed both by the trustees and the Executive Committee. By selling first those properties that were the least desirable, even at a loss on book values, the management could reduce the total account and at the same time retain the better property for a rise in market prices. The poorer properties were both more difficult to rent and involved greater expenditures for maintainance and repair. To implement the Examining Committee's recommendations, the trustees gave the Executive Committee authority to establish a special real estate division within the mortgage loan department. A Company officer, acting under the direction of the president, was to be given the responsibility for this division, and was directed to sell "as speedily as possible real estate obtained by the Company upon foreclosures of mortgages." [18] In 1881 Matthew Keenan was transferred from the agency department and made director of the new division, which had been organized the previous year. While the volume of special real estate

was kept from rising during 1880 and 1881, the task of liquidating was carried over into the next period.

The Mortgage Loan and Bond Accounts

Despite the growing volume of special real estate, mortgage loans remained the principal market into which Company funds flowed. The Company made loans in seventeen states during the period, but by 1880 it ceased lending in New York and Alabama, and had only token loans in Pennsylvania and Tennessee. The overwhelming bulk of its loans, as indicated in Table V-2, was made in eight states in the East North Central and West North Central regions. In 1874, for example, 90.5 per cent of total loans outstanding were in Wisconsin, Illinois, Indiana, Iowa, Michigan, Minnesota, Ohio, and Missouri; in 1877 loans in these same states accounted for 92.7 per cent of the total, and at the end of 1881 for 96.3 per cent.

The Company's experience with foreclosed farms apparently prompted the management to make more of its new loans on urban properties. Detailed information on the extent of this shift is not available, but as of December 31, 1874, it was reported that about 52 per cent of the Company's total mortgage loans of about $9.5 million were on city prop-

TABLE V-2

Northwestern Mutual: Regional Distribution of Mortgage Loans, 1874–1881

YEAR	MIDDLE ATLANTIC [a]	SOUTH ATLANTIC [b]	EAST-SOUTH CENTRAL [c]	EAST-NORTH CENTRAL	WEST-NORTH CENTRAL [d]	MOUNTAIN [e]
			(In thousands of dollars)			
1874	$0.7	$118.8	$235.6	$6,602.7	$2,466.3	$ 74.3
1875	1.7	173.2	219.9	7,246.3	2,878.1	82.3
1876	1.5	146.2	180.2	8,273.9	2,922.2	81.5
1877	1.5	120.9	130.7	8,877.1	3,054.8	123.1
1878	1.5	103.4	76.2	8,263.8	2,941.7	109.9
1879	1.5	90.2	63.4	7,380.9	2,811.1	83.7
1880	1.0	84.4	41.8	7,300.8	2,510.0	64.7
1881	1.0	65.1	34.6	8,024.7	2,788.1	129.7

[a] New York and Pennsylvania.
[b] Georgia.
[c] Alabama, Tennessee, and Kentucky.
[d] The Company did not lend in the Dakota Territory.
[e] The Company lent only in Colorado in this region.

SOURCE: *Executive Committee Minutes*. The data was contained in the reports of executive officers given to the Committee at each January meeting (1875–1882).

YEAR	NEW LOANS AND ADDITIONS	REPAYMENTS AND REDUCTIONS	NET CHANGE IN MORTGAGE LOAN ACCOUNT
1874	$2,229,739	$717,686	$1,512,053
1875	2,273,584	1,170,504	1,103,080
1876	2,039,256	1,035,097	1,004,159
1877	2,309,898	1,607,273	702,625
1878	1,111,912	1,923,488	−811,576
1879	1,103,888	2,169,580	−1,065,692
1880	1,752,868	2,181,123	−428,255
1881	3,200,822	2,160,323	1,040,499
Totals:	$16,021,967	$12,965,074	$3,056,893

SOURCE: Company records.

erty.[19] A sampling of new loans indicates the following percentages of urban loans to the total for selected years: 1875, 69 per cent; 1877, 59 per cent; 1879, 64 per cent; 1881, 81 per cent.

The magnitude of the Company's mortgage lending and the variation in the loan account is shown in the table above.

The general policy followed in making mortgage loans was to accept all applications which met the standards set by the Executive Committee at a relatively high scale of interest rates, which varied according to the place, type, and size of the loan. Residual funds were put into bonds which bore a lower rate of interest, or deposited in banks which paid 3 per cent. Indeed, with the events of the Panic of 1873 still fresh in mind, there was a tendency to build up cash balances quite rapidly throughout 1875 and 1876.

In January 1875 the Examining Committee raised the question of whether liquidity could not be combined with a higher return than the 3 per cent currently being paid on bank deposits. The Committee recommended that the Company place a total of $250,000 in federal bonds, $100,000 "as soon as practicable," the remainder "as the funds of the Company may justify without interfering too largely with the normal loans on real estate." They believed this necessary to guard against the possibilities of a panic such as that of 1873, as well as to provide payment of $1.5 million in endowment policies which were due in 1877. Such bonds, it was thought, would provide the necessary reserves in the event the "Company should not succeed to have the same large business as heretofore."[20]

The Executive Committee was in no hurry to act on the recommendation. It was not until 1877 that holdings began to move up, but subsequent in-

creases were more rapid and by 1881 the total amounted to nearly $2.5 million. There was also an expansion in the amount and proportion of municipal bonds during the last few years of the period. These changes are indicated in the following tabulation:

YEAR	TOTAL BONDS	U. S. BONDS	STATE & MUNICIPAL BONDS
	(In thousands)		
1874	$345	$327	$18
1875	382	352	30
1876	375	339	36
1877	753	581	172
1878	1,200	1,018	182
1879	1,914	1,764	150
1880	2,460	1,752	718
1881	2,486	1,664	822

SOURCE: Company records.

In 1875, the Examining Committee raised the fundamental question as to whether the management should not lower the rates of interest on its mortgage loans. As expressed by the Committee,

[We] would venture an opinion that because money can be loaned at 10 per cent it is not certainly the best policy of a large corporation like ours to take advantage of it and doubt the policy of seeking investments in out-of-the-way places in small amounts as in an emergency they could not be made available to help the Company. . . . large sums loaned on productive bits of property at a rate of interest as low as 8 per cent [are] much more desirable . . .

in the case it should be necessary to realize upon them.[21]

This subject was extensively debated by the trustees at their meeting in January 1876 and was only adopted after some modification. A year later the Examining Committee again took up the question, stating: "There is no good reason for fixing an arbitrary rate below which the money of the Company shall not be loaned to applicants." [22]

While these recommendations had some effect on mortgage lending procedures, chiefly in the size of individual loans, the Executive Committee was most reluctant to make any drastic change in interest rates. As shown in tabulation below, the modal or typical rate on new mortgage loans, 8 per cent, remained unchanged through 1879. The Executive Committee apparently was justified in maintaining rates because the mortgage loan account increased from 1875 through 1877. While the combined bond and cash accounts also grew to over $1 million by the latter date, this amount was not considered excessive.

YEAR	LOWER	MODAL	UPPER
1876	6.0%	8.0%	12.0%
1877	6.0	8.0	10.0
1878	7.0	8.0	10.0
1879	6.0	8.0	10.0
1880	6.0	6.5	10.0
1881	5.0	6.0	8.0

SOURCE: New Loan data from annual reports of officers to the Executive Committee, made each January. *Executive Committee Minutes.*

Beginning 1878, however, the mortgage account began to decline and the cash and bond accounts grew sharply. Moreover, in 1879 the interest rate on bank balances was reduced from 3 per cent to 2.5 per cent. Even in the face of these developments the Executive Committee was still reluctant to lower rates on mortgage loans. The members were uncertain whether this weakening of the mortgage loan market at current interest rates was temporary or represented a more permanent adjustment of the market. So long as there was doubt they felt it more prudent to keep the Company's funds in more liquid form, even at lower rates, than to invest in long-term mortgages.

By 1880, the Executive Committee was convinced that conditions in the mortgage market were more than a mere temporary response to depression, and that a reduction in the scale of interest rates was necessary. While the range of rates charged during 1880 was between 6 and 10 per cent, the modal rate dropped to 6.5 per cent, and during the following year to 6 per cent. At these rates the Company increased the amounts lent on mortgage security.

Investment Earnings

On the whole, management had good reason to be pleased with the handling of its mortgage loans. The modest drop in interest charges through 1879, plus the continuation and renewal of loans made earlier at higher rates, combined to maintain the income from the total mortgage account at over 9 per cent through 1879. As shown below, it was only after that year that lower interest rates charged were reflected in the Company's earnings:

YEAR	RATE OF RETURN	YEAR	RATE OF RETURN
1874	9.3%	1878	9.1%
1875	9.8	1879	9.3
1876	9.8	1880	8.2
1877	9.6	1881	7.5

SOURCE: Lester W. Zartman, *Investments of Life Insurance Companies*, 78-79.

Furthermore, the Company's success with its mortgage lending was reflected in its total investment income. As indicated in Table V-3, compared with eight of the leading life insurance companies in the industry, Northwestern, with the exception of 1881, showed the highest rate of income from its investments.

Establishment of Loan Agents

Of major importance in improving the efficiency of the mortgage loan department and the quality of loans made during this period was the introduction of salaried loan agents. This move was made largely in response to the issue of separating insurance sales from lending operations. Heber Smith's defeat had confirmed the principle of separation, but it did not solve the problem of finding new borrowers.

The president, the agency director, and a majority of the trustees were aware of these difficulties, and they moved slowly to effect a complete separation of investment and sales. Again the trustees' Examining Committee took the immediate initiative, although it is possible that Palmer and the other executives may have made the original suggestion. In 1877 the Examining Committee recommended that all loans of $10,000 or more be made only after the property had been examined by someone other than a soliciting agent, preferably a trustee or an officer, and that a full written report be made to the Executive Committee. The Examining Committee further suggested:

> that the business of placing loans be entrusted to other persons than the Agents of the Company, where it can be done without too great expense and without prejudice to the general interests of the Company. This will relieve the agents of a class of business which is unremunerative but which makes considerable demand on their time, and will enable them to devote themselves exclusively to their regular duties.

With this encouragement, President Palmer began combing the territories where the Company most heavily loaned for persons of integrity and ability who could serve as loan agents. Ideally, a loan agent ought to be experienced in the real estate business, possessing a knowledge of property values, both local and general, and willing to improve his knowledge of such values. Further, he should be able to make appraisals, have a knowledge of real estate law, and be devoted to the interests of the Company. The president believed it would be a mistake to remunerate such agents on a commission basis. Rather than make income depend on the volume of business and encourage applications for loans on dubious security, the better solution, he believed, was to place these agents on straight salary.

Sometime during 1878, President Palmer hired three men whom he called special loan agents, assigned them territories in Illinois, Ohio, and Minnesota, and thus launched a major innovation.* The loan agency system received its first official recognition in the report of the Examining Committee to the trustees in January 1879. The examiners specifically requested that the monthly reports of department heads include the progress of "the several loan agents in the examination of property offered as security for loans." [23]

In June 1879 Palmer suggested that the territory in which the Company was lending be reduced and

that the loan agents examine all properties offered as security for loans.[24] The Executive Committee accepted the recommendations and authorized Palmer to appoint special loan agents in each of the fields he suggested. During the following year five new loan agents were appointed, bringing the total to eight.

Although Palmer's plan for the divorce of loans from insurance was supported by a majority of the trustees, it stirred up some resentment among the agency force. In November 1879, for example, the large Dean and Payne general agency in Chicago requested that Northwestern place all loans in Illinois or, as a minimum, all those made in Cook County, through its office. A committee appointed to consider this demand reported that it could not "recommend any variation in the present general policy of the Company." [25]

A report of the Examining Committee in January 1880 strongly endorsed the new policy of loan offices and, as a result, assured the continuance of the practice.

> The methods adopted by that [Executive] Committee to obtain reliable information in regard to the character of the property offered as security, are commendable, and are resulting in a great improvement in the character of our loans in every respect, and the increased expenditure in that direction is money right well expended.[26]

Taxation

Probably no more than a handful of persons, corporate or real, enjoy the prospect of taxation, and life insurance managers have always insisted that theirs is a special case. As Stalson has observed, these men regard life insurance as "an institution which protects the family and which is essentially a savings fund ... to be above taxation." [27] But their pleadings have rarely impressed legislators and insurance companies have been taxed in one form or other throughout the history of the industry. Understandably, the Northwestern management shared the belief of the industry respecting the inappropriateness of taxes on life companies, although there was little to concern them prior to 1874.

Northwestern, because it was far the largest company in Wisconsin, had a particular stake in tax legislation affecting "domestic" insurance companies. Its strong financial position made it a tempting source of revenue for the state. The management was also vitally concerned with the Wisconsin leg-

---

* These agents were Redmond Prindiville of Chicago, A. B. Alden, and Clum Drew. Prindiville was easily the most picturesque agent Northwestern ever hired. At the time he was employed, at the age of 43, he had helped build the first railroad in the city of Chicago; had served as assessor, councilman, and commissioner of public works; and lost his entire personal property and home in the fire of '73. Cf., Tyrrell, 363.

islature's tax policies as applied to "foreign" (out-of-state) life companies. This concern was prompted not by a benevolent regard for the welfare of competitors, but because of the presence of so-called retaliatory laws in states where it conducted a life insurance business. These statutes, troublesome for the entire industry, provided that if another state imposed a tax upon foreign companies which exceeded the rate applied by the subject state on out-of-state companies, the local rates would be automatically raised to the same level.

In general, relations were reasonably cordial between the Company and the Wisconsin legislature. The Company from the outset paid license fees for its agents doing business in the state. In 1867 the legislature passed a bill (Chapter 179, Laws of 1867) charging foreign life insurance companies operating in Wisconsin a $500 first-year license fee, plus 3 per cent of all premiums they collected in Wisconsin. It was initially proposed that domestic life companies should pay the same premium tax, but Palmer, who had just been elected to the senate, persuaded the legislature to reduce the rate on domestic companies to 1 per cent of their Wisconsin premiums, plus an exemption from all other state taxation.[28]

Wisconsin's adoption of a life insurance premium tax was similar to laws enacted about this same time in several other states. This tendency raised questions regarding equitable treatment of policyholders, for not all states levied such taxes, and those which had them applied different rates. Payment of premium taxes, of course, reduced the earning assets and, therefore, the dividends. For this reason it was argued that it was unfair to pay the same dividends to policyholders in states which applied such taxes as to those in states which did not.

No particular effort was made to remedy the situation until 1871 when the National Convention of Life Insurance Commissioners (state officers) recommended that such taxes be charged against the dividends of policyholders residing in states where they were levied. In 1874 the National Chamber of Life Insurance recommended the same program to its members. In the following year, together with other companies, Northwestern put this recommendation into effect.

The objective of this procedure was to cause affected policyholders to bring pressure on the various legislatures to reduce or eliminate such taxes. One or two states did reduce their rates, but this was more than offset by increases elsewhere. Emory McClintock observed some years later, "What may be called the legislative argument in charging taxes against dividends has [since] been found of no

value." Moreover, he noted that the practice had led to "discrediting comparisons between the dividends in different states when the parties who read the comparisons are not acquainted with the cause of the difference." By the late 1880's the imposition of taxes on premium income was so general that "the practice is virtually continued for the benefit of members residing in [the non-taxing states of] New York, Illinois, and Kansas." [29]

Notwithstanding these arguments, and even after its principal competitors had abandoned the practice, Northwestern continued to deduct taxes from dividends until 1894. The principal reason for maintaining this policy was to treat the Company's members on an equitable basis. The defection of the other companies from their initial understanding was an important factor in Northwestern's long continued policy of isolating itself from the national associations of life companies.

Meanwhile, the management was alert to any proposed changes in Wisconsin legislation which might increase its tax burden or put it at a competitive disadvantage in selling insurance. In 1876, the Company faced a real threat in both respects when a bill was introduced in the legislature designed to increase taxes for all life companies operating in the state. On foreign companies the proposed tax was 2 per cent of their gross Wisconsin revenues, including premium notes; for domestic companies it was set equal to 1 per cent of the value of all property, plus 2 per cent of their gross non-Wisconsin receipts.[30]

Northwestern's management went into immediate action. In February a remonstrance was drafted, several thousand copies printed, and bundles of these expressed to all agents in the state. The agents were instructed to circularize the protests to policyholders in their areas, obtain petition signatures, and dispatch them to representatives of the policyholders in Madison. When the Company representatives arrived in Madison they were bolstered in their fight by a flood of these petitions. The measure was overwhelmingly defeated.

The same procedure was followed two years later, again with success, when a new tax bill was introduced. This time, however, an accompanying circular outlined the Company's position in some detail. Northwestern Mutual was not a "rich company," the circular noted; its assets were offset by liabilities to policyholders. The proposed legislation would, by cutting dividends, put the Company at a competitive disadvantage in selling insurance, especially in competition with companies domiciled in New York, Massachusetts, Pennsylvania, Missouri, Illinois, and Michigan—states which levied no such "excessive taxation of their companies." Finally, it was emphasized, under the Company's current plan of deducting state premium taxes from dividends, the entire dividends of Wisconsin policyholders would be wiped out. Even if the burden were "divided among the whole membership throughout the whole country, there would still be a decrease in all dividends amounting on the average to about one-sixth."

A further effort was made to tax Northwestern in 1880 which, although unsuccessful, persuaded numerous friends of the Company, in and out of the legislature and including the state revenue authorities, to suggest that, in view of the growing sentiment for increased taxation, the Company should volunteer to pay more taxes. In their opinion the best way of forestalling the introduction of future bills as unsatisfactory as those already defeated would be for the Company to agree to an increase of the Wisconsin license tax from 1 to 2 per cent of domestic premiums. To this proposal management reluctantly agreed, and a bill incorporating this increase was introduced and passed. This legislation (Chapter 256, Laws of 1878) continued to govern taxation of life companies in Wisconsin for the succeeding twenty years. It was by no means the end of agitation for changing the tax laws affecting the Company, however, and the management found it increasingly necessary to rally its friends in order to block the enactment of additional tax measures.

Eight Years' Operations in Review

By the end of 1881 there was no question that Northwestern had successfully met the challenge of the "troubled seventies." Not all life companies had survived. Of the fifty-six firms reported in operation at the end of 1873, only forty-four remained in 1881.[31] How important sound investment policies could be in affecting the financial health of life companies is shown by the experience of a number of those which had succumbed during these years. The first large insurance company to fail during the period was the North American Life of New York, which had most of its funds invested in New York City real estate that proved to be highly speculative. When real estate values dropped sharply after 1873, these loans were foreclosed at such a loss that the company became insolvent.[32] Continental of New York failed in 1876 for much the same reason as, in 1877, did Universal of New York and New Jersey

Mutual. New Jersey Mutual's management had evaded strict state laws governing investments, and put the company's funds into speculative ventures from which they personally profited.[33]

The failure of the Life Association of St. Louis in 1878 showed what could happen if investments were tied to a policy of loaning only in the area from which the premiums were collected. This procedure was followed by the St. Louis management with the result that

> assets were scattered in every state where the company did business. The rate of interest income for a while was exceedingly favorable, but the additional expense and trouble of managing the investments was fatal to the plan . . . insecure loans were made and those, coupled with other weaknesses in the company, produced insolvency.*

Against this background Northwestern's record stands out in bold relief. Even in comparison with the operations of some of the giants which survived, the philosophy of Palmer and his associates shows a marked contrast. A legislative inquiry made in New York in 1877, for example, brought out the dictatorial control exercised by the presidents of Mutual Life and the Equitable Society. The former had absolute control of Mutual Life through thousands of proxies secured by the agents; the latter owned a large share of the capital stock of Equitable and controlled a number of proxies of close friends.[35] The intense competition between these two individuals, their high salaries, their raiding of one another's agency forces by extravagant commissions, and loose accounting or auditing practices, all tended to cast doubt upon the soundness of life insurance. One writer speaking of the 1870's said, "But for the stand of the heads of [Connecticut Mutual and Mutual Benefit], Colonel Greene and Anzi Dodd, the trustee conception of life insurance would have come to nearly total eclipse." [36]

Public recognition that the Northwestern management should be included in this select circle came in 1877. In the summer of that year the insurance commissioner of Maryland arrived in Milwaukee and announced his intention to investigate the Company. This was the first time that outsiders had examined Northwestern, and Palmer suggested that

---

* Other prominent life companies to fail because of reckless financing were the Globe of New York in 1879, the Knickerbocker Life in 1881, and the Charter Oak. While this last company managed to survive until 1886, it was already in serious trouble by the end of the 1870's.[34]

TABLE V-3

Northwestern Mutual and Selected Other Life Insurance Companies: Aggregate Benefits to Policyholders, 1859–1881

	(1)	(2) TOTAL	(3)	(4)	(5)	(6) DIVIDENDS	(7)
COMPANY	GROSS PREMIUMS RECEIVED	PAYMENTS POLICY-HOLDERS	NET INCREASE ASSETS	COL. (2) + COL. (3)	COL. (4) ÷ COL. (1)	PAID TO POLICY-HOLDERS	COL. (6) ÷ COL. (1)
		(Dollar Amounts in Millions)					
Northwestern	$39.52	$26.88	$18.80	$45.68	115.6%	$8.62	21.8%
Mutual Benefit	83.83	67.84	38.72	106.56	127.1	26.89	32.1
National Life (Vt.)	4.15	2.57	2.40	4.97	119.8	0.69 [a]	16.6
New England Mutual	38.88	31.19	14.74	45.92	118.1	9.69	24.9
Connecticut Mutual	117.20	92.19	46.05	138.24	117.9	36.80	31.4
Mutual Life (N.Y.)	225.45	174.40	89.13	263.54	116.9	53.11	23.6
New York Life	95.11	60.02	45.45	105.47	110.9	19.76	20.8
Massachusetts Mutual	17.42	11.27	6.91	18.18	104.4	2.94	16.9
Germania (N.Y.) [b]	21.56	12.74	9.26	22.00	102.0	2.17	10.1
Equitable (N.Y.)	104.45	61.42	43.98	105.40	100.9	20.28	19.4

[a] National Life's total benefits to policyholders are understated. Prior to 1865, dividends were declared every five years and computed as reversionary additions or used in reduction of future premiums. While most other companies followed similar practices during the early years, they carried these as a credit in the dividend account; National did not. The time periods accounted for here are not precisely comparable since the companies used different fiscal years, particularly before 1870. The discrepancies resulting from this variance, however, are not sufficient to significantly alter the above computations.

[b] Germania was renamed The Guardian Life of New York during World War I.

SOURCE: *Insurance Year Book*, 1912, (Financial History Section, 142-275).

the examination be broadened to include the insurance commissioners of Wisconsin, Illinois, Massachusetts, and New York. This was accepted and representatives of the five departments spent six weeks going over the records of the Company.

In their report the commissioners noted that upon a basis of their own independent evaluation, Northwestern's mortgage loans were secured by property worth nearly three times their value. They reported that premium notes were well secured; that policy reserves were in excess of the amount required by a 4 per cent basis; that the surplus was sufficient to cover any probable contingency; and that dividends had been unusually large. In view of what was happening in some of the New York companies at the time, it was interesting that they should strongly commend the "degree of accuracy" of the record books and accounts and the fact that the Company's management received nothing but a fixed salary. This report was most gratifying to the management and to the trustees, for it resulted in favorable newspaper publicity and confirmed, by nonpartisan insurance commissioners of four important eastern states, that Northwestern could compete on favorable terms with eastern institutions.

Over the succeeding years the management had even more reason to be pleased with the progress of the Company. In 1882, after being guardedly optimistic for a number of years, the Executive Committee reported:

The Northwestern is the strongest of the ten largest companies in the United States, and since 1873 has paid larger dividends than any other while maintaining the highest reserves required, thus furnishing the best insurance at the smallest cost. With such a record the policyholders may, in view of the business prosperity of the country, confidently expect the year 1882 will be one of the most prosperous in the history of the Company.

These were strong claims, but in several instances they could be demonstrated. In terms of insurance in force the Company ranked seventh in the industry. Its policy reserves were among the highest

TABLE V-4

Northwestern Mutual and Selected Other Life Insurance Companies: Persistency of Insurance in Force, 1859-1881

COMPANY	(1) In Force, 1858	(2) Sales, 1859-1881	(3) Col. (1) + Col. (2)	(4) In Force, 1881	(5) Col. (4) ÷ Col. (3)
	(In Millions of Dollars)				
Northwestern	0	$250.11	$250.11	$74.50	29.8%
Mutual Life of New York	$32.58	707.96	740.54	315.90	42.7
Mutual Benefit	19.11	308.49	327.60	127.41	38.9
Germania (N.Y.)ᵃ	0	95.65	95.65	36.37	38.0
National Life (Vermont)	1.54	23.76	25.30	9.52	37.6
New York Life	13.58	445.23	458.81	151.76	33.1
New England Mutual	10.41	172.57	182.98	57.80	31.6
Equitable (N.Y.)	0	638.22	638.22	200.68	31.4
Massachusetts Mutual	2.50	102.65	105.15	30.14	28.7
The Industry ᵇ	141.50	6,663.85	6,805.35	1,676.93	24.6

NOTES:

ᵃ Germania did not begin operations until 1860. While most companies listed here had common accounting periods, the year ending on December 31, a few, particularly before 1870, ended their accounting year on various dates. The discrepancies, however, are minor and do not impair the above comparisons in any serious way.

ᵇ The data included here for the "industry" actually represents the overwhelming proportion of all United States life companies, as reported by Stalson. Complete data for the industry at the time is not known. The amount given for insurance in force for the industry in 1858 is actually the 1859 volume; data for the previous year has not been classified.

Connecticut Mutual, one of the largest and most conservative companies, and Penn Mutual, could not be used in this comparison because of the gaps in data on insurance in force and sales during the early years.

SOURCE: *Insurance Year Book*, 1912, 142-275.
Stalson, *Marketing Life Insurance*, 816, 820.

maintained by any United States life company, and its investment earnings and dividend rates compared favorably with the most formidable of its competitors. Beyond these items the management had reason to believe that the Company's marketing costs were relatively low and administrative expenses moderate.

A better measure of performance, however, would indicate more precisely what the Company was able to provide in total benefits to its policyholders in return for the premiums they paid. In other words, what was the value of benefits as a ratio of premium income? An application of this "yardstick" indicates that Northwestern's performance for the years 1874-1881 was excellent. Total premium receipts for the period were $18.3 million; total payments to policyholders (death claims, matured endowments, surrenders, and dividends), $19.41 million; and the increase in assets (reflecting policy reserves and surplus), $4.77 million. Thus

the total benefit to policyholders, $24.18 million, was equal to 132.2 per cent of policyholder premiums. Dividends, all paid in cash, amounted to 35 per cent of premiums.

The most valid use of this "yardstick" is in comparing different periods in the development of an individual life insurance company, but it can, with caution, also be applied in comparing the performance of one company with others. There are many considerations that qualify the application of this measure: the types of insurance plans offered, the age of the company and of its risks, premium rates charged, and the distribution of risks by type of plan. For the years prior to 1881 there is additional reason for being cautious in drawing conclusions about relative performance. For several years many companies did not pay dividends in cash, but computed them as reversionary additions to insurance. It was so also with surrender values. The companies following this practice were able to increase assets more rapidly than would have been true had dividends been on a cash basis.

Even with these limitations Northwestern, which began paying dividends in cash in 1871, compared favorably with other life companies, large and small, in the matter of benefits to policyholders. For the first twenty-three years of its existence, as is shown in Table V-3, the Company provided a total of almost $45.7 million in aggregate benefits to its policyholders in return for premiums of $39.5 million, or 115.6 per cent. Dividends, both cash and additions to insurance, amounted to almost 22 per cent. This performance, although substantially below the record of Mutual Benefit, compared favorably with the records of older and larger companies such as Connecticut Mutual and Mutual Life of New York, and was better than those of four other companies, including New York Life and Equitable. These companies, in addition to the others listed, offered plans of insurance comparable to those of Northwestern, and there is little reason to believe any of them differed significantly in the distribution of risks by type of insurance plan. In retrospect, therefore, the management of Northwestern had real reason to take pride in the accomplishments of its first twenty-three years. There could be no question that the Company deserved a place among the "best" and "lowest cost" members of the industry for that period. Whether Northwestern, or any other company, was the "leading" institution in the industry, as measured by this criterion, cannot be demonstrated.

Still another indicator of performance of a life insurance company is the tendency of insurance once sold to remain in force over time. Because the costs of putting a policy into force are greater than those involved in keeping it on the books, it is apparent that persistent business is more profitable both to management and the body of policyholders alike than is business with a relatively short duration. During its first twenty-three years of operation Northwestern wrote $250 million of life insurance, of which $74.5 million (29.8 per cent) was still in force at the end of 1881. The Company's persistency record was somewhat superior to that of the industry as a whole, but below that of several of its competitors, as is shown in Table V-4. This measure, like the benefit yardstick, is an imperfect criterion in that it does not precisely indicate the length of time the policies still in force in 1881 had been on the books. However, all companies during these years were subject to similar forces, and while some were more liberal in the treatment of policyholders in the matter of forfeitures, this factor did not significantly affect persistency. Northwestern's managers in the years to come were to place great emphasis upon persistency; thus while the achievement before 1881 required no apologies, its improvement would become a continuous objective for the Company.

The successful policies of this troublesome eight-year period placed Northwestern in a strong position. The initial principles had been tested and proved by internal struggle and economic depression. Although there would be economic fluctuations over the next quarter century to produce new problems and intensify old ones, the dominant theme would be growth and expansion, built upon the firm foundations that had been established by 1880. Northwestern was ready for an even more prominent role in the history of life insurance in America.

CHAPTER SIX

Marketing Problems in a New Era:

1882-1907

DURING the period 1882–1907, in contrast to the preceding decade, Northwestern Mutual operated in prosperous times. The insurance industry itself underwent a tremendous expansion and Northwestern Mutual worked diligently to maintain its position as leader in the field. Competition was keen, so vigorous indeed that certain firms in the industry engaged in practices that were brought under severe public criticism by the end of the period. Northwestern Mutual, on the other hand, operating along conservative lines, yet adjusting to the needs of the new era, retained its vital concept of trusteeship.

A New Era

In 1882 the United States was on the threshold of a quarter century of remarkable growth. Population which numbered some 52.8 million at the middle of 1882 grew to 87 million in 1907. National income expanded from an estimated $6.6 billion in 1879 to $22.1 billion thirty years later.[1] Allowing for changes in the price level, real income per capita rose during the same period from approximately $310 (measured in 1926 dollars) to over $525.[2] Economic progress, to be sure, did not proceed without interruptions. There was the severe depression of 1893–96 and the panics of 1903 and 1907; but their effect on the insurance industry was much less profound than the deep depression of the 1870's.

It is an impressive fact that between 1882 and 1897 expansion in the life insurance industry far exceeded the growth of the economy. Whereas national income was some three and one-half times as large, and income per capita about 70 per cent greater, the total amount of life insurance in force in American companies was over eight times as large in 1907 as it was in 1881. It had grown from around $1.7 billion to over $14 billions.[3]

The challenge of these years in the life insurance industry was not so much for survival as for leadership, identified by sheer size and volume of insurance, income, and assets. Marketing became noted for its ferocity, and investment practices in parts of the industry, particularly in view of the continued decline in interest rates, were characterized by the development of new outlets for funds, and, in some instances, failure to distinguish between individual and company interests. The result was a growing public suspicion of the industry, and, in 1905, a penetrating examination into the conduct of life insurance in the United States.

Management Personnel

The immediate responsibility for meeting the challenges that lay ahead remained with Henry L. Palmer, whose reputation as an able executive, established during his first eight years in office, remained unshaken. Despite Palmer's long tenure and great prestige, Northwestern did not become a "one-man" company. The president was careful to preserve both the letter and the spirit of the committee system which had been developed during the preceding decade, and the Executive Committee continued to exercise the main responsibility for top management decisions.

In 1882 Northwestern's official family, in addition to President Palmer, included Mathew Keenan, vice president; J. W. Skinner, secretary; Emory McClintock, actuary; David Hooker, legal counsel; Dr. Lewis McKnight, medical director; and Willard Merrill, agency superintendent. All of these men had been in the service of the Company for some time. With few exceptions they continued as officers over the succeeding twenty-four years. (See Table VI-1.) During this time the growing magnitude and complexity of operations, however, led to an expansion of staff and the creation of the positions of second and third vice presidents.

General Marketing Developments

It was in sales that Northwestern felt the major impact of the changes that marked the character of the industry after 1881. Competition became especially intense. Only fifty-eight firms survived the 1870's but by 1907 one hundred ninety firms were in operation.[4] Moreover, the intensity of competition and many of its excesses stemmed largely from the battle among the Big Three: Mutual Life of New York, Equitable Life Assurance Society, and New York Life, frequently described as "racers" in the industry.

While some of the less commonplace competitive devices became standard practice after 1882, there were few practices introduced which were wholly novel to the period. This was especially true of the highly disturbing selling tactics of twisting (getting a policyholder to change policies from one company to another, principally for the purpose of a commission) and rebating (returning to the purchaser a part of the agent's commission). There was also a tendency to rely increasingly on sheer numbers of agents and the proliferation of general agencies to get new business, sometimes, as in the case of the Big Three, with secret compensation paid to attract agents.[5] Piracy among rival agency forces was not uncommon; and some companies, like the Connecticut Mutual, substantially lost their entire agency force during this period. Selling techniques with a new emphasis on advertising were used extensively,

sometimes to make comparisons based upon highly questionable data, sometimes to build the reputation of their respective companies at the expense of others.

In the atmosphere of this era, the geographically isolated Northwestern Mutual was in a strategic position to expand. The Middle West and West, vastly important marketing areas for Northwestern, were growing rapidly in population, income, and economic activity. Concentration of its investments in Middle Western mortgages provided the Company with sound assets yielding higher rates of interest than were available along the Eastern seaboard. A limited variety of life insurance plans, rigorous selection of insurance risks, and initially higher interest earnings all enabled the Company to offer insurance to qualified policyholders at a lower net cost than could its rivals.

On the other hand, the Company had been selling in the Eastern markets only a relatively few years. It sought to expand its sales in the lucrative New York, New Jersey, Pennsylvania, and Massachusetts markets in the face of intense competition from the already entrenched Eastern companies. To meet this challenge, adaptation to the competitive ethics of the period appeared necessary, together with more attractive benefits to policyholders.

Insurance and Agency Committee

In 1881 general responsibility for all phases of Northwestern's insurance program was given to the newly established Insurance and Agency Committee. The bylaw creating this committee originally named only the Company's president, vice president, secretary, and actuary as members, but shortly thereafter the general counsel, superintendent of agencies, and medical director were added. Coordinating all insurance and agency matters through one committee was a sound forward step in administrative practice.

The initial impetus for the formation of this committee appeared to be a feeling on the part of certain trustees that Keenan exercised too much discretion in agency matters, especially with respect to the negotiation of agency contracts. In fact, for some months prior to April 1881 a ruling was in force that called for a review and approval by the full Board of Trustees of all agency contracts before they became valid. As the Board met only once every quarter, this ruling made it impossible for the agency department to negotiate contracts effec-

TABLE VI-1

Northwestern Mutual: Executive Officers, 1882–1907

PRESIDENT	
Henry L. Palmer, 1882-1907	

VICE PRESIDENT	SECOND VICE PRESIDENT
Matthew Keenan, 1882-1894	Willard Merrill, 1883-1894
Willard Merrill, 1894-1905	William McLaren, 1894-1904
George C. Markham, 1905-1907	George C. Markham, 1904-1905
	J. W. Skinner, 1905-1907

THIRD VICE PRESIDENT	GENERAL COUNSEL
William McLaren, 1893-1894	David Hooker, 1882-1888
George C. Markham, 1901-1904	Charles E. Dyer, 1888-1905
P. R. Sanborn, 1904-1907	George Noyes, 1906-1907

ACTUARY	SECRETARY
Emory McClintock, 1882-1889	J. W. Skinner, 1882-1905
C. A. Loveland, 1889-1907	C. H. Watson, 1905-1906
	A. S. Hathaway, 1906-1907

SUPERINTENDENT OF AGENCIES	MEDICAL DIRECTOR
Willard Merrill, 1882-1902	Lewis McKnight, 1882-1896
Henry Norris, 1902-1907	John Fisher, 1896-1907

SOURCE: Company records.

tively; nor did it seem advisable for the Executive Committee, already burdened with work growing out of increased investments, to assume any added responsibility.

The titles of the members of the Committee suggest their individual functions. While the Company's general counsel, Judge Dyer, was needed to advise on all legal matters affecting insurance and its sale, policy forms, agents' contracts, and the validity of claims, his duties were comparatively light. By contrast, the bulk of the secretary's work involved correspondence with the Company's insureds or their beneficiaries with regard to the payment of premiums, policy changes, certificates of death, and the payment of claims. He had to conduct his correspondence with a combination of tact and firmness.

This was a task that James W. Skinner, elected to the post of secretary in January 1882 to succeed Willard Merrill who became superintendent of agencies, was well equipped to handle. A native of Warren, Pennsylvania, Skinner came to the Company in 1865 as a clerk and was promoted to assistant secretary in 1872. Skinner had few interests outside Northwestern and his management of the

secretary's department was careful and efficient. In recognition of his long service Skinner was elected second vice president in 1905.

It was the function of the actuary (first the extraordinary Emory McClintock and later Charles Loveland when McClintock accepted an attractive offer from Mutual Life) to determine dividends, to develop new policy contracts, to review and advise on all suggestions of changes in policy forms, and to make the necessary actuarial calculations as to the types of acceptable risks, the terms of endowment policies, and the probable rate of interest return. The medical director, Dr. Lewis McKnight, who contributed so vitally in establishing reliable risk standards (and after 1896 Dr. John Welton Fisher), was largely responsible for seeing that the standards for the selection of risks were enforced by agents and medical examiners in the field, and to evaluate and relay to the actuary any information on mortality experience he might acquire.

Of all the key positions on the Insurance and Agency Committee, that of superintendent of agencies consistently commanded the highest salary and rank among the officers. From 1882 to 1902 this important post was held by Willard Merrill, who became one of the ablest directors of life insurance sales in the history of the industry.

At the time of his appointment to succeed Matthew Keenan in December 1881, Merrill had already served Northwestern some sixteen years. He brought an unusual background to his new position—experience as a lawyer, an insurance solicitor, and an officer in the Company. Merrill held his position as superintendent until 1902 when, at his own request, Henry F. Norris was appointed to succeed him. Sympathetic to the problems of the agents, diplomatic in handling men, Merrill contributed significantly in building a stable, effective sales force. His important role in the Company was recognized in 1885 when he was elected second vice president and in 1894 when he succeeded Keenan as vice president, a position he held until his retirement in 1905.

Restoration of the General Agency System

One of the basic policy matters that had to be decided after 1881 was whether the Company should continue to contract directly with local, special, and district agents. Keenan's moves in this direction, it will be recalled, were designed to strengthen the Company's sales efforts in those areas where the general agents were not operating effectively, yet where it was felt insufficient grounds for cancellation of contracts existed. By 1882, however, most of the general agency contracts signed prior to 1874 had automatically come up for renewal. This had permitted the management to weed out undesirable agents by not extending their contracts. It thus seemed appropriate to return the full responsibility for negotiating agreements with all persons working in their sales territories to the general agents.

While the shift was slow and not a matter of announced policy, there was a definite trend to abandon direct contract with all but general agents. Whereas in 1882 the Committee on Insurance authorized 144 new contracts of which seventeen were with general agents, by 1887 twenty-four of the thirty-four new contracts were with general agents, and in 1890 all agreements (except one with a special agent) were of this type.

A sampling of general agency contracts for the 1882–1905 period indicates that a few agreements were made for one year, with the obvious intent of trying out inexperienced agents. Over 60 per cent were made for five years and the remainder for ten years. With the bulk of the contracts coming up

automatically for review and renewal at the end of five years, it was possible to dispense with the services of unsatisfactory agents within a reasonable time and with the least embarrassment. The longer-term contracts, understandably, went to agents who had proved themselves, and a satisfactory record virtually insured an automatic renewal.

The extent to which the general agency system of 1895 was restored to its 1873 status is shown by the following letter written to an agency applicant in 1895:

> Under the system of work adopted by this company there is no way by which the company can make a contract direct with solicitors and new work is conducted entirely by general agents who have entire charge of their respective fields so far as new work is concerned.[6]

The Company did not, however, relinquish its rights to take action if necessary on problems which might arise between a local and a general agent.[7]

Structure of the Agency System

How Northwestern's field force was organized after the restoration of the general agency system had been completed is shown in Chart VI-1. As the classifications used by the Company at the time were in a state of flux, present-day descriptions have been used in identifying different types of agents.

Under direct contract with the general agents were district and special agents. The latter usually sold insurance only in the territory controlled or reserved by the general agent. Not all general agencies utilized district agents, but when a general agency had a territory too large for personal supervision, portions would be assigned to one or more district agents who operated to a considerable degree in their respective districts as general agents.*

Working under district agents were subagents or soliciting agents. Special agents also might subcontract with soliciting agents to assist them in selling. General or district agents would occasionally enter into brokerage contracts with individuals or firms that provided customers with insurance from various life companies or with different types of insurance such as life, fire, or casualty.

Size and Composition of the Agency Force

In 1893 Northwestern began listing the general agents in its annual reports. The estimated number of general agents prior to 1893, and the reported number after that date, are shown in Table VI-2. These figures indicate a fairly sizable expansion between 1882, when the Company restored the general agency system, and 1891. Following 1891 there was a period of relative stability until 1904, after which another expansion occurred.

While the steady increase in the total number of agencies in operation reflects Northwestern's determination to expand its selling activity and to develop better sales territories, the aggregate number of contracts negotiated indicates that rigorous standards were imposed. This involved considerable experimentation with both the size of particular general agencies and with the capabilities of particular agents. For example, some 176 contracts were signed with general agents during 1882–1890, although the number of agents under contract at the

---

* It should be noted that all types of agents, including general and district agents, might have supplementary contracts that permitted them to sell in territories controlled by other general or district agents.

CHART VI-1

Structure of Northwestern's Agency Force

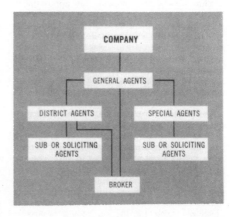

TABLE VI-2

Northwestern Mutual: General Agents Under Contract, 1882–1907

Year Ending December 31	Number
1882-1884	54-64*
1885-1890	64-75*
1891-1892	65-73*
1893	72
1894	78
1895	77
1896	75
1897	73
1898	74
1899	78
1900	74
1901	71
1902	78
1903	77
1904	76
1905	84
1906	91
1907	91

* Estimated.　　　　SOURCE: Company records.

end of each year over the whole period varied only from fifty-four to seventy-five.

Apparently if a general agent failed to produce within a few years following his appointment, Northwestern refused to reappoint him and chose someone else, or the Company merged his agency with another. In a few cases, failure to develop adequately a particular territory was cause for the management to appoint a second agency in the area and subdivide the territory. The Company experienced special difficulty in adjusting its general agency system in Ohio where no less than seventeen contracts were negotiated for the five-year period 1885–1890.

The period of experimentation had apparently run its course by 1893, for there was a marked reduction in numbers of contracts signed. Between 1893 and 1904 the number of general agencies operating varied from seventy-one to seventy-eight. After 1904 there was a further subdivision of several large territories into smaller units, which resulted in some fifteen new agencies. This brought the total to ninety-one at the end of 1907, where it remained relatively stable for the succeeding twenty-five years.

There were, of course, continued changes in personnel among the agents. Many of the changes over these ten years occurred as a result of death or retirement; others represented replacements. It is noteworthy, however, that twenty-five of the sixty-one general agents of record for 1885 were still active in 1895. In contrast to the "marginal group," these men were a part of the hard core of thirty-five or forty consistent producers among the general agents whose volume of business grew steadily over the years.

There is no way of estimating the growth of Northwestern's total agency force beyond what can be implied from a report in 1882 of a "600 man field force" and Henry Norris' statement in 1905, "We have issued licenses for nearly 4,000 agents . . ., [but] I would not like to be quoted that there were 2,000 who were giving their entire time to our work." [8] If this same ratio applied in 1879, the best guess would be that Northwestern's full-time field force had grown at least five-fold over the intervening quarter century.

Recruiting and Training of Agents

Under a fully developed general agency system, of course, responsibility for development of individual territories was assumed by the general agents. They were expected to live up to the standard clause in their contracts which specified that "within a reasonable time and as soon as practical they will at their own expense, employ a sufficient number of subagents to thoroughly canvass and develop the entire field embraced in the contract."

Since this provision was also contained in the contracts between general and district agents, the former could effectively delegate the responsibilities for recruiting and training subagents to the district agents. Delegation of authority, however, did not relieve general agents of their responsibility to the Home Office for the successful execution of the recruiting function.

This situation clearly made the selection of capable general agents by the Company a matter of primary importance. For this reason, during his first few years as superintendent of agencies, Merrill was keenly interested in obtaining the services of general agents who were successful with other companies; but by the late 1880's it was no longer necessary to recruit from the outside. H. F. Norris, writing in 1905, said: "It has been our practice for a good number of years to make appointments to general agencies from among our own agents, exclusively, and no exceptions to this rule have been made." [9] The practice of recruiting from its own force produced higher morale, better advancement opportunities, and better informed and oriented personnel.

In 1882, as today, the problem of selection was fundamental among the difficulties involved in the recruiting of life insurance agents. There existed no easy way of determining in advance which candidate would become a successful insurance solicitor and which would fail. Furthermore, of equal importance to the management was the uncertainty which existed in the selection of general agents. A successful record of insurance soliciting was, as experience proved, no guarantee of equal success in the management of a body of agents or in the development of a territory. Each general agent, of course, applied his own methods in selection, sometimes with the advice of the Home Office. Lacking the tools and techniques of a later day which, though not infallible, have improved the selection process, the general agents and the agency department apparently performed this difficult task better than the industry average. This is indicated by the size of the agency force during these years which, while relatively smaller than those of the Company's major rivals, produced an enviable volume of new and persisting business.

Aside from general agents, the agency department itself played no direct role in recruiting and selecting sales representatives. Its personnel was willing, however, to advise both general agents and persons who applied directly to the Home Office for employment. The latter were warned of the difficulty of predetermining success in insurance selling and frequently advised to "test yourself in a known area to see whether or not selling insurance is to your liking before striking out in a distant region."[10] Typical of the assistance the Home Office was ready to give general agents in recruiting a selling force was the program followed in the case of Llewellyn Miller. Miller, who was given a general agency contract for the Baltimore area in 1889, found it difficult to obtain qualified special agents. He almost buried the Home Office with mail requests for information and advice. With infinite patience and good humor Alonzo Kimball, assistant superintendent of agencies, did his best to help Miller. He was advised to send a circular letter to life insurance agents within his district, along with an offer to negotiate a "liberal contract." Kimball remarked,

> As a rule we dislike the proselytizing business and do not commend it. At the same time we find that all other companies are trying vigorously and persistently to secure our best agents and it has got to be the fashion, I believe, to make overtures to any desirable man working for any other company.[11]

This approach was apparently unproductive, for within a month Miller was again soliciting advice. This time Kimball recommended the insertion of a small advertisement in the local newspapers. Kimball further suggested that possibly a title such as "City Agent" might be offered to applicants, even though they would have the same duties as special agents.[12] This approach was evidently more successful, for eighteen years later Miller was still the Company's Baltimore general agent.

With growing stability of the general agency system after 1890, the Home Office administrators of the agency department had less and less occasion to participate in the recruiting and training of subagents for the general agencies. New generations of general agents served their apprenticeship in the service of other Northwestern general agents and were thoroughly acquainted with the business philosophy of the Company. According to Tyrrell, "Of the ninety General Agents now under contract [1908] less than 20 per cent, and of the four thousand agents a still smaller proportion, have been connected with any other company."[13]

As was true earlier, the pattern of training continued to be highly informal, and varied in effectiveness and administration with the individual general agent and his resources. The methods and techniques were about on a par with those employed by most United States life companies. A common procedure was for the general agent to hire a man, give him a desk, and send him out to solicit. In certain instances new agents were provided with lists of potential customers, but this was exceptional. Some of the general agents tried to teach the new agents the techniques and methods of selling insurance by accompanying them into the field or by joint work on the trainee's early cases. In other cases a new agent would be sent into the field accompanied by a more experienced salesman who attempted to show him the rudiments of insurance soliciting. Just as frequently, according to a sample of general agents' correspondence with the Home Office, the agent started with a list of relatives and friends hoping thereby to maintain himself over the critical first few years until renewal commission income accrued. Although data on turnover for new agents are nonexistent, there is every reason to believe that, in common with other life companies, it was high.

The Home Office management supplemented the training of local agents in various ways. Early in the 1890's Merrill instigated the preparation of a limited series of booklets which in essence were the forerunners of training manuals. These dealt with such concepts as principles of life insurance, basic types of life plans offered by the Company, and reasons for a man to buy insurance, especially with Northwestern. The booklets were distributed to the general agencies as they were published until the series was concluded; thereafter general agents could order complete sets for distribution to their agents.

The educational booklets were supplemented by other literature urging agents to develop methodical systems of procedure, to establish plans for making calls and recording the high points of interviews, and to develop broad contacts which would constitute a source of future business. In addition, the assistant superintendents developed a pool of sales talks, arguments, and methods which individual agents could use with effect.

Beginning with the publication of *Field Notes* in 1901 the agency department was equipped with another convenient tool for training agents. Issued quarterly, *Field Notes* typically contained reports of agents from the field, notes concerning selling techniques, information about competitors' marketing activity, and technical articles on life insurance. This publication, with its lively style and its appeal to the field men, marked a certain maturity and stability in recruiting and training agents.

Agents' Compensation

Northwestern's success in building an effective selling force after 1882 was accomplished in the face of intensive competition from rivals. Equally important, this record was achieved without letting the cost of acquiring insurance reach levels which, from the management's point of view, were unreasonably high. Moreover, under Merrill's superintendency, the Company moved to put its agency contracts on a more uniform basis, to eliminate all forms of compensation except commissions, and to introduce a more complex commission rate structure, adjusted to an increasing variety of insurance plans.

By the mid-1890's virtually all agreements with agents calling for salaries and expenses had been terminated and contract forms with general agents standardized. Typically, arrangements between the Company and the general agents provided for a base commission rate of 40 per cent on new business, with extras that would bring the total to 50 per cent provided that the amount of sales met the quotas established by the management for the year. Renewals were set at 7.5 per cent so long as the insurance was in force and the agent remained with the Company.

Compared to the reported practices of the Big Three of granting commissions of 100 per cent or more of the first-year premiums,[14] Northwestern's payments to agents were modest. The management was conscious of this differential, but expected larger sales by its agents to maintain their incomes at satisfactory levels even at lower commission rates. In fact, the Home Office became concerned when general agents paid what appeared to be excessive commissions to special or district agents. Merrill cautioned one general agent in 1882:

> We fear that you are not leaving enough to properly sustain yourself and we are anxious, not only that you should do a large business, but that you should make some money out of the commissions provided by your contract. You must remember that your commissions may vary from year to year, but it may not be easy to reduce the commission of your agents.[15]

Aside from sales of insurance which they personally solicited, the general agents derived the bulk of their income by retaining a share of the renewal commissions on business that was sold in their territories and remained in force. While the general agents could frequently retain a small portion of first-year commissions, in order to stimulate sales effort, they were willing, if necessary, to turn over the entire amount of first-year commissions allowed them by the Company to the agents working under them, frequently with the provision, however, that sales in a given year be larger than in the preceding year. (Brokers, it should be added, were usually paid the first-year rate with no renewals.)

What portion of renewal commissions went to special and district agents depended upon a number of considerations. On occasion a district would receive the entire sum for a time if it seemed especially needed to build sales in a particular district. On the other hand, part-time special agents might receive no renewal commissions. Highly productive or full-time special agents, especially those who in turn employed subagents, received renewal commissions that ran as high as two-thirds, or 5 per cent of the 7.5 per cent paid the general agent by the Company on renewals. These could be collected by the agent, however, only if the insurance sold remained in force and the agent remained under contract.

Around the turn of the century Northwestern re-examined its policy of compensating agents, especially as it involved perpetual renewals to general agents so long as the business remained in force and they remained with the Company. It had long been felt that perpetual renewals were necessary to attract and hold agents. It was also assumed that so long as general agents' incomes depended largely on renewals, they would be encouraged to write the type of business that would stay on the Company's books.

Experience over the years had shown, however, that the first few years in the life of policies were critical; that the lapse rate after policies had been in force for five years or more was relatively low. Moreover, the management also suspected that a number of its general agents, whose renewal interest had grown large under the perpetual renewal system, had lost the incentive to push sales vigorously in their respective marketing areas.

It was against this background that after protracted study and consultation with its agents Northwestern, in 1902, made a momentous decision. Effective that year, the vested commission period was limited to eleven years. To provide a margin for certain agency expenses, including some of the costs of recruiting and training new agents, a non-vested collection fee of 2 per cent of premiums beyond the commission period was authorized.

In terms of the cost of insurance to policyholders, this decision was instrumental in strengthening the Company's competitive position. On business persisting in force beyond the commission period, the servicing costs were reduced by amounts up to 5.5 per cent of premiums.

Since these provisions applied only to insurance issued thereafter, a vexing question arose regarding the adjustment of renewals on business written under contracts made prior to 1902. Agents were given the option of continuing their renewals under the old plan on such business provided they remained in good standing and, in the judgment of the management, were "productive," or they could take a fixed number of renewals on pre-1902 business, regardless of their record of productivity.

Restricting the commission period to eleven years focused attention on the anomaly of applying the same commission rates to all insurance plans without regard for variation in the length of the premium-paying period. Up to this time the only exceptions to this rule were for single payment life and endowment policies. Such policies yielded a relatively small commission rate, calculated to offer about as much total income to agents as a whole life or limited payment contract. Otherwise, assuming no special bonus or commission was introduced to stimulate the sale of a particular type of plan, the type of policy written made little financial difference to the agent. Larger annual commissions on limited payment plans would be offset by a longer collection period on whole life policies. Restricting the number of renewal commissions, however, changed this situation; after 1902 there could be a material difference in an agent's compensation, depending upon the proportions of his business written on whole or limited payment plans.

The executives responsible for Northwestern's agency and insurance affairs were, of course, cognizant of this problem, and the 1902 compensation plan included an elaborate schedule of first-year and renewal commissions, graded up or down from the basic whole life and long-term endowment plans. Generally, the shorter the premium payment period the smaller was the first-year commission rate.

Early meeting of the Association of Agents held in a "tent constructed of boards and canvas" on the roof of the Home Office

TABLE VI-3

Northwestern Mutual:
External Operating Expenses, Including Agents' Compensation, 1882–1907

Year	Agents' Compensation	Med. & Risk Inspection	Adver-tising	Taxes	Legis-lative	Legal	Hotel & Travel	Total
			(in Thousands)					
1882	$391.7	$25.8	$5.6	$39.4		$16.1	—	$478.6
1883	397.6	25.5	7.0	58.5		13.0	—	501.6
1884	419.6	26.3	8.3	59.7		10.7	—	524.6
1885	490.0	34.7	7.5	65.2		16.5	—	613.9
1886	633.1	46.2	7.1	79.4		16.3	—	782.1
1887	753.8	54.3	6.6	82.0		19.3	—	916.0
1888	949.5	72.7	7.2	90.8		16.6	—	1,136.8
1889	1,121.5	86.6	6.8	99.8		22.2	—	1,336.9
1890	1,396.4	103.8	6.3	115.1		27.7	—	1,649.3
1891	1,539.7	116.8	5.8	133.0		25.3	—	1,820.6
1892	1,709.4	126.7	6.5	152.4		30.5	—	2,025.5
1893	1,472.0	91.7	6.4	163.4		41.2	—	1,774.7
1894	1,410.8	103.5	6.0	163.9		58.3	—	1,742.5
1895	1,544.7	119.7	14.5	194.3		48.0	$1.5	1,922.7
1896	1,619.5	119.2	6.0	231.4		40.0	—	2,016.1
1897	1,689.4	121.7	6.3	269.3		74.0	6.3	2,167.0
1898	2,028.4	142.2	3.2	328.5		58.6	7.1	2,568.0
1899	2,475.6	160.1	3.9	563.0		70.8	9.4	3,282.8
1900	2,548.3	147.5	6.2	675.7		33.3	8.1	3,419.1
1901	2,688.7	158.2	4.8	605.7		19.4	8.5	3,485.3
1902	2,870.6	171.3	5.6	634.3		20.8	11.2	3,713.8
1903	2,928.3	183.8	6.1	670.5		19.6	11.3	3,819.6
1904	3,094.0	187.4	6.8	700.6		24.4	12.5	4,025.7
1905	3,393.4	203.0	7.9	719.7		22.9	12.4	4,359.3
1906	3,535.0	198.6	8.2	780.9	$6.6	22.1	17.4	4,568.8
1907	3,708.3	207.9	7.1	803.2	21.4	6.2	4.5	4,758.6
Totals	46,809.3	3,035.2	173.7	8,479.7	28.0	773.8	110.2	59,409.9

Source: Appendix F, Table 3.

Renewal commission rates were also graded, but not to the same degree.*

* The principal adjustments were made on first-year commissions, which ranged from 55 per cent to the general agent for the whole life contract down to 5 per cent on single payment life policies. Rates on endowments followed a similar pattern ranging from 50 per cent on contracts not maturing before thirty years down to 2 per cent for the single payment plan. The renewal rate for whole life policies and long-term endowment contracts remained 7.5 per cent; limited payment life and short-term endowment plans offered 5 per cent.

The annual aggregate compensation of agents, as shown in Table VI-3, grew from about $400,000 during 1882–1884 to over $3.5 million for the years 1905–1907. By itself this expansion offered some real attraction to those agents who measured up to the requirements of soliciting life insurance for Northwestern. For general agents, the growth of insurance in force and increasing annual sales during the period meant steadily improving gross and net incomes.

A rough estimate indicates that the gross income of the average Northwestern general agency was $20,000 in 1893; in 1907 it was about $41,000. On the assumption that approximately one-third of the gross income of the general agency remained in the hands of the general agent, in 1893 the average general agent's gross income was about $6,667, and in 1907 it was around $13,600.* From this amount the general agent had to pay the operating expenses of his agency, and make some investment in development work such as advancing money to his agents, recruiting new men, and sales promotion before arriving at his net personal income.†

Since the foregoing estimates are only averages, it is apparent that at least a substantial minority of Northwestern general agents were more successful financially. With the steady development of territories, as reflected by increasing sales and insurance in force, the position of general agent became an attractive and legitimate goal for ambitious Northwestern agents.

The remaining two-thirds of the total payments to agents were distributed to the variety of special, soliciting, and brokerage personnel engaged in marketing Northwestern policies. Based upon information available at the close of the period, it is possible to estimate average incomes for the Company's field men, but the distribution around the average cannot even be approximated. For the year 1882 the average compensation per agent fell within a range of $400 and $870; by 1907 the range of average compensation was from $600 to $1,000.**

Even though an accurate distribution of agents' incomes during these years cannot be made, it is apparent that Northwestern, like other life companies, had a small group of "star" agents whose production and income were greatly above that of the average. Based upon later information, it is not unreasonable to assume that about 5 per cent of Northwestern agents consistently produced from 15 per cent to 25 per cent of total annual sales. Projecting such estimates back to the 1882–1907 period, it would appear that the average income for this elite group would have been in the range $1,300–$2,000 for the early years, rising to the range $3,700–$5,900 around 1907. Typical agent incomes, however, would have been closer to the average of the entire force, which was close to the estimated average national family income for those years in the United States.‡ It is also probable that Northwestern agents fared somewhat better than their contemporaries serving other companies in the industry for, as Stalson has observed, life insurance agents were generally not particularly affluent.[16]

The Association of Agents

After 1881 Northwestern's association of agents continued to serve as a useful link between the members of the field force and the management. Various officers appeared before the agents to outline Company policies and frequently participated in discussions on how best to meet competition from rivals. The suggestions of the agents with respect to the election of trustees were presented through the association for consideration by the trustees, who nominated the "official" list. The association was also used to present formal requests to the Company for changes in policies or procedures which the agents believed were handicapping them in their selling efforts. One notable change occurred in 1884, for example, when the Company agreed to pay the fee of the medical examiner instead of collecting it from the applicant for insurance.

---

* These figures are derived from the following data:

	1893	1907
Total Commissions Paid by Northwestern Mutual (in Millions)	$1,432	$3,708
Number of General Agents	72	91
Average Commission Return per General Agency	$20,000	$41,000
Average Gross Return per General Agent	$6,667	$13,600

SOURCE: Company records.

† The greater proportion of this income. as already noted. was derived from renewal commissions, the maximum rate on which was 7.5 per cent. Of this percentage, general agents received a minimum of 2.5 per cent. Actually, because of turnover among agents, the general agent's share of renewal commissions was probably much higher, which, added to income from business he personally sold, could bring the proportion to a third of total commissions passing through his hands.

** In 1882 the Company reported six hundred selling agents under contract. If all were full-time men, the estimated $261,000 available for distribution to the non-general agents would yield an average income of about $400. If only one-half this number were full-time salesmen, the average would be greater, but the amount would depend upon the proportion of the business sold by this group. Assuming that the full-time men were responsible for 80 per cent of the total sales of the Company, the average income per full-time agent would have been $870.

Of the 4,000 agents under contract in 1907, only about half were believed by Superintendent of Agents Norris to be full-time salesmen. Using the same assumptions as developed in the preceding paragraph, it would be evident that the available funds for salesmen's compensation, $2.46 million, would yield average incomes of $600 and $1,000 respectively. The estimate of proportion of business done by full-time men is based upon performances after 1908.

‡ The United States census shows a population of 87 million for 1907, which would mean about 22 million family units. National income for that year is estimated to have been around $18 billion. Thus average national income per family would have been slightly over $800. *Historical Statistics of the United States, 1789–1945*, 26, 15.

While the agents initiated a number of suggested changes which would liberalize the policy contracts of the Company, the management moved slowly in accepting or adopting their recommendations. It was not uncommon for the same resolutions to be presented by the agents year after year, only to meet total or partial rejection. Often the suggestions of agents were accepted because of other pressures, particularly those which came when a leading competitor featured a change in policy contracts or developed a new selling technique. These differences in opinion, however, did not develop into any serious division between the basic interests of the agents or the Company during this period. The revocation of perpetual renewals produced some bitterness on the part of agents, but even as fundamental a change as this did not essentially disturb the morale of the field force.

Marketing Expenses

As shown in Table VI-3, agents' compensation between 1882 and 1907 constituted the bulk of Northwestern's marketing expenses. Of the remaining external outlays associated with marketing, medical examinations, inspection of risks, legal costs, and taxes made up the overwhelming majority. Taxes were consistently greater than 8 per cent of such total external costs, and rose sharply after 1897 due to a changed basis for taxation in Wisconsin. Since taxes were usually imposed upon the base of premium income by most states, they are included here as a cost of selling. The costs of medical examinations and special medical studies designed to improve the standards of risk selection varied only slightly as a percentage of marketing costs, increasing in dollar amounts as the volume of new sales went up. Legal expenses included the fees of legal talent employed outside the Home Office, and evidently the majority of such costs were applicable to the insurance and marketing side of the Company's business. Until 1906, when the management made a direct accounting for legislative expenses, these costs were apparently included with legal expenses. The extent of these outlays was usually quite modest, with the peak reached during the 1895–1899 period, at a time when the Company was actively combating tax legislation in Wisconsin.

Although aggregate marketing expenses increased some nine-fold between 1882 and 1907, the conservative philosophy of the management is reflected by a refusal to permit such costs to increase at a faster rate than did premium income. The following tabulation shows that marketing expenditures as a percentage of premium income were not only moderate, but show a downward trend during the entire period.

By the end of the period the Company had developed a larger sales force, restored the general agency system, and instituted a system of compensation more consistent and equitable than had existed previously. At the same time the Company moved to make its policy contracts more attractive and to improve its mortality experience by applying higher standards of risk selection.

Years	Average Annual Premium Income	Average Annual Expenses	Expenses As Percentage of Premiums
	(In Millions)		
1882-1884	$3.0	$.50	16.6%
1885-1889	5.4	.98	18.1
1890-1894	10.9	1.80	16.5
1895-1899	15.5	2.40	15.5
1900-1904	24.6	3.70	15.0
1905-1909	31.7	4.55	14.2

CHAPTER SEVEN

Marketing – Insurance Plans, Risk Standards, and Geographical Changes: 1882-1907

VIGOROUS competition was the key characteristic in life insurance during most of this quarter century of prosperity. It figured strongly in the new lines of insurance that were being advocated and in the question of underwriting standards. It arose when expansion in the market area was under consideration, especially in making sales outside the United States. It was intimately involved in the relationship between agents in the field and in the tendency, on the part of some firms in the industry, to carry on practices that attracted unfavorable comment.

Northwestern usually approached most of the new developments in life insurance with the basic conservatism inherent in its fundamental principles of sound underwriting and simplified methods. There was a marked tendency in the industry to promote old plans under new guises, particularly to introduce a "speculative appeal" to prospective buyers. While the Company followed the industry trend by adopting so-called tontine or deferred dividend policies, it customarily refrained from using the new merchandising techniques, relying instead upon lower net cost to attract prospects. The management steadily tightened already high underwriting standards when competitive pressures were causing many life companies to move in the opposite direction. At the same time Northwestern liberalized the terms of its policy contracts in light of experience and followed similar tendencies in the industry.

At a time when some American companies expanded their geographical markets to include Europe, Mexico, Cuba, and Canada, Northwestern restricted itself to only the "healthiest" regions of continental United States. In the area of sales promotion and practices Northwestern was troubled by most of the problems which beset the industry through unrestrained competition. Although it was impossible for a single life company to prevent fully its field organization from engaging in certain excesses, the management determinedly resisted dubious and unethical tendencies with as much success as it was possible to attain in the absence of industry-wide action.

Yet it would be a mistake to assume that Northwestern was content to follow tradition slavishly. Following careful study, and anticipating reforms which were imposed on the industry after 1905, the management introduced a new element in the life insurance contract: optional forms of settlement. In the area of promotion Northwestern developed a number of effective techniques which, combined with the advantage in net cost, provided vigorous competition for rivals. It was seeking to serve a select market with a relatively simple set of insurance plans. Although these self-imposed restraints restricted Northwestern to a given market, through the skillful use of a good field organization and the cost advantages inherent in rigorous underwriting practices it effectively exploited this market to such an extent that before the end of the period it had become the fourth largest company in the industry.

Expansion of the Home Office Agency Staff

When Willard Merrill became superintendent of agencies he had only two department assistants— Thomas W. Buell in the Home Office and, supervising the Eastern agencies, another carry-over of Keenan's administration, J. S. Gaffney, whose headquarters were in New York City. When Gaffney left the Company in 1882 Merrill began to experiment with the supervisory system. George Hilliard was hired as a special agent in the Eastern states, with the dual responsibility of soliciting insurance and "aiding our general agents in the establishment of their agencies."[1] This practice of using an on-the-spot supervisor for the Eastern agencies continued until 1894.

Meanwhile, in anticipation of the restoration of the general agency system and the expansion of the Company's field force west of Pennsylvania, Merrill asked Charles B. Coe, Northwestern general agent in Indianapolis, to become assistant agency superintendent at Milwaukee. A man of great persuasiveness, Coe enthusiastically entered into the work of developing the Company's Western agencies and streamlining the agency system. When, for reasons of health, Coe left Milwaukee in 1884 to take a general agency in Denver, he was succeeded by Alonzo W. Kimball, a partner in the Kimball and Libbey agency at Green Bay, Wisconsin. An excellent organizer, quick-witted and able, Kimball soon became Merrill's key lieutenant in the area of sales management, remaining in Milwaukee until 1894 when he was appointed general agent in Chicago.

The gap in the agency department left by Kimball's departure was filled by Henry F. Norris. Norris joined the Company in 1886 when, after a career as wholesale salesman and store proprietor, he became a soliciting agent with the general agency in Rochester, New York. A man of considerable forcefulness, he quickly won recognition from the Home Office. In 1892 he was appointed assistant superintendent and assigned as a special agent and coordinator for the Eastern territories. After succeeding Kimball, Norris carried out his responsibilities with such success that Merrill later recommended him for the post of superintendent of agencies.

The year previous to Kimball's resignation George E. Copeland, Northwestern's general agent at Davenport, Iowa, accepted a position at the Home Office. Because of a flair for systemization, Copeland reorganized the Company's purchasing department on a sounder basis and also acted as an assistant to Merrill. In 1894 Copeland was promoted to second assistant superintendent, a position he held until 1902 when, with Norris' appointment as superintendent, he became the first assistant.

Northwestern's Life Insurance Plans

As of 1881 Northwestern's "product line" (that is, the group of life insurance plans and contracts offered to the public) included several variations of term insurance, standard life policies, standard endowment plans, and two annuity plans. The management, particularly those members in the actuarial and underwriting divisions, strongly opposed adoption of plans which could not be actuarially defended. This attitude placed Northwestern's agents at somewhat of a disadvantage. On the other hand, the simplicity of the insurance line, combined with strictly enforced underwriting standards, meant that administrative and clerical costs could be kept low and a solid "gain from mortality" achieved. Coupled with investment earnings that were relatively high, lower expense and lower mortality resulted in reduced cost of insurance, an element of great importance for Northwestern.

While the overwhelming number of Northwestern's policies outstanding participated in the distribution of dividends, the Company did offer a number of nonparticipating contracts, including a whole life policy and five- and ten-year term contracts. Although such policies had lower premiums than the participating varieties, none became important sellers and were never aggressively promoted. The anomaly of a mutual organization—one that prided itself on being the "policyholders' company"—actively promoting nonparticipating insurance evidently put the management in an uncomfortable position. Eventually such contracts were completely discontinued.

Deferred Dividend Insurance

Probably the most significant, and certainly the most dramatic, innovation in American life insurance during this period was the deliberate introduction of a speculative element into the contract. With this aspect of "product competition," Northwestern's managers, although reluctant, went along. What was essentially involved was an alternative to the conventional annual dividend contract whereby the insured could elect to have his dividends deferred for a longer period, such as five, ten, twenty, or more years.

Deferred dividend or tontine insurance received its name from a scheme first advanced in the 1680's by Lorenzo Tonti, a sycophant at the court of Louis XIV of France. Tonti proposed that the king persuade a multitude of people to subscribe to a perpetual loan to the government, interest on which would be paid the subscribers as long as they lived, with the provision that as each member died his rights to interest reverted to the surviving members in the group. The plan was adopted and widely publicized; tontine schemes subsequently became popular as promotional devices in France and England, but by the end of the eighteenth century were in disrepute, largely because of mismanagement and the dishonesty of many promoters.[2]

After a hiatus of some seventy years the idea was revived, this time by Henry B. Hyde, president of

the Equitable Life Assurance Society of America. In 1867 Equitable introduced the so-called "full-tontine" plan, under which a policyholder could buy a ten-, fifteen-, or twenty-year endowment policy, during which time he paid premiums but received no dividends. If he died during the interval, his beneficiary received the face value of the policy. If the policy lapsed, he received nothing; but if he lived to the end of the selected period, he shared in the accumulated dividends and forfeited reserves of all policies originally in the group. The "full tontine" plan never became widely popular because of the complete forfeiture of all reserve values in case of lapse.

A modified contract was subsequently devised applicable to life as well as endowment policies. Called a "semi-tontine" or deferred dividend contract, this plan stipulated a surrender value but in all other respects was like the full tontine. No dividends were paid to policyholders during the tontine period. Those holders who died before the specified date of distribution, or let their policies lapse, forfeited all rights to their accrued dividends. These were paid instead to the holders of policies still in force at the end of the period. Hyde introduced this new plan in 1871 and it became instantly popular. Many leading companies, imitating Equitable, soon discovered that this type of insurance constituted the largest part of their sales.[3]

The debate over the merits and demerits of deferred dividend insurance was long and acrimonious.[4] There can be no question that the plan was subject to abuse, especially under the administration of executives like Hyde, although Equitable was not alone in exaggerating the possible gains to survivors in an attempt to meet competition for sales. The gains, even under the semi-tontine form, were obviously at the expense of those policyholders who were unfortunate enough to die before the end of the tontine period or who could not afford to keep up their payments. Yet it can be, and was, argued that individuals who wished and could afford to undertake these risks were not being deceived by the terms of the contract.

The first suggestion that Northwestern adopt tontine policies was apparently made by Mathew Keenan, then superintendent of agencies, who argued,

> our plans of insurance do not meet with demands or commend themselves to the public; they are less imaginative, and promise less to the applicant. The two companies most successful in their volume of new business for many years, the Equitable and the New York Life, offer their tontine policies

with extravagant promises subject to rigid and unbending rules.

Keenan proceeded to advocate "some new feature or change"—tontine insurance.[5]

Although there was little support for Keenan's idea in the 1870's, by 1881 his eloquence was effective, and a subcommittee was appointed to consider the feasibility of adopting tontine insurance. On the evening of January 25, 1881, using the opportunity offered by the annual gathering of trustees and agents, an unprecedented joint meeting of the Board of Trustees and the Association of Agents was called to consider the question. At this meeting Keenan argued for the proposal, Willard Merrill took a negative stand, while Emory McClintock "spoke on both sides of the question showing the advantages and disadvantages."[6] A vote taken on the question of adoption resulted in a division of twenty-two for and thirty-three against.

This decision was not binding, however, and the committee gave the matter further intensive study. On April 13, 1881, it reported to the Executive Committee: "It is deemed expedient for the Northwestern Mutual Life Insurance Company to add to its system what is usually known as the tontine plan and to receive applications and issue policies accordingly." While Secretary Merrill did not concur on the report, he assured the Committee that he would "cheerfully and cordially cooperate in carrying the system out if adopted." The Committee's decision quickly afforded him this opportunity.

Curiously enough Northwestern adopted the full tontine plan, already being abandoned by most other companies. Naturally, few policies of this sort were sold, and it was not until after 1883, when the semi-tontine was introduced, that deferred dividend sales became important,

Keenan, who anticipated difficulty in getting the Company's agency force enthusiastically to promote tontine plans principally because they had for so long been using opposing arguments, was not the one to undertake the task of persuasion and education. If the agents were to be equipped with effective selling arguments Willard Merrill, who had opposed the whole concept, would have to accomplish it. Despite his own reservations Merrill did his job well; by 1885 nearly 18 per cent of Northwestern's total insurance in force was on the semi-tontine plan. This percentage grew until, in 1893, it amounted to over three-fifths of the total, after which the proportion declined until by 1905 it was only one-fourth. In part this expansion was stimulated by an extra 5 per cent first-year commission

offered on semi-tontine policies by the Company between 1885 and 1894. More important was the enthusiasm with which Northwestern's agents pushed this type of policy and its favorable reception by applicants.

Despite the success achieved with deferred dividend policies, the Northwestern management became increasingly concerned about selling this type of insurance, especially after the middle 1890's. This reaction stemmed from a number of considerations. One important factor was the growing disparity between estimates made to buyers and results to survivors. In general, the Home Office made a determined and conscientious effort to keep within bounds the claims made by its agents for Northwestern's policies, but with only partial success. The task of policing a far-flung agency force was difficult, especially in the case of tontine policies which were sold in the face of vigorous competition. How to restrain the selling force from making overly optimistic claims for these policies, particularly when professional actuaries were unable to make precise estimates, was not an easy problem.

Even the more modest claims for this type of policy proved to be misleading because of two trends which could hardly have been foreseen during the 1880's: one was the increasing life expectancy in the United States, the other the continued fall in the rate of interest. Increased longevity permitted a significantly greater number of insureds to survive the period of dividend deferment, resulting in smaller average per capita shares for the survivors. Lower interest meant that the accruing dividend surplus earned less, at compound interest, than was originally estimated. Calculations for five-year periods were reasonably accurate, but over longer intervals survivors ultimately collected much smaller dividends than they had been led to expect.

Although not immediately involved the Northwestern management may also have been impressed with the position of Colonel Jacob Greene, president of Connecticut Mutual and an implacable and articulate enemy of deferred dividends, especially as marketed by Equitable and New York Life.[7] Northwestern's officers generally disapproved of the intense competition engaged in by the so-called Big Three, even though Mutual Life did not initially offer deferred dividends.

In any event Northwestern began to de-emphasize tontine insurance, the first step coming in 1894 when the 5 per cent premium commission on the sale of such policies was withdrawn. Shortly thereafter the Company offered all holders of new tontine policies two years within which to decide whether they wanted to enter a particular tontine class or to accept an annual dividend arrangement. The results were startling; about 95 per cent of the continuing policyholders favored the annual dividend plan.[8] Based upon this sample of policyholder attitude, the management prepared to abandon the sale of deferred dividend insurance altogether. Their determination was stiffened in early 1905 when the Wisconsin legislature prohibited deferral of dividends for periods longer than five years. In June 1905 the Company ceased issuing all tontine-type policies.[9]

This event came some months before the Armstrong Investigation of insurance in New York State which resulted, among other things, in legislation barring tontine policies. In view of the severe criticisms directed against this type of insurance by both the New York and Wisconsin investigations of 1905–1906, the fact that Northwestern voluntarily withdrew from tontine was of considerable public relations value to the Company.

One further fact deserves attention in regard to Northwestern's experience with deferred dividend insurance. The Company achieved a remarkable record in maintaining "an individual account with each deferred dividend or tontine policyholder and . . . from this account they are able to furnish a full statement of all apportioned dividends provisionally credited throughout the life of each policy."[10] Such care was uncommon, according to the testimony of several life company managements made before the New York investigating committee in 1905. By its careful apportionment of accumulated dividends to specific groups of tontine policyholders, Northwestern clearly avoided the reprehensible practice followed by a number of companies which used their accumulated but unallocated tontine accounts to build high-powered sales organizations through excessively high commission rates and other expenditures.

Meanwhile, Northwestern took steps to increase the appeal of its conventional policies. The most important move in this direction came in 1900 with the introduction of an option settlement plan. Under this arrangement policyholders could choose as an alternative to the standard lump sum payment any one of three other methods of settlement. Option A provided that the Company would retain the proceeds and pay interest on them to beneficiaries. There were, of course, limits on the retention period. Option B provided for the payment of principal and interest in a specific number of annual installments. Under Option C the beneficiary would receive fixed annual installments throughout his or

her life with payments guaranteed to continue for a specific number of years in any event.

Northwestern was the first life company in the United States to introduce the option settlement plan, which proved to be increasingly important as a selling point in future years. Coming as it did when the Company's sales of tontine insurance were declining, it provided an attractive substitute and helped materially to maintain total sales. Probably nobody in the Company anticipated the future popularity of the life income options or the problems which this would in turn pose.

Liberalizing the Policy Contract

From 1882 to 1907 Northwestern's management cautiously moved in the direction of more liberal terms in regard to forfeitures for failure to pay premiums, restrictions on travel, occupations, and place of residence of its insureds. In general, changes followed the industry pattern fairly closely and came in response to public demand and competitive pressures (frequently transmitted from the agents). All prohibitions regarding travel and occupation became inoperative after a policy was in force for three years. Simultaneously, it provided that if the age of the applicant was correctly given, and if death had not occurred within three years of the date of contract, no policy could then be cancelled for reason of mis-statements in the application. An exception was obviously made when misinformation was given with intent to defraud.

The nonforfeiture provisions cited did not apply in the matter of intemperance. The contract provisions, just as earlier in the Company's history, clearly stated that in cases where a policyholder became intemperate Northwestern could cancel the contract by repaying the amount of the reserve, computed according to the then existing standards of the state of Wisconsin.

In 1892 all restrictions on travel and occupation were removed after the second anniversary date of the policy. During the same year new policies contained a revised intemperance clause, limiting the period within which the Company could cancel the policy for habitual intemperance to five years, on the same terms as previously applied.

Beginning in 1884 contracts contained still another important liberalization. Earlier policies imposed a strict interpretation of forfeiture for nonpayment of premium or interest in which the policy-

Home Office—1886 to 1914
N.W. corner, Broadway and Michigan Streets

holder was left virtually without recourse. The new contracts limited the forfeiture period to three years. Further, if the policyholder defaulted after paying at least three *cash* premiums, he would receive "a paid-up policy for such sum as the reserve on the policy by the now-existing standard of the state of Wisconsin will then purchase as a single premium at the Company's published rates, but without further participation in dividends."

Until 1892 any policyholder desiring to obtain paid-up insurance after his policy lapsed was required to make application in writing within three months, later lengthened to six months, from the date of premium default. In 1892 the "automatic paid-up policy provision," applicable to all policies then in force with the Company, wiped out all con-

ditions and secured such paid-up insurance without requiring action by the lapsed policyholder. The basis of this move was declared to be that policyholders were entitled to paid-up insurance by reason of the premiums paid prior to lapse; the failure to surrender the original contract within six months following date of lapse could not be recognized as sufficient reason for the destruction of that right.

The process of liberalization was greatly accelerated in 1896 when, for the first time, Northwestern adopted guaranteed cash, loan, and paid-up policy values which were incorporated in the policy contract in easily read, tabular form. At the same time the insured was given the privilege of changing the beneficiary in the contract. Furthermore, the long-established practice of permitting restoration of annual dividend policies within one year after default of premium payment was made a contractual right.

Prompted in part by the insistence of agents, the Company agreed to adopt rules which made policy contracts incontestable after being in force for a given time. The principal argument for this change was that some immaterial or unintentional error in the application could make the policy contestable and possibly void at any time after it went into effect. In 1892 the Company deleted the policy provision which stated, "If any statement made in the application for this policy shall be found untrue, this policy shall be void." In 1905 this provision was again modified to read,

after one year from the date hereon the liability of the Company under this policy shall not be disputed unless it relates to some fact material to the risk and shall have been intentionally made. Misstatement of age made without fraudulent intent, will be adjusted by the Company in accordance with the published premium rate now in use for the correct age.

Another source of agent dissatisfaction with the policy contract was the so-called "suicide clause." Again the agents were successful, although it took from 1900 to 1903 to get the change providing that policies were not void if the insured committed suicide after one year instead of the previous two-year limit.

New Mortality Table and Interest Assumption

During the years after 1880 American life insurance executives became increasingly concerned with two major tendencies affecting the safety of life insurance reserves on the one hand and the terms of policy contracts on the other. The first of these was the declining trend of interest rates, the second was the lengthening life expectancy of individuals. In computing premium rates most domestic life companies, before the 1890's, used the Combined Experience or Actuaries' Table of Mortality and assumed or guaranteed an interest rate of 4 per cent or higher in accumulating policy reserves. Until 1890 this assumed rate of interest was quite conservative, as actual earned rates customarily exceeded it by most comfortable margins. For example, Northwestern, which had gone to 4 per cent in 1870, had an earned rate ranging from 6.8 per cent to 8.5 per cent during the decade 1870–1879. Over the following ten years

margins between assumed and earned rates contracted significantly, and by the late 1890's the differential for many companies was approaching zero; for Northwestern the earned rate was about 4.8 per cent. (See Appendix G.)

This trend was the subject of intensive study by Northwestern's executives. One solution was to move to a lower reserve rate, using the old mortality assumptions which Connecticut Mutual did in 1882, much to the astonishment of the industry.[11] Northwestern's officers, like those in most other companies, were convinced that, based on later experience of American life companies, the Actuaries' Mortality Table was outdated. The American Experience Table of Mortality, first developed in 1868, had been improved over the years through the pooling of mortality information by the actuarial societies and various commissioners of insurance, and provided a better basis for determining premiums and estimating life expectancy.[12]

Early in 1898 the Company's Executive Committee accepted the recommendations of a special committee which had these subjects under study, and announced that effective January 1, 1899, Northwestern would issue insurance based on the American Experience Table with an assumption or guarantee of 3 per cent interest.[13]

The decision, particularly the 3 per cent interest assumption, once again indicated the inherent conservatism of the Company and its concern for the security of policyholders. To provide policy reserves under the new interest rate assumption necessitated an upward adjustment of premium rates. While this move might make it more difficult for Northwestern agents to compete with companies that kept their reserve rates higher than 3 per cent, the management feared that a continued reduction in interest rates earned would once again place reserves in jeopardy and require a further reduction in the reserve assumption within a few years. Thus Northwestern's entire pattern of premium rates was increased, the greatest rise taking place at the younger ages. On ordinary life, for example, the new premiums at age thirty-five were 5.43 per cent higher than on the corresponding 4 per cent policies; at age fifty-five, however, the differential was only 0.5 per cent. On limited payment policies the increase was substantially greater. For twenty payment life contracts, at age thirty-five, the increase amounted to over 11 per cent; at age forty-five the differential was only 5.66 per cent. The higher differential at younger ages was apparently accounted for by new loading features.

The increase in premiums, while undoubtedly affecting the Company in marketing competition, had no net effect upon the position of policyholders. Dividends increased during the subsequent years on a comparable basis, leaving the net cost of insurance relatively unaffected. Northwestern agents, while facing a somewhat more difficult task in selling, benefited to the extent that commission rates on the increased premiums produced a higher absolute commission income. With this change the Northwestern premium structure was essentially set for the next forty-seven years.

Underwriting Standards

The success of the actuarial and medical departments of the Company in maintaining and improving the underwriting standards of selection which had been attained by 1882 is demonstrated by the record of the succeeding twenty-five years. As might be expected, this process of improving standards frequently brought protests from members of the agency force, especially when an adverse report from the Home Office resulted in the loss of a commission. At the same time improved mortality experience led to higher dividends and lower net premiums for Northwestern policyholders. With minor changes in wording and the addition of further questions, the detailed and searching medical examinations worked out during the first decade of operations also remained unchanged. Local medical examiners were still admonished to make their examinations "thorough, exact, and circumstantial."

From time to time Northwestern insured the lives of Negroes. In 1885 the problem of getting a full medical history on Negro applicants raised the question as to the advisability of continuing this practice. Kimball made it clear, however, that "we have no prejudice against insuring colored men growing out of the mere fact of color." [14] In 1902, after research by the actuarial and medical staffs showed a substantially higher death rate among non-whites than whites, Northwestern refused to accept further applications from the former group, although later in its history the Company reversed this decision.

Undoubtedly the most striking feature of the Company's effort to maintain the quality of its risks during these years had to do with the consumption of alcoholic beverages. The rule followed earlier, of rejecting not only those who consumed liquor but all who were in any way associated with its manufacture or distribution, was even more rigorously enforced after 1882.

In 1895 Merrill wrote a letter to an agent in West Virginia which succinctly expressed the philosophy of the underwriting management of the Company with regard to the use of alcohol by applicants and insureds. The occasion was the rejection of an application by the medical department because of the applicant's frequent use of beer. The general agent, in protesting the decision, angrily wrote, "If the company proposes to run a temperance society, please advise me, and I will have Mr. Douglas [the sub-agent] leave his field, for everybody here uses beer as far as I know, though none of them uses it to excess." Merrill replied that he was a total abstainer himself, and that he was convinced that even drinking of beer, particularly by young men, was usually the first step toward intemperance and bad insurance risks. He continued, "The Northwestern is not running a temperance society. We are trying to avoid running an *intemperance* society." [15]

It was undoubtedly propitious that an atmosphere of personal freedom existed within the Company's management hierarchy. All veterans of the Home Office staff knew of President Palmer's custom, in the company of Judge Dyer, to pay two dignified visits daily to a reputable saloon near the Company's Home Office on Broadway. Here, totally unaware that they were becoming bad insurance risks, each drank a single neat whiskey and returned, apparently unimpaired, to his respective duties. [16]

Apparently Dr. McKnight's medical controls and McClintock's tightened actuarial standards found the Company's agents particularly sensitive during 1885–1886. In 1885, for example, the general agent in Vermont, Lumen P. Norton, resigned when an eighteen year old applicant was rejected because of a rheumatic knee. About this same time the highly successful John I. D. Bristol, Northwestern's general agent in New York City, became so incensed over a medical department rejection that it required a half dozen letters, including one of twelve pages, before he abandoned his assault on risk selection practices. [17]

Although the Home Office generally assumed a conciliatory attitude toward the agency force, these illustrations demonstrate their determination not to deviate from standards of selection acceptable to the Company's management. In fact, this determination to maintain standards was not confined to actions of agents and medical examiners, for these years were marked by an enlargement of the inquiry department of the Company, first established in 1878 "to acquaint itself with the moral hazard of applicants and those already insured." [18]

Beginning in 1888, Dr. E. J. Stone, a Company medical examiner in New York, was appointed head of this department. Under his direction a small staff of investigators toured the territories of the various general agencies to assist in field checks and investigations of doubtful risks, the maintenance of relationships with local credit associations, and the preparation of dossiers on policyholders whose health, character, and personal habits made them, in the medical department's estimation, doubtful risks. The records of such risks were then marked, and notice sent to the respective general agents that if, and when, the policyholder submitted his premium after the final due date, it was not to be accepted without approval from the Home Office. Since all policies were cancellable in the event premiums were not paid on time, the Company was within its rights in applying this policy. As management generally permitted the late payment of premiums without penalty, this convention was definitely effective in culling out "nondesirables" and raising the Company's risk standards.

This practice, however, was severely criticized during the Wisconsin insurance investigation in 1906. (See Chapter IX.) The use of what might be termed a home-grown detective bureau to obtain health data which could be used to cancel policies whenever a legitimate opportunity arose struck some of the investigators as indefensible and discriminatory. The Company justified itself on the grounds that such measures were necessary to keep the quality of its risks at acceptable standards; that in fairness to the bulk of its policyholders those persons who became bad risks due to a change in habits after securing insurance should be dropped whenever the opportunity offered. It was difficult, however, to justify similar action with respect to those whose health deteriorated for other reasons. Presumably this was one of the hazards prompting the purchase of insurance in the first place.

What influence the operations of the inspection department may have had is impossible to measure, but the general effect of the Company's stringent selective standards on the mortality experience was striking. Calculations by Northwestern's actuaries indicated that the death rate, as a percentage of the average amount of the Company's insurance in force for the 1875-1879 period, was 1.21 as compared with an industry rate of 1.24. For the 1890-1894 period the rates were 0.93 per cent and 1.39 per cent, respectively.

The Geography of the Market

In broad outline the areas covered by Northwestern agents between 1882 and 1907 were confined to those parts of the United States lying north and west of the southern coastal states of Florida, South Carolina, Mississippi, and Louisiana. These last four states were excluded because of the evidence of relatively poor mortality experience.

Within this general area there were both additions and subtractions. For example, Northwestern established agencies for the first time in the territories of Wyoming in 1886, Arizona in 1890, and Oklahoma in 1891 because of the growth of population in these regions. The other changes in sales territory were associated either with state legislation unacceptable to the Company, or with evidence of improved or deteriorated mortality experience in particular places. This latter consideration led to the re-establishment of agencies in Tennessee and Arkansas; the question of unacceptable legislation was important in Missouri, North Carolina, Alabama, and Texas.

To take one example, legislative changes led to the withdrawal and subsequently the re-entry of Northwestern agents in North Carolina. Company agents began selling in the Tarheel State in 1869, during the hectic era of Reconstruction, and one of the Company's most distinguished agents, Colonel John B. Cary of Virginia, represented Northwestern in this region. In 1899, however, the state legislature passed the so-called Craig Law, aimed principally at the railroads but affecting other industries as well. The intent of the bill was to prevent the removal of suits from state to federal courts; to achieve this it required, for all intents and purposes, all corporations doing business in North Carolina to become domestic corporations in the state. As President Palmer remarked: "The provisions of the said act requiring this corporation to be a corporation in North Carolina, the same as if it had been originally created by the laws of that state, are, to say the least, novel." [19] Because of the uncertainties of the interpretation and the possible complications involved, Northwestern discontinued its agencies in North Carolina in June 1899. With the repeal of the Craig Law two years later, local agencies were re-established.

The Company abstained from participating in what has been described as "the most astonishing single aspect of American life companies in these years, 1868-1905" [20]—the invasion of overseas markets, led by the Guardian (then Germania), Equitable, New York Life, and Mutual Life, all of New York City. There is no evidence that Northwestern's management ever gave serious consideration to entering that market. A district agency contract had been issued in 1874 which included Honolulu and the Hawaiian Islands, but since this was part of a contract with a Georgia general agent, it is apparent that neither he nor the Company seriously considered the possibility of foreign business. It is probable that because of personal contacts there, the agent was merely seeking Company permission to secure legal applications in the territory. This interpretation is strengthened by Merrill's position in a similar matter some twenty years later. Replying to a request for the right to represent the Company in the Hawaiian Islands, the superintendent observed:

> We have no doubt as to the healthfulness of your climate or the fact that there is a desirable class of business that might be written, but for some years past we have done no business outside of the United States, and the fact that we limit our business to the United States has been so helpful in our soliciting business that nothing would induce us to open an agency outside the United States.[21]

In similar vein Merrill rejected a request for a Canadian agency, and for precisely the same reasons: "we have found it to our advantage to advertise the fact that Northwestern does not go out of the United States. The idea has entered so largely into our canvassing, that we would be unwilling to return to Canada even though the law should be changed."[22]

There seems to be little question that the Company's management felt the United States market offered sales opportunities sufficient for them to share in a healthy and vigorous growth of insurance. As a result, with but three exceptions, the 1907 sales territory of the Company shown on the accompanying map was maintained for the following half century. These exceptions were the addition of New Mexico in 1912, the re-entry into Alabama in 1950, and re-entry into South Carolina in 1954.

Sales Promotion and its Control

In their selling activities the Company management and agents stressed the growth of Northwestern, its record in establishing sound reserves, including contingency funds, while maintaining a high dividend rate, and the liberality of its policy contract. But the basic appeal, and the one most vigorously pushed, was the low net cost of Northwestern's insurance.

The most important, certainly the most usual method of acquainting prospects with Northwestern insurance plans was through personal solicitation by the Company's agents. These sales efforts were supplemented by advertisements and printed sales brochures, pamphlets, and broadsides; a reflection of the growing intensity of competition. Public advertisements were used only—and an annual budget of $6,000 shows how infrequently it occurred—when the Company wished to assert the truth where falsely attacked by advertisements of competitors.[23]

While the Company's direct advertising remained modest and circumspect, its agents advertised more extensively and at their own expense. As part of a more general policy of controlling all publications bearing the Company name, advertising copy had to be sent to Milwaukee for approval before publication. This supervision was not always easy to enforce and required constant attention. Early in 1882, for example, Merrill felt obliged to caution the general agent in Troy, New York, against making statements in an advertisement which implied that policyholders would receive 4.75 to 5 per cent compound interest, in addition to their insurance, by taking Northwestern endowment policies. Merrill said that though this had been true in the past, the suggestion should not be made that it would always be so; it would depend upon the interest rate earned, and upon other factors as well. In 1889 Kimball refused permission to an agent in St. Paul, Minnesota, to publish a scathing reply naming the company which had been circularizing his territory with anonymous pamphlets "exposing" Northwestern, explaining that, "An anonymous attack bears on its face its own character. Our company does not issue such and very seldom pays much attention to them when aimed at ourselves."[24]

The claims made by agents for Northwestern's tontine policies were especially difficult to control. This was illustrated by the Company's experience with J. I. D. Bristol, who had his own ideas on most aspects of life insurance, including effective selling tactics. During 1884–1886, when Northwestern was establishing its Eastern business and employing deferred dividend as the principal policy feature, Bristol advertised extensively in the New York newspapers. Copy for these advertisements contained estimates of tontine dividends which were Bristol's own, and which were considered by McClintock grossly optimistic. After repeated (and unheeded) advice and warning, Merrill silenced Bristol's promotional schemes by ordering him to withdraw his advertisements. Meanwhile, because of Bristol's reputation for success and his leadership in the Association of Agents, word of his fruitful employment of these advertisements soon spread. Bristol's copy, with its sanguine estimates of benefits, was quickly publicized by other Company general

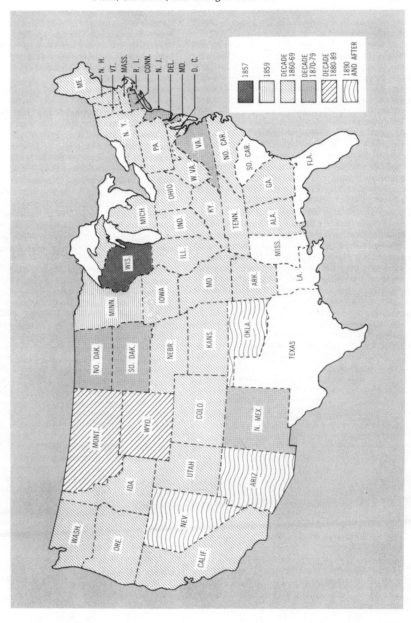

Growth of Northwestern Service in the United States

agents. In 1886 management restored order in the promotional field by forbidding all agents to use Bristol's circulars.[25]

In contrast to its attitude toward newspapers and magazines as media, the management enthusiastically pushed the use of sales brochures, booklets, and pamphlets. If the Company did not originate the use of comparative cost-ratio promotion, it was quick to respond to the device, and developed the technique to a remarkable degree. By the early 1880's the Company had already made available to its agents a series of booklets entitled "Accumulated Evidence," containing comparisons of Northwestern policies with those of other companies. This use of direct comparison, naming specific companies, became widespread over the industry. A typical example was the pamphlet prepared by the agency department in 1885 called "The Mutual Life Insurance Company of New York vs. The Northwestern Mutual Life Insurance Company." The pamphlet was designed to show that by a comparison of the operating ratios of the two firms, actual dividends paid, and net costs to policyholders, the prospective insured could not fail to benefit from insurance with Northwestern rather than with Mutual Life.

Other pamphlets, equally effective, were subsequently issued. One, containing some three hundred examples of the records of its policies, was issued in 1887 to prove that holders of Northwestern policies received benefits that could not be met by other companies. The following year thousands of copies of a booklet were distributed to agents for direct competition with Equitable. On each left-hand page was the heading, "Attack," with quotations from Equitable's sales literature claiming features and advantages of an Equitable policy. On each opposite page was printed a "Reply," with information and analytical data representing the absurdity of these claims; how Equitable was misinforming the public; how unfounded were the charges against Northwestern; and how ill-advised was the Equitable management to make these statements. A few years later another series of pamphlets, entitled "Over Their Own Signatures," was especially effective. Each issue contained the personal testimonials of scores of prominent policyholders, telling why they purchased Northwestern insurance and describing the benefits enjoyed from membership in the Company.

One especially troublesome competitive practice involved what the industry called "twisting," i.e., inducing a policyholder to cancel one policy and acquire another one, usually with another company. There were occasions where such a shift might be in the best interests of a policyholder; it might offer benefits better suited to his needs, or it might offer lower net costs. Industry complaints centered largely on those cases where it was alleged that agents, solely for the commission received on newly issued policies, "sold" the insured on the idea of changing his policies.

Obviously transactions of this type could be harmful to some people. Equally obvious is the difficulty of proving the intent of the insurance agent, and in a market characterized by a growing number of insurance plans it was no easy matter to determine whether the individual had been harmed or benefited by the switch. While the Northwestern management was inclined to the view that it was a public service to persuade individuals to switch from the policies of certain other companies to those issued by the Company, it was opposed to agents exceeding the bounds of reasonable claims in making the effort. For example, as early as 1885, when corresponding with an agent in Pennsylvania, accused by a rival of twisting, Merrill wrote:

> We know there are times when the agents of companies make attacks of such a character that a sharp comparison of the two companies becomes unavoidable, but we are sure that whatever is said by any solicitor prejudicial to the integrity or financial condition of a rival company is very detrimental to the entire business. We hope the charge made in this case against you and Mr. Fleming is entirely false, for we cannot state in too strong terms our disapproval of that class of soliciting and we are unwilling to believe that, even in the heat of sharp competition, you have gone so far as reported.[26]

Another competitive measure, even more pernicious during these years, was rebating, or the return to policyholders by the agent of part of the commission. As a device to encourage sales, rebating had long been troublesome; with the introduction of deferred dividend insurance and the spread of ruthless marketing tactics, the practice became nearly universal. In 1888 the Life Underwriters' Association of New York called for concerted industry action to halt rebating; President Palmer was an active member of a committee created by the association to formulate anti-rebate legislation. Legislation prohibiting the granting of rebates by agents was enacted by a number of states, including New York in 1889 and Wisconsin in 1891,[27] but experience soon demonstrated that legislation was not by itself the answer. As the Massachusetts insurance commissioner explained in 1890, no one company could by itself refuse to give rebates and long remain in competition.

Meanwhile, it became increasingly obvious that the rebate problem was largely a function of the all-out drive for increased sales by the life companies. This in turn led to larger agency forces and higher rates of compensation. The higher the commission rates, the greater was the pressure on individual agents to give rebates. Informed buyers soon came to expect them as a condition for the purchase of insurance.

Northwestern's attitude toward rebating was, essentially, pragmatic. Merrill wrote to one agent in 1882:

> The whole practice of giving off commissions is exceedingly demoralizing, not only to the agent, but also to the party solicited. . . . The moment a merchant gets a reputation of depreciating his own goods and giving discounts according to the emergency, he loses his standing and people are afraid to trade with him. It is precisely so with an insurance solicitor.[28]

By 1886 Northwestern's agents were sufficiently concerned about rebating to pass the following resolution at their annual meeting in July:

> Whereas, We believe the rebate system, practiced to a wide and deplorable extent by the representatives of the different life insurance companies, is a great and despicable evil, and demoralizing in the extreme to the profession of life insurance; therefore,
>
> Resolved, That we will show our condemnation of this evil by emphatically denouncing it in every possible manner and doing all in our power, in action and influence, to overcome it.[29]

This action stimulated the management to adopt a stronger stand regarding the practice. In that same year a circular sent to all agents on the subject of rebating closed with the statement, "We cannot too strongly state our disapproval of giving away commissions."[30] In February 1893 Merrill notified the Company's representatives in states having anti-rebate laws that it would cancel the contract of any agent found guilty of rebating in those states. Five months later the Executive Committee, acting on Merrill's suggestion, adopted a resolution making Northwestern's anti-rebating policy binding upon all Company agents.[31] In the same year, 1893, an anti-rebate clause was made a part of the standard contracts with agents.

Northwestern did more than merely adopt resolutions and place toothless clauses in agents' contracts. When certain Company agents became implicated in a number of rebating cases around 1895, their contracts were cancelled by the Home Office. In addition, the Company refused to renew contracts with others who, while not officially convicted of rebating, had aroused management's suspicions.[32]

Thus the attitudes and actions of Northwestern's management significantly pre-dated the general condemnation of rebating which followed when the Armstrong Investigation uncovered the full extent of the practice in 1905. In the opinion of Northwestern's officers, rebating could not be effectively controlled until the managements and general agents of all companies behaved as those of Northwestern —by refusing to accept business which had been written on a rebate basis.[33]

After becoming head of the agency department, Merrill developed and consistently followed a practice of writing letters of praise and encouragement to agents whose work improved from year to year. Furthermore, this practice became so deeply ingrained in the administrative habits of his lieutenants that Norris, who succeeded him as superintendent of the department, continued it after Merrill's death. Having been an agent himself, Merrill recognized the morale problem facing the individual salesman in the field, separated from the Home Office and his fellow employees. Typical of the letters which went out to the men in the field, and one which aids in explaining the respect and affection in which he was held by the Company's sales agents, was the following, written in 1882: "I notice with great pleasure your increase for the month of January. If you will keep up your successful efforts through the year the result will be profitable to you as well as to the company. So fine a start promises well for the future."[34]

This letter, moreover, is indicative of another administrative control by the agency department under Merrill's management, the close inspection of new business reported by each agent on a monthly basis. This information provided Merrill and his lieutenants with the data needed to supervise more effectively the force in the field. In addition to enabling Home Office personnel to compliment the successes of the field men and to reward meritorious individual effort, this intimate first-hand knowledge of its field men enabled the management to goad and prod agents who failed to come up to expectations, and to rid the Company of their services when failure became too flagrant. In 1885, for example, Merrill noted that the local agencies in the Wisconsin territories consistently failed to write the volume of new business he believed possible. To the Neenah agent he wrote:

> We feel that for a number of years that most of the Wisconsin agencies have been asleep. I have just been looking over the record of your agency and find that in 1882 we issued $3,000 of insurance for you; in 1883 $1,000; and in 1884 $3,000. I find that the entire renewal premiums of your agency amount to less than $5,000. Of course you know, without my saying it, the high esteem in which you are held by the officers of the company, and certainly by no one are you esteemed more highly than by myself. At the same time the agency department must be handled with a view to business, and I think we ought not to be satisfied with a small amount received from so thriving a place as Neenah.[35]

There was no question that by 1907 the sales agencies were closely integrated with over-all management policy.

The Sales Record

The real achievement of the agency force, as developed and administered by Willard Merrill, can be measured by the sales record of Northwestern from 1882 through 1907, and by the absolute and relative growth of the Company's insurance in force. As shown in Chart VII-1, the annual new business grew from about $20 million at the beginning of the period to more than $100 million in 1907. This rate of sales growth closely paralleled that of the industry as a whole. Total Northwestern sales of insurance during these years of $1.5 billion,

CHART VII-1

Deferred Dividend (Semi-Tontine) Insurance in Force Compared with Total Insurance in Force: Northwestern, 1885–1907

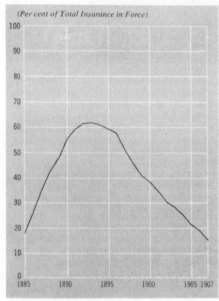

(Per cent of Total Insurance in Force)

SOURCE: Company Records.

while somewhat less than one-half the average sales of each of the Big Three ($4.17 billion), represented the fourth largest volume produced by an ordinary life company for the period.

The volume of sales alone reflects only a part of Northwestern's marketing record. The Company's self-imposed limitation of selective underwriting and refusal to match the high pressure selling tactics

	(1) IN FORCE, DEC. 31, 1881	(2) SALES 1882-1907	(3) 1881 IN FORCE PLUS SALES 1882-1907	(4) IN FORCE, DEC. 31, 1907	(5) IN FORCE, DEC. 31, 1907 AS PERCENT OF COLUMN 4
	(In Millions)				
NORTHWESTERN	$74.5	$1,505.6	$1,580.1	$881.6	55.8%
Big Three (total)	668.2	12,498.3	13,166.5	4,798.2	36.4
Industry	1,644.0	24,437.3	26,081.3	14,063.0	54.3

SOURCE: *Insurance Year Book*, 1910; Appendix E.

CHART VII-2

Sales of Insurance: Industry and Northwestern, 1882–1907

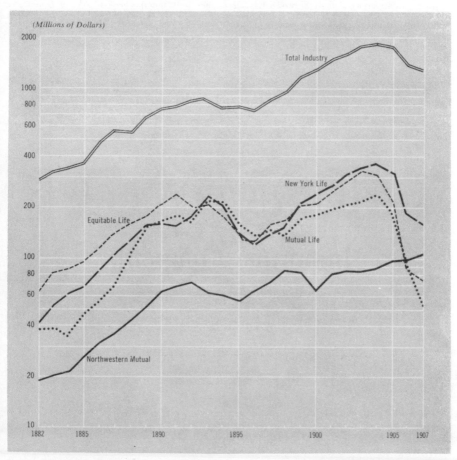

SOURCES: Industry data: Stalson, *Marketing Life Insurance,*
pp. 813-14. Company data: *Insurance Year Book,*
1910, financial history section.

of its rivals were undoubtedly reflected, through low mortality and low lapse and surrender rates, in the relative amount of its total sales that remained in force during the period. As shown in the preceding page, judged by this standard, Northwestern did somewhat better than the industry as a whole, and considerably better than the Big Three.[36]

In terms of its own stated objectives in the marketing of insurance—to be not the biggest company but rather the best—Northwestern Mutual, under the Palmer administration, was highly successful. Its share of the market had been enlarged during the period, particularly in relation to the ordinary life insurance market. In 1880, measured by insurance in force, Northwestern had ranked seventh in the industry; in 1905 it stood sixth. If the two leading sellers in the field of industrial insurance, Metropolitan and Prudential, are excluded for the latter year, the Company's size rank was fourth.[37] Not only had selling costs been lowered per dollar of premium income, but quality standards of selection had been improved and the general agency organization firmly established. These results constituted an impressive achievement.

Heading used on policy forms from July 15, 1896 to February 1, 1899

CHAPTER EIGHT

Investment and Public Relations in a Prosperous Quarter Century: 1882-1907

THE quarter century after 1881 was, with specific exceptions, a period of vastly expanded
investment activity for United States life insurance companies. For Northwestern the increase
in the amount of investment funds was striking, and
required management to devote a larger share of
time and Company resources to find investment opportunities and secure the best returns commensurate with safety. While investment opportunities un-
folded at an astonishing rate, this growth was more
than matched by the increase of funds seeking employment and the type and number of financial
institutions competing for outlets. One of the results
of this development was a gradual but steady reduction in interest rates, probably due, at least in part,
to the reduction of "risk" in a nation which had survived the ordeal of union and was engaged in intensive industrialization. The Northwestern investment
portfolio reflected most of the changes which were
dictated by the course of economic development,
but it was still characterized by the basic policies
continued by management from an earlier epoch. It
was these principles more than any other single factor which made Northwestern distinct from most
firms in the industry. Together with its role as a
capital-forming and tax-paying institution, Northwestern's investment patterns and problems are reviewed in this chapter, which concludes with a final
evaluation of its achievements and progress during
the quarter century.

Investment Management: Procedures and Personnel

During the twenty-six years following 1881, several important procedural changes were introduced
in the management of Northwestern's investments.
These included the grooming of responsible personnel to administer the loan department and the growing system of branch loan offices, and the appointment of executive officers to direct and coordinate
the policies and practices. In addition, further division of trustee responsibility for operations was required to cope with the greater demands upon the
Executive Committee as new investment opportunities were explored and exploited.

At the beginning of the period investment management continued to be but one of the major functions of the Executive Committee to which its chairman, President Palmer, devoted a steadily greater
proportion of his time. The rapid increase in the
number of loan applications coming to its attention
quickly placed the Executive Committee under a
most onerous burden that soon required relief. In

1887 the trustees created a Finance Committee to function along lines similar to the Executive Committee, while restricting itself to purely financial and investment matters. This committee was made directly responsible to the Executive Committee and the Board. In theory its creation was supposed to establish a logical division of functions and at the same time to preserve the principle of direct control of the Company by the trustees. In practice, however, the advantages were less readily apparent. Duplication in the membership of the two committees was so extensive that it can hardly be said to have saved time and energy.*

Within the Finance Committee itself the evolution of the investment portfolio and the problems associated with business depressions caused a further subdivision of responsibility. By 1894, with the growing importance of bonds in Northwestern's portfolio, two subcommittees were appointed: one responsible for the maintenance, rental, and sale of real estate obtained through foreclosure; the second to supervise the purchase and disposal of bonds.[1]

The needs of insurance marketing and systematic administration of the Company's foreclosed real estate resulted in the reshuffling of top management, thereby shifting Willard Merrill to the agency department and transferring Keenan to responsibility for special real estate and other investment matters. From 1881 until 1890 Keenan and Palmer administered the loan department with only supervisory assistance. Growth of mortgage investments, with the commensurate increase in administrative and record-keeping activity, obviously required additional management personnel and resulted in the promotion of P. R. Sanborn to the newly created post of superintendent of mortgage loans. Sanborn was the only Northwestern investment officer during these years who had come up through the employee ranks, starting as a clerk in the loan department in 1875. Sanborn, born in Appleton, Wisconsin, in 1853, had received a good general education, and matured in a tradition of dominant business personalities, jealous of the prerogatives of office. This training, in addition to excellent administrative abilities, won for him a steady progress in the Company; he was elected third vice president in 1904 and obtained the second vice presidency four years later.

The continued expansion of investments revealed

other gaps in the hierarchy of investment management after 1890, and to fill the most apparent the trustees persuaded William P. McLaren to emerge from semi-retirement. Since the retirement of Matthew Keenan was imminent, an experienced businessman was sought to supervise loan agents and understudy the vice president. McLaren, a native Scotsman, possessed the kind of successful business background the Company desired. This, and his active interest in Milwaukee affairs, had resulted in his election to Northwestern's board in 1877; he subsequently devoted much time to the Company as a member of the Executive and Finance Committees. In 1892, at the age of fifty-nine, McLaren undertook the management of Northwestern's branch office loan system and assisted in supervising foreclosed real estate. After his election as third vice president in 1893 he succeeded Keenan as chief investment officer under Palmer the following year.

The pattern of management succession, which had taken both Keenan and McLaren from the Board of Trustees and the standing committees and appointed them to the professional officer group, was apparent again in 1901. With additional assistance needed in the investment division, President Palmer obtained the election of George C. Markham as third vice president. Markham, a native of New York and a highly successful attorney, had been a Northwestern trustee since 1895 and a member of the standing committees since 1896. Vigorous and forceful in personality, he assumed many of the burdens of Palmer and McLaren, enabling the latter to devote more attention to the investigation of railroad investments. Following McLaren's death in 1904, Markham was promoted to succeed him, and, when Merrill died a year later, he became vice president and apparently heir-apparent to Palmer.

Other structural changes in investment management during the years after 1890 involved appointment of a supervisor for the loan agencies, who also reviewed lending territories, and of an assistant superintendent of mortgage loans to assist Sanborn. Record keeping and administrative routines for bond holdings were also the responsibility of the loan department.

President Palmer, demonstrating his alertness to the changing needs of the investment organization by appointing able personnel and delegating authority, remained the great central stabilizing force in Northwestern. Although the men he selected as his lieutenants and potential successors formed a diversified but capable group, their effectual coordination into a disciplined organization was ample testimony to the president's skill as administrator and leader.

---

* At the time of the 1887 move, the Executive Committee was composed of seven members, including President Palmer and Vice President Keenan. Five of these men, including the latter two, were named to the Finance Committee. In 1892, after the Executive Committee had been increased to nine trustees, all seven of the Finance Committeemen also sat on the Executive Committee.

General Developments
in Investments to 1907

In contrast to the previous period, investment opportunities from 1882–1907 expanded rapidly. The rate of capital formation in the United States increased from an average of about $2 billion per year for the decade 1879–1888 to nearly $4.3 billion annually for the decade 1899–1908.[2] Transportation and manufacturing facilities were improved and extended, agriculture was marked by an increasing mechanization, and urban communities grew at an accelerating pace. Interestingly enough, however, investment opportunities did not expand sufficiently to prevent interest rates from continuing the long-run downward trend that began in the 1870's; and what proved to be particularly significant for Northwestern was the increasing nationalization of capital markets, which narrowed regional differentials in interest rates that had always been to Northwestern's advantage.

More specifically Northwestern's investment managers were confronted with three sets of problems during the 1882–1907 period. The first had to do with the adjustment of interest rates and maturities of mortgage loans, as well as the allocation of funds between rural and urban loans. The second involved the handling of special real estate. Finally, there was the problem of analysis and selection of municipal and railroad bonds. Most of the problems in the first and second category were similar in kind, if differing in degree, to experiences previously encountered. Bond investments, particularly in railroads, represented a new field for the Company.

Northwestern's premium income, which expanded some thirteenfold from 1882 to 1907, continued to be the most important source of funds for the Company. Moreover, as sales increased after 1882, the contribution of premium income to the total income rose from 60 to 70 per cent. Coupled with interest on investments and rentals from real estate, which expanded nearly eight and one-half times over the same period, Northwestern's total gross annual income increased from $3.8 million in 1882 to over $43.5 million in 1907. The total for the entire period amounted to almost $503 million. As indicated in Chart VIII-1 the net funds available for investment grew at about the same rate as gross income, from an annual average of about $1.21 million for the years 1882–1884 to over $13.8 million for 1905–1907, or an aggregate of some $212.4 million.

In reality these net amounts substantially understate the magnitude of the investment problem. The repayment of loans and exchanges within the invest-

CHART VIII-1

Income, Expenditures, and Net Available
for Investment: Northwestern,
1882–1907

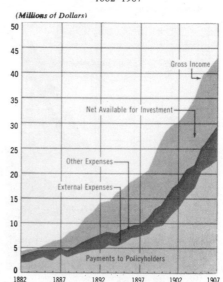

(*Millions* of Dollars)

SOURCE: Appendix F, Tables 1-4.

ment portfolio probably brought the totals to be invested annually to roughly twice the size of the net figures.

The reaction of Northwestern's investment managers to the problem of finding satisfactory outlets for these funds is reflected in the shifting pattern of the Company's investment portfolio. (See Chart VIII-2.) Not only did the three primary types of investments—mortgage loans, bonds, and loans to policyholders—greatly increase, but following the onset of the 1893 depression a significant shift occurred in the distribution of the Company's assets. The most striking change, as shown in Chart VIII-3, came in the relative importance of mortgage loans which, after reaching a high point of about 84 per cent of the total in 1890, dropped to approximately 50 per cent by 1907. The decline in the proportion of mortgage loans was largely offset by increases in bond holdings and policy loans.

Real estate, acquired through foreclosure, constituted a troublesome problem for the Company during these years. In absolute amount the value of

CHART VIII-2

Distribution of Admitted Assets:
Northwestern, 1882–1907

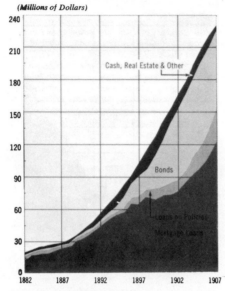

(Millions of Dollars)

SOURCE: Appendix F, Table 5.

business slump, principally because of sudden contractions in the demand for loans. Similar tendencies can be noticed in the accrued and deferred accounts.

The Policy Loan Account

The policy loan account, made up of premium notes, bills receivable, and loans on policies, increased from $1.5 million in 1881 to over $30.5 million at the end of 1907. Of these three types, the receivables were already insignificant in 1882 and totally extinguished by 1892. The decreasingly important role of premium notes in the Company's marketing policy was reflected in the diminishing magnitude of this account from about $1.5 million in 1882 to $288,000 in 1899, although it rose slightly after that date. Thus the over-all growth was largely a result of the demand by insureds for policy loans which were first made available by the Company in 1894.

Before 1893 Northwestern was prohibited by Wisconsin law to lend to policyholders on the security of their policy reserves, and anyone wishing to borrow on his insurance was forced to turn to sources other than the Company for funds. So many requests were received by the Company to make such loans, however, that an attempt was made by management to locate lenders in the Milwaukee area willing to accept an assignment of insurance as security. Among the Company's own officers and trustees, and among friends of officials and employees, were persons with money and knowledge of the negotiable nature of an insurance policy. Such persons soon were involved in this kind of lending, some of them on a rather large scale. As an added service, records of these loans were kept in the secretary's department of the Home Office, and regular assignment forms prepared there for use by policyholder borrowers. The expense of keeping these records and notifying the lender if interest or principal payments were not forthcoming was borne by the Company as a service to policyholders.

Under legislation passed by the Wisconsin Legislature in 1893 Northwestern was allowed, at its own discretion, to lend policyholders up to 90 per cent (later 95 per cent) of the policy reserves, at interest rates not to exceed 6 per cent. Northwestern had sponsored the legislation as a step in liberalizing its policy contracts, and in practice such loans were ordinarily made automatically at the request of policyholders. Coming in 1894, just as many of the Company's insureds were feeling the impact of the

such properties on Northwestern's books diminished rather steadily from about $1.3 million in 1882 to only $243,000 at the close of 1892. Between 1892 and 1907 the cyclical pattern of the depression period of the 1870's was repeated; the account reached a peak of $3.86 million in 1900, then declined continuously to a level of $1.44 million by the end of the period. It was notable that during both the 1873 and 1893 depressions the high point in distressed real estate owned by the Company was reached some time after the nadir of depression had been passed and the economy was well along on the road to business recovery.

The other assets, cash and accrued items, increased at a nominal rate during these years. The principal characteristic of these accounts was not growth, but a considerable degree of variation, again a reflection of cyclical fluctuations in business conditions. The amount of cash, for example, was increased more than proportionately to the growth in total assets during periods of financial crises and

1893 depression, a large number of policyholders took advantage of the new borrowing privilege; policy loans grew from $79,000 in 1894 to $1.9 million in 1895. Over the succeeding years the amount continued to expand, increasing with characteristic rapidity following the panics of 1903 and 1907.

While most insurance companies making policy loans handled the transactions in one or another of the insurance departments, Northwestern chose to administer them as part of the functions of its mortgage loan division. The decision was not based on objective evaluation, but was made largely because President Palmer felt that since money was to be loaned the responsibility for it should be vested with the investment department. Not until 1929, in fact, was this function transferred to the actuary and a reduction in duplication of records made possible.

Northwestern policy loans were distinctive in the life insurance industry in still another way. Terms tended to follow those made on mortgages, for one, three, or five years, and were renewable at the end of the specified period. Interest was due on the anniversary of the loan instead of on the policy anniversary, a practice which is probably unique in the business. Should the borrower default on the interest, within the terms of the contract the Company could cancel the policy and remit the difference between the amount of the debt and the cash value, if any. The management, however, generally exercised this right only after permitting a period of grace. Not for many years did Northwestern provide, as part of its policy contracts, for the automatic addition of unpaid interest to principal for as long as any value remained in the policy.

Loan practices were somewhat different, however, for holders of semi-tontine policies. The Company refused, for two reasons, to lend more than a nominal amount of the estimated reserves behind these policies. One was the uncertainty of the amount of these reserves until the termination of the tontine period. The other involved the question of ethics: should the Company help individuals in a tontine group to keep their policies in force when the participants counted on the occurrence of lapses? The management, however, saw no apparent inconsistency in continuing to refer applicants for loans on semi-tontine policies to private lenders in the Milwaukee area and maintaining the practice of handling these loans through the Company. This procedure, although explained as a needed service to policyholders, proved a source of some embarrassment to the Company management at the time of the Wisconsin insurance investigation in 1906.*

---

* See Chapter IX.

Mortgage Loans

As the magnitude of the account suggests mortgage lending remained the principal concern of Northwestern's investment managers. Despite the decline in the relative importance of mortgage loans to total assets after 1890, the account grew impressively, from $14.3 million in 1881 to $121.7 million in 1907. As shown in Table VIII-1, including the investment of repayments, the total sum allocated to this type of lending during the period amounted to $290.5 million. The solution of the problem of how best to allocate these funds in the face of greater competition for outlets and decreasing interest rates depended on the development of new lending areas and a careful weighing of the advantages of other types of securities.

The decline in average interest rates obtained by Northwestern on new mortgage loans was moderate from 1882 through 1889, varying between 6.6 and 5.8 per cent, with 6 per cent the most frequently quoted rate. After 1890 this rate dropped from 6 to 5 per cent. The average rate obtained on new loans fell from about 5.8 per cent to 4.5 per cent in 1902, rising again to around 4.7 per cent in 1907. As might be expected with a decline in interest rates, the return on the entire mortgage loan account on the whole averaged somewhat higher than the returns on new loans. From 6.5 per cent in 1885 the average interest rate earned fell to 5.6 per cent in 1895, and declined to 4.6 per cent in 1905.

The Company followed no set pattern in adjusting to changing conditions of competition for investment outlets. Differentials were maintained by the size of the loan, the geographic location, and the varying size of the communities. During 1884 loans were made at rates under 5 per cent on urban commercial properties valued at $200,000 or more. Generally, over the entire period interest rates on loans of $3,000 or less exceeded those made on higher valued properties by one-half of 1 per cent to 1 per cent. Interest rates on property loans made in the West North Central states and Colorado before 1895, as well as in the Tennessee-Kentucky-Georgia areas, were 1 per cent or more higher than the charges applied in the East North Central zone. Over the succeeding years the differential was reduced to about one-half of 1 per cent.

Decisions concerning the length of the loan periods were closely correlated with the change in interest rates. During 1874–1881 when the investment managers thought the decline in interest rates was temporary, they attempted to protect earnings by shortening the length of loans in anticipation of renewals or reinvestment at higher rates. After 1882 when it was apparent that rates were unlikely to rise and possibly might continue to decline, they gradually lengthened the terms of loans. The average loan period, as a result, grew from a little under four years in 1881 to four and three-quarter years in 1889, and to just under six years by 1900.

In attempting in this fashion to protect earnings, the management encountered a further problem, the

TABLE VIII-1

Northwestern Mutual: New Loans, Additions, and Repayments of the Mortgage Loan Account, 1882–1907

YEAR	NEW LOANS AND ADDITIONS	REPAYMENTS	TOTAL MORTGAGE LOANS AT YEAR-END
	(In Millions)		
1882	$5.3	$2.0	$14.3
1883	3.1	1.8	15.7
1884	3.3	1.6	17.4
1885	3.9	2.1	19.2
1886	4.2	2.3	21.1
1887	5.7	2.6	24.2
1888	5.5	2.3	27.4
1889	6.1	3.4	30.0
1890	9.9	4.5	35.5
1891	10.3	5.0	40.7
1892	10.2	5.9	45.1
1893	11.3	5.0	51.4
1894	10.5	6.1	55.8
1895	11.2	8.0	59.0
1896	13.7	5.9	66.9
1897	9.5	9.6	66.8
1898	16.4	11.2	72.0
1899	10.8	12.3	70.6
1900	10.3	8.3	72.5
1901	11.7	11.6	72.6
1902	14.3	10.4	76.5
1903	17.1	7.9	85.7
1904	17.0	9.3	93.4
1905	20.5	14.8	99.0
1906	25.2	13.3	110.9
1907	23.5	12.6	121.7
Total	$290.5	$179.8	

NOTE: Repayments include repayments and transfers to Special Real Estate as well as other reductions.

SOURCE: Annual Report of Officers, *Executive Committee Minutes* (January), 1883-1908.

prepayment of loans. As long as interest rates were advancing borrowers had little reason to pay off their debts before maturity, but when rates declined and more funds became available, borrowers often found it advantageous to repay loans to one lender with funds provided from other sources at lower rates of interest.

It was with great reluctance that Northwestern adjusted its lending policies to meet this problem. Until 1886 the Company permitted no prepayment, except under unusual circumstances. After that date the privilege was granted only on specific request and usually with the imposition of a penalty rate of from 1 to 3 per cent for the unexpired period, depending upon the amount of the loan.[3] By the mid-1890's, prepayment provisions became a standard lending practice, although they were not incorporated in the loan contracts except at the request of the borrower, and continued to bear a penalty rate.

Throughout this period Northwestern was predominantly an urban loan company. Except for a few years, from 1882 until 1896, new loans on city property absorbed 80 per cent or more of funds placed in mortgage investments; only after the 1893 depression was there a reversal of this trend. At their peak in 1902 urban loans comprised roughly 84 per cent of the total mortgage investment.[*] Thereafter the proportion dropped steadily to 60.5 per cent in 1907. (See Chart VIII-3.)

Various reasons may be assigned to both the earlier trend toward urban mortgages and the reversal which came after 1902. During the 1880's the rapid development of cities and towns of the Middle West and some plains states created a substantial demand for capital and a general increase in the value of the property which secured the loans. The latter phenomenon, of course, resulted from rising values of both land and buildings as population and business activity increased in the urban areas. Agriculture, on the other hand, while recovering from the severe depression of the 'seventies, prospered less than the rest of the economy until 1897. As a result farm loans were considered somewhat riskier than urban mortgages by the Company's management.

Experience during the post-1893 depression, combined with improved conditions in agriculture and increasing value of farm lands in the upper Mississippi Valley by the late 1890's, evidently convinced Northwestern's investment officers that farms offered security comparable to that of urban properties. Furthermore, with some unimportant excep-

---

* Prior to 1897 the *Annual Statement* of the Company did not include schedules of mortgage loan distributions.

CHART VIII-3

Mortgage Loan Investments, Average Interest on New Loans and on Total Loans: Northwestern, 1882–1907

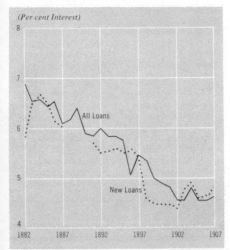

SOURCES: New loan rates all years and realized rates 1905-1907 from: Annual Reports of the Officers to the Executive Committee, *Minutes of the Executive Committee,* January, 1882-1908. Realized rates 1882-1904 from Lester W. Zartman, *The Investments of Life Insurance Companies,* New York, Henry Holt and Co., 1906, pp. 89-91.

Rates on new loans between 1888-1891 not available.

tions, farm loans offered a slightly better rate of interest, an important consideration in a period when interest rates as a whole were moving steadily downward. Because the foreclosed properties which were acquired by Northwestern in the 1890's were overwhelmingly urban in location, quite understandable in view of the distribution of the Company's accounts, the management evidently believed that the foreclosure rate on urban properties was disproportionately large. This belief undoubtedly influenced the later distribution of loans, although this was nowhere clearly stated by responsible officers.

From 1882 through 1907 Northwestern's lending area was expanded from fifteen to twenty-three states, although the actual amount loaned in several of the states was relatively insignificant. The heavy concentration of Northwestern mortgages in the North Central States throughout the period is shown

in Table VIII-2. The five states of Illinois, Indiana, Ohio, Michigan, and Wisconsin absorbed over 60 per cent of the Company's loan funds until 1903; thereafter the principal markets were in the West North Central states, Washington, and Oregon. New York was the only Middle Atlantic state in which Northwestern made loans during these years, and Georgia was the principal South Atlantic market. A few loans were made in Texas, but California and all Mountain states, with the exception of Colorado, were avoided. The single most important state for Northwestern was Illinois. Largely because of the rich investment opportunities in Chicago and vicinity, over 34 per cent of the Company's outstanding loans were concentrated in Illinois until 1907, when the proportion fell to about 25 per cent.

In New York, in the South Atlantic and East South Central states, and in the Northwest the Company's loans were overwhelmingly urban in location. The one-crop agricultural practices of the South were not highly regarded by the Company's loan officers, and when farm loans were made in Kentucky and Tennessee they were restricted to the most prosperous agricultural regions. Colorado loans also were exclusively urban. Northwestern farm loans were distributed broadly across the North Central states from Ohio to eastern Nebraska and Kansas, with the elite territory lying in the states bordering the Mississippi River.

In contrast to its broad and successful invasion of the Eastern insurance markets, Northwestern almost completely avoided this area in mortgage lending. The urban loan markets, except for certain towns and cities in western New York where the Company did lend, were already dominated by other lenders, including insurance companies. The interest rates available to the Company were considered too low to permit the heavy investment necessary to establish loan agencies. Although Eastern agriculture was sound and prosperous, the typical farm in the area was comparatively small by Western standards, and, although the value per acre was high, the total value of farms was, on the average, lower than for those in the North Central regions. Furthermore, the Company was limited as to the amount of loan it could make; in no case could it lend more than 50 per cent of the value of the underlying real estate. Thus farm loans made in the Eastern states would have to be for relatively small amounts, the cost of which was considered by management to be too high to yield competitive net earnings.

Changing conditions in the capital markets around the turn of the century required major ad-

TABLE VIII-2

Northwestern Mutual:
Regional Distribution of Mortgage Loans by Selected
Years, 1882–1907

	1882	1887	1892	1897	1902	1907
		(In Millions of Dollars)				
Middle Atlantic[a]	—	—	—	$0.01	$1.22	$1.69
South Atlantic[b]	$0.06	$0.01	$0.01	0.03	0.45	1.57
East North Central	10.32	15.32	24.90	41.29	47.34	53.61
West North Central[c]	3.36	8.58	14.76	17.89	20.39	53.76
East South Central	0.07	0.01	1.25	2.71	2.35	3.11
West South Central[d]	—	—	—	0.01	—	0.06
Mountain[e]	0.53	0.30	4.16	4.49	3.61	3.26
Pacific[f]	—	—	—	0.36	1.19	4.67
Total	$14.34	$24.22	$45.08	$66.79	$76.55	$121.73

[a] New York.
[b] Principally Georgia; North Carolina after 1900.
[c] North and South Dakota added in 1907 and 1892.
[d] Texas.
[e] Colorado.
[f] Company did not loan in California.

Source: *Executive Committee Minutes* (January), 1883-1908.

justments in the composition of Northwestern's investment portfolio. The effect of this change on the mortgage loan account was to reduce its relative importance in the Company's aggregate assets. In 1902 mortgages comprised roughly 46 per cent of assets; this increased to about 52 per cent in 1907, but never thereafter would such investments constitute over 55 per cent. In absolute dollar amounts, however, mortgage loans were to increase greatly over the succeeding twenty years.

Special Real Estate

Although the problem of special real estate continued throughout the period, it was acute only from 1894–1901. Before 1894 the problem centered on farm property acquired, for the most part, as a result of the depression of 1873–77; after 1894 most special real estate consisted of urban property acquired during the 1893 depression.

It was difficult to dispose of farm property between 1881 and 1886 because of the general agricultural depression and the competition of cheaper lands to the west.[4] Keenan, who was in charge of the account, suggested that prices on the less desirable properties be reduced, taking whatever losses were necessary to avoid maintenance costs, while retaining the better properties until there was a market recovery.[5] The management was at first reluctant to

accept such losses and the poorer properties were retained, even though this required both special permission of the Wisconsin insurance commissioner and a modification of the state investment statute.* By 1887, however, Keenan's counsel was followed so that during the ensuing four years the least promising holdings were sold.†

After 1893 the properties acquired were principally urban in location. In addition, while the total value of foreclosed real estate was much greater than had been true earlier, the ratio of special real estate to the aggregate amount of mortgage loans was much lower, being only 5.3 per cent at the 1900 peak, compared with 15.6 per cent at the previous high point in 1880.

Little effort was made to push the sale of special real estate in the years immediately following 1893, but with the business recovery after 1900 the rate of sales increased noticeably. The Company's loan agency system was sufficiently widespread by the early 1890's so that individual loan agents could effectively manage, rent, and develop prospective pur-

---

* See *Executive Committee Minutes,* Jan. 30, 1883, and Aug. 24, 1887. The statute which permitted domestic life companies to hold real estate acquired through foreclosure for six years was changed by *Wisconsin Legislation: Acts of 1885,* Ch. 199, to permit ten years' retention.
† Prices were sufficiently low on 1887 sales to cause the net earning rate of the combined realty account to fall to −7.5 per cent. Cf. Lester W. Zartman, *Investments of Life Insurance Companies,* 84.

chasers. Farms were promptly disposed of at satisfactory prices.[6] From 1895 through 1904, in fact, the earning rate on all real estate owned ranged from 8.4 per cent to 11.6 per cent.[7] By the end of 1907 the total value of the Company's foreclosed real estate was slightly over $1.4 million.

Public and Corporate Investments

The residual character of Northwestern's bond account prior to the early 1890's is evident from an examination of Table VIII-3. Until 1887 mortgage

loans were sufficiently attractive to absorb increasing amounts of the Company's funds and the bond account was reduced from about $1.25 million to $670,000, reaching the low point of 2.1 per cent of total assets in that year. As competition for real estate loans stiffened after the mid-1880's, it was recognized that bond purchases would, in the future, become a more important outlet for Company funds. Starting in 1888 the municipal bond account grew rapidly, reaching a peak of over $20.4 million in 1898. Because of relatively lower return there was no corresponding purchase of federal bonds until 1895, but following the panic of 1893 the need

TABLE VIII-3

Northwestern Mutual: Bond Investments, 1882–1907
(In Thousands)

Year	Federal	Municipal	Railroad	Total	Per cent of Total Assets
1882	$332	$915	—	$1,247	6.3%
1883	285	912	—	1,197	5.7
1884	144	718	—	862	3.8
1885	144	507	—	651	2.7
1886	142	465	—	607	2.3
1887	136	471	—	607	2.1
1888	140	976	—	1,116	3.4
1889	134	1,943	—	2,077	5.6
1890	131	2,833	—	2,964	7.0
1891	130	2,839	—	2,969	6.1
1892	126	4,504	—	4,630	8.2
1893	110	5,180	—	5,290	8.2
1894	110	7,061	—	7,171	9.8
1895	1,960	9,811	—	11,771	14.2
1896	1,950	11,822	—	13,772	14.9
1897	2,150	16,845	—	18,995	18.4
1898	1,350	20,431	$745	22,526	19.5
1899	540	19,408	15,519	35,467	28.0
1900	139	19,676	25,885	45,700	32.8
1901	137	13,880	43,059	57,076	37.6
1902	135	11,464	54,235	65,834	39.9
1903	132	10,390	56,927	67,449	37.9
1904	131	9,569	61,231	70,931	36.4
1905	130	8,879	69,862	78,871	37.8
1906	130	8,766	68,405	77,301	35.0
1907	128	8,144	65,169	73,441	31.5

Source: *Annual Statement*, Northwestern Mutual Life Insurance Co., 1882-1907.

for liquid assets to make possible policy loans and pay for surrenders prompted the acquisition of United States Government bonds amounting to $2 million. With the passing of the emergency the government bond account was reduced to a nominal $139,000 by 1900. Meanwhile, a growing demand for municipals by other lenders raised the price of these securities to the point where they no longer offered a satisfactory rate of return.

Forced by competitive pressure to seek alternative outlets for its continuously expanding investment funds, Northwestern again adjusted its program and moved into the corporate field, specifically railroad securities. In anticipation of this step the management sponsored a bill in the Wisconsin Legislature providing for a revision of the state investment code. The bill was enacted in 1893 permitting domestic life companies to acquire, among other assets, the mortgage bonds of specified types of railroads.*

Before Northwestern could exercise its new investment privilege, fluctuations in the price of railroad bonds and defaults by certain carriers following the panic of 1893 made their immediate purchase inadvisable. Not until 1898, when prospects improved, did Northwestern acquire its first railroad bonds. The initial acquisition included first mortgage obligations of five operating divisions of the Chicago, Milwaukee & St. Paul Railway. These securities had a book value of $325,000 and were purchased to yield a rate of 3.75 per cent. The rail account was rapidly developed after 1898, amounting to almost $70 million by 1905, the peak for the period. The predisposition toward the securities of western railroads continued over the following two decades, comprising over 60 per cent of the Company's corporate security portfolio at the end of 1907.

The purchase of railroad securities was sufficient to increase the proportion of the bond account to the Company's total assets, even though municipal holdings were cut by some $12 million between 1898 and 1907. The ratio of bonds to total investments reached a peak of almost 40 per cent in 1902, dropping off to some 31.2 per cent by the end of 1907.

Data on the earnings of Northwestern's bond account from 1882 through 1904 are shown in the tabulation below. Because gains or losses from the sale of securities are included, the year-to-year rates frequently show considerable variation.

The acquisition of corporate securities created

one important difficulty for Northwestern's management. As long as mortgages and municipal bonds comprised the bulk of its assets, the Company was relatively immune from problems involving a valuation of assets; after 1898 this was no longer true. The various state departments of insurance were required to place an annual value on the securities owned by life companies, and a uniform practice developed of taking the year-end prices from the organized security markets and assigning these to the respective holdings of the life companies.

For many life insurance companies, including Northwestern, this method of evaluation proved vexatious. The reasons were twofold: the first concerned the relationship of surplus to total reserves; the second involved the nature of the life company as a going institution. State insurance laws established a maximum surplus or contingency reserve for the companies; this surplus served as a cushion to absorb changes in asset values or in sudden adverse mortality experience. Thus a sharp reduction in the price of corporate securities could, if these comprised a substantial proportion of a company's assets, wipe out the surplus and even render the institution insolvent. The companies took the position that they invested for long-term purposes, were unconcerned with speculative investment, and, since they were going to operate over time, should not be bound by the same liquidation standards applicable to other kinds of business.

President Palmer had this consideration in mind when early in 1903 he requested the Wisconsin Legislature to adopt an alternative method of valuation, using the average market price of such securities over a period of from six to twelve months rather than of a single day.⁸ Endorsed by the commissioner of insurance, the proposal was passed by the legislature and the valuation period set at six months.⁹

The foresightedness of Northwestern's management in requesting this change was demonstrated at the time of the financial panic in 1907. The critical situations faced by many life companies, as a result of the sudden drop in security prices at the time, prompted the industry to call for assistance and the life insurance commissioners to provide it. A leading authority said that "the interest of both policyholders and the public required a sensible view of the total situation.... The commissioners, meeting in 'convention,' decided, therefore, that securities should be valued according to a formula of averaging which they then devised." ¹⁰ This unified action, following the pattern recommended by Northwestern in 1903, enabled many companies to pass the crisis and protect policyholders' interests.

---

* *Wisconsin Legislation: Acts of 1893*, Ch. 115. *Executive Committee Minutes,* February 21, 1893, mention this proposal for first time.

Year	Earnings Rate	Year	Earnings Rate	Year	Earnings Rate
1882	3.8%	1890	5.2%	1898	5.8%
3	5.2	1	4.4	9	3.0
4	1.5	2	5.4	1900	4.9
1885	1.9	3	5.0	1	3.2
6	4.9	4	6.1	2	2.3
7	4.4	1895	3.4	3	4.0
8	2.9	6	4.0	1904	6.7
9	8.3	7	5.0		
				Average	4.4%

Even so the fluctuations of bond prices worked some minor hardships on Northwestern in 1903 and again in 1907. In the former year Northwestern agents, suffering real or imaginary losses of sales to rival companies which were not hit by the depression of security values, complained to Vice President Merrill about the Company's bond holdings. A minor storm, leaving bruised feelings but no material damage, flared within the executive hierarchy over security selection. In 1907, to meet the rise in demand for policy loans, some $3.2 million in rail bonds were sold at depressed prices. These losses, however, were balanced by profits earned by sale of high-priced securities in 1901, and by the differential in interest rate charged on policy loans.[11]

The Investment Record

A comparison of Northwestern's investment portfolio with those of the ten largest life insurance companies in the United States, shown in Table VIII-4, indicates the extent to which the Company followed the pattern of the industry. In spite of the trend toward a larger proportion of bond holdings, it is clear that Northwestern, with the exception of one year, kept a larger share of its assets in mortgages than any of the other leading companies. It is also noteworthy that the Company at no time made collateral loans, a practice that was to come under severe criticism in the New York investigation in 1905.

Northwestern added to its assets at a somewhat faster rate than the average of its major competitors until 1900, and faster than the industry from 1890 (when data are first available for the industry) to 1900. More precisely, the proportion of industry assets owned by Northwestern grew from an estimated 5.3 per cent in 1882 to 8 per cent in 1900, and was 7.6 per cent in 1907. These holdings were sufficient to make the Company fourth in size among United States life companies in terms of assets owned.

Northwestern's net annual investment earnings rates for the 1882–1907 period are shown in the table below. The effect of the downward trend in interest rates up to 1904 is clearly visible. The upward shift after that suggests that the low point in the long-run course of interest rates may have been reached in that year.*

The skill of Northwestern's investment managers in adjusting their policies to changing conditions is also shown by a comparison of its earning rates with those of other companies. Judged by this standard

* SOURCE: Zartman, *Investments of Life Insurance Companies,* 75. Years 1905–7 from the Company's own estimates based on statements in officers' report to Executive Committee made each January.

Year	Rate	Year	Rate	Year	Rate
1882	5.8%	1891	5.1%	1900	5.0%
1883	6.1	1892	5.7	1901	4.5
1884	5.5	1893	5.7	1902	4.0
1885	5.9	1894	5.4	1903	4.0
1886	5.6	1895	5.7	1904	5.7
1887	5.4	1896	5.3	1905	4.7
1888	5.9	1897	5.3	1906	4.7
1889	6.3	1898	5.6	1907	4.8
1890	5.8	1899	4.6		
				Average	5.3%

SOURCE: Zartman, 74-75.

TABLE VIII-4

Ten Largest United States Life Insurance Companies: Distribution of Assets, Selected Years: 1882–1907
(As a Percentage of Total Admitted Assets)

COMPANY	BONDS	STOCKS	MORTGAGE LOANS	LOANS ON POLICIES	COLLATERAL LOANS	REAL ESTATE	CASH	ADMITTED ASSETS
				(1882)				(In Millions)
NORTHWESTERN	6.3	-0-	72.4	7.5	-0-	7.8	3.1	$19.8
Aetna	27.7	4.8	40.6	8.9	2.2	1.6	9.8	28.0
Conn. Mutual	22.1	0.3	39.8	6.0	0.7	23.4	5.1	51.6
Equitable	21.2	2.7	23.7	-0-	21.8	19.4	6.1	47.8
Metropolitan	27.1	-0-	27.3	9.4	5.5	16.0	1.1	2.0
Mutual Benefit	21.4	-0-	18.3	10.7	34.3	6.8	2.4	36.3
Mutual Life	18.2	-0-	48.5	-0-	17.5	12.4	2.8	97.7
New York Life	32.8	2.9	38.2	1.0	8.5	8.2	2.5	50.6
Penn Mutual	42.5	0.5	24.2	9.2	5.9	9.8	0.8	8.5
Prudential	30.8	-0-	50.3	-0-	-0-	-0-	16.8	0.4
				(1892)				
NORTHWESTERN	8.2	-0-	80.2	0.9	-0-	1.8	5.6	$56.2
Aetna	30.3	3.3	46.1	3.3	1.0	1.4	10.4	38.6
Conn. Mutual	20.6	0.6	59.9	2.4	0.1	11.5	2.2	60.8
Equitable	34.4	9.4	14.1	-0-	3.8	24.4	7.9	150.6
Metropolitan	23.6	1.2	55.0	0.8	-0-	16.1	1.3	16.5
Mutual Benefit	21.6	-0-	53.2	10.7	7.9	1.7	1.6	51.4
Mutual Life	31.6	3.6	40.0	-0-	6.0	9.0	5.7	173.2
New York Life	56.7	2.7	17.6	0.8	2.8	9.1	3.1	137.5
Penn Mutual	29.8	0.1	43.6	6.7	7.5	5.1	0.7	21.0
Prudential	19.2	-0-	46.8	0.1	-0-	22.2	9.7	8.8
				(1902)				
NORTHWESTERN	39.9	-0-	46.4	6.7	-0-	2.6	1.8	$165.2
Aetna	29.6	6.3	40.9	4.4	1.6	1.1	8.4	63.4
Conn. Mutual	38.8	1.2	36.7	1.0	0.0	18.2	0.9	65.6
Equitable	46.3	4.1	21.0	4.2	5.3	1.1	7.7	334.1
Metropolitan	40.4	7.1	28.8	1.7	-0-	12.6	5.6	89.2
Mutual Benefit	22.2	-0-	50.8	14.1	3.8	3.7	1.0	82.9
Mutual Life	39.9	11.1	21.4	3.8	2.7	8.6	4.1	382.4
New York Life	67.5	-0-	8.1	7.7	0.1	4.0	6.9	322.8
Penn Mutual	34.2	0.6	37.0	9.7	6.8	5.4	1.0	54.4
Prudential	33.4	4.8	18.2	1.8	7.9	18.5	8.2	60.2
				(1907)				
NORTHWESTERN	31.5	-0-	52.3	13.1	-0-	1.0	0.7	$232.8
Aetna	28.4	5.9	47.8	7.3	1.6	0.7	6.5	86.4
Conn. Mutual	42.3	1.3	37.7	4.4	0.0	13.9	0.7	65.0
Equitable	49.1	10.3	22.2	11.6	1.8	6.6	2.7	427.3
Metropolitan	41.8	5.0	37.6	3.3	1.8	10.0	2.6	198.3
Mutual Benefit	27.2	-0-	48.3	16.8	1.1	3.3	1.1	111.8
Mutual Life	45.5	9.4	25.4	10.5	2.4	6.0	1.3	494.2
New York Life	72.3	-0-	10.1	14.8	0.2	2.6	1.9	494.4
Penn Mutual	38.7	1.5	42.4	13.7	2.0	2.3	0.6	89.6
Prudential	53.2	2.0	18.2	5.1	5.4	8.3	8.2	145.2

NOTES: -0- indicates holding of zero.
    0.0 indicates holding of greater than zero but less than 0.045 per cent.
SOURCE: *Annual Statement*, Northwestern Mutual Life Insurance Company, 1882, 1892, 1902, 1907. Other companies: *Twenty-fourth, Thirty-fourth, Forty-fourth* and *Forty-ninth Annual Report of the Superintendent of Insurance of New York*.

Palmer and his associates could be proud of their record. While the margin was not high, as shown in the following tabulation for the 1882–1907 period, the Company ranked second among eleven leading life companies in the United States.

RANK	COMPANY	AVERAGE RATE
1	Penn Mutual	5.46%
2	NORTHWESTERN	5.31
3	Mutual Life	5.21
4	Connecticut Mutual	5.20
5	Aetna	5.19
6	John Hancock	5.16
7	Mutual Benefit	4.93
8	Metropolitan	4.90
9	Equitable	4.79
10	Prudential	4.77
11	New York Life	4.73

SOURCE: Zartman, 74-75; *Insurance Year Book*, 1910, 295.

Northwestern's Role in the Regional Flow of Funds

Measured in terms of the areas from which the Company drew its income (sold insurance) and made investments, Northwestern moved through four broad stages in its evolution as an investment institution. During the first stage the Company functioned as a local marketer of insurance and a local investor; during the second, as a regional marketer and a regional investor; during the third, as a national marketer and regional investor; and during the fourth, as national marketer and national investor.

From 1858 until about 1865 the Company sold insurance and made its investments almost exclusively in the state of Wisconsin. Its investment funds came largely from premium income—from payments of individuals who, if they had not purchased insurance, would have been unwilling or unable to make the money available for investment. For this reason the increase in the assets of the Company from nothing to over $900,000 by the end of 1865 largely represented a "net" addition to the capital supply of the state. By making these funds available to farmers and small businessmen in the form of mortgage loans, the Company made an important contribution to the economic growth of a "capital-scarce" area.

Beginning about 1866 and ending around 1880 Northwestern supplied the same investment functions for Wisconsin and its neighboring states, prin-

cipally Illinois, Indiana, Ohio, Michigan, Minnesota, and Iowa. Although insurance marketing had been extended on a national basis, these states provided the bulk of premium income. They also absorbed the greater part of the Company's investment funds, principally in the form of mortgage loans. By the end of 1880 net investment funds and re-investment of earnings brought Northwestern's total investments over these years to over $18.3 million, about $17.4 million more than the total reported for 1865.

The third phase of Northwestern's evolution as an investment institution began about 1881 and extended into the 1890's. By the early 1880's Northwestern was firmly established as a national marketer, and a considerable portion of its premium income was drawn from outside the group of states that had earlier supplied the bulk of such income, especially from the Eastern markets and California. At the same time the Company's investments continued to be concentrated in the same group of states as before. Therefore, during this period the Company derived a greater share of its income from outside the region in which it made its investments than at any time in its history.

Fortunately Northwestern's records make it possible to measure, with considerable accuracy, the extent of this movement for the 1881–1897 period. Northwestern's total investments during these years increased by about $83 million, from approximately $19 million to over $103 million. Of this amount, some $46 million represented "net additions" to capital made possible by an increased volume of premium income, and $40 million from investment earnings that went into the investment account. It is not possible to trace the exact origin of the investment earnings. On the whole they came largely from the same areas where they were reinvested. In the discussion that follows, therefore, it is assumed that they did not enter into the inter-regional flow of funds.*

For purposes of analysis Northwestern's insurance and investment markets have been divided into four major regions, shown on the accompanying map. Column 1 in the following tabulation shows the gross premium from each region for the period. From these amounts all expenses (agents' commissions, medical fees, etc., and a pro rata share of the Home Office costs) and policyholder benefits (death claims, matured endowments, etc.) were deducted to derive net premiums, shown in column 2. Column

* For an explanation of the method used in obtaining premium estimates, expenses, payments to policyholders, and net investment during this period, see Appendix D.

REGION	GROSS PREMIUMS	NET PREMIUMS	NET INVESTMENT IN REGION	NET FLOW OF FUNDS TO (+) OR FROM (−) REGION
Atlantic	$46.0	$15.2	$4.1	−$11.1
Great Lakes	40.2	9.6	41.0	+31.4
Western	29.2	9.8	27.6	+17.8
Other	21.3	7.4	9.3	+1.9
Total	$136.7	$42.0	$82.0	+$40.0

SOURCE: Appendix D.

3 indicates the net new investments in the respective regions, and column 4 shows the net inflow or outflow of funds for each region.

From the data shown in the table it is obvious, for example, that the "Atlantic" region transferred to Milwaukee net premiums amounting to $15.2 million, of which only $4.1 million were re-invested in that area, making the net outflow of funds $11.1 million. In the case of the remaining areas, net premiums were less than net investments by some $51.1 million. The difference between this amount and the $11.1 million received from the Atlantic region was made up by reinvested earnings.

In acting as a transfer agent Northwestern added

Regional Flow of Net Policyholder Premiums and Net Northwestern Investment, 1881–1897

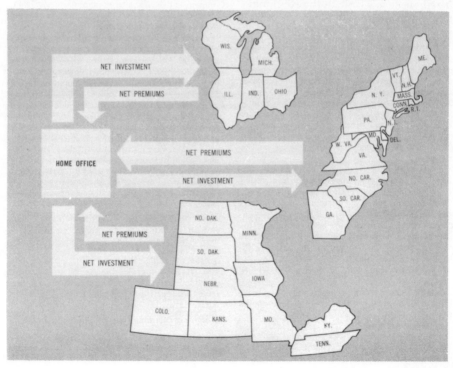

significance to its role as a regional gatherer and investor of funds, and it contributed to the resources of the region by drawing on areas where investment funds were comparatively more abundant. For Northwestern policyholders the higher rate of interest earned on these investments contributed to a lower net cost of their insurance.

With the first purchase of railroad securities in 1898 Northwestern moved into the last phase of its evolution as an investment institution. It is true that mortgage loans were not made throughout the marketing area, but the rise in the proportion of the bond account to total investments sharply modified the regional character of the Company's loans. In this sense Northwestern became a full-fledged national institution.

Public Relations, Legislation and Taxes

Like most life companies of its day Northwestern usually enjoyed cordial relations with its body of policyholders. In general, so long as dividends were regularly paid and the cost of insurance did not rise unduly, most policyholders paid little attention to the company in which they were insured. There were, of course, the occasional attempts at fraud by policyholders which plagued all companies. The Company contested claims in cases where suicide or misstatements on the application were considered to have abrogated the contracts; and, as has already been noted, the major dissatisfaction of policyholders with the results of deferred dividend benefits was met by the voluntary abandonment of semi-tontine insurance by Northwestern in 1905.

To make sure that relations remained satisfactory Northwestern's field force was urged to devote several weeks each year to making the rounds of Company policyholders to offer the services available to members and assist them in reviewing their insurance. These visits were undoubtedly beneficial to Northwestern as an organization, in addition to providing opportunities to sell more insurance or develop new prospects.

Outside its own policyholders the Company's principal contact with the public, during this period, was generally limited to state insurance commissions and state legislative bodies. Occasionally Northwestern was involved in specific legislative inquiries about the broader aspects of life insurance and the public; but until the full-scale investigations of the industry after 1900 the Company's main con-

tact with legislative groups involved taxation, investment, and insurance. With respect to investment and insurance the problem was generally to obtain modification of statutes considered unreasonably restrictive, or to prevent the imposition of laws that seemed to be immoderate, ineffectual, or likely to impair the Company's competitive position.

While there were other important duties attached to the office, Northwestern's legal counsel played a particularly significant role in all matters involving the Company and the various state legislative bodies. Following the death of David Hooker in 1888, Palmer and the trustees persuaded Charles E. Dyer, judge of the United States District Court (Eastern Wisconsin), to become the Company's legal counsel. Judge Dyer was elected a trustee on July 17, 1888, and the following day became a member of the Executive Committee. Judge Dyer had a distinguished career as a lawyer and on the bench, and was prominent in Republican party circles in Wisconsin; he improved and expanded the legal department.

Until the late 1890's the management still relied heavily upon its good name in Wisconsin, the public interest of its policyholders, and the common sense of a majority of the legislators to protect its interests within the Wisconsin Legislature. To keep informed of bills presented in the legislature affecting taxes, investments, or insurance, the Company followed the routine procedure of having copies of such bills mailed to Milwaukee by the clerk of either the assembly or the senate. If members of management wished to initiate modifications in the insurance or investment codes applicable to life companies, they would customarily bring their arguments directly to the attention of the various state departments of insurance, with the request that they be approved and sponsored by the insurance commissioners in the legislatures. In the event bills were introduced into the Wisconsin Legislature which were considered contrary to the Company's interest, to obtain support for Northwestern's point of view the management followed the pattern, established during the 1870's, of mobilizing opposition.

Northwestern not only actively opposed imposition of high tax rates upon Wisconsin companies by the state legislature, but also other than token taxation of out-of-state companies. The latter concern arose because of the retaliatory laws in many of the states where it was doing business. In the legislative session of 1897 a bill was introduced which would have sharply increased the tax burden of domestic companies and the license fees for foreign companies; but it was eventually defeated after vigorous opposition by the Company, including the employment of two lobbyists, a Milwaukee lawyer and the Oshkosh postmaster, whose political connections were expected to carry weight in the state. Early in 1899 a new tax bill was introduced by an assembly-man, Philo A. Orton, then a member of the rapidly growing Progressive Republican wing of Robert M. La Follette. This bill specified that, except for minor exemptions, the total receipts of domestic life companies would be subject to a tax of 1 per cent. The bill also provided that the license fee on foreign life companies, excluding assessment and fraternal organizations, be set equal to 1 per cent of the annual premiums collected by those companies from policyholders residing in Wisconsin.* Despite a vigorous campaign to defeat the bill, which included extensive advertising, hiring of lobbyists, rallying agents and policyholders, and employing special legal counsel, Northwestern was unable to persuade the legislature of its view. The Orton Bill passed.[12]

The immediate effect of the Orton Bill on North-western's expenses is shown in Table VIII-5. Not only was the Company's tax burden in Wisconsin considerably increased, but the amounts paid to other states, largely as a result of retaliatory laws, moved up sharply. The latter point had been stressed during the hearings. Judge Dyer, in 1900, pointed out the shortsightedness of any group which, in order to obtain a tax revenue of $8.52 from the one life insurance company incorporated in Illinois doing a Wisconsin business, imposed a tax increase upon Northwestern of $7,200, the amount the insurance department of Illinois collected from the Company because of the automatic operation of the retaliatory law.[13]

The Northwestern management was determined, if possible, to secure the repeal of the Orton Bill, and if that was not possible, to modify the high tax on out-of-state insurance companies. Just prior to the reconvening of the Wisconsin Legislature in 1901 the Company employed Thomas W. Spence, a partner in the distinguished Milwaukee law firm of Quarles, Spence, and Quarles, to take charge of the campaign.

Spence believed that Northwestern's public relations had been handled ineffectually during the previous struggle over the bill.[14] He employed a staff, located in Madison, whose principal duties were to study insurance tax legislation and to see that arguments favoring Northwestern's position, documented with the appropriate research data, were printed and distributed to legislators. Spence and

his staff consulted legislators, including Philo A. Orton, who agreed to support an amendment of the "foreign company" license tax. A compromise, however, was still necessary. In exchange for the substitution of a nominal license fee for the 1 per cent tax on the Wisconsin premiums of foreign companies, Northwestern agreed to pay a Wisconsin tax equal to 3 per cent of its gross income from all sources, except rents on real estate and premiums collected outside the state.[15]

Northwestern had good reason to be pleased with the results of the compromise bill. Even though in 1901 its Wisconsin taxes were approximately $2,000 larger than for the preceding year, the Company's out-of-state tax bill was reduced by some $46,000. The general increase in both sets of taxes in 1902, and afterward, reflected the increase in the Company's total insurance sales and the consequent increase in income. Without the modification of the Wisconsin license tax, total tax outlays would have been substantially higher.

Over the succeeding six years the Company made further attempts to get a reduction in taxes, but without success. On the other hand, the management contributed to the defeat of a bill offered in 1905 which proposed a gross premium tax ranging from 7 to 14 per cent on all companies doing business in the state.[16]

At the end of 1905 Northwestern's management had accumulated some thirty-five years of experience with legislative bodies. On the whole it had been quite successful. The tactics devised in dealing with the Wisconsin Legislature were also reasonably effective in opposing objectionable laws or proposed bills in other states. Where these efforts were not effective, it was always possible to stop doing business in the state in question; this was done in a number of instances. The characteristic attributes of Northwestern's policy were independence of operation, acting only when the interests of Northwestern seemed threatened, and avoiding efforts in concert with other companies.

The Company's experience with the Orton Bill, however, raised some doubts as to whether it was sound policy to continue to deal with legislative problems on an *ad hoc* basis. Actually Spence was asked if he would accept the full-time responsibility of handling the Company's relations within this area; when he declined the matter was dropped. The Company's experience before the Wisconsin legislative investigating committee in 1906 resolved all doubts about the advisability of this step, however, and within two years Henry F. Tyrrell was appointed legislative counsel.

---

* See *Wisconsin Legislation: Acts of 1899*, Ch. 326; for the bill was passed substantially without modification. (Assembly No. 14, 1899).

TABLE VIII-5

Northwestern Mutual: Total Taxes as Per Cent of Total Income;
Wisconsin Taxes as Per Cent of Total Taxes; 1882–1907
(Dollars in Thousands)

YEAR	TOTAL INCOME	TOTAL TAXES	TOTAL TAXES AS % OF TOTAL INCOME	WISCONSIN[a] TAXES	WISCONSIN TAXES AS % OF TOTAL TAXES
1882	$3,796	$39	1.0%	$6	15.4%
1883	4,209	59	1.4	7	11.8
1884	4,652	60	1.3	8	13.3
1885	5,104	65	1.3	9	13.8
1886	5,871	79	1.3	11	13.9
1887	6,860	82	1.2	12	14.6
1888	8,001	91	1.1	14	15.4
1889	9,380	100	1.1	17	17.0
1890	11,119	115	1.0	20	17.4
1891	12,545	133	1.1	22	16.5
1892	14,557	152	1.0	24	15.8
1893	14,964	163	1.1	27	16.5
1894	16,250	164	1.0	28	17.1
1895	17,514	194	1.1	29	14.9
1896	18,538	231	1.2	31	13.0
1897	19,981	269	1.3	33	12.3
1898	22,126	296	1.3	34	11.5
1899	24,558	507	2.1	192	37.9
1900	27,159	625	2.3	247	39.5
1901	29,472	581	2.0	249	42.8
1902	31,642	634	2.0	259	40.9
1903	33,663	671	2.0	268	39.9
1904	36,453	701	1.9	284	40.5
1905	39,067	720	1.8	316	43.9
1906	41,926	781	1.9	340	43.5
1907	43,595	803	1.8	368	45.9

[a] Does not include property taxes paid by Company on Realty.

SOURCE: Total Income, Total Taxes: *Annual Statement*, 1882–1907; Wisconsin Taxes: Brief of George H. Noyes before Finance Committee, Wisconsin State Senate on hearings on Senate Bill No. 5, 1909.

A Quarter Century in Review

A review of Northwestern's operations during 1882–1907 suggests that few administrators in the life insurance industry were more worthy of acclaim than the president, Henry L. Palmer. Nor had many companies more reason to congratulate themselves upon achievement than Northwestern. In the critical areas of marketing and investment of policyholder funds the Company was highly successful.

Among ordinary life companies, measured by insurance in force, Northwestern advanced from seventh in size to fourth. It strove to safeguard policyholders' interests by improving standards of underwriting, and marketing costs were held to reasonable levels. Northwestern policyholders were more persistent in keeping their insurance alive than was true for the industry as a whole.

Policyholder funds were invested prudently. Not only was the principal of the reserves carefully conserved, but the assets acquired by Northwestern earned an income sufficient to yield a rate of interest that put it near the top among the eleven largest firms in the industry. Northwestern's rate of earnings, favorable mortality experience, and low expense rate offered its policyholders insurance at net costs that few competitors could match.

In terms of the benefits policyholders enjoyed in return for the amounts paid by them in premiums during these years, the Company's record was also substantially above average. Total premium income between 1882 and 1907 amounted to $387.8 million. In return $148.7 million went out to policyholders and beneficiaries in settlement of claims, matured endowments, payment for surrenders, and annuities. Another $63.7 million was distributed to policyholders as dividends, which amounted to 16.4 per cent of premium income. And finally, the total assets of the Company, the legal reserve plus surplus, were increased by $214 million. For the whole period the aggregate of these items equaled 110 per cent of policyholder premiums.

This record compared favorably with that of the major competition (excluding the industrial companies). Only two rivals, Connecticut Mutual and Mutual Benefit, contributed more to policyholders from premium income received. The record of the Big Three was much less impressive. Policyholder benefits for six ordinary companies are shown below.[17]

For Northwestern this record of policyholder benefits was significantly smaller than had been true for the years 1874–1881, but it was superior to that earned for the years preceding 1874. Apparently the benefit to policyholders, using this measure, was greater in periods of depression than during periods of expansion. On the other hand, it is also apparent that during these years the policyholders of com-

panies with a pronounced market orientation and aggressive sales policies benefited less than did those following more restrained merchandising and selling programs. Connecticut Mutual and Mutual Benefit were the only companies among the industry leaders that did not sell deferred-dividend insurance.

Members of Northwestern's management were probably not particularly concerned with these criteria in judging their own performance as stewards of the Company during these years. Such standards have been established only recently, and even today there is no unanimity in the industry concerning their applicability between companies. They were, however, aware of such criteria as the accumulation of surplus and its distribution, the net cost of insurance to policyholders, investment earning rates, and investment policy. Northwestern insurance contracts, while liberalized with respect to nonforfeitures, policyholder loans, and travel and occupational restrictions, were conservatively underwritten. The Company's gain from mortality more than completely offset the narrowing differential in interest earned on investment, and produced low net cost insurance for policyholders despite the increase in gross premiums which followed the shift to the American Experience Table of Mortality and the 3 per cent interest assumption.

Management believed its performance had been good and its business and ethical judgment excellent, but it was less certain concerning the extent to which this feeling was shared by policyholders and the public generally. In 1905–1906, however, as a result of the major investigations of life insurance conducted in New York and Wisconsin, both Company officers and the public were to have opportunities to evaluate this performance against that of other major insurers, and to draw their own conclusions.

Company	Premium Income	Paid Policyholder Benefits	Change in Total Assets	Total Policyholder Benefits	Total Policyholder Benefits as a Percentage of Premium Income
Equitable	$931.5	$546.3	$383.2	$929.5	99.8%
Mutual Life	953.0	603.2	396.4	999.6	104.9
New York Life	997.8	525.3	447.4	992.7	99.5
Connecticut Mutual	126.3	158.0	16.2	174.2	138.6
Mutual Benefit	222.1	179.4	76.0	255.4	115.0
Penn Mutual	170.1	91.6	81.8	173.4	101.9
Northwestern	387.8	212.3	214.0	426.3	110.0

SOURCE: *Insurance Year Book*, 1910; Appendix F, Tables 1, 2, 5.

CHAPTER NINE

Public Investigations of the Industry

A T the end of 1904 the United States life insurance industry could point with considerable pride to a quarter century of expansion. An ever-increasing number of persons had been provided protection under insurance in force, which grew from about $1.56 billion in 1880 to over $12.5 billion. Through their investments the life companies had contributed much to America's material growth, the industry having expanded its investment holdings at an impressive rate from about $77 million in 1890 to some $2.5 billion in 1904.

Superficially there was little to suggest any impending agitation for sweeping reforms of the industry's methods of doing business or any widespread public condemnation of the administration of its most prominent executives. Beneath the surface, however, there was a growing dissatisfaction with the operations of the life companies which resulted in a sweeping examination of the industry. Known as the Armstrong Investigation, this inquiry in New York laid bare abuses and malpractices by companies constituting the elite of the insurance business. Although Northwestern was not primarily involved in the Armstrong Investigation —most of the fire was directed toward the Big Three: Equitable, Mutual Life of New York, and New York Life— the indictment against the industry provoked a Wisconsin legislative investigation, which was aimed more directly at the Company. Although this second investigation revealed some

practices that proved embarrassing, Northwestern emerged from the searching public scrutiny with its reputation unimpaired, an achievement of some distinction during this stormy decade of public dissatisfaction.

Background of the Armstrong Investigation

Ironically the provocation to investigate life insurance was gratuitously supplied early in 1905 from within the industry itself, as a result of the "violent warfare within the Equitable on the part of different investment banking interests over access to company funds."[1] It began in 1889 with the death of Henry Baldwin Hyde; extended over the succeeding twenty-five years it involved various New York investment banking groups, the Gould interests, J. P. Morgan, E. H. Harriman, and Kuhn, Loeb. The board of Equitable split over a demand that James Hazen Hyde, son of Henry Baldwin, be ousted and the company mutualized; one group of directors, under the chairmanship of Henry Clay Frick, initiated an investigation.* The

---

* Cf., North, "Entrepreneurial Policy and External Organization," 150. See also, Marquis James, *The Metropolitan Life,* 139. The account of the trouble from the point of view of the best of the then current reports is Burton J. Hendricks, *The Story of Life Insurance* (New York: McClure, Phillips and Co., 1907).

report of the Frick committee was sharply critical of the Equitable management, charging that accounting practices were improper, that company money was used to support the price of securities where the officers had a personal interest, and that excessive payments were made to acquire new business. A majority of the board, however, rejected the report, a decision which caused such prominent members as Frick, E. H. Harriman, and Cornelius Bliss to resign.

Despite attempts to restrain the growing tide of public indignation, such as creating a three-man voting trust headed by ex-President Grover Cleveland, the management was soon under intensive public investigation.[2] The insurance department of New York, under pressure from an aroused public interest, began its own inquiry into the operations of Equitable. Its report, issued in June 1905, was even more critical of the management than that of the Frick group and it recommended that stringent investment regulations be incorporated into the state insurance code. Although the legislature was not scheduled to reconvene until 1906 the metropolitan press demanded immediate action; the governor responded by calling a special session on July 20, 1905, in which a joint legislative committee was appointed under the chairmanship of state Senator William W. Armstrong to conduct an investigation into the operations of all life insurance companies doing business within the state. In August, Charles Evans Hughes, fresh from a triumphant investigation of the Consolidated Gas Company and later to become one of the most distinguished public figures of his era, was appointed counsel. Public hearings began on September 8, 1905, and ended on December 30, fifty-seven public sessions later.

The Investigation

The public atmosphere, the thoroughness of the inquiry, and the unimpeachable conduct of Charles Evans Hughes gained national attention and respect for the investigation; and it resulted in a serious indictment of a substantial portion of the American life insurance industry. Few representatives left the witness stand with the reputation of their companies completely untarnished or without revealing practices and business methods that were embarrassing to disclose in public hearings. As the hearings progressed the chief interest of the committee and of the public was centered more and more on the Big Three. The specific charges brought against

them served to indicate the nature of the indictment against the industry, and it represented a check list against which companies could measure their own records.

One of the first points brought out in the hearings was the great concentration of control in the three large companies, where one or two officers held votes (shares or proxies) to establish executive autocracies that were "maintained without challenge."[3] Such control led to grave abuses. Large sums were spent for lobbying activities at Albany and at the capitals of other states; in one election year alone, for example, the Big Three contributed $120,000 to the Republican Party. The officers paid themselves large salaries, hand picked appointees in key positions within the management hierarchy, and enthusiastically sponsored the idea of a family dynasty for management succession.[4] As one commentator has since noted,

It was this personal identification with the company not only on the part of the chief executives but also of the entire business control group which resulted in a blending of the personal profit-seeking activities of the officers with company affairs. As a result it was hard to distinguish where their activities in the role of executives left off and as private individuals began. Not only did they

look upon the company as the avenue of business activity for the rest of the family, but also as a vehicle for further profitable activity individually to the extent that such opportunities presented themselves.[5]

Personal rivalry among the heads of the Big Three prompted them to engage in vigorous competition in the sales of insurance, and sheer size, rather than benefits for the policyholders or security for the company, became a prime objective. The members of the Armstrong Committee took a dim view of the sales record of the Big Three.

> The business of the *Mutual,* the *Equitable* and the *New York Life* has grown beyond reasonable limits. Notwithstanding the fact that they have long since passed the point where further enlargement can benefit their policyholders, they have resorted to every effort to obtain new business, regardless of the expense which is reflected in diminishing dividends. Fearful of losing prestige, the chief concern of each has been to keep up with the others . . . while the huge accumulations of the companies and the great responsibilities involved in their management have furnished pretexts for increased salaries and extravagant administration.[6]

Much of the selling success of the Big Three stemmed from their promotion of semi-tontine policies. A good example of this "extravagant" administration, the investigation revealed, was the management of the semi-tontine policies where the reserves, for which there was no immediate accounting, were used to finance aggressive selling campaigns, with the expectation that they would be recouped from future earnings.

This frightening rivalry extended to investment as well as sales and led to further abuses. Because mortgage securities could not, for one reason or another, absorb the rapid accumulation of investment funds, there was an increasing reliance on securities. It was possible, of course, for the investment managers of these companies to buy securities in the open market; but there was an alternative—to join forces with large investment banking houses in underwriting the issue of new securities. As one authority has noted about the heads of the Big Three, "Life insurance leaders of this stamp came in time to see that they held command over a money power sufficiently great to make them the natural associates of the ranking business men of their day."[7] More specifically, participation in underwriting syndicates offered company officials not only the

chance to purchase securities at bargain prices but also to gain immediate personal profits.

In forming an alliance with the bankers, however, the life insurance executives surrendered a good deal of freedom in the management of the investment funds of their respective companies. While the amounts of money they brought to the alliance were large, they were not sufficient to make the life company officials more than junior members in the agreement. As George Perkins, vice president of New York Life, testified before the Armstrong Committee, J. P. Morgan and Company sold more railroad bonds in four and one-half years than the Big Three had purchased over a sixty-year period.[8] Thus in joining various underwriting syndicates in some instances, the life officials bound themselves to share only in underwriting profits, without the privilege of purchasing their companies' own shares at less than market prices. In other cases they agreed to retain their holdings until a "market had been established" by the bankers.

The financial relations between the insurance companies and the investment bankers were not confined to syndicate underwriting. The Armstrong hearings also brought out that the companies commonly maintained large, ostensibly idle, balances with the bankers that paid a low rate of interest. In reality these funds were not held as cash balances but were put into subsidiary and trust companies affiliated with the bankers. These affiliates held speculative securities, made collateral loans, and engaged in syndicate operations which the life companies were legally prohibited from doing. In return for permitting the use of their companies' funds for these purposes, the life insurance managers were allowed to purchase stock in the affiliates on their own account and share personally in the profits.

Immediate Results and Remedial Legislation

The top executives and directors of the Big Three had entered the arena of public investigation secure in the belief that, aside from a temporary inconvenience and momentary embarrassment, there was nothing to fear. The metropolitan press of New York, however, emblazoned the testimony taken by the Armstrong Committee in headlines, editorialized its own conclusions, and dispatched these to newspapers all over America. None but the professional insurance papers saw much to admire in the conduct of the insurance giants, and the influence of these journals was most limited. The attitudes of the leaders of the major New York companies began to change from arrogance to apprehension even before the taking of public testimony was concluded. There was a mass resignation of key officials from the Big Three, and both civil and criminal suits were filed against the discredited leaders for funds illegally expended. In several instances voluntary restitution was made.

Of more importance to the institution of life insurance than the report of malpractices were the specific legislative recommendations of the Armstrong Committee, designed to end the abuses revealed by the investigation. These recommendations applied to three areas of life insurance: actuarial and marketing practices; investment conduct; and business controls, including elections, accounting, and legislative and political relations.

The actuarial agenda sought the abolition of deferred dividend plans by requiring annual distribution of dividends and the limitation of surplus. Furthermore, the committee recommended uniform nonforfeiture provisions for all policies, other than term, after the payment of three annual premiums, and advocated that each company doing business in the state be limited to four standard forms of policy contracts.

While the life companies bridled at all of these restraints, they had much more reason to be concerned with two other provisions designed to curb the extravagant marketing policies of the recent past. The first of these proposed to limit the insurance a com-

pany could issue in any single year to a fixed percentage of its paid-for insurance of the previous year. The second imposed a ceiling on the acquisition costs of new business: expenses could not exceed first-year loading plus "the present value of probable mortality savings in the ensuing five years."[9] Other limits were imposed on selling costs by prohibiting bonuses, prizes, special compensation to agents, and advances to agents and brokers. If the proposed legislation became law, agents' renewals would be restricted to four 7.5 per cent commissions.[10]

The Armstrong Committee sought to provide greater protection to policyholders from fraudulent marketing devices, and to restrain severely where it could not prevent collusive relationships between insurance companies and other financial organizations. Rebating would become a criminal offense; discrimination between policyholders of the same class was proscribed; uniform values on surrendered policies were established; and officers and employees misrepresenting the terms of insurance contracts to the public were to be made subject to serious penalties.[11] Carefully defined proposals forbade the ownership of corporate stocks and provided for divestiture of those already in company portfolios; types of real estate which could be legally acquired were clearly defined and specifically limited.* Syndicate participation in security underwriting was made illegal for life companies, and their officers were to be denied direct compensation for negotiation of loans.

In the matter of the control of life companies, particularly the mutuals, the committee recommended the elimination of permanent proxies and the provision for full access to company membership lists by policyholders desiring to propose a slate of director or trustee candidates different from that proposed by the management.†

Other important recommendations were made by the committee. These included a ban on political contributions; the compulsory registration of lobby-

---

* *Armstrong Committee Report* (Assembly No. 996, Sec. 94). Proxies were to be limited to a single election and were to be voted by any of three proxy voters appointed under direction of the New York insurance department. Any one hundred or more policyholders, by petition to the superintendent of insurance at least three months prior to an election, would be assured of having their list of candidates published on the notification of election form required to be mailed to all participating members. (See also, Assembly No. 964.)

† *Armstrong Committee Report*, Vol. X (Assembly 996, Sec. 101, 20, 36). Divestiture of all corporate stocks then in portfolio was to be completed within a period of five years following December 31, 1906, with full report of the transactions and valuations to be made to the insurance department.

ists with the state; the clarification and modification of bookkeeping and accounting practices where dummy accounts or misleading entries had invited deception; the requirement of more detailed reporting to the insurance department and more frequent and careful examinations by that office. Furthermore, the procedure whereby a stock company could become mutualized was to be simplified, and such reorganizations encouraged.[12]

The life companies which did business in New York, particularly the domestic companies, were appalled by the proposals of the Armstrong Committee, and their representatives crowded into Albany in early 1906 to dissuade the legislature from enacting them. Their efforts, however, were without effect; the disclosures were too recent and the public reaction too strong to provide for a legislative "time out" for a cooler, more judicious consideration of the recommendations. Moreover, the industry's program failed to concentrate on those elements of the proposed reforms which it considered the least defensible from the point of sound actuarial and operating requirements. Instead they opposed everything without discrimination, without apparently sensing the changed climate of opinion which then existed. The shotgun techniques of opposition failed miserably; the major recommendations of the committee were consolidated into nine separate bills and duly enacted by the legislature, with only slight modifications.[13]

Northwestern was, like the other out-of-state companies, only modestly involved in the New York investigation. The Armstrong Committee had neither the time nor the resources to examine in detail each company which did business in the state, concentrating instead on the most obvious target, the Big Three. The Company forwarded certain records and statistical exhibits to New York, at the request of the committee, but none of the officers was called upon to testify publicly.[14] A few kind words were spoken concerning the relatively low expense rate which Northwestern had achieved, but that was about all. As was true of agents of other companies, the less thoughtful Northwestern agents advanced some rather extravagant claims for accolades presented the Company by the investigators. The committee, however, would have been astonished to learn that it had found such virtues in Northwestern or most of the other members of the industry. The investigation was no exoneration for Northwestern, nor for any company not carefully examined. The winds of reform, however, had not died away with the 1906 New York legislation. Before the year was over, and in direct consequence of the Armstrong Investigation, Northwestern was facing a full-scale legislative inquiry in its home state.

Background of the Wisconsin Legislative Investigation

The ink was hardly dry on the report of the Armstrong Committee when the governor of Wisconsin, Robert M. La Follette, decided to conduct a similar investigation of life insurance in the state. Several members of the Wisconsin Legislature, at the invitation of the Armstrong Committee, attended the public sessions in New York and benefited from the discussions of the evidence and the proposed legislative recommendations being considered by that body. The governor, about to be elected to the United States Senate, had several reasons for his course of action. As he explained to the legislature, which he called into emergency session in January 1906: "With the exception of the corporations which control the transportation facilities of the commonwealth there is no class of corporations more in need of careful and economical administration than those which make a business of life insurance." Since the newspaper accounts of malfeasance and mismanagement of life insurance companies in New York, as revealed by the investigation, caused much public anxiety, it was

> due to our home companies, their policy-holders, and the people of the state, that Wisconsin takes such action as shall make impossible a repetition in this state of what has occurred in New York, and, at the same time, satisfy the people as to the condition of Wisconsin companies.[15]

Legislative approval of the governor's request followed quickly and a joint committee was appointed to conduct the investigation.* It decided to limit its inquiry to two domestic companies and one from out of state. Wisconsin Life of Madison and Northwestern Mutual, home-state companies, were obvious choices; Union Central Life of Cincinnati was the third selection. Union Central, which like Northwestern had not been seriously interrogated in New York, conducted an extensive farm loan business in the Middle West and was among the twenty largest Companies in the United States.

The executive officers and key trustees of Northwestern had no reason to fear any inquiry re-

---

* In addition to Senator James Frear, the chairman, the committee included Senators Julius Roehr and Jacob Rummel, Assemblymen Herman Ekern, W. S. Braddock, George Beedle, and B. S. Potter.

garding investment and financial manipulation. Management, however, did perpetuate itself through a proxy system; and the agency officials were aware that a certain amount of twisting and even rebating continued, despite official resolutions condemning both. Paid lobbyists had been employed in the struggle over the Orton tax bill, and at times there was discrimination between policyholders. These practices, the management believed, were not reprehensible; rather they were actions that officers of a large life company, operating in an era of fierce competition, were forced to take.

The investigation got under way in a spirit that in no way could be described as serene. The disclosures of the Armstrong Committee had caused many persons to prejudge the inquiry, at least to the point of a feeling on the part of some that it was a case of "letting the Northwestern prove itself innocent." Although several newspapers attempted to maintain a non-partisan attitude, notably the *Journal* and the *Evening Wisconsin,* the *Milwaukee Daily News* strongly supported the investigation, while the *Milwaukee Sentinel* just as vigorously opposed it. In addition, the Progressive element in the Republican Party, led by the restless reform spirit of Robert M. La Follette, was in control of the state political machinery, which was strongly reflected in the membership of the committee as well as its counsel, James L. O'Connor. To make matters worse a number of Northwestern's prominent trustees, though Republicans, vigorously opposed La Follette's wing of the party.

In view of this situation it was rather remarkable that the hearings were fairly, and even courteously, conducted. Although the opportunities for demagoguery were frequent, the forbearance of the committee was admirable. President Palmer, who in spite of his advanced age insisted on retaining his office as president while the Company was under fire, was treated in the manner of an elder statesman. Most of the witnesses evidenced willingness to testify, yet were understandably reluctant to advance opinions. When passions did flare, the instances were occasioned by committeemen who became irritated over what they considered evasiveness, or by executives restive under the questioning of "outsiders." In general, the fear that committee members would reflect a political bias in their conduct of the investigations was unfounded. Judge George H. Noyes, Northwestern's general counsel, stated at the conclusion of the hearings that the committee members "were men of intelligence and honesty, against whose probity and character nothing has been said or can be said." John M. Olin, Northwestern trustee

and witness, observed that the members "were attentive, showed great patience—even forbearance—and Senator Roehr proved a model chairman."[16]

The Investigation Gets Under Way

The investigation of Northwestern Mutual began on April 12, 1906, and continued for twenty-three days of public testimony, to the end of June. Officers, trustees, and employees were closely interrogated in open sessions, as the committee conducted its examination along lines made famous by the New York inquiry. Investments, financial relationships with other companies, discrimination, semitontine experience, managerial perpetuation, and nepotism were unsparingly probed by the committee.

Closely following the lead of the Armstrong Committee the Wisconsin legislators opened their examination by an inquiry into the structure of managerial control in Northwestern and the apparatus used to maintain that control. Testimony brought out the fact that prior to each election ballots were expressed to each general agent for distribution to the policyholders residing in their respective territories, and that the ballots of policyholders electing to exercise their franchise were either collected by the agents and forwarded to the Home Office, or mailed directly to Milwaukee by policyholders. The

ballots were voted by proxy holders appointed by the Company's officers. While no provision was made on the ballots for candidates other than those nominated by the existing management, the Company did provide for election inspectors from among the policyholders. Like the New York mutuals, however, no provision was made for inspection by the state department of insurance. Unlike the New York companies the Northwestern proxies were not perpetual, but had to be renewed each year. Since the nominations for candidates for trustee were made by the trustees and executive officers, and since the officers were in turn elected by the trustees, the machinery to insure self-perpetuation was effective.

Counsel for the committee made much of the fact that the proxy voters were frequently not insured in the Company, implying that the results perhaps might have been different had they been policyholders. He also pointed out that since the Company would not make available the names and addresses of policyholders to any member of the Company requesting them, policyholders dissatisfied with an existing management had no opportunity to elect trustees satisfactory to them. With respect to perpetual control by a given Northwestern management, it was, in the eyes of the committee, in the same class as the much criticized New York companies. The committee was hardly surprised when most management witnesses denied that the current procedure was essentially undemocratic or that it resulted in the perpetuation of the management.[17]

Although Northwestern abandoned issuance of deferred dividend policies in June 1905, the committee probed the semi-tontine experience as part of its inquiry into the Company's marketing practices. Evidence was brought out that Company estimates of probable benefits from these policies were frequently exaggerated. It was also charged that the cost of acquiring new business, primarily because of the agent's first-year commission, exceeded the regular expense loading. The evidence was plain that, for the year 1904 at least, the expense of new business to the Company was 134 per cent of the regular loading on first-year premiums.[18] If the Armstrong evidence was correct, then the cost of the new business was financed from the deferred dividend surplus or charged against future renewal premiums; in either case it was considered too high.

Like the Armstrong Committee, the Wisconsin body recognized that Northwestern's ratio of actual expense to "loading" was low when compared to those incurred by the Big Three; however, it was still considered as discriminatory to semi-tontine policyholders. The committee, furthermore, was firm

in its belief that this excessive cost was directly due to the fiercely competitive struggle the Company had been waging for a market. It professed to see little sense to this competition, and no valid reason why rapid growth was necessary for the welfare of policyholders. The committee also strongly implied approval of those Armstrong recommendations that limited new business and expense loading. It argued that since the struggle for new business resulted in increasing commissions to agents, which in turn increased the loading expense, a limitation on the volume of new business a company could write would remove the need for these incentives. Commissions would decline and expense ratios would be reduced. One member, Senator Jacob Rummel, was willing to go so far as to recommend the elimination of selling agents by the creation of a state-operated insurance fund, which in fact was subsequently established by the state of Wisconsin.[19]

In view of the abandonment of semi-tontine business by Northwestern in 1905 and the New York legislation prohibiting this type of insurance in 1906, most of this discussion was academic. It served chiefly to confirm the conclusions about deferred dividend insurance that had already prompted Northwestern to halt the issue of such policies.

The Wisconsin investigators were interested in other marketing practices, especially as they related to the drive for new business. Devices such as twisting and rebating came under special scrutiny. The testimony brought out certain contradictions between the avowed policy of Northwestern and the practices of its agents. On the matter of twisting, for example, Northwestern's superintendent of agencies, Henry F. Norris, vehemently stated that it was "reprehensible—wrong—[and we] have not hesitated to say so in any case where the agent would not, with his knowledge of the business . . . take exactly the same action which he recommends a man to take." As interpreted by the committee counsel this statement merely indicated that the criterion was to be "the agent's judgment in a particular case of how far he may twist."[20] Although Norris protested against this interpretation, he was unable to make a strong case, especially in the face of a letter sent by J. I. D. Bristol, Northwestern's general agent in New York City, to Charles Evans Hughes during the course of the Armstrong Investigation. At that time Bristol wrote:

Is it possible that a law against twisting is really seriously contemplated to prevent such men [owners of policies in the Big Three] giving their families a much larger amount of life insurance, in better companies, for the same outlay now paid to the most costly companies, with paid-up insurance in the latter companies as an added value? I have no fear that you or any member of the Armstrong Committee will be misled by the deceptive clamor of men notorious as rebaters who seek to continue their high cost policies in force without the possibility of a comparison being made by the representatives of conservative companies, proving that in many cases cheaper, safer, and better insurance is elsewhere obtainable. Such restricted salesmanship in life insurance would tend to a high cost monopoly utterly at variance with the best interests of the business.[21]

The staunch official position of management against rebating was a matter of record, but even here certain contradictions existed. An examination of several of the Company's agents in the Milwaukee area, together with a number of policyholders, indicated that a certain amount of rebating was carried on. One policyholder, a prominent Northwestern trustee, refused to testify fully on this matter on grounds of possible self-incrimination; the other policyholders and the implicated agents quickly followed suit.

With respect to political activity, the committee concluded that, unlike the major New York companies, the management of Northwestern had carefully avoided using policyholders' money for contributions to political parties or campaign committees, "or given aid in the election or defeat of any candidate for public office." [22] The closest approach to direct political activity was the occasional circularization of Wisconsin policyholders in order to bring pressure upon representatives in the legislature concerning particular issues of special concern to the Company. Furthermore, it was made clear that Northwestern followed the policy of taking independent action whenever the Company's interests were at stake, whether or not such action coincided with efforts of other insurance companies to influence legislation. Where Company interests were not directly involved, it either abstained from interference with legislative processes or lent its cooperation to the other life insurance interests.

The committee was critical of Northwestern's use of hired representatives rather than its own officers in its relations with the Wisconsin Legislature, as well as the lack of detail in the financial records for payments made to legislative agents.[23] In this area,

where members of the committee were particularly sensitive, the investigators indicated a desire for tighter control of legislative expenditures, and more detailed reporting by life companies to the state insurance authorities concerning the nature and purpose of the outlays.

The Wisconsin investigators dug deeply into Company records for evidence with respect to irregular treatment of policyholders in such matters as surrenders, contested claims, lapses, forfeitures, and restorations of policies. On the basis of testimony, they were critical of the Company in several respects. It was found, for example, that Northwestern paid a number of death claims when the evidence clearly indicated suicide within the initial two years following the filing of the policy. In other instances, when management believed a claim of suicide could not be legally upheld, the Company sought to compromise the claim.[24] It was the committee's judgment that these cases reflected discrimination among policyholders.

The committee also made public the existence of the Company's "inspection department," whose functions, as explained in an earlier chapter, were to investigate the character, health, and personal habits of policyholders. In cases where the inspection department unearthed information indicating that a policyholder was using alcohol or narcotics, or that he was in poor health, note of it was made on Company records. A notice was then sent to the general agent in whose territory the policyholder lived, with instructions not to accept premiums if received after the due date, unless so instructed by the Home Office.[25] This practice, Secretary James W. Skinner maintained, was followed in the interests of all the policyholders.[26] The committee denied this saying, "Subsequent examination of the books and records of the company clearly indicates that he [Skinner] was mistaken, and that such caution marks were placed against policyholders and notices thereof given to the agents because of ill-health as well as intemperate habits." [27]

The chief defense by the Company for the "inspection department" was that it improved the mortality record of Northwestern and thus enabled it to pay higher dividends to policyholders.[28] The committee seriously questioned whether such improvement was justifiable, either ethically or in terms of the costs, and expressed doubt as to whether it actually had been accomplished.

On all cases involving variations in the treatment of policyholders the committee insisted that Northwestern was a mutual organization and, therefore, that management possessed no power of discretion which could lead to a differentiation between policy-holders. More specifically, the committee stated:

> We find no provisions of the charter which warrant the officers in exercising a discretion which leads to discrimination between policyholders. The discretion which they exercised in this respect was conferred upon them by themselves, and in the exercise of this self-conferred discretion we find that the officers have discriminated against policyholders in the matter of restoring their policies when lapsed or cancelled and likewise discriminated against the beneficiaries in settling claims.[29]

Probing the Company's Financial Practices

As far as financial practices were concerned the committee reported that the records of Northwestern, Wisconsin Life, and the Union Central were excellent, quite in contrast to what the Armstrong Investigation had revealed about the New York companies.

> There is no evidence that any of said companies has engaged, directly or indirectly in any syndicate operations, or that any officer of said companies has had any interest in any such syndicate operations.
>
> There is no evidence that any of said companies, or any officer thereof, has ever had any interest in the flotation of securities, and we find there has been no investment of the company's funds, except in income bearing securities and real estate, all properly listed in the assets of the companies, as provided in their charters and the laws of the state.
>
> We have found no evidence of any misappropriation of these companies' funds or manipulation of the business of these companies for personal gain, except as it may be inferred from facts hereinafter specifically set forth.[30]

The one area of financial operation which evoked bitter condemnation from the committee involved loans made to policyholders by a number of the Company's personnel, or by members of their families or friends. This development evolved, as was reported in Chapter VI, from the Company's inability to make such loans prior to 1893, and because of the conviction that, as a trustee, it had no right to interfere with the final distribution of semi-tontine results.

After 1893 policyholders were able to make policy loans directly from the Company, but despite the rapid growth in this account the bulk of it was on annual dividend insurance rather than on deferred dividend plans. With the latter policies the Company refused to lend more than 90 per cent of the reserve value of deferred dividend policies, a decision that was fully justified on moral and legal grounds. This procedure, of course, excluded dividends which had accrued to each account or had been accumulated as a result of deaths or lapses among the particular tontine class. Semi-tontine policyholders naturally wanted to borrow on the basis of the entire estimated value of their policies rather than the smaller reserve values; but private lenders were loath to undertake the risk that if the policy did lapse, forfeiture of accumulated dividends would reduce the surrender value below the amount loaned. If, however, the lender was kept fully informed of the status of the policy and had the privilege of paying premiums himself if necessary, he had nothing to lose and a generous rate of interest to gain. It was precisely this position which the group lending through the Company enjoyed.

As of January 1, 1906, when the total amount of loans from all sources outstanding against Northwestern's semi-tontine policies was $1,375,386, "private loans made by officers, agents, and employees of the company and their relatives reached the sum of $807,581,"[31] over 58 per cent of the aggregate. Included in this group were a majority of the Company officers, a number of trustees, relatives of both, and Company agents.[32] The view of this group was expressed before the committee by Vice President Markham when he asserted: "It is perfectly legitimate business—it is something that I have no apologies to make [for] to this committee or anybody else." When he further testified that he was keeping one-third to one-half of these policies alive by paying the defaulted premiums to avoid a forfeit which would jeopardize his loans, the committee counsel made his most telling point:

> Now then, when you and other officers are keeping alive these policies, because of your loans, keeping them alive until maturity, when they otherwise would be forfeited, are you not depriving that class of their share of the accumulated surplus in one-third to one-half of your policies?[33]

In retrospect it appears that initially Northwestern fostered private lending to its policyholders in good faith. Over the years, and especially after 1893, there was no attempt to reappraise the practice in terms of an obligation to policyholders; the result was the most devastating criticism of the management for discrimination between policyholders advanced during the entire investigation.

The Wisconsin committee, alert for signs of nepotism, found scant fare at Northwestern. Of the ten citations of alleged nepotism in the Home Office five involved men classified as clerks, none of whom earned salaries over $3,000 annually, including President Palmer's son. Three others earned within the range of $4,000–$6,500, and only two had incomes over $8,000. The highest salary was paid to Dr. John W. Fisher, the medical director, who received $12,000, but Dr. Fisher was one of the most prominent figures in the medical underwriting profession of his day.

The Armstrong Committee had uncovered some truly large-scale nepotism in its investigations, not the least of which was the practice of giving the president's son in one company a general agency, and later a percentage of the premiums on overseas business. The Wisconsin investigators believed they had exposed a similar situation when they revealed that Charles D. Norton, a partner in the Chicago general agency and nephew of Judge Charles Dyer, had received as his share of the agency income nearly $70,000. This amount, however, was gross income and included the value of Norton's personal business.[34] Furthermore, Norton was a highly able man who subsequently won acclaim both as a banker and as Assistant Secretary of the Treasury in the cabinet of President Taft.

Salaries of the executive officer group, as an indicator of the relative dominance of a business-control group in the Company, were comparatively modest. President Palmer, after thirty years as chief executive, received $25,000 per year; Vice President Markham, $18,000; Second Vice President Skinner, $15,000; and C. A. Loveland, actuary, $12,000. Salaries of the general counsel, the third vice president, and the other executive officers ranged below $12,-000.[35] For an organization as large as Northwestern these salaries were hardly excessive. In most instances they were substantially less than those paid in the Big Three, or for similar positions in financial institutions of comparable size and responsibility.

The committee found that several of the leading bankers in Milwaukee were members of the Board of Trustees and the key standing committees. They also learned that the trustees carefully reviewed the rates of interest paid by Milwaukee banks on Company deposits, and that Northwestern's business was scrutinized by examining committees of trustees.

The investigators, however, were dissatisfied with Northwestern's investments and portfolio policy on several counts. First, they regarded the investment earnings rate as being lower than that which could have been earned with a different investment policy. Second, they criticized the Company for lending such a small proportion of its available funds on Wisconsin real estate, particularly on farm properties.

With respect to earnings, the committee called particular attention to the rate earned by the Union Central, which apparently exceeded that of Northwestern by 25 per cent.[36] It was the committee's contention that the differential existing in favor of the Ohio company was due to the higher proportion of mortgage loans made by the Union Central (about 80 per cent compared to 50 per cent for Northwestern). Furthermore, Union Central's loans were principally upon farm real estate, typically in amounts of less than $5,000 per loan.

Northwestern witnesses pointed out that while both companies utilized a system of loan agents, those of the Union Central were compensated on a commission basis, thus placing their interest somewhat at variance with that of the company in the matter of security. They further insisted that the Union Central's higher interest rate was obtained because of greater risk, and that Northwestern refused to lend on many of the properties regarded by the Ohio firm as acceptable. In fact, Northwestern avoided certain of the Union Central's lending territories altogether. They further explained that the variance between the two companies in the sheer amount of money to be invested had to be taken into account. Northwestern, seeking to minimize risks, accepted only the better real estate mortgages and developed other outlets of a long-term nature for its funds, principally railroad bonds. The Union Central, on the other hand, was prohibited by statute from acquiring corporate securities.

The subsequent discussion over the relative merits of farm loans, especially in Wisconsin, and urban loans did little to reconcile the basic differences between a number of committee members and the spokesmen for the Company. The committee generally reflected the rural or small-town orientation of its membership. The Progressives had a basic suspicion of the power of corporations and their ability to affect the welfare of small farmers and tradesmen. The committee also reflected the widely current resentment against "drawing money out of an area with no reinvestment." Company officers, on the other hand, argued that many rural areas of Wisconsin did not provide a sufficient volume of attractive mortgages to warrant the cost of a loan agent. They also pointed to the growing proportion of farm mortgage loans in the Company's portfolio. It was their contention that the management's first responsibility was to the policyholders, and not to local interests of potential borrowers.

Summary of the Investigation

Compared with the sensational disclosures of the Armstrong Investigation the results of the Wisconsin hearings were a distinct anticlimax. They were not followed by management reorganizations, group resignations, or dismissals on the part of any of the three companies under investigation. No suits had to be filed for the recovery of misappropriated funds and none of the officers or trustees found it advisable to take up residence in foreign countries, as happened with several firms in the New York investigation.

Northwestern management felt, with considerable justification, that it came through the investigation with its reputation comparatively unshaken. It was clear that the management was essentially self-perpetuating, but no small group had taken over control from the trustees. The Company was completely absolved from any claim that its funds were used to further private interests; there were no shadowy relationships between the officers and investment bankers or members of other financial institutions. The committee's criticisms of Northwestern's investment policies involved matters of judgment. In terms of the Company's over-all investment problems, its policies in this area were quite defensible.

The most serious criticism of Northwestern's management by the investigating committee was in reference to certain discriminatory treatment of policyholders. Here the Company did not put up a very strong defense. There was some substance to the claim that certain of these practices were necessary to meet competition, but the arguments advanced by the Company seeemed to reflect a spirit of benevolent paternalism, an attitude that the management should decide what was best for the majority of its policyholders. On principle this position was hard to defend, especially in view of the letter and spirit of the Company's charter.

The findings of the investigating committee un-

doubtedly prompted the Company to make a belated reappraisal of a number of its operations. Subsequent examinations by public authorities, particularly by the insurance commission, brought out no further criticism of the type made in 1906. This led to minor changes, but there seemed no reason to question the basic soundness of practices developed by the Company over the preceding quarter century. It was too soon, perhaps, to anticipate a number of changes that were to mark the industry in the years that lay ahead. The successive managements might well have paid more attention to President Palmer's remark at one stage of the investigation when he said, "The Company may have outgrown the methods which suited it in the past." [37]

Legislation Produced by the Investigation

Although the legislative investigation was completed in the summer of 1906, the official committee report and transcription of the testimony was not published until January 1907, a tense and uncertain interval for life insurance companies operating in Wisconsin. Included in the report were twenty-four bills recommended to the attention of the legislature which would substantially modify the state insurance code. These, however, were only a part of the mass of legislation which would occupy that body for the ensuing several months. The attention which had been focused upon life insurance by the Armstrong Investigation, the Canadian and New Jersey inquiries, and the Wisconsin probe resulted in wholesale efforts by a broad variety of interests to remodel the legal framework which controlled the industry. To the twenty-four committee bills were added another seventeen submitted by interested officials of several states.* Before the legislature adjourned a grand total of seventy-two insurance bills had been introduced, most of which were killed in committee or combined with other proposals for formal consideration.

A substantial proportion of the bills which emerged from the legislative committees for consideration by the whole legislature closely resembled the laws passed in New York the previous year. For

---

* These officials, governors, attorneys general, and insurance commissioners had formed an informal vehicle for joint action which was known as the Committee of Fifteen. The committee, organized early in 1906, formulated its own model insurance legislation which, as Stalson points out, was not entirely in agreement with the new New York insurance laws. Its work was beneficial to many hard-pressed legislatures in seeking to improve the legal framework of insurance. Stalson, *Marketing Life Insurance,* 557.

example, new forms and requirements for annual reporting to the state by the life companies were recommended, including detailed gain and loss exhibits, schedules of employees and agents receiving a minimum of $5,000 per year, and the amounts spent on legislative and political activity. In addition there were bills prohibiting discrimination, misrepresentation, and rebating.[38]

Several of the recommendations of the investigating committee clearly had Northwestern in mind. These included a stipulation prohibiting proxy voting in the elections of trustees and directors in domestic life companies and guaranteeing access to lists of policyholders by members of the companies dissatisfied with a given management. Also proposed were a limit on salaries and the appointment by the governor of the state of an additional director or trustee to the board of domestic mutual companies.[39]

While Northwestern and other members of the industry were critical of many of these proposals, they were much more concerned with a suggested change in the state insurance code. This would have (1) established the incontestability of all policies after one year, (2) provided for a cash surrender value payable on demand after two years, (3) made the terms on policy loans more lenient, and (4) prohibited policy loans (except in the case of automatic premium loans) from constituting a lien against any or all policies unless a memorandum was specifically attached to the policy and approved by the borrower.[40]

The greatest antagonism, by Northwestern and all industry representatives, was reserved for three recommendations which proposed to compel certain investments, circumscribe premiums, and limit expenses. The first of these would require all companies selling insurance in the state to deposit certain securities with the secretary of state equal in value to the total liabilities on their outstanding Wisconsin policies. Northwestern had withdrawn from Canada rather than conform to a similar compulsory investment act; when passed by the Texas legislature in 1907 another such law resulted in the departure of all the major life companies from the state.[41] The proposed limitation on the amount of premiums which could be charged was damned by

the insurance companies as ambiguous and actuarially unsound.*

Out-of-state companies insisted that their own actuaries failed to understand the meaning of the premium and expense limitation bills. They informed Governor J. O. Davidson that the loading and expense provisions would force them to withdraw from Wisconsin.[42] Northwestern spokesmen were equally unhappy about the prospect of operating under these provisions, but withdrawal posed much more serious problems.

Most of the legislators believed that the announced intention of withdrawal by the foreign companies was a bluff, designed to obtain gubernatorial veto of the insurance bills. When Governor Davidson, however, signed them, the reaction was not long in coming. By December 1907 eight out-of-state companies had withdrawn from Wisconsin, including Mutual Benefit, which had operated in the state since 1846; Mutual Life of New York; Equitable Society; Massachusetts Mutual; and Phoenix Mutual. Before the objectionable features of the legislation were modified or revoked in 1915, a total of twenty-three non-Wisconsin companies left the state.[43]

The Northwestern management, rather than exploit these withdrawals, sided with the industry and urged policyholders of those companies to continue their policies. Henry F. Norris wrote to all Wisconsin agents, informing them of the behavior the Company's management expected:

> Every company that has withdrawn is perfectly solvent and just as able to protect the interests of its policyholders as it ever was; but all these companies will be embarrassed by serious difficulties arising from disorganized agency forces, severing, in large measure, the existing reciprocal interests between agent and insured, and menacing the general business by causing lapses due to withdrawal of agency cooperation and advice, coupled with the natural reluctance of persons to conform to novel requirements and disconcerting inconveniences.
>
> Your opportunity is this: To impress upon every policyholder of every one of

---

* According to the proposal the premium was to be set so that it would not exceed the sum of: (a) the net single premium, which, excluding the expense factor, would mature the policy according to its terms; (b) an amount for expenses equal to one-fourth of the net single premium calculated on the basis of the American Experience Table of Mortality at 3 per cent interest assumption, and based on an ordinary life policy taken at the same age. The

third proposal specified that the expense charge was not to exceed: (a) the first year, on the difference between the premium and the mortality charge for the first year; (b) the second through the fifth years, the mortality charge for such years, or one-half the difference between the premium and the mortality charge for such years, whichever was greater; and (c) sixth and subsequent years, the expense provision of any previous year of the policy.

these companies that his policy is just as good as it was before the withdrawal of the companies; that his interests in every way are just as safe and that he would make a serious mistake to drop his policy.[44]

This unusual stand was an unexpected and pleasant surprise to rival companies. As President Peabody of Mutual Life, who had previously dreaded what would happen, said,

> It is with peculiar pleasure, . . . that we note the high stand taken by our great competitor, the Northwestern Mutual Life Insurance Company of Milwaukee, in urging its agents to advise the policyholders of all withdrawing companies to maintain their insurance in force, and admonishing them under no circumstances to disturb the existing business of these companies.[45]

The rate of Wisconsin business for Northwestern did increase, however. Despite a lag in the first quarter Wisconsin business was up 29 per cent in 1908, while the remainder of its field increased by only 7.4 per cent; during the next two years the rate of increase in new business written in Wisconsin by Northwestern was greater than its respective rate for the entire country.[46] This increase does not mean that the Company was guilty of cynical behavior; rather the explanation lies in the circumstance that, with the withdrawal of many of its competitors from Wisconsin, Northwestern found itself the principal seller in the state. Insurance prospects in these years simply did not have a large number of companies from which to purchase insurance.

The Investigations and Legislative Remedies in Retrospect

The interval which elapsed between the appointment of the Armstrong Committee in New York and the departure of the Eastern companies from Wisconsin was only a few days under two and one-half years. Yet within that brief period changes of a revolutionary nature to American life insurance were wrought. The legal framework of the business was tightened, more clearly defined, and provided with a more effective apparatus for the exercise of public control. The immediate effects, it is true, were evident only in New York, Wisconsin, and New Jersey, but the importance of those markets, particularly in New York, was such that the repercussions

were felt in almost every state. The companies licensed to do business in New York possessed over 80 per cent of the industry's insurance in force and about an equal proportion of its assets. To withdraw from this market, the richest in the country, was unthinkable for companies already well established there. Thus the large out-of-state companies modified their practices and methods to conform to the revised New York insurance code, exactly as if they had been incorporated within that state. The changes in New Jersey and Wisconsin, while here or there more or less stringent, generally followed the initiative of the Empire State, in effect extending the insurance reforms to still other companies.

Some of the new rules, as could have been expected, had to be changed again in the light of further information and the basic requirements of the business. The attempt to place restrictions on sheer corporate size ran into serious difficulties almost from the beginning. The Armstrong Committee and the legislature were unable to offer a working definition of optimum size for life insurance companies; the limitations they imposed in 1906 (that is, a fixed percentage rate of growth based upon existing insurance in force) temporarily penalized the Big Three. Because industrial companies like Metropolitan Life were accorded somewhat different treatment, no such restrictions applied to their sales volume, and one of the results was the rapid capture of a vast segment of the market by such companies.

Like the restriction on growth, limitations regarding expenses and the agents' renewal commission period were subsequently modified. Yet the purpose of such legislation was to give policyholders, particularly those with insurance in force for some time, more equitable treatment than the old marketing practices had given them. Predatory marketing, the outgrowth of greater-than-optimum expansion, required expenditures in excess of the revenue from new business, and such market invasions implied reduced profits and consequently lower dividends for older policyholders.

A further effect of the remedial legislation that followed 1905 was the acceleration and greater uniformity of the slowly growing tendencies to liberalize the policy contract which had gone on for decades. Nonforfeiture provisions were improved and became more standardized, incontestability periods were shortened, and cash surrender and policy loan features likewise became more liberal and more generalized as a result of the 1906–1907 legislation.

The investigations and the accompanying legislation had salutary effects upon the attitudes of the insuring public, public control groups, and the professional managers of life companies alike. While no law could compel a body of policyholders to exercise their voting franchise, and certainly men of the stamp of Charles Evans Hughes were not so naive as to believe that it could, the legislation at least provided that if it were desired, adequate machinery for its implementation would exist. As a result the opportunities for small, ruthless groups to seize and maintain control in mutual organizations were substantially reduced, as was also the temptation to further dynastic ambitions. In a certain sense the climate of opinion regarding the trusteeship ethic in life insurance was altered and the questionable practices of certain managements abruptly terminated.

The legislation of reform was not perfect. The investigators and legislators were not omniscient. Life companies after 1907 would continue to contest for market shares, and personal self-aggrandizement of insurance executives would continue to spur the contestants in the race. The future would continue to pose the problems of seeking and maintaining efficiency, flexibility, and good morale in giant-sized companies. The imperious manipulation of the funds of policyholders by arrogant officials, which

had been accomplished chiefly through opportunities to acquire and deal in equity investments, resulted in the withdrawal of these rights. In future years, when investment opportunities were altered and the income of life companies hugely expanded, these revised investment codes would rise to complicate the problems of effective financial administration of life insurance funds. The investigations, however, came at a particularly strategic moment for the life insurance business. Curiously there were apparently few, if any, life company officers ready to admit the weaknesses and deficiencies of the business, or to seek reform from within the industry. That reform had to be imposed from outside, over the protests of the industry. One of the major results was that the altered climate of opinion, wherein the industry was to a large degree cleansed of public suspicion, provided a vehicle by which new generations of insurance officials could offer better insurance service to the public than had their predecessors. It is somewhat doubtful if this would have been true, at least to the same degree, had there been no investigations and no reform legislation.

CHAPTER TEN

The Trend Toward Specialty: 1908-1918 Management and Marketing Organization

D URING the spring of 1905 Henry L. Palmer once again announced his intention to retire from active office. This time he evidently did not mean to be deterred from his purpose by the trustees, no matter how flattering their insistence that he remain chief executive. Age—he was eighty-eight—and the cumulative strain of thirty-two years of presidential responsibility had exhausted and weakened him. The appointment by the New York legislature of the Armstrong Committee just a week before Northwestern's annual meeting abruptly shattered Palmer's plans. If, as seemed likely, the Company were to come under the spotlight of investigation, the president believed it was his duty to personally defend the policies and practices followed during his stewardship. The Wisconsin investigation caused a further postponement of his contemplated retirement, but by the spring of 1908, with the storms abating, he informed his colleagues that a successor would have to be chosen at the annual meeting in July.

The clearly defined lines of managerial succession established over the preceding thirty years, combined with obvious professional ability and experience, made the selection of George C. Markham self-evident. The vice president also had the advantage of an established position in Milwaukee society, long membership on the Board, and since 1904 the experience of being Palmer's lieutenant with its attending responsibilities. On July 15, 1908, the Board of Trustees elected Markham president of the Company, and promoted James W. Skinner and P. R. Sanborn to the first and second vice presidencies respectively. By virtue of a change in the by-laws Judge Palmer was named chairman of the Executive Committee, but this was more a reflection of the desire to secure his continued relationship with the Company than a belief he would actively participate in the management of Northwestern.[1]

Physically, by manner and temperament, George C. Markham was probably a *beau idéal* of the successful American executive of his era. A contemporary who was associated with the president throughout his administration observed that he was

> a gentleman of the old school, tall, well-built, with big, strong shoulders and a large well-formed head. He had keen, steady eyes, a grey mustache, and the suggestion of a goatee. A firm, strong mouth, large, well-formed hands and altogether in his looks he reflected a powerful personality.
>
> He was a man of strong convictions, and he was not always diplomatic in their expression. Because [he was] inflexible in his opinions he appeared arbitrary at times, but when business proceeded unruffled, he was a kind, considerate gentleman. The arbitrary rules required by modern methods often irked him and there were times when

George C. Markham

he was disregardful of those exact amenities which are expected from a diffusion of responsibility in a corporation. President Markham was more concerned with the results than with methods. While he remained in office as its titular head, there was no room for doubt as to who was president of the Company, and as the years crept upon him this fact became more and more apparent.[2]

While a man of these characteristics might prove somewhat difficult to work with or for, it was probably less important in this period than in later years. Of more pressing concern to Northwestern personnel was what President Markham had in mind for the future. Considering that only a very few could remember a chief executive other than Henry L. Palmer at Northwestern, this concern was understandable.

Any apprehension that the new administration might plan disruptive changes was quickly allayed when, the day following his election, Markham addressed the Company's Association of Agents. "I can assure you gentlemen of the agency force," he announced, "that there will be no radical change; in fact, I today do not conceive of the necessity for any change whatever." The role the Company would play in the life insurance business in the future was clear:

> The president [Palmer] believed, and I believe, that it is far better that we have the best and safest company in the world rather than the largest.... You have my assurance that the good work will be carried on in the same conservative lines that have always been maintained by my predecessor.[3]

President Markham, of course, did not intend that his announcement of "no change" should be interpreted literally. What he did mean was that Northwestern would meet future challenges in the same way they had been met in the past—by application of the three basic principles which had guided the Company for fifty years and raised it to its current position in American life insurance. Adherence to the first of these principles, conservative underwriting standards, meant resistance to any tendencies that would impair criteria of individual risk selection and favorable mortality experience. It also meant resistance to insurance schemes which were not actuarially sound as demonstrated by experience. Adhesion to the second principle, simplicity of operation, implied several things, not the least of which was a low expense rate. Included would be the restriction of the number of insurance plans offered by the Company, abstention from new methods of mass distribution, and continued reliance upon the pure general agency system for marketing insurance. The last principle, conservative investment policy, inferred sound portfolio distribution and intelligent geographic dispersal of assets, with adequate safeguards for both the amount at risk and the Company's earning position.

All this indicated that Northwestern was to find itself developing as a specialty company in the changing insurance markets which materialized in the years after 1906. Although this would not make it unique in the life insurance business, it would certainly differentiate it significantly from most of the very large companies in the industry. Markham's policy statement indicated that Northwestern would select its own markets and restrict its growth to that rate which its principles, due regard for policyholders' interests and the changing nature of the economy and society, would set.

Despite the sporadic nature of business conditions during the years 1908–1918, the economic growth of the United States continued without serious check. The aftermath of the panic of 1907 caused a sharp but brief depression which ran its course by the end of 1908. The mild recovery of 1909 was succeeded by recession for the next two years, and a more substantial prosperity in 1912–1913. Outbreak of war in Europe in August 1914 contributed to panic and economic slump; but with a correction of maladjustments and indications of prolonged hostilities, business recovered in 1915. Under the stimulus of allied war orders and American involvement, business boomed over the following three years.

Productivity and income followed the same general vicissitudes, but the American people substantially improved their material position over the period. Population rose by approximately 7 per cent, from 97 million to over 104 million; the annual average net product for the 1909–1918 decade was $36.3 billion, about 84 per cent higher than that for the previous decade.[4] While part of this improvement was dissipated by steeply rising prices after 1915, real per capita income increased from about $510 in 1907 to almost $600 in 1918.[5] Gross capital formation for these years rose by almost 90 per cent from the average level enjoyed in the ten years 1899–1908. Although the level of personal and business savings also increased, the demand for capital was so great that the long-term downward tendency of interest rates was reversed. A heavy program of construction stimulated by the rapidly expanding urban population materially assisted the mounting level of investment. In fact, for the first time the United States had more people residing in urban communities than lived on farms or in rural villages.

These developments had important implications for American life insurance. Not only did accelerating urbanization, industrialization, and rising income serve to broaden the market for life insurance both quantitatively and qualitatively, but the expanding investment opportunities readily absorbed the increasing funds accruing to the life companies. At the close of 1907 the 190 legal reserve companies comprising the United States life insurance industry had in force an aggregate of approximately $14 billion; eleven years later 295 companies had almost $30 billion in force. During the period expansion of life insurance coverage had encouraged the formation of 233 new companies while, for a variety of reasons, 128 firms had discontinued operations.[6]

Influence of Policyholders on the Company Management

Northwestern's growth and the geographic spread of its market had made it a national institution long before 1908. Following 1900 the management had grown more aware of the desirability of having the Company's twelve non-Wisconsin trustees represent the areas where its business was most concentrated. In an effort to have at least one trustee from the most important of these regions represented on the Board, the general agents were drawn upon for suggestions of men in their territories who possessed the qualifications considered important by the Company. Usually these included the possession of some prominence, particularly in business; mature judgment and the respect of his community; and an enthusiastic belief in Northwestern. Furthermore, the management did not want men on the Board merely because of the prominence of their names. Under a State law passed in 1906 if a trustee were absent from three consecutive meetings he was automatically removed from the Board. This provision effectively excluded the presence of uninterested and non-participating trustees. During Markham's administration Northwestern's trustees outside Wisconsin were drawn largely from heavily populated urban areas, although smaller communities were by no means excluded. While most trustees were drawn from the ranks of commerce, banking, transportation, and manufacturing, two prominent jurists were included. It was noticeable, however, that the Company did not have members of the investment banking fraternity on the Board, evidently preferring to avoid any embarrassment in the exercise of investment decision.

From its very earliest years Northwestern had provided for periodic examinations of the management and Company operations by a committeee of three trustees, not themselves members of the Executive Committee. Since both the New York and Wisconsin investigators had urged greater representation of policyholders in the management of life companies, the Company responded by changing its bylaws to provide that this committee be composed of three policyholders, whether or not they were trustees. In 1909, two years after this modification, the Executive Committee provided that the Examining Committee could have as many as five members. The members of the committee were selected from a list of candidates which had been suggested by the general agents; and membership was frequently a prelude to selection as a trustee, depending

upon the impression the member made upon the management.

As originally conceived the Examining Committee had the responsibility of conducting an audit of the Company's securities, books, and accounts, and for evaluating the performance of the management. Valuable suggestions were frequently forthcoming from these committees, as has been shown in an earlier chapter. In 1912, at President Markham's suggestion, the bylaws were changed to permit the employment of an audit company in lieu of an examining committee in any year; but later, in the face of vigorous opposition by several members of the Executive Committee, the former scope of its interests was fully restored.

Executive Management Personnel

George C. Markham inherited a veteran group of executive officers when he became president (see Table X-1), all but one of the seven officials having been with the Company longer than he. Judge George H. Noyes, legal counsel, was the only newcomer, having been appointed in 1906 upon the death of Judge Dyer. Charles Loveland had been actuary since 1889 and Dr. John W. Fisher, the medical director, had occupied that position since 1896. The other officers were more recent appointees. Henry F. Norris became superintendent

of agencies in 1902, James W. Skinner and P. R. Sanborn were elected vice presidents in 1904 and 1905, respectively; and A. S. Hathaway was appointed secretary in 1906. Hathaway's immediate predecessor had been Charles H. Watson, who became secretary in 1905 when Skinner had been promoted to vice president. Watson served only a few months, and his death signalled the promotion of Hathaway who had then been in Northwestern's service for twenty years.

During Markham's tenure of office each of these operating officers was directly responsible to the president for the administration of his own department. Practically, however, Vice President Skinner absorbed many of the responsibilities associated with the insurance departments, both in his own office and through the Insurance and Agency Committee. The superintendent of agencies was also a member of this committee. Indeed there was some indication that Norris was a rather dominating member, but like the general counsel and P. R. Sanborn, for the most part he worked directly with the president.

Markham had no reason to alter either the personnel or the structure of the management hierarchy in his first year as president. During that time, however, he became aware of a lack of top level administrative assistance such as he had furnished during the last few years of the Palmer administration. In August 1909 the Executive Committee was requested to appoint a person to act as a vice president and who would be responsible to the president and the Committee.

While there were several trustees, particularly members of the Executive Committee, who possessed both business acumen and a vital interest in the Company, most of them were already too heavily committed to business and professional careers to devote all their time to Northwestern. One, however, who was willing to undertake the challenge and had the endorsement of the trustees and the president, was William Duncan Van Dyke. Son of the former Northwestern president, Van Dyke had been elected a trustee in 1904 and subsequently appointed to the Executive and Finance Committees. In addition to assisting his father in the management of the family business interests, he was a practicing attorney, with a particular interest in insurance law. The Executive Committee, which could only make temporary appointments at this level, named Van Dyke chairman of the Committee, this position being temporarily vacant due to the death of Henry L. Palmer.⁷ On October 20, 1909, the Board of Trustees elected him a vice president.

TABLE X-1

Northwestern Mutual: Executive Officers,
1908-1918

PRESIDENT
George C. Markham
1908-1918

VICE PRESIDENT
James W. Skinner
1908-1912*
William D. Van Dyke
1909-1918

SECOND VICE PRESIDENT
P. R. Sanborn
1908-1918

ACTUARY
Charles Loveland
1908-1915
Percy H. Evans
1915-1918

SECRETARY
A. S. Hathaway
1908-1918

GENERAL COUNSEL
George H. Noyes
1908-1915*
John Barnes
1916-1918

SUPERINTENDENT OF AGENCIES
Henry Norris
1908-1916*
George E. Copeland
1916-1918

MEDICAL DIRECTOR
Dr. John Fisher
1908-1918

* Died in office.

Home Office Administration

The great expansion of Northwestern's business during the previous decade, and through the first four years of Markham's administration, resulted in a substantial increase in the Company's clerical force and subsequent overcrowding of the Home Office building. Methods of organization and routines which had been adequate when Northwestern was smaller were no longer effective with increased size and more intensive division of labor. In addition the matter of employee morale gained in importance and necessitated a more systematic approach to personnel problems generally. With the construction of newer and larger headquarters the management undertook to solve many of these problems, a fair start having been made by 1918.

The total Home Office staff, which numbered 422 in 1908, had grown to 562 in 1914 and to 618 at the end of 1918. The Company's outlays for Home Office compensation grew at about the same rate, from $646,000 to $943,000 from 1908 to 1918. Working hours prior to 1910 were from 8:30 a.m. to 5:30 p.m. five days per week, with ninety minutes for lunch, and four hours on Saturdays. At that time, in response to employee requests for an earlier quitting time, the management reduced the lunch period to thirty minutes, leaving the thirty-nine hour week and the half-day on Saturdays undisturbed.

Despite improved efficiency of the work force through introduction of more modern equipment and systems in 1908–1909, the headquarters building became so overcrowded that the trustees approved a management request for a new and more commodious building. In 1910 an entire block was purchased near the northeast end of Wisconsin Avenue overlooking Lake Michigan, and a structure began which would occupy the south half. The building was designed so that in the event of future expansion an additional building could be erected on the vacant land to form a single structure. Besides housing all operations under one roof, with a commensurate improvement in operating efficiency, the new building was designed to provide for the comfort and convenience of employees. Space was set aside for lounge and game rooms; and in 1916, after the construction of kitchen and dining facilities, the Company furnished lunch to all personnel at its own expense. Formal dedication ceremonies accompanied the official opening of the new Home Office in October 1914.

Increasing quantity of work and additional employees brought the usual problems of adding to the staff of supervisors and middle management personnel. In addition the management became more concerned with the establishment of salary scales and job classifications. The advisability of a formal study was first considered in 1910, but it was not until 1912 that consultants were employed to survey the needs and recommend a program.[8] The plan which was finally adopted did establish salary ranges for comparable jobs in the Company, and made some attempt to classify and describe the various tasks. How thorough and systematic the plan was is not definitely known; but as future events would show it was not effective in improving Northwestern's personnel relations.

With a growing number of senior employees on the Home Office staff, in 1915 the management acted to provide for their retirement from active service. The pension and retirement program adopted by the Company provided neither for employee contributions nor a vesting of rights; and, to conform to the New York insurance code, it was not applicable to officers or insurance agents. All persons employed for fifteen years or longer were, upon retirement, to receive an annual pension equal to 1 per cent of the terminal year's salary for each year of service, up to a maximum of thirty years. For male employees the retirement age was optional after sixty-five and compulsory at seventy years. For women the optional retirement age was fifty-five and compulsory at sixty years.

The effects of the military draft and the employment opportunities offered in the booming industries of Milwaukee created difficulties for the Company in retaining the services of its younger clerks and recruiting new employees during 1917–1918. To overcome this problem a permanent salary committee was appointed to review proposed adjustments in salary. In January 1917 the Executive Committee authorized payment of bonuses up to $100 per year. Although not called such, these were clearly cost-of-living bonuses; under the instructions of the Executive Committee they were not to be considered as permanent additions to salaries.[9]

Insurance and Marketing

The action of the state of New York to prohibit deferred dividend insurance and to restrict the companies to four standard policy forms was intended to reduce the great variety of policy features which had blossomed in the post-Civil War era and to eliminate the speculative element in life insurance. The discretion granted the insurance department by the legislature, however, made the actual restriction of policy forms much less onerous than the industry originally feared. During the years after 1906 there was a gradual resumption of merchandising and increased diversity of insurance plans.

Northwestern's rapid growth after 1880 was the result of several causes, not the least of which was the emphasis given to deferred dividend insurance. More solid bastions of strength, however, were an able agency force, conservative underwriting practices, and the simplicity of operations and of the plans offered to policyholders. The substantial savings effected by favorable mortality experience and the difference between actual expenses and the charged loading factor produced a substantial portion of the Company's earnings. When the favorable yields on investment were added, the dividend returns to policyholders enabled them to provide insurance protection at a net cost which was the envy of most of the industry. The success of this pattern was too obvious to prompt any serious consideration for change by the Company's management in the decade after the Armstrong investigation.

The introduction of optional modes of settlement of policy proceeds in 1900 had given Northwestern the means of providing flexibility in its standard contracts, a fact which largely obviated the need to design specialized plans. During the subsequent years of changing social and business conditions, option settlements would grow in popularity because of the opportunities they offered to persons and institutions with financial plans which could be benefited by the use of life insurance.

Northwestern officials believed there was even less need to alter the Company's method of distribution than to add to the number of insurance features and plans which it had to offer. The reform legislation, with its limitations on acquisition expenses and the elimination of the speculative appeal, posed some distinctly new challenges to life company marketing organizations. The entire agency compensation structure had to be revised downward, with reductions in commissions and the prohibition of bonuses and extra payments. For many companies these changes had the effect of forcing the general agents to devise new appeals and new approaches to replace those outmoded by the revised situation. For many reasons most general agents found themselves unable to cope with the new marketing problems, not the least of which was financial. To sell insurance on the basis of appeal to policyholder needs required the selection of soliciting agents able accurately to ascertain these needs and recommend a plan to meet them. This in turn implied an organization of adequately trained agents. Careful selection and training, however, was an expensive investment for a general agent; furthermore, it grew in importance just at the time when agency margins and acquisition allowances were being seriously curtailed.

With respect to both the challenges and revisions of life insurance marketing after 1906, Northwestern was in an excellent position. Modification of the agents' compensation plan and limitation of the commission period had been undertaken earlier.

Disgruntled agents had already left the field, and no substantial changes were necessary to make the compensation plan conform to the New York and Wisconsin codes. Furthermore, Northwestern general agencies were larger, on the average, than those of many competitors. Most of the Company general agencies produced sufficient business to provide the general agent with a liberal margin of profit, if he was enterprising and a good manager, and had capital to invest in agency development and induction of new men. Unless it were proved wrong by the greater efficiency of another method, the management had no intention of giving up the advantages of the general agency system, or of tampering with it as many other companies began to do.

Agency Organization: the Home Office and the Field

Perhaps to even a greater extent than had Palmer, President Markham was content to delegate authority for the marketing of Northwestern insurance to his subordinates. In general he was not disposed to interfere with the officers responsible for insurance and agency matters provided, as he expressed it, "they got results." Results, so long as the traditional underwriting standards were maintained, could be measured pragmatically by the volume of new business issued, the persistency and increase of the amount in force, and by the absolute and relative levels of marketing costs. These were the criteria by which Markham and his associates would judge the administration of the agency department and the effectiveness of the general agents.

Operationally, of course, administration of the field organization was more complex. Success depended upon the abilities of the general agents to manage their agencies, and the skill of the Home Office agency department in selecting competent general agents and assisting them, where possible, to meet the problems of the field. Certain of these problems could be met by encouraging investment in the agencies by the general agents, investments which required time before they could be recovered or realized. Others involved questions of morale, and a harmonious blending of the interests of the general agent and the Company. Diplomacy, an appreciation for the problems of general and soliciting agents, and the ability to rally the loyalty and devotion of the field were qualities which Willard Merrill had possessed in full measure; he was convinced they were shared by Henry F. Norris when he rec-

ommended his appointment as superintendent of agents in 1902.

Sixty years of age when Markham became president, Norris retained the vigor and zealous interest in Northwestern and its field organization which had earlier attracted Merrill's attention. It was no secret that Norris believed the Northwestern field force to be without equal in the industry, a pride which he reflected in his descriptive report to the Executive Committee on July 11, 1911:

> The Northwestern has been perfecting its sales system for half a century and its field organization is the envy of all its competitors. The fact that during the trying years of 1905, 1906, and 1907, the Company was able to hold its agency force practically intact while other companies were losing their field men by the thousands, reflects great credit on the agents as a whole. The loyalty of the agents to the Company and to the principles of correct life underwriting for which the Company has so persistently stood, and the results accomplished augurs well for the future of the Company's business.

This pride was accompanied by a determination that the agency force produce all the business which was compatible with the Company's underwriting philosophy. In striving for this goal Norris frequently found himself in conflict with his associates, the secretary, actuary, medical director, and Vice President Skinner, all of whom were concerned with the maintenance of high underwriting standards. As a result the relationship within which the Insurance and Agency Committee operated was sometimes strained. Norris was, however, evidently regarded highly by a majority of the general agents who believed him to be the only member of executive management to have a sales orientation.

Two lieutenants, George E. Copeland and Percy H. Evans, assisted Norris in administering the agency department and coordinating the activities of the field force. Copeland, until he succeeded Norris as superintendent in 1916, was concerned principally with administrative procedure and methods, and because of his own previous experience as a general agent, in assisting the agencies with advice on induction and development. Evans, who had originally promoted and founded *Field Notes,* edited that publication, analyzed competition, and concerned himself with relations between Home Office and the field force.

Northwestern's general agency structure during

the period was characterized by a high degree of stability. The number of general agencies never fell below eighty-nine nor increased beyond ninety-one. As the following tabulation shows, however, there were some small but important shifts in geographical distribution, with an increase in the number operating in the Northeastern and Pacific Coast regions and a reduction in the North Central states. This stability extended to the general agent personnel, for of the more than ninety individuals under contract in 1908 fifty-four, or almost 60 per cent, were still active in 1918. The loss of general agents through death, retirement, and other termination of contract averaged less than four per year.

REGION	1908	1910	1915	1918
New England	10	9	9	9
Middle Atlantic	19	21	21	22
South Atlantic	6	6	6	6
East North Central	26	26	22	23
West North Central	17	16	15	15
East South Central	2	2	3	3
West South Central	3	3	2	2
Mountain	4	4	5	4
Pacific Coast	4	6	6	7
Total	91	93	89	91

SOURCE: *Annual Statement*, Northwestern Mutual Life Insurance Company, 1908-1918.

Within the general framework of stability, however, there was considerable shuffling of the general agencies. Seventeen agencies were closed or transferred to other locations, while fourteen new agencies were opened. This activity enabled the Company to obtain more effective market coverage and took into account population shifts and trends. As had been true earlier those agencies located in rural districts used district agents most extensively to develop their territories.

District, Special, and Soliciting Agents

For the years prior to 1915 no record of the number of agents under contract to general agents is available. The best estimate indicates that their number rose from about 4,500 in 1908 to nearly 5,500 in 1914. In 1915 there were 5,925 agents under contract and in 1918, 5,723.

Information regarding the distribution of the Company's agents according to the various contract classifications for these years does not exist. By this time, however, most of the contracts offered by general agents were with special and district agents. Special agents, in turn, frequently made contracts with what were then termed "subagents," persons who were willing to develop prospects. While some subagents conducted a sale in its entirety, the more customary procedure was for the special agent to carry on most of the negotiations and to compensate the subagent by some percentage of the first commission. District agents' contracts, on the other hand, were usually made with soliciting agents. The general and district agents also issued brokerage contracts to fire and casualty insurance agents, but this was apparently not a very common practice.

The proportion of agents devoting their whole time and energy to the sale of Northwestern insurance is also unknown, particularly for the years before 1915. Company officers with long experience in agency matters believe that only about 40 per cent of the total agents under contract could be considered as full-time insurance solicitors; and it is probable that, aside from district agents, special agents accounted for the biggest share of these. Turnover of life insurance agents was heavy during all these years for the entire industry. At Northwestern, judging from the number of new and terminated contracts filed with the Company, the turnover rate must have ranged between 25 and 40 per cent.

Contract Relations with Agents

The uniform contract made with general agents by the Company during the previous administration remained in effect, with some moderate changes, during 1908–1918. The insurance legislation of 1906–1907 limiting expenses and payments to agents necessitated reducing the commission period for Northwestern agents from eleven to ten years. In 1908–1909 the New York code was modified to permit quality and quantity standards of production to affect agents' compensation, and also to provide for varying the size of individual renewal commissions as long as the original gross amount permitted was not increased. In consequence life companies discounted 3 per cent commissions for the eleventh through the fifteenth years of a policy, and added 5 per cent to the first renewal commission. For Northwestern general agents this change provided for a first-year commission of 50 per cent on the ordinary whole life policy, one renewal of 12.5 per cent, and eight of 7.5 per cent. In 1910, to eliminate tedious bookkeeping, the 2.5 per cent renewal commissions due general agents were thereafter credited to those in whose territories the policyholder resided, regardless of the geographic origin of the business. No such standardization applied to contracts made by general agents with other agents, although there was probably greater uniformity in certain aspects of the agreements.

Commission arrangements between general and district agents varied with the men involved, the territory to be developed, and other factors. Some general agents permitted the district agents to retain most or all of the margin on first-year commissions, and a share of the general agent's renewal interest. Others were less liberal, reserving a margin on first commissions and the renewal interest to themselves. The ability of district agents to finance the development of a territory depended largely upon the margin between what he had to pay his soliciting agents and what was allowed him by his principal, plus the forfeited renewals of those of his agents who terminated their contracts and the proceeds of his own production.

Essentially the same arrangements characterized the commission relations of general agents with special agents. While there was some variation, the special agent usually received between 40 and 45 per cent of the first-year premium, 10 per cent of the second premium, and 5 per cent of each of eight subsequent premiums, provided he met the terms of the production quota under which he customarily worked. Contracts with brokerage agents generally specified payment of a single first-year commission of about 37.5 per cent of the premium on all business turned over to the general agent, the latter collecting the renewal commissions. Failure of special and soliciting agents to attain production quotas in any single year was cause for forfeiture of renewal commissions on the insurance he had sold. Furthermore, variation existed in the rate of renewals paid to such agents, for general agents did not always grant the full 5 per cent. On the other hand many general agents were extremely liberal, permitting full renewal rates to these agents and furnishing office space and stenographic services.

Although the majority of special agents operated within a single territory and contracted with only one general agent, a few special agents sold insurance over a broader market area. Such men contracted with all general or district agents in whose exclusive territories they sought business; and commission terms of these contracts were, of course, similar to those issued to conventional special agents. While a few general agents were reluctant, or even refused, to contract with these special agents, no major issues arose over the practice.* Northwestern's leading special agent during most of these years was Dr. Charles Albright of Milwaukee, who consistently wrote better than $1 million of insurance annually; in fact by 1918 Dr. Albright had more business personally in force than did many life companies.

Induction of Agents

The selling situation which faced the life insurance industry in the wake of the Armstrong Investigation and its accompanying reforms was in startling contrast to that which existed prior to 1906, particularly for the larger companies with national selling organizations. The familiar pattern of appeals based upon the speculative aspect of semi-tontine, comparative costs, prices, and dividends had been abruptly removed. Agency development, based upon inordinately high acquisition expenses and financed by accumulated deferred dividends, was no longer possible in view of the legal limits on expense. With the prohibition of bonuses and extras and the restriction on commissions, the general agents were limited in what they could offer agents. Furthermore, the criticism of life insurance practices lowered the prestige of soliciting agents in the public's mind. The initial limitation on the number of policy forms which could be issued cut sharply into the merchandising aspects of insurance marketing, although the effect of this was more temporary.

While the implications of change were not lost upon home office agency officials the more vulnerable position of general agents made them particularly sensitive. New appeals were necessary to replace those which had been rendered illegal or obsolete, and in these confusing times certain general agents perceived the opportunity of evolving sales patterns to fit various needs of insurance prospects. Traditionally life insurance had been marketed on the premise of providing a lump sum settlement; depending upon the size of the settlement and the needs of the beneficiary, this sum could be spent at the discretion of the latter. There were, however, any number of financial objectives which could be realized by the purchase of life insurance: clean-up funds to take care of immediate obligations, including burial; income for a widow or other dependents;

---

* That the Company did intercede with general agents in the arrangement of terms for this class of special agents is indicated by the letter of Percy H. Evans to the E. J. Stone agency at Cleveland, Nov. 21, 1910, suggesting an upward adjustment in the commission rate offered a special agent by Dr. Stone.

money for the education of children; and savings for old age. Business enterprises, moreover, could utilize life insurance to provide, in part at least, for emergencies brought about by the death of a proprietor, partner, or key official.

Exploitation of these opportunities required agents able to diagnose needs and recommend plans to fit them; but only a few agents were equipped for the task. Believing that life insurance salesmanship was a teachable art, the ablest and most perceptive general agents—and there were only a few of them —set about training men in their own agencies, urging upon their home offices adoption of similar programs. Although there was some precedent for educating the life insurance agent—a few universities had introduced lectures and formal courses in life insurance around the turn of the century—no great attention was given to the matter by home office agency officials in the life companies during this period. The reason for this was in part that under the general agency operation responsibility for induction was the general agent's, and in part that the need for more systematic training was only dimly perceived.

Because training of agents would be expensive, recruiting and selection acquired importance. It would be a waste of resources to provide extensive training for men who were not adapted to a career of life insurance selling, a fact that implied a restriction of the mass recruiting methods of the past. More careful selection, however, was expensive, requiring improved interviewing and other screening techniques. In the absence of direct or indirect assistance from the life companies themselves, the number of general agencies with the resources, managerial skills, and will to undertake such an induction program were few. As a result the new patterns were to have a most uneven development, and before 1917 were barely perceptible in most companies.

What was true of the industry responses to the changing selling situation applied to Northwestern as well. The Company's sales in force and persistency records indicated the effectiveness of its general agency organization, and the management was willing to rely upon it during these years. The induction functions were the responsibility of the general agents, and while agency department officers assisted in such matters whenever their help was needed, this assistance was necessarily restricted to the resources permitted them.

The Company's program for selection and training was directly concerned with only the general agents. Under its civil service rule the sole source

from which Northwestern general agents could be supplied was the body of district, special, and soliciting agents already under contract. From this group the superintendent of agencies sought men who were believed to possess certain leadership qualities, administrative abilities, and resources of capital or credit. Although in the future a record of successful personal selling was to diminish in importance as a necessary prerequisite for appointment as a general agent, during these years it was of some consequence. One of the places where a man could demonstrate leadership and management abilities in the field organization was in a district agency; many of the general agents appointed during these years came from the ranks of district agents.

There is substantial evidence that most general agencies during this period functioned effectively. The general agents, by and large, were conscious of the need for able selling agents. Although the pattern of assistance varied considerably between the ninety-odd agencies, the help given new agents by the general agents was apparently not ungenerous. Furthermore, there was some evidence that the general agents were under pressure by their own agents to provide improved supervision, planning, and training. More fundamental as stimuli for effective agency development were the self-interest and ambition of the general agent. A reasonable investment in new agents, including the costs of selection, training, and occasionally the advance of financial assistance to new men during the learning period, could become profitable from the renewal interest on the volume of new and persisting business they produced.

The general agency system in operation in most companies during these years was subject to several weaknesses: one of these involved the problems of financing new general agents or those with inadequate capital; the second pertained to the older general agent and his terminal interest. Northwestern was probably less affected by these handicaps than were most companies. The relatively larger size of its general agencies, and the 2 per cent collection commissions on premiums for business which had passed out of the renewal commission period, combined to guarantee to the new general agent revenue to meet his regular operating expenses. Furthermore, the financial assistance which general agents extended to newly recruited agents in that period was quite limited in amount and extent, and income taxes did not exist before 1913 and were modest thereafter. Northwestern general agents were expected to stand on their own feet financially; in that era most of them, new and old, employed their own capital, or borrowed from banks using their renewal interest or other property for collateral. In certain cases the Company advanced funds for investment in the agency, but these were loans and not subsidies.

The problems associated with the older general agent concerned "coasting," that is, his tendency to ride along on his renewal commissions and collection fees without continuing to further develop his agency by recruiting and maintaining an effective selling force. Most of the coasting problems for Northwestern in this period—and they were not numerous—arose from the desire of prosperous older general agents to enjoy their incomes and avoid the irksome task of finding and selecting new agents. In later years, and under changed circumstances, the Company's problems with the "coasting" general agent were concerned with general agency capital formation and the more intense need for providing financial assistance for newly recruited agents. But even under these conditions there were limits to what the management could do about "coasting," barring direct Company subsidies or a curtailment of vesting renewal commissions. During the years 1908–1918 the management obviously had no intention of dislocating its effectively functioning system by resort to either of these alternatives. By no means could all or even a majority of the older general agents be accused of inactivity during these years. Many continued to develop their territories energetically and to recruit extensively; as a result they could point to excellent production records. The problem, in fact, had always existed. It became somewhat more important during these years because of the effects of decisions made thirty years earlier, when resumption of the pure general agency system was undertaken. Many of the general agents, put under contract by Merrill during the 1880's and early 1890's, had reached advanced age during the period of the Markham administration.

Either excessive "coasting" or inadequate financial investment by a new general agent could result in deterioration of a territory, because fewer effective agents were under contract than was warranted. With the older general agents the management was customarily very lenient, unwilling to dismiss them after long service. With the newly appointed agents, however, there was necessarily less patience. Although by no means ruthless in applying this policy, the management terminated the contracts of those general agents who, after what was considered a reasonable time, failed to increase the volume of sales.[10]

Other than making available the series of educa-

tional booklets written by Alonzo Kimball twenty years earlier, the Home Office took no direct part in the training of its field force. The training undertaken by the general agents, of course, varied in intensity, duration, and effectiveness from agency to agency. Some general agents evidently continued to let the new agent go into the field with no formal preparation; others insisted upon joint work for the new men, a method which had much to recommend it and is still used in many Northwestern agencies; while a few apparently combined joint work with the requirement that the new man study the educational booklets provided by the agency. Just how much attention was paid to selection cannot be determined, but there were indications that those general agents who were most progressive in the training of new men also devoted the most time to interviewing and screening candidates.

The sources from which new soliciting and special agents were recruited were many and varied. It is known that during these years Northwestern general agents used newspaper and trade paper advertising to attract the attention of candidates, that Northwestern policyholders and business contacts provided leads, and that men with experience in direct selling in other fields were issued contracts. In addition some of the general agents persuaded school teachers to enter the business, customarily on a part-time basis to begin with, frequently changing to full-time soliciting as they experienced some success and acquired a taste for selling life insurance.

Compensation of Agents

The total income earned by Northwestern's field force during this period increased substantially as the volume of annual production rose together with the total amount in force. Furthermore, the increase in aggregate agents' compensation exceeded the rise in the number of agents under contract. This indicated, in addition to the general expansion of insurance coverage taking place nationally, that the skills and sales capacity of the average agent under contract exceeded those of earlier periods. What was true of the agency force as a whole was applicable to the Company's general agencies. Of equal importance, however, was a narrowing of the gap which existed between the earnings (and production) of the strongest and weakest agencies. During 1908, for example, the Company's ten most productive general agencies were responsible for about 42 per cent of the year's sales; in 1918 the leading ten agencies could claim only 30 per cent of aggregate production. By contrast the ten agencies on the other end of the scale produced only 1.5 per cent of the Company's sales in 1908, while in 1918, with double their 1908 volume, the ten lowest wrote 2 per cent of gross production.

The increase which took place in general agency revenues and its distribution between the strongest, weakest, and middle agencies, as estimated from Company production records, is indicated for 1908 and 1918 in the following tabulation:*

	1908	1918
Leading ten agencies	$1,620,000	$2,160,000
Middle seventy-one agencies	1,840,000	3,365,000
Lowest ten agencies	59,000	143,000

SOURCE: Company records.

While the lowest ten agencies included some of the Company's long-established agencies located in areas of sparse population, several for each of these years were newly opened organizations; between the two years, most of the latter included in the 1908 tabulation had moved out of the group before 1918.

Among the most productive of Northwestern general agencies, and those enjoying the highest revenues, were metropolitan organizations located in New York City, Chicago, and St. Louis; also included were such dispersed agencies as those headquartered in Omaha, Denver, Nashville, Aurora, and Oshkosh. These last developed their extensive territories through the use of district agencies.

It is impossible to make more than a rough estimate of the incomes of individual agents during these years. However, by careful interpolation of accurate net agency incomes available subsequent to 1923 it has been estimated that the net income from all sources enjoyed by the ten leading agencies in 1918 was in excess of $25,000 and probably averaged close to $50,000. The total net income of the

---

* Records for the period are fragmentary. The agency department supplied a copy of the production records of Northwestern general agencies for these two years; based upon a general assumption that production was related to previous sales achievement and thus to insurance in force, these data were projected to estimate total commissions earned.

middle group probably ranged from $7,000 to $25,000, with an average of approximately $14,000. In respect to the ten lowest producing general agencies the income range was between $3,600 and $7,000, with an over-all average of about $5,500. The comparable average incomes for the year 1908 have been estimated as 75 per cent, or an average of $36,000 for the ten leading agencies; $10,000 for the middle group; and $4,100 for the lowest ten agencies. In the smaller agencies, such as those in northern New England and in some of the Rocky Mountain territories, personal business constituted a considerable portion of total agency production. In metropolitan agencies personal production by the general agent was less customary.

For all agents other than the general agent group, the estimate of average income for 1908 was about $520 and for 1918 about $700. A more realistic estimate, however, based on the assumption that only about 40 per cent of the agents worked full time for the Company and that they were responsible for at least 80 per cent of all insurance in force, would be an average of $1,050 in 1908 and about $1,400 in 1918 for full-time agents. In view of the fact that approximately half the full-time agents made less than these incomes, some of the causes for high turnover of agents are apparent.

The possibility of achieving the financial success of the Company's most productive agents was undoubtedly prominent among the motives that attracted men to a selling career. The leading one hundred Northwestern agents sold $28.7 million of insurance during the years 1914–1915, equal to almost 24 per cent of the Company's aggregate sales. If the individuals composing this group were consistently among the leading producers in earlier years, as was probably the case, their average annual commissions would have been around $7,000. Of course at the top were the "star salesmen," those who consistently produced an annual volume of $500,000 or more. Incomes for the members of this elite group ranged upward of $12,500 per year.

Sales, of course, involved more than organization. Whether or not Northwestern would achieve its objectives—continuing its conservative approach to insurance underwriting while maintaining a high record of sales—would depend upon the types of policies offered and the effectiveness of the Company's relations with its agency force.

Interior of the 1886–1914 Home Office
N. W. corner, Broadway and Michigan Streets

CHAPTER ELEVEN

Sales Management and Legislative Relations: 1908-1918

N ORTHWESTERN'S special role in the life insurance field, as it developed between 1908–1918, was reflected in its underwriting and sales policies. Where many firms in the industry relied heavily on innovations, some of which were designed merely to promote sales, Northwestern clung to its traditional policies. When disability and double indemnity clauses became the newest offerings in the insurance field, for example, Northwestern's management refused to join their advocates, despite strong pressure from its sales force to conform. In the instance of disability income, the Company's judgment was later vindicated when actuarial experience demonstrated that many disability clauses were unsound. Even in legislative relations the Company revealed its independent approach by formulating its own policies on the national and state levels when in disagreement with the position taken by the other members of the industry.

The Company's conservative approach to sales brought less happy results in management's relations to its sales forces. The lack of response to agents' requests and unwillingness to follow competitors into new fields did little for agents' morale. This shadow, however, should not obscure the obvious: that a distinguished sales record was compiled between 1908–1919.

Underwriting Policy and Insurance Plans

The post-Armstrong insurance markets were characterized by several novel developments with respect to underwriting practices and contract features. In spite of the temporary public suspicion, a host of new life companies were formed, heightening the inter-industry competition. Avidly seeking a foothold in the market, the new companies introduced several new features to older insurance plans; longer-established firms scrambled for advantages of their own. As a result, certain unique qualities were combined with more familiar insurance plans which appealed strongly to several of the buyer's motives. Most important of the innovations were disability and double indemnity features. The greatest innovation, with tremendous implications for the future, was the introduction of group underwriting wherein whole bodies of individuals could be insured under the same certificate. This plan was significant not only because it opened a previously unexplored channel of distribution, but also because it generally waived such traditional devices for risk selection as individual medical examinations. Throughout the period there was also a continuation of the tendencies to liberalize the policy contract and extend the rights and privileges of policyholders. Finally, national involvement in World War I prompted an industry-wide attempt to guard against adverse selection and introduced federal government life insurance.

The refusal of Markham and his associates to commit the Company to most of these novelties and innovations was to be expected in view of their determination to adhere to basic Northwestern principles of conservative underwriting and simplicity of operation. The already existing contract forms and insurance plans were deemed sufficient to meet the challenges of the market, particularly since the optional settlement feature permitted great flexibility in meeting the insurance needs of individuals and business organizations. The few new insurance plans and benefits that were adopted were prompted by a desire to assist policyholders to keep their policies in force, and to meet more precisely certain needs of prospects. The actuarial soundness of these had either already been demonstrated or could be logically projected.

Undoubtedly the most popular of the new benefits offered policyholders by Northwestern competitors during the period was the disability guarantee. Put in the form of a clause or rider, this feature had first been introduced in life insurance about 1896, and originally provided that in return for a small additional premium the policy would remain in force in the event the insured was totally and permanently disabled and future premiums waived. Apparently it had never been aggressively promoted in the turbulent years before 1906, but this oversight was quickly remedied by offering a guaranteed income to the disabled insured as well as waiver of premiums. Beginning about 1907 a few life companies guaranteed to provide an annual income, in the event of disability, of $100 for each $1,000 of insurance held by the insured; within a few years other companies began offering monthly income benefits in amounts up to 1 per cent of the face value of the policyholder's insurance in force. By 1915 contracts containing both guaranteed income and waiver of premium disability clauses were common throughout the industry—assisting the sales of companies promoting them, offering formidable competition to those which did not. The agents of the latter companies were soon demanding similar features in the insurance they were marketing; Northwestern agents were no exception.

Although the president found the agitation for a disability feature distasteful, he consented to a thorough investigation of the subject. Percy H. Evans, the newly appointed actuary, was made responsible for the study, which he conducted with as sweeping and objective a treatment as the limited data then available permitted. His report, indicative of the future distinction which would mark his career, concluded that while a woeful lack of information on the incidence of total and permanent disability existed, a life company was relatively safe in offering the waiver of premium clause in its contracts. Furthermore, he contended that this was within the legitimate purview of a life company since its effect would be to protect only the basic insurance contract from lapse in the event of disability. A guarantee of income, however, introduced a health and accident provision which was logically divorced from simple life insurance protection. The absence of adequate experience data, he warned, made the disability income clause a pure gamble. Evans recommended neither type of benefit to the management, but indicated he would not oppose inclusion of a premium waiver clause or rider in future contracts.

The Executive Committee considered the Evans report at length, then voted to include the premium waiver clause for those who desired such protection in the Company's 1916 contracts.*[1] The concession, however, did little to satisfy many of Northwestern's agents who continued to urge adoption of the disability income feature. Despite this pressure, which grew in intensity, the management remained firm in its decision.

It took almost fifteen years before the management's position was fully vindicated, a time lag during which a statistical body of experience was accumulated from which probability estimates could be projected. In 1926, as a result of industry experience with disability income provisions, new incidence tables were introduced; by this time, however, it was already too late to be of use in preventing problems for business already issued with such clauses. With the great depression of the 1930's came a great increase in the number of claims of total disability, and companies learned just how broadly juries could interpret the definition of "total and permanent." For many people disability insurance came to be unemployment insurance, and the costs to the life insurance industry ran into hundreds of millions of dollars; obviously only a fraction of this amount had been covered by the extra premiums. By contrast the depression experience of insurers which restricted themselves to waiver of premium benefits

---

* The privilege of obtaining the waiver of premium benefit was not, however, extended to those engaged in occupations which required the payment of extra premiums to obtain Northwestern insurance protection. Furthermore, like most insurers, the Company refused to pay agents commissions on the additional premiums which had to be paid to obtain disability coverage. See *Circular to Agents*, No. 100, Feb. 1, 1916.

was generally good, an experience shared by Northwestern. In effect the management's position in 1915 had been sound; its courage in resisting the market blandishments and the demands of its agency force had saved its policyholders from substantial losses.

Although there was some desire by agents for Northwestern to offer a double indemnity clause during this period no serious attention was paid to the device by the management. In the opinion of Company officials at the time, and over the following generation, double indemnity lacked even the virtue of protecting the basic contract against lapse, being a sales promotion device whose basic attraction consisted of offering double the face value of the contract in the event of accidental death. This additional benefit was evidently considered well worth the price of the small extra premium charged, for double indemnity proved popular.

Evidently group insurance received no more consideration from Northwestern's management than did double indemnity, although the market potential of providing insurance protection for millions of employees never before covered, or inadequately protected, was tremendous. Interestingly enough, Northwestern was offered the opportunity of insuring the three hundred employees of a firm in Syracuse, New York, a full year before Equitable Life Assurance Society issued its first group insurance in 1911. Acceptance of risks without the rudimentary control of medical examinations had no appeal to a select-risk company; neither did the prospect of adopting new channels of distribution, nor the establishment of a special group department which management regarded as being essentially a new line.

The only new insurance plans to be adopted by Northwestern were the "65 Life" and "Endowment at 65," first issued in 1918, and the five-year convertible term contract with no renewal privilege offered in 1916. The first two of these were evidently prompted by an increase in the tendency to retire at age sixty-five and to provide a fully paid policy for the insured at that time. In view of current thinking the concept was a fresh approach to the whole ordinary insurance philosophy, for among the disappointments of men retiring at the present time is that they cannot afford to continue the premiums on whole life contracts, and the amounts of converted paid-up insurance are substantially below the face values of original policies. The new term contract was a substitute for the Company's previous renewable term and ten-year convertible term policies.[2] On the other hand, Northwestern reduced the number of plans it offered by withdrawing deferred annuities, return premium, and modified life policies.

The most important step taken by Northwestern in further liberalizing the terms of its insurance contracts was the elimination of restrictions on residence, travel, and with certain exceptions, occupation. Taken in March 1910, this action was made retroactive to all previously issued policies. In February 1908 the management extended to all insurance contracts the privilege of thirty-one days of grace in the payment of premiums; a few months later it also waived interest charges on late premiums. In December 1909 the Executive Committee voted to make it possible for policyholders to obtain policy loans and surrender policies for cash after two years rather than three. When there was evidence that its privileges could impair mortality experience, however, the management did not hesitate to apply new restrictions. Such a step occurred in 1914 when, as a result of a study of the results of forty-three United States and Canadian life companies, the Company tightened its regulation for insurance of persons employed in the mining industries.[3]

Northwestern's War-time Experience

The greatest single restrictive action taken by the Company between 1908 and 1918 was the renewed application of military service or war risk clause in new policies. Northwestern had never accepted members of the regular armed services for insurance, and before 1900 every policy contained a clause voiding the contract if the insured, without prior consent of the Company, entered active military or naval service except during time of peace. Beginning in 1900 a two-year restriction on such service was inserted in newly issued contracts, reduced to one year in 1907. In 1910 all restrictions of this type were stricken from new contracts. By May 1, 1914, when the Mexican border troubles began, the Company had about $1 billion of insurance outstanding which was subject to no limitation on military service.

The outbreak of war in 1914 signaled the start of steadily mounting concern by all United States life companies regarding military risks, and a variety of restrictive and extra-premium clauses were introduced. Northwestern had adopted certain modest restrictions before 1917, but with the formal declaration of war on April 7, 1917, it quickly applied a full-scale military clause. By its terms all persons who might enter the armed forces were acceptable for insurance, but only if they paid additional premiums equal to $50 per thousand dollars of insur-

		CLASSIFIED AGE GROUPS			
	UNDER AGE 26	AGES 26-31	AGES 32-35	AGES 36-44	OVER AGE 45
Married Men	$5,000	$10,000	$50,000	Regular Limit	Regular Limit
Single Men	2,000	5,000	10,000	$50,000	

ance; to obtain the benefits of the disability clause still another $50 per thousand was required.

The competition with regard to war clauses had caused the Association of Life Insurance Presidents to seek adoption of a uniform model clause somewhat earlier, but there was little enthusiasm for such in the industry before April 1917. With United States involvement the atmosphere suddenly changed. State insurance commissioners and various life company officers urged all companies to send representatives to New York City during the week of April 27, 1917, to consider a uniform war clause for the industry. The clause submitted was the result of the work of a joint industry-commissioners committee whose members included Percy H. Evans and the Wisconsin insurance commissioner, Michael J. Cleary. It proposed an annual extra premium of $37.50 per thousand of insurance, with all premiums not actually required to meet losses returnable to the insureds; a proviso limited company liability to simple return of premiums in cases of military mortality where the extra premiums had not been paid.[4]

While there was some delay by various companies, most of the industry responded affirmatively and promptly. Northwestern accepted all the provisions recommended by the committee but insisted on its original, higher extra premium, cheerfully accepting a relatively disadvantageous competitive position in exchange for greater safety. At Evans' request limits were imposed on the amount of insurance that the Company would issue according to the age and marital status of the applicant. The above tabulation provides some indication of the nature of these limits imposed to restrain selection against the Company by high-risk age groups.

With the introduction of conscription Company agents were instructed to refuse applications from men in the highest priority draft class; other draft classes were scaled with a maximum of $25,000 for single men and $60,000 for married men.[5] In October 1917 when Congress amended the War Risk Insurance Act of 1914 to provide life and disability insurance coverage for members of the armed forces up to a maximum of $10,000, President Markham directed the agents to contact families of servicemen and urge that their sons apply for the government insurance.[6]

On December 2, 1918, Northwestern cancelled all war clause restrictions on outstanding policies with the exception of disability benefits, and all war service premiums were subsequently refunded.[7] The total amount of such extra premiums was only $49,-000 on $750,000 of insurance, an indication of the inability or unwillingness of the affected policyholders to take advantage of the full coverage provisions of the war clause. Seven of the service deaths incurred by Northwestern policyholders were subject to the war clause limitation of return of premium only; in all these cases, however, the Company waived its rights and paid the claims in full.[8]

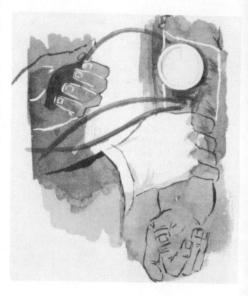

Risk Selection

Northwestern's efforts to achieve and maintain high standards of risk selection were continued during this period. They were materially assisted by the work of Dr. John W. Fisher, the medical director, and after 1914 by Actuary Percy H. Evans. While the liberalization of policy contracts removed many of the earlier controls on selection, those responsible for the quality of risks intensified their search for information with which to improve Northwestern's mortality record.

Under Dr. Fisher's guidance an increased staff of Home Office medical men gathered data on Northwestern and industry experience. Relationships between mortality and such factors as heredity, weight, blood pressure, and personal habits were observed. From other significant studies, made frequently in cooperation with other life companies, results were used in altering the standards of acceptability of applicants. During this period the Company, and ultimately the industry, experienced the first observable benefits of Dr. Fisher's greatest single contribution to medical underwriting. This was his insistence that a blood pressure test be made part of the regular medical examination of insurance applicants, and that recordings above the maximum determined for different age groups be cause for rejection. Dr. Fisher, after exhaustive research, discovered that as a person's blood pressure increased above the 15 mm. margin allowed by the Company for his age group, he became a poorer risk for insurance. Using control and experimental groups, with the former composed of men whose blood pressure was within the limits set by the Company, Dr. Fisher found that his hypothesis of a meaningful relationship was verified. Whereas for the control group the rate of actual to expected mortality was 49 per cent, for the experimental group, whose systolic pressure averaged 20 mm. above Northwestern's limit of acceptance, the rate was over 120 per cent.[9] In the face of this kind of evidence the insurance industry was convinced; within a few years use of the sphygmomanometer in making systolic pressure readings became an integral part of medical examinations in scores of life companies.

PERIOD	NORTH-WESTERN	AVERAGE OF FIFTY-SIX COMPANIES	AVERAGE OF ONE HUNDRED COMPANIES
1908-1909	0.92%	1.21%	
1910-1913	0.96		1.16%
1914-1918	1.03		1.18

The Company's mortality record during these years reflected the devoted efforts of Dr. Fisher and other Company personnel concerned with standards of underwriting selection. How favorably it compared with those of competitors is indicated in the table on page 164 which shows the death rate based on the average amount of insurance in force.[10]

Because of the effects of war and the great influenza epidemic which raged in 1918-1919, Northwestern's mortality and claim experience is of special interest. Among the Company's policyholders there were a total of 963 service deaths; of these 361 were killed or mortally wounded in combat, the rest were attributable to nonbattle injuries or disease, principally influenza. Total service losses from all causes amounted to $2.1 million. Much more serious was the influenza epidemic which resulted in claims of $5.8 million and increased the ratio of actual to expected mortality for the Company in 1918 from 54 per cent to 78 per cent.

Like other life companies, however, Northwestern discovered that its military mortality experience had offsetting compensations. The average age of the Company's insureds was about forty-five. Some 80 per cent of the Northwestern service deaths in 1918 occurred in the group under age thirty which, in general, tended to have less insurance. Furthermore, general population health was apparently improved as a result of more restricted diet, greater temperance, and more exercise; an additional offset was the improved persistency of outstanding insurance. The Company noted that once the most virulent phase of the influenza epidemic had passed the mortality ratio greatly improved, dropping to below 50 per cent.

Guiding the Sales Effort:
The Movement Toward Specialty

In general, Northwestern's basic approach to the problem of marketing its insurance contracts was reliance upon the personal sales effort of its corps of agents. The total advertising effort, that made by general agents as well as direct Company promotion, was minor. Company outlays on advertising for the entire period aggregated only $96,000, less than 1 per cent of Northwestern's total acquisition expense. The effects of the new market situation were apparent in Northwestern's promotional policy, however, for comparative claims and ratios were reduced in the Company's own literature and strongly discouraged in that of general agents, who, as in preceding years, were required to submit advertising copy to the Home Office before making it public.

Typical of the management attitude were the instructions given one general agent in 1910 that he was not to use the phrase, "If it's not in the Northwestern Mutual it's not good." He was further advised, "Don't emphasize cash surrender value. Tone down, 'Its policies cost less.' Don't call attention to our honesty, thus suggesting dishonesty in others."[11]

The management continued its efforts to stamp out rebating and twisting, although one general agent, as late as 1910, observed that most agents were still under repeated pressure to rebate from prospects who hinted or openly suggested such payment.[12] Whenever evidence of rebating came to the attention of the Home Office, however, the official action was prompt and forthright—the agent's contract was cancelled.[13]

Transcending these activities in importance was the stress placed by the Home Office and the general agents in selling to the needs of prospects, and particularly in developing life insurance for the satisfaction of certain business requirements. Because of its early and aggressive penetration of this field Northwestern established the foundations which would characterize it as a specialty company in the life insurance industry.

Prior to 1909 Northwestern had issued policies on the lives of proprietors, business partners, and corporation executives; but except in a few cases the intent of such insurance had been the protection of families rather than for needs of the business enterprise itself. Like other firms in the industry it had issued joint policies on the lives of partners, but except for the substitution of the business partner as beneficiary instead of one or more members of an immediate family such contracts were routine insurance transactions and constituted a negligible portion of the Company's sales. After 1908 several firms initiated the practice of issuing a separate contract on the life of each partner, the other partners as beneficiaries; by 1912 a number of Northwestern agents were reporting considerable success in promoting this plan.

But it was in the area of providing protection for the financial plans and needs of corporations that Northwestern perceived its greatest opportunity in the whole field of business life insurance. Whereas group underwriting, double indemnity, and disability income contracts were directly contradictory to Northwestern's underwriting philosophy, no such objection could apply to business insurance; the Company quickly jumped ahead of most of the field in this area. Beginning in 1909 some of the Company's more imaginative agents began soliciting insurance from various corporations for a variety of purposes. One of the more obvious corporate insurance needs was in providing for the loss of "key men," since the death of leading officials could have as serious an effect on the success of a corporation as that of one member of a partnership. Late in that year the agency department reported that an agent had negotiated the purchase of a sizeable endowment contract, the funds from which would provide for the retirement of the corporation's bonds.[14] During the ensuing three years other corporation policies were sold to provide for stock and mortgage retirement, and working capital requirements.

At the present time the provision of life insurance to meet multiple corporation needs is so commonplace that it is difficult to believe that a company which first offered it incurred definite risks. In 1909, however, there was no certainty that a corporation had an insurable interest in the life of its officers. The Company had taken a calculated chance that the law, as devised by legislators and interpreted by the courts, would ultimately support its position; at the time only two states, North Carolina and Pennsylvania, provided expressly for corporations insuring their own executives.[15]

Neither Northwestern nor any other life company had more than a small cadre of insurance agents sufficiently trained and technically equipped to intelligently conduct these new ideas of "advanced underwriting" in this area of business. The opportunities, however, were great, as were those just dawning in the areas of providing insurance to protect inheritances and provide for the establishment of estates and trusts. Because of the general superiority of Northwestern's several hundred career agents, the Company gained some early advantages in these fields of underwriting, providing the base for an even greater development as a specialty company in the future.

The success of Northwestern's "business insurance" campaign was evident before the end of 1918. Although no division of insurance sales according to the classifications of "business" and "nonbusiness" was made before 1911, over 7 per cent of the $137.5 million of insurance issued in that year was in corporate and partnership form. Between 1910 and the end of the period the total sales of partnership and corporation insurance exceeded $100 million, or about 8.7 per cent of aggregate Company sales.

Relations with Agents: Management and Morale

Among the major factors in Northwestern's success prior to 1908 had been the development of its field organization to some ninety general agencies, directing the efforts of more than 4,000 agents. In comparison to those of its largest rivals Northwestern's agency organization was relatively small, but this "deficiency" was offset by the efficiency of the operation. The majority of Northwestern general agencies, as previously indicated, were large enough to offer excellent opportunities for income sufficient to provide for territorial development and the personal profit of the general agent. The terms of the contracts for all classes of agents satisfied a number of Company marketing objectives: vesting of renewals provided special and soliciting agents with a steady income, provided the business persisted in force and the agents met their minimum qualification quotas of production. Business which persisted in force beyond the ten-year commission period was inexpensive for the Company and policyholder alike, subject as it was to only small administrative expenses and a mere 2 per cent "collection" charge. Thus it was to the agent's advantage to sell insurance which persisted over time; this, in general, could be attained only by an intelligent diagnosis of the prospect's needs and selection of plans to fit them. In effect, Northwestern's stable general agency organization, the general terms of its contracts with agents, including liberal vesting of renewals, and the persistent nature of its insurance in force tended to attract better-than-average qualified insurance solicitors.

These elements of strength were capable of sustaining Northwestern's position in the insurance market and in selling a large volume of business even when the calibre of sales management at the Home Office lagged somewhat behind the developments taking place in the field. During the years of the Markham administration the number of agents in the field increased by about one-fourth, a growth which placed some additional strains on the administrative and financial resources of the general agencies. This growth and the new market situations, with their ever-changing problems, placed a premium upon a mutually sympathetic understanding between Home Office and the agency force, including good two-way communication.

The management of Northwestern's marketing program could not be described as bad, particularly in comparison with competitors, nor were the Company's relations with its agents ever threatened by a serious breakdown. There just seemed to be a comparative absence of the skill and tact which had characterized the Company's sales management under Merrill's guidance, and a definite deterioration in the cooperation between the agency department and the other insurance divisions which had been a bench mark of the Palmer regime. There were a number of incidents arising to reveal a lack of mutual understanding and respect in the relations of the Home Office and the field, some of which no doubt were inevitable. Several, however, got badly out of hand and resulted in a lamentable depreciation of cooperation and morale.

One area of this depreciation was apparent in the Association of Agents. This organization had been originally promoted as a forum and channel of communication wherein agents and Company officers could make personal contact, introduce plans and policies, and discuss issues of mutual interest, including agents' complaints and suggestions. Some time prior to 1908 the association had come to be dominated to a considerable degree by the general agents. This was a logical development, reflecting not only the key role played by the general agents in the marketing system, but also the Company's pre-1908 policy of paying expenses of agents who produced a given amount of new business to the annual meeting. These quotas were flexible and customarily included the whole corps of general agents, leading inevitably to the election of many of their number to the key offices of the association year after year. Justifiably or not the other agents came to feel that the organization was growing less representative of the whole field force. As this feeling spread, with a consequent loss of confidence, the usefulness of the association as a communicating forum was impaired.

The disaffection of the nongeneral agents crystallized about 1909 with the organization of the District and Special Agents' Association. This group had as objectives representation of the interests of its members in their relations with the general agents; they had, of course, no direct relationship with the Company itself. During these years this association had no apparent success in obtaining whatever goals it set as to terms of contract and conditions of work. Several observers described it as "strongly antagonistic to the general agents," a condition hardly conducive to smooth harmony in the field.

In addition to the influential role the general agents played in the Association of Agents, they were represented by their own special group, the General Agents' Association, founded about 1889. During the years through 1918 the annual meetings of this association were only perfunctorily attended by the members, and the real organizational work was delegated to its executive committee. Even before 1908, according to one contemporary member, this executive committee came under the control of a strong minority of general agents who were not particularly representative of the whole association.[16] The same observer noted that during the period of the Markham administration relations between Home Office executives and the executive committee of the General Agents' Association were conducted in an atmosphere of mutual hostility; the committee members accusing the Home Office of a lack of "sales-mindedness," while the latter considered the general agents' committee to be willfully lacking in any understanding of the over-all operations and problems of the Company.

While these divisions among the various agency groups made effective sales management more difficult, there were a number of positive achievements to the credit of the management. One of these involved the establishment of a new system of awards to the more successful agents. Under the expense-limiting legislation of 1906–1907 Northwestern abandoned the practice of paying expenses of its agents to annual meetings. No attempt was made to introduce a substitute method of acknowledging exceptional selling achievements until 1915, when the "Honor System" was adopted, followed the next year by the "Marathon Club."

Under the "Honor System" the agents were grouped into nine different classes, stratified principally according to the amount of insurance they sold in the past. Monopolization of prizes was avoided by excluding the winner of any single class from competing in any other class. Annual membership in the "Marathon Club" was open to all soliciting agents who wrote insurance on one hundred lives or more. Prizes consisted of pins, plaques, cups, certificates, and publicity in *Field Notes*. The awards

were made on the occasion of the agents' dinner held during the week of the annual meeting.[17]

To bridge the gap between the agent in the field and the Home Office an effort was made to provide management representation at regional gatherings of agents. Depending upon the importance of the assembly, Home Office delegates might include such members of executive management as the president, Van Dyke, Dr. Fisher, Hathaway, Evans, or Noyes. For smaller groups an officer or junior management representative of the agency department was usually assigned.

In addition, agency department representatives kept in direct touch with the field force for other reasons. One was to inspect agencies and evaluate their operations. Another was to meet Company agents, canvass their attitudes, opinions, and estimate their potential as future general agent candidates. Finally there was the task, usually unpleasant, of cancelling a general agent's contract. Until 1917 field trips by Home Office agency personnel were made only when the occasion warranted, but after Copeland became superintendent there was more systematic contact with the field.

Some of the general agents also grew more concerned with the problem of relations with the Company and expressed a desire for division of the general agencies into zones. The chief proponent of this viewpoint was Franklin Mann of the Omaha agency, who became president of the General Agents' Association in 1919. Not only would division of the field into two or three general agency zones permit more frequent meetings of general agents and make for a better exchange of views, Mann argued, but it would "make the executive committee of the Association more representative, so that they could go to the Company without a chip on their shoulders."[18] While management gave serious consideration to the proposal, it was not put into effect for several years.

Although relations were not entirely satisfactory during the early years of Markham's term of office, several conflicting interests were resolved without much difficulty. One concerned the payment of commissions on policies agents wrote on their own lives. Pre-1909 rulings of the New York and Wisconsin insurance departments forbade companies from paying such commissions. The management protested, as did officials of other companies, and when the commissioners reversed their interpretation Northwestern quickly restored these commissions to its agents.[19]

A second problem which confronted the Company arose out of the practice of accepting premium notes by the field force. While Northwestern itself did not accept notes in partial payment of premiums except on those old policies whose terms contained the privilege, there was no rule prohibiting a general agent from extending this favor, particularly on new insurance applications. Insurance solicitors would accept notes from applicants up to one-half the initial premium; general agents would make the proper credits and transmit the cash collections to Milwaukee. Since the notes were interest bearing, the business was not inherently unprofitable, but it did have the effect of impairing the cash position of the general agencies.

During the first four years of Markham's administration the extent of this note business was astonishing, for according to Vice President Van Dyke's observation, "about 50 per cent of our new business is paid for by agents taking the note of the insured for the first premium."[20] Hard pressed for cash, the general agents requested the Company to either discount the notes for them or lend them funds against the security of the notes. Not wishing to re-enter the premium note business through the back door and pointing out that the note practice was a self-imposed risk which the general agent himself had to bear, the management firmly refused to commit itself to this aspect of agency financing.

Relations with agents were also somewhat strained when management forbade payment of commissions on policies which the Company regarded as substitutes for insurance surrendered or lapsed by policyholders. While such substitution had occurred before 1907, the statutory requirement giving a demand status to policy loans evidently increased the tendency of policyholders to lapse old contracts and apply for new insurance with the Company. The management began to suspect "internal twisting," that is, that some of its agents were encouraging the practice by persuading policyholders to borrow up to the full limit of their reserve, apply for a new policy, and then surrender the original contract. To unscrupulous agents the advantages of exchanging several renewal commissions for a first-year commission were obvious, even on policies they had themselves originally sold; even more obvious if the new policy were substituted for policies sold by others.

Growing discontent with internal twisting on the part of some Northwestern agents prompted the management to introduce a "substitution rule" in 1910. Under this rule any insurance application dated within ninety days of lapse or surrender of insurance by the same individual was regarded as a substitution of one policy for another, and no commissions were paid to the agents. On principle the rule was sound, but it was almost impossible to enforce. Directed at the Company's less conscientious agents, it actually hit hardest at the most conscientious salesmen. The latter might obtain applications from individuals who genuinely wished to surrender their policies and reinsure within three months, which would deprive the agent of his commission. The unscrupulous agent, adequately forewarned, could obtain a commission merely by advising the policyholder to postpone his surrender until after three months following the date of his application.

The unpopularity of the substitution rule among the agents was soon made known to the management. One agency partnership reported that,

> it is unquestionably a signboard to the agent without conscience, and very, very many times, a gross injustice to the agent with a conscience. We do not know of a single rule emanating from the Home Office that has more unqualifiedly demonstrated its undesirability than this Three Months' Rule.[21]

This response was somewhat perplexing to the management which was convinced that the practice should be checked, but could find no practical method for determining the merits of particular cases.[22]

It was only after three years that a compromise solution was reached which shifted the responsibility from the Company to the general agents. As explained in a communication to the agents, in any case which apparently involved substitution, the general agents were to make a careful investigation of the facts and report them together with their recommendation to Milwaukee.[23] The decision had the merit of having the investigation conducted at close range by an individual more familiar with the agents and the circumstances than the remote agency department. It also rechanneled the flow of agents' complaints.

Before the difficulties of internal twisting could be resolved, however, the Company was involved in a situation with an agent that became a source of considerable embarrassment. As a management problem the episode was of no great importance, but the handling of the case reflected adversely on Northwestern's sales management.

The Rose Case

The episode in question concerned a special agent of the J. I. D. Bristol Agency named Bernard R. Rose. Rose became a Northwestern agent in 1896, joined the Bristol Agency in 1902, and resigned three years later to join the agency force of a competitor. During the turnover of agents experienced by the life insurance industry in the years of the insurance investigations, Rose returned to Bristol.

The Rose case had a tangled history; but one development is evident, that as time passed and feelings became more intense Rose's charges, which at first were selective, became increasingly indiscriminate and extravagant. The problem began about 1911 when Rose wrote Secretary Hathaway complaining of "twisting" practices used by other agents. This letter was submitted to the Committee on Insurance and Agencies, which in turn asked Norris, the superintendent of agencies, to investigate. Though Norris communicated and met with Rose, the latter came away with the impression that Norris was blocking him from seeing other key officials. As a result Rose sent a long communication directly to President Markham and the Executive Committee. Entitled the "Voice from the Field," it not only was highly critical of the Company's practices in agency matters but also charged that the agency department was under the domination of a small group of general agents, a direct assault on Norris.

This communication ushered in a new stage. Some preliminary investigations by Vice President Van Dyke revealed that some general agents supported Rose's charges on Company practices, though all were guarded and equivocal in discussing the accusation against Norris and the domination of a clique in marketing management. A second letter from Rose, this time more outspoken against Norris, prompted a now quite annoyed President Markham to set up a special committee, including himself, to investigate the entire matter. By this date Rose's charges were an odd mixture. They ranged from a review of the Company's difficulties with dividends during the 1870's and its failure to stamp out twisting more effectively before 1905, to criticism of a number of current actuarial and insurance practices. The general theme that the Company was being run by a clique of general agents under the leadership of Norris was explicit throughout. The historical references could easily be dismissed as irrelevant, but on actuarial and insurance matters Rose seems to have raised questions concerning which there was a considerable difference of opinion among the officers. Apparently some of the committee members also suspected that Norris and a small group of general agents did exercise an undue influence on Company policies. At least Rose claimed to have been encouraged by several Company officers in his attempts to bring about a "reform."[24]

Years	Premium Receipts	Total Acquisition and Certain Other External Costs	These Costs as a Percentage of Premiums
		(In millions)	
1908-1909	$72.4	$9.4	13.0%
1910-1914	215.6	29.5	13.7
1915-1918	214.0	28.3	13.2

On May 19, 1914, fifteen months after its appointment, the committee made its report. Rose's charges against Norris were dismissed as "unbecoming of an agent." The report stated that some of the actuarial and insurance matters were unfounded and others had been remedied after further study. Officially, Northwestern had considered the Rose complaints and had rejected them.

The Company considered the matter closed; Rose did not. He wrote President Markham that the investigation was a "whitewash," that Norris was a "sinister politician," and that a thorough and complete reform was necessary. To obtain this he threatened to lay the case before the state commissioners. For President Markham this was the last straw. He had Rose's license as an agent revoked, writing him that his letter was "insulting and impudent." Rose sued for damages, charging that he had been deprived of a means of earning a living. The matter was finally settled out of court in 1919 for $30,000, even though it was the opinion of the general counsel that Rose could not win.

Any hope that the settlement would silence Rose was premature. In 1923, at his own expense, he published a book, *The Northwestern Unmasked.* Here he repeated his earlier charges; purported to describe the machinations of Norris, Van Dyke, and other Company officers; and he accused the Company of many crimes against policyholders. In 1929 he repeated his accusations in a second book, *The Northwestern More Completely Unmasked.* The Company met these attacks in silence, although a special committee of the National Association of Insurance Commissioners in 1929 rejected Rose's charges and exonerated Northwestern.

A more market-oriented group of Company officers and executive committeemen might have become concerned with the symptoms of agent dissatisfaction which the Rose episode tended to dramatize. For top executives, largely preoccupied with investment problems, however, such an incident was accepted as the product of the twisted mind of one man. An examination of the Company's marketing record for the 1908-1918 period indicates why,

judged by the pragmatic tests of sales volume and relative standing in the industry, the executive group had little reason to assume that the agency administration was anything but successful.

The Sales and Marketing Record

Just how impressive the marketing record was between 1908 and 1918 is indicated by the total sales for the period which exceeded $1.5 billion, rising from $114 million in 1909 to $166 million in 1918. Northwestern's total insurance in force, as a result, increased from the $881.5 million on the books at the end of 1907 to $1.68 billion at the end of 1918. The Company began and ended the period as the sixth largest life insurance firm in the United States, and its total sales were exceeded by only five companies, two of which, Metropolitan and Prudential, were selling in different markets. The annual volume of insurance sales by the whole industry and for various groups of companies is shown in Chart XI-1.

This record of sales was even more pleasing to the management in that it was obtained without an inordinate increase in acquisition costs. Although the total outlays associated with Northwestern marketing and other external activities rose by approximately 50 per cent between 1908 and 1918, the relative costs declined as compared to the previous period.

Total marketing expenses incurred amounted to $54.6 million, with agents' compensation accounting for $51.7 million, medical examinations for $2.8 million, and advertising for only $96,000. Of the remaining outlays shown, taxes of $12.4 million made up the overwhelming proportion. Total external outlays amounted to $67.3 million. The relative costs, that is, the ratio of the above expenses to the Company's premium receipts, as shown by the above tabulation, averaged 13.4 per cent for the whole period as compared to 14.8 per cent for the eight years 1900-1907.

Excellent as the record of sales was during these

CHART XI-1

Sales of Insurance: Industry and Northwestern, 1908–1918

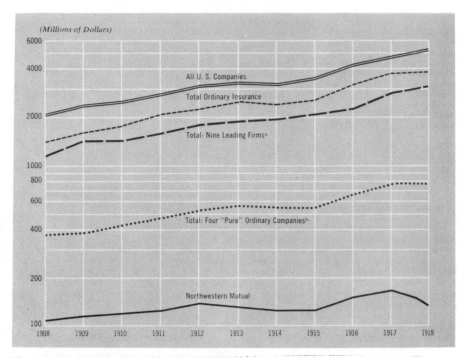

(Millions of Dollars)

All U. S. Companies

Total Ordinary Insurance

Total: Nine Leading Firms[a]

Total: Four "Pure" Ordinary Companies[b]

Northwestern Mutual

[a]Aetna, Equitable (N. Y.), John Hancock, Metropolitan, Mutual Benefit, Mutual Life (N. Y.), New York Life, Penn Mutual, Prudential.
[b]Mutual Benefit, Mutual Life (N. Y.), Penn Mutual, New York Life.

SOURCES: Appendix E; *Insurance Year Book,* 1920.

years, it is clear that Northwestern's underwriting policies were not hitched to the goal of pure volume. Although Northwestern managed to market almost 6 per cent of the total amount of ordinary insurance sold during this period, the aggressive drive of such companies as Metropolitan, Prudential, Equitable, John Hancock, and Aetna, that sold a variety of insurance lines, overshadowed the life insurance market. It was clear that in the future the dominance of these "combination" companies would become even greater.

Northwestern's market philosophy, as has been indicated, was founded on the basis of conservative underwriting, simplicity of operation, and excellence of an agency force which believed in the value of these things. Part of the Company's inherent strength was the tendency of the business it wrote to remain in force over time; a basic element in its ability to attract and keep an efficient agency organization was this persistency. With respect to persistency the Company continued to perform excellently. As indicated in the tabulation on page 172, only one company, Mutual Benefit, had a better record during these years.[25]

COMPANY	(1) SALES	(2) INSURANCE IN FORCE 1907	(3) INSURANCE IN FORCE 1908	(4) 1907 INSURANCE IN FORCE PLUS TOTAL SALES	(5) COL. (3) ÷ COL. (4)
NORTHWESTERN	$1,501.3	$881.6	$1,680.9	$2,382.9	70.5%
Aetna	879.8	271.0	673.2	1,150.8	58.5
Mutual Benefit	923.4	440.7	987.5	1,364.1	72.4
Penn Mutual	874.4	425.9	802.2	1,300.3	61.7
Equitable	1,601.9	1,340.1	1,712.1	2,942.1	58.2
Mutual Life	1,700.1	1,452.7	1,861.9	3,152.9	59.0
New York Life	2,005.3	2,005.3	2,838.8	4,583.6	61.9
John Hancock	1,478.5	456.9	1,061.1	1,935.4	54.8
Metropolitan	6,083.4	1,804.9	4,429.5	7,888.4	56.2
Prudential	5,790.0	1,337.4	3,891.7	7,127.4	54.6
Ordinary	27,637.0	11,486.1	23,954.7	39,123.1	61.2
All Insurance	37,574.3	14,063.4	29,870.3	51,637.7	57.8

Legislative Relations

Sales and investment were intimately related to legislative regulations, state and national. The emotional intensity in this area, roused by the Armstrong and Wisconsin Investigations, had noticeably subsided. But the need for continual vigilance was demonstrated by Northwestern when it created the post of permanent legislative counsel within the legal department and by the type of individuals who occupied the office of general counsel. As in former years the Wisconsin Legislature was regarded as the main arena of action; but relations with governments of other states continued, while those with the Congress of the United States acquired a new importance.

After 1908 Northwestern's legislative interests remained the major responsibility of the Company's general counsel, Judge George H. Noyes, who continued to serve the Company in this capacity until his resignation in 1915. The importance attached to this office by the Company was reflected by the selection of another distinguished jurist for the post, Judge John Barnes of the Wisconsin Supreme Court. Born in Manitowoc County, Wisconsin, in 1859, Barnes was a person of unusual charm. As a contemporary described him: "He always had a fitting story to illustrate his point and his drawling, whimsical repartee was delightful."[26]

Northwestern had two primary objectives in dealing with the Wisconsin Legislature during this period. One was to modify that part of the 1907 legislation which limited the loading charges included in premiums; the second sought modification of the structure of Wisconsin's taxes on life companies. In 1915, after exhaustive effort, legislation was passed which partially achieved both objectives.

A modest relief from the 1901 tax burden was also granted the Company by the 1915 legislature. Of greater importance, however, was the revision of the tax base to be applied to domestic Wisconsin life companies. In essence, the modified structure provided that these companies pay a tax equal to 3 per cent on aggregate income, but exempted premiums and income from real estate upon which property taxes had already been paid.[27]

The most serious legislative threats confronting the Company in states outside Wisconsin came in Iowa in 1913; and Illinois, Missouri, and Pennsylvania in 1917. When the Pennsylvania legislature was considering a tax bill which would have affected life companies, Markham offered to assist the managements of companies domiciled in that state in resisting it. The Pennsylvania companies, however, believed they would be more effective without the intrusion of "outsiders," and requested Northwestern not to become involved, a position that President Markham appreciated and to which he was sympathetic.[28]

Because the United States Supreme Court had declared in 1868 that issuing a life insurance policy did not constitute interstate commerce, the life industry's experience with federal legislation was confined exclusively to revenue measures enacted during periods of wartime emergency. While many in the industry would have preferred federal control to the confusing pattern of multistate regulation which existed, all companies resisted attempts to impose national taxes on life insurance except in crisis conditions. In 1894 Congress had considered an income tax on life companies as part of the tariff bill, but withdrew the objectionable clause in the face of unified industry opposition.

When in 1909 Congress enacted an excise tax on corporations, including life companies, it raised a hornets' nest of opposition from industry members. The companies were disturbed both by the imposition of a tax in a nonemergency period and by the tax base used. There was no question that income was the base, but Northwestern, like other companies, did not accept the government's ruling that dividends applied to payment of premiums or for the purchase of paid-up insurance should be considered as income. Northwestern decided to test the government's interpretation, and after paying its 1909–1910 taxes under protest, filed suit to recover that portion considered by the Company's general counsel to have been illegally collected.[29] In 1918 the United States District Court upheld the Company's contention; the government's appeal was rejected, and nearly $170,000 in taxes and interest recovered.[30]

The Company was also deeply concerned when, in 1913, an income tax proposal was submitted to Congress. Having no apparatus on hand to conduct a legislative campaign in the Washington arena, Company strategy and planning was devised by the general counsel and President Markham. As in Wisconsin prior to 1908, principal reliance was placed upon building up popular pressure against those portions of the revenue bill which applied to life insurance, and particularly to mutual companies. A circular letter was addressed to policyholders explaining the Company's viewpoint, and these were expressed to the general agents for distribution in their fields. In addition, the agents, loan agents, and trustees were urged to protest the inclusion of mutual companies in the bill to their congressmen, and to influence policyholders to take similar action. Judge Noyes personally led the fight to defeat the objectionable section in the Senate, for he believed that policyholder remonstrances would have little

effect in the house. The Company effort, like that of the industry generally, had little discernible effect; the income tax was approved by Congress.

Until the United States entered World War I it appeared that the Company would have been wiser had it supported the income tax bill. Whereas federal taxes paid by Northwestern for 1912 and 1913 aggregated $206,000, under the application of the 1913 law only $2,800 was paid during the years 1914–1916. In early 1917, however, Congress imposed a tax of 8 per cent on net corporate profits over $5,000; and a few months later it doubled this rate, plus imposing a special tax of eight cents per one hundred dollars of insurance issued. The Company's federal tax bill went up sharply, totaling $332,000 for 1917–1918.

The 1917 tax legislation called forth renewed life industry opposition. The Northwestern again reverted to the type of campaign that had been conducted four years earlier, and with the same results. Judge Barnes contended that the 1917 tax proposal specifically exempted mutual savings companies and like consideration should be extended to mutual life companies.[31] This view was first advanced by him in a paper given before the Association of Life Insurance Counsel, then printed by the Company and distributed to its policyholders. The general counsel's argument had considerable merit, but neither his logic nor his energetic representation of Northwestern's interest in Washington made any apparent impression during the tumultuous weeks following the declaration of war.

Although not successful in exempting itself or other mutual companies from the federal corporate income tax, the Company's experience in the national capital was useful in planning future relations with Congress. The management recognized the parallel between its Washington experience and that which had existed in Wisconsin before the legislative counsel was established. In the future less reliance would be placed upon "crisis measures" and more on a continuous policy of "educating" congressmen as to the nature of life insurance in general and mutual life companies in particular.

CHAPTER TWELVE

Investment: 1908-1918

THE fact that three of the leading executives of Northwestern, including President Markham, were primarily investment men indicates the continued emphasis placed upon this phase of the Company's operations. Although the fundamental theme of these years is one of preserving the pattern of investment established earlier, there were numerous developments that caused management to review and alter its decisions. There was, for example, an astonishing variation in the demand for policy loans and in interest rates, the result at times of localized phenomena but more often the effect of short-term general trends, brief downturns in the economy in 1910 and again in 1914, or the shock produced when the United States entered the first World War in 1917. A vigorous debate was also carried on during this period with respect to farm loans as opposed to loans on urban property, a question that became vital in view of the rapid inflationary trend in the value of real property and the swiftly moving mortgage market. Such were the investment questions confronting management during this eventful period.

General Development in Investments

In the administration of the Company's investment activities President Markham assumed personal responsibility for securities. The Bond Committee was dissolved in 1908, and with the assistance of Henry Whitcomb, a member of the Finance Committee, Markham selected the issues to be presented to that committee. Vice President Van Dyke took over Markham's former duties as supervisor of the Company's loan agents. Vice President Sanborn remained in charge of the mortgage loan department. All three, of course, were members of the Finance Committee, and each was capably assisted by key subordinates.

Northwestern's aggregate income during the years 1908–1918 amounted to slightly over $675 million, about 75 per cent of which came from premiums, and most of the remainder from earnings on investments. While, as shown in Chart XII-1, payments to policyholders and expenses varied from year to year, the Company was able to allocate about a quarter of its total income to investments. This meant that, in addition to receipts from repayments of loans and the role of securities and real estate, the management had to find outlets for some $172.5 million of new investment funds. These funds, plus an approximate $10 million appreciation in the value of securities held, enabled the Company to increase its total assets some two-thirds, *i.e.,* from $232.8 million to $414.8 million during 1908–1918.

Examination of Chart XII-2 shows that over the whole period there were few significant changes in the distribution of assets by major types. Mortgage loans continued to be the chief form of investment, varying between 50.8 and 55 per cent of total invest-ment. Bond investments made up 30 per cent of as-sets both at the beginning and end of the period. The only important increase in the amount of the bond account came in 1917–1918 with the purchase during the war of United States Government secu-rities. Northwestern's total loans on policies in-creased steadily for the entire period, growing from $34 million in 1908 to $59.8 million at the end of 1918. As a component of total assets they increased from 13.7 per cent in 1908 to a peak of 16.8 per cent in 1914.

Several smaller accounts varied with circum-stances. Relative to total investment, real estate holdings did not exceed 1.5 per cent at any time, the construction of a new and larger Home Office build-ing valued at over $4.4 million marking the only sig-nificant change. The Company's cash balances con-tinued to follow a business cycle pattern, rising in periods of financial crisis and diminishing with re-covery. The greatest amount of cash was reached in 1915, equal to 1.3 per cent of assets.

CHART XII-2

Distribution of Admitted Assets:
Northwestern, 1908–1918

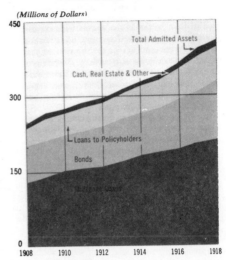

SOURCE: Appendix F, Table 5.

CHART XII-1

Income, Expenditures, and Net Available
for Investment: Northwestern,
1908–1918

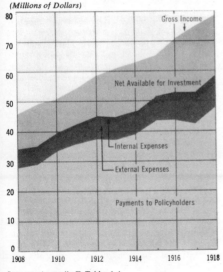

SOURCE: Appendix F, Tables 1-4.

Loans to Policyholders

During the 1908–1918 period the Company had three types of loans on policies available to policy-holders. These included the familiar premium notes and policy loans, in addition to a new type called automatic premium loans. While the Company did not accept premium notes on policies sold after 1907, holders of policies issued before that date con-tinued to exercise the privilege. The result was a growth in this account which reached a peak of over $1 million in 1915–1916.

Under the automatic premium loan provision in-troduced in 1908 a policyholder could elect to have premiums charged automatically up to an amount equal to the cash surrender value of his policy, less interest. Such loans made it possible for the insur-ance to be continued in force and for the insured to resume premium payments at any time without having to furnish evidence of insurability. They were favored by management largely because they involved only a transfer on the books and put no cash drain on the Company. For the policyholder who intended to maintain his insurance in force but was temporarily short of funds, such loans were beneficial. Automatic premium loans grew steadily after 1908, although they did not exceed $1 million until 1918.

The relatively slow growth of the account may have been in part due to the unpopularity of this type of loan so far as the agents were concerned. Under the rules of the Company, no renewal commissions were paid agents for the year or years in which the loans were outstanding. Despite protests by the agents the rule remained in force with the result that wherever possible the agent urged the policyholder to take a policy loan rather than exercise the automatic loan privilege.

Policy loans, as shown in the chart, were by far the most important type of advance to policyholders. This account grew from $33.4 million to nearly $58.2 million during the period, with the heaviest demands coming in 1910 and again in 1913–1914.

The effects of policy loans on Northwestern's other investments were especially troublesome during 1913–1914 when they coincided with vigorous demand for mortgage loans and temporarily depressed security prices. To meet the increased demand for cash from policyholders the Company was forced to curtail its mortgage loans sharply and also to dispose of some railroad bonds.

The management was much disturbed about the situation in 1913–1914, not only because of foregone investment opportunities, but because borrowing against policies was frequently a prelude to lapse or surrender. President Markham thought the banks were largely responsible for increased policy loans. As he put it,

> When money is tight the banks raise their rate of interest and cut down their credit, and advise all their customers who have insurance in force to go to their companies and borrow instead of taking it out of the banks, and this is very largely done. So you see that the insurance companies are constantly used as buffers to really protect the calls upon the banks when credit is most needed.[1]

The effects of meeting heavy policy loan demands on planned investment were made clear by Vice President Van Dyke in a letter to one of the Company's general agents:

> This policy loan feature of our business is a most unfortunate one in many aspects, for when money becomes tight and the opportunity is presented to buy bonds at a very favorable income producing rate, then the opportunity is lost to us, for we are brought face

to face with the enormous demand for policy loans, and are obliged to conserve our funds very carefully to provide for the same.[2]

As early as 1909, largely at Markham's insistence, Northwestern had attempted to protect itself against unusual demand for policy loans by inserting a clause in all new policy contracts which gave the Company a ninety-day leeway period before it was forced to grant a requested loan. The management realized that the rule could not be invoked except in periods of extreme panic without bringing criticism from policyholders. The president repeatedly sought, during 1913–1914, to get other life companies and the state commissioners of insurance to impose some similar restraint on policy loans. He hoped, through joint action, to obtain legislation which would impose some general restrictions on policy loans which would avoid possible resentment against particular companies.[3] He received some encouragement from other company officials, but with the easing of demand for policy loans after 1914 he no longer attempted to push the idea.

Bond Investments

Northwestern's bond investments not only remained virtually constant as a percentage of total investments, but as shown in Chart XII-3, there was little change in the relative importance of the items within the account. Railroad bonds continued to be, as they had in the decade prior to 1908, the largest item in the portfolio. The amount invested in state, county, and municipal bonds more than doubled, although it remained a small part of the total. The principal change was the addition of United States Government bonds during 1917 and 1918. The Company supplemented this aid to the allied war effort by purchases of Canadian securities during the same two years. In 1915 the Company added railroad stocks for the first time to its holdings, but this was a temporary acquisition resulting from a railroad reorganization. The small amount of commercial bonds were also acquired in settlement of a debt.

There were, in fact, only three problems associated with the Company's security investments between 1908 and 1918 that were of real concern to the management. One had to do with the question of security valuation. The second came in connection with the default on railroad bonds. The third involved public relations growing out of the Liberty Bond drives.

CHART XII-3

Bond Investments: Northwestern, 1908–1918

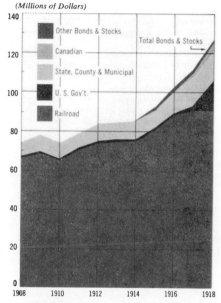

(Millions of Dollars)

SOURCE: *Annual Statement* (Convention Form), Northwestern Mutual Life Insurance Company, 1908-1918, inclusive.

The problem of proper security valuation was one of the unresolved questions that had first appeared in the 1890's. As already noted, the Company had obtained a change in Wisconsin law in 1903 which allowed a six months' average to be used for evaluating securities rather than a year-end market price. During the panic of 1907 a number of state insurance commissioners, in consultation with various life insurance officers, devised a similar formula which, with slight modification, was adopted by the National Association of Insurance Commissioners in 1911.[4]

The officers of life companies were not satisfied with the maintenance of even a modified market value system, but no further action of importance was taken until the United States entered World War I and many security prices fell sharply. The National Association of Insurance Commissioners

again acted to ease this dangerous situation for the life companies by permitting them to elect either (1) the market formula valuation already in force, or (2) an amortization valuation.

The amortization valuation was something new. It applied only to bonds not in default on which amortization values were obtained by referring to the relation between the acquisition price of a security and the par value. Bonds purchased at a premium, if eligible for amortization, were valued at the purchase price less the percentage of the premium which was written down during the year; bonds purchased at a discount were valued at the purchase price plus the percentage of the discount written up during the year. Since this method made no direct reference to market prices, life companies using it were not subject to the rapid fluctuations of asset values which characterized a market value method. The sanction of the commissioners for amortized valuations was extended through 1918 and into 1919, then withdrawn only to be reintroduced in the 1930's.

The Northwestern management shared most of the industry's dissatisfaction with the market formula of evaluating securities and had supported the efforts to get it changed. When the opportunity came in 1917, President Markham promptly chose the amortization method.

A much more immediate and pressing problem for the management than security valuation came in connection with defaults on certain railroad bonds held by Northwestern. This was a new experience, for the Company, by delaying its railroad bond purchases until 1898, had escaped the numerous default cases that occurred during the 1893 depression.

Northwestern's initial case of this sort occurred in 1915 when the Cincinnati, Indianapolis and Western Railroad and one affiliate line, the Decatur and Western, were unable to pay the interest due on their bonds. These securities were fairly widely held and a bondholders' protective committee was formed which represented various institutional investors, including the Chase National Bank and a number of insurance companies in addition to Northwestern. Henry F. Whitcomb represented the Company on this committee; Albert H. Wiggin, who represented the Chase, was also a Northwestern trustee. The committee foreclosed the mortgages of the railroads, bought in the properties, and carried on operations with a management appointed under the terms of a reorganization plan.

As a result of the writedown of the original debt Northwestern exchanged bonds having a par value of $1.6 million for new mortgage bonds valued at $489,600 and equal amounts of common and preferred stocks with a total par value of $1.96 million. The Company carried the stocks during 1915 and 1916 at values equal to par for the preferred and zero for the common. Then early in 1917 the valuation committee of the National Association of Insurance Commissioners placed the values equal to 15 per cent for preferred and 8 per cent for common, and ordered the Company to reduce its valuations accordingly. Markham protested the decision and managed to convince the Wisconsin commissioner to set the values at 19 and 9 per cent.*

The Pere Marquette Railroad Company experienced difficulties in 1915-1916 and it also defaulted on certain securities. On the protective committee, formed in 1917, H. F. Whitcomb again represented Northwestern, and was named to the reorganization committee. After the customary disputes between conflicting parties-at-interest were resolved, the debt structure of the road and its affiliates was scaled down by exchanging new bonds and stocks for the old bonds. Northwestern surrendered mortgage securities of a book value of $750,000 in exchange for new mortgage bonds of a book value equal to $556,900. The stock included 955 shares of common and 1,910 shares of preferred; par values were equal to $100 per share, but the insurance commissioner's committee on valuations set the values equal to $70 per share for the preferred and $20 per share for the common.†

In contrast to the seriousness of the reorganization case Northwestern's experiences with the Liberty Loan drives of 1917-1918 had an almost ludicrous aspect. Despite this quality, however, they illustrated a vital facet of the character of management: an intense resentment, particularly by President Markham, with what was considered—with some justification—by the Home Office to be an unreasonable outside interference with the administration of the Company's affairs.

The question simply was: where should Northwestern make its purchases of government bonds during the Liberty Loan drives? The answers, however, involved sensitive areas of public relations and were much more complex. The Finance Committee,

believing it to be a conventional investment decision, subscribed for $2 million of the bonds offered during the first Liberty Loan drive through Chase National Bank of New York. There was an immediate protest from the banks in Milwaukee and the Federal Reserve Bank in Chicago, which succeeded in changing this decision so that the purchase was divided equally between the Chase and the Milwaukee banks.*

The Home Office decided that all future subscriptions would be placed entirely through the Milwaukee banks, but reckoned without the fervor of state officials, its own general agents, policyholders, and various public-spirited individuals who were not insured in the Company. Management was besieged with requests to place its subscriptions in a score of states and hundreds of districts. The reasons for the requests were understandable. Agents were eager to have this material demonstration of the Company's patriotism made in their own communities where the action would enhance their status and opportunities to sell insurance. Public officials and patriotic citizens anxious to make an impressive record in loan subscriptions neglected few opportunities to achieve the goal, not always diplomatically. The Company, on the other hand, desired to avoid the added expense and administrative difficulties associated with the fractional amounts involved in a broad geographic distribution of the subscriptions. During the next two Liberty Loan drives the management grimly resisted all such suggestions and subscribed for its $7 million of war bonds through the Milwaukee area banks.

With the fourth Liberty Loan drive, however, and following the lead of other life companies, Northwestern reversed its policy and agreed to purchase $3.25 million of its $10 million subscription in the forty-two states outside Wisconsin in which it did business. But the acceptance by management of a policy more closely geared to the delicate public relations problems inherent in the situation probably did not anticipate the extent of the ambitions of some of the general agents.

According to Markham's plan the Company's subscription was to be allocated to the individual states and territories in the proportion to which the insurance produced in these regions bore to the total allotment. The president suggested that general agents place their allotments in one or two banks in their territories. For several general agents,

---

* The Company lost rather heavily as a result of this default, for while the bonds were disposed of at about book values, the stock was finally sold to the Baltimore and Ohio Railroad for $372,096. Thus the final loss, aside from interest and dividend earnings, was in the neighborhood of $800,000. (*Annual Statement,* Schedule D, 1924, 1926, 1927.)

† The new bonds were eventually disposed of at prices slightly over their book values. The stock was disposed of through sale to bond houses in 1924 and 1927 at a price of $372.096. This represented a net profit on the entire transaction of about $5,700. (*Annual Statement,* Schedule D, 1924, 1927.)

* The Milwaukee banks complained that the annual balances kept by Northwestern contributed to the amount of the allotment assigned them by the Seventh District Federal Reserve Bank; it was only fair, therefore, that the Company's subscriptions be placed in Milwaukee. (George C. Markham to Albert H. Wiggin, Chase National Bank, June 12, 1917.)

however, there were pressing reasons for having their shares of the allotment distributed somewhat more broadly. One optimistically suggested that the subscription for his territory be divided into small amounts so as to cover all the fields of his several district agents; a second proposed that his allotment be placed through fourteen different banks such that each could boost its private subscription; while a third requested that the subscription for his state be split into tenths. With each such request the temperature in the office of President Markham rose several degrees; rejecting all such proposals and by alternately placating and scolding, the president drove his original plan through without modification. When the Victory Loan drive was launched in 1919 Northwestern quickly allocated one-half its allotment to the states outside Wisconsin, the operation was completed smoothly and with none of the earlier complications.

Mortgage Loans

It was the field of mortgage lending that absorbed the principal attention of the investment officers during 1908–1918. One reason was the size and relative importance of the account in the Company's total investment. A second was the controversy that arose over the wisdom of expanding farm rather than urban loans. Finally, these years presented particular difficulties because of rapidly changing conditions in the supply and demand for mortgage funds, years that tested the management's skill to the utmost in adjusting interest rates and loan requirements to maintain an orderly flow of investments.

Northwestern's mortgage account not only expanded by some $81 million from 1908 through 1918, but the $210.5 million at the latter date put the Company second only to Metropolitan as a mortgage lender among American life companies. As shown in Chart XII-4, the trend toward farm lending continued. This movement was sufficient to make the Company the largest farm mortgage lender in the industry by the end of the period.

Northwestern's urban and rural activities were concentrated largely in the same areas that had attracted their investments before 1908. Nearly two-thirds of the loans were in the six states of Illinois, Iowa, Missouri, Minnesota, Ohio, and Indiana. California was added as a loaning territory in 1909, with loans being confined largely to urban mortgages in San Francisco and Los Angeles.

Unsettled conditions during this period caused frequent changes in interest rates. Beginning in 1908 the Company set its rates on first-class large

CHART XII-4

Mortgage Loan Investments:
Northwestern, 1908–1918

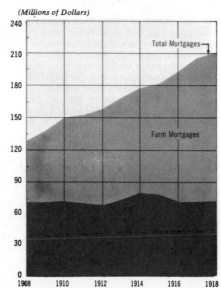

(Millions of Dollars)

SOURCE: *Annual Statement* (Convention Form), Northwestern Mutual Life Insurance Company, 1908-1918, inclusive.

urban loans at 4 to 4.5 per cent, with 4.5 to 5 per cent being charged for smaller loans less well secured. The basic farm loan rates in the best territories of Iowa, Minnesota, Illinois, Missouri and southern Wisconsin, as well as in Ohio and Indiana, were 5 per cent for loans of $2,000 and over, and 5.5 per cent for loans under that amount. These rates remained unchanged throughout 1909 and into 1910, even though the Company was pressed by the demand for policy loans and an increase in farm loan applications. As a result investment funds were insufficient to meet the demand and in June 1910 the Finance Committee increased interest rates generally, raising farm rates in many territories to 6 and 6.5 per cent. This action so sharply reduced loan applications that within four months the Finance Committee again reduced rates to 5.5 per cent on all loans, including renewals. Immediately requests for farm loans poured into the Home Office. When loan commitments had reached $9 million the Company's loan agents were notified that the Company would accept no applications until further notice. To control investment expenses during this "moratorium" the Company discharged a number of assistant loan agents.[5]

These recurrent fluctuations in demand and interest rates continued. During 1911 demand again slackened and the loan agents began to encounter heavy resistance to the average 5.5 per cent rate on acceptable farm properties, much of it caused by increasing competition from Eastern life companies. The Finance Committee responded by permitting renewals and extensions of farm loans at a 5 per cent rate, but insisted upon 5.5 per cent for new loans. Markham indicated that he hoped to obtain a sufficient number of good farm loans at the higher rate but was prepared to lower rates if necessary to satisfy borrowers and absorb investment funds;[6] by August 1912 he was seriously disturbed by the decline in applications, and the Finance Committee was finally persuaded to reduce rates by ¼ to ½ per cent.

About the same time, in an effort to increase the average maturity of loans, the Committee lengthened the period of the prepayment privilege, a decision disapproved by Vice President Van Dyke and President Markham. The "prepayment privilege" meant that borrowers could pay in advance all or a portion of their loans. The Committee's action continued the privilege but increased the time lapse before it could first be exercised to three years. Van Dyke opposed it because he feared borrowers would turn to competitors who would allow shorter prepayment terms. The competition for farm loans was so great that he believed any restrictions placing the Company at a disadvantage were unwarranted.

President Markham, however, also made known his doubts about the advisability of trying to compete in the farm mortgage area altogether. He pointed out that between 1908 and the end of 1912 Northwestern's farm loans had increased by over $33 million while city loans were reduced by $2.7 million. Looking to the future, he said,

> in the last ten years farm values all over our field have more than doubled. It is generally conceded that farm lands are too high, that there must be a considerable falling off in values in the near future. I have called the attention of the Finance Committee to this phase of our business a good many times; called attention to the fact that we were loaning the same percentage upon this increased valuation of farms that we did when the farms were valued at half of what they are today. While I think that our farm loans are reasonably safe, nevertheless, if from a failure of

crops for two or three seasons, or other reasons, there should be a considerable shrinkage of farm values, this Company might suffer. In fact, I do not think we should crowd this farm loan business at the same ratio as we have heretofore, but rather foster our city business upon the kind of security and favorable terms that we are now able to control.[7]

Markham was convinced that most of the Company's loan difficulties could be terminated by a change in policy. Urban land values had not increased as fast as the prices of farms and lands in the Middle Western territories; while farm mortgages still commanded a slightly higher rate of interest, the expenses of city lending were substantially lower per dollar loaned. In addition, despite the increasing competition of other insurance companies and banks, Northwestern was one of the few firms able and willing to make large loans in Middle Western and Pacific Coast cities. Markham concluded that since the larger portion of the expenses of lending

> is made necessary on account of our farm loan business and it has been a question in my mind, and is yet, whether or not we could not reduce the farm loan business and increase city business and, therefore, reduce the cost and still have left all the farm business we need, and also have satisfactory security that would, on the whole, yield us as great, and perhaps a little greater, return than we can get upon this vast sum loaned upon farm securities.[8]

The president's arguments were well formulated, and if his recommendations had been followed the Company would have avoided a number of difficulties encountered with its farm mortgages during the late 1920's and early 1930's. But the reluctance of the remaining members of the Finance Committee to accept Markham's suggestions is also understandable. To make them effective would have required discontinuing the greater portion of the twenty-five loan agencies then operating. Furthermore, the Company would have been forced to sharply revise relationships with the large and effective group of loan correspondents built up by the loan agents over many years, most of whom were country bankers in strategic positions to receive loan inquiries. An unwillingness to disturb the effectiveness of the loan agency-correspondent source of loan applications, plus the fact that farm loans continued to command a higher rate of return than urban loans, largely account for the unwillingness of the Finance Committee to implement Markham's suggestions.

While the farm and urban accounts were increased in about equal amounts (approximately $10 million) during 1913 and 1914, events during those years brought about a renewed emphasis on farm loans beginning in 1915. During the first four months of 1913 the management was so flooded with loan applications that in May it was again obliged to cease lending.[9] It also prompted an increase in interest rates: with 6.5 per cent charged on farm loans of $3,000 or less; 6 per cent on farm loans over this amount; and 5.5 on city loans, except for those particularly well secured.[10]

The sudden cessation in loaning once more brought into bold relief the problem of maintaining cordial relations with loan correspondents. Northwestern was in a position where, in the face of a temporary inability to make loans, action was necessary to prevent the permanent loss of correspondents and a consequent decline in the efficiency of its whole loan apparatus. To meet this contingency the Company, in November 1913, established a system of quotas under which loan agents were given monthly or quarterly allotments of loan funds against which they could submit applications. The amounts allocated varied according to the past business and desirability of the territories, with some flexibility to insure the best reception for particularly good applications.

Following entry of the United States into World War I the Company found it no longer necessary to utilize this quota system. The principal reason for the decline of demand for mortgage money was the Federal Government's creation of a system of twelve regional Federal Land Banks, bolstered by the incorporation under Federal charter of privately owned joint stock land banks.* Designed to help farmers to meet the production requirements of the war effort, these banks made funds available at interest rates ranging from 5 to 6 per cent and for periods of from five to forty years. Under these circumstances the Company was prepared to consider all good loan applications. As a result the total mortgage account was increased by some $16.5 million during 1917-1918, mostly on farm security.

The Company took extra precautions, however, against lending too heavily on farm properties whose values were rising rapidly as a result of the war demands for agricultural products. Whereas the Company had earlier loaned up to 40 and 50 per cent on appraised values, during 1917 and 1918 the maximum loan was under 40 per cent.[11] This practice

proved to be essentially sound even though some business was lost as many farmers turned to more liberal lenders. Late in 1917 the management also raised the rate on farm loans approximately one-half per cent in most territories.[12]

During the 1908-1918 period the Company also purchased a few mortgages directly from banks and mortgage brokers. The first of these transactions occurred in 1909 and involved the purchase of about $150,000 of mortgages from the Iowa National Bank at Des Moines, whose president, H. A. Miller, was a Northwestern trustee. Markham outlined the Company's requirements in the proposed purchase, which had been fully approved by the Finance Committee:

> [we] would expect generally, in furtherance of your suggestion, that whatever mortgages the Company would buy from you would be subject to inspection, and if there were any, in the judgment of our Finance Committee that were not perfectly satisfactory, you would replace them with such other securities as would meet our requirements.[13]

In 1912 a second purchase of mortgages valued at $641,800 was made, followed in 1918 by the acquisition of another lot worth $800,000, both from the same bank. By these transactions the Company acquired mortgages at prices which yielded a net return equal to that currently obtainable by direct lending. The 1918 transaction, for example, was made at a price which netted the Company slightly over 5.5 per cent.

During 1916 and 1917 mortgage purchases were also made from the Markham and May Company, a mortgage brokerage concern in Milwaukee. The total value of these mortgages, chiefly on Wisconsin farms, amounted to $952,200. Examination of the security behind these mortgages was made by the Company's general loan agent, and with the same guarantees to Northwestern that applied to the Iowa National purchases. Later inquiry revealed, however, that these purchases were never brought to the attention of the Finance Committee or authorized by that group. This by-passing of the Committee by President Markham in acquiring these mortgages caused serious criticism by the trustees and, as will be noted below, hastened his retirement.

The Investment Record

An examination of the investment portfolios of the ten largest American life companies, shown in Table XII-1, indicates the relative emphasis Northwestern placed upon mortgage lending. It is also

---

* The Federal Farm Loan Act was passed in 1916 but was not fully operative until 1917-1918. It provided for twelve Federal land banks which were to finance themselves by issuing tax-exempt bonds.

TABLE XII-1

Ten Largest United States Life Insurance Companies: Distribution of Assets, 1908–1918
(As a Percentage of Total Admitted Assets)

COMPANY	MORT-GAGE LOANS	BONDS	STOCKS	LOANS ON POLICIES	REAL ESTATE	CASH	OTHER	ADMITTED ASSETS
				(1908)				(In Millions)
NORTHWESTERN	52.20	30.14	-0-	13.70	0.85	1.28	1.83	$248.0
Aetna	47.43	27.67	4.19	8.39	0.71	6.30	5.31	87.1
Equitable	21.08	47.13	9.01	12.33	5.93	2.81	1.71	462.8
John Hancock	31.34	50.75	-0-	6.27	6.47	1.67	3.50	56.8
Metropolitan	38.32	39.85	4.29	3.90	9.47	2.02	2.14	236.9
Mutual Benefit	44.78	27.72	-0-	17.60	3.04	1.09	5.77	121.1
Mutual Life	23.14	45.33	8.49	11.57	4.81	0.72	5.94	544.9
New York Life	10.53	67.74	-0-	15.67	2.27	1.66	2.13	557.3
Penn Mutual	39.46	37.44	0.37	14.76	2.16	0.40	5.41	99.7
Prudential	18.17	54.38	1.64	5.79	6.97	6.56	6.49	173.7
Average:	23.82	49.37	4.49	11.69	4.74	2.17	3.72	$258.8
				(1912)				
NORTHWESTERN	53.55	28.61	-0-	14.95	0.97	1.16	0.75	$297.8
Aetna	44.90	24.50	3.72	8.07	0.51	2.92	15.38	112.8
Equitable	19.26	53.29	3.40	15.17	5.65	1.33	1.90	513.3
John Hancock	42.81	39.97	-0-	7.15	4.44	1.33	4.30	93.6
Metropolitan	40.11	42.64	2.04	5.09	5.96	1.42	7.60	397.9
Mutual Benefit	48.02	26.68	-0-	17.45	1.74	0.78	3.56	158.1
Mutual Life	23.29	51.60	4.77	13.35	3.92	0.37	2.70	599.7
New York Life	19.62	59.27	0.04	16.80	1.40	0.69	2.18	735.9
Penn Mutual	38.47	36.63	0.25	16.26	1.90	1.38	5.11	135.6
Prudential	24.66	53.72	1.00	6.97	6.11	2.83	4.71	297.8
Average:	27.42	49.45	2.03	12.74	3.77	1.17	3.32	$334.3
				(1915)				
NORTHWESTERN	53.10	27.13	0.27	16.62	1.50	1.25	0.13	$343.6
Aetna	44.03	23.33	4.42	9.68	0.88	3.63	14.03	124.4
Equitable	19.96	52.23	3.03	17.82	3.20	2.24	1.52	545.9
John Hancock	48.77	35.51	-0-	8.27	3.29	1.01	3.15	127.1
Metropolitan	43.44	41.28	1.03	6.76	3.44	1.12	2.93	539.4
Mutual Benefit	48.42	24.00	0.02	19.45	1.54	1.28	5.29	192.7
Mutual Life	17.99	55.84	4.48	14.91	3.50	1.87	1.41	616.6
New York Life	18.72	56.69	0.03	19.02	1.43	2.35	1.76	852.3
Penn Mutual	38.19	34.83	0.19	18.62	2.60	1.67	3.90	162.0
Prudential	26.81	53.54	0.70	8.40	4.45	3.60	2.50	393.3
Average:	27.89	48.48	1.65	14.38	2.81	2.11	2.68	$389.7
				(1918)				
NORTHWESTERN	50.84	30.29	0.10	14.44	1.08	0.51	2.74	$414.8
Aetna	45.17	30.59	5.42	9.47	0.87	3.12	5.36	128.5
Equitable	18.08	58.56	2.74	14.75	3.20	0.86	1.81	611.8
John Hancock	49.94	36.34	0.22	7.52	1.61	0.81	3.56	171.3
Metropolitan	35.85	48.37	0.95	7.24	3.50	0.31	3.78	775.3
Mutual Benefit	40.67	36.65	0.01	16.10	1.13	0.85	4.59	253.5
Mutual Life	15.75	63.17	3.93	12.99	2.59	0.33	1.24	675.6
New York Life	16.69	61.39	0.01	15.59	1.35	2.11	2.85	995.1
Penn Mutual	36.82	41.86	0.21	15.74	1.09	0.41	3.87	206.8
Prudential	23.08	61.14	0.70	7.15	3.42	1.27	3.24	571.5
Average:	25.42	54.91	1.42	12.04	2.42	1.06	2.73	$480.4

SOURCE: *Annual Statement*, Northwestern Mutual Life Insurance Company, 1908, 1912, 1915, 1918. Other companies: *Fiftieth, Fifty-Fourth, Fifty-Seventh,* and *Sixtieth Annual Report of the Superintendent of Insurance of New York.*

TABLE XII-2

Ten Largest United States Life Insurance Companies:
Distribution of Bond Investments, 1908–1918
(As a Percentage of Total Bonds Owned)

COMPANY	U. S., FEDERAL	FOREIGN	CANADIAN	U. S. A., MUNICIPAL	RAIL-ROAD	PUBLIC UTILITY	INDUSTRIAL & MISC.	TOTAL BONDS
				(1908)				(In Millions)
NORTHWESTERN	0.2	-0-	-0-	11.1	88.7	-0-	-0-	$74.8
Aetna	0.4	1.9	17.2	15.3	54.1	7.5	3.5	24.1
Equitable	-0-	3.9	1.3	1.4	84.1	6.1	3.1	218.1
John Hancock	-0-	-0-	-0-	23.0	74.6	2.5	-0-	28.8
Metropolitan	-0-	-0-	6.2	1.8	64.7	21.6	5.6	94.4
Mutual Benefit	0.3	-0-	-0-	10.8	83.4	5.1	0.5	33.6
Mutual Life	-0-	5.6	1.3	2.0	80.0	4.9	6.2	247.0
New York Life	0.3	11.0	1.4	7.9	76.6	1.5	2.2	377.5
Penn Mutual	-0-	-0-	-0-	9.7	60.0	24.1	6.3	37.3
Prudential	0.1	-0-	-0-	12.6	65.1	19.5	2.8	94.5
				(1912)				
NORTHWESTERN	0.1	-0-	-0-	12.8	87.0	-0-	-0-	$85.0
Aetna	0.4	1.7	15.4	25.6	46.0	1.8	9.1	27.6
Equitable	-0-	4.7	1.1	7.4	79.8	5.3	1.4	273.6
John Hancock	-0-	-0-	-0-	19.9	78.3	1.8	-0-	37.4
Metropolitan	-0-	-0-	4.3	5.5	64.7	23.4	2.2	169.7
Mutual Benefit	0.2	-0-	-0-	11.1	84.5	3.8	0.4	42.2
Mutual Life	-0-	4.7	0.9	2.6	81.2	4.3	6.3	309.4
New York Life	-0-	10.5	0.7	10.0	76.6	1.6	0.7	436.2
Penn Mutual	-0-	-0-	-0-	15.4	58.0	19.4	7.2	49.7
Prudential	0.1	-0-	1.0	8.6	54.9	13.5	2.0	160.0
				(1915)				
NORTHWESTERN	0.1	-0-	-0-	12.8	87.1	-0-	0.0	$93.9
Aetna	0.4	1.5	18.3	28.0	43.9	7.1	0.8	29.0
Equitable	-0-	4.1	2.8	6.2	80.2	6.1	0.6	285.1
John Hancock	-0-	-0-	-0-	27.4	70.6	2.0	-0-	45.1
Metropolitan	-0-	-0-	6.9	5.7	67.4	17.5	2.5	222.7
Mutual Benefit	0.2	-0-	-0-	9.5	86.5	3,4	0.4	46.2
Mutual Life	-0-	5.3	1.1	3.6	80.7	3.9	5.4	344.4
New York Life	-0-	12.7	1.9	11.3	72.1	1.4	0.6	483.2
Penn Mutual	-0-	-0-	-0-	17.9	59.9	14.8	7.4	56.4
Prudential	0.1	-0-	1.7	9.3	72.9	14.5	1.5	210.6
				(1918)				
NORTHWESTERN	11.9	-0-	2.3	13.9	72.0	-0-	0.0	$125.8
Aetna	18.5	1.4	15.0	27.2	31.5	5.7	0.8	39.3
Equitable	16.5	5.3	4.8	3.8	63.2	5.8	0.5	358.3
John Hancock	17.8	-0-	-0-	25.3	53.6	3.4	-0-	62.2
Metropolitan	14.3	0.0	8.4	3.9	59.3	12.2	1.9	375.0
Mutual Benefit	40.9	-0-	-0-	4.2	53.0	1.8	1.2	92.9
Mutual Life	14.9	5.4	0.7	2.6	69.4	3.1	4.0	426.8
New York Life	11.4	15.9	2.5	10.2	57.6	2.1	0.3	610.8
Penn Mutual	23.1	-0-	-0-	14.2	47.1	10.2	5.4	86.6
Prudential	23.6	-0-	2.4	7.7	53.2	11.0	2.2	349.4

NOTES: -0- signifies absolutely no holding; 0.0 signifies holding of less than 0.045 per cent.

SOURCE: *Annual Statement*, Northwestern Mutual Life Insurance Company, 1908, 1912, 1915, 1918. Other companies: *Fiftieth, Fifty-Fourth, Fifty-Seventh* and *Sixtieth Annual Report of the Superintendent of Insurance of New York*.

clear that Mutual Life, John Hancock, Metropolitan, Aetna, and Penn Mutual were important mortgage lenders. Of these Aetna, Mutual Benefit, and John Hancock greatly expanded their farm loans during the period; all three in fact were aggressive lenders in the territories formerly almost exclusively dominated by Northwestern. The urban lending of the Eastern companies, however, remained largely concentrated in the metropolitan areas of the New England and Middle-Atlantic states.

The most striking difference between Northwestern's investment holdings and those of a number of its principal rivals was in the composition of security investments. Table XII-2 shows that while railroads dominated the bond holdings of all companies several, especially Metropolitan, Penn Mutual, and Prudential, invested substantial amounts in public utilities. These holdings were chiefly bonds of gas and electric power and light companies, considered by the managements of the purchasers as sound investments. The other major difference was in the field of foreign bonds. Of those companies making foreign investments New York Life was most heavily committed, owning securities not only of governments and municipalities, but also bonds of railroad companies, including those in Russia.

On the whole the Northwestern investment managers had little reason to question the soundness of their policies and showed no inclination to follow the example of other companies in entering new investment fields. Even though the Company was permitted under legislation passed in 1917 to acquire public utility bonds, no purchases were made.[14] In part this may have been the result of large purchases of government bonds, but more basically it represented a wait-and-see attitude.

Although Northwestern expanded its assets impressively from $232.8 million in 1907 to $414.8 million at the close of 1918, the Company failed to

maintain its relative ranking among the largest companies in the industry. As shown in the tabulation below, Northwestern, measured by assets owned, was fourth in 1907; in 1918 it stood sixth, having been passed by Metropolitan and Prudential.[15]

| COMPANY | 1907 | | 1918 | |
	ASSETS	RANK	ASSETS	RANK
	(In millions)			
Northwestern	$232.8	4	$414.8	6
Aetna	86.4	9	149.6	10
Mutual Benefit	111.8	7	253.5	7
Penn Mutual	89.6	8	206.8	8
Equitable	427.3	3	611.8	4
Mutual Life	494.2	2	675.6	3
New York Life	494.4	1	995.1	1
John Hancock	48.1	10	171.3	9
Metropolitan	198.3	5	775.3	2
Prudential	145.2	6	571.5	5

The total investment of the industry was also increasing over these years at a slightly greater rate than were those of the Company, rising from $3.05 billion in 1907 to $6.47 billion in 1918.

In general the Company's investment earning record for the 1908–1918 period confirmed the effectiveness of the management's investment policies. (See Table XII-3.) While the 4.93 per cent average was slightly lower than the 5 per cent achieved for the entire twenty-six years 1882–1907, it was above the 4.76 per cent earned for the ten years 1896–1907.

The management was not especially concerned by the fact that compared with the ten largest companies Northwestern stood sixth in the rate of interest earned on investments; the marginal differences between it and the top five companies were small. Of primary importance was the feeling, based on long experience, that the security of the Company's loans had not been sacrificed for the sake of higher returns that could prove illusory.

The Resignation of President Markham

There were good reasons why President Markham should have thought of retiring at the end of 1918. At the age of seventy-five he could look back over twenty-four years of association with the Company and a record as president that compared favor-

TABLE XII-3

Ten Largest United States Life Insurance Companies: Average Investment Earning Rates, 1908–1918

COMPANY	RATE	COMPANY	RATE
John Hancock	5.10%	Northwestern	4.93%
Aetna	5.03	Prudential	4.74
Penn Mutual	5.03	Mutual Life	4.70
Mutual Benefit	4.96	Equitable	4.57
Metropolitan	4.95	New York Life	4.57

SOURCE: Derived from data in *Insurance Year Book*, 1919, 292.

ably with his distinguished predecessor. Yet there is little question that his retirement was hastened, if not forced, by criticism that arose out of the purchases of mortgages from the Markham and May Company during 1916–1917.

Attention was first drawn to these purchases during the course of a regular examination of the Company in 1917 by the insurance departments of Wisconsin, New York, Illinois, Missouri, and Minnesota. It was noted that the mortgages were on farm properties located in the peninsula country of Michigan and Wisconsin (territory in which the Company did not regularly loan), and that some of the papers connected with the mortgages had not been properly filed or the assignments recorded. The fact that one of the partners of Markham and May, Stuart Markham, was the oldest son of the president and a Northwestern trustee appeared suspicious to the examiners. They found, upon the basis of an independent sample appraisal of the Company's mortgages, that those obtained through Markham and May had been overvalued.[16] At the request of the other examining states the Wisconsin department was asked to make a full investigation of the Markham and May mortgages, including appraisals of the security and inquiry into the nature of the brokerage firm.

The Wisconsin report, prepared by Commissioner Michael J. Cleary, clearly refuted the implied criticism in the original report. The reasons Northwestern purchased the mortgages, according to Markham and other officers, were primarily political. The Company had not previously loaned to farmers in the peninsula region and, as the commissioner stated,

> This policy has been the subject of comment and adverse criticism by newspapers located in the State. Members of the legislature from that section have made this policy the subject of comment and threatened retaliation. The insurance company defended its policy upon the grounds that the loans were small and desirable property was widely scattered, making the expense of direct loaning prohibitive. According to testimony offered in the investigation of this subject, the fact is disclosed that this criticism from the newspapers and legislative representatives was persistent at about the time the 1917 session of the legislature in Wisconsin was convened. The officers of the insurance company at that time, wishing to meet the demand of this territory and avoid if possible harmful criticism, even adverse legislation, took up the subject with the Mark-

ham and May Company. . . . Out of this discussion and negotiation the purchase of these loans resulted.[17]

A discrepancy of 1 per cent lower interest charges, according to the commissioner, arose because certain services were being provided by Markham and May, and of course there was a brokerage fee. The commissioner did not believe the 1 per cent excessive.[18]

Since the original examination had questioned the valuations of the properties securing the Markham and May mortgages, the Wisconsin department conducted independent appraisals of the properties. The earlier appraisal had been made during the winter, when the snow conditions made it impossible to determine the character of the soil or the condition of the area. The commissioner submitted a sample of seven properties, all of which originally were estimated to be in violation of the Wisconsin law requiring loans to be no greater than 50 per cent of the appraised value of property. In each case of this sample, the report stated, as well as in all other cases, "all of these loans are amply secured."[19]

The commissioner's report made it clear that there was no basis for the suggestion that the purchases of mortgages from the Markham and May Company involved a financial sacrifice to Northwestern. But this was not enough to offset the growing dissatisfaction on the part of a number of trustees with the administration of the president.* The fact that the insurance commissioners of five important states had raised the question at all brought some unfavorable publicity to the Company. Some felt that, like Caesar's wife, the president of Northwestern Mutual should be above suspicion; that in authorizing the purchases from his son's company without clearing them through the Finance Committee, Markham had violated the spirit of trusteeship so proudly defended during the Wisconsin investigation of 1906. Pressure for his resignation mounted.

It was not in character for Markham to accept this situation without a fight; and he was not without friends among the trustees and others closely associated with the Company. Had Markham been ten years younger he would have met the challenge, but the prospect of internal turmoil that could well bring further adverse publicity to the Company was repugnant to him. In December 1918 he resigned and retired to California where, in 1930, he died at the age of eighty-six.

---

* No specific bill of complaints was drawn up, but conversation with several of Markham's fellow officers suggest the nature of this discontent.

CHAPTER THIRTEEN

Facing Prosperity and Depression: Insurance, Sales, and Sales Management, 1919-1932

URING the years 1919–1932 the American economy experienced the full gamut of prosperity and depression. Following the feverish post-war boom of 1919–1920 business toppled into the slump of 1921, then recovered quickly and maintained a high plateau of prosperity through 1929. From 1930 through the end of the period economic activity contracted at an accelerating pace into what became the most disastrous depression in the country's history.

National income varied directly with the general level of economic activity, with an over-all increase during the 1919–1929 decade of from $64.2 billion to $87.2 billion. During the three years of depression, however, national income fell to a mere $41.7 billion. The changes in per capita income corresponded closely with those occurring in the economy generally. Population increased from 105 million to nearly 125 million over the period, a rate of growth substantially slower than that of income. As a result per capita income rose from $610 in 1919 to $715 in 1929; by 1932 it had sagged to only $334.

The national economic prosperity was fully shared by the life insurance industry, where the volume of sales was unprecedented. In the eleven years ending 1929, 284 new companies were organized and 141 went out of business, leaving 438 life companies in the United States by 1930 compared to 295 in 1919.[1] The influx of new entries into the industry was largely a function of the tremendous volume of insurance sold; during the years ending with 1929 more than $140 billion of insurance was marketed, increasing the total in force from around $36 billion to over $103 billion.[2] Assets owned by the industry rose by almost as great a proportion, from about $6.5 billion in 1918 to nearly $17.5 in 1929. The growth in the popularity of life insurance was much greater than that which occurred in population or in national income. Per capita insurance in force in the United States was about $340 in 1918; by 1929 it exceeded $800. In 1919 the total premiums paid to United States life companies were $1.2 billion, almost 1.7 per cent of national income; in 1929 premiums were $3.3 billion, equal to 3.8 per cent of national income. In fact, during the eleven years 1919–1929 life insurance sales exceeded by 35 per cent the total insurance marketed during the fifty-nine years ending in 1918.

The economic debacle after 1929 did not spare the life insurance industry. During the years 1930–1932 the number of firms in the industry was reduced from 438 to 392. While only fifty-one new companies entered the field, ninety-seven failed or were absorbed by other firms; losses to policyholders, however, were negligible.[3] The depression had equally serious effects upon the members of the industry which survived 1932. While the market still absorbed over $48 billion of insurance between 1929 and the end of 1932, total insurance in force remained virtually unchanged because of the rapid rise in lapsed and surrendered policies.

The effects of business depression were as grave for the investment policies and operations of life insurance companies as they were for their underwriting and marketing programs. After 1929 opportunities for successful investment dwindled to a trickle while at the same time managements faced mounting problems of foreclosure, property management, and the general preservation of asset values. As the depression deepened the increasing demand for cash by policyholders placed the life companies under new and perilous strains.

Northwestern had reason to be proud of its record during past fluctuations in the American economy; the challenge to the new management was unmistakable: how skillfully could it operate a life company possessing distinctive sales and investment policies during a period marked by unprecedented extremes of prosperity and depression.

The Management Structure

There was no question concerning who would succeed George C. Markham as president of Northwestern, for even before Markham's resignation the qualifications of William D. Van Dyke were recognized by the trustees. On January 29, 1919, the Board officially elected him chief executive. Van Dyke, sixty-two years of age at the time, possessed a remarkable constitution and great powers for concentrated effort. He firmly subscribed to the fundamental conservatism of Northwestern's underwriting and investment philosophy, and was thereby a lineal descendant of Palmer and Markham.[4]

In other respects, however, Van Dyke contrasted sharply with his immediate predecessor. If Markham had been devoted to the Company, the new president, according to one observer, "was a zealot on its behalf . . . [who] could not have been more fervent had his obsession been a religious one."[5] In a most literal sense Northwestern was his life; he rarely took a vacation, was among the first to arrive at the Home Office mornings and among the last to leave at night. By virtue of family background and the prestige of his office Van Dyke occupied a secure place in the upper stratum of Milwaukee society, but he engaged in no political or fraternal activity.

In temperament Van Dyke was cautious and investigative; he also tended to view events and propositions in terms of black or white: "That which was not altogether right in his estimation was altogether wrong."[6] In addition to this pronounced sense of right and wrong and a pervading consciousness of grave responsibility, Van Dyke had definite

William D. Van Dyke

convictions concerning the management of the Company. One was that the staff was to be used to a limited degree; he relied principally upon his own personal investigations and the counsel of a select group of associates to provide the basis for decisions. Another was that he insisted on holding the reins of authority in his own hands, delegating responsibility sparingly. While the desire to participate personally in all aspects of the Company's business was admirable, its execution was suited to a smaller organization; with nine or ten heads of departments reporting to him directly, the administrative and coordinating tasks of the president were vastly multiplied.

Like Markham, Van Dyke's particular interest was in finance and investment; he was, however, more engrossed in insurance and agency matters, an area where he felt more qualified than his predecessor because of his interest in insurance law and his earlier work with the Insurance and Agency Committee. His contributions in this field (the application of a standardized system of general agency accounting over the whole field organization, steadfast resistance to a market expansion that could be purchased only by what he regarded as an unwarranted increase in acquisition costs, and firm adherence to traditional Northwestern underwriting principles) were a logical extension of his personal attributes and characteristics. His associations with his colleagues in the Home Office were marked by courtesy and kindness, within the framework of formal dignity. Although this gentlemanly courtesy was also extended to the field force it was difficult for him to convey to the agents any sense of personal warmth and enthusiasm.

The Structure and Composition of Executive Management

Soon after his election to the presidency Van Dyke recommended several changes in the Northwestern management structure, and obtained the appointment of a highly qualified insurance vice president. Thereafter, during his administration, changes among the top management personnel occurred only as a result of retirement, death, and the need to provide specialized skills in the field of investment. (See Table XIII-1).

Foremost on the priority list was the need for an insurance vice president of proven experience and ability. James M. Skinner had been the last Northwestern insurance vice president, and since his death in 1913 this gap in the organization had been growing steadily more apparent. To fill the post a special committee, composed of the president and two trustees, carefully screened the qualifications of many able persons before ultimately recommending the appointment of Michael J. Cleary, then Wisconsin's commissioner of insurance. On the basis of his experience and reputation in life insurance Cleary offered all that the management could desire. He had been a member of the insurance committee in the Wisconsin state assembly which had systematized the flood of insurance bills in 1907 into basic legislation, and had served as insurance commissioner since 1915. His extensive knowledge of life insurance and warm personal leadership in the National Association of Insurance Commissioners had won him election as president of that body in 1918. Cleary was elected a Northwestern vice president in April 1919.

Following a thorough examination of the Company's organizational needs the Executive Committee endorsed Van Dyke's recommendation that no more than two trustees be Northwestern officers, employees, or agents. This action, approved by the Board in July 1919, was a significant departure from tradition in the Company, and was taken to termi-

TABLE XIII-1

Northwestern Mutual: Executive Officers, 1919–1932

PRESIDENT
William D. Van Dyke, 1919-1932

VICE-PRESIDENTS
P. R. Sanborn (Mortgage Loan) 1919-1932
Michael J. Cleary (Insurance) 1919-1932
Frederick W. Walker (Bond) 1926-1932
Percy H. Evans (Actuary) 1929-1932

GENERAL COUNSEL
George Lines, 1919-1929
Sam T. Swansen, 1930-1932

ACTUARY
Percy H. Evans, 1919-1932

SECRETARY
A. S. Hathaway, 1919-1923
Evan D. Jones, 1923-1932

MEDICAL DIRECTOR
John W. Fisher, M.D., 1919-1932

SUPERINTENDENT OF AGENCIES
George C. Copeland, 1919-1925
Charles H. Parsons, 1925-1932

COMPTROLLER
Shepard E. Barry, 1932

nate a situation wherein officers would be placed in the position of judging their own performance. Furthermore, in an institution which prided itself upon being the "policyholders' company," it was sound policy to guarantee that the ultimate control of Northwestern reside in the hands of policyholders who were not members of the official staff. The timing of the move minimized the embarrassment which could have resulted from numerous resignations. Only Percy H. Evans had to surrender his Board membership; P. R. Sanborn continued as the second member of the staff on the Board.

At this same time the Board also approved two other Van Dyke recommendations designed to provide more effective administration of the Company. The first of these formally created a bond department, effectively separating the basic investment functions; the second clarified the titular designations of the executive and middle strata of management and more specifically defined their functions.

The core of the executive organization which served Van Dyke during the fourteen years of his administration was inherited from his predecessor. Of the five officers of executive rank thus acquired three continued their responsibilities throughout this period. These were P. R. Sanborn, Percy H.

Evans, and Dr. John W. Fisher. The other two, George C. Copeland and A. S. Hathaway, were replaced before 1926. Copeland, who resigned, was succeeded by Charles H. Parsons, whose long experience as Northwestern agent and general agent particularly qualified him to head the agency department. Evan D. Jones, a career employee with long service in the secretarial department, replaced Hathaway, who died in 1923. Jones directed the complex and growing functions of his department with a smooth and quiet efficiency which contributed much to the Company's ability to serve competently policyholder and administrative demands at modest cost.

The second major gap which the new president had to fill immediately was that of general counsel, vacant since the death of Judge Barnes on January 1, 1919. To succeed Barnes the management departed from the tradition of selecting an eminent jurist when it appointed George Lines. Lines, sixty-five years old, was a member of a prominent Milwaukee law firm, with forty years of corporation law experience in Wisconsin and the District of Columbia. In this respect, of all those who had occupied the office, he was probably the best equipped to serve the requirements of a large and growing enterprise such as Northwestern. Lines delegated departmental responsibility shrewdly, initiated the practice of regular weekly meetings with his assistants, and brought his entire unit to a high level of efficiency.

Over the remaining years of his administration Van Dyke directed the Company's activities with only three further changes in executive personnel. Frederick W. Walker joined Northwestern in 1926 to manage its bond investment program; and the death of George Lines in late 1929 resulted in the appointment of Sam T. Swansen as his successor. Swansen had entered Northwestern service as assistant to Judge Barnes, and was the first Company general counsel to gain this position by promotion from within. In 1929 the actuary, Percy H. Evans, was elected a vice president. In 1932 the Examining Committee recommended the appointment of a comptroller for the Company, and the first occupant of this new post was Shepard E. Barry, who had been assistant to the president since 1928.

Underwriting and Agencies: Management Policies

It was consistent with Van Dyke's interpretation of the functions of a chief executive that throughout his administration he involved himself directly

in all phases of underwriting and agency management. To a much greater extent than had been true in the past Van Dyke assumed the responsibility for coordinating the activities of the Insurance and Agency Committee by having each member report personally to him. He also played the leading role in the formulation of the major policy decisions affecting these phases of the Company's business.

This procedure, especially as it involved coordination of the activities of committee members, placed a heavy burden on the chief executive, a burden that might have been delegated to the newly appointed insurance vice president. Fortunately, however, Van Dyke had an able, even brilliant, group of underwriting and insurance officers to draw upon for advice and counsel. Nor did this procedure impede Cleary's development into an excellent insurance officer. He not only acted as advisor and counselor to the president on insurance and underwriting questions, but became absorbed in the operations of the Company's field force and developed a deep and sympathetic understanding for the problems confronting the agents.

The Company was fortunate that Cleary demonstrated the same sure touch in performing his new duties as he had in his earlier career. He was vitally interested in the need for better education and training of life insurance agents; and he was impressed with the contributions in this area being made by the newly founded Carnegie School of Practical Insurance Salesmanship and later in the work of the American College of Life Underwriters. He persuaded President Van Dyke of the need for a more systematic program of training Northwestern agents, including the establishment of a training division in the Home Office. Cleary was also a firm advocate of the district agency method of developing large territories; his enthusiasm and ability to win cooperation positively affected the great expansion of the district agency plan during this period.

Cleary's sympathy for the field force, and his belief that they should be provided with "a full kit" of selling tools and methods to enable them to market Northwestern insurance more effectively, did not include the surrender of strong convictions and principles. Like the president and the actuary he refused to yield to expediency on such matters as disability income and double indemnity benefits.

One of the principal policy questions that had to be resolved during these years was how best to adapt the Company's insurance and selling program to meet the challenge of a rapidly expanding market and the competition of rival insurance companies. Within the life insurance industry after 1918 there was a continued emphasis upon contract features such as disability income and double indemnity, an increase in the tendencies to merchandise plans, and the development of so-called "special" policies and extra dividends. In terms of the agency organization, the industry made more effective provision for the training of solicitors, devised means of "programming" the life insurance needs of prospects, and experimented with methods and techniques of sales organization and management. Group life insurance, only four years old in 1919, developed rapidly during these years; with sales of over $13 billion, the amount of group insurance in force increased from $630 million to over $9.9 billion between 1918 and the end of 1931. As had been true in the previous decade, the companies which enjoyed the greatest market growth and sold the greatest volume of life insurance were those combining two or more "lines" of contracts, group and ordinary or industrial and ordinary; occasionally they combined a life business with health and accident or casualty coverage.

With most of these rapidly growing firms which, because of the complexity of their operations and marketing expenses, could not offer low "net cost" policies, Northwestern rarely came into direct competition. The Company's most formidable-competition came from rivals that followed more conservative practices or combined simplicity of operations with merchandising and special feature selling.

In the light of Northwestern's experience during the years following the Armstrong investigation none of the insurance and agency executives had reason to consider any basic alterations in the Company's underwriting and marketing framework. There were, however, some differences of opinion within the managerial hierarchy regarding the volume of insurance which Northwestern should sell during these years. Certain officers, including Cleary, evidently believed that without surrendering any essential part of its underwriting and operating principles the Company could obtain a much greater share of the ordinary life insurance market. Since the national prosperity of the 1920's was benefiting the men in the income and occupational strata which Northwestern regarded as its natural market, on a scale at least proportionate to the whole society, these arguments had much to support them. These insurance and agency officers were convinced that a more intensive exploitation of sales territories by a larger force of agents, better trained and with greater promotional support from the Company, could accomplish this end.

Other members of management, particularly the president, viewed the vastly expanding insurance markets of the period somewhat less enthusiastically. Van Dyke questioned both the soundness and the permanence of the wave of prosperity that lay behind the expansion of insurance sales during the 1920's, and he was reluctant to undertake any special steps to expand the selling effort.

Until the mid-1920's Van Dyke's judgment prevailed, and a respectable volume of sales was produced without special stimuli or substantial augmentation of the field force. George C. Copeland, the incumbent superintendent of agencies, was well qualified to carry out this program. Industrious, devoted, and thoroughly ingrained in Northwestern tradition, he tended to interpret his functions rather narrowly. He was satisfied with the system as he had known it, did not regard the assumption of responsibility for agent training by the Company with much enthusiasm, and concerned himself largely with the details of administration and the application of modest changes in supervisory techniques.

Copeland resigned in 1925. After a thorough canvass of the field, Charles H. Parsons was appointed his successor. Although there might have been some reservation as to the advisability of assigning so demanding a post to a man nearly sixty-five years of age, there could be few doubts regarding Parsons' qualifications. He had spent most of his adult life as a member of Northwestern's field force, first as a special agent, then as a successful general agent. A leader in the General Agents' Association and the Association of Agents, Parsons knew the problems and needs of the field intimately. Genial, and a strong advocate of the Company's principles and methods of doing business (all important attributes for a sales manager), he had the sympathy of the men in the field.

When he became superintendent of agencies on November 1, 1925, Parsons' comments gave promise of some fresh and welcome responses to the new era of competition in the industry, while retaining the basic foundations of Company principles. He observed that,

Supremacy in the field of competition depends upon the character of the men who make up the field force. The growth and expansion of the business has been great, but its future possibilities are yet beyond our imagination. No field has as yet been developed to anything like its possibilities. More men than ever are inquiring what the business of life insurance has to offer, yet the outstanding need is manpower. It is no longer so much a problem of finding agents, as one of better selection, equipment, and training.[7]

During the first few years of his tenure of office Parsons displayed concrete evidences of real leadership. He urged an accelerated program of induction upon the general agencies and the number of agents under contract perceptibly increased. He added to the ranks of middle management in his department, brought the educational division under his aegis, and obtained a more systematic and efficient operation. In cooperation with the secretary a standardized system of audits and administrative procedures was introduced throughout the general agencies. In 1927–1928, in collaboration with M. J. Cleary, he devised methods for implementing the desire for greater production. When applied in 1929 this program included the establishment of territorial and individual agent quotas, and the provision of accurate and pertinent information to agencies regarding the market potentials of the regions in which they were located. Parsons' appointment laid the groundwork for an increased sales effort and for better relations with the field.

Insurance Plans and Underwriting Standards

Whatever the differences among the members of the insurance and agency group over the extent to which new sales of insurance should be pushed, they fully agreed that Northwestern should continue its conservative underwriting policies. This position was maintained in the face of growing experimentation by a large portion of the industry with contract merchandising and new appeals to insurance prospects that had begun during the previous decade. Essentially, such merchandising was undertaken by life companies in response to demands from the field for contracts which could be sold to fit one or several of the insurance needs of prospects. In this class belonged income-maintenance, family income, modified life, and term-expectancy policies. In addition, certain companies, principally those which combined industrial and ordinary life insurance, began to promote "preferred risk" or "special" contracts of the type that had originated before 1910. The logic of the "special" policies for such companies stemmed from the fact that most of their sales of ordinary insurance were produced by industrial insurance agents. Since the conventional market for industrial insurance was confined largely to

occupational groups with modest incomes, the average size of the ordinary insurance contracts sold by these agents was considerably lower than those sold by ordinary companies. As the unit costs of small face amount policies were typically higher than those of larger sized contracts, these companies found themselves unable to compete effectively for the larger sized policies. To overcome this competitive disadvantage they attempted to "wall off" their large policies and emerged with the "special." By requiring the payment of annual premiums and by paying lower commissions to agents, they were able to offer these special policies at rates that were frequently below the premium rates charged by purely ordinary competitors.

While not a form of contract competition, it was during this period also that the life insurance industry received its first experience with so-called extra or special dividends. These posed a problem that threatened to get out of hand after 1932. After 1906 the New York insurance department permitted life companies to distribute extra dividends to policyholders so long as such disbursements did not recur regularly. This ruling enabled company managers, from time to time, to reduce surpluses from levels which exceeded the statutory maximum of 10 per cent of policy reserves, or which were considered unnecessarily high. The New York insurance officials did not object if the "irregular" intervals coincided with the termination of policies by death, surrender, or maturity.[8] When attention was called to the practice of one large competitor of calculating such terminal dividends into estimates of costs of insurance to prospects, Company officers strongly suspected that something more than a rational adjustment in accumulated surplus was involved. In 1928 Percy H. Evans replied to one of the Company's district agents, who had protested the use of this type of promotion, that there was nothing to "justify the practice of maintaining a minimum dividend scale and supplementing it by periodical special dividends because such practice creates what is in effect a tontine fund."[9] A tontine fund, of course, was illegal, but the New York insurance department, which had to decide between attempts at illegal subterfuge and legitimate adjustments in surplus accumulations, did not see it as such. Northwestern insurance agents desired some competitive measure to counter extra-dividend estimates in the market, but the management stayed with the straightforward annual distributions.

In the face of these developments Northwestern made only modest changes in its policy contracts and insurance plans. The management was convinced of the competitive superiority of the option settlement features of its standard contracts. It believed these could meet the newly recognized needs for income replacement rather more satisfactorily than the so-called income contracts of other companies. The size of the premium units of its outstanding contracts was eminently satisfactory since all insurance had been sold on a quarterly, or longer, premium basis and the Company's acquisition and servicing costs were among the lowest in the industry. Under such circumstances the management felt no compulsion to offer preferred risk "specials," or to extend the number of its insurance plans unless new life insurance needs of sufficient importance arose to require such addition.*

Only five new insurance plans were added to the Company's series during this period. In 1919 two new limited payment life policies were introduced: one for twenty-five years, the other for thirty years. In 1930 a special retirement endowment at age sixty-five was offered, and two years later a similar contract was introduced, effective at age sixty. The Company also issued a five-year convertible term plan.

The special retirement endowment policies deserve particular attention because of their importance in the development of Northwestern's huge employee pension trust business in the late 1930's and thereafter. Designed to provide retirement income, the principal change between these contracts and the standard endowment at sixty-five policies was an increase in premiums which was necessary to provide a minimum guaranteed life income of $10 per month per thousand of the face amount of the policy.

In its efforts to meet the needs of prospects for life insurance more satisfactorily, Northwestern also made certain adjustments in its optional settlements. In 1922, for example, provision was made whereby insureds could elect monthly as well as quarterly or annual installments in the settlement of policy proceeds under all three options. In September 1932 a fourth settlement option was introduced which was also geared to income needs by offering

payment in monthly installments. Under this option the insured could elect that all or any portion of the value of the policy at time of settlement be retained by the Company at 3 per cent interest, payment to be made in fixed amounts until the fund was exhausted.

From 1919 until 1932 there was a moderate but steady liberalization of the Company's insurance contracts. In 1919 the suicide and aviation clauses restricted the Company's obligation to a return of the reserve value only in the event of the insured's death during the first policy year as a result of suicide or aviation accident. In 1930 the aviation clause was stricken from the contract. With the introduction of the new policy series in 1922 policy loans were somewhat liberalized as a result of the increase in cash value, as was the cash surrender benefit. On surrenders the charge per $1,000 face amount, after payment of the second annual premium, was reduced; and the time during which the Company could exact surrender charges was shortened. In 1932, however, when the effects of depression had greatly increased the number of surrenders and the costs of such transactions, the charge was again increased and the penalty period lengthened. The Company's practice of charging extra premiums in the case of particular occupations was discontinued on new policy issues beginning September 1, 1925.[11] Twelve years later Northwestern discontinued such extra premiums for all outstanding policies.

The 1932 policy series tightened other features of the Northwestern contracts. The suicide period was lengthened from one to two years, as was the incontestability period. Cash surrender values were reduced from the second through the ninth policy years, while the first-year dividend was made contingent upon and proportionate to premiums due and paid for the second policy year. The period of presumption of total and permanent disability, following the tightening of state legislation, was increased to six months. Two years earlier Northwestern had increased the amount of the extra premium charged for the disability waiver privilege.

As the tendency toward issuing larger amounts of insurance on a single life accelerated during the 1920's, Northwestern limits also went up, but not to the same extent as those of many of its competitors. Between 1918 and 1929 the single life limit was increased from $100,000 to $150,000, then raised again to $250,000. In the meantime the agents persistently demanded that the lower and upper age limits on risks be modified so as to make more prospects eligible for Northwestern insurance. As a result of

---

* There was no question, for example, regarding the dominant position Northwestern held with respect to the amount of its business which carried optional settlement of proceeds. In 1941, long after other companies had emulated Northwestern in featuring option settlements, the Company had about 16 per cent of all the life income options in effect among the industry.[10] During the 1920's, as a result of its pioneering and strong sales emphasis, the proportion would have been much higher. The fact was that the management believed strongly that the merchandising activities of rivals were undertaken to attempt to reduce Northwestern's advantages in the ordinary insurance market.

these demands in 1924–1925, the Company reduced the lower age limit to fifteen years and increased the upper limit from age sixty to age sixty-five. Although agents pressed for a further reduction in the lower age limit, President Van Dyke was unwilling to go below age fifteen.

During these years the management continued to resist the pressure from the field to adopt disability income and double indemnity features. In 1921 the Executive Committee, in response to requests from agents, asked Actuary Percy H. Evans to study the experience other companies had with insuring women. Basing his conclusion on the relatively unfavorable mortality and lapse experience of other companies, and the indication that the market for women would be less than 5 per cent of that for men, Evans recommended that Northwestern continue to refuse insurance to women. Much to the annoyance of the agents this recommendation was endorsed by management.

Northwestern's management resisted excessive contract merchandising with good reason. What its members were attempting was the orientation of the agency force to the strength of conservative underwriting and the principle of simple market operation. A fair summary of this position was given to a member of the Policyholders' Examining Committee in 1926 by Charles H. Parsons:

> There is no doubt but that the introduction of these things [merchandising features and special benefits] has made it harder for the agents of this Company to obtain business; but there is no doubt also but that the position of the Company, when known to its policyholders, will be greatly strengthened because of its courage in refusing to do things that other companies are doing for the sake of increased volume.[12]

Market Territory and Size and Structure of Field Force

Except for certain minor modifications in the states within which the Company had previously done business, the boundaries of Northwestern's geographical market remained unchanged. The Company accepted no business from the Gulf States or the coastal areas of the south Atlantic region; nor did it market insurance in the lowlands bordering the Mississippi River in Arkansas, southern Missouri, Kentucky, and Tennessee. Within the traditional limits of its market, however, the geo-

graphical center continued its slow shift toward the West.*

During the Van Dyke administration the basic structure of the Company's field organization remained virtually unchanged. The number of general agencies varied within a modest range, the minimum in any given year being eighty-five, the maximum eighty-nine. The personnel of the general agents' group was also highly stable; of the over one hundred general agents active in 1919 (including partners), forty-one were still under contract in 1932. The principal change in the field organization during this period came after Parsons' appointment and involved a much more intensive utilization of the district agency plan. The number of district agencies was doubled, making possible the increased delegation of responsibility for territorial development from general to district agents. The district agency plan was somewhat more demanding of the administrative and financial resources of general agents, but when intelligently directed usually more than repaid the latter through a larger volume of sales, an increased amount of insurance in force, and thus a larger base for renewal income and collection fees.

In contrast to the number of general agents, the total agency force varied considerably. From 1919 to 1925 the number dropped from 5,843 to less than 5,300. The trend was reversed after 1925, and by the close of 1932 the Company had over 7,000 agents under contract. It should be noted, however, that a substantial portion of this gain occurred after 1929 when reduced employment in other fields caused many men to turn to life insurance selling in desperation.

The number of agents who were classified as devoting full time to life insurance before 1927 is unknown; in that year 2,413 agents, or 43 per cent of the aggregate sales force, were listed as full-time personnel; by 1932 the proportion had increased to 47 per cent, which was probably also a depression effect. It is doubtful, however, that all of the agents who held full-time contracts actually devoted all their attention to life insurance. Company

*	Number of General Agencies	
Geographic Region	1919	1932
New England	9	7
Middle Atlantic	21	17
South Atlantic	5	7
East North Central	23	24
West North Central	15	16
East South Central	3	3
West South Central	2	2
Mountain	5	5
Pacific	6	7
Total	89	88

agency officials estimate that no more than 40 per cent of the total agency force have ever been truly full-time agents. The distribution of special and soliciting agents is not known for these years, but in view of the trend toward district agencies in the rural fields it is probable that the proportion of soliciting agents under contract increased over the whole period.

Other than the infrequent addition and elimination of general agencies, the one important structural change in the agency organization was the modification of the metropolitan New York market in 1931. Prior to 1931 the greater New York City area had been served by three general agencies, each of which had exclusive territorial rights to a particular segment. These agencies were located in Brooklyn; Manhattan; and Newark, New Jersey. The problems of jurisdiction in this market had been painfully evident for some time. With the impending retirement of John I. D. Bristol the management sought to eliminate them by making the metropolitan territory open, without restriction, to the agents of all general agencies in that area. Two general agencies were opened in New York City to replace the Bristol agency; with four general agencies operating in the metropolitan market the Company believed it was getting a maximum development of the territory. This experiment set a precedent for the subsequent establishment of similar programs in other major cities where a more intensive sales effort was believed necessary.

Agent Induction: General Agents

The process of selecting new general agents practiced by Northwestern during this period differed little from that followed during the previous decade. Success in the selection of general agents depended on the skill with which the Home Office diagnosed relative attributes and the response of new general agents to the challenge and opportunity of their jobs. The expansion in the number of district agents did, however, affect the selective process in two ways. First, it put more emphasis on the ability of the general agents to supervise their respective sales organizations; second, it provided a large number of better-qualified candidates from which new general agents could be selected.

Throughout the 1920's there was a trend in the life insurance industry toward larger investment in the training of soliciting agents, including some financial assistance during the beginning stages of their careers. This trend put an added financial burden on general agents, a burden that in many instances had to be shared by the companies with whom they contracted.

While most of Northwestern's general agents followed the practice of their competitors in financing their agents, with few exceptions they had no serious difficulty in providing for the necessary financing without help from the Company. There were several reasons why this was the case. First, the Company infrequently established a new general agency in a new territory, so the newly appointed general agent rarely had to start the agency from scratch. Generally, he inherited a going business with some experienced agents under contract, numerous sources of contacts among existing policyholders, and the reputation of the Company well established in the territory. Second, all general agencies received a collection commission of 2 per cent of premiums on business in their territory which had passed out of the renewal period, plus 1 per cent on business still in the renewal period. These fees were usually sufficient to provide the new general agent with the means of covering such out-of-pocket operating expenses as rent. Even more important, the previous general agent had usually established a line of credit with local banks. Though the Company did not itself guarantee a new general agent's credit, the banks were familiar with the nature of renewal interest as security, a vital element in meeting the financial needs of new general agents.

The solid base on which these advantages rested was the fundamental nature of the Company's general agency operation and its contracts with general agents. The stability of the organization, with relatively large size and good prospects for growth for each general agency, was an integral part of Northwestern's field superiority. The great extent to which renewal commissions were vested with the general agent was of equal importance, and contrasted sharply with the practices of many competitors. To a large extent this practice drew the Company and the general agent into a tighter partnership; it also provided the new general agent with stronger incentives to invest more heavily in his own enterprise, whether with his own or with borrowed capital. Many other companies, with more numerous and correspondingly smaller general agencies and with more limited vesting of renewal commissions, sought alternative solutions. One choice available was the branch-office system, first adopted by New York Life in the 1890's and copied wholly or in part by other companies. Under this method a salaried manager directed the agency, and the company itself provided the financing; soliciting agents, however, were compensated by commission. In still other companies general agents were required to plow non-vested income back into agency development, and the companies underwrote certain other financial requirements. In such organizations, however, the companies themselves controlled the field operation to a much greater degree than was true in a general agency structure like Northwestern's; the general agent or branch manager did not have the same opportunities nor the same incentives.

Not all of Northwestern's new general agents escaped financial difficulties, nor were all successful in the financial administration of their operations. In one instance the agency department reported of a general agent,

> he had started out with $10,000 and that was nearly gone. He had borrowed on his life insurance and secured a mortgage from the Company on his home. . . . He is now trying to sell his home . . . and hopes that the money he will get out of it will tide him over until he reaches a turning point in his agency.[13]

In another instance the Company recognized it had erred in selecting a general agent, but was forced to postpone cancellation of his contract until his bank debt had been materially reduced. The principal reason for the delay was fear of imperiling the credit resources of his successor if the dismissed general agent still had heavy obligations owing at local banks.[14]

Only under exceptional circumstances did the Company directly assist a general agent in financing his operations. In 1922 Salt Lake City bankers were unwilling to extend necessary credit to the resident general agent unless Northwestern waived its right of first claim against his renewal commissions. Unwilling to accede to this demand, the management authorized the general agent to utilize a portion of the premium collections in his territory for the purpose of development. The original amount of this advance was for $5,000 to run for two years—actually the loan was extended for five years and then increased in amount.[15] For different reasons a somewhat similar arrangement was made in 1925 with the newly appointed general agent in Oakland, California.

In extending financial aid to newly recruited solicitors, a procedure used in some general agencies was to "establish a line of credit" after which "advances were made to [him] at an agreed rate; when this line of credit had been exhausted a new look was taken of the progress that had been made."[16] The selection process applied, as well as the "line of credit" advanced to the new agent, however, varied

with the individual general agent. John I. D. Bristol, for example, set very high standards; in 1927 he considered only those candidates having a minimum of $3,000 of cash assets and who gave promise of producing at least $150,000 of business annually.[17] Although not liberal in advancing money to new agents against the security of their renewals, Bristol was more generous in the matter of furnishing office space and services to agents under contract and in giving an extra 5 per cent commission on the first renewal premium. Other general agents were less selective, extended a more liberal line of credit to new men, but applied more restrictions on contract rights and office space privileges.

Although the ability to advance money to newly recruited agents was one of the induction responsibilities of general agents, it was by no means the only one. The general agent's personality, age, experience, and leadership qualities, together with the characteristics of his local market, all played a part. The morale of any agency force varied with these factors, although not in any easily predictable way, and would naturally influence a prospective solicitor. One general agent, liberal in advancing funds to new agents, might have a body of agents under contract whose morale was low; another, more penurious, could have very high agency morale. There was no single determining factor in the situation.

Agent Induction: Selection and Training of the Field Force

The tentative movement of a few general agents and students of life insurance toward providing better selected and educated agents, which had begun during the previous decade, gathered speed and force during the years following 1919. As indicated earlier, the initial impetus for improving the selection and education of agents came from the field. Response by the companies themselves was apparently negligible until late in the 1920's, for as a leading scholar of life insurance marketing has observed, when seeking to enlist the help of home offices the pioneers of the new movement encountered a rather complacent acceptance of things as they were.[18]

The experience of those who pioneered better methods of selection and training gradually forced even the most reluctant home offices to adopt some of these measures. Insurance which was better sold tended to remain longer in force; and the face value of policies sold by well-trained agents was much higher, on the average, than that of unqualified men. These two factors by themselves tended to result in greater earnings from insurance and lower unit costs—vital elements in the success of a company.

Although Northwestern's Home Office agency officers were aware of the new developments taking place in the field of agent selection, until 1925 they remained principally concerned with the selection and supervision of general agents. After that date the agency department acted more vigorously to provide information, and even rating scales and interview forms, to general and district agents to assist them in screening out less desirable candidates for agent contracts.

Even the most advanced techniques of selection, however, fell far short of providing any adequate tests of predetermining the success of candidates as insurance solicitors, and Northwestern's sources of new agents continued to be many and varied. Although a few recruits had previous selling experience in other fields, and a number had previous training with other life companies, most men came into the field force innocent of life insurance or the techniques of its sale. During the period some of the general agents began systematically to recruit recent college graduates or young men still in undergraduate training. In 1922 an agency department officer observed that in the Minneapolis general agency he had,

> been impressed with the large group of very young men. . . . Most of these boys are recent graduates of the University of Minnesota and all seem to be members of a group who were acquainted during their college days. . . . From present indications, practically all of the group . . . will make good.[19]

While the Home Office somewhat feared that this agency had recruited more young college men at one time than were readily assimilable, this was viewed as "certainly an error in the right direction."[20] Most of the other Northwestern general agencies that followed similar patterns were not so aggressive as in the Minnesota example, but they generally profited from the inclusion of better-educated men in the ranks of agents.[21]

With the advent of the great depression Northwestern, like other life companies, was besieged with applications from individuals who had lost jobs in other fields. Of those who obtained contracts with Northwestern general agencies, a considerable number came from investment banking and security brokerage firms. Contrary to what might have been expected of men with this background, these individuals did not, as a group, enjoy much success as life insurance agents.[22] The failure rate, however, applied as severely to engineers and other technically skilled people who tried to make the switch to life insurance soliciting under recession conditions. Such circumstances could hardly provide a fair testing ground for the life insurance sales aptitude of those trained in other occupations.

While it was evident that chance still played an important role in the selection of successful agents, there was a mounting appreciation that the inherent selling talents of those who were chosen could be improved by better training methods. Like recruiting and selection, the education and training of Northwestern's soliciting and special agents remained the primary responsibility of the general agents; the type and extent of training varied widely between agencies. Until early 1924 the Company, other than making available its series of educational booklets, took no active part in the program. After that date, however, the Home Office played an increasingly active role in extending educational aid to the members of the field force.

The impetus for this change came from the experience a few of the Company's general agents had with graduates of the Carnegie School of Practical Life Insurance Salesmanship. This school, an outgrowth of the Carnegie Bureau of Salesmanship Research founded several years earlier, enrolled its first class in October 1919. The initial class was limited to one hundred students whose tuition and expenses were paid by scholarships sold to general agents and life insurance companies. While only forty-three "graduates" emerged from this class, three eleven-week courses were offered in 1920. Students were taught organized sales presentations; the practices, functions, and principles of life insurance; and were given "practical laboratory" training by soliciting insurance in Pittsburgh during the course of their instruction.[23]

If the experience of Northwestern general agents who sent men to this school for training was a criterion, the graduates must have made a deep impression upon their sponsors, as did the concept of practical agent training programs. The West Virginia general agency had sent two young agents to the first Carnegie class, both of whom were soon made district agents. Early in 1920 a Home Office representative visiting the agency reported:

> I never met two more intelligent, upstanding, and promising young men. They have a wonderful vision of the possibilities of the busi-

ness and their enthusiasm and determination is unbounded.[24]

Almost a year later the agency department was advised that because of the success of these and subsequent graduates in the field force, "plans for Carnegie-trained, full-time men, in small territories" seemed to be materializing for the West Virginia agency.[25] A similar attitude was reflected by the general agent in Washington, D.C., who underwrote the tuition and expenses of several of his new men for the Carnegie courses.

Not all Northwestern general agents shared this enthusiasm for Carnegie-type training, possibly because men they had sponsored were trained in branches in different parts of the country where the "faculties" were less skilled than those in Pittsburgh. On the other hand, the advantages of good training and a more centralized program appealed strongly to Vice President Cleary and several of the junior officers in the agency department. Cleary, in fact, addressed one of the earliest graduating classes at Carnegie, while one of the Company's staff spent some time in Pittsburgh studying the program.[26]

Convinced of the need for adopting a more systematic program of agent training, Cleary undertook to persuade the rest of top management. What had to be overcome was not opposition to better-trained agents, but a reluctance to introduce elements into the Company-general agent relationship which might weaken the general agents' independent contractor status. Following long and careful study, in October of 1923 a final program was adopted which obviated such fears. The training plan was geared primarily to the educational needs of new agents and consisted of study material to be prepared in Milwaukee and administered in the field by the general agents. The Home Office established an educational department and appointed a training director with the rank of junior officer.[27] The lack of enthusiastic support for the program by the agency department was reflected by the independent status of the training director, who was not made responsible to the agency department.

To fill the new post the management selected a young man, John P. Davies, who had achieved remarkable success in a somewhat similar role for the Company's Brooklyn general agency. Davies quickly justified the judgment shown in his selection and developed a correspondence course that was introduced in 1925–1926. It consisted of a series of twenty-four booklets, each devoted to a particular topic, thoroughly and imaginatively prepared. The content of the booklets ranged from such basic matters as the functions of life insurance, the policy

contract, and use of the rate book, to the ways life insurance could serve particular personal and institutional needs. The final volume of the series included an introduction to partnership and corporation insurance.

The program itself was developed around the educational booklets and an earlier tract entitled the "Agents' Prospectus." The latter, subsequently retitled, was compulsory reading for all new agents. All training material—quiz and examination forms as well as the educational booklets—was provided to general agents at cost. The general agents, in turn, were expected to assist agents in mastering the subject matter, to review progress, and to forward the completed examinations to Milwaukee for evaluation and suggestion. Most general agents gave full endorsement to the course, cooperated warmly, and used the materials singly or as a supplement to similar activities carried on in their own agencies.*

Following Parsons' appointment as superintendent of agencies the educational department was transferred to his control, and the educational director was given additional responsibilities. Although Davies resigned several years later, his successors continued the training operation along the lines he had originated.

In 1931 an experiment in visual education, initiated by the General Agents' Association, was attempted. While some of the materials were subsequently utilized in different training situations, the program was not successful.[29]

In the light of modern developments the training activities of the Company during these years appear minimal, but in the period when they were introduced they greatly benefited both new men and those desiring to improve their selling efficiency. In the hands of conscientious general agents who appreciated the relationship between well-trained agents and an increased volume of business which persisted because it was well suited to the needs of policyholders, the training course was a highly effective marketing instrument.

There was, however, a need for advanced training of agents to fit them more adequately to diagnose and prescribe for the more complex life insurance needs of the times. Northwestern agents, like their counterparts elsewhere in the industry, were also conscious of the advantages of the professional status accorded to such highly trained

---

* The calibre of the program was very good, for more than thirty years later Northwestern's training director commented that "even in the light of today's publications it would still qualify as a very well-done course. It must undoubtedly have been the outstanding publication of its kind at the time."[28]

groups as lawyers and physicians. In 1927, in response to these needs, the National Association of Life Underwriters sponsored the Chartered Life Underwriter movement and the American College of Life Underwriters. In the ordinary meaning of the word this latter organization was not actually a college, but rather an institution established by life insurance field men with the power to "prescribe examinations and grant degrees to successful candidates."[30] In an effort to help eligible life insurance agents to qualify for its "degree"—the C. L. U. designation—the college outlined an organized course of readings in such subjects as economics, life insurance theory, finance, business law, sociology, sales psychology, and selling techniques. A number of Northwestern general agents and agents were among those who took the first examinations given by the college in 1928. Of the thirty-five candidates who were examined only twenty-one received the Chartered Life Underwriter designation; of these two were from Northwestern. Thus from the very inception of the C. L. U. program, Northwestern agents won a high percentage of the designations awarded, and have held a leading position to the present day.

During the four years after 1928 the Company's interest in the advanced underwriter training offered by the college steadily grew. One of the original chapters of C. L. U. was organized by agents and agency department personnel in Milwaukee; it has

sponsored its own publication, "Time and Money," since 1934.[31]

Sales Promotion

For life insurance generally, sales promotion after 1919 continued to be primarily directed toward the objective of making the personal selling efforts of the agents more effective. A number of companies supplemented this program by increasing their advertising expenditures; some began advertising on a national scale. Perhaps the most distinctive characteristics that marked sales promotion during the 1920's, however, was the growing emphasis on "selling to needs," "programming" and "auditing," all devices to aid the agents in increasing sales and improving the quality of service. Among the most important stimuli in calling attention to the possibility of adapting life insurance programs to the needs of individuals during these years was the growing imposition of inheritance, estate, and gift taxes by the federal and state governments.

While Northwestern and its general agents continued to advertise during these years, it was not done on a national basis and expenditures remained on a relatively modest scale. What the agents spent is not known, but the Company's total advertising bill for the 1919–1932 period aggregated $319,000. Media employed included the trade magazines, but primary reliance was placed on brochures, booklets, and pamphlets which were usually distributed to the general agencies for use in direct-mail promotion or personal presentation to prospects. The management continued to maintain control of the advertising copy of the general agents, such censorship being exercised both for the Company's own protection and in compliance with the statutes of several of the states.[32]

In preparing agents to sell to the needs of insurance prospects, however, Northwestern was undeniably in the vanguard of the industry. The Company was initially well equipped for this effort, having in its arsenal both an unusually effective agency system and the great flexibility of its settlement option contracts. During the early 1920's the field men in the industry placed great emphasis on selling to meet individual needs. The home offices later followed their lead. As a prominent authority on life insurance marketing has explained, such selling suggests that certain needs are more pressing and universal than others, that intelligent marketing must attempt to provide for the priority of needs, and that the policies should be carefully appraised to see that they in fact provide for the objectives they are meant to serve.[33] Thus the task of the conscientious agent was to ascertain the priority of needs of the prospect—his income and resources—and develop a program.

While a score or more states had death and gift taxes before 1916, it was the enactment of a permanent inheritance levy by the federal government in that year which first made the sale of life insurance to provide for death tax needs important. Thereafter, taxation of gifts and estates spread to other states, and by the end of 1932 only Florida and Nevada applied no levy on inheritances.[34]

Even though the rates of the federal tax on inheritances were, judged by current standards, moderate, and the exemptions generous (including up to $40,000 of life insurance), the universal nature of the tax provided a new need for insurance. In 1919, when the inheritance tax schedule was somewhat revised, Northwestern strongly urged agents to use the tax as an argument to wealthy clients, illustrating how purchase of life insurance could protect the principal of their estates at time of transfer.[35] Many of the Company's agents who had already acquired valuable experience in selling to business needs and had gained familiarity with legal and tax aspects of this variety of insurance, moved readily into the estate planning and tax insurance field. Well before federal death tax rates were substantially raised in the 1930's the Company had developed a small but compact corps of agents, skilled and experienced in fitting insurance to such needs.

In providing their customers with insurance programs designed for particular needs Northwestern's agents were quick to adopt devices that would make their job more effective. Two such devices that proved quite popular were evolved by members of the Northwestern agency force. The first of these was contributed by Urban H. Poindexter, a partner in the Company's Kansas City general agency. The inventor, a trained engineer, originated a series of audit sheets and program schedules wherein the specific needs of a client could be formalized and the premiums needed for protection at each stage balanced against his income and budget of regular expenditures. Poindexter utilized this technique in his own personal solicitation and assisted other agents in applying it. News of the method was spread through the agency force by such channels as the Association of Agents' meetings, zone conferences of general agents, and the reports of agency department personnel visiting agencies. At the request of the agents the Company reproduced Poindexter's "kit" in quantity and, upon request, distributed it to general agencies at cost.

A similar process followed the contribution of another Northwestern field man several years later. General Agent B. A. Million of Evansville, Indiana, worked out a systematic method of showing premium outlays, policy costs, and policy values which was highly useful to agents in working out programs with prospects. After introducing it in his own agency Million publicized it to other general agents; the Home Office soon reproduced thousands of copies of the "Million Book" and distributed it to the field at its own expense. In zone conferences and meetings of the Association of Agents, and by visits of Home Office personnel to agencies, this book and the Poindexter kit were promoted, and systematic programming, income canvassing, and organized presentations were urged upon the agents.

In the development of systematic organization of the time and effort of its agents, the management of the agency department and the general agents used still other devices. An integral part of the program was the establishment of specific and attainable goals, such as the number of contacts to be made in a given time period and the number of lives upon which insurance was to be placed. How successful such programming could be was demonstrated by the achievements of those agents who annually attained membership in the Marathon Club. Marathoners, each of whom annually had to write insurance on a minimum of one hundred lives, accounted for a significant proportion of total Company production. In 1921, for example, the sixty-two agents who qualified for membership were responsible for more than $22 million, or 9 per cent of Northwestern's total new business for the 1920–1921 agents' year.[36] During the previous year, however, before the onset of the 1921 depression, the eighty-six Marathoners sold $41 million of insurance, almost 12 per cent of the Company total;[37] and this was the typical performance before the steep sales decline of 1931–1932.

In 1932 a new promotional device, based on the same concept, was formed which was entitled the "Four Lives Club." Membership in this group required an agent to submit paid-up applications on at least four lives each month. In the depth of depression this was a more reasonable goal for the great majority of Northwestern agents than was membership in the Marathon Club; but even in more prosperous periods it provided a stimulus for many agents and has continued to be a regular part of the Company's system of awards.

Despite the great volume of insurance which had been purchased from the Company in the years 1919–1928, Northwestern's share in the ordinary insurance sales of the industry had steadily diminished.

In 1919 the Company had written almost 4.7 per cent of the total ordinary issued in that year; by 1928 its proportion was down to 3.1 per cent. Whether this trend played any important role in the determination of promotional policy of the management in 1929 cannot be verified. Whatever the reason, the most determined and systematic program ever undertaken for increasing the volume of sales and the Company's share of the ordinary market was put into operation in that year. The plan was devised by Cleary and Parsons, organized and sold to the general agents by one of Parsons' lieutenants, and applied across the Company's entire field.

In simplest terms, the expansion program set up volume quotas for each agency territory in accordance with data provided by an intensive program of market analysis. Criteria upon which the quotas were based included insurable population, estimates of purchasing power, per capita wealth, banking facilities, relationship of Northwestern coverage to the total insurance in force in the territory, and relative rank of the agency in the Company. A canvass of the manpower resources of each agency was conducted and individual agent quotas assigned; when available manpower was deemed insufficient to achieve the territorial quota, general and district agents were urged to step up the rate of induction of new agents and to intensify agent training. Agencies were pressed to provide more effective supervision and the more experienced agents spurred to organize study groups in preparation for C. L. U. examinations. The issuance of agency bulletins, establishment of more frequent regular meetings within agencies, and contests, inter- and intra-agency, were likewise encouraged.

By all indications the expansion program was well conceived and enjoyed the support of the field generally, and of the junior officers in the agency department. Induction of new agents increased, and sales rose during the year. The program, however, had barely gained momentum when it ran into the problems associated with the depression. The ultimate objective of the program had been to market approximately $2 billion of insurance in a five-year period; at the half-way point, June 30, 1931, the field had achieved 88 per cent of the quotas assigned them up to that date. Considering that this span included over eighteen months of depression, it must be regarded as a significant accomplishment.

With the gathering force of depression it soon became evident that a more realistic quota would have to be substituted for the remainder of the period. By the end of 1932 the adjusted quota for the four years had been 81 per cent fulfilled by sales of insurance which exceeded $1.25 billion.[38] In terms of improv-

ing the Company's share of the ordinary insurance market, the success of the program is less clear. In 1929 Northwestern's share of aggregate ordinary sales was 3.04 per cent, up slightly from 1928; but it fell to 2.76 per cent in 1931, recovering to almost 3 per cent at the end of 1932. It is probable that the program prevented it from falling even more.

Compensation of Agents

Conservative underwriting and the more careful selection and training of agents provided the Company with definite competitive advantages. These advantages, however, were not restricted to policyholders or members of management, but were shared by the men of the field force. One measure of the success enjoyed by the Company's agents was the amount of income earned, and in this respect there was ample evidence of progress.

For the entire life insurance industry during the 1919–1929 period the level of agent compensation tended upward. The factors causing the increase were the astonishing rise in the aggregate sales of life insurance, and the improved technical skills of life insurance agents resulting from more careful selection and better training.

Northwestern's experience was typical of the general tendency, although the level of income earned by Company agents was probably higher than for the industry as a whole. For the fourteen years ending December 31, 1932, the Company paid agents an aggregate of $147.85 million. The annual outlays rose from $7.9 million in 1919 to $12.75 million in 1929, then fell to $10.3 million in 1932. Continuing the trend of the previous period the gap between the incomes of the Company's most productive and least productive general agencies narrowed. For the overwhelming majority the income position was very good. The average revenue for the Company's general agencies for 1929 and 1932 is given in the following tabulation:

	1929	1932
Gross revenue	$12,751,000	$10,298,000
Number of general agencies	87	88
Average gross revenue per agency	$161,494	$117,000
Revenue retained by agency	$53,831	$39,000
Average agency expenses	$29,300-32,300	$20,500-23,500
Net income of general agent (or partners)	$21,500-24,500	$15,500-18,500

The share of gross commissions received from

the Company which was retained by the leading ten general agencies probably lay within a range of $100,000 or more per year; for the ten least profitable agencies the range most likely varied from $20,000 to $100,000.

The compensation of Northwestern's special and soliciting agents also tended upward during this period. For this entire group of agents the average compensation rose from about $900 in 1919 to $1,340 in 1929, then fell to $950 in 1932. For full-time agents, however, the average annual compensation was about twice this estimate, rising from about $1,850 in 1919 to over $2,800 in 1929, then dropping to slightly under $2,000 in 1932. Considering the large number of men who came into the agency force after 1929, the figure for 1932 is probably least representative of all. Those agents who had been under contract for several years prior to 1930 benefited from renewal income which somewhat offset the loss of first-year commissions and had a braking effect upon the decline in income.

The actual range of incomes of Northwestern full-time agents cannot be accurately estimated, but for the solid corps of producing agents—men who made a career of soliciting life insurance—it is probable that the Company's elite group averaged over $10,000, while those full-time agents with earnings clustering more toward the center of the top half most likely averaged over $3,000.* Part-time men, principally soliciting agents under contract to district agencies, earned much less on the average, although there were some notable exceptions.

From this data it is clear that whatever the problems confronting the general agents, lack of revenue was not principal among them. Not only did most general agents have sufficient funds to meet expenses, including the costs of induction of new men, but the agents under full-time contracts earned incomes which were at least comparable to those of men of similar training in other occupations. In the absence of more comprehensive information it is uncertain that Northwestern agents were, as a group, the highest compensated in the industry. It is certain, however, that they were among the leaders in this respect, and that the principal reasons for this included the better-than-average care with which they were selected, trained, and supervised.

---

* Company data indicates that an agent received about $2,500 for each $100,000 of life insurance he had sold and of which 65 per cent still remained in force at the end of 10 years. This commission is composed of both first-year and renewal income. Thus for an agent who produced $500,000 of new business per year for a period of ten years the total income he would receive in the tenth year would be about $12,500. For the "elite" group of agents, men who annually produced from 18 per cent to 22 per cent of the Company's new business, this level of income was not unusual.

Relations with the Field Force

One of the notable advances during the 1919–1932 period was an improvement in the relations between the Home Office and members of the agency force—relations that had reached a low ebb in 1918. Much of this improvement was the result of a more sympathetic understanding by members of executive management of the problems faced by agents. Communication between the agents and the Home Office was improved by a reorganization of the various groups of agents.

One such change involved the establishment of a zone system for the general agencies during the early 1920's. This move, taken in response to numerous requests from the field, particularly from Franklin Mann, new president of the General Agents' Association, divided the Company's general agencies into three zones: eastern, central, and western. Over a decade later a fourth zone was set up by a subdivision of existing zones. All general agents in a particular zone gathered annually for a meeting. To these meetings, at which general and specific problems and issues were discussed, Home Office personnel were invited and usually addressed the agents on matters of common interest.

That the general agents were eager to improve their relations with Northwestern's management was further evident from changes which occurred in their association, both in organization and orientation. The old executive committee was reorganized to include at least three members from each zone, with one of the three to be zone vice president. The president of the association could designate one committee member from each zone, the rest being elected. The executive committee held a general session each year at the Company's headquarters to consider recommendations and problems presented by members from the respective zones, and to strive for solutions in conference with the Company's officers.[39] Not only was the committee more representative, but there was a notable moderation of the earlier antipathy.

Modification of the General Agents' Association and its relations with the management was followed in the late 1920's by changes in the composition and structure of the District and Special Agents' Association. Rapid development of the district agency system increased the number of district agents and, combined with the nature of their special problems and interests, led to the creation of a separate organization. Following the formation of the District Agents' Association, the special agents invited soliciting agents to enter the older group which was retitled the Special and Soliciting Agents' Association.

Special and soliciting agents, of course, had their particular problems, including conditions of work, terms of contract, utilization of part-time agents, training, local promotion, and financial assistance from general agents. By the very nature of their contracts their relations were largely with general and district agents and not directly with the Company. Through their association, however, these agents brought problems and requests directly to the Home Office. They attempted to persuade management to take certain actions which they believed would benefit them, for example, to modify general agent contracts in such ways as would permit greater liberality of treatment of men under contract to the general agent. In such attempts the Special and Soliciting Agents' Association was usually not successful, a situation which caused some of its membership to believe, probably erroneously, that "the Company doesn't listen to us because they don't think we are very strong."[40]

The Association of Agents, the principal forum and fraternity for all Northwestern agents, continued to function along the same lines and for the same purposes as it had in the past. Its annual meeting, held at the time of the Company's annual meeting each July, was attended by all agents who desired to go, but they paid their own expenses regardless of the status of their production record. This in itself was a remarkable factor in a major marketing organization. The banquet was the occasion for presentation of awards and official recognition of agents for achievements in production during the past year. The awards were purely honorary, but the expenses for the banquet were paid by the Company.

The inherent advantages of the Northwestern general agency organization were founded on the pillars of financial strength and the stability of the general agent force. The financial position of the great majority of the general agencies, as has been indicated, was strong throughout the period. Because of the 2 per cent collection fees paid on business which was in force longer than ten years, the general agents in 1929 first began to enjoy the collections on the great volume of insurance sold during the decade. As a result, and despite the increase in lapsed and surrendered policies, the general agencies were in a much stronger position to ride out the depression than were the agencies and branch offices of most of their rivals. The basic stability of the general agent force is indicated by the fact that during 1919–1929 only thirty-two of the eighty-nine general agencies were affected by a complete change of general agent personnel. In fifty-seven agencies the original proprietor

(or a partner) was still under contract to Northwestern.

Some problems did arise, of course, with the general agencies. Among them was that of the older general agent who coasted, content with a substantial renewal and collection fee income. When the Company encountered this problem before 1930 the management had been noticeably benevolent. There was no compulsory retirement age for general agents, and the Company patiently refrained from abruptly terminating contracts of such men. One result was that in Boston, Detroit, New York, and San Francisco agency productivity and efficiency were seriously retarded. These agencies were rebuilt only by the strenuous efforts of successor general agents. After 1929 there was evidence of less management tolerance in such situations. The turnover rate, under the spur of depression and the five-year expansion plan, rose. Thirteen general agent contracts were terminated during 1930–1932, including those of two whose small Pennsylvania agencies were closed.

The Company's consideration for longer-service agents was also reflected in 1926 with the inclusion of a "veteran's clause" in contracts. Affecting general, special, and soliciting agents, this clause provided that after an agent had been under contract for twenty consecutive years or had attained age sixty-five with ten consecutive years under contract, he was entitled to nine renewal commissions regardless of the volume of insurance produced.[41] The liberalization of the renewal commission conditions for veteran agents naturally had beneficial morale effects on the whole field force.

Changes in the organization of agents and more sympathetic attention to agents' problems alone did not account for the degree of improvement in the relations between agents and the Home Office. What really marked the difference from the situation in 1918 was the improved morale that characterized the entire selling organization. Parsons, of course, had made an important contribution to morale, but the agents, particularly the general agents, gave Cleary the chief credit. Should the opportunity arise, the general agents would have liked nothing better than for a market-oriented leader to head the Company; and Cleary fitted their concept of such a leader. This feeling required only a catalyst.

Sales and Marketing Record

Soon after his appointment as superintendent of agencies Charles H. Parsons succinctly phrased the Company's basic attitude toward sales, "We of course want enough volume to hold our place in the procession, and we are getting it without undue pressure or added expense."[42] In 1932, looking back over the record of the previous fourteen years, the members of management had good reason to feel that these objectives had been attained. Measured in terms of the Company's own past accomplishments and against the record of its chief competitors in the field of ordinary life insurance, Northwestern's marketing achievement was impressive. During the period the Company sold more insurance than it had during its entire history prior to 1919, while its insurance in force rose from $1.68 billion to almost $4 billion.

In terms of the management's further objective of selling high-quality insurance at moderate costs, the Company's record was also excellent. Table XIII-2 shows that among the largest eleven American life companies Northwestern was first in respect to the persistency of its insurance in force. While the margin over its nearest rival was small until 1929, during the succeeding three years the gap was considerably widened.

The total direct cost of acquiring the $4.4 billion of Northwestern's new business for the period increased substantially over the amount spent during the administration of George C. Markham. Aggregate "external" costs for the entire fourteen years were $196.3 million, of which $153.8 million involved direct acquisition expense. Of this total, $147.8 million was paid out in commissions and collection fees, $5.7 million went for medical examinations and inspections, and $319,000 was spent on advertising. In addition, Northwestern paid taxes of $41.4 million, hotel and travel expenses involved $482,000, legal expenses $307,000, settlement of contested claims took $142,000, and legislative outlays, $25,000. The actual proportion of such costs which could be charged to marketing is not known; they are included here because some sales and marketing element was involved in all of them.

Relative to premiums collected by the Company, however, it remained about the same, 10.9 per cent for the 1908–1918 period and 10.8 per cent for 1919–1932. Equally encouraging to the management was the fact that the level of relative direct acquisition costs was steadily forced downward. For the five years 1919–1923, for example, such costs constituted 12 per cent of premiums received; for 1924–1928, only 11 per cent; and for the last four years only 9.5 per cent.

Whether Northwestern in respect to sales did in fact hold its "place in the procession" rests largely on a definition of terms. Compared to total industry sales of almost $200 billion, Northwestern's share of the market dropped off sharply during the greater part of the period. (See Chart XIII-1.) This was true even in respect to the amount of ordinary insurance, about $137 billion, marketed from 1919 through 1932. It may be noted, however, that the larger companies that kept pace with industry sales were combination companies. The "procession" in which Northwestern was primarily interested included the large ordinary companies such as Mutual Benefit,

TABLE XIII-2

Persistency of Insurance in Force, Selected Companies, 1919–1932

COMPANY	(1) IN FORCE DEC. 31, 1918	(2) SALES 1919– 1929	(3) SALES 1919– 1932	(4) IN FORCE DEC. 31, 1929	(5) IN FORCE DEC. 31, 1932	(6) COL. (1) + COL. (2)	(7) COL. (4) ÷ COL. (6)	(8) COL. (1) + COL. (3)	(9) COL. (5) ÷ COL. (8)
				(Dollar figures in millions)					
NORTHWESTERN	$1,681	$3,560	$4,449	$3,913	$3,999	$5,241	74.7%	$6,130	65.2%
Mutual Benefit	987	2,353	2,877	2,435	2,335	3,340	72.9	3,864	60.4
Penn Mutual	802	2,216	2,881	2,002	2,009	3,018	66.3	3,683	54.5
New York Life	2,839	8,584	10,745	7,266	7,342	11,423	63.5	13,584	54.0
Mutual Life	1,862	4,960	6,100	4,299	4,227	6,822	63.0	7,962	53.1
Equitable	1,835	9,962	13,145	6,761	6,665	11,797	57.3	14,980	44.5
Prudential	3,892	21,298	30,664	14,313	15,305	25,190	56.8	34,556	44.3
Metropolitan	4,430	28,445	40,185	17,934	18,981	32,875	54.6	44,615	42.6
John Hancock	1,061	4,817	7,157	3,308	3,457	5,878	56.3	8,218	42.1
Travelers	754	8,648	10,850	4,735	4,369	9,402	50.4	11,604	37.6
Aetna	673	7,625	9,811	3,790	3,457	8,298	45.7	10,484	33.0

SOURCE OF BASIC DATA: Northwestern, *Annual Statement*, 1918–1932, incl. Other companies: *Insurance Year Book* (The Spectator Company, New York, 1927, 1934; Life Insurance History Section).

New York Life, Mutual Life of New York, and Penn Mutual. In 1919 these four companies sold about 19 per cent of the aggregate ordinary insurance reported for the industry; Northwestern's share was approximately 4 per cent. In 1932 the proportions were 13 per cent for the four companies noted and 3 per cent for Northwestern.[43]

Thus in terms of self-imposed limitations on the types of policies offered and the selling methods used, Northwestern's record remained highly creditable. And even with these restrictions, although the Company ranked tenth in the industry in new sales from 1919 through 1932, measured by insurance in force it dropped only one place, from sixth to seventh position, and so far as assets were concerned maintained its sixth place in the industry.

CHART XIII-1

Sales of Insurance: Industry and Northwestern, 1919–1932

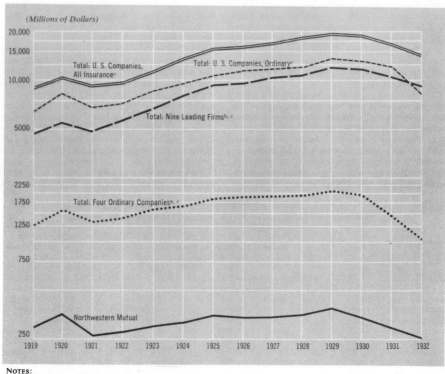

(Millions of Dollars)

NOTES:
[a]Mutual Benefit, Mutual Life of New York, New York Life, Penn Mutual.
[b]Aetna, Equitable Society, John Hancock, Metropolitan, Mutual Benefit, Mutual Life of New York, New York Life, Penn Mutual, and Prudential.
[c]"Insurance Written," which was somewhat larger than the amount actually purchased since it included issues not taken by policy applicants.

SOURCES: For Northwestern and industry totals, see Appendix E. For individual companies, *Insurance Year Book,* 1926, 1933, financial history section.

CHAPTER FOURTEEN

Investment During a Period of Extremes: 1919-1932

THE extremes of prosperity and depression brought challenging problems in the investment field, for the swift changes in the investment market placed an extra premium upon prudence and wisdom. Although Northwestern remained the leading farm mortgage lender among the life companies, the rapid changes in interest rates and in the mortgage market frequently compelled the Company to modify its policies. Moreover, there were some decided shifts in emphasis during these years: the sharp increase in urban loans after 1925; the move toward larger loans, a trend in which Northwestern led the field; and the increasing problem of foreclosures after 1929. In addition, weaknesses appeared in Northwestern's investment program during these years: the hesitation to invest in utilities and the declining value of its railroad holdings. Investment problems such as these, however, should not overshadow Northwestern's achievements, for despite the fluctuations in the economy which sorely tested the management's judgment, Northwestern's rate of earnings was superior to that of any other life company. This achievement reflected the continuing vigor and prudence of the Company's investment policy.

Home Office Administration

The expanded scale of investment and insurance activities not only made necessary an increase in Home Office personnel but it also added to the complexity of the organization. The number of officers and employees rose from 618 at the end of 1918 to over 1,200 in 1932, and wages and salaries from about $900,000 to over $2.3 million. Even with this expansion Northwestern's Home Office salaries and wages were less, proportionately to the insurance in force, than other companies in the industry. When the Executive Committee in 1932 announced the results of its survey of wages and salaries paid by the twelve largest life companies, this fact became evident. Using the industry's standards of measurement, total payrolls of these companies were compared with results as shown in the table on the following page.[1]

Despite the excellent showing on costs the depression made it advisable to introduce further economies in 1932. Lengthening the work week had the effect of adding the time of one hundred fifty clerks to the work force.

The Company, however, supplemented the base salaries and wages of its employees in various ways. During the years 1919–1922, for example, a total of $615,000 was paid in cost-of-living bonuses, while over the whole period pension plan payments amounted to $381,000. The expense of operating the Company restaurant, where all personnel were served free lunches, totaled almost $1.1 million.

Other costs associated with the administration of the Home Office included compensation to trustees that ranged between $48,000 and $57,000 per year

	AVERAGE OF TWELVE COMPANIES	HIGHEST COST COMPANY	NORTHWESTERN
Per $1,000 of Assets	$3.94	$5.83	$2.49
Per $1,000 of Insurance in Force	0.84	1.05	0.59
Per $1,000 of Premium Income	24.55	34.65	18.75
Per Policy in Force	3.06	4.05	2.31

annually, and $204,000 for examinations and audits, which, added to amounts paid for supplies, office equipment, printing, postage, and the like brought total costs for the entire period to about $13.4 million.

Underlying the mere expenditure of payrolls and overhead costs, however, lay the host of administrative problems characteristic of a large and growing institution. One evidence of management's concern with this new complexity was the development of the "Salary Committee," appointed originally by Markham, into an "Office Committee." The latter group, like the committee on agencies and insurance, was composed of Company officers and employees appointed by the president. In contrast to its predecessor, which was limited to reviewing salary adjustments, the Office Committee dealt with a wide range of activity: establishment of salary scales, classification of jobs, personnel transfers, promotions, and other problems of personnel administration. In addition, it considered such subjects as business methods, equipment, supplies, and coordination of administrative activities in the various departments. To an extent many of the powers of the Office Committee were more shadow than substance because the president's confidential assistant, Shepard Barry, though officially listed as auditor undertook most of the hiring, and in consultation with the president strongly influenced salary scales, personnel decisions, and the operation of the Home Office building generally.[2] When Barry was appointed comptroller in 1932 many of these responsibilities came directly under his supervision.

Certain benefits were given to a larger number of Home Office employees between 1919–1932. The pension system, for example, was extended in 1921 to include building service employees, and in 1925 to loan agents.[3] In 1920 the Home Office clerks were encouraged to form a cooperative association "to foster, establish, and encourage activities along intellectual, social, and economic lines."[4] It was a fraternal-recreational association, not a trade union, company or otherwise. Not only did the management make the Company's facilities available to this

group, but it regularly made contributions to its social activities' fund.[5]

As the rising volume of Northwestern's business required a larger office and management force, so the sheer increase in the number of employees in turn required more space. Before the Home Office building was ten years old it was already proving to be inadequate to the needs of the Company. In 1927 the president recommended construction of an addition to be built on the vacant half block fronting Mason Street. The work was begun under the supervision of a committee of trustees and officers, and in 1930 the new structure was ready for occupancy. Constructed of marble, granite and limestone, the addition was similar to the original building, but more utilitarian in design. Although limited to eight floors, it was so constructed that an additional sixteen floors could be added if the need arose. Most of the operating functions were housed in the addition, with the original structure being largely devoted to executive offices, quarters for middle management personnel, and facilities for employees and trustees. By 1932 the total valuation of the Home Office property was over $4 million.

Background to Investments and Investment Policies

Under Van Dyke the investment organization was essentially the same as developed by Palmer and followed by Markham. Control over investments and investment policies remained in the hands of the Finance Committee, subject to review by the Board of Trustees. As president and a member of the Finance Committee, Van Dyke helped formulate policies and had the principal responsibility for carrying out the decisions of the Committee, although he was assisted by a number of able subordinates including vice presidents P. R. Sanborn and Frederick W. Walker.

Moreover, an expansion in the investment departments demonstrated the increasing complexity of the investment problems. In 1919 a separate division charged with servicing the bond accounts was formally designated as a department. In the same year two new positions, manager of mortgage loans and superintendent of mortgage loans, were created; and in 1923 the position of manager of mortgage loans was abolished and replaced by two new posts, a manager of farm loans and a manager of city loans. In 1926 a separate position was created charged with responsibility for foreclosed farm properties, and two years later the job was redesigned to include responsibility for supervising farm loan agents and the management of real estate. In 1928 two assistant managers were appointed to aid the farm loan department in handling the problems of a growing volume of foreclosed farm properties.

This reorganization and expansion reflected the need to invest the growing sums of money. How Northwestern's gross income grew during this period is shown in Chart XIV-1. Premium income, as had been true earlier, contributed between 70 and

CHART XIV-1

Income, Expenditures, and Net Available for Investment: Northwestern, 1919–1932

(Millions of Dollars)

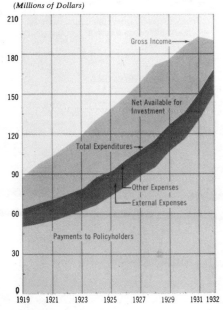

SOURCE: Appendix F, Tables 1-4.

CHART XIV-2

Distribution of Admitted Assets: Northwestern, 1919–1932

(Millions of Dollars)

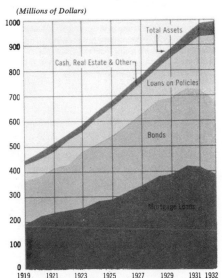

SOURCE: Appendix F, Table 5.

75 per cent of annual totals that expanded from about $87.4 million in 1919 to over $189 million in 1932. Out of an aggregate gross income of $2 billion over one fourth, or nearly $564 million, was added to the Company's new investment funds.

Some impression of what this amount meant in terms of the investment problems of management is indicated by the fact that outlets had to be found for new funds that averaged $485,000 per week in 1919, $790,000 per week in 1923, and over $1 million per week in 1928. Repayments, as before, brought total investable funds to amounts nearly double these figures.

The Company's new investment funds were sufficient to expand total assets from $414.8 million at the end of 1918 to just under the billion dollar mark at $996 million by the end of 1932. (See Chart XIV-2.) Until 1928 the distribution of assets among the major categories remained remarkably stable; the principal shifts came after the onset of the depression in 1929. Mortgage loans, for example, as a proportion of the total varied between 42.7 per cent (1925) and 45.4 per cent (1919); they dropped to 39.6 per cent in 1932. The bond account was kept within even narrower limits prior to 1929, from a high of 38 per cent (1923) to a low of 35.9 per cent (1928); it fell to 29.9 per cent in 1932. Loans on policies grew slowly from 13.4 per cent (1919) to 15.6 per cent (1928), moving up to 24.9 per cent by the end of 1932. Other assets (including real estate, cash, and accrued rent, interest, and premiums) made up 4.1 per cent of the total in 1919, 4.3 per cent in 1928, and 5.6 per cent in 1932.

Loans on Policies

The growth and distribution of Northwestern's loans on policies are shown in Table XIV-1. The steady expansion in the account from 1919 through 1928 was followed by a rapid rise that increased the total by more than $117 million by the end of 1932. Of the three types of loans made to policyholders, premium notes comprised but a small part of the total, reaching their peak in the post-war depression of 1920–1921. Automatic premium loans on policies issued after 1907 grew steadily, rising at a somewhat faster rate in 1932.

During Markham's administration Van Dyke had expressed concern over the steady growth of policy loans because he thought that they not only inter-

fered with orderly investment planning, but were frequently the first step toward the surrender of insurance policies. At the end of his first year in office he was pleased, therefore, to report that for the first time since 1894 loans on policies "show a commendable decrease for the year of $666,624."[6] As the subsequent growth of this account after 1919 shows, the president had to reconcile himself to the fact that these loans would normally grow roughly in proportion to the amount of insurance outstanding, and that in a period of economic crisis the volume would increase sharply, as it did after 1929.

Throughout these years the Company maintained the interest rate on policy loans at 6 per cent. To policyholders who protested that this was an excessive charge for the privilege of borrowing "their own money," Van Dyke replied,

A fixed uniform interest rate for policy loans, available with certainty, practically on demand at any time or times over a period which may exceed fifty years, from every standpoint clearly seems preferable to an uncertain and indefinite variable interest rate based upon the current general rate of interest at any particular locality where the policy loan may be desired. . . . The adoption of any such uncertain varying interest rate would create a condition which would be undesirable for the policy-

TABLE XIV-1
Northwestern Mutual: Loans on Policy Accounts, 1919–1932
(In millions)

YEAR	PREMIUM NOTES	AUTOMATIC PREMIUM LOANS	POLICY LOANS	TOTAL LOANS ON POLICIES	LOANS ON POLICIES AS PER CENT OF TOTAL ASSETS
1919	$0.45	$1.16	$57.50	$59.11	13.44
1920	0.38	1.23	64.61	66.22	14.01
1	0.84	1.54	76.18	78.56	15.49
2	1.09	1.97	81.42	84.48	15.46
3	1.06	2.40	87.07	90.47	15.36
4	0.93	2.83	93.17	96.93	15.34
1925	0.74	3.29	99.55	103.58	15.37
6	0.66	3.88	107.18	111.72	15.33
7	0.59	4.59	115.46	120.64	15.43
8	0.52	5.32	124.74	130.58	15.56
9	0.45	6.09	149.02	155.56	17.51
1930	0.45	7.25	171.96	179.66	19.16
1	0.42	8.60	205.99	215.01	22.00
2	0.46	10.74	236.73	247.93	24.89

SOURCE: *Annual Statements*, Northwestern Mutual Life Insurance Company, 1919-1932.

holder while from the Company's standpoint it would obviously be un-mutual, unworkable, impractical, and result in unjust discrimination.[7]

The growth in policy loans from approximately $125 million in 1928 to over $236 million in 1932 put a heavy cash drain on the Company. Despite this outflow, which was augmented by payments for surrenders, the Company's cash income exceeded outflow by some $165.7 million for the 1929-1932 period.[8] The Company's total cash holdings at their peak in 1932 were only $5.3 million, or one-half per cent of total assets. Thus at a time when other sources of funds were rapidly drying up, Northwestern's management was able to meet the cash needs of its policyholders without being under heavy pressure to sell securities in a depressed market.

Security Investments

Although securities remained substantially unchanged as a percentage of Northwestern's total investments, the account grew impressively from about $163 million in 1919 to over $297 million at the end of 1932. As shown in Chart XIV-3 railroad bonds consistently made up between 50 and 60 per cent of the total. United States government bonds were gradually reduced, reaching a low point in 1927, after which the trend was reversed. Holdings of state, county, and municipal bonds were steadily expanded throughout the entire period. By contrast, purchases of Canadian governmental, provincial and municipal bonds moved up sharply through the early 1920's, reaching a peak of about $42.5 million in 1927, and dropping off only slightly over the succeeding years. The most striking change was the addition of public utility bonds, which increased from $65,000 in 1923 to nearly $28 million in 1930, and were reported at just over $21 million at the end of 1932.

The continued attraction of railroad bonds as the foundation of the Company's security holdings is explained by the relative prosperity of the railroad industry during the period. Although meeting increased competition from alternate methods of transportation, an increase in rates in 1920, coupled with lowered operating costs after that date, enabled most of the Class I railroads in the United States to improve their operating ratios and earnings through the 1920's. It was this situation that prompted the management to add rail bonds valued at $87 million to the account from 1919 to 1928.

CHART XIV-3

Bond Investments: Northwestern, 1919-1932

(Millions of Dollars)

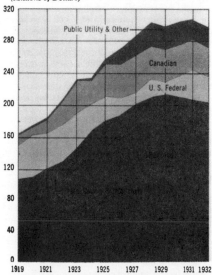

SOURCE: *Annual Statement* (Convention Form), Northwestern Mutual Life Insurance Company, 1919-1932, inclusive.

This action was taken even though between 1922 and 1926 railroad bonds held by the Company with a par value of $8 million were defaulted through a failure to pay interest. The first of these defaults came in 1922 and involved the Missouri, Kansas and Texas railroad. In the reorganization that followed Northwestern gave up bonds originally valued at $475,000 for common and preferred stock, which was subsequently sold for $272,000. The same year the Minneapolis and St. Louis, the Des Moines and Fort Dodge, and the Iowa Central also defaulted. The Company held some $3.38 million of these carriers' bonds. In all three cases settlement was slow and the securities were still in default by the end of 1932.

The Company fared somewhat better with its $4 million (par value) of Chicago, Milwaukee and St. Paul Railroad bonds after that road went into receivership in 1925. After complicated negotiations among the rival claimants, the railroad was reorganized in 1928. President Van Dyke became a director, and Northwestern received mortgage bonds valued at $795,000 and income bonds in the amount of $3.18 million.

Compared to the Company's total holdings of railroad securities the losses incurred through default prior to 1930 were small, amounting to less than 2 per cent, but after 1930, when the effects of the depression began to hit the railroads, the situation changed. In 1931 the issues of two railroads held by the Company, the Florida and East Coast and the Seaboard Airline, went into default. The next year the securities of three more railroads held by Northwestern were similarly affected when The Wisconsin Central, the Central of Georgia, and the Wabash all went into receivership. By the close of 1932 railroad bonds made up the larger portion of the Company's $19.5 million (par value) securities then in default. It was clear that the management's experience with protective committees and reorganization problems, up to this point, was only a preview of what lay ahead.

The ebb and flow of United States bonds in Northwestern's security portfolio was in response to both the government's management of the public debt and the relative attractiveness of alternative investment opportunities. Following the conclusion of World War I the policy of the Treasury was to reduce the public debt as fast as circumstances and annual surpluses allowed. At the end of 1919 the total federal debt amounted to some $25.5 billion; by 1930 it was reduced to $16.2 billion.[9] Prior to 1929, as portions of the Company's holdings of government bonds matured or were called, the funds were invested in other types of securities. Following the stock market crash government bonds were again acquired, partly for greater liquidity of the Company's assets and partly because other investment opportunities were greatly reduced.

During the 1920's local and municipal governments in the United States and Canada borrowed extensively to finance public improvements. Northwestern, together with other life companies, participated in this financing; the Company increasing its state, county, and municipal portfolio from $17 million in 1919 to over $40 million in 1929.

Although a 1917 statute permitted the Company to invest in public utility bonds, the first purchase of this type of securities was not made until 1923, emphasizing once again management's essential conservatism. The initial venture was a modest one, involving $65,000 of 5 per cent mortgage bonds of the Hydraulic Power Company of Niagara Falls, New York. Two years passed without further acquisitions; but following Walker's appointment in 1925 the Company bought $5.2 million of the bonds of

three companies that were a part of the Bell telephone system. By the end of 1932 public utility bonds valued at over $21.3 million made up some 8 per cent of the security holdings.

Mortgage Loans

As the most important part of the Company's total investments, the mortgage loan account grew impressively from $210.5 million at the end of 1918 to $394.5 million in 1932. The most striking feature in the account, as shown in Chart XIV-4, was the growing proportion of farm to urban mortgages up to 1925, followed by a reversal in the trend after that date. The handling of mortgage investments that brought about this shift is indicated in Table XIV-2, which shows that from 1919 through 1925 new farm loans exceeded repayments by a substantial margin, whereas the urban mortgage portfolio was barely maintained. After 1925, although new farm loans were still large, repayments were even larger in con-

CHART XIV-4

Mortgage Loan Investments:
Northwestern, 1919–1932

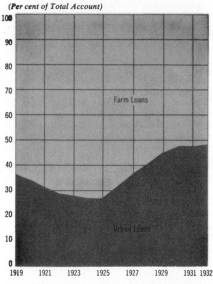

(Per cent of Total Account)

SOURCE: *Annual Statement* (Convention Form), Northwestern Mutual Life Insurance Company, 1919-1932, inclusive.

TABLE XIV-2

Northwestern Mutual:
Changes in Mortgage Loan Account,
1919–1932

	FARM MORTGAGES	URBAN MORTGAGES
	(In Millions)	
1919-1925		
New Loans	$230.3	$55.8
Less Repayments	143.1	55.4
Net Additions	$87.2	$0.4
1926-1932		
New Loans	$137.3	$174.3
Less Repayments	143.1	64.3
Net Additions	−$5.8	$110.0

trast to the urban loan account, which grew rapidly.

In emphasizing farm loans during the first seven years of Van Dyke's administration, Northwestern investment officers followed the policy adopted prior to 1900. Until the mid-1920's the same reasons that had prompted the Finance Committee to reject Markham's recommendation to concentrate on urban lending still carried great weight. The loan agency system was intact, the loan agents were skilled in picking high-quality farm loan prospects, and until 1923 interest rates were considerably higher on farm mortgages than on urban properties. The reasons for the shift toward more vigorous urban lending were rooted in part in the changing fortunes of American agriculture after 1919 and the nature of competition in the farm mortgage field.

The wartime prosperity of American agriculture, as shown in Table XIV-3, continued through 1919. It was abruptly halted by the post-war depression of 1920–1921 when farm incomes fell over 40 per cent, the index of parity prices dropped some 31 per cent, and farm debt rose nearly 45 per cent. Although agricultural prices made a substantial recovery by 1923, they did not rise to the point of restoring the price-cost relationship that existed during the war. Throughout the 1920's land values gradually declined, reflecting lower farm incomes. This decline, coupled with debts acquired by farmers during and immediately after the war, reduced the equity of many farm owners and led to distress transfers (foreclosures or assignments to creditors to avoid foreclosures) that increased from a rate of around four per thousand in 1920 to eighteen per thousand in 1926.[10] Compared to the difficulties faced by American farmers in the 1920's, however, the problems after 1930 were catastrophic. By the end of 1932 it was increasingly apparent that only drastic measures could bring relief, not only to farmers, but to the entire American economy.

The general role played by life insurance companies as a group, and Northwestern in particular, in farm financing during these years is indicated in Chart XIV-5. Total farm debt increased rapidly from 1918 through 1921 as farmers borrowed against equities to meet short-term obligations. By 1923 the peak of emergency borrowing was reached, and over the succeeding years total farm debt was gradually reduced. After some hesitation the life insurance industry more than doubled its holdings of farm mortgages between 1920–1926, with about half the increase coming after the 1923 peak in total

TABLE XIV-3

United States: Data on Agriculture, 1919–1932

DATE	FARMERS' GROSS INCOME (In Billions)	PARITY PRICE INDEX* (1910-1914 = 100)	INDEX OF VALUE OF FARMS PER ACRE (1912-1914 = 100)	TOTAL FARM DEBT (Billions)
1919	$17.7	109	170	$7.1
1920	15.9	104	157	8.5
1921	10.5	75	139	10.2
1922	10.9	80	135	10.7
1923-1929	13.2	88	124	10.0
1930	11.4	80	115	9.6
1931	8.4	64	106	9.4
1932	6.4	55	89	9.1

* Ratio of prices received by farmers to prices paid including interest and taxes.

SOURCE: *Historical Statistics*, 95, 99, 111.

CHART XIV-5

Life Company Holdings of United States Farm Mortgage Debt, 1919–1932

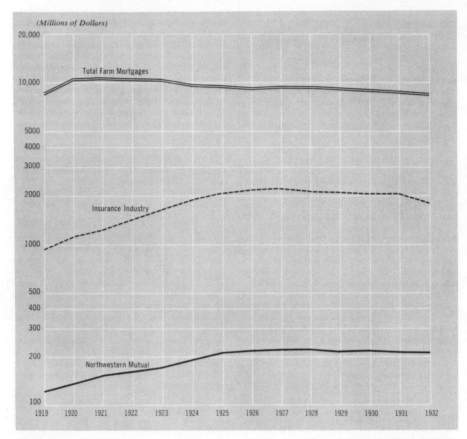

NOTES: Beginning in 1930 life insurance company account, except Northwestern, includes purchase-money mortgages and sales contracts.

SOURCES: *Annual Statement* (Convention Form), Northwestern Mutual Life Insurance Company, 1919-1932, inclusive. *Historical Statistics of the United States, 1789-1945*, p. 111.

farm loans was reached. While Northwestern began adding to its farm loan account in 1920, its farm mortgage portfolio increased at a less rapid rate than that of the life insurance industry through 1926. Even so, the Company remained the leading farm mortgage lender in the industry with 14.4 per cent of the industry total in 1920, 10.8 per cent in 1925, and 10 per cent in 1932.

A more detailed account of the Company's lending activities will indicate why farm loans remained relatively attractive until 1925, and why the management shifted its emphasis to urban lending after that date. During 1919, when land values were pushed to then record highs, the Northwestern management wisely refused to loan up to the 50 per cent limit allowed by statute; instead the maximum limits were generally set at about 40 per cent of appraised values. With borrowers able to obtain greater percentage loans elsewhere, the amount of new money loaned was about $7 million less than farm loan repayments. Lending increased during the first half of 1920, but following the onset of the depression the management raised rates and virtually stopped making loans, except for authorizing extensions. The combination of falling prices and over-extended short-term credit by country banks resulted in bankruptcy for many of these institutions. Despite the actions of federal land banks and some insurance companies to increase mortgage lending, over 1,400 small banks failed in the farm areas during 1921.[11]

In this situation, when farmers turned to other sources of funds, Northwestern's loan applications increased sharply. Although interest rates ranged (depending on the location of the property and the size of the loan) from 6.5 to 7.75 per cent, the Company's new farm loans during 1921–1922 amounted to $65.5 million. In 1922, confronted with increased competition for mortgages from other life companies, management reduced interest rates slightly and made loans more attractive by liberalizing the prepayment privilege. In 1920 Van Dyke had persuaded the Finance Committee to adopt his earlier suggestion of extending the city privilege to farm loans, thereby permitting borrowers to pay up to one-half the principal amount of the loan at any time after one year.[12] In June 1922 a further change permitted borrowers to repay the entire loan at any time after the expiration of two years, provided an additional sixty days' interest was paid the Company.[13]

From this date on there were rapid changes in the market. The concessions made to borrowers brought a flood of new loan applications during the first seven months of 1923, compelling the Company to place its loan agents on a quota basis; but by the end of the year the flow of applications sharply declined as competition with the big Eastern life companies became more vigorous.[14] Different statutory requirements in the states where each was incorporated frequently enabled competing firms to make larger loans per acre than Northwestern, whose standard practice was to make "forty-twenty" loans, *i.e.,* 40 per cent of the value of the real estate and 20 per cent of the value of the farm buildings. To compete successfully, in September 1923 Northwestern reduced its rate to 5.25 per cent for new loans.[15] Since the Company, unlike most lenders, absorbed servicing fees and performed its own legal services, this rate actually constituted a preferential price in competition.[16] With such attractions the Company's loan agents were able to submit applications in sufficient quantities to permit new farm loans of $37.6 million in 1924 and $38 million in 1925.

Considering that the margin of interest rates on farm loans over urban loans had been sharply reduced by 1923 (see Table XIV-4), it is difficult to understand why Northwestern placed more emphasis on urban lending prior to 1925. Apparently the management expected agriculture to recover more than it did after the major readjustment of 1920–1921. The rising number of distress transfers by farmers, plus growing competition from other life companies, brought about a change in policy. The $137.3 million new farm mortgages acquired from 1926 through 1932 were sufficient to keep the farm loan agents busy, but did not quite equal repayments for the period.

Even before 1925 the Northwestern management became concerned about the difficulties that farmers were experiencing in adjusting to post-war condi-

TABLE XIV-4

Northwestern Mutual:
Interest Rates on New Mortgage Loans, 1919–1932

DATE	FARM		URBAN	
	High	*Low*	*High*	*Low*
1919-1922	7.75%	—6.50%	6.25%	—5.75%
1923	6.50	—5.25	6.00	—6.00
1924	6.25	—5.25	5.50	—5.50
1925	6.25	—5.00	5.50	—5.00
1926-1932	6.25	—5.00	6.00	—5.50

tions. During 1923 and 1924 the most distressed agricultural areas were located in the South and the Pacific Northwest. While Northwestern's Southern loans were restricted to a few areas in Tennessee and Kentucky, the Company was more heavily involved in the Northwest. Late in 1923, in response to complaints from agricultural and political interests from that section of the country, President Coolidge called a conference to consider the area's problems and to make legislative recommendations. Northwestern was invited to participate together with other life insurance companies, and President Van Dyke was named chairman of the committee on mortgage indebtedness.

The committee's report accurately presented the problems and made recommendations for their solution, but these were apparently beyond the powers or will of the administration in Washington to implement.[17] Beyond calling further attention to the difficulties of the area and the eventual creation of intermediate credit banks to finance farmers by short-term loans on livestock and commodities, the contribution of the Coolidge conference was imperceptible.

How significant the declining agricultural situation was for Northwestern with its substantial investment in mortgages can be seen when, in 1924, the Company initiated a program of mortgage loan

agent conferences. These conferences were usually held during July of each year in conjunction with the annual meeting of trustees and insurance agents.[18] At the sessions loan agents had the opportunity to compare problems and alternative solutions, and were made to feel more a part of a team operation. Farm loan agents were also encouraged to improve their knowledge of farm problems, methods, and techniques by attending special summer seminars, at Company expense, given by agricultural colleges. Other services were provided farmers through Company cooperation with agricultural experiment stations, agricultural colleges, and government organizations. For example, when the corn borer ravaged crops in Ohio, Northwestern printed and distributed a booklet to inform farmers how to combat the pest.

By 1927 the amount of delinquent interest payments on farm loans had become quite serious. The management was willing to permit farm borrowers to postpone interest payments temporarily, but as Vice President Sanborn wrote the loan agents,

We are not willing to continue to waive our right to funds which belong to this Company, to the end that junior lienholders, judgment creditors and local money lenders may take all while this Company takes nothing and pays

the delinquent taxes for the general benefit of all concerned.[19]

In most instances local creditors had an advantage over the mortgagor because they were in the area, and when their loans were in jeopardy they urged borrowers to place chattel mortgages on crops and stock to guarantee repayment. This advantage was substantially overcome by Northwestern's branch office system whereby agents could keep closely in touch with borrowers and act quickly to protect the Company's interests. Such attentiveness did improve the delinquent interest record before 1929.[20]

When the full impact of depression was felt after 1929, the problems of protecting the Company's farm loans multiplied. The management was loathe to foreclose farms when there was any chance the owners could work out of their difficulties. As H. D. Thomas, Northwestern's farm loan manager during these years, explained,

We always followed the policy in our delinquent loans of nursing the man who was doing his best, and who was a capable farmer and not allowing his farm to depreciate in value. With prices as low as the farmer was then receiving, it was just impossible for him to pay his taxes and running expenses and meet his interest obligations. If he was getting out of his farm all that was humanly possible we were very lenient with him as long as he played fair with us.

Our trouble was that there were second mortgages on some of these farms; there were local debts to implement dealers and to stores. They [the junior lienholders and other creditors] would take chattel mortgages so that when the farmer sold his crops they would take all of the receipts and he had nothing left with which to pay taxes or mortgage interest.[21]

In such cases, particularly those involving default of interest on junior liens, Northwestern in self-defense was forced to resort to foreclosure, even though the preference of the farm loan managers was to continue the loan. In other instances farmers, overwhelmed with the burdens of the depression, preferred to surrender their farms rather than continue.[22] By 1932 the problems involving mortgage loans had reached monumental proportions.

Special Real Estate

Northwestern's difficulties with farm mortgages were reflected in an upward trend in the Company's holdings of special real estate after 1923. As the following tabulation shows, the account reached a low point of about $300,000 in 1923, after which it expanded slowly through 1929, rising rapidly during the following three years; all but a small proportion were farm properties.

As a percentage of total mortgages, special real estate did not exceed 1 per cent until 1930, this being due in part to the quality of the loans and in part to a determined effort to avoid foreclosures wherever possible. In 1925 the Company began to expand its Home Office staff in order to handle the growing number of farms under the administration of the mortgage loan department. In cooperation with the loan agents the job of the mortgage loan department was to sell the property if possible; otherwise they were to obtain tenants and see that the properties were kept in repair or improved in anticipation of eventual sale.

In 1929 several new loan agencies were opened

Year	Special Real Estate	Ratio of Special Real Estate to Total Mortgage Loans	Year	Special Real Estate	Ratio of Special Real Estate to Total Mortgage Loans
			(Dollar data in Millions)		
1919	$0.5	0.25%	1926	$1.4	0.43%
1920	0.5	0.23	1927	1.9	0.57
1921	0.4	0.18	1928	1.2	0.57
1922	0.4	0.17	1929	3.0	0.75
1923	0.3	0.12	1930	4.3	1.05
1924	0.6	0.21	1931	6.7	1.64
1925	0.9	0.30	1932	14.3	3.62

SOURCE: *Annual Statements*, Northwestern Mutual Life Insurance Company, 1919-1932.

in Iowa. Their main function was not to expand farm loans, but to manage farm properties owned by the Company and help borrowers who were in difficulties. By the end of 1932 the Company was well into the administration of special real estate, a burden that was to become even greater in the years that lay immediately ahead.

Urban Loans

From 1919 to 1925 the Company's urban loan account was barely maintained, but with the shift to urban lending in 1925 this situation was suddenly and dramatically changed. Early in that year the president took the initiative by submitting to the Finance Committee a proposed construction loan of $17 million on the Palmer House, a noted Chicago hotel, which was approved on April 1.* A month later Van Dyke sent a memorandum to W. E. Griswold, the city loan manager, stating that the Finance Committee was of the unanimous opinion that every effort should be made to increase the volume of urban loans in the major cities, particularly in the central western states. Griswold was instructed to explore the feasibility of opening a city loan office in Detroit and to investigate the need of developing a corps of "good city loan agents."[23]

It was soon discovered that the urban account could be greatly increased with no addition to the number of city loan agencies, and with little added cost. Reduction of interest rates to 5 per cent on good urban property and numerous large-scale loans on newly constructed office and mercantile buildings greatly increased the city loan account during the next five years. The Company was particularly suited to make these loans because of its large income and preferred market position in the Middle West. As a result, new city loans in the amount of $174.3 million were made between 1924 and the end of 1932, adding a net of $110 million to the account.

The large loan pattern established by the Company during the 1890's was resumed with the Palmer House loan. In the years following 1925 a score of loans in amounts exceeding $1 million was consummated. By the end of 1932 approximately 74 per cent of urban loans, by dollar amount, were concentrated in six cities, with almost 40 per cent of that amount being invested in Chicago. This great increase in urban loans was accomplished largely by

---

* *Minutes of the Finance Committee,* April 1, 1924. The loan was made at a rate of 5.5 per cent for twenty years. Partial amortization was required with a balloon payment of $8.8 million due in 1944.

the efforts of only one full-time and five part-time loan agents.

At the end of 1932, although the account had diminished somewhat from the 1931 high, urban loans amounted to $189.6 million and equalled 48.1 per cent of total loans and 19 per cent of admitted assets. The average size of the 552 urban loans on Northwestern's books as of January 1, 1932, was $348,000.[24] This greatly exceeded the average urban loan in the portfolios of all life companies which for the 1920–1924 period was $47,500 and for the 1925–1929 period $70,000.[25]

Among the problems facing city loan agents were those concerning the location of business property with respect to trends in the movement of business activity, value of property, income earned, and the quantity of existing and prospective space relative to its demand. Company practice, in these respects, was very good. Although offered the mortgage on the Civic Opera House in Chicago, the Company's loan agent advised its rejection, being convinced that the trend in business location was not in a westerly direction.[26] Some mistakes, of course, were made. It was difficult in some cases to calculate proper allowances for depreciation and obsolescence of older office buildings where the major value was in improvements rather than in land, or in other instances to fix an accurate valuation of the land itself. Nor was it always possible to predict how the income from particular properties would be influenced by changes in the rentals of neighboring property.[27]

Mistakes and errors of judgment of this type, however, were almost inevitable in a loaning business conducted on Northwestern's scale. On the whole the decision to aggressively resume urban lending was a wise one, although in retrospect it is clear that the delay in making the decision was unfortunate. A large proportion of the funds loaned after 1925 went into construction loans for which applications were accepted although structures were not completed for one or two years. During the interval between the commitment of funds and the completion of the buildings, and before the Company could begin collecting interest on the full investment, the ratio of available space to the demand for such space was subject to rapid change. It became apparent that, on the average, the later in the 1920's a large loan was made the greater was the probability of foreclosure during the 1930's. Of the amount loaned in 1928, for example, Northwestern acquired as special real estate 44.8 per cent during the 1930's. For the entire 1919–1932 period of urban lending,

11.6 per cent by dollar volume was eventually taken over under foreclosure; for the amount loaned during the four years 1926–1929, however, 17.8 per cent was foreclosed.[28]

Comparative Investment Policies and Investment Earnings

With few exceptions Northwestern's investment policies from 1919 through 1932 generally conformed to the pattern followed by the largest companies in the industry. As indicated in Table XIV-5, the Company's holdings of securities, with two exceptions, were quite typical. The most obvious departures from the pattern followed by its leading competitors were in the absence of public utility bonds prior to 1927 (when they exceeded 1 per cent for the first time) and the lack of industrial bonds throughout the period.* In respect to the distribution of its assets by major categories, Table XIV-6 shows that Northwestern was neither the highest nor the lowest in any class. Even in terms of the proportion of farm mortgages to total investments the Company was a consistent third in the group. A further division of urban lending would show, however, that Northwestern made more loans on office and mercantile properties than on residential property. Unlike Northwestern most of the other companies engaged heavily in residential lending, although the largest firms, such as Metropolitan, also loaned extensively on office, banking, and industrial properties.

The Northwestern management had reason to be proud of the Company's investment earnings record during Van Dyke's administration. Not only was an average net return on investments of 5.05 per cent above the 4.9 per cent achieved during 1908–1918, but, as indicated in the tabulation above, this rate placed the Company third among the largest companies in the industry.

It is noteworthy that the first six companies, measured by rates of earnings, maintained a relatively high percentage of their investments in mortgages, while the lowest four invested primarily in bonds. The earning rate on bonds was lower than that on mortgages for securities acquired during the 1920's. Whether this differential would be compensated for by less frequent and less serious difficulties could only be answered by the experience of the subsequent six years.

* Wisconsin law did not permit investment in industrial securities until 1935.

Company	Average Net Earnings	Company	Average Net Earnings
Metropolitan	5.15%	Prudential	4.81%
Penn Mutual	5.14	Equitable	4.78
Northwestern	5.05	Travelers	4.74
John Hancock	5.00	New York Life	4.61
Mutual Benefit	4.94	Mutual Life	4.59

Source of Basic Data: *Sixty-First* through *Seventy-Fourth Annual Report of the Superintendent of Insurance of New York*, (Life) 1920–1933; *Insurance Year Book*, 1920–1933.

Note: Formula used: $\text{rate} = \dfrac{y_1}{\dfrac{(L_0 + L_1) - y_1}{2}}$

where: y_1 = investment earnings current year;
L_0 = ledger assets as of Dec. 31, previous year;
L_1 = ledger assets as of Dec. 31, current year.

Summary of the Administration of William D. Van Dyke

When William D. Van Dyke assumed stewardship of the Company in 1919 Northwestern was the sixth largest company in the United States industry, both according to the amount of insurance in force and by the amount of assets owned. Its basic strength included a limited, if strong, line of insurance contracts, a well-established marketing apparatus, a cadre of veteran executive officers, and an investment portfolio which earned a rate of return comparable to most companies of similar size. But there were weaknesses as well. Other than the actuary the management included no outstanding insurance executive. It also lacked effective coordination between the underwriting and sales departments, a situation that had led to a deterioration in relationships between the Home Office and the field force.

By 1932 much had been done to eliminate these defects. Management was strengthened at all levels by the appointment of promising executives. Relationships between the Company and its agency force were much improved and Northwestern's agents were generally better selected, better educated, and better trained than had been true a decade earlier. Sales had been maintained at levels that were, on a whole, consistent with the underwriting and insurance policies of the Company; and while Northwestern lagged behind the industry generally, in 1932 among the large companies it still ranked sixth

TABLE XIV-5

Ten Largest United States Life Insurance Companies: Distribution of Bond and Stock Investments, 1919 –1932
(As a Percentage of Total Admitted Assets)

COMPANY	U. S. FEDERAL	U. S. A. MUNICIPAL	CANADIAN	FOREIGN	RAILROAD	PUBLIC UTILITY	INDUSTRIAL & MISC.	CORPORATE STOCKS
				(1919)				
NORTHWESTERN	10.2	3.9	2.0	-0-	20.9	-0-	0.0	0.1
Equitable	12.9	2.2	2.9	3.4	36.9	3.1	0.2	2.6
John Hancock	10.1	8.2	-0-	-0-	17.8	0.9	2.1	0.2
Metropolitan	13.4	1.9	4.4	0.0	25.2	5.6	1.2	0.6
Mutual Benefit	16.7	1.5	-0-	-0-	19.4	0.8	0.0	0.0
Mutual Life	15.2	1.3	0.4	3.5	44.1	2.0	2.1	3.5
New York Life	10.5	6.3	1.8	7.5	35.2	1.2	0.2	0.1
Penn Mutual	11.4	5.7	-0-	-0-	17.4	4.7	0.3	0.2
Prudential	16.3	4.5	1.9	-0-	31.3	6.9	1.6	0.6
Travelers	7.4	3.5	4.7	0.2	10.9	1.4	0.2	0.9
				(1924)				
NORTHWESTERN	5.3	4.5	5.2	-0-	22.2	0.0	0.0	0.1
Equitable	6.0	0.4	1.0	1.2	30.2	6.6	0.4	0.7
John Hancock	5.4	8.1	-0-	-0-	13.1	3.1	-0-	-0-
Metropolitan	10.3	1.3	5.0	0.0	22.2	5.8	1.9	0.3
Mutual Benefit	9.5	1.3	-0-	-0-	21.3	0.6	0.1	-0-
Mutual Life	12.1	2.0	0.3	1.5	42.0	1.5	1.8	3.0
New York Life	7.8	5.8	2.4	1.8	31.2	4.0	-0-	0.0
Penn Mutual	5.3	4.9	-0-	-0-	13.4	3.8	1.7	0.1
Prudential	8.3	3.2	2.4	-0-	21.5	8.3	2.0	0.2
Travelers	11.4	3.7	7.0	0.1	8.3	2.4	0.1	1.6
				(1930)				
NORTHWESTERN	2.7	3.9	4.2	-0-	18.8	3.0	-0-	0.0
Equitable	0.6	0.1	0.5	0.4	18.2	11.4	0.7	4.4
John Hancock	0.3	5.4	-0-	-0-	8.4	10.6	0.2	3.8
Metropolitan	1.1	1.5	4.0	0.0	20.2	9.2	2.8	1.9
Mutual Benefit	1.1	1.6	-0-	-0-	17.8	8.2	0.7	1.1
Mutual Life	4.6	1.6	1.3	0.3	33.3	7.2	1.3	1.7
New York Life	0.8	5.6	1.8	0.4	21.3	8.7	1.0	4.1
Penn Mutual	2.2	5.7	-0-	-0-	11.5	5.9	2.2	1.8
Prudential	1.8	3.3	3.6	-0-	15.7	10.7	3.9	2.7
Travelers	8.0	3.9	8.0	0.0	8.5	7.9	1.4	4.9
				(1932)				
NORTHWESTERN	3.2	3.9	3.8	-0-	16.8	2.2	-0-	-0-
Equitable	0.8	0.1	0.5	0.3	16.6	10.1	0.7	5.2
John Hancock	1.9	5.0	-0-	-0-	7.9	10.5	0.2	4.2
Metropolitan	1.1	2.6	4.1	-0-	18.4	9.1	3.3	2.1
Mutual Benefit	0.7	2.0	-0-	-0-	16.6	5.8	0.6	1.1
Mutual Life	3.6	1.5	1.3	0.1	30.2	7.9	1.1	2.0
New York Life	2.8	6.5	1.7	0.4	19.1	7.7	1.0	3.8
Penn Mutual	3.2	5.7	-0-	-0-	8.8	7.5	1.8	2.3
Prudential	2.3	5.2	3.7	-0-	13.9	11.0	3.6	2.7
Travelers	9.1	3.1	8.9	0.0	7.7	7.3	1.4	3.1

NOTES: -0- indicates holding of zero.
   0.0 indicates holding of more than zero but less than 0.045 per cent.

SOURCE: *Annual Statement*, Northwestern Mutual Life Insurance Company, 1919, 1924, 1930, 1932. Other companies: *Sixty-First, Sixty-Sixth, Seventy-Second*, and *Seventy-Fourth Annual Report of the Superintendent of Insurance of New York*, 1920, 1925, 1931, 1933.

TABLE XIV-6   219

Ten Largest United States Life Insurance Companies: Distribution of Assets, 1919 –1932
(As a Percentage of Total Admitted Assets)

Company	Bonds and Stocks	Mortgage Loans Farm	City	Loans on Policies	Real Estate	Cash	Other	Admitted Assets
				(1919)				(In Millions)
NORTHWESTERN	37.1	29.1	16.2	13.4	0.9	0.5	2.7	$439.9
Equitable	62.2	4.3	12.9	14.2	3.1	1.2	2.2	599.4
John Hancock	37.1	42.3	6.8	7.4	1.5	1.0	4.0	186.6
Metropolitan	52.3	2.0	31.5	6.7	2.6	1.2	3.8	864.8
Mutual Benefit	38.4	35.0	2.4	16.1	1.1	0.8	6.3	257.7
Mutual Life	68.0	0.0	15.2	12.5	2.3	0.3	1.7	662.4
New York Life	62.6	3.9	12.8	15.1	0.9	2.2	2.6	961.0
Penn Mutual	41.5	8.1	28.6	15.8	1.0	0.5	4.6	208.9
Prudential	63.1	13.1	9.3	7.2	3.1	1.2	3.8	598.1
Travelers	29.2	18.3	7.3	8.3	3.2	2.2	31.5	169.0
				(1924)				
NORTHWESTERN	37.3	31.3	11.9	15.3	0.4	0.6	3.2	$632.0
Equitable	46.4	17.4	15.2	13.7	2.9	0.6	3.8	725.6
John Hancock	29.9	48.9	4.6	8.1	2.9	0.7	5.0	333.2
Metropolitan	42.6	9.9	33.6	7.0	1.7	1.0	4.2	1,628.2
Mutual Benefit	32.8	39.7	2.6	18.8	0.8	0.6	4.6	388.9
Mutual Life	63.8	0.0	19.2	13.3	1.5	0.7	1.5	714.1
New York Life	53.0	6.5	21.8	13.9	0.7	0.6	1.6	1,055.9
Penn Mutual	29.1	9.5	37.7	13.9	0.6	1.0	8.3	291.0
Prudential	46.0	16.4	25.9	6.4	1.3	0.9	3.2	1,196.3
Travelers	34.6	20.7	4.8	10.0	2.5	1.1	26.3	329.1
				(1930)				
NORTHWESTERN	32.6	23.4	20.5	19.2	0.9	0.5	3.0	$937.7
Equitable	36.3	14.5	25.6	17.4	1.8	0.7	3.9	1,284.4
John Hancock	28.7	31.4	19.8	11.4	3.6	1.0	4.2	584.1
Metropolitan	40.7	5.8	38.1	10.0	1.3	0.5	3.7	3,310.0
Mutual Benefit	30.4	27.7	13.0	22.0	2.4	0.5	4.1	571.8
Mutual Life	51.2	0.0	28.5	16.1	0.9	0.4	3.0	1,052.2
New York Life	43.8	1.7	30.7	18.2	1.9	0.4	3.3	1,789.1
Penn Mutual	29.2	4.1	40.5	15.7	1.2	0.8	8.5	458.7
Prudential	41.7	8.2	36.6	7.2	1.7	0.8	3.9	2,491.8
Travelers	41.0	12.4	6.4	13.8	2.8	1.5	22.1	635.5
				(1932)				
NORTHWESTERN	29.9	20.6	19.0	24.9	2.1	0.5	3.0	$996.0
Equitable	34.2	13.0	22.4	20.8	2.6	3.2	3.8	1,471.7
John Hancock	29.7	25.6	18.4	14.5	6.4	1.0	4.5	639.5
Metropolitan	40.6	4.4	34.4	12.4	2.8	1.7	3.7	3,769.3
Mutual Benefit	26.7	23.3	13.0	26.7	5.3	0.8	4.2	588.9
Mutual Life	47.6	0.0	26.7	19.6	1.8	1.4	3.0	1,127.2
New York Life	43.0	1.1	26.8	19.7	2.4	1.4	5.4	1,974.1
Penn Mutual	29.2	2.9	34.7	19.2	3.9	0.9	9.2	514.6
Prudential	42.3	7.3	32.9	9.2	3.3	1.2	3.8	2,773.8
Travelers	40.6	10.0	6.0	18.0	4.0	2.1	19.3	678.1

NOTES: -0- indicates holding of zero.
    0.0 indicates holding of more than zero but less than 0.045
    per cent.

SOURCE: *Annual Statement*, Northwestern Mutual Life Insurance
Co., 1919, 1924, 1930, 1932. Other companies: *Sixty-first,
Sixty-sixth, Seventy-second,* and *Seventy-fourth Annual
Report of the Superintendent of Insurance of New York.*

measured by assets and seventh measured by insurance in force. Its earning record placed the Company first among its peers.

Judged by benefits to policyholders the Company also fared well, better indeed than the record of the earliest decades of the twentieth century. Aggregate premium income for the 1919–1932 period was almost $1.43 billion. In return policyholders received the following benefits: dividends of $412 million (28.8 per cent of premiums); death claims, matured endowments, cash surrender values, annuities, and waiver of disability premiums, $732 million; and dividends and policy proceeds left with the Company at interest, $43 million. The addition to assets, representing principally the legal reserve of the insurance in force, amounted to $581 million. Thus total benefits to policyholders for these fourteen years were almost $1.77 billion, equal to 123.7 per cent of premiums paid to the Company.

Judged by the benefits received by policyholders, the Company's performance during the twenty-five years 1908–1932 was outstanding. Aggregate income from premiums during these years was $1.93 billion. In return policyholders received the following benefits: dividends of $548 million (28.5 per cent of premiums); death claims, matured endowments, cash surrender values, annuities, and waiver of disability premiums, almost $1 billion; and dividends and policy proceeds left with the Company at interest,

$48 million. The addition to assets, representing principally the legal reserve of the insurance in force, amounted to over $760 million. Thus total benefits to policyholders for this quarter-century amounted to $2.36 billion, equal to 122.3 per cent of premiums paid to the Company.

President Van Dyke, who reached his seventy-second birthday in 1929, found his job as chief executive an almost intolerable burden, especially in face of the demands created by the catastrophic economic decline after that year. Moreover, the death of his wife shook his spirit. Not easily bowed, the president drove himself, keeping late hours at the offices on Wisconsin Avenue, often watching the special force of night clerks prepare the checks for policy loans and cash surrender of policies that flowed out from Milwaukee in mounting volume.[29] But his health finally broke, and failing to recover from a severe cold, he died on June 7, 1932.

In view of the momentous decisions to be faced at the depth of the depression in 1932, the question of Van Dyke's successor had special significance. Would the tradition be continued of selecting a person whose primary interest and training was in investment and finance? Indeed, would the selection be made from Van Dyke's closest advisers?

For a time the issue was in doubt. Among those most prominently mentioned as Van Dyke's successor was Vice President Frederick W. Walker, who

TABLE XIV-7

Eleven Largest United States Life Insurance Companies: Aggregate Benefits to Policyholders, 1919–1932

COMPANY	(1) GROSS PREMIUMS	(2) TOTAL PAYMENTS TO POLICYHOLDERS	(3) NET INCREASE IN ASSETS	(4) COL. (2) + COL. (3)	(5) COL. (4) ÷ COL. (1)
	(Dollars amounts in billions)				
NORTHWESTERN	$1.93	$1.60	$0.76	$2.36	122.3%
Mutual Benefit	1.16	0.89	0.48	1.37	118.1
Mutual Life (N.Y.)	2.46	2.29	0.61	2.90	117.9
Penn Mutual	1.00	0.74	0.42	1.16	116.0
New York Life	3.94	3.03	1.48	4.51	114.5
Equitable	3.07	2.37	1.05	3.42	111.4
Aetna	0.92	0.64	0.36	1.00	108.7
Travelers	1.15	0.60	0.63	1.23	107.0
Metropolitan	7.51	3.72	3.57	7.29	97.1
Prudential	5.97	3.08	2.63	5.71	95.6
John Hancock	1.47	0.81	0.59	1.40	95.2

SOURCE: *Insurance Year Book* (Financial history section), 1923, 1927, 1934.

not only received the strong endorsement of the Executive Committee but also the support of many trustees; in fact, his selection for a time seemed certain. Several latent forces in support of Michael J. Cleary, led by the General Agents' Association and by key trustees, gradually gathered strength, however. Their tactic was to postpone the selection of a president until the field was more thoroughly canvassed, thereby giving those who favored Cleary a chance to rally support. Actually the Board, recognizing the importance of the decision to be made, approved of the canvass and a committee was appointed to make it. The climax came on October 18, the eve of the Board meeting. Charles Q. Chandler, one of the trustees supporting Cleary, invited all members of the Board to a dinner held in a private room of the Pfister Hotel. Chandler announced that they were going to have to elect a president and that it was intolerable for the Company to continue any longer to operate without a formal head. He then asked each member in turn to rise, state his choice of candidate and the reasons for supporting him. At the conclusion he distributed blank paper and asked that a ballot be cast. The result was seventeen votes for Cleary, thirteen for Walker, and one for L. J. Petit, a trustee. At this point it was requested that a unanimous vote be cast for the majority candidate.[30] When the Board met the next day to make the selection official, a letter from Frederick W. Walker asking for unanimous support for the president and withdrawing his candidacy was read into the record.[31] It was a generous gesture and set a standard for management cooperation that was to typify relations in the troublesome years that lay ahead. Because of his background, and because of his interest and primary responsibility with sales, Cleary's selection signified a break in the Northwestern tradition of selecting chief executives oriented and experienced in the field of investment.

CHAPTER FIFTEEN

A Critical Era of Marketing Management: 1932-1946

EW periods in the history of the United States witnessed such momentous changes as those that occurred between 1932 and 1946. The problems of a depressed economy, complicated by social, political, and economic reforms that persisted for the entire decade of the 1930's, were not entirely solved when the nation became involved in the grim trials of global conflict and the responsibilities of a world power. World-wide economic depression posed obstacles so great that the conventional solutions of the past appeared powerless to redress them. In the United States the government undertook economic policies which either were new or had previously been applied only during wartime. To such antidepression measures were added reform policies, not entirely economic in character, such as social security, compulsory collective bargaining between labor and management, and attempts to conserve human and natural resources.

Economic Change and the Life Insurance Business

When Michael J. Cleary became president of Northwestern the depression phase of the business cycle was still gathering force. Price levels were lower than they had been for twenty years, estimates of unemployment varied from 20 per cent to 30 per cent of a labor force of fifty million persons, and the national income was down to about $40 billion. The business failure rate was mounting, while the crisis in private banking, where failures had already wiped out deposits of almost $800 million, loomed just over the horizon. The economic wastes of depression had exacted huge tolls in the nation's human resources; with its patience wearing thin, the nation indicated its dissatisfaction with the administration by electing Franklin D. Roosevelt president of the United States in November 1932.

Under Roosevelt's leadership the country halted the retrograde economic drift, partially recovered its lost prosperity, and substantially modified the bases of economic and social change in the United States. If the actions of the new administration were not always coordinated toward the achievement of specific goals, they did possess the merit of being vigorous and bold attempts to combat fear and pessimism.

The economic recovery of the United States was spurred by such instruments as monetary devaluation; banking reform; national spending for public works and work relief; deficit financing; and subsidies to farmers, low-income groups, and special segments of business. It moved steadily forward through 1936, faltered into recession, and recovered again by the end of the 1930's. By 1939 the national income had been raised to over $72 billion, but unemployment remained close to the eight million level and private investment spending still lagged. The outbreak of war in Europe, culminating with the Nazi victories in 1940, provoked a substantial

American commitment to rearm and to assist nations resisting aggression. By December 1941, when the Japanese attack at Pearl Harbor plunged the United States into the war, national income was over the 1929 level and unemployment down to about two and one-half million persons. The unprecedented scale of production during wartime drove national income to previously unknown heights. Despite wage stabilization and price control policies income rose to $183 billion during 1945, slipping back slightly in 1946 as a result of the process of retooling and change-over from military goods to consumer and industrial goods production.[1]

The companies which comprised the United States life insurance industry shared fully in all the problems experienced by the economy in depression and war. The size of the industry as measured by the number of companies was one indicator, and the 1933–1946 pattern closely resembled the experiences during the depression of the 1870's. From 392 companies at the end of 1932, the number fell to 368 during 1937; by 1945, however, the industry consisted of 463 firms; and during 1946 forty-six new companies commenced operations.[2] Over one hundred life companies went out of business during the years 1933–1940, but no company of major importance failed to survive the disturbances of the 1930's. The companies that failed were small concerns, and many of them were absorbed into stronger organiza-

tions that preserved the greater proportion of policyholders' funds.

During the seven years 1933–1939, United States life insurance companies marketed $82.1 billion of insurance—ordinary, group, and industrial. Due to such factors as the extraordinarily high rates of policy lapse and surrender, however, the total amount of insurance in force rose by only $10.8 billion. This rate of growth of 11 per cent was the slowest the industry had experienced since the calamitous 1870's. For the seven years 1940–1946 aggregate industry sales were $101.7 billion, and the growth of the amount in force was $60.6 billion, an increase of 52 per cent. The total insurance in force at the end of 1946, $174.5 billion, was sufficient to provide an average coverage of more than $1,200 for every American citizen. The superior rate of growth of insurance in force for the 1940–1946 period reflected the improved economic condition of the country as lapse and surrender of policies dropped abruptly, and the huge increase in personal savings during the war years included a substantial increase in life insurance purchases.

The value of the assets owned by United States life companies, as shown in Chart XV-1, increased at a steadier and more impressive rate than did the volume of insurance in force. For the seven years 1933–1939 industry assets rose from $20.75 billion to $29.24 billion, an increase of 40 per cent; for the remaining seven years assets went up to $48.19 bil-

CHART XV-1

United States Life Insurance Companies: Assets, Sales, and Insurance in Force, 1932–1946

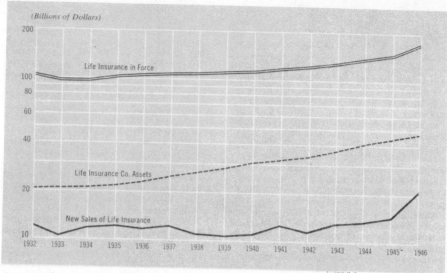

SOURCE: *Life Insurance Fact Book,* New York: Institute of Life Insurance, 1956,   13, 60, and 21.

lion, a 64 per cent rise. The quantitative increase in assets, however, masked important shifts in the investment portfolios of life companies. The effects of depression cut heavily into construction and greatly reduced the rate of aggregate private investment. Life companies, as a result, were forced to seek new outlets for investment; the securities of the United States government, loans to policyholders, and the bonds of public utility companies replaced mortgages and railroad bonds in company portfolios. With the coming of the war government bonds became the principal investment outlet for the industry.

The conditions of marketing life insurance and investing policyholders' funds were greatly altered during the 1930's; the problems and challenges posed by the changes differed both in kind and degree from those which had existed during the previous decade. Managerial soft spots, concealed by the unparalleled insurance sales of the 1920's, became obvious in the harsher atmosphere of the depression. In applying corrections, in shifting to meet the altered conditions of public control and in pro-

viding more adequately for the needs of individuals and institutions, the life insurance industry attained a new level of maturity. The task of guiding Northwestern during these fateful years provided enough tests to challenge the skill, ingenuity, and courage of any management.

The Turning Point: 1932–1933

During the six months that followed his election as president Michael J. Cleary faced emergencies about as grim as could be envisioned. The difficulties which beset Northwestern applied impartially to almost all financial institutions in the United States, but the fact that they were of such a nature that no single corporate management could modify them by independent action was of small consolation.

The peak of the financial crisis was reached in the late winter of 1933 when thousands of banks, unable to meet their obligations, were faced with ruin. Even before this, however, the life insurance companies had been subjected to unprecedented demands for cash by policyholders. The cash demands of surrenders and policy loans were greatly intensified by the imposition of banking moratoriums in state after state. As people were abruptly denied access to time and demand deposits they turned to whatever sources of cash remained. The insurance companies suddenly found themselves functioning as commercial banks, and subject to the same risks. Even under these abnormal conditions life companies could satisfy the cash demand from premium and investment income, but only for a limited time. If the conditions of February-March 1933 had been continued for much longer conventional revenue would have been insufficient to meet cash needs; and the sale of assets would have become necessary. The prospect of attempting to sell securities in wholesale lots under such circumstances was forbidding. To absorb heavy losses in the sale of assets would be fatal to the solvency of many companies; unless the panicky demand for cash could be halted it was certain that a major catastrophe would sweep the life insurance business.

At the very brink of disaster came deliverance— the federal government intervened directly to avert the banking debacle. The national moratorium was applied immediately following Roosevelt's inauguration in March, and was succeeded by such measures as devaluation of the dollar, minimum insurance of bank deposits, and formal abandonment of the gold standard. Whatever the individual merit of these actions the new administration's campaign against panic had the desired effect. Slowly, but unmistakably, the wave of fear abated; the threat to the financial structure of the nation passed.

In the meantime, the menacing situation confronting the life insurance companies also had to be solved, but because the industry was not subject to federal regulation the solutions emerged from individual states. Shortly after the imposition of the federal banking moratorium several states applied similar measures to the life companies. Under these actions the companies were prohibited from paying more than a fraction of the amounts demanded by policyholders through surrenders or loans. While there were no restrictions imposed concerning the payment of death claims, several companies were unable to meet their claims promptly in full; policyholders were assured, however, that all claims would ultimately be honored. Many of the state emergency measures were prompted by the requests of life company managements, others were initiated by individual legislatures or insurance commissioners. By the end of March 1933 twenty-one states had adopted emergency legislation;[3] by the end of July,

with the pressures on the cash resources of the life companies substantially eased, the restrictions were almost entirely removed.

The crisis, even when its worst phase had passed, had pronounced effects within the life insurance industry. Sales continued to fall, the amount in force diminished, and thousands of citizens were skeptical concerning the intrinsic worth of the life contract itself. The morale of life insurance men, agents and home office personnel, already shaken by three years of depression, had suffered considerably by the financial crisis and the state restriction on payments of cash to policyholders. The task of bolstering that morale and encouraging personnel to new efforts was met by all life companies, in various ways and with varying degrees of success.

At Northwestern there were many sources from which strength could be drawn to meet these challenges, and possibly the greatest single contribution came from the new president. All during the months of the crisis "M.J." epitomized the calm, confident, cheerful leader; only a few intimates knew the strains of this effort, of his fears for the future of the industry had one or more of the major insurance companies failed. President Cleary was extrovertive, completely informal, possessing a genuine affection and respect for his fellow men. He had high regard for Northwestern values and principles, and admiration for the contributions of his predecessors in developing these characteristics. In addition to a quick and able mind, an intuitive sense of the fundamental elements in the problems confronting him, Cleary was contemptuous of sham and pretense, impatient with customs and habits which kept men apart or uncomfortable. He quickly eliminated the last vestige of tradition: the wearing of formal attire at meetings of the Board of Trustees, where men in swallow-tailed coats and striped trousers had once sat stiffly as the full minutes of the Executive and Finance Committees for the previous quarter were monotonously read. It was his opinion that physical discomfort was not necessarily equated with business customs or personal respect. He also discouraged the old custom of officers addressing one another as "mister." Cleary lived and worked without pretension; he managed to infuse into his organization many of the same qualities.

At the Company's annual meeting in July 1933, speaking as usual without notes, President Cleary reviewed the days just past, expressed his gratitude for the patience and cooperation of agents and Home Office staff during the crisis, and indicated ways in which the strength shown by the Company could be utilized in the future. Northwestern, he pointed out,

Michael J. Cleary

did not ask for the moratorium, but it supported it! We did not seek to make the public believe that we did not need it. If any life insurance company of major importance had crashed, God knows what might have happened to all life insurance in this country.

The problems which had been faced, however, had been collective and not individual. The industry and Northwestern had much to be proud of, he explained, for,

> life insurance has emerged with its record intact, with its vigor and strength intact, stronger than it was when the public officials took the action that they did. Now let me say to you: there never was a time in all these trying months that the Northwestern could not have met every demand that was made upon it with business promptness, in full, and without the sacrifice of a dollar of its securities.

And how, Cleary asked, were agents to convince those who questioned the soundness of the insurance contract?

> Tell men the story of life insurance over this past period of three and one-half years. Do not let them forget that life insurance was

functioning from October 1929 until the third day of March 1933. Ask them what else they owned functioned as life insurance did. . . . Do not let them forget that even if they had to wait ten days or two weeks or four weeks for some money, even though they needed it; that nobody, with a few very minor exceptions, has asked them to take one penny less than their contracts called for.

As to the future, President Cleary held out hope and promise. The events of the past months, he stated, emphasized more than ever before that management would be the vitally important factor in life insurance. These events would underline the need for firmness and soundness of policy and stress those elements which indicated safety and stability to the intelligent purchaser of insurance. The Company's agents should look forward with confidence because,

> You have seventy-six years of integrity behind you, you have seventy-six years of stability of policy behind you; and I say to you, now, that at least to the extent that my word goes, those policies and that integrity will continue to back you up in your selling.

Cleary's rapport with his audience, principally agents, was perfect. The editor of *Field Notes* reported that the crowd "gave him such an ovation . . . as this reporter has rarely, if ever, witnessed on such an occasion."

Strengthening the Management Structure

Cleary's concept of the presidential function was inherently simple: to select men in whom he had confidence, assign them responsibility, delegate authority, and leave them alone to execute their tasks. He was eminently successful in appraising men, and his selections were frequently brilliant. While all department heads reported to Cleary directly, according to the formal table of organization, in practice the procedure was more simplified and effective. Vice President Evans had Cleary's unreserved confidence, and he skillfully developed a pattern of coordination among the Company's insurance and agency executives which contributed significantly to the effectiveness of the organization. In turn, this relieved the president of many responsibilities, permitting him to direct his attention to other and more pressing problems. Among the latter, particularly during the early years, were financial and investment matters, about which he was less experienced than either of his two predecessors. Cleary, however, learned quickly and profited greatly from the tutelage of his investment officers and the members of the Finance Committee alike.

The president, despite his quickness of mind, did not believe in making decisions rapidly, and this quality he also impressed upon his colleagues. While his philosophy of management required that his subordinates be granted full freedom of action, Cleary was too much of a realist to assume that all his officers possessed equal ability, either in thinking creatively or in the execution of administrative responsibilities. The stimulatives, or, more rarely, the disciplinary correctives which he felt compelled to apply were invariably subtle, gentle, and demonstrated a high regard for the dignity and feelings of the men involved.

One of the characteristics of life insurance companies during the great depression was that employment, both in home offices and in the field, did not decrease proportionately to the reductions occurring in other fields of business. In many cases, in fact, the opposite was true; Northwestern was one of these cases. In the Company's agency force, as has been shown, there was a noticeable increase in numbers between 1929 and 1933. The huge increase in policy loans, surrenders, term extensions, and option changes expanded the Company's paper work significantly and resulted in additional clerical employment. In the investment fields, even though conventional opportunities were contracting, the problems of foreclosure, management of properties acquired through such process, and those pertinent to the bankruptcy of corporations in which the Company had invested required additional personnel with experience and skill in these areas. Unemployment, and the blocking of opportunity to men in various fields during these unfortunate times, made available large numbers of persons with the type of training and experience needed by the Company. This situation was used to the advantage of Northwestern and the men it recruited. One indicator of the quality of those hired by the Company during the first two years of Cleary's presidency was their progress made within the organization. Seven of these men were to become executive officers, including a president and four vice presidents.

President Cleary began his administration with the full complement of executive officers who had served Van Dyke, with the single exception of the mortgage loan vice president, Howard D. Thomas. The most pressing need, in the upper echelon of management, was for an executive capable of providing immediate assistance to the president in meeting the pressing problems of cash demands and defaulting investments. Late in December 1932 Cleary persuaded Edmund Fitzgerald, a young vice president of the First Wisconsin National Bank in Milwaukee, to provide such assistance on a part-time basis. The procedure followed was reminiscent of the Palmer-Markham eras of the Company's history. Fitzgerald was recommended as a trustee, duly elected at the Board meeting in January 1933, and appointed to the Finance Committee as a substitute member.[4] He served in this capacity, or as an unofficial member of the Committee, until July 1933 when, at the age of thirty-eight, he was elected a vice president.

The confidence Cleary had in this newest member of the executive group was quickly evident. To a very large degree Fitzgerald was left free to create his own job, and to identify and assist in the problems most vital to the welfare of the Company. Between 1933 and 1937 he provided valuable assistance in the areas of finance and investment, particularly in special real estate, bond default and reorganization cases, and in working out satisfactory solutions to troublesome mortgage situations. But he was no solitary specialist; when problems of advertising, public relations, and associations with business organizations within and outside the life insurance industry became increasingly important, he turned his attention to these. In 1937 the Home Office clerical force formed an independent union, demanding, among other things, that Northwestern organize a personnel department and improve its wage and job classification policies. M. J. Cleary recognized the grievances and the opportunities. Collective bargaining was accepted, a personnel section was established and put under the jurisdiction of Fitzgerald.

In effect, Fitzgerald became the executive vice president, although no change in title was made. That he was marked to succeed Cleary was apparent and officially emphasized during 1943–1944 when he was elected to the Board and appointed to the Executive Committee. In line with Company policy Fitzgerald had resigned from the Board after his appointment as vice president in 1933. During his tenure as vice president Fitzgerald provided the same kind of coordination in specific areas as Percy H. Evans provided in the insurance and underwriting field. He directed and harmonized the work of the treasurer, comptroller, and director of personnel, and was responsible for building maintenance, allocation of space, and supply, in addition to the previously indicated functions.

The only other addition to the structure of executive management in the Company came toward

TABLE XV-1

Northwestern Mutual: Executive Officers, 1933–1946

OFFICE	INCUMBENT	DATES OF INCUMBENCY		
President	Michael J. Cleary	1932		
Vice Presidents:	Edmund Fitzgerald	1933		
Bond	Frederick W. Walker	1926		
Mortgage	Howard D. Thomas	1932	1945	R
	Howard J. Tobin	1945		
Actuarial	Percy H. Evans	1929	1945	R
Agency	Grant L. Hill	1946		
Actuary	Percy H. Evans	1915	1945	R
	Elgin Fassel	1945		
Comptroller	Shepard Barry	1932		
Director of Agencies	Charles H. Parsons	1925	1933	D
	Grant L. Hill	1933		
Director of Underwriting	Joseph N. Lochemes	1945		
General Counsel	Sam T. Swansen	1930	1943	R
	Gerald M. Swanstrom	1943		
Medical Director	John W. Fisher, M.D.	1896	1936	R*
	D. E. W. Wenstrand, M.D.	1936		
Secretary	E. D. Jones	1923	1935	D
	G. L. Anderson	1935	1942	Res
	Ralph E. Perry	1943		

R—Retired   D—Died   Res—Resigned   * Continued to serve as emeritus functionary

the end of the period when the "Underwriting Department" was formed. Originally entitled "New Business Issue," this department was organized in 1942 and renamed three years later. It was responsible for the clerical functions concerned with the issuance of new policy contracts, the nonmedical aspects of underwriting controls, and was established to permit a more effective administration of this aspect of the Company's work. The first head of the underwriting department, Joseph Lochemes, a Northwestern career employee, was appointed an executive officer in 1945.

While these were the only additions to the executive management structure during the Cleary administration, there were, of course, several changes in personnel. As shown in Table XV-1, death and retirement caused executive succession in the agency, medical, and secretarial departments before 1937; while four other officers were replaced by the end of the period.

Throughout these fourteen years there was a continuous expansion of the Company's middle man-

agement personnel (junior officers) from forty-three at the end of 1932 to fifty-six at the close of 1946. The greatest increase took place in the bond, legal, actuarial, and agency departments. A treasurer was appointed in 1933, but this was primarily a change of title from cashier and involved only a minor change of function. A similar expansion took place in the lower echelons, both because of the expansion of the Company's activities and because, following unionization of the clerical staff, all personnel classified as "specialists" or higher were designated as members of management.

Sales Management and the Selling Organization

The election of M. J. Cleary provided the basis for a strengthened organization to market the Company's insurance plans and for a continued improvement in the morale and efficiency of the field force. To a significant extent his election had been a victory for the agents, particularly for the general agents. There was sound reason for them to assume that the general orientation of the Home Office would be closer to the market than had been the case in the past, and that certain underwriting limitations would be relaxed. Some of the field men undoubtedly hoped for much more, but those who knew Cleary best recognized his devotion to sound underwriting principles and simplicity of operations. While they knew that he favored equipping them "with a full kit," they also realized that the kit did not include policy contracts, insurance plans, Company subsidization of agents, or channels of distribution which violated those principles.

It appeared clear that Cleary's own ideas of successful marketing included the maintenance of the general agency system, the continued development of district agencies within that framework, and steady improvement in the selection, training, and management of agents. He desired that Northwestern agents should be the best in the industry and that their earnings should be proportionate to their skill. Since he believed that the field force had already achieved this distinction, he wished to maintain it by eliminating those of its members who were ineffective agents and by recruiting men capable of selling the type of insurance in which the Company specialized. This concern for quality extended to the Company's general agents and those responsible for sales management in the Home Office.

The Home Office Agency Department

The focal point of the Company's general agency apparatus was, of course, the individual general agent. Coordination of the agency organization, as well as the direction of the marketing effort, was the responsibility of the Home Office agency department and the director of agencies, as the position of superintendent of agencies was retitled in 1933. The director of agencies was responsible directly to the president, but his work was coordinated, through the Insurance and Agency Committee and Vice President Evans, with that of the Company's insurance and underwriting divisions. When Cleary became president Charles H. Parsons was the incumbent director, operating with a large and functionally organized staff. His death in June 1933 posed the problem of providing a well-qualified successor to this important position. The specifications for an ideal director of agencies were clear. The Company needed someone who could combine marketing experience, administrative skills, and vast energy with the ability to imbue the whole agency organization

with enthusiasm. Moreover, this had to be an enthusiasm for Northwestern Mutual and its way of doing business.

The president's search for a successor to Parsons was patient and unhurried; he knew what he wanted and it was a matter of finding the man to fit the specifications. After a thorough canvass he made his selection: Grant L. Hill, production manager of the McMillen general agency in New York City. Hill, born in Des Moines, Iowa, was thirty-six years old and had already achieved an enviable success in life insurance marketing. A man of extensive selling and management experience, and a United States Marine officer in World War I, he became convinced Northwestern offered the best life insurance for the buyer. After McMillen became a general agent in New York City, Hill joined him as production manager. His selling record before coming with Northwestern was brilliant, while his administrative skills and flair for promotion won general acclaim in the New York field. His reluctance to surrender the freedom and income that were already his for the responsibilities and fixed salary of agency director was understandable, but President Cleary was not to be denied—he was no mean salesman in his own right. Convinced of the opportunities of the proffered position, and intrigued by its challenges, Hill accepted Cleary's offer and assumed his new duties in September 1933.

There can be no doubt that challenges confronted him. His youth, his brief experience with the Company, and his assumption of a position to which others in the agency department aspired subjected Hill to the old skepticism of "let's see what he can do."[5] The new director of agencies met the situation with poise and reserve; within a few months he was ready to execute those steps which, in the opinion of Cleary and himself, required prompt action. Certain of these pertained to territorial realignment of various general agencies to permit more efficient development. Hill was also determined to cull nonproductive agents from the field force so that the sales management resources of the Home Office and the general agencies could be more effectively utilized. He made a tour of the field to acquire a first-hand view of general agency resources, personnel, and problems; assessed needs, and solicited ideas from many sources on how Northwestern could best meet these needs without violating the integrity of its independent contractor system. In his own opinion, there were "no bad times for good ideas," and by example he demonstrated that this was not an idle adage. He also advocated changes in some of the Company's underwriting limits affecting age and sex.

At the time Grant L. Hill became director of

agencies the department staff, in addition to the complement of clerks, specialists, and supervisors, consisted of six assistant directors of agencies. While these officers, as has previously been explained, kept in touch with the general agencies by field trips, conferring with the general agents, and evaluating the operations and personnel of each agency, Hill believed that the system could be tightened and improved.[6] After this reorganization each assistant director was responsible for specific agencies within a definite zone, the number of field trips to be made each year was established, and each general agency was kept in direct personal contact. In addition, Hill made certain changes in the functional responsibilities of his assistants, shifting men to those tasks best suited to their special talents.

The increasing specialization of the functions of sales management resulted in the need for more personnel, and by 1946 the agency department staff of assistant directors had been increased to eight men. An indication of Hill's concepts of the role to be played by his department assistants in the development of the Company's agency organization was their rate of turnover. Fourteen men served as assistant directors of agencies during these years, five of whom became general agents. Hill knew that the attributes he sought in a general agent included administrative and managerial ability. One of the ways of providing experience, as well as a testing ground for determining a man's ability to work harmoniously with others toward given goals, was to bring promising agents into the Home Office to assist him. Here they could absorb Home Office viewpoints, administrative training, and a concept of the functioning of the entire field, all of which would be highly valuable for a man appointed as a general agent. At the same time, the continual infusion of men from the field into the agency department would keep that organization sensitive to the real problems in the field and more alert to provide the essential services needed in the market.

Hill applied an unwritten rule that consideration would first be given to the agents in the field when a general agency opening occurred, and that if it were not filled from that source, an appointment would be made from the ranks of assistant agency directors. The degree to which this policy was followed is clear: the five men appointed general agents from Hill's staff during this period comprised less than 10 per cent of the total appointments made.

The direction and strength of Grant Hill's characteristics and interests were forcefully reflected in the emphasis placed on the various aspects of the operation of the agency department and the general

agency field. He was promotion-minded and thoroughly convinced of the benefits of sound underwriter training. A man of intense loyalty to the Company, to his colleagues and subordinates, he expected—and exacted—reciprocal faithfulness in others. He fought hard for the interests of the Company's agents, insisted upon and obtained freedom of expression for his and their viewpoints. At the same time he insisted that when the Company made its decisions, whatever his own opinion, that policy be carried out in the field and in his own department.

As a result of these qualities Northwestern's relations with the agents and the efficiency of its marketing organization were greatly strengthened. Agent education and training, sales promotion and advertising, and agency accounting and finance were emphasized. Local, regional, and national meetings of agents were characterized by new levels of enthusiasm; communications between Home Office and the field were steadily improved, and with mutual profit. The Company contributed much more, in time and money, to such organizations as the Life Insurance Sales Research Bureau, the Association of Life Agency Officers, and the American College of Life Underwriters. In turn, it drew more heavily on the services and information these organizations offered in such matters as the training, recruiting, selection, and supervision of agents.

Hill's contributions to Northwestern were evidenced by the improvement in agents' morale, increased productivity per agent, and the tightened efficiency of the whole apparatus. He was rewarded by a degree of agent loyalty and a warmth of personal affection from the field which the Company had not experienced since the era of Willard Merrill. Northwestern's management and trustees recognized this in 1946 when he was elected a vice president.

Size and Structure of the Agency Force

The basic structure of Northwestern's agency organization remained unchanged throughout this period of its history, although a minor modification was made in the district agency framework. More than 99 per cent of the new business issued was the result of the direct sales effort of the Company's own agents, with the rest being insurance accepted from agents of other companies where the insured already had the limit allowed by those companies.*

The earlier constancy in the number of general agencies in operation was continued during the period. The number of general agencies varied from year to year within a range of eighty-four and eighty-eight; during the previous fourteen years the variation had been between eighty-five and eighty-nine. From 1933 through 1937 the number of agencies in operation did diminish, but over the following six years it increased to eighty-seven. During the first three years of Cleary's administration Northwestern closed four general agencies (Dubuque, Iowa; Worcester, Massachusetts; Asheville, North Carolina; and Racine, Wisconsin; while one of the two in Cleveland was transferred to Akron, Ohio). In 1938 a second Nebraska agency was opened at Lincoln, and four years later a contract was issued for a general agency in Albuquerque, New Mexico so that the Southwest could be more effectively developed. During the following year the Company advanced another step toward making Chicago into a metropolitan territory similar to New York City when a second general agency was opened there.

No important alteration was made in the regional distribution of the Company's general agencies. The New England-Middle Atlantic and South Atlantic regions each lost one agency during the period; at the end of 1946 these had, respectively, twenty-three and seven general agencies in operation. The East and West North Central regions had twenty-four and sixteen general agencies, respectively, at the close of 1932; each lost one agency during the 1930's, and after 1939 each recovered one agency. The East and West South Central, as well as the Pacific Coast regions, incurred no change, having, respectively, three, two, and seven agencies in operation throughout the period. In the Mountain region there was an increase from five to six agencies.

The Company's force of general agents was also characterized by a high degree of constancy. Of the ninety-seven general agents (including partners) under contract at the close of 1932, forty-four were still active fourteen years later. The average annual rate of new general agent appointments was about 4 per cent, slightly above that recorded during the years of the previous administration.

In contrast to the stability of the general agent personnel the total number of district, special, and soliciting agents was greatly reduced during this period as the Company cleared nonproducers from its

force. In 1932 the aggregate number of these agents was 7,100; eleven years later the sales force was reduced to 3,633. During 1946 the number rose to 4,090; this was principally because of the return of men from the armed services.

The over-all reduction of the agency force affected part-time agents to a somewhat greater degree than it did full-time men. The number of the former fell from 3,718 to 1,962; the latter fell from 3,382 to 2,127. As a result the proportion of full-timers rose from 47 per cent in 1932 to 52 per cent in 1946. Part-time agents continued to be recruited in the rural territories, while in the city agencies their number was greatly reduced. In all territories general agents were strongly urged to renew contracts only with agents who produced sufficient new business to qualify for renewal commissions.

Induction of Agents: Old Problems with New Intensity

The sources of Northwestern agents during these years remained virtually unchanged from those which had produced members of the selling force in earlier periods. The continued trend toward specialization in the larger insurance cases, such as trust and estate planning, business and corporation insurance, and pension fund underwriting, strongly emphasized the need for better-educated personnel among the agents and in turn strengthened the tendency to recruit college graduates. This emphasis, when added to the enhanced training of new and older agents alike, intensified certain problems for the general agents and the Company. While no permanent solutions to these problems were forthcoming, a start was made in that direction which gave promise for the future. In the field of agent training the Company steadily improved its program. By the close of the period Northwestern had established the framework for the intermediate and advanced training of agents which placed it well up among the most progressive companies in the industry.

For the years prior to the United States' participation in World War II there was, in general, no seriously acute problem of financing the general agencies. Here and there, of course, when specific problems of financing arose the Home Office acted promptly to assist the affected general agents within the framework of the independent-proprietor relationship. As suggested in a previous chapter, one of the fundamental reasons for the generally strong financial position of the Company's agencies was

---
* In such cases the business was not accepted unless the company for whom the agent was under contract verified that such was the situation. In cases of this kind a "one-case commission agreement" form of contract was used by Northwestern.

that the great volume of insurance sold in the 1920's tended to persist in force; and as this business began to pass out of the renewal commission period in the 1930's the general agents received collection fees from it. In addition, new general agents received a 1 per cent collection fee on the business of their predecessors which was still within the commission interest period. During 1936, for example, the average amount of all collection revenue per agency was about $13,000, sufficient to finance approximately two-thirds of all agency expenses. The average investment in a general agency, including operating surplus, advances to agents and policyholders, furniture and equipment, and other items, was not excessive. Even in 1945 it amounted to only $13,500, of which $8,500 represented the general agent's own capital or his reinvested earnings.[7] With the war and sharply increased income taxes, the difficulty of accumulating capital intensified for men who were appointed general agents. The problem of financing new general agents correspondingly increased.

To assist new general agents in cases where their capital resources and collection income were insufficient to permit the adequate development of an agency, the Company provided assistance in two ways. First, beginning in 1933 it increased the scale of loans to general agents; second, in special cases an additional collection fee was granted. The loans made by the Company were secured by the general agent's renewal interest, were to be used only for investment in the agency, and bore the going market rate of interest for such types of risk.[8] Since the management believed that a general agent should have his own funds invested in his own agency as early as possible, the Company tried to secure amortization of its loans as quickly as agency revenues were sufficient to provide for new capital requirements and still yield a surplus for the repayment of indebtedness. In the cases where extra collection fees were permitted these were strictly limited as to amount, and were terminated when the management was convinced that the agency's development would not be imperiled by the withdrawal of such revenue.

Agency development, of course, depended to an important degree upon the efficient induction of new agents, particularly in mid-decade, in view of the diminishing proportion of new business being produced by men who had been under contract prior to 1930.[9] Because they were becoming more selective in choosing new agents, the Company's general agents found it necessary to provide more interim financing of recruits during the induction period, both for living expenses and to supply adequate training. For many general agents this problem was not particularly pressing; for others the opposite was true. Important among the reasons for the difficulties confronting the latter was the degree of variation in the contracts between general agents and special and soliciting agents. Because of the lack of uniformity, general agents who gave less than others came under pressure to be more liberal; while others, hoping to modify earlier arrangements in view of changed circumstances, came under other pressures to preserve the status quo. The Company brought the representatives of all the different agents' associations together in 1938, seeking to achieve greater uniformity and understanding in this matter, particularly as concerned distribution of the first renewal commission. The management believed that the extra 5 per cent commission of the first renewal should be devoted to agency development and used as an incentive for increased production. Had such a proposal been universally acceptable it is probable that a substantial part of the induction-financing problem would have been solved; but this agreement was not achieved to the degree desired by the Home Office.

After 1941 manpower shortages and alternative employment opportunities, at attractive rates of remuneration, added to the induction problems of the general agents and increased the necessity of financing newly recruited agents. With their own resources being seriously affected by the greatly increased scale of income taxes, the general agents asked the Company to assist in meeting the induction problem. In 1943, following joint conferences of the General Agents' Association and agency department officials, the Executive Committee approved a plan which it believed would alleviate the difficulties while preserving the letter and spirit of the general agency system.[10] The Company agreed to advance funds to general agents based upon the number of new men inducted, the advances to be secured by the general agents' renewal interest and the loans to be amortized within three years. Each general agency could receive up to $200 per month for each new man placed under contract, up to a maximum of three agents for a single year. The general agent would recoup from the agents' commissions. The program, as initially conceived, was to last four years, and the Company's maximum aggregate commitment was set at about $700,000. General agents, of course, were not restricted to recruit only three agents annually or to limit the amount of their own advances; this was merely the limit of the Company's assistance. In March 1946 it was necessary to increase the amount of the advances to $300 per month per agent to attract the class of new agent desired.[11]

During the first twelve years of the period Northwestern's agent educational material was continually revised, but the basic format and pattern of agent training remained virtually unchanged. The correspondence feature was abandoned, and the Company's "Short Course to a Northwestern Career" was introduced in 1935. This course became the first stage in training Northwestern agents. For advanced training of agents Northwestern relied principally upon the work of the American College of Life Underwriters, the cooperative efforts of many of its general agents, and members of the Home Office agency staff. By 1933 sixty-one of the Company's agents had earned the coveted Chartered Life Underwriter designation; five years later there were 136 such agents in the field force.[12] While this number constituted less than 3 per cent of the total agents under contract, it amounted to more than 10 per cent of all agents in the industry who had earned the designation; and according to estimates of the agency department, the Company had more CLU members under contract than did any other life company during these years. Although possession of the designation was not by itself a guarantee of an agent's success, there was significant evidence that the productivity of CLU agents substantially exceeded the average for the Company's entire agency force.

In addition to the constant modification of its own training materials and encouraging its agents to prepare for the Chartered Life Underwriter examinations, Northwestern contributed to organizations engaged in activities associated with improved agent training and education, including the training of teachers of life insurance.[13]

Beginning in 1946 the Company's educational program was considerably expanded and revised, both in content and emphasis. These changes had their beginnings in 1945 when, as the war drew to a close, the director of agencies proposed that the Company provide a refresher course for the 250 full-time agents who were expected to return to Northwestern upon demobilization. The Executive Committee approved a plan which provided that the Company would underwrite the travel costs of such agents as desired to attend the course in Milwaukee, while the general agents were to pay all other expenses for those they sent.[14] The first course for returned veterans was held in the summer of 1945, and before the program was completed the following June seven separate sessions had been conducted.[15] At the same time a series of refresher courses for more experienced Company agents was begun, the content of which concentrated on such matters as tax problems, estate planning, business

insurance, and pensions. These "Advanced Training" courses were conducted both at the Home Office and in different geographical regions, and included seminars for which Northwestern engaged prominent legal authorities from all parts of the United States.

From these refresher programs agency department officers responsible for agent training developed the plans which were to characterize the Company during the ensuing decade. The integrated plan began with the "Short Course," which was compulsory for every Northwestern agent, and was followed by the "Reporting Program," a thirteen-week course developed several years earlier during a time when reduced staff and restrictions on travel had limited its application. Thereafter, agents could progress to the newly developed "Intermediate Course" and ultimately to the "Advanced Course." In addition, the Company set up the "Career School," patterned on the original refresher course structure; and continued to hold regional seminars in taxes, business insurance, and estate planning for more advanced agents. The Career School was conducted in the Home Office semi-annually for a period of two weeks. Originally general agents paid all the expenses of agents they sent to the school, but because this imposed differential travel costs the Company assumed transportation expenses after 1947.

Certainly the most important contributions to the development of agent education were the intermediate and advanced underwriting programs. These courses were not formally begun until 1947, but the integral planning, course content, and organization had been set up in 1946. The intermediate program contributed several important new techniques in training life insurance agents, the most significant of which was the case-study method.[16] Subsequently this method formed the prototype from which the National Association of Life Underwriters developed an equivalent program. The advanced underwriting course undoubtedly was among the most progressive developments taking place in the industry at the time; like the other elements of the Company's educational program it was closely geared to the Chartered Life Underwriter movement.

Underwriting Standards: Stability and Change

During the fourteen years following 1932 the underwriting practices of United States life insurance companies continued to develop within the same general framework that had evolved after 1906, but were complicated by the effects of increased human life expectancy and a steadily falling pattern of interest rates. The number of insurance plans offered by the industry grew as companies devised new appeals to the life insurance needs of the public, many of which were altered and intensified by the Social Security Act. Group underwriting increased significantly, as did the number of persons covered by such plans, while the steeply increased personal income tax and estate taxes after 1941 greatly broadened the appeal of life insurance for large segments of the population. By the end of the period the interaction of increased longevity and falling interest rates had caused the adoption by most life companies of revised mortality and interest assumptions, and resulted in somewhat higher premium and annuity rates.

At Northwestern the modifications which occurred in insurance plans offered were few in number, but important in effect. Similarly, the standards of risk selection were adjusted in the light of further experience. While these adjustments constituted no important departure from traditional underwriting standards, they did extend the range of the Company's market and improved the selling and income opportunities of its agents. The effects of falling interest rates and greater life expectancy were matters of deep concern to the management, particularly because of the high percentage of policies in force under life income settlements. During the period the Company took necessary steps to protect itself against adverse selection, and culminated these attempts by adopting the newly authorized Commissioners' 1941 Standard Ordinary Mortality Table, with a 2 per cent interest assumption.

For years Northwestern agents had campaigned to have the Company accept women as risks, reduce the lower age limit on all risks, and adopt some type of family-income plan to offset certain merchandising appeals of competitors. After intensive investigation, in 1933 the management responded favorably to all three of these requests. In February the Company announced that it would insure males down to attained age ten, the limit on a single life to be $5,000, increasing by equal amounts annually to a maximum of $25,000 at age fourteen.[17] Several months later a family-income plan was introduced. This plan was similar to those being marketed by competitors in that it consisted of an ordinary contract with a term insurance rider; but unlike other plans the preliminary term rider provided for twenty annual installments following

the death of the insured instead of the period of income coverage beginning with the original policy date. Promptly promoted by sales literature and special effort, the family-income plan soon became a valuable new tool in the hands of agents. By early 1934 *Field Notes* commented on the plan's popularity and reported that the Company was "issuing more than $250,000 a day, on the average, on upwards of twenty lives."[18]

While certainly no more important in terms of sales volume than lowering the age limit and introducing the family-income plan, the decision to again accept women as risks was historically more dramatic. Fifty-eight years after it had ceased insuring women, and less than ten years since the preceding administration had rejected a similar proposal, the Company reversed itself on the basis of the great changes which had occurred in the economic status and methods of selection of women since 1918. *Field Notes* explained that

> The growing importance of women in the investment, business, and professional fields has been carefully watched by the Company in its constant effort to keep abreast of changing conditions. Rapid advance in these fields, both in number and in directions which indicate increased responsibility and earning power, has established them as desirable life insurance risks.[19]

The Company imposed several limitations on female risks: the maximum amount which would be carried on a single life was only one-half that permitted men, while the extra premiums for the disability benefit were double. Restrictions on finan-

cially dependent women were even more stringent.* The Company expected that despite the limitations imposed on feminine risks, this move would result in increased business such as had been the experience of other insurers.[20] This expectation was realized.

In August 1933 the Company introduced its single-premium life annuities. This move was made in spite of misgivings on the part of Percy H. Evans, who was disturbed by the longevity trends and fearful that interest rates would continue to fall. He foresaw only trouble if the management committed itself further to the annuity business. The members of the Executive Committee, however, believed it to be one of the services which Northwestern should offer to its market. The following year the number of insurance plans was increased again when a special retirement endowment, maturing at age fifty-five, was introduced. This plan was similar to the types previously issued which matured at ages sixty and sixty-five.[21]

By 1936 Evans' reservations about annuities were being confirmed. Late in the previous year he called the management's attention to the heavy volume of single-premium annuities and limited-payment endowments being issued, and upon which Northwestern had assumed interest rates of 3.8 per cent and 3 per cent, respectively. Pointing out the obstacles to the actual realization of such rates, he suggested three modifications to be applied to future issues of these contracts: that premiums on single-payment endowments be raised, with a higher expense loading and lower interest assumption; that single-premium annuities on one life be limited to $25,000; and that joint-and-survivor refund annuities be discontinued. These suggestions were quickly adopted.[22]

In 1937 Northwestern revised certain terms of all its policies to become effective the following year; the representatives of the various agents' associations were invited to participate in the contract modifications and several of their suggestions were adopted. Most important of the new features adopted were the extension of the disability benefit to term policies and the introduction of an initial term contract.[23] In addition, the dual-income option, which provided a life income on two lives, was revived. During the course of preparing

the new contract series Evans expressed his view that the downward trend of interest rates made it imperative to modify certain privileges available to policyholders, particularly by limiting the income options to reasonable periods of time. Cogent though his arguments were, the management did not believe the time was appropriate for so fundamental a change.[24] During the following year, however, the Company announced that the rates it would guarantee to pay on dividends and settlement option funds left with Northwestern at interest would be reduced from 3 per cent to 2.5 per cent on policies issued after 1938.[25] Annuity premiums were further modified by increased expense loading.

Prior to 1940 Northwestern had added materially to the number of endowment plans offered the public. In addition to the special retirement endowments a series was introduced in 1936 with a period of payment ranging from ten to forty years, and in 1938 a single-payment endowment was made available, as was a single-payment life contract. Development in the marketing of endowments was accelerated, beginning 1938, by the expansion of employee pension plans in American business firms. This expansion was stimulated by the introduction of social security in 1937, and by rulings of the Bureau of Internal Revenue which permitted the deduction from income of employer contributions to pension plans. Northwestern entered the pension trust field in 1938, and its special retirement endowments formed the basis for plans set up by its agents. In 1940, in response to certain problems arising out of pension trust cases, the Company issued a deferred-retirement annuity plan which was followed in 1941 by a single-premium, deferred-retirement annuity.[26] These annuities, however, were restricted to pension trusts and not offered in the general market.

The effects of increased life expectancy and falling interest rates became more serious after 1939; and Northwestern met the problems to the extent of its ability. Nothing, of course, could be done about contracts already in force, but for contracts to be issued in the future, adjustments could be made to provide for lower expected interest earnings. In June 1940 premium rates on annuities were revised on the basis of a 2.5 per cent rather than a 3 per cent interest assumption, together with a slight reduction in the loading.[27] This move was helpful, particularly in terms of the Company's life income options; but the tendency in the industry was also toward lower interest assumption and certain competitors increased annuity rates to the extent that Evans became alarmed. In 1943, claiming

---

* Such women were limited to $5,000 of life insurance, and were not eligible for the disability benefit or term insurance. In all cases of women applying for insurance and naming the husband as beneficiary, agents were instructed to refuse the application "unless the husband carries a satisfactory amount of insurance payable to the applicant." *Field Notes,* Nov., 1933, Vol. XXXIII, No. 3 (Supplement).

that the effect of such competitive moves was to place the Company in the position of offering a preferential price on annuities and the life-income options, he recommended the adoption of a new life-income option table with interest assumption at 2 per cent.[28] As adopted by the Executive Committee in April 1944, this meant a higher maturity value for retirement-endowment, retirement-annuity, and single-premium retirement-annuity policies.[29]

The only other addition to the number of Northwestern's insurance contracts were ten-, fifteen-, and twenty-year convertible-term contracts, issued in 1941. These nonrenewable policies were adopted "to meet certain problems of the agency force in competition."[30]

The outbreak of war in Europe in 1939 was, like its precedent twenty-five years earlier, an indication that United States life insurance companies would eventually have to apply war-risk riders to contracts. It was not until the fall of France, however, that Northwestern executives considered a war clause necessary. In October 1940 the president was given discretionary power to apply the war-risk limitation to new contracts, after obtaining approval from the several state departments of insurance.[31] The Company did not actually put the clause into effect until December 24, 1941, two weeks after Pearl Harbor.[32]

United States life companies did not adopt a uniform war clause as had been done during World War I, but all companies did conform to the rules adopted by the state insurance departments. There was some competition between companies on the basis of extra charges, benefits, and assumption of full liability, but this was held within reasonable bounds. Northwestern underwrote full liability for insureds who paid extra premiums on contracts subject to the wartime limitation; for those who did not, the liability was for return of premium only. The vast proportion of Northwestern insurance out-

standing, however, was not subject to the clause. As in the previous war Company agents campaigned to familiarize prospects and policyholders liable for military service with the advantages of National Service Life Insurance.

The Company's mortality experience during World War II for both military and civilian risks was better than it had been for the years preceding the war, including the experience during the depth of the depression.[33] Of the $915 million of insurance issued by Northwestern between December 24, 1941, and September 1, 1945, all of which was subject to war and aviation restriction, death losses due to war service totaled only $340,325.[34] The mortality record of the Company for civilian risks was superior to that of World War I, even when the effects of the 1918 influenza epidemic are discounted, and as indicated by the following tabulation:[35]

WORLD WAR I				WORLD WAR II	
RATIO OF ACTUAL TO EXPECTED MORTALITY	YEAR			YEAR	RATIO OF ACTUAL TO EXPECTED MORTALITY
55.87%	1914	Outbreak of European War		1939	52.40%
60.31	1915			1940	54.63
63.62	1916				
54.23	1917	United States Entry		1941	50.25
				1942	50.44
				1943	51.97
				1944	55.42
78.12	1918	End of War		1945	48.99

The Company continued to enjoy a favorable total termination rate during this entire period. The ratio of actual to expected mortality fell from about 56 per cent in 1933–1936 to about 46 per cent in 1946. The lapse and surrender rate was well below the industry average and few, if any, companies equalled or exceeded Northwestern's aggregate termination rates on a year-to-year basis.[36] In 1941, for example, the Life Insurance Sales Research Bureau reported that the Company's termination rate of 3.9 per cent for the first nine months of that year was the lowest ever reported by a United States company for a comparable period.[37]

The steadily increasing life span in the United States would, by itself, have caused a revision of the basis of life expectancy as measured by insurance mortality tables. This had occurred near the turn of the century when the American Experience Table was adopted by the life insurance industry. Whether the adoption of a new mortality table would have been accompanied by the assumption of a lower rate of interest, and correspondingly higher premiums, depended upon the nature of investment opportunities and the income investments could earn. The sharp reduction of investment opportunities for life companies during the years of depression, when combined with federal fiscal and monetary policies aimed at reducing interest rates, was cause for serious concern among the nation's insurers. The life companies were committed, on existing contracts, to rates of 3 per cent or higher; as interest rates were driven lower during the war and approached 3 per cent, the concern became even more grave. With expenses consuming 0.25 per cent or better, the margins between the contract and actual net earning rates tended to disappear entirely.

In 1939 the National Association of Insurance Commissioners appointed a committee to propose a new mortality table, the chairman of which was Alfred N. Guertin, now actuary of the American Life Convention. Between 1930 and 1940 Guertin, as actuary in the New Jersey insurance department, had conducted studies of the mortality experience of United States companies; and this combined experience was reflected in the mortality table proposed by his committee.

This new "Commissioners 1941 Standard Ordinary Mortality Table" involved the recognition of the actual industry experience, including a margin for safety. The use of the table, in effect, would result in a lower net level premium at any rate of interest assumption than would the American Experience Table.[38] Although the C. S. O. table could be used with any rate of interest assumption, it was quite obvious that most companies were ready to move to lower rates. At Northwestern, for example, the excess of interest earned over the 3 per cent assumption had narrowed from 2.3 per cent in 1923 to 0.7 per cent in 1940, and by all indications would diminish even further.[39] As this trend continued, the management became eager to make the Company's 3 per cent policies a "closed group" and to write future business on a lower interest basis.

While there was no division among the members of management at Northwestern about the advisability of adopting the C. S. O. table once it had been accepted by the various states in which the Company did business, this unanimity did not extend to the rate of interest which the Company should assume. Percy H. Evans and Elgin G. Fassel, who was scheduled to succeed Evans as actuary, were convinced that the long-term interests of the Company would be served best by a 2 per cent rate. In their opinion the true net costs to policyholders in a mutual company would, on the average, be identical, regardless of the reserve basis used for calculating reserve values and gross premiums.[40] The lower rate would provide greater security in the event that interest rates, for any reason, were driven even lower. Other management members, however, were apprehensive about the marketing effects of premium rates which might be higher than those of competitors. Northwestern agents, who participated in the discussions of the problem, were particularly sensitive on this account. There was the further possibility that the greater margin of income that the 2 per cent base would provide might subject the Company to higher income taxes.

In April 1946 President Cleary, after an agonizing consideration of the rival contentions, recommended to the Executive Committee that the 2 per cent basis be adopted by the Company for policies to be issued in 1947.[41] The Company's two life-income option settlements, however, being in effect annuities, would be based on the Standard Annuity Table with a 2.5 per cent interest assumption.[42] Cleary's decision was typical of those of Northwestern presidents when confronted with similar situations, and one of the most difficult he believed he had ever been called upon to make.

Corollary to the 1941 mortality study, the insurance commissioners investigated the practicability of adopting new standard valuation and nonforfeiture provisions for the life insurance industry. The committee to which this study was assigned was also directed by Alfred N. Guertin, and in December 1940 presented several model bills for consideration. Following study by a joint committee representing the membership of the Association of Life

Insurance Presidents and the American Life Convention, the model bills were revised and finally adopted by the commissioners in 1942. The purpose of the two bills was to divorce nonforfeiture benefits from policy reserve liability, adjust the premium method to be used in defining the statutory minimum for benefits, and to apply a modern mortality table in the computation of reserve liabilities and nonforfeiture benefits.[43] The adjusted premium was calculated on the basis of a preliminary term formula, using the 1930–1940 experience, and with interest assumption of not more than 3.5 per cent.

The commissioners recommended that the legislation to be introduced into state legislatures be permissive after July 1, 1943, and should not become mandatory until 1948 at the earliest.[44] Actually, by the end of 1946 thirty-five states had adopted the valuation and nonforfeiture bills, and the remaining states and the District of Columbia were being pressed to join them.[45] Some of the delay in the remaining legislatures was due to certain differences between the bills being recommended by members of the industry and those recommended by the Guertin Committee, but this was reconciled before 1948. By that year Oklahoma was the only state which had not enacted the standard bills; and more than 95 per cent of the insurance being issued was on the new mortality and reserve bases.[46] Northwestern had endorsed the Guertin proposals, and the Company's legislative counsel had successfully campaigned for their adoption by the Wisconsin legislature in 1943.

Sales Promotion

With a smaller, better trained and supervised agency force and with a more flexible array of insurance plans, Northwestern also undertook a more extensive and aggressive promotional campaign throughout the period. The agents had frequently requested the Company to advertise nationally, but until 1933 the management had always backed away from such suggestions. During 1933 the point was again raised, this time by Merle Thorpe, editor of *Nation's Business,* at that time a member of the Company's Policyholders' Examining Committee. Following numerous subcommittee meetings and consultations with various advertising agencies, the Executive Committee approved a plan in 1934 which had several objectives. These were the bolstering of agent morale, the furnishing of new leads for agents, the provision of uniform direction to sales effort, and assistance in reducing lapse rates and confirming sales in process of closing.

The first advertisement to appear in a nationally distributed consumers' magazine featured the appeal of the "Billion Dollar Estate." Variations on this theme touched upon the major purposes of life insurance. Media included seven magazines, among them two farm periodicals. In this and subsequent campaigns the national program was supplemented by local campaigns in the various marketing territories, where adaptations of the national advertising copy were used.[47]

National advertising absorbed the greatest proportion of the Company's annual promotional budget after 1933; but through the special division which was set up in the agency department, from 25 per cent to 50 per cent of the promotional outlays were channeled into planning aids, special literature, and other selling aids. As a result of this program much of the heterogeneity of promotional material that had previously marked agents' "kits" disappeared.[48] The total amount spent by Northwestern on advertising and promotion during the fourteen years was $3.4 million.* This exceeded past Company budgets for promotion, but still amounted to only 2.2 per cent of Northwestern's direct acquisition expense, and less than 0.2 per cent of premium revenue. In comparison with similar budgets for major competitors in the industry, these expenditures were modest.

The role of the Honors Program and the Marathon Club in the production of sales continued to be as important after 1932 as had been true earlier. With the improvement of business during 1934–1938 the number of members of the Million Dollar and Half-Million Clubs increased. The importance of these heavy producers in the success of Northwestern's marketing program was indicated in 1938 when the twenty-three agents who had sold at least $500,000 of insurance during the agents' year had averaged more than $722,000; and approximately 1 per cent of the Company's agents were responsible for almost 6 per cent of the total insurance then in force.[49]

As already indicated, the augmentation of employee pension plans in many industries received particular impetus by the enactment of social security and the favorable tax rulings concerning employer contributions to such plans. During the war and immediate post-war years steep corporate taxes and strong union pressures contributed even further to the growth. In establishing pension plans industry had a number of institutional and personal serv-

---

* Agents, of course, continued to spend substantial amounts on advertising and other promotional activities.

ices upon which it could draw for assistance, including independent actuaries, trust companies, and life insurance companies. The latter, during the years immediately following 1937, were in a particularly advantageous position because of their unique ability to grant guarantees, something neither trust companies nor independent actuaries could offer.

Northwestern's management was divided concerning the desirability of entering the pension trust field. Company sales were at the lowest point since 1933; its agents had contacts in hundreds of the smaller, closely held businesses where they had been selling key-man, business, and personal insurance to officers; and members of the field force were concerned about the effects upon these clients if other companies moved in to underwrite pension plans.[50] These considerations argued for Northwestern participation in the pension trust field. On the other hand, some officials were anxious that acceptance of such business would adversely affect the Company's basic underwriting philosophy and impair its excellent record of low cost, low lapse rate, and careful selection of risks.[51] There was also some apprehension that acceptance of pension business would bring Northwestern, at least partially, into the group field and complicate the simplified structure of internal operation.

The several management viewpoints were reconciled when Northwestern entered the pension trust field during the years 1939–1941. Each employee covered in plans underwritten by the Company was insured by individual special-retirement endowment, deferred-retirement annuity, or other contracts; a complete medical examination was required for each. The Company provided limited help to agents pioneering in this field, but, unlike group companies, sent no specialist-helpers to the field. During 1941 Northwestern prepared what was probably the first manual on individual pension trusts in the business, and conducted a special seminar for those agents desiring more intensive instruction in pension trust agreements and their problems. * A pension trust division was subsequently established in the secretarial department, and the Home Office worked out routines, methods of subjecting policies to pension agreements, and special forms required to make the cases effective.

Invaluable as the Home Office contribution was

---

* Members of the secretarial and agency departments, with assistance from the actuary and general counsel and three members of the field force who had gained early prominence in installing pension systems, are credited with the preparation of this manual. These same persons were also reponsible for conducting the seminar, as well as for subsequent contributions to the development of training agents in pension agreements.

to the success of Northwestern's pension trust business, it was the agent in the field who had to sell and administer the plan and provide the continuous and demanding service to his clients. The Company allowed the regular pattern of commissions on pension cases, and during the early 1940's a dozen or more agents had developed exceptional skill in the marketing and administration of pension trust agreements. Furthermore, the advantages of Northwestern's competitive contracts, particularly in pension cases of small and medium-sized firms, attracted some especially qualified agents of other companies. Before the end of the war many agents in such commercial and industrial centers as Detroit, New York, Chicago, Milwaukee, Cleveland, Minneapolis, Los Angeles, and St. Louis were specialists in the field and had developed resources of their own to implement the Company's contribution, including tax, legal, and government-relations consultants.

While Company agents succeeded in installing pension plans in a number of the very large American corporations, the basically individual nature of Northwestern plans was probably better suited to the needs of smaller firms. In this field the Company's success was remarkable. During the twenty-two months ending August 31, 1942, Northwestern set up 185 of the aggregate 1,288 government-approved pension plans established. By the close of 1944 the Company had installed 548 such plans, equal to 7 per cent of the almost 7,800 government-approved pension arrangements which had been introduced in the years after 1920. The extent of the pension trust business in Northwestern's own marketing was also astonishing. In 1944, for example, pension trust contracts accounted for over 20 per cent of the total insurance issued, and included in these plans were agreements ranging from buyers with fifty employees or less to the Chrysler Corporation case with almost 2,500 policies.

During 1945–1946 two factors caused a retardation of the expansion of Northwestern's pension trust business. First, management was growing more concerned regarding the absolute magnitude of its outstanding insurance which was included under pension agreements. As a result, further underwriting restrictions made pension policies somewhat more difficult to market.[52] Second, there was a marked slowdown in the number of pension plans installed.[53] There were several causes for this deceleration, including the uncertainties arising from the conclusion of the war, repeal of the excess profits tax, the Supreme Court decision which ruled that pension plans were subject to collective bargaining, the termination of wage stabilization, and possible modifications to the Social Security Act. Even these factors, however, did not seriously detract from the impressive pension trust business in force in Northwestern. At the end of 1946 the Company's pension insurance amounted to nearly 8 per cent of the total number of government-approved plans which had been installed in American business up to that time.

The executive group was not particularly happy about the proportion of the pension business concentrated in the large cases, for nearly one-fifth of the insurance involved in pension plans was gathered in only eight of the more than seven hundred trusts. For reasons stated earlier, however, it was obvious that the Company would continue to do a pension business, but the natural market would be among smaller companies. There were several indications that the management would make no special effort to sell the huge industrial organizations, or even struggle to retain such cases which it had in force.

Relations with Agents

Morale of Northwestern agents reached the lowest ebb during the dreary months of the financial crisis of 1932–1933, for not only was personal income affected by declining sales and increased lapse and surrender of policies, but the fears for the future of life insurance penetrated the ranks of the men in the field. With the forceful leadership exerted in the Home Office, the obvious desire on the part of management to give the field force all the assistance which was compatible with Northwestern's basic principles of operation, and with the improving economic environment, morale quickly recovered and remained high throughout the rest of the period. The loyalty the agents gave M. J. Cleary personally became indistinguishable from that rendered Northwestern. The field force felt itself to be a more integral part of the total Company effort than ever before; representatives of the various agents' associations participated in management examination of questions which particularly affected their interests, and this had a beneficial effect upon the degree of enthusiasm with which they helped carry out policy. In addition, because of improved training, better selection and supervision, and Company promotional assistance, the men in the agency force became steadily more competent and better able to sell persisting, profitable insurance. Loyalty, high morale, and identification of interest were also im-proved when the Company set up a retirement plan for agents in 1942.

Company actions to widen the market by modifying the limitations on certain risks and promoting the family-income plan during the first few years of Cleary's administration served to bolster morale and provide additional bases for income. The prompt responses to the needs of general agencies for revenue during the height of the financial panic of 1933, and the assistance rendered to some of the more hard-pressed agencies by Company loans and additional collection fees had still further beneficial effects, as did subsequent management actions. In 1935, for example, the Company permitted the extra premiums charged for disability-waiver protection to be included in aggregate premiums when computing agents' commissions. Four years later, when sales slumped to the lowest point of the decade, the management revised its former policy respecting premiums waived under the disability clause and permitted these to be subject to commissions as well.

When preparation of the new policy series to be issued in 1938 was in progress, the Company also undertook to re-examine the structure of compensation of its agents. In the process the compensation plan was revised in several important aspects, the decision being reached only after exhaustive consultation with representatives of the general, district, and special and soliciting agents' groups. Among the most important objectives of the revised compensation arrangement was the provision of additional funds to the agencies for development purposes. Other objectives included liberalization of the production requirements that determined an agent's eligibility to earn full renewals and a liberalization of the "veteran's clause."[54] For special agents the volume requirements for renewal commission qualification were reduced approximately 15 per cent; and all agents were helped by the revised veteran's clause which reduced the number of years agents had to be continuously under contract before they could qualify for full renewal commissions without regard to production requirements.*[55]

To provide for agency development the Company left to the discretion of the general agents the determination of the distribution of the extra 5 per

---

* The benefit for special agents was accomplished by granting credit when and as first-year premiums were paid by policyholders, and by permitting one-half credit for term insurance as it was written and the other half at the time of conversion. Previously credit was given only upon conversion. The revised volume requirements for renewal commission qualification were set on a graduated basis which probably was more beneficial to agents who produced less than $100,000 annually than for any others.

cent first renewal commission, suggesting that it be paid for development effort only. In cases where general agency territories used district agents, volume requirements were eased respecting qualification for renewals, and provision was made for standard district agent over-rides on the new business of soliciting agents.[56] In addition, a "district agency experimental plan allowance" was authorized to apply specifically to district agents in cities of 50,000 or more population. An extra collection fee allowance was granted to such agencies, payable on a fixed sum per month basis, and was related to the program for eliminating part-time agents in cities of this size. In authorizing the experimental plan for district agencies of this type the Executive Committee limited the amount of these allowances to $100,000 annually beginning in 1941.[57]

Congressional enactment of the Social Security Act in 1935, together with subsequent state legislation and rulings of the Bureau of Internal Revenue, created great uneasiness in life insurance circles concerning the employment status of agents. In June 1937 Northwestern's contention that its agents were independent contractors, and hence not taxable for social security purposes, was upheld by the Bureau of Internal Revenue. While this decision relieved the Company of a substantial tax bill, it also meant that the Company's agents were not eligible for federal old age benefits. During 1939–1940 representatives of the agents' associations suggested that a retirement plan be set up to provide them with the type of protection which had been accorded Home Office employees and loan agents for over twenty years. Under the direction of Percy H. Evans an extensive investigation of such a plan was conducted, including the opinions of federal and state authorities as to the tax status of the Company's contributions.

The Wisconsin insurance department approved the Company's proposal in 1941, and following authorization of the Executive Committee, the agents' retirement plan went into effect in 1942.[58] The plan, self-administered by the Company, provided that all agents with fifteen or more years of service with Northwestern would be eligible for retirement benefits upon attaining age sixty-five. The program was to be financed through the joint contributions of agents and Company, and administered by a special retirement committee in the Home Office. Agents' contributions were set at an amount equal to 4 per cent of their annual first-year and renewal commissions, with the option of making additional deposits in equivalent amounts. Northwestern's contribution was 10 per cent of the renewal commissions and fees earned annually by agents. This base was chosen

because it accentuated the value to agents of persistent business. During the first five years of the plan's operation the Company contributed a total of $936,000.

General agents, however, were not included in the agents' retirement plan, and the Company came under strong pressure to establish a similar program for these men. The management embarked on this study with great reluctance, not because it was adverse to contributing to the welfare of general agents, but because of the fundamental underlying differences of its relations with the general agents. Because of these differences the approach to the whole question of retirement for general agents was much more complex than had been the case of the agents' retirement problem. The differences received their most obvious expression in the application of different tax laws, and it was these which constituted an important obstacle to a solution of general agents' retirement questions in a manner consistent with the management's desire to retain the general agency system as it then existed. Nevertheless, the Home Office, with the assistance of a committee of general agents, developed the framework for a retirement plan which was submitted to the trustees for approval in early 1947.

During this entire fourteen-year period it was evident that among the reasons for improved agent morale and for the steady improvement in the relations of the Company with the field force was the level of income earned by the men with the rate books. Despite the fact that Company sales during the years before Pearl Harbor were generally below those attained during the 1920's, the revenues of the general agencies and the incomes of full-time career agents did not suffer a proportional reduction. This was fundamentally due to the persistent nature of Northwestern insurance which was productive of renewal commissions and collection revenue to a degree higher than the industry average. That the average level of agent income did not decrease greatly during the period was due also to the greater selectivity practiced in choosing new agents and to the rigorous policy of separating poor producers from the agency force.

Total compensation of agents for the period amounted to $146.2 million, including Northwestern's contribution to the retirement plan. The annual amount paid to the field force ranged broadly around the average of $10.5 million, the low point being $8.8 million in 1940 and the high being $15.3 million in 1946. Over 70 per cent of these amounts was ultimately paid to the district, special, and soliciting agents, and the rest constituted the general agency revenue. Of this amount between 50 per cent and 60 per cent went to pay the operating and other expenses of the agencies.

The gross revenues for all Northwestern general agencies rose during the middle 1930's from the 1932–1933 low, fell again during the 1938 recession, and then increased steadily through 1946. Actual data for five selected years for all general agents under contract for the full calendar year is given in the tabulation below on an average basis.

The range of gross and net agency income around the averages shown here was somewhat narrower than during earlier decades, but was still enough to result in fairly wide variation. Reasonable estimates for the net revenues of the smaller agencies would range from $10,000 in such years as 1933 and 1940, to over $12,000 in the more prosperous years. As in former years, the net incomes of the general agents in the Company's most productive agencies were probably twice the Northwestern average.

Compensation for nongeneral agents followed about the same trends. The average income for all such agents, other than revenue earned from other activity, was approximately $1,300 in 1933, $1,900 in 1940, and $3,700 in 1946. Data based on retirement plan records indicate, however, that the average compensation of full-time agents participating under the plan was about $6,600 for 1946; and if those agents receiving less than $780 of income during the year were excluded as being really part-timers, the average would approximate $6,900 per agent. For the depression years the averages were probably within the range of $2,400 to $3,600. Since many Northwestern agents earned commissions from other life companies through placement of insurance not accepted by the Company, even these estimates would tend to understate the actual average income per full-time agent under contract. As in earlier years, the earnings of Northwestern's most productive agents were much greater than the averages indicated. During the entire period the leading one hundred agents produced between 18 per cent and 24 per cent of the Company's annual volume of new business. Assuming consistent performance by the members of this group, their income from selling Northwestern life insurance would

have been four or five times higher than the average of all full-time agents.

The record of Company-agent relations during the period of Michael J. Cleary's stewardship was impressive. The management had demonstrated its desire to provide the men in the field with the best marketing tools, educational facilities, and supervisory skills. Coordination of field and Home Office interests in making decisions affecting the Company's market position and the agents' welfare had been brought to the highest level in its history. As reflected by agents' income data, the economic interests of the field force had been protected at the same time that the strength of the general agency operation had been preserved. Agents had been shown that Home Office sales management could be depended upon to represent their grievances and support their legitimate hopes for the future. The desire of agents for recognition as an integral part of Northwestern was verbalized by a representative of one agency group in 1935 when he argued for continuing to have the Association of Agents meet during the week of the Company's annual meeting:

> the agents are what make a life insurance company, in spite of theories that the agents are merely a necessary nuisance. . . . We want to impress the trustees of this Company with what the agency force is and the calibre of the men there, and just incidentally, we may impress them with the fact that we are a vital force in the Company.[59]

By 1946 there was no question in the minds of any member of the Northwestern family that this had been achieved.

The Marketing Record

The effects of a better-directed force of well selected and trained agents were apparent in Northwestern's record of sales, insurance in force, and acquisition costs during the fourteen years ending December 31, 1946. The Company issued insurance, other than revivals, increases, and dividend addi-

	1933	1936	1940	1943	1946
Gross Revenue	$34,023*	$33,921	$36,193	$42,045	$53,635
Expenses	18,169*	20,456	20,437	20,865	29,136
General Agents' Net	$15,854	$13,465	$15,756	$21,180	$24,499

* The gross revenue and expense averages are estimated for 1933; the general agents' net revenue, however, is actual.

tions, with a face value of $3.56 billion; insurance in force increased from almost $4 billion to slightly over $5 billion; while aggregate direct acquisition expenses for the period were $155 million. Total marketing-associated expenses amounted to $212 million. These included: agents' compensation and Company contributions to retirement, $146.2 million; medical examinations and risk inspections, $5.6 million; advertising and promotion, $3.4 million. Total taxes paid were $55.0 million; legislative expense, $62,000; legal outlays, $279,000; hotel and travel expenses, $1.2 million; and costs associated with the settlement of contested claims, $412,000. Measured by insurance in force Northwestern remained the eighth largest life insurance company in the United States.

Because of the prolonged effects of economic depression the value of the insurance sold by the Company during this period was about $880 million, or 20 per cent less than the volume marketed during the previous fourteen years. This, however, was an experience common to the entire industry, for the total of $116.3 billion of ordinary insurance purchased in 1933–1946 was about $20 billion less than that purchased for the years 1919–1932; and the aggregate sale of all classes of life insurance of United States companies was $183.8 billion, down $14 billion from the level of the previous period.[60]

While Company sales did not increase as rapidly as did aggregate sales of all types of life insurance during the period, Northwestern continued to market almost the same proportion of ordinary insurance issued by the industry as it had during the years 1926–1932. For the entire fourteen years Northwestern issued almost 3.1 per cent of the aggregate ordinary insurance purchased through United States companies, and its insurance in force at the end of 1946 amounted to 4.3 per cent of aggregate ordinary in force in United States companies. Fourteen years earlier it had amounted to 5.2 per cent. By comparison with four of its traditional rivals, all ordinary companies, this was a most impressive achievement. Aggregate sales of Mutual Benefit, Mutual Life of New York, Penn Mutual, and New York Life, all of which were included among the ten largest firms in the industry, were equal to about 12.3 per cent of total ordinary sold during the period, and substantially below the comparable achievement for the previous fourteen years. The insurance in force for these four companies fell from 21 per cent of total ordinary in 1932 to 15 per cent at the end of 1946, a relatively greater rate of decline than that experienced by Northwestern.

The cyclical effects of prosperity and depression

are indicated in Chart XV-2 showing the sales of Northwestern, the ten largest life companies, and the entire industry.

Two basic factors of Northwestern underwriting policy and sales programming were also evident from the record of the Cleary administration. These were cost and persistency. The absolute amount of the Company's acquisition and other market-associated expenses is not significant unless related to the Company's income base. For the period, direct acquisition expenses constituted only 7.8 per cent of premiums collected by the Company; the total of all externally incurred expense, some portion of which was associated with marketing effort, amounted to only 10.7 per cent of premiums. When combined with the savings effected due to favorable mortality experience and low Home Office expenses, this kind of restraint in the acquisition of new business resulted in the type of low-cost insurance that was a Northwestern trademark.

Life insurance that was well sold, fitted to the needs and resources of prospects, and properly serv-

TABLE XV-2

Eleven Largest United States Life Insurance Companies: Persistency of Insurance in Force, 1933–1946

COMPANY	(1) 1932 In Force Plus 1933-1946 Sales	(2) In Force 1946	(3) Col. (2) ÷ Col. (1)
(Dollar Figures in Millions)			
Northwestern	$7,777	$5,046	64.88%
New York Life	14,211	8,543	60.11
Equitable	17,767	10,564	59.46
Mutual Benefit	4,307	2,462	57.17
Penn Mutual	4,182	2,376	56.82
John Hancock	14,949	8,306	55.60
Metropolitan	62,035	34,422	55.50
Travelers	13,313	7,360	55.29
Prudential	49,211	26,072	52.98
Mutual Life	7,666	3,949	51.51
Aetna	13,672	6,314	45.88
Total:	$208,873	$115,414	55.26%
Total of United States Companies	$288,443	$174,553	60.52%
Ordinary Only	$194,020	$116,110	59.84%

Source of Basic Data: Northwestern, *Annual Statement*, 1932-1946, incl. Other companies, *Insurance Year Book*, 1941, 1950. Industry, *Life Insurance Fact Book*, New York: Institute of Life Insurance, 1953.

CHART XV-2

Sales of Insurance: Industry and Northwestern, 1933–1946

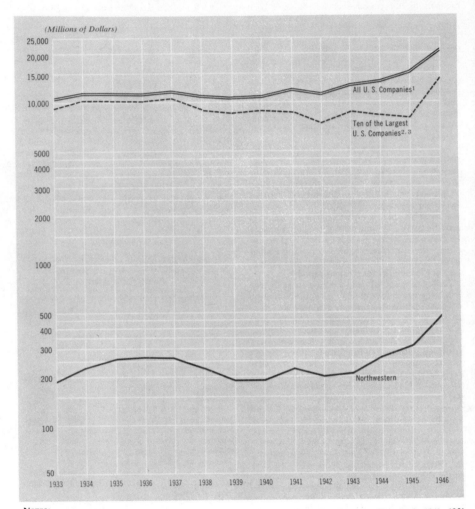

(Millions of Dollars)

All U. S. Companies[1]

Ten of the Largest
U. S. Companies[2,3]

Northwestern

NOTES:
[1]Exclusive of dividend additions, revivals, etc.
[2]Inclusive of dividend additions, revivals, etc.
[3](Metropolitan, Prudential, Aetna, Equitable Society, Travelers, John Hancock, New York Life, Mutual Life, Mutual Benefit, and Penn Mutual)

SOURCES: Companies: *Insurance Year Book,* 1941, 1951.
Industry: *Life Insurance Fact Book,* 1955, p. 22.
Annual Statement, Northwestern Mutual, 1933-1946, inclusive.

iced tended to remain in force more persistently over time. Thus persistency was one measure of the competence and skill of agents, and the effort which produced persistent business was rewarded by greater agent commission income, a stronger general agency operation, and was profitable to companies and policyholders alike. The persistency performance, as indicated by Table XV-2, demonstrates clearly the Company's advantages in this respect. While subject to the caveats specified earlier, of the total insurance sold between 1933 and 1947 plus that in force at the end of 1932, nearly 65 per cent was still active at the close of 1946. This achievement not only exceeded those of the other life companies shown in Table XV-2, but was significantly better than that of those companies which marketed only ordinary insurance.

There can be no doubt that by relaxing certain principles, by spending the full amounts on acquisition of new business which were allowed by the New York insurance laws, by subsidization of the marketing apparatus, and by increased selling pressures, Northwestern could have sold a much greater volume of insurance than it did in 1933–1946. Neither can there be any real doubt that if these steps had been followed policyholders would have paid more for their protection, and that Northwestern would be a different company. The management and field force accomplished their marketing goals without that pressure, with due consideration for the interests of old and new policyholders alike, and retained the fundamental principles and operating policies which had permitted Northwestern to develop into the high-quality, specialty company it was. The principal differences between Northwestern during this period and the previous quarter century were attitudes and the quality of leadership, both of which were functions of social and economic change and a deepening maturity concerning the Company's role in American society.

CHAPTER SIXTEEN

Home Office and Legislative Relations: 1932-1946

Legislative Relations

THREE factors were primarily responsible for the increasing importance of legislative relations within the full sphere of Northwestern's activities. One, of course, was simply the prominence of the Company in the life insurance industry; as a leader, it had certain responsibilities. A second factor is reflected in the Company's budget. Aside from the compensation paid to agents, taxes constituted the Company's largest expenditure, an obvious indication of the importance of the Company's legislative relations. A third factor, directly related to the times, was the deep depression that provoked a rapid expansion of federal action in the economic life of the nation. Each of these factors, as this chapter will attempt to show, had a profound effect upon Northwestern.

With only a few exceptions, until 1933 the legislative experience of Northwestern had been confined to the individual states in which it conducted business. Similarly, the Company's experience with public bodies charged with the control of life insurance had been limited to the insurance departments of the states, to the various commissioners of insurance, and to the National Association of Insurance Commissioners. The exceptions were confined principally to federal revenue measures as they affected insurance company income. After 1930, however, the life insurance industry was directly affected by the far-reaching changes caused by the great depression and the important federal enactments of the "New Deal," especially fiscal and monetary policies, and the role of government in social welfare.

Indicative of the direction of this shift was the Company's activity in 1932 during the enactment of the revenue bill in Congress. The bill proposed to raise the corporation tax from 12 per cent to 13.5 per cent and—this was of particular interest to the life insurance industry—to reduce the allowance for maintenance of reserves on policies from the 4 per cent authorized by the 1921 Revenue Act to 3.5 per cent.* In urging that this lowered allowance for reserve maintenance be adopted, Northwestern subscribed to the position taken by representatives of the Association of Life Insurance Presidents;[1] but the American Life Convention, representing many of the smaller companies in the industry, was opposed to a flat rate being applied for maintenance of reserves.[2] This intra-industry controversy was evident, in one form or another, throughout the debates and hearings. At one stage the Senate Finance Committee adopted such a position that the tax bill of an insurance company like Northwestern would have been increased 180 per cent.[3]

Understandably enough, Northwestern fought

---

* H. R. 10236. This reduction was intended to restore to the government an estimated $4.5 million per year which had been lost as a result of the Supreme Court's decision in the National Life case in 1928, which declared that interest from tax-exempt securities was not to be included in excess interest aggregates (277 U. S. 508).

vigorously against this proposal, enlisting the help of Senator Robert M. La Follette, Jr. As finally enacted on June 6, 1932, the law was a compromise which set the corporate income tax at 13.8 per cent of net income, which for life insurance companies meant gross investment income less specified exemptions. These exemptions were: interest from tax-exempt bonds; investment expenses, real estate expenses, and rental value of occupied real estate; amounts equal to 4 per cent of the mean reserve funds required by law, except that a rate of 3.8 per cent would apply in any case where these reserve funds were computed at a lower assumption of interest; and a deduction of 2 per cent of funds reserved for deferred dividends.[4] Although Northwestern and the entire life insurance industry, as the result of this bill and subsequent revenue increases, paid substantially higher taxes to the federal government, it had succeeded in defending a basis for application of the tax which protected the interest of its policyholders and its competitive position to a much greater extent than would have been possible had the alternative method been adopted by Congress.

In essence, the 1932 tax legislation affecting the life insurance companies remained in force until 1942, when wartime financial needs of government brought about a general revision of federal tax legislation. In anticipation of pressure for a new tax base each of the two major life insurance associations, the American Life Convention and the Life Insurance Association of America, proposed tax programs that had the support of the majority of its members. Initially some American Life Convention companies, while not enthusiastic, apparently were willing to back a premium tax in preference to many other proposals; L. I. A. A. companies, in the main, preferred an excess earnings tax in which net investment income less the interest necessary to maintain policy reserves would constitute the base.[5] The tax committees of the two associations, however, agreed to work for a compromise solution which both memberships could endorse. After protracted negotiation with the Treasury Department, a compromise plan was submitted and enacted by Congress which contained the basic elements of the "free interest"[1] theory advocated in the fight over the 1932 revenue bill.

Briefly, the so-called "McAndless formula" imposed a 40 per cent tax (24 per cent on normal tax income, 16 per cent surtax income) on all net interest earned by life companies in excess of the amount

required to maintain reserves. The tax base was determined on an industry-wide scale. Each life company submitted data on its investment income, investment and real estate expenses and depreciation, tax-exempt interest, and the interest necessary to maintain its reserves. The Secretary of the Treasury then calculated a ratio (Secretary's ratio) with an over-all industry allowance of 3.3 per cent interest rate. This ratio, when applied to each company's net investment income after deduction of tax-free interest, comprised the company's tax base.*

Although Northwestern executives favored a tax based upon premiums, M. J. Cleary supported the McAndless proposal and the Company's legislative counsel in Washington rallied Congressional support for the compromise plan. What the management wanted—what many other companies wanted also—was a unified industry position on federal taxes, even though many would have been individually better off with another formula. No such compromise was reached, however, either during the war years or within the decade following the end of the war.

While the life insurance industry paid more in federal taxes during the war years than it had previously, the McAndless formula produced less revenue than was anticipated. The principal reason for this was "that it predicated tax payments on bases which assumed adequate conservatism in the rates of interest in calculating reserves, and that no substantial changes in interest assumptions would be made."[6] Fundamentally, this was the same weakness that underlay all federal taxes on life insurance beginning in 1921. As the structure of interest rates steadily declined investment receipts of the life companies were reduced; and life insurance executives were forced to revalue reserves on a lower base. The net interest rate earned for the overwhelming majority of companies was too low to place them in an excess profits bracket. This situation led to a reconsideration of the tax base in the postwar period.

In general, the life insurance industry received the initial New Deal legislation and executive orders with mingled emotions. Many companies took the position that the moratorium extended to life insurance companies in 1933 was unwarranted, while others accepted it as offering a breathing space that permitted public panic to abate. Agreement regard-

---

* That was, the interest earned above that necessary to maintain the legal reserve and other contract commitments.

* The formula was, Tax Base $= (N - E)(1 - R/N)$. N, net income, was gross investment income minus investment and real estate expenses and depreciation. E represents tax-exempt interest; R represents reserve interest allowance. See Buley, *The American Life Convention*, II, 901n; Revenue Act of 1941 (*United States Statutes at Large*, 56, Part 1 [77 Cong., 2 sess., 1942], Ch. 619.)

ing the abrogation of the gold clauses in all contracts and the decision to devaluate the dollar was more general; only a handful of insurance executives believed that some things might be more disastrous than inflation.[7] During a time when over ten million persons were unemployed and the productive facilities of the country were operating at half capacity, the life insurance industry's preoccupation with inflation appeared somewhat curious. Strong inflationary tendencies, if protracted, could do irreparable harm to life insurance contracts; but the depth of a deflationary period seemed hardly the most propitious time to raise the issue.

Like other managements, Northwestern executives were concerned about the possibility of a code for the life insurance industry during the period of the National Industrial Recovery Act, and Northwestern accepted the President's Re-employment Agreement in the late summer of 1933. In addition, Company legislative representatives closely followed the hearings on the Securities Act in 1933 and the Securities and Exchange Act during 1934. It was not until the Frazier-Lempke Farm Bankruptcy Act was up for Congressional consideration in 1934, however, that the Company took an active and direct part in attempting to influence federal legislation. Northwestern's newly appointed legislative counsel, Clarence C. Klocksin, worked vigorously to modify or defeat the bill, but without success.

The management found the Frazier-Lempke Act especially objectionable. Under this legislation a farmer might petition in bankruptcy that his entire property be appraised and that he retain possession; following appraisal by a district court, if amenable to the creditors, he could pay 1 per cent interest on the outstanding balance. Should the creditor refuse to agree, the farmer could gain a stay of five years during which he could occupy the premises at a "reasonable rental."

The Company quickly challenged the constitutionality of the Frazier-Lempke Act in the lower courts. President Cleary explained Northwestern's opposition on two grounds. First, in addition to its alleged illegality, it was detrimental to the indebted farmer who needed to "adjust his financial structure," and tended to impair "the future credit that is a necessity to prosperity in agriculture."[8] Just as strongly he resented the dangers which this legislation implied for the effective cooperation between the Farm Credit Administration, Federal Land Bank officials, state and local committees, and representatives of institutional lenders in meeting the distressed mortgage problems. This cooperation, which had followed passage of the Farm Credit Act

in 1933, had functioned, according to Cleary, "in a way that was producing results beyond the hope of any of us twelve months ago."[9]

In May 1935 the Supreme Court of the United States found the Frazier-Lempke Act unconstitutional since it deprived persons of property without due process or just compensation.[10] This decision came just four days after the Court had nullified the National Industrial Recovery Act in the famous Schechter case. Together with other life company managements the Home Office greeted this decision with approbation.

In the same year Congress passed the Social Security Act, another measure that provoked opposition in the life insurance industry, including Northwestern. Many life company officials regarded the act as being destructive of personal initiative, self-reliance, and other virtues. Creation of a $50 billion insurance reserve, as originally proposed, which would be invested in the bonds of the United States excited many others, including Percy H. Evans, who questioned whether politicians could refrain from using this planned reserve for ulterior purposes.[11] Michael J. Cleary somewhat misread the willingness of the American public to accept social security when he informed the Company's agents that "the idea of social security through legislative decree and political machinery has not clicked with the American public, and anyone who thinks it has should look at the record. . . ."[12] In J. Owen Stalson's opinion, however, among the reasons for passage of the bill was the failure of the life insurance industry to meet popular demands for "low-outlay, low-cost, long-term, bare-protection contracts."[13]

Subsequent modification of the Social Security Act somewhat calmed the uneasiness of the life insurance leaders. For example, the proposed reserve to be "invested in government debt" was modified. Furthermore, the amendments of 1939, although providing for benefits payable to "beneficiaries" of the insured employees in event of death, did not have the effect feared by the industry of reducing the demand for regular, privately issued life insurance. Instead, as a leading insurance authority has explained, the effect was just the reverse,

chiefly because the maximum benefits which can be obtained under O. A. S. I. are no more than sufficient to provide a bare subsistence so that many insured employees, who might not have purchased insurance at all, are interested in supplementing the government benefits by taking additional insurance in the private companies. This need has, in fact, opened up a new field in insurance selling.[14]

The Social Security Act had an additional effect upon life insurance companies: were agents "employees" to be covered by the act, or were they independent businessmen? The Company held to the latter view, while the Social Security Board, at least for a time, interpreted the law to include agents. The result was a period of indecision on a state as well as national level which was not finally resolved until June 15, 1937, when the Bureau of Internal Revenue ruled:

> that the Company here does not exercise the control prescribed by the Regulations under such Titles [VIII and IX of the Social Security Act] as being necessary to establish the relationship of employer-employee for the purposes of . . . the Act. It is concluded, therefore, that the agents of the Northwestern Mutual Life Insurance Company are not employees of the company within the meaning of . . . the Social Security Act.[15]

In January 1938 the Bureau buttressed this decision with an informal ruling, given to the manager of the American Life Convention, that "companies whose contracts were similar to those under which agents were exempted might assume similar exemption for their agents."[16] Thus Northwestern agency contracts became models for other companies seeking exemption of agents from the tax provisions of the Social Security Act.

State officials tended to follow the Treasury's lead in the matter of agents' status. In 1939 Northwestern again had cause to be disturbed when the House of Representatives passed a Social Security Board bill intended to alter the construction of the term "employee" from the traditional common-law meaning to one of "economic reality." Clarence C. Klocksin and other Company executives strongly represented their views to the Senate committee holding hearings on the amendment, which was ultimately defeated. Even so, Northwestern and the other life companies had other occasions for concern during the next seven years. Not only did the Social Security Board support the House of Representatives' viewpoint by administrative interpretation, but many federal courts did likewise. Beginning with its decision on the Hearst case in 1944, the United States Supreme Court also tended to construe the term "employee" to conform to the concept of "economic reality."[17] While it was initially assumed that the Court was dealing exclusively with this interpretation of economic relationships in terms of labor law, the decision in June 1947 was extended to include the Social Security Act.[18] But the final interpretation lay in the future; at the end of 1946 the subject was in a state of uneasy equilibrium.

Federal Investigation of Life Insurance: The TNEC

The resounding re-election of President Roosevelt in 1936 reflected both popular support for the New Deal and its reforms and for the steady economic recovery which had begun in 1934. Despite the intensive drive of the Committee for Industrial Organization in the automobile plants, including the dramatic sit-down strikes, automobile production in 1937 exceeded the level of the previous year. Steel production in March 1937 was only slightly below that of 1929, and the industry was operating at 90 per cent of capacity. Price levels had risen at a faster rate than payrolls, but even the latter were up nearly 30 per cent over the corresponding level of 1936. While over eight million persons remained unemployed, an estimated five million had been reabsorbed into the labor force.

At this point Congress and members of the administration were persuaded to reduce expenditures, balance the budget, and inspire the kind of business confidence that would permit a rapid return to full prosperity. Congressional appropriations, beginning early in 1937, were cut by almost $1 billion; the Public Works Administration and Reconstruction Finance Corporation activities were tapered off sharply by early fall; and Federal Reserve Board actions tightened the supply of credit. Instead of the rapid return of prosperity these steps were followed by a slump in prices, curtailment of business spending, reduced payrolls, increased unemployment, and legislation inimical to the traditional concepts of vigorous competition.

Administration leaders, smarting under these reverses, suspected that not a little of the responsibility for the recession was due to monopolistic practices of industry. By April 1938 President Roosevelt was sufficiently convinced by his advisors to ask Congress not only for an expanded program of public spending, but also for a study of the concentration of economic power in the United States among which the vast pool of "investment funds controlled by our great insurance companies" was specifically named.[19] As finally organized, the "Temporary National Economic Committee for the Investigation of Concentration of Economic Power" was composed of three members from the Senate, three from the House of Representatives, and six nonlegislative appointees representing the Treasury, Securities and Exchange Commission, Labor, Justice, Commerce, and the Federal Trade Commission. Senator Joseph C. O'Mahoney of Wyoming became chairman, with Hatton W. Sumners of Texas, member of the House Judiciary Committee, as vice chairman.* Leon Henderson was named executive secretary, and responsibility for the insurance probe was assigned specifically to the Securities and Exchange Commission. Committee counsel for this phase of TNEC's inquiry was Gerhard A. Gesell, while financial advisor for the commission was Ernest J. Howe.

Pertinent information regarding the operations of life companies was available from the convention-form annual reports, but the SEC also required data not covered in these statements. Consequently, detailed questionnaires were sent to industry members pertaining to management, control, administration, sales, investments, expenses, and other financial aspects. Some industry members completed these questionnaires only reluctantly, for their preparation required considerable outlays in time and money. A minority responded with alacrity, and foremost among this minority was Northwestern.

President Cleary learned from a friend in Chicago that a representative of the TNEC staff had been making inquiries about the Company. Sensing the importance of good public relations, Cleary greeted the representative with cordiality and friendliness upon his arrival in Milwaukee. Vice President Fitzgerald was also called to the conference, and Cleary repeated the requests for information made by his visitor. Fitzgerald recalled that the president was warmly sympathetic to the problems of the investigator, frequently patting his shoulder. Although this was a Friday afternoon, with the Company due to be idle over the week-end, Cleary proposed to work members of the clerical and administrative staff overtime so that the TNEC emissary could return to Washington early the following week with all the requested data and exhibits. Although in sympathy with neither the TNEC investigation of life insurance nor with the national administration, Cleary realized that the probe was going to be held and that it was therefore only sensible to comply with com-

mittee requests gracefully and promptly. Furthermore, with his characteristic affection for individuals, he saw little reason to humiliate a rank-and-file employee who was merely doing his job. As a result, the TNEC representative left for Washington early the next week with his mission pleasantly accomplished, many pounds of questionnaires and exhibits in the baggage car, and a warm respect and admiration for M. J. Cleary. Without question this feeling was conveyed to SEC officials and was to materially affect their treatment of President Cleary at the hearings.

The Hearings

The committee began hearings in December 1938, their initial target being the relation of patents to the domination of markets by a few sellers. While germane to the over-all purposes of the inquiry, the almost academic procedures of this phase of the investigation lacked drama.[20] The insurance industry sessions began February 6, 1939, and continued for ten days. Following a three-month respite, the insurance phase of the investigation resumed in June, and additional sessions were held in September, October, and December. Final hearings were concluded in March 1940.

From the outset there was an obvious mutual antagonism between industry representatives and the SEC participants, with the Congressional members of the committee striving to maintain the inquiry on a dignified level. In many aspects the SEC was in the position of the Armstrong Committee a generation earlier. Since funds and time were limited, only a selected handful of companies and their executive officers could be carefully examined. If a case really existed which would support a thesis that the large size of sellers was correlated with restraints of competition and with results inimical to the best interests of the community, it would have to be tested in terms of the giant firms in the life insurance industry. If the thesis could be proved, then the recommended reforms would apply to all sellers in the business.

The committee's approach closely followed the practices of the Armstrong Committee. The questions of absolute size, self-perpetuating managements, costs to policyholders, interlocking directorates, and abuses of policyholders' interests reminded the observer of 1905. In addition, the committee was concerned with such matters as the magnitude of lapses and surrenders, industry "cooperation" on such matters as premium rates, control of

---

* Other committee members included Senators William E. Borah and William H. King, and Representatives E. C. Eicher and B. Carrol Reece. The committee representatives from the various departments and commissions consisted of William O. Douglas from SEC; Isador Lubin, Department of Labor; Thurman W. Arnold, Department of Justice; R. C. Patterson, Commerce; Herman Oliphant, Treasury; and G. S. Ferguson, Jr., FTC.

investment funds entering the capital markets, and selling and agency practices. William O. Douglas announced at the beginning that he had no doubts concerning the adequacy of the reserves of any company, and he assured the industry that the standards of the Armstrong Committee would be closely followed. This failed to calm the doubts that plagued life insurance men, not the least of which was a fear that the investigation was but the opening gun in a campaign to bring life insurance under federal regulation, perhaps even to merge industrial insurance with the social security program.* Industry people were also disconcerted by the attitudes of the committee counsel. Gesell was not a Charles E. Hughes; he was a determined inquisitor who had assisted Thomas E. Dewey when the latter had prosecuted a former chief of the New York Stock Exchange on a charge of fraud. His relentless cross-examinations prompted Ralph Ingersoll's innovative *PM* to remark, "he sometimes went after the big shots of the insurance business as though they were underworld characters brought to book for pandering."[21]

Northwestern Wins Commendation

The major exception to Gesell's standard examinations was the treatment accorded President Cleary of Northwestern. Although Northwestern's management was no less self-perpetuating than those of the vast majority of the life insurance companies, the Company's practices in the selection of trustees, its use of the Policyholders' Examining Committee, its scrupulous abstinence from having men on its board who might embarrass the management because of associations with other insurance firms, and the Wisconsin rule that three consecutive absences by a trustee automatically caused his removal, impressed the counsel and the committee, particularly the non-Congressional members. Several of the Congressmen were, in fact, absent when Cleary stated Northwestern's policy regarding working trustees. "We have always," the president observed, "taken the position that the law requires attendance at meetings, that the trusteeship carries responsibility, and naturally we don't want to put men on who may be forced off by failure to function."[22]

Although the counsel, both in his interrogation

and later in his report, produced little tangible evidence in connection with the matter of interlocking directorates and their effect on life management decisions, Northwestern was singled out for special commendation as an example of the absence of such a tendency. It was pointed out, for example, that when the securities of the Chicago and North Western Railroad Company went into default, the president of that carrier, Fred W. Sargent, was a member of the Northwestern Board of Trustees. The Company wished to avoid the embarrassment of finding itself handicapped, in protecting policyholders' interests by participation in bondholders' protective committees and reorganization plans, by having a railroad official in a position of influence on its board. His resignation followed. The investigation disclosed no similar action on the part of the Company's largest rivals, although identical circumstances existed.[23]

The committee noted many instances of what it termed "dubious interlocking connections" on the boards of several life companies. Although executives of other large companies insisted there was nothing wrong in this practice, and in fact that it was a necessary price to be paid for having men on the board who had the qualifications deemed desirable, Northwestern was held up by the committee as a shining example of a different ethic. To the question,

> in the process of eliminating people who might have an interlocking interest, has it ever been necessary for you to turn down a man that you regarded as superbly qualified and accept somebody whose qualifications seemed to you to be inferior to those that you could have had if it were not for that interlocking relationship,

President Cleary replied: "I wouldn't say that. My experience is that there is no superman. You can always find a duplicate."[24] Furthermore, the counsel found that in the selection of directors, Northwestern had been scrupulously careful to avoid conflicting interests.

> One individual was not chosen simply on the ground that Northwestern Mutual had a large investment in the company of which he was the chief executive officer. Another, who was active in the real estate field, was eliminated on the ground that his extensive activities in the Chicago area where the Northwestern Mutual had substantial holdings might bring him into conflict with the company's interests. . . . It also appeared

---

* James, *The Metropolitan Life,* 358. Also, Buley, *The American Life Convention,* Vol. II, 844, who states, "After the first round of hearings was over, life insurance men were relieved but somewhat puzzled as to the next step. Would the Securities and Exchange Commission recommend legislation to give it control of life insurance investment? . . . What purpose other than federal regulation could there be in continuing the investigation?"

that as a matter of general policy the Northwestern Mutual discouraged the inclusion of members of banking or investment banking institutions on its board since it sought to be perfectly free from 'any embarrassment in buying and selling securities,' and in the placing of its deposits.[25]

In several other respects Northwestern's performance was cited in comparison to the overwhelming majority of the insurance industry. One of the best examples was the matter of lapse and surrender rates, a point that the committee and counsel emphasized and that the industry, by and large, sought to minimize. Using a period extending from 1928 to 1937, the investigators pointed out that whereas insurance in the amount of $146.6 billion was sold, the net increase of insurance in force was but $16.1 billion. On the other hand, the amount of insurance terminated, $126.7 billion, was almost eight times the magnitude of this gain, and of that amount less than 22 per cent was accounted for by death, maturity, disability, decrease, or expiry. This exceedingly high percentage of insurance which was "terminated in a manner which did not fulfill the principal purposes for which it was intended" was also deprecated by the industry. Evidence on lapse rates for individual companies, prepared by the Life Insurance Sales Research Bureau, indicated that for some firms the rate was as high as 65 per cent of total terminations and as low as 9 per cent for others.[26] Northwestern's ratio of lapse to total terminations, while not the lowest for the period covered, compared favorably with other conservative companies.[27]

Of even greater gratification to the Northwestern management were the comparisons made by SEC specialists of net cost of insurance. One of the most difficult problems in competitive life insurance marketing was the matter of net cost. Yet it was largely on the basis of its low net cost to policyholders that Northwestern had attained its position in the industry. While admitting the obstacles in comparing costs, the committee staff applied what was probably a satisfactory method of showing the contrasts between life companies in the net cost of insurance to the body of policyholders. The results, calculated on a discounted base and employing the 1939 dividend scale, projected on the basis of policy continuation and policy discontinuation, respectively, placed Northwestern at the forefront of a representative selection of the industry. The comparative record of twenty-three companies is shown in Table XVI-1.

For decades the management of Northwestern had

regarded the Company as being, in essence, the competition for the rest of the industry, operating from such positions of strength as careful risk selection, a conservative number of insurance plans, and a low expense rate. The TNEC findings, like those of the various service and reporting agencies auxiliary to the industry, not only tended to publicize and confirm this belief but also brought out another characteristic of Northwestern—its competitive position with respect to price. Although to most companies the idea of competition on rates and net cost was abhorrent and to be avoided, Gerhard Gesell, who prepared the monograph on the life insurance section of the inquiry, noted that Northwestern, in contrast, believed it stimulated business.* To prove his point Gesell cited the Company's instructions to its agents.

> The important thing to realize, first of all, is that competition is not an unmitigated curse, as the comments of some agents would occasionally lead us to believe. It is not a curse at all. Active competition stimulates public interest and increases the sales of the best products. An experienced salesman offering a product of unusual merit prefers a highly competitive market because he knows that he will profit by the public attention which competition always directs toward the best product in its class.[28]

General Results of the Investigation

In many important respects the TNEC investigation of life insurance was frustrating, both to the public and to the industry itself. Like the Armstrong Committee before it, the TNEC was unable to develop a workable concept of effective size for a life company. Several of the very largest corporations appeared as able to offer low-cost insurance to the public as were middle- and small-sized firms. The committee, particularly the SEC segment, charged that various efforts at pricing agreements had been resorted to, particularly on annuities and nonpar-

---

* TNEC, Monograph No. 28, 235–238. Examples of instructions to avoid a competitive company approach in selling life insurance, included the following: "An excessive desire to establish a superiority of your own company may sow the seed of doubt in your prospect's mind, and perhaps make him feel that he can make a serious mistake by buying life insurance from the wrong company"; "Selling life insurance as a mere commodity instead of a service brings up the question of price, and that makes comparison necessary"; "All companies use the same or very similar tables in figuring actual rates for protection. You will get only what you pay for in every company. No company can give you greater protection for your money than another."

TABLE XVI-1

Twenty-three Selected Legal Reserve Companies: Net Cost of Life Insurance to Policyholders, as Shown by Temporary National Economic Committee Investigation, 1939

Participating Policies Only, Taken as of age 35, at end of 20 years, in amount of $1,000 or more

COMPANY	DISCOUNTED[a]		BASED ON ACTUAL DIVIDENDS	
	20-YEAR NET COST, POLICY CONTINUED	POLICY SURRENDERED END OF 20TH YEAR	20-YEAR NET COST, POLICY CONTINUED	NET COST, POLICY SURRENDERED END OF 20TH YEAR
Northwestern	$290.04	$125.41	$367.56	$39.98
Metropolitan	291.39	116.13[b]	370.15	37.31[f]
Prudential	303.50	134.14	361.69	50.69
Penn Mutual	300.77	136.14[c]	364.06	56.48
Provident Mutual	291.79	127.45	371.79	61.79
New York Life	301.67	137.33[d]	373.83	46.83[g]
National Life	294.00	129.66	393.88	66.30
New England Mutual	309.75	145.12	387.58	60.00
Equitable (Iowa)	304.25	139.41	389.44	78.44
Mutual Benefit	311.05	146.42	388.10	60.52
Equitable (New York)	311.76	147.42[e]	396.12	69.12[h]
Connecticut Mutual	310.69	146.06	405.04	77.40
Massachusetts Mutual	313.56	148.93	392.45	64.67
State Mutual	312.45	147.82	398.79	71.21
Phoenix Mutual	306.71	146.39	410.38	78.93
Pacific Mutual	306.54	141.70	435.36	132.36
Connecticut General	313.43	148.59	404.03	93.03
John Hancock	314.78	148.43	410.11	99.11
Mutual Life (New York)	342.96	178.33	404.08	76.50
Aetna	317.17	152.33	414.73	83.73
Banker's Life	320.03	153.45	408.05	97.30
Union Central	322.42	158.08	407.72	97.72
Guardian Life	324.67	160.04	410.16	82.58

NOTES:

[a] Policy discounted on a base of 3.5 per cent.

[b] Includes $9.92, the discounted value of "cash settlement" dividend, payable in addition to guaranteed cash value of policy, in event policy is surrendered at end of 20th policy year.

[c] Includes discounted value of "extra" dividend payable at end of 5th policy year.

[d] Includes discounted value of "extra" dividends payable at end of 10th, 15th, and 20th policy years as follows: 10th year, $5; 15th year, $10; 20th year, $20.

[e] Includes discounted value of "extra" dividend payable at end of 5th policy year.

[f] Includes "cash settlement" dividend of $18.84, as per note b, *supra.*

[g] Includes "extra" dividends, as per note d, *supra.*

[h] See note 17, page 244, Monograph No. 28.

SOURCE: Temporary National Economic Committee, *Study of Legal Reserve Life Insurance Companies, Monograph No. 28.* United States Government Printing Office: Washington, 1940, 243.

ticipating insurance; but this evidence appeared relatively unimportant when compared to the vast area of competition based on different rates and disparate costs. What the investigators apparently felt most uncomfortable about was the size of the industry's largest companies and what they believed this very size *could* mean in terms of economic power.

The growth of life insurance coverage had resulted in a great increase of institutionalized savings and had transformed insurance companies into vast investment organizations. The nature of the insurance contract, and the development of the legal framework within which insurance investments had to be made, forced reserve funds to flow into debt securities. During periods of prosperity with high levels of national income, the percentage of such income used to pay insurance premiums might be as low as 1 or 2 per cent, but in times of depressed economic activity this ratio had gone as high as 8 per cent. That this type of economic leverage *could* be misused, to the detriment of the public, there seemed little question. That it had not been misused, that insurance company managements with rare exceptions had been circumspect in their dealing with debtors, was in effect a tribute to both life company managements and state officials charged with public control of the industry.

In other ways, however, the satisfaction of many insurance men at the failure of the government to prove a case of monopoly and restraint of trade appeared short-sighted and premature. The excessively high lapse rates indicated that a need existed for better training and preparation of life insurance agents and a modification of industry emphasis on high pressure selling. There could be little doubt that growth for growth's sake was a strong motive among many company managements, as Gesell's monograph observed.[29] The chairman of Metropolitan's board, Frederick H. Ecker, indicated that if his company stopped growing—not just selling enough insurance to maintain its then current size —his field organization would "go to a company where they will get paid, and that whole organization will disintegrate."[30] There were other views expressed, some advocating vigorous growth and others urging some restraint.

Although Northwestern did not publicly express itself at this time, the attitudes of its executives on the matter of sheer volume and size were clearly expressed in the record. Percy H. Evans believed that a volume of new sales sufficient to produce a net growth at 3 or 4 per cent of insurance in force would give all the vitality necessary for a company, while providing sound policyholder services. Growth beyond that point, in the estimation of Northwestern officers, merely aggrandized company presidents and agency directors.

The investigation of the life insurance industry drew one clear conclusion, comforting to the insurance-owning public: that in the aggregate, the industry was sound, well managed, and fully able to meet its contractual obligations. It also demonstrated that, despite the distrust, suspicion, and mutual recrimination, the investigations were important to the policyholder and the community. There were few responsible persons either in the government or in the industry, however, ready to make the acknowledgment that the investigation had accomplished much good. In this respect the observations of one veteran insurance man were exceptional:

> I remember the Armstrong Investigation . . . and I remember the discussion there was in the public press in regard to it. Life companies generally were opposed to it then as now and about the same statements were made regarding the harm it would do the business and the lack of confidence it would create, etc., yet that investigation is primarily responsible for the progress and development of life insurance since that time because the laws enacted in various states as a result of it made possible the organization and growth of practically all the companies that have since been chartered. . . .
>
> I cannot believe that men of the standing and character of the men who are conducting that investigation would have any desire to interfere with or retard the progress of any business or industry that means so much to the people of our land. If the management is right, if the record is good, the companies have nothing to fear from the verdict of the public.[31]

For the Northwestern's managers, trustees, and policyholders the investigation had been a source of immense pride. From this inquiry, carried on in a national arena, Northwestern emerged with enhanced reputation for its enviable record of corporate ethics and genuine service to its policyholders.

Other Public Relations and Legislative Matters

With the death of Henry F. Tyrrell in February 1935 Northwestern lost an able and devoted servant; he had effectively performed the complex and difficult duties of legislative counsel since that position was created in 1907. Tyrrell was succeeded by Clarence C. Klocksin, who had served as his assistant since late 1930. Because Klocksin spent most of his time in Washington, the Company required a legislative assistant to operate on the state level. Orville Ware was appointed to this position, following a career as life insurance agent and legislative representative in Oklahoma.

During the 1930's the Company's legislative counsel, on a state basis, was concerned with two issues: to resist the spread of compulsory investment legislation and to keep taxes among the states as uniform and as low as possible. On the first issue his efforts were entirely successful; as to the second, a few failures were mixed with the triumphs. Most irritating for Northwestern was a 4 per cent premium tax passed in Oklahoma in 1941. Convinced that a unified effort by life companies could cause the tax rate to be lowered, for it was the highest levied in all the states, Northwestern began to organize a group of independent companies to reduce it. The Association of Life Insurance Presidents, however, persuaded Northwestern's management to follow its lead rather than pursue its own strategy; in the end this proved unsuccessful and the Oklahoma tax remained in force.

Taxes, as shown earlier, remained one of the major expense items for the Company throughout this period. Total taxes paid during these fourteen years amounted to $55 million, exceeded only by agents' commissions among the Company's outlays. State premium and federal income taxes accounted for about $43 million of this sum, federal old age insurance and state unemployment levies for almost $1 million, and real estate taxes for the rest.

Undoubtedly the amount would have been greater had the Company, in 1927, not been able to bring about a modification in the Wisconsin tax formula. This change had been accomplished with the cooperation of a joint legislative committee representing the Association of Life Insurance Presidents, the American Life Convention, and the Wisconsin Life Convention; it also had the approval of the state commissioner of insurance. In effect, this modification caused the outmoded $300 license fee for foreign companies to be abandoned and a flat 2 per cent tax on Wisconsin premiums substituted for it. Since the reduction in rate for domestic companies resulted in revenue losses which exceeded the gains obtained by the tax on foreign companies, the Wisconsin companies agreed to accept a 3 per cent rate on total income, less various deductions for themselves. The savings for Northwestern in terms of Wisconsin taxes were partially offset by increased taxes in other states through the operation of the retaliatory laws. Nevertheless, the gross tax savings for 1927 had amounted to more than $200,000; this saving increased in subsequent years.

While comparatively unknown to the public, the efforts of Northwestern's legislative counsel and the management's basic policies in public and legislative relations were recognized and respected in the insurance world, in legislatures, and among the insurance commissioners. In 1940 a trade publication rather succinctly summarized both the policies and

the ability with which policy was implemented. It reported that:

> This company does not camouflage its activities in the way of legislation, but properly designates those who handle such affairs as its legislative agents. It is not trying to procure some peculiar benefits, but merely to obtain for its policy owners and others similarly situated what is rightfully theirs. Its legislative representatives are imbued with the integrity of its management and its high ideals.[32]

Although Northwestern had been a national marketer of insurance and a national investor of funds since the previous century, in several important ways it remained a regional institution until the years following the great depression. Its independence in the field of legislation and isolation from the trade associations was an important indication of its character. The rapid expansion of federal government functions in taxation, public control of business, labor relations, social security, and national defense involved Northwestern more fully in the national scene than ever before. During 1933–1937, when uncertainty concerning administrative and Congressional intentions was widespread, the management hired the services of a consulting economist in Washington to keep them informed of legislative trends and political shifts.[33] Furthermore, during this period the Company greatly extended its contributions to and association with such professional and business organizations as the National Industrial Conference Board, United States Chamber of Commerce, and the Committee for Economic Development. In 1938 there was an indication that the Company's sixty-year old isolation from life industry associations would finally be breached when Northwestern became one of the initial subscribers to the newly formed Institute of Life Insurance.[34]

Home Office Problems

The depression years created new problems for management in employee relations, personnel management, and the development of more effective systems of work organization. The numbers of the Home Office staff rose and fell inversely to the degree of economic prosperity in the nation, and the Company's hiring policies during the years of deep depression had a significant bearing on the organization of a union of clerks in 1937 and the creation of a personnel department within the Company.

The increase in the number of clerical employees which occurred the last few years of the Van Dyke administration continued until 1934, when the force totaled 1,391, the Company's all-time peak. Thereafter the number of clerks fell steadily until at the end of 1946 there were only one thousand such employees on the payroll. Due to depression-induced pressures to hire heads of families, the Company added a disproportionate number of men to the clerical staff during 1930–1934. Although a clerk's job at Northwestern was preferable to relief, married men found that salary scales designed for single women were inadequate for the support of families, particularly after prices began to rise in 1935.

Working conditions at Northwestern, under the usual labor force ratio of more than two women to one man which existed until the 1930's, had been good. In addition to providing lunches for the staff, the Company had a pension plan, paid vacations, and was noted for its reluctance to discharge employees. With a labor supply readily available, it was not surprising that the management became somewhat complacent during these years regarding employee relations, salary administration, and wage and job classifications. Wage boosts based upon seniority, and the degree of autonomy granted to departments in setting salaries and classifying jobs, occasionally resulted in stenographers being more highly paid than the men from whom they took dictation. With the unusually large number of men on the staff the lack of job integration caused a considerable degree of employee frustration as human skills were not fully exploited, transfers prevented, and what was psychologically vital, hopes for advancement blocked. When such conditions were aggravated by the inadequate earnings of family heads, repercussions were inevitable.

Unable to obtain consideration for themselves on an individual basis, a hard core of Home Office clerks began actively to consider collective bargaining as the only effective alternative. When the Supreme Court of the United States upheld the constitutionality of the National Labor Relations Act in April 1937, the stage was set for such action. A delegation of clerks presented demands upon the management for pay increases, the elimination of Saturday work, and the introduction of a job-classification system. A mass meeting of employees heard their leaders report on the progress of negotiations with the Company, and opinion was sampled so that a program could be determined in the event their demands were rejected. While no final decision

was made regarding the advocacy of affiliating with the American Federation of Labor, it was evident that most employees would prefer an independent status for their union. A determined minority, however, meant to obtain acceptance of their demands and were convinced that affiliation with a large international union would guarantee that result.

To the relief of almost everyone the Company did bargain. Although Cleary did not favor a union, he believed that the employees had to work out their problems as they saw fit. The union, subsequently chartered as the "Independent Union of Northwestern Mutual Employees," elected as president William B. Minehan, the present secretary of the Company. A total of twenty-five directors representing the various units around the Home Office were also elected, and from these a bargaining committee was chosen.

The new organization, with the overwhelming support of the Company's rank and file, presented its demands firmly and skillfully. An across-the-board increase based on salary was granted. In addition, Saturday work, except for a "skeleton crew," was eliminated tentatively; and all personnel who had been with the Company for twenty-five years or more were excused from "punching the clock." The Company also agreed to study the matter of a personnel department and the introduction of job classification and wage standardization systems. The Office Committee was skeptical about the clerks' insistence that the half-day work on Saturday was unnecessary and that it was possible to complete the weekly work load in five days. They did agree to a fair trial with the proviso that a small force be on hand in the event the plan failed. Within a few months the union had proven its contention. Subsequently, it won further concessions regarding the maximum work week and the setting of overtime payments for Saturday work.

Although there were some added costs (for example, the payroll increased 10 per cent), the management profited from the collective bargaining arrangement because of the great improvement in employee relations. Responsibility for personnel relations was taken from the comptroller and vested with Vice President Edmund Fitzgerald. A study of the Company's needs indicated the desirability of establishing a professional personnel department, and on August 1, 1937, one was established with a long-time Northwestern employee as director. The new personnel director, however, had no professional training or experience in the technical aspects of modern personnel management such as job classification, job specifications, merit rating, and employee evaluation. On September 16, 1937, Miss Louise Marie Newman was engaged as assistant personnel director, having had ten years' experience in similar work with other life companies. Not only did Miss Newman's skills answer the Company's principal needs, but she subsequently became director of personnel and in 1951 was made the first woman officer in Northwestern's history.

In essence, the clerical union remained a Northwestern institution. Relations with the management were, on the whole, excellent. In 1944–1945, however, it was deemed advisable by the membership to abandon its wholly independent status and affiliate with the Associated Unions of America, an organization representing white collar employees in financial and commercial companies. The reason for this decision was that with the exception of a few determined, well-informed, and able employees, the clerical bargaining representatives found it embarrassing to negotiate with Company officers for whom they worked. It was felt that a professional business agent could carry on such negotiations with greater freedom.[35]

Total compensation, including payments of trustee per diem, grew slowly between 1937 and 1941, then more rapidly throughout the remainder of the period. In part this was a result of union action; in part it was due to management decision. In 1937, for example, after a year of study and completely independent of the organization of the clerical employees, the pension plan was modified. The plan provided for increases in the amounts of retirement benefits and in addition became an employee right, whereas formerly the Company could withhold it. Beginning in 1941 and continuing for a decade, the Company began payment of a cost-of-living bonus for employees based on a National Industrial Conference Board index, later changed to that of the Bureau of Labor Statistics. In essence this plan, like others adopted by American business during these years, provided for bonus payments geared to changes in living costs, and further provided that a reduction of 2 per cent in the index was necessary before any downward change would take place.

Between 1932 and 1946 total outlay for employee compensation amounted to $44.8 million, rising from $2.5 million in 1933 to almost $4.1 million in 1946. During the latter year there was a rise in total compensation expenditures of about $550,000 over

that of 1945. This increase reflected not only the sharp rise in the cost of living but also benefits granted to returning servicemen. In addition to direct wages and salaries, retirement benefits, and Company-furnished lunches, Northwestern also contributed $938,600 in state unemployment and federal old age insurance taxes between 1936 and 1947.

Aside from investment expenses and bookkeeping adjustments of assets, the total internal expenses incurred by the Company during this period were $74.5 million, and of this amount compensation outlays constituted 60 per cent. The rest was allocated to Home Office rental and maintenance, $14 million; supplies, equipment, printing, and communications, $7.4 million; expenses for examinations and audits, $250,000; and a variety of miscellaneous expenses which aggregated $8 million. Yet despite the over-all rise of 52 per cent in the aggregate of such expenses between 1933 and 1946, the extremely low Home Office and internal expense ratio per million dollars of insurance in force showed only a modest increase. In 1933, with $3.8 billion in force, the Home Office expense ratio was just $1,100 per million; at the end of 1946, with $5.05 billion in force, it had increased to only $1,230 per million. Thus, while the wholesale price index for all items in the United States had risen by 84 per cent between 1933 and 1946, Northwestern's Home Office expenses, one important element in the cost of insurance to policyholders, had increased by only 11.8 per cent.[36]

Perhaps the most obvious conclusion to be drawn from Northwestern's record in legislative, personnel, and public relations was that these activities were destined to play an increasingly important role in the history of the Company. What is more important, Northwestern had demonstrated great skill in meeting the problems that arose in those areas. It had proved its worth before a governmental investigating agency; it demonstrated its calm persuasiveness when issues of monetary and tax policies or legislative enactments related to the welfare of the Company and its policyholders; it had shown its good will in Wisconsin by its compromise on taxation; and it had satisfactorily met an uncomfortable situation in its Home Office. This experience would be invaluable in preparing Northwestern for its continuing role in these areas.

CHAPTER SEVENTEEN

Investment Problems During Depression and War: 1932-1946

ROM 1932 through 1946 Northwestern's investment managers faced a series of problems that in dimension and complexity were unprecedented in the history of the organization. There was the immediate task of adjusting operations to the impact of bank failures, agricultural distress, defaults on urban mortgages, the financial difficulty of the railroads, and mass unemployment that affected the economy generally. While the recovery that began late in 1935 marked the close of the emergency period, it by no means brought an end to investment problems.

By this time the management was fully aware that, compared to the 1920's, the structure of the capital markets had undergone significant changes. It was clear that for some time to come the government's fiscal policy would probably prevent any return of interest rates to the levels typical of the 1920's, that many of the sharp distinctions between various types of loans had largely disappeared, that competition for investments would be vigorous, and that to maintain earnings at reasonably acceptable levels required a flexibility and willingness to invest in new areas that were in sharp contrast to the situation prior to 1933. Even the American involvement in World War II failed to produce an expansion in investment opportunities comparable to the expansion of the economy as a whole, largely because of the direct financial aid given to war industries by the government. Moreover, the immediate postwar boom after 1945 was full of uncertainties, for no one could predict its strength or duration.

Investment Management and Personnel

The responsibility for guiding the Company through these difficult years rested primarily upon the Finance Committee, of which the new president, Michael Cleary, was chairman.* Although relatively inexperienced in this field, Cleary soon familiarized himself with the investment problems and, according to his associates, "learned fast." Unlike Markham and Van Dyke the president took no direct responsibility for the administration of the investment activities; securities were delegated to Vice President Frederick W. Walker and mortgage loans to Vice President H. D. Thomas.

* As a result of death and one resignation, only two members of the Finance Committee, Howard Greene, prominent Milwaukee manufacturer, and Frederick L. Pierce, vice president of the Cutler-Hammer Corporation, remained of the group that had served under Van Dyke. New members, in addition to M. J. Cleary, included Louis Quarles, well-known Milwaukee attorney; Fred C. Best, president and treasurer of the Bankers Farm Mortgage Company of Milwaukee; Harold S. Falk, vice president of the Falk Corporation; Mitchell Mackie, investment counselor; and William D. Van Dyke, Jr., son of the former president and treasurer of the Mineral Mining Company of Wisconsin. In terms of experience and background, the Committee was well qualified to take over responsibility for guiding Northwestern's investment policies in the years that lay ahead.

One of the first steps undertaken by the president, in cooperation with the members of the Finance Committee, was to enlarge the staff and strengthen the personnel in the bond and mortgage loan departments. After a careful survey of prospective candidates, the first of a series of appointments came in October 1933 when Philip K. Robinson and Philip N. Cristal were added to the bond department staff. Robinson accepted the newly created position as Northwestern's director of municipal bond research while Cristal was chosen to handle the Company's research in the field of railroad bonds.

A third appointment, made in October 1934, went to Donald C. Slichter as director of public utility investment research.

A fourth appointment late in 1934 added Howard J. Tobin to Northwestern's mortgage loan department. In 1936 Tobin was appointed assistant manager of city loans, becoming manager a year later.

During the same year Karl Maier, Jr. was named superintendent of residence loans.

These appointments gave Northwestern a young, competent, and vigorous investment staff that compared favorably with any of the large institutional lenders. Working closely with Gerald Swanstrom of the Company's legal department, its members had the temperament and ability to develop new investment opportunities and to carry through the complicated negotiations that these loans so often involved. As the members of the Finance Committee gained confidence in the skill and judgment of the research group, they showed an increasing willingness to make Northwestern a leader rather than a follower in pioneering new investment opportunities appropriate for a life insurance company.

Growth of Investment Funds and Changes in the Investment Portfolio

As indicated in Chart XVII-1 Northwestern's net investment funds started from about $8.8 million in 1933, within two years exceeded the previous peak in the Company's history ($54.6 million reached in 1929), and in 1946 amounted to approximately $130 million. These sums were sufficient to add over $1 billion to the Company's assets, which in 1946 were valued at approximately twice the amount reported for the end of 1932. In addition to new funds, repayments of loans and the sale of securities added at least another $500 million to the total amount for which investment outlets had to be found.

Northwestern, of course, was only one of a large number of institutional investors competing in the capital markets of the period. As already noted, the life companies alone increased their assets from approximately $21 billion in 1933 to over $48 billion in 1946. Some impression of the general characteristics of the investment markets in which Northwestern and other large investors were lending during these years may be obtained from Table XVII-1. In general, the period through 1945 was marked by a decline in the volume of private debt which was more than offset, however, by the expansion of the federal debt, especially after the entrance of the United States into World War II.

How Northwestern reacted to the investment opportunities of the period is shown in Chart XVII-2. Aside from the reduction of policy loans, over which the management had little control, the most striking change in the distribution of the Company's assets among the major investment categories was the relative decline in mortgages and

CHART XVII-1

Income, Expenditures, and Net Available for Investment: Northwestern, 1933–1946

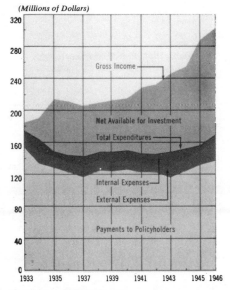

(Millions of Dollars)

Gross Income

Net Available for Investment

Total Expenditures

Internal Expenses

External Expenses

Payments to Policyholders

1933 1935 1937 1939 1941 1943 1945 1946

SOURCE: Appendix F, Tables 1-4.

CHART XVII-2

Distribution of Admitted Assets:
Northwestern, 1933–1946

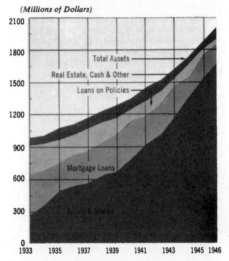

(Millions of Dollars)

SOURCE: Appendix F, Table 5.

the sharp expansion in security holdings. This shift from Northwestern's traditional role as primarily a mortgage lender reflected both the Company's experience with mortgage loans during the troublesome 1930's as well as the decline in investment outlets in the area, especially in the field of farm lending after the early 1930's. Within each of the major investment categories, as will presently be noted, there were adjustments of particular accounts as Northwestern's investment officers attempted to maintain income in the face of a downward pressure on interest rates.

Loans on Policies

The most urgent financial problem confronting the Company during late 1932 and early 1933 concerned the amount of cash the Company might be called upon to pay out to policyholders. During 1932 loans on policies had grown by some $70.3 million, bringing the total amount to over $236.7 million by the end of the year. At that time about one third of the Company's 629,200 policyholders had already borrowed on their policies.* Policies repre-

* It may be noted that only about $11 million of total loans on policies was in the form of automatic premium loans. The rest was made up of policy loans.

TABLE XVII-1

United States: Long Term Private and Public Debt, 1933–1946 (In billions)

| | | PRIVATE | | | PUBLIC | | TOTAL PRIVATE |
DATE	CORPORATE	FARM MORTGAGES	NON-FARM MORTGAGES*	TOTAL PRIVATE	STATE AND LOCAL	FEDERAL	AND PUBLIC
1933	$47.9	$7.7	$26.3	$81.9	$16.7	$24.3	$122.9
1934	44.6	7.6	25.5	77.7	15.9	30.4	124.0
1935	43.6	7.4	24.7	75.7	16.0	34.4	126.1
1936	42.5	7.2	24.4	74.1	16.2	37.7	128.0
1937	43.5	7.0	24.3	74.8	16.1	39.2	130.1
1938	44.8	6.8	24.5	76.1	16.0	40.5	132.6
1939	44.4	6.6	25.0	76.0	16.3	42.6	134.9
1940	43.7	6.5	26.0	76.2	16.5	44.8	137.5
1941	43.6	6.4	27.2	77.2	16.3	56.3	149.8
1942	42.7	6.0	26.8	75.5	15.8	101.7	193.0
1943	41.0	5.4	26.2	72.6	14.9	154.4	241.9
1944	39.8	4.9	26.1	70.8	14.1	211.9	296.8
1945	38.3	4.8	27.0	70.1	13.7	252.7	336.5
1946	41.3	4.9	32.4	78.6	13.6	229.7	321.9

* Non-Corporate borrowers.

SOURCE: *The Economic Almanac*, The Conference Board, New York, 1956, 99.

senting 7.6 per cent of the Company's insurance in force were surrendered in 1932, thereby adding $11.8 million to total cash outlays for the year.

As the banking crisis became more acute after January 1933, insurance companies became almost the only source to which people desperate for funds to meet debts and living costs could turn. During January and February Northwestern paid out in policy loans nearly $6.9 million, and in surrender values about $9.2 million. The Company was able to meet these demands out of income and cash on hand; but on March 3, in anticipation of still further need, the Executive Committee authorized the management to obtain a commitment for a $3 million collateral loan from the Chase National Bank of New York.[1]

The Company, however, did not have to borrow this money. The "bank holiday" that began on March 5 marked the peak of the financial crisis that had gripped the country. By the end of March most of the commercial banks had resumed operations and within a few weeks had received deposits of about $2 billion from individuals and business concerns. Over the next several months the restrictions on payments to policyholders by life companies were successively eased, and were entirely removed in September.

The passing of the crisis was reflected in Northwestern's policy loan account. From a peak of almost $250 million in 1933, which amounted to 25 per cent of total assets, policy loans declined steadily and were only $79.8 million in 1946, or 4 per cent of the assets owned by the Company at the end of that year. (See Chart XVII-2)

The excellent persistency record of its outstanding policies was probably the single most important reason for the magnitude of Northwestern's policy loans. The average Northwestern policyholder had maintained his insurance in good standing over a relatively long period of time. Since the average face value of Company policies was among the highest in the industry, this condition reflected comparatively high cash values which were available to policyholders.

Mortgage Loans

The decline in Northwestern's position as a mortgage lender for this period can be seen in Chart XVII-3. The total investment in mortgages fell from almost $378 million in 1933 to $158 million at the end of 1946. The most startling change in the composition of the Company's mortgage account occurred in the farm segment which fell by almost 80

CHART XVII-3

Mortgage Loan Investments: Northwestern, 1933–1946

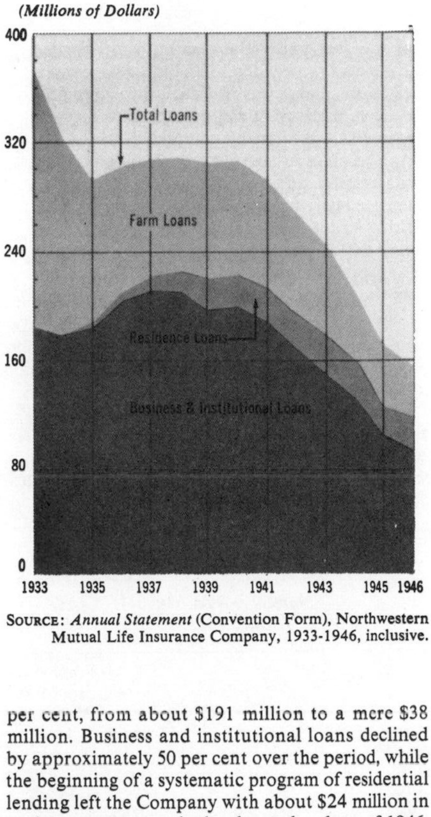

(Millions of Dollars)

SOURCE: *Annual Statement* (Convention Form), Northwestern Mutual Life Insurance Company, 1933-1946, inclusive.

per cent, from about $191 million to a mere $38 million. Business and institutional loans declined by approximately 50 per cent over the period, while the beginning of a systematic program of residential lending left the Company with about $24 million in such mortgages on the books at the close of 1946. The reasons for these shifts in emphasis and the over-all reduction in the mortgage investment can be best understood when examined against the background of Northwestern's experience with foreclosed properties during these years.

Special Real Estate: Northwestern as a Landlord

Compared to the situation affecting policy loans, the Company's problems of conserving and liquidating assets acquired as a result of the depression were of much longer duration. This was especially true in respect to properties acquired as a result of fore-closures. As shown in Table XVII-2, Northwestern's holdings of special real estate continued to grow after 1932, reaching their peak in 1939. As a percentage of total mortgages, special real estate in that year was just under the maximum proportion of 15.6 per cent recorded in 1880. Liquidation was relatively slow, and it was not until the United States had been involved in the war for over a year that the process was virtually completed.

As a result of its acquisitions of special real estate Northwestern continued in its role as landlord on an extensive scale throughout the greater part of the period. At the end of 1933 the Company owned some 1,600 farms; three years later the number was 3,318 (approximately 600,000 acres); and as late as 1942 the number was 1,473. By contrast, the number of urban properties owned at any one time never exceeded fifty-one, although some ninety-two different properties came into Northwestern's possession during these years.

The administration of special real estate was no new experience for H. D. Thomas who, for ten years prior to his appointment as vice president in 1933, had been manager of the Company's farm loans. The primary objective, of course, was to liqui-

date the properties as rapidly as possible without incurring loss. As the earlier experience of the Company had demonstrated, however, to sell such real estate at satisfactory prices meant that the properties had to be maintained or improved to make them attractive to buyers.

Because of the size of the farm account, the number of properties involved, and the economics of agriculture, the major effort and expense were associated with farm properties. In this area an enlarged Home Office staff and an expanded field force were responsible for the rehabilitation of farms held by the Company, for lease arrangements and the collection of rents, and for the pursuit of sales and the employment of special salesmen.[2]

For purposes of valuation and sale the farms were classified into three basic groups according to the criteria of soil, topography, drainage, fertility, buildings, water supply, location relative to markets, and access to roads and other transportation facilities. Class A farms were those which were considered to be above the average for the community in which they were located, Class B farms were regarded as average for their respective communities, while Class C were rated below average. The general policy was to hold the Class A and B farms until an improvement in prices would permit their disposal without loss. In the case of the Class C farms every effort was made to dispose of them as rapidly as possible, even at a loss, rather than incur the expense their rehabilitation and maintenance would necessitate.[3] The Company gave priority to original borrowers when disposing of farm properties.

Even in the higher classification groups a substantial number of the farms acquired during the 1930's were badly run down and urgently in need of repair and rehabilitation, The Company established a central organization to undertake the repair and painting of buildings; the installation of equipment; the construction of new buildings and fencing; the testing of soils, introduction of soil improvement through use of lime, legumes, and plant food; and the institution of strip and contour farming where feasible.[4] Centralized purchases of materials such as paint, shingles, fencing, lumber, and barn and dairy equipment, at wholesale prices and in carload lots, were worked out by the farm managers in cooperation with the special real estate field force.* Painters

TABLE XVII-2

Northwestern Mutual:
Special Real Estate, 1933–1946 (In millions)

DATE	FARM	URBAN	TOTAL	PERCENTAGE OF TOTAL MORTGAGE LOANS
1933	$21.9	$4.1	$26.0	6.9%
1934	26.2	5.5	31.7	11.7
1935	26.6	7.6	34.2	11.5
1936	28.1	8.6	36.7	12.1
1937	26.2	10.4	36.6	11.9
1938	25.3	11.8	37.1	12.0
1939	23.9	19.5	43.4	14.3
1940	21.1	17.6	38.7	12.7
1941	16.9	21.5	38.4	13.2
1942	11.7	21.4	33.1	12.7
1943	6.1	9.4	15.5	6.3
1944	3.0	5.9	8.9	4.2
1945	2.1	0.2	2.3	1.3
1946	1.2	-0-	1.2	0.8

SOURCE: *Annual Statement*, Northwestern Mutual Life Insurance Company, 1933-1946, inclusive.

---

* By 1940 the Finance Committee had authorized $343,432 for such materials. A. C. Fiedler (interview) related that the Company had effected substantial savings through centralized purchasing and shipment, as well as by the employment of specialists whose knowledge of substitute materials permitted adequate repair with limited expenditures.

were hired, equipped with sprayers, and deployed to Company farms for entire seasons; other teams were employed for repair and construction work, all under the general and personal supervision of the Company's field organization. Where electrification was feasible the management cooperated with private power companies and the Rural Electrification Administration. Field men were permitted to pledge Company farms to the cooperative soil building and crop restriction programs of the Agricultural Adjustment Administration, and the Company shared with its tenants the government payments forthcoming from such cooperation.

One important problem that faced the management during the early 1930's was determining the best method of operating the farms possessed by the Company. The long-established Company practice had been to lease on an annual basis at fixed rentals, but it became increasingly difficult to persuade tenants under such leases to adopt new methods which would increase the value of the properties involved. In addition to an inherent disinclination to abandon familiar farming methods, the techniques suggested by Northwestern personnel frequently called for additional short-term capital expenditures that tenants were unwilling or unable to undertake, especially when not convinced that such methods would increase output.

The Company experimented briefly with a plan of employing superintendents to manage several farm properties, using hired labor; but it soon discovered that this method was unsatisfactory and unduly expensive.[5] The management then adopted the system of leasing farms on a sharecrop basis, which proved much more satisfactory. Under this arrangement the Company furnished a portion of the seed, equipment, fertilizer and fuel in exchange for a share of the crop.

Even with this system it was necessary to engage in a good deal of "missionary" work to convince tenants of the need for fertilizers or the value of seed inoculation and selection. Many tenants, for example, had never used fertilizers and refused to pay any of the cost involved in introducing them on Company farms. In such instances Company representatives frequently agreed to fertilize particular strips of given fields, at Company expense, and let the tenant decide upon the value of the fertilizer when the crop was harvested. Similar arrangements were followed in the case of the inoculation of certified seed

and in the introduction of hybrid seed corn. In most instances farmers readily admitted the improvement that resulted and joined in the program in succeeding years. In cases of continued recalcitrance, the management had little choice but to terminate the lease upon its expiration.[6]

Undoubtedly the most profitable change in the use of the Company's farm properties during the period was the development of livestock feeding, first begun in 1935. By the mid-1930's the management noted that livestock and meat prices had improved more rapidly than other agricultural prices. Having acquired a number of large farms suitable for raising or feeding livestock, the managers decided to shift the nature of production on these properties, and tenants were recruited who possessed some experience or aptitude for stock farming.

An experienced cattle buyer was sent into the Southwest to purchase range stock for shipment to the Company's feeder farms; and between August 1935 and October 1942 the Finance Committee authorized outlays of $1.2 million for the purpose. Under the customary arrangements the tenants paid half the purchase price of the stock and shared the net revenues in a like proportion. Among the institutional holders of farm properties in its seventeen-state farm territory, the Company was the first to develop the stock-share lease and to convert crop farms to stock feeding.

The protracted drought conditions in the Dakotas, Nebraska, and Missouri during the early and middle 1930's caused severe hardships to the farmers of those areas, including tenant farmers on Company properties. With no income available from which rents could be paid, the management cancelled delinquent rents and advanced operating funds to tenants. In these hardship areas up to $150 per quarter section was advanced to meet costs of tractor fuel and feed, and local agents were permitted to make emergency advances before consulting Milwaukee. Between September 1933 and January 1941 over $61,000 of such rents and advances had been cancelled by management.

Northwestern's disposal of farm properties was closely related to the growing prosperity of agriculture after 1936. From the depression low of $6.4 billion in 1932, gross income to farmers moved up to $10.6 billion in 1936, where it was relatively stabilized through 1940. Thereafter, gross income rose sharply, being reported at $13.9 billion in 1941, $18.6 billion in 1942, $23.0 billion in 1943, $24.2 billion in 1944, and $25.4 billion in 1945.[7] Against this background the Company found it increasingly easy to dispose of its farm properties, especially after 1941.

There is no question that in farm rehabilitation, maintenance and management, as well as in humaneness and good business practice, Northwestern was an innovator among the life companies engaged in farm lending. The Company's program originated in the middle 1920's and expanded with the great wave of farm foreclosures during the 1930's. Other life companies developed their programs only after 1930, and those that followed the most enlightened practices appear to have copied Northwestern's program.* Company participation in farm conferences called by other life companies in 1938 and after, as well as the personal observations of Home Office and field personnel, indicated that other companies followed Northwestern's methods quite closely, in some instances even to the degree of adopting the branch office loan system.[8]

The administration of Northwestern's urban holdings was much less complex than that of the farm properties. The amount of real estate held was relatively small, and the purposes for which the buildings were designed were more limited. Although the Company made significant outlays for upkeep, and sometimes for remodeling to attract prospective buyers, it was seldom necessary to incur major capital expenditures; and the problem of persuading tenants to change their "techniques of production," as had been the case with farm properties, never arose.

Northwestern's program in disposing of its urban properties was first to contact the strongest tenant in a particular building, quote the going market price, and offer terms of 20 per cent down with the balance to be amortized within twenty years. Much to the disappointment of the management only a few tenants responded to these opportunities. In several instances such tenants had reason to regret their actions, for occasionally the new owners forced them to vacate the premises and the cost of moving heavy equipment exceeded the prices originally quoted by the Company. When tenants did not accept the Company's offer, contact was established with other realty investors who had purchased similar properties in the community. Real estate brokers were also contacted, but only on a selective basis. By use of these low-pressure methods, bolstered by a willingness and the resources to hold properties pending a more favorable market, Northwestern

---

* The Metropolitan was among the life companies that followed Northwestern's methods. For an excellent and detailed account of that Company's handling of the problem see Marquis James, *The Metropolitan Life*, 294–305.

was able to avoid excessive capital losses and in most cases earned rental income sufficient to meet operating expenses.

In contrast with the experience with farm properties, the urban real estate market did not recover until 1942. As shown in Table XVII-2, Northwestern's holdings of urban property reached a peak of $21.5 million in 1941. Once the market stabilized, however, the Company made rapid disposal of its properties, closing the account entirely by the end of 1946.

New Mortgage Loans

Experience with foreclosed farm properties made both loan agents and members of management increasingly doubtful, during the 1930's, about the long-run future prospects of American agriculture.[9] Although new loans were made to farmers, the general pessimism regarding future land values limited such loans to the very best quality properties, and then only in conservative amounts. During the late 1930's the renewed interest of other insurance companies, particularly Prudential, and the competition of federal and other private lending agencies, made funds available on terms more satisfactory than Northwestern was willing to offer. The result was the continuous contraction of the farm loan account.

Experience with distressed urban properties also made the management cautious about vigorously pushing this type of loan after 1933. New loans were made on a carefully selected basis from 1933 through 1938, and the account was expanded by some $32 million at a time when the construction of new business and commercial properties was slow. Between 1938 and 1941 the account declined as new loans were not sufficient to offset the reduction that resulted from final foreclosures on distress mortgages that had been continued in the hope that owners might improve their earning positions. After 1941 the account was further reduced. Wartime restrictions on the construction of new office buildings cut the demand for new financing; at the same time better earnings enabled a number of Northwestern's borrowers to repay their loans, either from increased incomes or with funds borrowed elsewhere on terms the Company was unwilling to meet.

The growth in Northwestern's residential mortgage loans represented both a change in policy and a response to an area of investment that was expanding during the late 1930's. One objective of the New Deal was to improve the level of housing in the United States. Under the National Housing Act of 1935 the Federal Housing Authority was empowered to guarantee residential loans in the expectation that this feature would encourage large institutional lenders to finance residential construction more vigorously.

Northwestern made a few residential loans during 1934 and 1935, but the management was reluctant to enter the field on any considerable scale. The principal reason was the relatively high rate of foreclosures on urban residential properties experienced by competitors during the early 1930's. Even the prospect of acquiring loans guaranteed by the government did not appeal to the majority of the management group, especially Vice President Thomas. Objections were in part based on a reluctance to accept the principle of government participation and in part on doubts regarding the quality of the loans offered under governmental guarantee.

It was finally decided to explore the possibility of making "conventional" residential loans not guaranteed by the government. Beginning with Milwaukee, a survey was made of several metropolitan areas to determine the market potentials. The results were sufficiently encouraging for the Company to establish a separate residential loan division in 1935 and to begin building the account which reached $27.6 million in 1942, when wartime restrictions reduced the supply of residential mortgage applications. In this manner the management was able to contribute to housing development without participating in the insured loan field. An exception was made in the case of a few large-scale housing loans, one of which did go into default but was repaid under the terms of the government guarantee.[10]

The end of the war brought a change in policy, largely as a result of the efforts of Howard J. Tobin, who succeeded H. D. Thomas as vice president in 1945. Tobin, born in Chicago, was for a time a student at the University of Chicago but dropped out of school in 1919 to take a job in the real estate department of the Standard Oil Company of Indiana. He continued his education by enrolling in the Kent College of Law in Chicago and received a master's degree in law in 1925, being admitted to the Illinois bar the same year. In 1933 Tobin left Standard Oil to join the real estate department of Montgomery Ward and resigned the following year to accept an offer from Northwestern. He was appointed assistant manager of city loans in 1936, becoming manager a year later.

Tobin was convinced that the field of guaranteed loans offered an attractive investment outlet. After a careful analysis of the experience with this type of investment, he recommended to the Finance Committee in June 1945 that modest sums be invested in F.H.A. and Veterans' Administration guaranteed mortgages.[11] Over the succeeding months additional loans were approved and guaranteed mortgages became an important part of the Company's loan activities.

Whatever promise residential loans held for the future, however, the decline in the total mortgage loan account by 1946 raised a serious question regarding the place this type of lending would play in Northwestern's investments in the post-war period. This was a major question that the succeeding administration would have to answer.

Security Investments

The changing pattern in Northwestern's security account, that grew from about $297 million at the

CHART XVII-4

Bond Investments: Northwestern, 1933–1946

(Millions of Dollars)

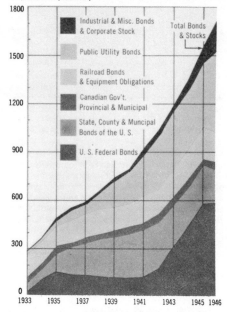

SOURCE: *Annual Statement* (Convention Form), Northwestern Mutual Life Insurance Company, 1933-1946, inclusive.

end of 1932 to over $1.7 billion in 1946, is shown in Chart XVII-4. Except for United States government securities during 1942–1945, the principal expansion came in state, county and municipal bonds, and public utilities and industrial obligations. Only in the case of railroad bonds and Canadian securities was there a relative decline.

In general, the Company bought United States bonds only when the supply of higher-yielding securities was limited. During the uncertain years from 1932 to 1935, for example, the account was built up rapidly; but from 1935 to 1941, when gradual economic recovery made other outlets more attractive, the holdings of government bonds were reduced. Following the United States entry into World War II, restrictions on the civilian economy, coupled with extensive governmental aid in financing the expansion of war plants and equipment, reduced the demand for private financing. These circumstances, plus the obvious obligation to contribute to the financing of the war, led to a rapid rise in the Company's government bond account to nearly $600 million by the end of 1945.

In the area of private financing the most startling change, compared to Northwestern's previous pattern of security investments, was the decline in the relative importance of railroad obligations and the expansion in public utility and industrial securities. As in the case of foreclosed mortgages, the Company's experiences with defaulted securities played an important role in shaping the investment pattern among the major security items in the portfolio.

Bond Defaults

That Northwestern's problem of protecting its assets was not confined to real estate acquired through foreclosures is indicated by the magnitude of the Company's defaulted bond account that grew from $19.5 million in 1932 to a peak of $53.2 million in 1938, when it exceeded the maximum level of special real estate by about $10 million. (See Table XVII-3.)

Of the $19.5 million (par value) of bonds in default at the end of 1932, some $5.1 million were state, municipal and county obligations. While new defaults by counties, municipalities, and Canadian provinces amounted to $10.5 million over the next four years, with one exception the Company experienced relatively little difficulty in coming to satisfactory agreements with the issuing authorities. The usual procedure was for Company officials to join with other institutional lenders in a bondholders'

TABLE XVII-3

Northwestern Mutual: Holdings of Defaulted Bonds, 1932-1945 (In millions)

| | TOTAL AT YEAR'S END | NEW DEFAULTS COUNTY, MUNICIPAL & | | |
YEAR		PROVINCIAL	RAILROAD	TOTAL
1932	$19.5			
1933	39.2	$2.8	$16.9	$19.7
1934	38.6	3.3	1.7	5.0
1935	40.8	.8	15.7	16.5
1936	50.3	3.6	8.5	12.1
1937	51.3		5.0	5.0
1938	53.2		8.5	8.5
1939	52.6			
1940	50.6			
1941	50.6			
1942	44.9			
1943	36.3			
1944	8.6			
1945	0			

SOURCE: *Annual Statement*, Schedule D, 1933-1945.

protective committee to negotiate for a settlement that either provided for a scaling down of interest payments, an extension of the maturity date of the loan, or both. By 1937, among the United States municipal and county bonds, only one issue with a par value of $60,000 remained unsettled.

The most troublesome default case among the municipal bonds began in 1936 and involved some $3.3 million (par value) of bonds of the Province of Alberta. The default resulted from an experiment in Social Credit administration, not from the inability of the province to meet its payments. This experiment prompted Alberta officials to announce that after June 1, 1936, they would pay only half the fixed interest charges, which ranged from 4½ per cent to 6 per cent on the eight different issues involved. The Northwestern management refused to accept this offer and negotiations were carried on for several years. Finally in 1945 a compromise was reached with the provincial authorities which provided for a scaling down of the interest rate and a payment of interest accrued over the intervening period. Eventually these securities were completely refunded.

Management problems arising from municipal and provincial defaults during the 1930's were insignificant when compared to the difficulties caused by the financial plight of the United States railroads. In 1938, the year in which the Company's rail portfolio contained the highest proportion of securities in default, over one third of the Company's rail bonds were in carriers which had defaulted in some portion of their obligations. Railroad default cases were usually difficult to settle because of the heterogeneity of interests of the creditors involved and the conflicts between creditors and stockholders. The life insurance companies soon found it desirable to form committees themselves, a technique made possible under the recently revised bankruptcy statutes, and attracted additional members from mutual savings banks and other institutions. Fundamental among the difficulties facing the defaulting carriers was the magnitude of fixed debt and the relationship of the burden of this debt to dwindling income.

Throughout, the insurance companies generally held firmly to their main objective of achieving sound reorganization plans with consonant credit recovery as well. Many times, this basic policy required some sacrifice in values on the part of participating institutional holders of weaker mortgages or unsecured positions as part of their rail portfolio. Strenuous opposition to this "sound plan" policy arose principally from the holders of the equity securities of the bankrupt carriers who, in many cases, were forced out through absence of capitalizable earnings values estimated under the institutional group plans.

It can also be noted that the reorganization plans were evolved and presented at relatively lower costs to the carriers, and consequently to the security holders, under the auspices of institutional groups than had been previously true.[12] Operating as interested parties under Section 77 of the Bankruptcy Act of 1933 insurance company representatives received no compensation for their services. In addition all expenses involving the employment of experts and travel were subject to approval by the Interstate Commerce Commission.

By 1941 the worst phases of the railroad bond defaults were over and the solid rise of railroad revenues during the war caused their securities to increase in value. The management took advantage of the improved market prices to dispose of all but underlying mortgage bonds and equipment trust securities. There was also a continuous effort to dispose of securities considered doubtful and to improve the quality of the portfolio. That area of management most concerned with transportation investment, however, remained dubious of the future place of rail bonds in the over-all investment portfolio.

Additions to the Railroad and Municipal Bond Portfolios

Reservations concerning the future of rail securities, it should be pointed out, did not extend to railroad equipment trust certificates and other obligations used to finance the purchase of equipment which could be repossessed by the holders of these obligations in the event of default. Unlike most railroad securities they were issued in series and were repayable within a relatively short period of time. Although Northwestern could legally have acquired such certificates at any time following 1925, when the Wisconsin statutes were amended, none were purchased. Low yield was the principal reason for excluding them from the portfolio.

With the rapid rise in the number of railroad bankruptcies in the early 1930's, trustees in bankruptcy for the rail carriers were in the unhappy position of being forced to operate the defaulted lines with obsolete, worn-out equipment. To meet this problem Section 77 of the Bankruptcy Act of 1933 was devised to permit trustees to issue equipment trust certificates that had a prior claim on railroad earnings. As a result, the volume of trust certificates offered for sale was sharply expanded. For several years, however, most life insurance companies were unable to purchase these obligations since the investment statutes of the important insurance states (outside Wisconsin) made it illegal for life companies to acquire securities of corporations that within a period of three years had defaulted on payment of principal or interest of their outstanding debts. Consequently, between 1935 and 1940 Northwestern was able to acquire extensive blocks of railroad equipment trust certificates at favorable yields.

In the judgment of its investment management, however, the most promising areas for an expansion of the Company's security holdings were state, county, and municipal bonds in the United States and the obligations of public utilities and industrial concerns. Instead of waiting for applications the Company sought out attractive loan propositions, contacting public officials, investment banking houses, and the officers of public utility and industrial companies. Northwestern, thereby, became one of the most aggressive competitors among life companies in the capital markets.

The Company's experience with municipal securities prompted a special management effort to build up this account throughout the 1930's and early 1940's. Northwestern was particularly effective in adding to its holdings of securities—including newly developed revenue bonds—issued by states, counties, and municipalities in the southern and southwestern parts of the United States. The personal contacts developed in these areas by Robinson and his associates were highly effective from 1933 through 1937 in enabling the Company to increase the account rapidly, at prices that yielded relatively attractive returns. From 1937 to 1940, when the account reached its peak of nearly $276 million, purchases were made in the face of growing competition from other institutional investors who somewhat belatedly began to recognize the potentialities of the market.

These same attractions did not apply, however, to Canadian provincial and municipal securities during this period. One reason was that the income from these bonds, unlike that from corresponding United States securities, was not exempt from taxation. In addition, there was some apprehension during the late 1930's that the Social Credit scheme, which had affected the Alberta bonds, might spread. While the account was increased between 1941 and 1945 by some $12 million, it was not until the postwar years that Northwestern considered a further expansion of its Canadian holdings.

Public Utility and Industrial Securities

Of all the investment areas public utility and industrial securities, largely because of their favorable showing during the depression and their future prospects, were the most attractive to the Northwestern management. Because this opinion was shared by other large institutional lenders, the Company faced intensive competition in adding to its holdings. Moreover, a substantial portion of the securities available did not represent new financing but was the result of refunding operations as corporations took advantage of lower interest rates to scale down the carrying charges on long-term debt. The extent of refunding operations from 1933 through 1946 is indicated by the tabulation of (non-governmental) security issues in the United States on the following page.

The limits of investment policy were determined by conditions over which the Company had only modest control. Within these limits, however, the investment managers sought to safeguard the capital values of Northwestern's assets and simultaneously to maintain investment income at levels consistent with the commitments of outstanding insurance contracts. There were many obstacles to the attainment of these goals—goals that were not always achieved. But in seeking these Northwestern be-

	Total Issues	New Capital	Refunding	Percentage Refunding
1933-1940	$33,392.1	$14,185.8	$19,206.1	57.5%
1941-1946	30,958.7	11,927.5	19,031.1	61.5%

Source: *Historical Statistics of the United States*, 281.

came one of the most vigorous competitors among the life insurance companies for a share of the security markets.

The record was impressive. Public utility bonds were increased from a modest $22 million in 1933 to nearly $495 million in 1946; and industrial bonds and stocks grew from nothing in 1934 to nearly $80 million twelve years later. By 1946 the combined account was equal to approximately one quarter of the Company's total assets.

During the period of extensive refunding operations by the public utilities that began in the 1930's, Slichter and his staff maintained close contact with the leading financial houses that handled such operations. From these contacts came opportunities to participate in refunding negotiations and to share in the new securities issued; opportunities that were later extended to include similar participation in the floating of public utility issues for new capital.

The Company also benefited by having its own research staff evaluate securities which had some unusual feature or were below a top rating. It was frequently discovered that improving factors behind these securities, not yet reflected in their prices, made them attractive investments.

In addition to developing the Company's holdings of public utility bonds, the management quickly responded to changes in Wisconsin legislation permitting the addition of new types of securities to the investment portfolio. Throughout the period the general trend in this legislation, frequently enacted at the suggestion of Northwestern's top management, was to broaden the range of securities that could be acquired by life companies domiciled in the state. In 1935 legislation permitted the Company to make its first purchase of the mortgage bonds of industrial and commercial enterprises.

Meanwhile, analysis indicated attractive investment opportunities in the form of industrial bonds not secured directly by mortgages. This was especially true of oil companies which did not ordinarily issue mortgage bonds; and when the Wisconsin investment code was modified in 1939 to permit life companies to acquire "evidences of indebtedness" of industrial corporations, the Finance Committee promptly authorized the acquisition of the debentures of the Shell-Union Oil Company ($1.1 million) and the Union Oil Company ($200,000).

The final important legislative change affecting security investments during this period came in 1945, a change that permitted the Company to hold preferred stocks of public utility and industrial corporations. Again management acted promptly, and by the end of the year had added the following preferred stock ($100 par value) to the Company's assets: 2,500 shares of the Wisconsin Power and Light Company, 400 shares of the Idaho Power Company, 10,000 shares of the Central Illinois Electric and Gas Company, and 2,436 shares of the Dictaphone Corporation.

Two innovations in Northwestern investment practices during this period were especially significant in contributing to the growth of the Company's security account, the first of which involved cooperation with commercial banks in what was called "term lending." During the mid-1930's, when good loan opportunities were scarce, commercial banks would cooperate with institutional lenders in loaning money to public utilities and industrial concerns. The banks would assume that portion of the loan that matured during the early part of the period—say the first five years—and the insurance company or other lender would assume the subsequent maturities—perhaps ten additional years. A major advantage of this kind of lending was its flexibility: the fact that it could be adapted to a variety of requirements of particular borrowers.

Because of close geographic proximity and a long association, Northwestern was asked by the First National Bank of Chicago to participate in term lending beginning in the 1930's. Working closely with Irving Porter and his successor James Buchanan of the Chicago bank, in the face of strong competition the Company was able to expand its security holdings on terms that were attractive.

The second innovation was the vigorous promotion of loans through direct placement. During the early 1930's there was a growing tendency by large public utility and industrial companies, because of abundant capital funds seeking employment, to sell their security issues directly to large institutional lenders. This not only reduced the cost of underwriting services but provided additional flexibility in working out particular financial problems. For lenders willing to seek out loan prospects and able to make arrangements that were often complex and drawn out, direct placements offered an opportunity to expand loans without waiting for underwriting organizations to take the lead.

Two examples illustrate the variety of problems encountered in the direct placement of securities. The first involved the Virginia Public Service Generating Company, located near Washington, D.C., which in 1938 desperately needed new electric generating facilities. An operating subsidiary of a holding company, the Virginia firm was in a poor credit position; its bonds were selling at a heavy discount and further mortgage borrowing could only be done at exorbitant cost. After surveying the situation Northwestern suggested the formation of a new company which would build the generating plant and lease it to the public service company. The Securities and Exchange Commission, however, withheld approval of this proposal for some months on the grounds that it would add another subsidiary to the holding company. Only after Northwestern representatives testified before the Commission, pointing out the feasibility of financing in this manner, was approval granted. A new company, the Virginia Electric Generating Company, was formed; its original first mortgage bonds, valued at $1.4 million and bearing interest of 4 per cent, were acquired by Northwestern. The plant was completed in 1940, just in time to meet the growing needs of the Capital's mushrooming population.

In 1938 the Company was asked to finance certain capital needs of the National Bulk Carriers. This organization owned some old tankers carrying gasoline and crude oil from Texas ports to the Atlantic Coast. Its president, D. K. Ludwig, proposed to add to his fleet by converting World War I Shipping Board vessels, using a new electric welding process developed by the Sun Oil Company. One of the complications involved in the financing was that because the vessels were engaged in coastal trade it was necessary that at all times they remain under United States registry, and that the owner qualify as a United States citizen under the technical provisions of the Jones Act. This meant that the mortgagor would have to qualify as a United States citizen, that is, that not less than 75 per cent of the policyholders and all the directors must be citizens of the United States. Obviously the major Eastern life insurance companies doing business in Canada and

having one or more Canadian directors could not qualify. Because Northwestern did all of its business within the United States and its trustees were all United States citizens, it clearly met the technical requirements.

Loaning on ships was a new and unfamiliar experience for the Northwestern investment group. Furthermore, National Bulk Carriers was not then in a strong financial position. It had, however, ingeniously worked out long-term charters with Pan-American Petroleum Corporation on a cost-plus basis, which included debt service charges. Ludwig was a capable and efficient operator, and extensive field investigation by Northwestern's investment staff, with the help of admiralty lawyers, indicated that a safe and desirable loan could be made. The $1.6 million advanced by Northwestern in 1939 added great impetus to Ludwig's enterprise and, coming as it did just prior to World War II, enabled his company to expand rapidly. Today his enterprise operates super-tankers and mammoth iron ore carriers throughout the world.

The importance of direct placements in the Company's operations in the security field is indicated by the fact that in each year beginning 1935, between 20 per cent and 70 per cent of public utility bonds, and from 65 per cent to 100 per cent of the industrial bonds and stocks were acquired in this way.

Comparative Investment Portfolios

During the years 1933–1946 all of the large life companies in the industry operated in an investment environment that brought a higher degree of uniformity in respect to the distribution of their assets than had previously been true. (See Table XVII-4.) A continuous flow of savings increased the aggregate investment of the ten largest companies to over $30 billion by 1947. By their very size these companies were confronted with investment problems more or less common to all, since they were generally restricted by legislation to approximately the same types of investments.

The primary characteristics of the investment portfolios of the largest companies during this time showed a decrease in the relative importance of mortgages, a consistent increase in the holdings of bonds, and a continued diminution of policy loans from the high of 1933. A significant and heavy increase in real estate from 1933 through 1936, after which the relative holdings of real estate slowly diminished through the war years, and a substantial proportion of assets held in the form of cash from

TABLE XVII-4

Ten Largest United States Life Insurance Companies: Distribution of Assets, 1933–1946
(As a Percentage of Total Admitted Assets)

COMPANY	BONDS AND STOCKS	MORTGAGE LOANS	LOANS ON POLICIES	REAL ESTATE	CASH	OTHER	ADMITTED ASSETS
			(1933)				(In Millions)
NORTHWESTERN	28.8	37.8	25.0	3.3	1.0	4.2	$998
Aetna	44.5	14.5	17.2	6.4	4.1	13.2	449
Equitable	38.7	30.4	20.0	4.7	3.2	3.1	1,521
John Hancock	31.0	39.5	14.7	9.0	2.4	3.3	656
Metropolitan	41.7	35.2	13.0	4.6	2.5	3.0	3,861
Mutual Benefit	27.5	34.4	24.7	8.2	1.3	3.9	570
Mutual Life	48.6	25.5	18.0	2.7	2.9	2.3	1,120
New York Life	44.2	25.5	20.6	3.6	1.6	4.6	2,011
Prudential	44.3	36.2	10.0	5.2	1.3	3.1	2,835
Travelers	43.5	13.8	18.2	5.6	2.1	16.6	681
			(1941)				
NORTHWESTERN	62.8	20.3	9.7	3.5	1.2	2.5	$1,440
Aetna	60.0	16.2	7.8	3.4	4.0	8.7	777
Equitable	69.8	13.5	7.2	4.7	3.0	1.8	2,741
John Hancock	69.1	14.3	7.2	5.4	3.6	0.5	1,116
Metropolitan	62.7	16.9	8.6	7.2	2.7	1.9	5,648
Mutual Benefit	62.4	14.5	9.1	8.0	3.0	3.1	796
Mutual Life	70.4	14.7	7.8	3.4	1.3	2.2	1,542
New York Life	68.6	13.9	9.6	3.1	2.7	3.1	2,987
Prudential	58.6	24.6	7.3	3.9	2.6	3.1	4,562
Travelers	60.4	10.9	8.8	3.9	1.4	14.6	1,162
			(1946)				
NORTHWESTERN	84.8	7.3	4.0	0.6	1.0	1.8	$2,019
Aetna	73.6	12.4	3.2	1.6	1.7	7.5	1,247
Equitable (NY)	81.9	11.8	2.7	0.8	1.5	1.3	4,193
John Hancock	84.6	7.8	2.9	0.9	1.7	2.1	2,038
Metropolitan	78.4	11.0	4.2	2.6	1.6	2.2	8,045
Mutual Benefit	79.3	12.5	4.0	1.1	1.5	1.6	1,069
Mutual Life (NY)	84.1	9.4	3.6	1.1	0.5	1.3	1,846
New York Life	84.8	8.3	3.9	0.6	1.0	1.4	4,027
Prudential	77.6	14.3	3.7	0.9	0.6	2.9	6,830
Travelers	67.5	10.2	4.0	1.0	0.7	16.6	1,595

SOURCE: Northwestern Mutual: *Annual Statement*, 1933-1946, inclusive. All other companies: *Seventy-Fifth Annual Report of the Superintendent of Insurance of New York* (Life), 1934. For later years, the annual statements of each respective company for the years 1941 and 1946.

1933 through 1941 were also typical of the portfolios.

After 1933 Northwestern tended more and more toward the general pattern followed by the other large life companies in their allocation of assets among the major investment categories. This development was marked by a shift of its relative position in several important respects. The most obvious change came in the proportion of mortgage loans to total assets: whereas in 1933 Northwestern ranked second highest among the ten largest companies, in 1947 it was second lowest. From having the lowest percentage of its assets in bonds and stocks the Company moved into third position during the same period. On the other hand, among the major life companies Northwestern continued to hold about the smallest proportion of its assets in United States government securities and in cash.

Investment Earnings

The long-range effectiveness of life insurance investment policies was put to an unusually severe test during the 1933–1946 period. By the very nature of their long-run financial commitments to policyholders the investment managers had to anticipate the possibility of a crisis such as affected the American economy during the 1930's. In placing their funds in anything except the most conservative investments (such as federal government bonds) the life companies assume that over a period of time, sufficient to cover a full cycle of prosperity and depression, net earnings would be at least as high, and probably higher, than if ultraconservative investment policies were followed.

How Northwestern fared in respect to earnings over the twenty-five year period ending in 1946 is shown in Table XVII-5. In essence, after taking into account all items of expense, depreciation, and capital gains and losses, the Company netted 4.3 per cent on its total investment portfolio for these years. Considering the fact that the average yield on United States government bonds for the 1922–1946 period was about 3 per cent, it is obvious that the Company was well advised to assume the "risks" of putting the bulk of its funds in other forms of investment.

A comparison of the return for each of the categories listed in Table XVII-5 shows the attraction of policy loans as a form of investment and reflects the difficulties encountered by the Company with properties acquired through foreclosure and with defaulted bonds. In respect to foreclosed properties (special real estate), operating expenses cut earnings by 0.35 per cent, and depreciation by another 0.11 per cent. Because in final liquidation there was a capital gain of 0.01 per cent, the net effect of special real estate on the earnings from mortgage loans was to reduce the total by 0.45 per cent. In the case of defaulted securities, final liquidation resulted in capital losses which exceeded capital gains sufficiently to reduce earnings on the combined security account by 0.06 per cent. It may be added that this loss was almost entirely the result of difficulties with railroad bonds.*

In itself this was an impressive financial record. It becomes even more impressive when compared with the average net earnings of the remaining companies that ranked among the ten largest in the industry.

---

* Capital gains on railroad bonds amounted to $8.8 million, capital losses to $36.1 million, or a net loss of $27.3 million. How this loss affected the net earnings rate of the railroad portfolio is shown in the following tabulation:

Gross Rate		4.12%
Investment Expense		0.05
Net Earnings Rate		4.07
Capital Gains	0.18%	
Capital Losses	0.78	
Net Loss		0.60
Net Earnings		3.47

TABLE XVII-5

Northwestern Mutual: Average Annual Investment Experience, 1922–1946

	Bonds & Stocks		Mtg. Loans & Special Real Estate		Policy Loans & Misc.		Total Assets	
Average Distribution of Assets		49.2%		34.2%		16.6%		100.0%
Gross Earnings Rate		4.10		5.02		5.59		4.66
Less:								
Investment Expense Rate	.05		.35		.35		.20	
Spec. Real Estate Operating Expense Rate	—		.35		—		.12	
Total		.05		.70		.35		.32
Net Earnings Rate		4.05		4.32		5.24		4.34
Less:								
Depreciation Rate	—		.11	.11	.07	.07	.05	.05
Net Earnings Less Depreciation		4.05		4.21		5.17		4.29
Capital Adjustments								
Capital Losses or [Gains]	.06		[.01]		—		.03	
		.06		[.01]		—		.03
Net Earnings Rate after Capital Items		3.99		4.22		5.17		4.26

As shown in the tabulation below Northwestern had the best earning record, both for the twenty-five year period 1922–1946 and for the period 1932–1946.

COMPANY	AVERAGE NET EARNINGS 1922-1946	1932-1946
NORTHWESTERN	4.34%	3.82%
Metropolitan	4.31	3.67
Mutual Benefit	4.16	3.57
Travelers	4.14	3.61
Aetna	4.02	3.59
Prudential	4.09	3.51
New York Life	4.06	3.57
John Hancock	4.10	3.44
Equitable	4.03	3.42
Mutual Life	3.87	3.33

The Passing of the Cleary Administration

Michael J. Cleary had begun to show definite signs of wear during the first years of World War II and was forced to slow his pace somewhat following a coronary attack in 1943. Evidently the tensions surrounding the decision to adopt a 2 per cent interest assumption on 1947 policies seriously taxed his strength during 1946. On February 19, 1947, he left his office preparatory to taking his annual vacation in Arizona. The following day he was stricken by another coronary and died on Saturday morning, February 22. The Executive Committee met the following Monday and named Edmund Fitzgerald acting president. This action was confirmed at the April meeting of the Board of Trustees which elected Fitzgerald Northwestern's tenth president.

Under Cleary's direction Northwestern had passed the critical tests which history, economic crisis, and a rapidly changing set of business-government-societal relations could pose. It had modified its practices to meet the profound problems of the depression and was ready for the new challenges of the national prosperity. Indeed no testimony to Northwestern's soundness and its adherence to the responsibility of trusteeship was more eloquent than the commendation of the TNEC investigation which found Northwestern's practices and policies unimpeachable.

This splendid record was also reflected in the Company's contributions to the welfare of its policyholders. As shown in Table XVII-6 aggregate policyholder premiums amounted to slightly under $2 billion, while total payments to policyholders and the increase of assets was over $2.8 billion. Thus aggregate benefits to policyholders amounted to 141.4 per cent of policyholder premiums. In both absolute

TABLE XVII-6

Eleven Largest United States Life Insurance Companies: Aggregate Benefits to Policyholders, 1933–1946

COMPANY	(1) PREMIUM INCOME	(2) PAYMENTS TO POLICYHOLDERS	(3) INCREASE IN ASSETS	(4) COL. (2) + COL. (3)	(5) COL. (4) ÷ COL. (1)
	(Dollar amounts in billions)				
Mutual Benefit	$1.023	$0.989	$0.480	$1.469	143.65%
NORTHWESTERN	1.988	1.789	1.023	2.812	141.44
New York Life	3.840	2.824	2.053	4.877	127.00
Penn Mutual	1.074	0.789	0.556	1.345	125.26
Travelers	1.653	1.100	0.915	2.015	121.87
Equitable	4.598	2.789	2.721	5.510	119.80
Mutual Life	2.083	1.719	0.719	2.438	117.04
Aetna	1.514	0.938	0.801	1.739	114.88
Metropolitan	11.183	7.654	4.276	11.930	106.68
Prudential	9.431	5.795	4.056	9.851	104.45
John Hancock	2.705	1.373	1.398	2.771	102.43

SOURCES OF BASIC DATA: Northwestern, *Annual Statement*, 1933-1946, incl. other companies, *Insurance Year Book*, 1941, 1950.

and relative terms this record was superior to that achieved by the Company for over the previous sixty years.

President Cleary made many contributions to Northwestern, ranging from an impressive improvement in Home Office-agent relations to the selection of superior personnel throughout the Company. Undel his direction Northwestern retained its relative position among the leaders of the life insurance industry in both insurance in force and the quantity of assets. This was achieved with a much smaller sales force and a continued low expense ratio. In addition, greater flexibility was introduced into investment; in some phases, such as the management of foreclosed real estate, the record was distinguished.

There was still much to do; the administrative structure needed streamlining and strengthening, and more efficient operation was desirable. Moreover, there were serious problems arising in the investment field, for by 1946 Northwestern no longer enjoyed the prospect of a continued superiority in earning capacity. To insure the continuation of its low net-cost position in this situation, the management would be pressed to keep its expenses as low as generally rising prices and wages would permit.

CHAPTER EIGHTEEN

Sales and Underwriting in the Tenth Decade: 1947 – 1956

IT was soon apparent that the decade following the end of World War II would not be marked by the "return to normalcy" which, however illusory, had typified the period that succeeded World War I. Indeed, the possibility of another global conflict was never absent in the planning of the government or far removed from the thinking of most Americans. It brought acquiescence, if not enthusiasm, for a continuation of peace-time conscription and support for a program of expenditures on military security which attained gigantic proportions.

Whatever other changes the postwar decade brought to the people of the United States, it was a period of vast economic expansion. Gross national product rose from about $232 billion in 1947 to over $400 billion in 1956, while personal income after taxes increased from an estimated $169 billion to more than $280 billion. Even with population rising by an unexpected 10 per cent from the level of 150.7 million of 1947, per capita disposable income increased from about $1,120 to over $1,600. Indeed, these years were marked not only by a startling growth in population, production, and income, but also by a continuation of income redistribution and a steady migration of people into the suburban areas surrounding the cities. The combination of these forces had powerful effects on the social and economic patterns of the national community. Heavy new investment by business enterprise in increased

productive and distributive capacity was strongly stimulated by the demand for new housing and durable consumers' goods, and by the huge government expenditures for foreign aid and military security. While the level of federal debt stabilized after the end of the war, private debt and that of municipal governments steadily expanded. Under these pressures, and modified by changes in federal monetary policy beginning in 1951, the long-term downward trend in interest rates was halted and then reversed.

All segments of American business enterprise shared in the economic expansion, although not to the same extent. The life insurance industry enjoyed the kind of prosperity which it had experienced during the 1919–1929 era, benefiting both from the effects of increased personal income and improvement in investment opportunities and interest rates. As shown in Chart XVIII–1, from the end of 1945 to the close of 1955 annual sales of life insurance rose from $22.9 billion to $50.2 billion, insurance in force from approximately $156 billion to $389 billion, and assets from about $45 billion to over $90 billion.

The vast expansion in new business during these years provided opportunities for the growth of the existing companies in the industry, and for new organizations as well. The number of life companies grew from 509 in 1946 to 1,060 by mid-year 1955. The new entrants were to an overwhelming extent stock companies, and increased their proportion among all United States companies to more than 84 per cent. Even so, in 1955 the 166 mutual companies continued to dominate the industry, having on their books more than 60 per cent of the total insurance in force.[1]

Prosperity brought other benefits and problems for the life companies. The huge demand for investment capital provided welcome new outlets for funds that were accumulating at an unprecedented rate. Expanding markets enabled agents to earn higher incomes, a factor which raised the morale of selling forces and attracted more effective sales personnel. Improvement in interest rates enabled companies to protect the margins between the rates assumed on older policies and those which could be earned in the market, and to increase the level of dividends to policyholders. This huge volume of sales, however, intensified many of the old problems of the companies and also created some new ones, the most serious being rising prices and costs, and steep rates of personal and business income taxes. With the expense of acquisition rising, and because heavy taxes made the accumulation of capital by agents more difficult, the problems of financing general agency systems of distribution became more acute. The expansion of employee benefits by business concerns, particularly the growth in group life insurance coverage, pension plans, and deferred profit-sharing schemes, was beneficial to many life companies and induced some to depart from traditional adherence to ordinary plans only. The extent and growth of these forms of coverage, however, were regarded by many life insurance agents with misgivings concerning the effects they might have upon the demand for individual insurance protection.

By 1956 the United States life insurance industry reflected the strength of these forces. Group insurance comprised 27.1 per cent of the total life insurance in force in United States companies as compared to only 12.8 per cent in 1940 and 14.5 per cent in 1945. The tendency for life companies to combine two or more classes of coverage was reflected by the fact that of the dozen largest firms in the industry in 1956, Northwestern alone continued to market only ordinary insurance.

Executive Management and Organizational Structure

Fifty-three years of age at the time of his election, Edmund Fitzgerald had the distinction of being the youngest man to head Northwestern since John

H. Van Dyke was selected in 1869. His fourteen years with the Company and his close association with Cleary had thoroughly imbued the new chief executive with the basic philosophy and management principles that were the distinguishing features of Northwestern. As he once said, "[We owe a] great debt for the status of the Company as we find it today to those who have preceded us here."

Just as Northwestern had been fortunate in the selection of the man so well qualified to guide it through the troubled times of depression and war, it was equally fortunate in choosing a leader whose abilities and temperament were suited to meeting the problems of the postwar period. As he visualized the Company's future, Fitzgerald observed,

> Our objective might well be to improve rather than to enlarge—in other words, to strengthen the base of the entire enterprise rather than broaden its reach. . . . The growth that is appropriate for us is that which still permits us to produce quality life

Edmund Fitzgerald

CHART XVIII-1

United States Life Insurance Companies: Assets, Sales, and Insurance in Force, 1947–1955

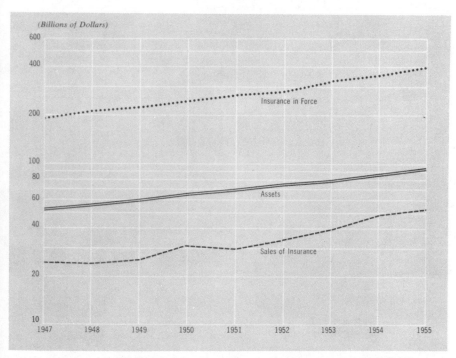

Sources: *Life Insurance Fact Book,* (New York: Institute
of Life Insurance, 1956), 13, 21 and 60.

insurance. That is the growth that we can justify. Our performance itself will tend to determine our size.[2]

In the president's estimation the two most pressing problems confronting the Company were to keep expenses low without sacrificing service and quality and to increase the yield on Northwestern's investments. There was no spectacular, bold solution to either of these problems. They could be met only by a continual strengthening in the personnel and operating efficiency of the Home Office, and by steady improvement in the selection and training of the members of the agency force. In short, the new president proposed to maximize Northwestern's potentialities as a specialized life insurance company within the framework of its basic characteris-

tics. External conditions would have strong influences upon Northwestern's behavior during the years ahead, but Fitzgerald's concept of the role of management was to prevent the Company from becoming a blind pawn of circumstance. To achieve this goal he considered it necessary to reshuffle and streamline administrative responsibilities, provide for a steady supply of new management personnel, and make the most efficient use of the talents of the executive group.

In Fitzgerald's judgment, one of the most important ways of improving the effectiveness of his executives was, so far as possible, to free them from the burden of routine administrative operation in order to provide time and opportunity to develop plans and suggest policies for the future. Reorganization of administrative structure, and the addition of

CHART XVIII-2

Structure of Executive Organization: Northwestern, 1955

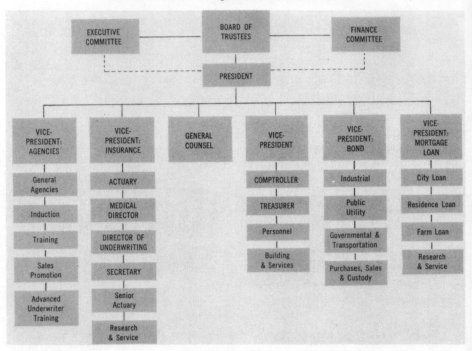

Note: Designations in capitals indicate heads of departments who are members of executive management. The Senior Actuary, while a member of executive management, is not chief of an operating department in the Company.

specialized service and research functions in the various departments, had been largely completed by 1955, permitting a significant realization of the president's goal. Aware of the various strengths and deficiencies of the members of executive management, the president reassigned functions and responsibilities when necessary. Not only was the flow of work expedited by these steps, with a commensurate saving to policyholders, but the delegation of authority resulted in a great reduction in the strains imposed on Fitzgerald himself. By the end of the Company's centennial year only six executive officers were directly responsible to the president: the five vice presidents and the general counsel. As shown in Chart XVIII-2, all other departments and functions were coordinated through and responsible

to one of these six executives. At the time Fitzgerald took office approximately twice this number of officers reported directly to the chief executive.

The objectives of the process of administrative streamlining which began in 1947 were to consolidate similar functions within the same operating department and to regroup departments performing correlated duties under single executives for better control, direction, and coordination. In early 1947, for example, collections from policyholders and payments to government units, agents, and employees were handled through several different departments. By 1953, through consolidation of functions and offices, all such activity was under the personal supervision of the treasurer and the comptroller, and coordinated under the direction of one of the vice presidents. Similar simplification of department processes occurred throughout the Company, and the changes were typified by the modifications made in the secretarial department. Over time this department had been given such varied responsibilities as premium collections; payment of dividends, premium taxes, agents' commissions and fees; endorsements of policies and option settlements; policy changes; title changes; and pension trust administration. Settlement of claims and options, however, were the responsibility of still another division, separate from the jurisdiction of the secretary. By 1953 the collection and disbursements sections had been transferred to the treasurer, the claims division integrated with the secretarial department, and the entire activities of the latter

consolidated in four sections. One of the most important results of these changes was the elimination of duplicate record keeping and services which resulted from the imposition of departmental barriers.

Like his predecessors President Fitzgerald inherited a group of operating executives when he assumed office in 1947. As can be seen in Table XVIII-1, only two of these, Howard J. Tobin and Elgin G. Fassel, had been in office for less than four years. Two problems immediately confronted him: the first of which was the need to select a replacement for his own previous vice presidency, the second involved a change of comptrollers. To succeed him as what could be defined as administrative vice president, Fitzgerald in April 1947 secured

TABLE XVIII-1

Northwestern Mutual: Executive Officers, 1947-1957

POSITION	OCCUPANT	YEARS	
President	Edmund Fitzgerald	1947-	
Vice President, Bonds	Frederick W. Walker	1926-1949	R
	Donald C. Slichter	1949-	
Vice President, Mortgage Loans	Howard J. Tobin	1945-	
Vice President, Insurance	Robert E. Dineen	1950-	
Vice President	Philip K. Robinson	1947-	
Vice President and Director of Agencies	Grant L. Hill	1946-	
Senior Actuary	Elgin G. Fassel	1953-	
Actuary	Elgin G. Fassel	1946-1953	T
	Victor E. Henningsen	1953-	
General Counsel	Gerald M. Swanstrom	1943-	
Secretary	Ralph E. Perry	1943-1951	R
	Robert E. Dineen	1951-1952	
	William B. Minehan	1952-	
Medical Director	D. E. W. Wenstrand	1936-1950	R
	Gamber F. Tegtmeyer	1950-	
Comptroller	Shepard E. Barry	1932-1947	R
	Victor E. Henningsen	1947-1953	T
	Charles G. Groeschell	1953-	
Director of Underwriting	Joseph N. Lochemes	1945-1956	R
	Paul K. Frazer	1956-	
Treasurer	Chester W. Adamson	1951-	
Director of Agencies	Grant L. Hill	1933-	

Dates include year in which appointed to office and year of termination.
R—retirement   T—transfer to another position

the appointment of Philip K. Robinson, North-western's director of municipal bond investment. To replace the ailing Shepard Barry, who retired in August 1947, the Company chose Victor E. Henningsen.

Robinson was initially placed in charge of the cashier's, comptroller's, personnel, and building maintenance departments. To these were subsequently added claims and the newly organized treasurer's department.* Henningsen, aged thirty-nine, had joined Northwestern in 1932, a year after his graduation from the University of Iowa. In 1933 he was appointed an assistant actuary and in 1946 he became associate actuary. Under his direction the comptroller's department contributed strongly to the Company's development in several ways, particularly through the expansion of its planning activities and their effects upon the systemization of work routines and methods. In 1953, when Elgin Fassel was given the newly created post of senior actuary, Henningsen succeeded him as chief of the actuarial department. His own successor was another member of the actuarial staff, Charles G. Groeschell, who had joined the Company in 1947. A native of Wisconsin and navy veteran, Groeschell had acquired actuarial experience with Metropolitan Life before entering Northwestern's service.

During the four years 1949–1952, the executive management hierarchy was affected by five changes which began when Donald C. Slichter, director of public utility bond investment, was elected a vice president to succeed the retiring Frederick W. Walker in 1949. During 1950 the Company acquired a new insurance vice president and a new medical director; the following year the title of treasurer was reactivated in executive management; and in 1952 a new secretary was appointed.

The selection of an insurance vice president was reminiscent of the Company's 1919 experience, both as to the reason for the appointment and the experience of the man chosen for the office. As shown in a previous chapter, Michael J. Cleary had not believed it necessary formally to appoint an officer to succeed him in the role of insurance vice president since Percy H. Evans had, for all practical purposes, the administrative flair for coordinating and directing the work of the operating departments in the underwriting fields. During the four years following Evans' retirement, however, it became apparent that none of the remaining insurance executives, regard-

less of their other merits, then had his background in the area of administration.

To obtain an administrator of proven ability, the Company went outside its own organization to employ Robert E. Dineen, the forty-seven year old superintendent of insurance for the State of New York. A graduate of Syracuse University's school of law, Dineen had practiced in his home state until 1943 when he was appointed head of the insurance department. Like Cleary before him, he had been elected president of the National Association of Insurance Commissioners. When he assumed his new position at Northwestern Dineen was given responsibility for coordinating the functions of the actuarial, secretarial, medical, and underwriting departments. To these were subsequently added the tasks of coordinating the Company's insurance research and service programs. For about a year following the retirement of Secretary Ralph E. Perry in February 1951, Dineen also acted as temporary secretary of the Company.

All subsequent appointments to executive management involved men who had made their careers with Northwestern. In 1950 Dr. Gamber F. Tegtmeyer became medical director, succeeding Dr. David E. W. Wenstrand who retired. Dr. Tegtmeyer had been educated at the University of Wisconsin and Oxford University before graduating from Harvard's medical school. He joined Northwestern's medical department in 1936, after practicing medicine in Milwaukee for several years. The following year Chester W. Adamson was appointed treasurer when that department was reorganized in 1951 and given executive management status. Adamson was a career employee with almost thirty years of service, including experience as an assistant secretary. Most of the functions for which he had been previously responsible were transferred to the new department, to which were added the cashier's duties and those pertaining to agents' compensation and retirement, and general agency audit. In 1952 William B. Minehan was elected secretary of the Company. Forty-two years of age, Minehan had joined the Company in 1931 following graduation from Dartmouth College. After years of service in the secretary's department he spent four years in the army during World War II before returning as executive assistant to Vice President Fitzgerald. Subsequently he became assistant and then associate secretary, preparatory to his new appointment. Still another career employee, Paul K. Frazer, was appointed to succeed Joseph N. Lochemes as director of underwriting when the latter retired in 1956 after forty-seven years with

---

* The claims department was later integrated with the secretarial department and the cashier's department consolidated under the treasurer.

Northwestern. Forty-eight years of age, Frazer was a graduate of the University of Iowa, joined the Company's actuarial department in 1928, and was transferred to the new underwriting department in 1942, becoming an officer the following year.

In 1951 the Company formalized its public relations functions with a division responsible directly to the president. They were to place particular emphasis on identifying Northwestern with the home community and upon more effectively publicizing the institution.

In addition to the streamlining of organizational structure and the appointment of new, and on the average, younger executives than the Company had previously used, Northwestern's committee apparatus was extended and research facilities improved. There were, moreover, certain modifications of policy, one of which was highly significant for the Company. This was the abandonment of Northwestern's traditional isolationism from the big trade associations of the life insurance industry. The question of joining either or both the Life Insurance Association of America and the American Life Convention had been raised in the Executive Committee a number of times before 1950, only to be rejected. Meanwhile, however, pressure for membership became stronger. While Northwestern had been kept informed of the decisions of the associations, particularly in the field of federal taxation of the life insurance industry, such information was always *ex post*, and in view of the uncertain atmosphere of the time it seemed desirable for the Company to participate more actively in the formulation of association policy. This position was strengthened by the impending retirement of Legislative Counsel Clarence C. Klocksin, generally acknowledged as one of the most effective representatives of life insurance in Washington. It was also recognized that Northwestern had already gone part way along this road by helping in the financing of the Institute of Life Insurance and by contributing substantially to the industry's anti-inflation program of national advertising.[5] The decision of the Executive Committee in September 1950 authorizing membership in both the associations not only brought an end to the Company's historical insularity from industry alliances, but to the standing joke among insurance circles that there were three major associations in life insurance—the Life Insurance Association, the American Life Convention, and Northwestern Mutual.

The changes in management personnel, organization, and policy suggested and put into effect under Fitzgerald, had the active support and endorsement of the standing committees of trustees and the full board. The board itself continued to be composed of distinguished policyholders who took their responsibilities seriously. Through its members on the Executive and Finance Committees, and an occasional representative on the Insurance and Agency Committee, the board kept in close touch with management policies and operations. As in prior years, an added check was provided by the annually appointed Policyholders' Examining Committee. One particularly noteworthy addition to the board occurred in 1955 when the first woman trustee, Miss Catherine Cleary, was elected.[4] Although Miss Cleary was the daughter of the Company's late president, she won the honor as a result of her own distinguished record as a lawyer, vice president of a leading Milwaukee trust company, and as an Assistant Treasurer of the United States.

Administration and Personnel

One administrative task the management set for itself was the improvement of employee productivity. This had to be accomplished if Northwestern was to retain its cost advantages in the face of steadily rising wages, salaries, and machinery and equipment prices. Operationally, this placed a premium upon effective employment and salary administration, efficient utilization of personnel, as well as skilled methods and procedures engineering. The record of the number of employees and their total wage and salary bill, compared to the amount of business done by the Company, gives a measure of how well this administrative goal was achieved.

The total Home Office staff, management, clerical, and service personnel numbered 1,369 in 1947; by the end of 1955 it had grown by about one-sixth, to 1,593.* This increase was more than completely offset by the growth of insurance in force in Northwestern, with the result that the number of Home Office employees per $100 million of insurance in 1955 was only 17.3 as compared to 21.4 in 1947, and more than thirty in 1940. Based on industry-

---

* Employment distribution for three selected years was:

	1947	1951	1955
Officers	70	70	79
Supervisors and Specialists	81	92	106
Total Management	151	162	185
Clerical	1,018	1,106	1,187
Service	200	217	221
Grand total	1,369	1,485	1,593

wide data, the average of all companies doing business in the United States in 1955 was about thirty-four persons per $100 million of life insurance in force.[5]

The Company's total wage and salary bill, however, went up by more than three and one-half times the increase in the Home Office staff, from about $5.1 million in 1947 to over $8 million in 1955. Total wages and salaries, including retirement and other Company contributions to employee welfare, amounted to $58.3 million for the nine years beginning 1947. Relative to the change in the Company's premium revenue, the increase in the aggregate compensation bill was no greater than the increase in the number of employees. In 1947 the compensation bill amounted to 2.45 per cent of premiums received; in 1955 it was equal to 2.85 per cent.

The management was confronted by several problems in improving employee efficiency, in addition to those posed by the upward pressure on salary rates. Some of these arose from decisions made during the 1930's when the Company had increased the number of male employees well beyond the proportions which had been customary before the depression. Because of the conditions of the 1937–1938 era, the management had greatly reduced the number of male employees hired, and by 1947 had substantially restored the predepression ratio of three women to each man on its staff. This policy, reinforced by the military draft during the war years, had produced a ten-year gap in the age distribution of male employees by 1947, and posed certain difficulties in terms of future replacement of managerial personnel. A program of recruiting at the college level implemented a systematic "personnel inventory" which, by the use of counselling and aptitude testing, sought to discover and use the managerial potential of men already employed. To encourage a higher level of education and technical skill, the Company also underwrote the tuition of those employees who enrolled in evening courses in the colleges and institutes in the Milwaukee area.

With the effects of the low birth rate of the late 1920's and 1930's becoming apparent in the smaller size of the graduating high school classes, the Company modified its policy regarding the employment of married women. With fewer girls seeking employment, the difficulty of replacing women who left Northwestern because of marriage increased. By 1956, after some experimentation, the policy was to retain women employees for five years after they married, but to hire no married women.

During these years the management extended and liberalized the employees' retirement plan. In 1947, concerned about the steady erosion of rising prices upon the living standards of retiring employees, the Company adopted a new plan under which retirement income would be a higher percentage of the employee's terminal salary.[6] In the same year short-hour maintenance and restaurant employees were brought under the plan. The Company's costs rose as a result of these improvements in employee welfare, particularly after 1950 when both the scale of Northwestern contributions and the Home Office payroll were increased.

The specialization of the Company's insurance business, as reflected by the growing proportion of business, estate, trust, and retirement plans to the total in force, added to the complexity of internal operation and placed a premium upon effective systemization of procedures and methods. New equipment, frequently designed by Company personnel, was substituted for direct labor where possible to offset personnel shortages, reduce expense, or eliminate dull, repetitive duties. As a result, the

CHART XVIII-3

Home Office Expenses: Northwestern, 1947–1955

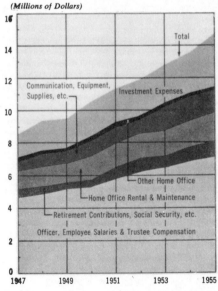

SOURCE: *Annual Statement,* Northwestern Mutual Life Insurance Company, 1947-1955.

amounts spent for equipment, internal communication, and supplies rose almost three-fold between 1947 and 1956; while a somewhat smaller increase was experienced in Home Office building rental and maintenance costs. Similar increases characterized the Company's expenses for investment, which rose from over $1.4 million in 1947 to more than $3.3 million in 1955. The magnitude and changes of these internal expenses for each year of the period are shown in Chart XVIII-3.

Despite the rise in expenses incurred at Northwestern during these years, the Company managed to retain its position among the leaders of the industry with respect to low cost. The Institute of Life Insurance reported in 1956 that "The increasing cost of doing business has affected all industries. . . [that] in general . . . all companies show a higher expense ratio today than a decade ago . . . [and] the increase in this ratio in the last ten years . . . has brought it to a level close to that of the late 1920's." The ratio of all life company expenses, except taxes, to total income was 17 per cent in 1947 and 16.9 per cent in 1955.[7] For Northwestern, for the same years, it was roughly 10 per cent. As measured by this criterion, at least, the low-cost objective of the management had been substantially achieved.

Underwriting and Marketing Development

Expanding insurance markets, the increase in group coverage, and the intensification of merchandising competition in the life insurance industry posed many new challenges for Northwestern in the 1947–1956 era. Particularly strong were the tendencies of competitors to get a larger share of the insurance market by: adding group, health, and accident coverage to their ordinary business; the growing resort to "special" contracts; company subsidization of selling organizations. The Company's responses to these challenges were, for the most part, not surprising. Concentration upon the more complex insurance solutions to human and institutional needs such as estate planning, and corporation and other types of business insurance, had already made Northwestern a specialty company. Effective underwriting in this area required an exceptionally trained agency force, ably directed by the general agents and the Home Office agency department. The management could see little point in abandoning policies, methods, and organization which had been successful merely because rivals were moving in other directions. As President Fitz-

gerald observed, the management could not believe that "certain elements of strength inherent in Northwestern methods and operating policies [were] suddenly wrong, or that all the others have suddenly found the key."[8]

Yet in other respects Northwestern responses to the post-1946 challenges were marked by some bold and new departures. Following intensive investigation of the substandard risk field, the Company began accepting the business of certain classes of such risks at extra premiums in 1956. Later that year the management took a major step forward with regard to the problems associated with the "special" policies of competitors. This decision, long under study, involved application of the principle of a scale of premiums graduated according to the amount of insurance purchased. It was made possible by rulings of the New York, Wisconsin, and other state insurance departments and action by the National Association of Insurance Commissioners in May 1956. For policies to be issued as of 1957, assuming comparable ages, the savings on premiums would be proportionately greater to those individuals who purchased contracts with large face amounts; Northwestern had met the single breaking point on one plan of insurance offered by competitors with multiple breaking points on all plans of insurance.

Essentially, Northwestern attempted to meet the market situations of the postwar period by the same basic methods with which it had achieved success in the past. Improvement of the agency system as a source of new business and a servicer of old business was sought within the framework of a true independent-contractor relationship. The agency force was made more effective by means of careful selection and training, particularly in the area of advanced underwriting. Additions to the number of policy contracts and plans offered were few, and the services offered by the Company to policyholders were increased. Although the experience with substandard business was too limited at the end of the Company's first century of operation to draw definite conclusions, there were several indications that the excellent mortality record would not be significantly impaired. The Company, however, was somewhat less successful in selling insurance relative to the expansion of ordinary insurance coverage which took place during these years.

Home Office Marketing Management

While the basic functions and responsibilities of the director of agencies remained unchanged, the nature of the insurance markets and the development of the Company's underwriting program during this period entailed a further specialization and extension of the marketing services provided by his department. Specifically, the increasing emphasis given to the more complex phases of underwriting caused Vice President Hill to add to his staff both a director of advanced underwriting training and specialists in the legal and tax aspects of advanced programming. In several instances members of the latter group moved out into the field to help in the development of trust, estate, and business insurance of various general agencies, and enjoyed a notable success. In general, however, marketing management at the Home Office continued to be concerned about sales promotion, the selection of general agents, financing of the agencies, training and compensation of agents, communication and relations with the field force, and effective supervision and motivation of its salesmen.

The organizational streamlining within the Home Office was reflected within the agency department where further delegation of responsibilities and an expansion of specialization were undertaken to relieve the director of the more routine supervisory duties. In addition, several functions, together with their administrative personnel, were transferred to the treasurer in 1952. These included responsibility for agents' financing and administration of the agents' retirement plan.

The number of Hill's assistant directors was slightly increased by 1956, and a substantial turnover of this staff had taken place as these men went back into the field force as general agents. New recruits for the staff of assistant directors continued to be selected from the agency force as in previous years.

Size and Structure of the Agency Force

While the numbers of Home Office employees grew by roughly 16 per cent during these years, the size of the Company's agency force was reduced, and the proportion of full-time agents under contract rose steadily. The structure of the agency organization remained basically unchanged from the previous period, except that the number of general agencies was increased from eighty-seven in 1947 to ninety-one in 1956. The number of district agencies, however, was somewhat reduced, falling from 241 in 1947 to 214 in 1951, then rising to 238

in 1956. The stability of the general agency organization during a period of steadily expanding sales resulted in a substantial increase in agency production and revenue. In 1947 only ten Northwestern general agencies enjoyed a five-year average production volume of $6.5 million or more annually; eight years later there were twenty-six such agencies. Whereas forty-one general agencies averaged $3 million or more in production per year for a span of five years in 1947, the number had increased to sixty-six in 1955. From 1951 on only three Northwestern general agencies produced less than $1.5 million per year, calculated on this same base.

As a result of medical, demographic, and socio-economic investigations the Company enlarged the geographic character of its market after 1946. In 1950 Northwestern agents re-entered Alabama following an absence of over fifty years.[9] Shortly thereafter the Company accepted Arkansas risks from the previously excluded Mississippi River country, and in 1952 obtained a license to sell in South Carolina. This decision was made to facilitate the administration of the pension trusts of businesses which had transferred personnel to newly opened plants in that state, however, and no drive for new business was contemplated in South Carolina.[10] In 1955, after careful study, the Executive Committee authorized business to be accepted from the thirty-three Georgia counties which had been excluded from the territory of the Atlanta agency.[11] The question of accepting Florida business and re-entering Texas was also investigated preparatory to establishing new general agencies in these states.

Excluding general and district agents, the size of the Northwestern agency force fell from 3,721 in 1947 to 2,948 in 1951, and then rose to 3,216 during 1956. Over the entire period there was a net reduction of seventy-six full-time special and soliciting agents as compared to a decrease of 429 part-time agents.* The proportion of agents under full-time

---

* The distribution of the Company's agents, by classification and type of contract, for the years 1947, 1951, and 1956 was:

	1947	1951	1956
Number of Agencies	87	89	91
General Agents	91	92	93
District Agents	241	214	238
Special Agents:			
Full-time	1,460	1,304	1,331
Part-time	751	533	548
Soliciting Agents:			
Full-time	441	395	494
Part-time	1,069	716	843
Total agents—all classes	4,053	3,254	3,547

SOURCE: Company records.

contracts, other than general and district agents, rose from about 51 per cent of the field force in 1947 to almost 56 per cent nine years later.

Two of the four new Northwestern general agencies opened during the 1947–1955 era were located in New York City and Milwaukee, respectively, following the retirement of veteran general agents in both cities. The other two agencies were established in territories where population and economic expansion made necessary a more intensive sales development. With four general agencies operating in New York City and two in Milwaukee (which was made a metropolitan open territory in 1949), policyholders' service bureaus were opened in both cities, the costs of which were prorated among the agencies involved.[12]

The stability which had characterized the Company's general agent personnel in earlier years continued after 1946, but with a modest increase in the rate of turnover. In addition to the four new general agencies opened, forty-five general agents were replaced following retirement, death, or termination for other reasons; and three agencies were affected by retirement of one member of a partnership. Replacement policy followed earlier criteria quite closely, with a clear indication that the average age of new general agent appointees was significantly lower than had been the case in previous years.

While district agencies continued to be the main method of territorial development in the larger rural general agencies, after 1953 the Company acted to permit the extension of the system in metropolitan territories with populations of at least 500,000. In the latter locations, district agents did not have exclusive territory privileges, but were used to develop outlying areas near the cities. In these cases the management was careful to establish safeguards to prevent a shifting of the responsibility for agency development from the general agent to the district men.[13]

Postwar Developments in Agent Recruiting and Training

One high priority objective of the management team was to maintain the advantages its agency force held over those of rivals. This could be accomplished by refining the selection process, improving and extending the Company's training program, and by effective supervision and incentives, developing the full potential of individual agents. The bases for Northwestern's intermediate and ad-

vanced underwriter training had been completed by 1947, and it remained only to put them into operation. To improve the recruiting process, however, several actions were required. These included a program to interest college students in a career as an agent, and the development of incentives for aggressive recruiting at the general and district agency level. The latter, however, had to be obtained without building new fixed costs into the acquisition-expense structure of the Company, which no field or Home Office management skill could overcome.[14]

The sources from which the Company obtained its general and district agents remained unchanged from previous periods, and except for the greater interest shown in recruiting college students, this was also true of special and soliciting agents. In an effort to assist the recruiting efforts of the general agencies, the agency department set up a college relations section to contact college placement offices, university teachers, and graduating seniors. Those interested were directed to the Company agencies in the location of their preference.

As indicated in Chapter XV, the steady rise in prices and high personal income taxes of the period made the accumulation of capital more difficult for newly appointed general agents. These difficulties were reflected in the development of the recruiting problems of the agencies, since an increasing percentage of new agents required financial assistance, and rising living costs intensified the difficulties. The problems were further aggravated by the competition of other business firms for manpower. One contribution which management made to assist the general agents in recruiting was the liberalization of the revolving loans which had been first introduced during the war. Under this plan general agents could borrow from the Company amounts which would permit them to advance up to $300 per month to new agents. The plan set a maximum limit on the total which could be owed by the individual general agent at any single time. Under the impact of rising living costs, the total amount of the credit was increased so that the maximum advance to agents could be raised to $450 per month. As originally introduced, this plan geared the amounts that could be loaned to each general agent by the Company to the production of the newly recruited agents. In 1955 this was modified to relate Company loans to commissions earned.[15]

In the life insurance business the inflationary pressures of the period were nowhere more evident than in acquisition costs, which had approximately doubled during the twenty-five years after 1925.* By 1951 the General Agents' Association requested the Company to provide further assistance to meet induction and training expenses. The management was sympathetic to these needs of general agents, and aware that a program of assistance which was limited only to successful agents could seriously retard recruiting and agency production. In advancing its assistance program, however, the Home Office refused to subsidize the induction losses of the general agents or to make other concessions which, in its opinion, would be inconsistent with the theory on which the general agency compensation structure continued to rest. Company assistance was divided into two principal parts—development fees for district agents and induction fees for general and district agents.

In introducing development fees in 1947 the Company substituted a systematic for the somewhat arbitrary program of subsidies and advances previously made to support the district agency system.[16] Management believed that the district agencies provided good opportunities for the testing and training of potential general agents and offered other advantages to the Company which warranted such extra subsidies. Among these was the service provided to policyholders by district agency offices. In 1954 induction fees were introduced. These also represented a refinement of an earlier program under which the Company had been paying the general agents fees related to the business of new agents winning certain awards based on production in the initial years. District agents were also eligible for a share in these fees. The specific purpose of the plan was to stimulate new agent production; it was not part of the contractual compensation of the general agent and the Company reserved the right to withdraw it at any time.

Other actions taken by the management to help general and district agents meet the financial burdens of more active recruiting included a modification of the rates of interest charged by the Company on loans and advances, and the privilege of commutation of commissions for new general agents. The change in the interest charge became effective January 1951, and the new rate was set equal to "the net rate earned by the Company" before taxes during the previous year.[17] Since Northwestern's annual earned rate during this period was con-

sistently below the rate which the Company had charged up to this time, the move benefited debtor general agents. The commutation privilege was extended to new general agents to permit them to collect part of their renewal interest during the second year of a policy's existence, and involved an increase in the first renewal commission with an equitable reduction of the subsequent four renewals.[18] At the same time that the commutation contract was authorized, the Company permitted payment of development awards to general agents based upon the production of agents under contract to them whose ability was demonstrated by winning gold, silver, and bronze buttons under the Company's honors program.[19]

The results of these management efforts, and the responses from general and district agents, were not always easy to measure; but by the Company's centennial year there were certain indications of success. For example, the number of agents under contract had not only risen from the 1951 low point, but the agents who had been under contract less than three years had produced about 20 per cent of Northwestern's total sales during 1955.

Development of the intermediate and advanced agent training courses, the planning for which had been largely completed in 1946, gave the Company an integrated and highly efficient system of agent education. Regardless of the excellence of the entire program, it was the development of advanced underwriter training which gave the management the greatest single satisfaction. The subject matter of this course has been previously described. To be eligible agents had to have completed the four previous courses in the training program, or have attended the career school; further, attendance was limited to those who had sold a minumum of $150,000 of insurance in any of the three years before enrolling. This course dovetailed with the Company's advanced underwriting specialization, and provided advantageous preparation for agents seeking the Chartered Life Underwriter designation.

The degree to which Northwestern agents qualified for this designation is one indication of the quality of the field force. By the end of 1956 the Company had 350 C. L. U.'s, equal to 16.1 per cent of all agents under full-time contract. By comparison, the total C. L. U.'s for the entire industry comprised less than 3 per cent of all full-time agents under contract in the United States.[20]

Additional indications of the quality of Northwestern's agency force during this period were the number of National Quality Award winners and

---

* Based upon studies conducted by the Life Insurance Agency Management Association and cited by Laurence S. Morrison to a Company committee. "Report Number Sixteen, General Agents' Compensation Committee," March 2, 1953, 1.

members of the Million Dollar Round Table among its agents. At the end of 1955 the Company had 726 of the former among its agents. This number constituted 5.4 per cent of the industry total, and over 32 per cent of full-time Northwestern agents. The 13,300 awardees in the United States comprised but 5.8 per cent of the national aggregate of full-time agents. Membership in the Million Dollar Round Table of the National Association of Life Underwriters was restricted to those agents who sold a paid-for business of one million dollars in a single year. Life memberships required that the agent meet this qualification for three consecutive years. Northwestern led all companies in total members until 1955–1956, when it was second. Even during the latter years, 172 and 208 agents, respectively, attained membership in the Round Table. This number amounted to about 9 per cent of Northwestern's full-time agents; the total membership in the Round Table, by comparison, comprised less than 1 per cent of the industry's full-time agents. In life memberships the Company's agents continued the leadership they had held since the Round Table was originated.[21]

Insurance Plans and Underwriting Standards

During the years 1947–1954, after the change to a 2 per cent basis January 1, 1947, there were few changes in the Company's insurance plans, although the lower age limit for accepted risks was reduced to five years and the maximum amount of insurance on a single risk was increased to $400,000. The principal additions to Northwestern's insurance plans were the family income policy in 1950 and the "65 Life Family Income" contract in 1954. Both of these contracts combined diminishing term insurance with a permanent plan, and differed from the Company's original income plan in that the guaranteed monthly income feature terminated twenty years from the date of the policy rather than from the death of the insured. Other modifications of the "contract line" included a revision of initial term policies, a reduction in the gross premiums of term contracts, and permission to policyholders to discount premiums in advance.[22] The Company also imposed the condition that the minimum amount for term policies would be $3,000 after 1954.

Beginning 1956, however, the changes which occurred in Northwestern underwriting had much greater significance. The two most important have already been indicated: the acceptance of so-called

"special class" or substandard risks in 1956 and gradation of premiums by size of policy. The latter plan was adopted in late 1956 for application in 1957 and made retroactive through dividends to policies issued after 1946. A further decision, retroactive to all business, had several objectives, including a more flexible approach to the problem of settlement options. In addition to these changes, the management further modified the age and face value limits with respect to risks. In 1956 the Company raised the maximum limit on a single risk to $600,000, and at the same time reduced the lower age limit to one month.

The decision to accept risks which had been regarded as substandard was a critical one for management, and was not taken without exhaustive investigation. Actuarially, there was no question of the soundness of the move; by the mid-1920's a host of companies had entered the field with satisfactory results. The key question for the management, therefore, was whether acceptance of such risks would impair the character of the Company and lower the level of moral and financial responsibility of its policyholders as a group. Elgin Fassel, who conducted the investigation, was convinced that by extending its coverage to impaired lives Northwestern would be more adequately filling policyholders' needs than it had previously, and could legitimately be regarded as a better company. In the opinion of a majority of executives and field force alike, the concept of "preferred risk" applied to the economic level of policyholders to a much greater degree than it did to social and medical standards. By medically grading impaired risks and providing proven safeguards such as extra premiums and more modest limits on the amount issued per risk, the Company could continue to solicit business from the same income strata which had enabled it to maintain its high-grade performance during the past.[23]

Although Company officers denied that the specific objective of the decision to accept substandard business was to increase the volume of sales, there can be little doubt that such was a factor. The experience of other companies indicated that special class business amounted to almost 10 per cent of total insurance issued, and on the basis of Northwestern's 1947–1954 sales would give the Company an additional $40 million to $50 million annually. Particularly attractive was the prospect of providing additional coverage to older policyholders who, because they could no longer meet the medical standards, were obliged to obtain insurance from other companies.

This decision, taken in July 1955, was popular with Company agents, since they would thereafter receive retirement fund and other credits, something not possible when they had to place substandard insurance with other life companies. General agents were also benefited since they received over-riding commissions and collection fees on Northwestern business; formerly, they received only some renewals or an over-ride on substandard business placed by their agents with competitor companies, and frequently nothing at all. Since the general agents housed their agents and paid many of their expenses, they were resentful that other companies got a substantial block of business without paying any of this overhead.

The competition of "special" policies and extra dividends grew more troublesome during this period and undoubtedly cut into Northwestern's sales volume. Many insurers had long contended that the use of terminal dividends in illustrating the costs of insurance to a prospect was misleading at best, while the systematic payment of extra dividends was a backdoor re-entry to the deferred dividend of the past. Northwestern executives were partly satisfied, therefore, when late in the summer of 1956 the New York insurance department decreed that in the future companies using terminal dividends in cost illustrations must state the conditions under which such dividends would not be paid as prominently as they did the conditions under which payment would be made. The Company, of course, desired a much stronger restriction in this matter, and hoped that the 1956 action was only the first step toward this end.

In the matter of the "specials," however, the management took direct action of its own. In December 1956 Northwestern announced that beginning in 1957 a gradation of premiums by size of policies would take place, applicable to all policies and retroactive through dividends to contracts issued after 1946. Since gross premiums on business issued during 1947–1956 could not be changed, larger dividends were to be adjusted on these contracts, the amount of the adjustment to be determined by the face values of the policies in force. Three groups were established and premiums graded accordingly. For permanent policies with face amounts of less than $5,000, the existing premium structure applied; for those between $5,000 and $9,999, premiums would be $1 less per thousand of insurance than for the first group; while for policies of face amounts of $10,000 or more, premiums would be $1.25 per thousand below those in the first group.[24]

In essence, this step carried the theory upon which the special policy was based, namely, the application of the gradation by size principle to a special class of policies, toward a more logical conclusion—the application of that principle across the board to all plans of insurance. The decision was based upon evidence that in the past smaller sized policies had been, to some degree, subsidized by larger policies; and that specific differences in administrative cost existed for policies of different face amounts. In approving this approach the National Association of Insurance Commissioners recognized that mortality, interest, and all other relevant factors should also be considered. Since management believed that price differences between amount groupings had to be substantial and that a reasonable percentage of total policies should be included in each grouping, only the three stated classifications were established.[25]

As in the decision made earlier on substandards, there was reason to infer that the use of premiums graded by policy size would substantially offset the competitive effects of the "special" policies and provide greater protection for the Company's self-defined market. To Company agents who had grown increasingly impatient over what they regarded as management insensitivity to the trends in life insurance underwriting, the decision was most welcome. The management, however, felt that price gradation to the buyer of one plan but not to the other was unjustified in those cases where the principle could be applied, and delayed action until the regulatory authorities permitted more uniform treatment.

The plans to adopt premiums graded by policy size and to accept substandard risks were prompted in part by a desire to strengthen the Company's market position. Such a consideration, however, was not behind the move to provide greater services and more equitable treatment of beneficiaries which occurred during 1955. In brief, these changes provided for a greater freedom of choice to beneficiaries in electing the settlement of proceeds after the insured's death, including a full year of grace within which to decide. These features, all of which where possible were made retroactive on all existing business, would prevent the recurrence of unnecessary hardships for beneficiaries which resulted from changed social, economic, and family conditions not anticipated by the insured.[26] In addition, the management inserted in these contracts protection against outmoded rates on a deferred-election basis. In future years, when a transfer from another option to the life-income option was made, the monthly payments per thousand would be those being assumed on like options in policies issued at the time.[27] This was an attempt to prevent a recurrence of the troubles which had beset the Company for years: a fixed interest rate commitment above that which economic conditions allowed it to earn, coupled with increased longevity of beneficiaries. In addition, because of the proportion of policies in force in which the insured and the owner were different persons, the Company issued an owner form of policy which extended certain ownership rights 60 days beyond the death of the insured. With some qualifications this was made available on request to older policies in force.

The remaining developments in the field of underwriting and the selection of risks pertained to the circumstances arising out of the Korean War and the decision to strengthen life-income option reserves of the pre-1947 insurance in force. The outbreak of military action in Korea in 1950 caused management to consider readopting the war and aviation clauses of 1942–1945; but this alternative was rejected in favor of imposing limits on the amount of insurance which Northwestern would issue to men of military age, and by restricting the insurance it did issue such men to higher-premium permanent plans. These measures prevented any perceptible distortion in the age distribution of Northwestern insureds during these years.

The implications of strengthening the life-income option reserves were nothing a life company management could contemplate with equanimity. By 1949 the Company was settling nearly $20 million annually of new proceeds under these annuity options, far more than had been estimated a generation earlier. The combination of lower interest earnings and lengthening life span of beneficiaries had already caused losses to be incurred on such settlements, and the Company had been funding these by policy classes as of the date of settlement. At this time the Company began to establish reserves of approximately $1,200 for each $1,000 of life income options for the settlement of older policies.

The decline in interest earnings—to a low of 3.01% in 1947—made a reduction in dividends necessary. Dividends paid by Northwestern fell from an amount equal to about 20 per cent of premiums, which had been the level in 1947–1948, to slightly under 17 per cent for the years 1949–1954. Total dividends paid for these six years were $249 million, whereas if the previous ratio had been

maintained the dividend payments would have amounted to about $295 million. This also enabled the Company to set up reserves to cover possible future losses under the options without reducing the relative size of the contingency reserve (surplus). In 1955, with strengthened reserves and interest earnings back up to 3.52%, Northwestern again paid dividends equal to 20 per cent of premiums received during the year.

In retrospect, Company decisions taken during the last few years of the post-1946 decade appeared to be more closely geared to the trends in life insurance underwriting than was true earlier in the period. In part this change could be explained by a growing managerial awareness that competitive modifications were making it more difficult to retain Northwestern's share of the market; in part it resulted from the activities and influence of the various agents' groups whose members were both more sensitive to market conditions and probably more aware of the effectiveness of competitors. Despite this growing awareness on the part of the Home Office, however, the Company still refused to issue policies carrying a double indemnity feature. Agent demands regarding such a feature continued to fall on deaf ears in Milwaukee, particularly on the ears of the most influential members of management who regarded double indemnity as a form of casualty coverage and did not want the Company to go into that business and, as a consequence, incur the possibility of greatly increased litigation in settling claims.

Relations with the Field Force

During the 1947–1956 decade relations between the Home Office and the men in the field force were characterized by a steady improvement in communications which permitted a greater knowledge of, and mutual understanding for, one another's problems. In this respect Northwestern was probably unique in the life insurance industry, for not only did the Company permit the various associations representing its agents great latitude in expressing recommendations and complaints, but policies which most affected the field force were worked out cooperatively between management and these representatives. The process was beneficial, if at times painful, to Company executives concerned with retaining the demonstrated advantages of its system of distribution and simple methods of operation. But for agents facing the competition of insurance plans and features with special appeal to prospects which were offered by aggressive rivals, the assurance of inherent Northwestern superiority appeared at times to be merely complacency. The adoption of graded premiums and acceptance of substandard risks was evidence that the management was, by the end of the Company's first century, anticipating the trends of life insurance in America and taking actions which would make better use of its field organization.

Many of the problems which confronted the Company in the operation of its general agency system during these years were carried over from previous decades, some of which became more intense as a result of rising costs and increased personal and business income taxes. This was particularly true of the financing problems of new general and district agents. As shown earlier, however, the management provided certain assistance in the solution of these problems through development fees, more liberal lending provisions, and induction awards. These, when combined with the basic fabric of general agency strength at Northwestern, continued to provide productive and profitable general agencies. As pointed out previously, the management had also established a retirement plan for general agents which went into effect in 1947. This plan was financed by joint contributions of general agents and Northwestern, and operated through 1952.* In 1952, however, Bureau of Internal Revenue rulings subjected to income taxes during the first year in which retirement benefits were received by a general agent "the total amount of Company contributions and interest credits" made on behalf of the pensioner. The management, at the request of the general agents, then terminated the plan.[28] The deposits of the general agents were returned and the graded 0.5 per cent margin in policy years seven, eight, and nine was restored effective January 1, 1953. The ninth renewal, however, was not restored.

By modification of its compensation plans for agents in 1947 and again in 1952, the Company attempted to provide greater incentives for the production of persistent insurance and for new agents to make a career with Northwestern. With the introduction of its 1947 policies, based on the Commissioners' 1941 Standard Ordinary Mortality Table with 2 per cent interest, all agents who came under

contract in the future, and any already under contract who elected to, would receive eight renewal commissions (if earned) and persistency fees in lieu of the ninth renewal. Persistency fees were paid agents in amounts equal to sixty cents for each one thousand dollars of premium-paying insurance which had been in force for more than nine years. To qualify for payment an agent was required to have produced, and have in force, a minimum of $200,000 of such insurance; the amounts due were determined at the close of each calendar year and prorated monthly over the ensuing year.[29] For agents who were near age fifty, however, the advantages of the persistency fee contract were doubtful, and many of these preferred the older nine-renewal contract. For those who made the change to the new plan, and for all new agents who joined the Company after 1946, the financial advantages to agents of persistency fees were obvious by 1957.

In August 1952, following protracted investigation of compensation plans, the management again modified the basic agent contract. Some of the changes, including the increase of first-year commissions to 55 per cent of premium on whole life policies and proportional grading for other insurance contracts, were necessitated by competition and a proposed change in the New York insurance code.[30] Other modifications were basically motivated by a desire to encourage agents to make a career of selling for Northwestern. Under the 1952 plan agents were permitted to elect a choice of eight vested renewals or a contract with nine renewals, only the first four of which were vested. If an agent elected the second alternative, however, full vesting would occur if certain conditions were met, such as fifteen consecutive years of service with the Company or upon reaching the age of sixty.[31] Persistency fees were continued under the revised contracts.

These changes finally enabled the management to achieve a long desired objective, namely, standardization of the Company position with respect to contracts between general agents and special and soliciting agents. Because of different local arrangements as to rent, secretarial and other expenses, and date of the agent's contract, agency practices had long differed as to the distribution of the extra 5 per cent first renewal. Some agents contended that the differences were discriminatory and because the resulting amendments to the basic contract were filed with the Home Office and recognized by it in determining retirement plan credits, it was asserted by agents not receiving the extra commission that the Home Office had become a party to the discrimina-

---

* The over-riding commission of the general agent on the seventh and eighth renewals was reduced, a 2 per cent collection fee was substituted for the ninth over-riding commission, and the Company contributed an amount roughly equal to 3 per cent of the total general agent renewals per year.

tion. These agents argued that all agents should have the extra 5 per cent.

To meet this problem the Home Office announced it would no longer file and recognize such contractual amendments made to reflect local situations. In order to avoid any possible participation in the alleged discrimination, the Company also refused the use of Home Office facilities in making payments on such local arrangements after termination of a general agent's contract. To satisfy agents resentful of this latter refusal, which they regarded as technical, the Company subsequently agreed to make its payment facilities available after termination but not during the lifetime of the general agent's contract, while reaffirming its basic position.

Although disagreement occasionally arose between general agents and agents under contract to them with respect to specific problems in individual agencies, the relations between the associations representing these two groups were probably warmer and more cooperative than ever before. When the board of directors of the Special Agents' Association drew up proposals and requests to submit to Milwaukee, the cooperation of general agents was sought and usually forthcoming. Both groups, while respecting the advantages of belonging to the field organization of Northwestern, were interested in having the Home Office take a position of leadership in the industry with respect to anticipating developments, rather than to follow where others had led. Further, they believed that the management did not take as complete advantage of the knowledge and experience of the men in the field as it should have, particularly as such knowledge would improve the extent of the Company's market. These sentiments were communicated to the Home Office; and in 1952 the Company established a policyholders' research and service division and began to publish *The Milwaukee Letter,* a bulletin containing Home Office news and viewpoints on various matters of interest to the field. Such management responses to field force criticism and suggestions were welcome to the agents and contributed much to the evolution of profitable mutual relations.

In 1950 Congress broadened the application of the Social Security Act to provide old age coverage for thousands of persons formerly excluded, including life insurance agents. Northwestern could claim some primary credit for the development of the amendment which made agents eligible for federal old age benefits because of the efforts of Clarence C. Klocksin, its legislative representative. Because of the ruling that agents who had a "large investment

in rent" and other facilities were not covered by the meaning of the amendment, general agents were not eligible.

During the years 1947–1955 Northwestern agents earned a total of $174 million in commissions, to which were added Company contributions of $3.8 million for the retirement plans and almost $417,000 in Social Security taxes. Commission income ranged from a low of $17.5 million in 1950 to a high of $23.4 million in 1955, with an average annual agent compensation for the whole period of $19.3 million.

As a result, Northwestern's field force enjoyed the highest level of compensation in the Company's history (although because of higher taxes this was not the highest take-home pay ever earned) and probably continued to be the best paid field organization in American life insurance.

An examination of the results of three representative years of this period indicates why, although bothered by reduced margins and generally rising prices, general agents enjoyed an excellent financial position and had the incentives to provide effective local leadership of the field organization. As shown below, gross commissions per agency rose steadily from 1947 through 1955, as did the amounts retained by the agency and the net income of general agents. As a result of increased expenses, however, the net average income of the general agents increased less rapidly than the total revenues of the agencies.

	1947	1951	1955
Gross commissions per agency	$196,000	$207,600	$257,300
Amount retained by agency	58,800	62,280	77,190
Net general agents' incomes after payment of agency expense	26,356	26,565	32,449

Since the amounts are only averages, it is apparent that approximately one-half of the ninety general agents enjoyed net incomes in excess of the amounts shown above; and for the leading agencies in the Company the net general agents' income would be several times these amounts.

The average level of compensation for agents other than general agents also rose during the period. On the basis of payments from business placed with the Company alone, the average commission income for agents under full-time contract was probably over $6,000 in 1947 and around $10,000 in 1955. In addition, agents who placed business rejected by Northwestern prior to 1955 received commissions from the companies accepting these risks. One of the reasons why agents welcomed the Company's acceptance of substandard business was that henceforth they would receive credit for such sales in the determination of the renewal rates and get Company contributions toward the retirement plan.

As in former years, of course, able agents who produced a consistently high volume of business and enjoyed the general Company persistency experience earned incomes double or more that of the fulltime agent average. In one large metropolitan agency which was checked by the authors in 1956, fifteen of the fifty special agents under contract had made over $20,000 in commissions the previous year. While hundreds of agents were just making ends meet, the Home Office and general agents were concerned with the effects of poor production on the morale of these men and the agencies alike. Where further training and careful supervision were unavailing, sales management was not loath to refuse to renew contracts of ineffective agents.

The Marketing and Insurance Record

With respect to the volume of insurance sold and the increase of insurance in force, Northwestern's record for the nine years 1947–1955 was much superior to the achievement of the preceding fourteen years. Total sales exceeded $4.6 billion, and insurance in force rose from $5.05 billion to $7.93 billion, a gain of 57 per cent. Among the largest ten firms in the industry during the period, the Company's sales and insurance in force ranked eighth in size.

There were, however, other aspects of the marketing picture which appeared less favorable. One of these was the decline of Northwestern's share of the aggregate amount of ordinary life insurance issued during these years. During the years 1919–1932 the Company's sales amounted to 3.24 per cent of the total ordinary insurance sold by United States companies, while during the next fourteen years this share fell to 3.03 per cent. For the eight years 1947–1954, however, Northwestern's proportion of the total ordinary insurance marketed was reduced to 2.5 per cent.[32] One important reason for the decrease in Northwestern's share of the ordinary market should be mentioned. During this period great numbers of so-called blue-collar workers were moving into income brackets where they could purchase ordinary insurance whereas formerly their

purchases fell into the so-called industrial brackets. The big industrial companies began to experience large increases in their ordinary business through the up-graded activity of the large existing sales forces which had been writing the industrial accounts, weekly and monthly premium business. Conversely, industrial sales in these companies began to fall off. In comparisons adjusted for the effect of this change in nature of the market, or in comparisons eliminating the three large industrial companies, Northwestern's relative drop in production of ordinary is much smaller. At the end of 1946 Northwestern had 4.34 per cent of the aggregate ordinary insurance in force in the industry; at the close of 1955 this share had been reduced to 3.52 per cent.[33] It is probable that the management entered the substandard field and adopted graded premiums as steps toward recovering their former share of the ordinary market.

Of real concern to the Home Office was the rise in total acquisition costs which characterized this period of expanding insurance sales. Direct acquisition expenses—agents' compensation, medical examinations, and advertising—amounted to $188.6 million for the nine years 1947–1955, an average of almost $21 million per year. For the fourteen years 1933–1946, the annual average had been about $11 million. Other expenditures, some part of which must be attributed to the Company's insurance and marketing activity, totaled about $2.4 million, and Northwestern's tax bill, other than for Social Security, amounted to $66 million. While Northwestern's absolute costs of acquisition rose, on the average, by nearly 90 per cent above those of the previous period, the relative increase was much smaller. Total premium income for 1947–1955 was over $2.18 billion, and direct acquisition expenses constituted only 8.65 per cent of this amount. This was only 10 per cent greater than the ratio of acquisition costs to premiums recorded during the Cleary administration, and was substantially below the increase in the general price level during the period.

The Company's sales for these years followed closely the changes in general business conditions in the United States, and corresponded roughly to the pattern of the other giant companies in the industry. As shown in Chart XVIII-4, the brief slumps of 1948–1949 and 1951 were followed by a steady increase in the sales of ordinary insurance, total life insurance, and those of Northwestern. Aggregate sales of nine of the giant firms in the industry, while conforming to this pattern through 1953, experienced a moderate decline in 1954. Northwest-

CHART XVIII-4

Sales of Insurance: Industry and Northwestern, 1947–1955

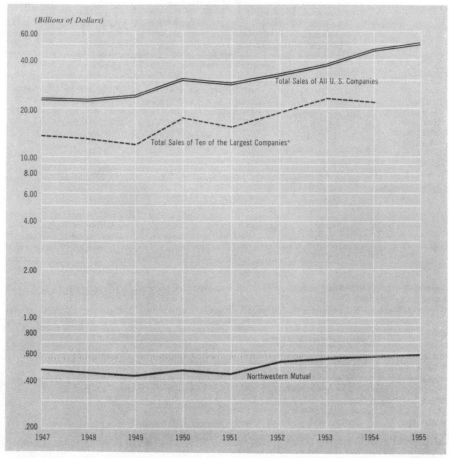

Sources: Individual companies. *Insurance Year Book* (New
    York: Spectator Co., 1955); *Annual Statement*, North-
    western Mutual Life Insurance Company, 1947–1955;
    Life Insurance Fact Book (New York: Institute of Life
    Insurance, 1956), 21.

ern sales in 1947 were close to $500 million, a figure not again reached until 1952; in 1955 a new Company record of almost $600 million was attained.

A further source of satisfaction with the marketing record for the period was Northwestern's persistency of insurance in force. A comparison of Northwestern with three of the large ordinary com-

TABLE XVIII-2

Selected Life Companies: Persistency of Insurance in Force, 1933–1954

COMPANY	(1) AGGREGATE IN FORCE 12/31 1946 + SALES, 1947-1954	(2) IN FORCE, 12/31 1954	(3) PERCENTAGE COL. (2) OF COL. (1)	(4) AGGREGATE IN FORCE 12/31 1932 + SALES, 1933-1954	(5) PERCENTAGE COL. (2) OF COL. (4)
	(Dollar data in millions)				
Northwestern	$9,055	$7,551	83.4%	$11,786	64.1%
Aetna	17,793	14,802	83.2	25,151	58.9
Equitable	26,779	22,976	85.8	33,982	67.6
John Hancock	21,180	15,832	74.7	27,813	56.9
Metropolitan	71,483	59,968	83.9	99,615	60.2
Mutual Benefit	4,531	3,558	78.5	6,376	55.8
Mutual Life (N.Y.)	6,625	5,042	76.1	10,342	48.8
New York Life	17,448	13,638	78.2	23,116	59.0
Prudential	60,759	46,143	75.9	83,898	55.0
Travelers	18,455	15,375	83.3	24,408	63.0
Total United States Companies	424,905	348,141	81.9	535,327	65.03
Total Ordinary Only, U. S. Companies	274,286	206,197	75.2	343,168	57.8

SOURCE: Company data: *Insurance Year Book* (New York: The Spectator Company), 1941, 1950, 1955. Industry data: *Life Insurance Fact Book* (New York: Institute of Life Insurance), 1956, 21, 23.

panies and the total ordinary insurance market, shown in the following tabulation, clearly indicates the persisting nature of the Company's insurance:

Proportion of Insurance in Force Dec. 31, 1954 to:

	1947–1954 Sales + Amount in Force on Dec. 31, 1946	1933–1954 Sales + Amount in Force on Dec. 31, 1932
NORTHWESTERN	83.4%	64.1%
Mutual Benefit	78.5	55.8
Mutual Life (N.Y.)	76.1	48.8
New York Life	78.2	59.0
Total Ordinary	75.2	57.8

Since so much of the Company's promotional effort was directed to marketing insurance which would remain in force over time, and since a substantial source of the strength of its agency organization depended upon a persistent business, these achievements were exceptionally important.

Looking back over the decade which began in 1947, there was ample reason for gratification. A substantial segment of the administrative structure of the Company had been streamlined and made more efficient, the field force had benefited from im-proved selection and training practices, and it had produced an unprecedented volume of new business. Furthermore, the general effectiveness and morale of Home Office and insurance agents had been strengthened, in part because of management's wise approach to the problems of rising prices and cost of living. Growth had taken place in a way which presented the new insurance prospect with a bargain that had not been purchased at the expense of existing policyholders. Backing its able agency force with the advantages of lean, simplified, and low-cost operations, Northwestern could look forward to the problems of its second century of life with well-justified confidence.

Relations with Government

Northwestern's relations with government during these years followed the same general pattern established during previous decades, with activities being divided between the federal arena and the legislatures and insurance departments of the individual states, principally Wisconsin and New York. In one important respect the Company apparatus for meeting legislative problems was modified; this involved the use of the legislative organization of the Life Insurance Association of America and the American Life Convention on the national and various state levels outside of Wisconsin. In the home state, however, Northwestern's legislative representative continued to look after the interests of the Company, and in addition represented the major national associations.

The principal problems which confronted the Company on the national scene involved the taxation of life insurance and modification of the Social Security Act. In Wisconsin the Company was principally concerned with modifying the state investment code to permit greater flexibility in investment such that the earning position could be strengthened and protected, and with obtaining more equitable tax treatment for all life companies operating in Wisconsin. Northwestern, with other companies, resisted the efforts of several state legislatures to apply restrictive and oppressive statutes which would discriminate against nonresident concerns or distort the pattern of competition; and pressed to gain permission to introduce such insurance features as gradation of premiums by policy size.

The problems of federal taxation of life insurance companies during this decade concerned both the absolute amount of taxes paid by the industry and individual companies and the lack of unity among the companies seeking an equitable and reasonable base for taxation. When the effects of reduced interest rates became serious for life companies and the necessary revaluation of reserves was made, the taxes which the industry paid to the federal government fell to only $3 million during 1947–1948; and several companies, including giant-sized firms, paid no federal taxes. Greatly disturbed by the loss of revenue, the Treasury Department proposed to recoup the deficiency by new legislation which would not only be retroactive to cover the years 1947–1948, but would apply substantially increased rates to a broader tax base for all life companies. While opposing higher rates, industry representatives were divided on the questions of tax base and retroactivity; Northwestern and Equitable Life Assurance Society fought vigorously against retroactive taxes, and the Senate Finance Committee proved sympathetic to their objections during the hearings on the so-called "stopgap" tax provision of the Revenue Act of 1950. As a result, the modified formula which was accepted applied a tax comparable to a flat levy on investment income which was below the 3 per cent recommended by the Treasury Department. Even

so the tax proceeds by the new secretary's ratio greatly increased the burden on life companies. Applying to the tax years 1949–1950, federal tax yields from the life insurance industry were $42 million and $72 million respectively; Northwestern's federal taxes for the two years aggregated over $4 million.

Life insurance officials were dismayed by the results of the 1950 tax bill; and as investment income rose following increased earning rates after 1950, the dismay deepened. Opinion regarding a just tax base varied sharply as small companies complained that the large firms were avoiding payment of a just share of taxes by strengthening settlement-option and other reserves through reduction of dividends. In 1951 enough unity was achieved among the companies to produce an industry-recommended formula which was believed to be more equitable among the various classes of companies than the 1950 measure. Essentially this proposal, which was adopted by Congress and later extended to cover the year 1952, provided the equivalent of a flat tax of 3.75 per cent on the first $200,000 of adjusted net income, rising to a 6.5 per cent maximum.*

The effects of the 1951 legislation included a steep rise in the industry's tax bill and more eloquent expressions of dissatisfaction from many companies. The total federal taxes in 1951 were $125 million and rose to $141 million in 1952. While Northwestern's federal tax payments increased by over 100 per cent between 1950 and 1952, reaching over $5 million in the latter year, the management was grateful that an industry-wide, instead of a company-by-company, formula was in use. Had the reverse been true the Company's tax bill would have made its competitive position more difficult.

From 1953 to the end of 1956 Congress made several further modifications in the life insurance taxation formula, none of which met with the full approval of all life insurance officials. The most important change came in 1953 when a net investment income formula was substituted for the flat tax provision, with an 85 per cent deduction allowed for reserve maintenance. The taxable income was

---

* Thus not only was consideration given to smaller companies, but succor for firms having trouble maintaining reserves was obtained by a provision for "reserve interest credit." If the ratio of adjusted net income to the amount of interest required to maintain reserves was less than unity for any company, then that firm would be credited with an amount equal to one-half its normal tax net income. This latter amount was defined as "adjusted net income" plus "eight times the amount of the adjustment for certain [health and accident] reserves . . . and minus reserve interest credit."[34]

levied upon at the regular corporation tax rates. An intracompany squabble resulted in the removal from the final bill of certain additional deductions for investment income on pension funds, annuities, and settlement options.[35] Responsible industry spokesmen were deeply concerned whether continuing company bickering would not cause an impatient Congress to approve Treasury Department proposals to apply a total income base to the whole industry. Such a formula could raise the total taxes paid by life companies to the federal government to more than double the $250 million burden of 1955.

While Northwestern executives were not happy with the $8 million paid in federal taxes in 1955 or the prospects of a 25 per cent rise for the following year, they were mindful of the fiscal needs of government and were prepared to pay a fair tax. They were much more concerned, however, with having the industry reach and maintain a common principle which could be presented to Congress. Like other large company managements, the officers wanted a tax base which would not completely disrupt the competitive structure of life insurance and Northwestern's position within it. There was no indication, however, that in the situation of 1956 any of these goals would be achieved.

Northwestern's legislative counsel and other management representatives participated actively in the Congressional arena in matters other than federal taxes, particularly in the hearings preceding the extension of the Social Security program in 1950. Life insurance spokesmen vigorously opposed much of the administration-backed plan which would have greatly broadened the extent of social security coverage, increased the tax and benefit base from $3,000 to $3,600, and provided for total and permanent disability benefits under the Old Age and Survivors' Insurance program.[36] In several respects, particularly the opposition to disability benefits, the industry position was based solidly on experience. In other areas it was more assailable in view of the persistent warnings of its spokesmen that each extension of the Social Security Act was one more insidious step toward socialism; and some suspicion arose that the industry was seeking merely to protect its own economic interest. Although Congress refused to include the disability-income feature, the amendment was passed without other substantial modification.

Coverage under the Old Age and Survivors' Insurance program was granted to "full-time life insurance salesmen," whether or not they were included under the common law interpretation of employee. By virtue of the "Klocksin amendment" to the revenue act in 1951, life companies would be protected from adverse tax rulings in the event they established pension or other types of employee benefit plans for those agents included under the Social Security Act.[37] According to the act, however, certain full-time agents were still considered independent contrators and eligible for O. A. S. I. protection only as "self-employed" individuals. These, including Northwestern general agents, were not eligible for the tax treatment given the contributions by companies to pension or retirement plans, and in Northwestern's case this situation led to Company abandonment of the general agents' retirement plan.

On the Wisconsin scene several pieces of legislation were passed which positively affected the Company's operations. In the opinion of several members of the management, the single most important act approved by the legislature was the revision of the method of taxing domestic life companies. For decades the Company had paid its Wisconsin taxes under the guise of a "license fee," although in effect it was a levy on investment income not too dissimilar to the income tax of the federal government, including an allowance for maintenance of reserves. Furthermore, the so-called "valuation fee" had, because of the improvement in life insurance company accounting, become for all real purposes an annual tax.

All the inherent deficiencies of applying an income tax to life insurance which the federal government was encountering held true on the state level. Because of the variations in interest rate structure before and after 1950–1951 and the transference of surplus to bolster reserves, the Company's Wisconsin tax bill fluctuated widely. With the generally higher earnings after 1950, management began to experience a scale of Wisconsin taxes which was both substantial in amount and potentially damaging to its competitive position in the industry. In an effort to obtain tax relief during a period when the state revenue needs were expanding, the Company undertook the task of persuading the other Wisconsin life companies to accept a premium tax and to present the entire program to the insurance department and the legislature.

The Company contended that Wisconsin companies should be taxed at no higher rates than were applied to out-of-state companies licensed by the state; this was equal to a 2 per cent charge on Wisconsin premiums less a deduction for dividends. Other domestic companies, however, had fared very well at the hands of the legislature, and their reaction to a proposal to terminate this happy position was not enthusiastic. To obtain agreement of the other Wisconsin companies, Northwestern proposed that the income tax section be amended so that the existing formula be retained while limiting the Company's total tax and valuation fees to an amount equal to 2 per cent of its Wisconsin premiums. Since agreement by the legislature to this proposal would abruptly reduce the state's tax revenue, Company representatives offered a further proposal: that a graduated scale of revision be applied. According to this schedule Northwestern would pay the equivalent of a 3 per cent tax in 1953, 2.5 per cent in 1954, and 2 per cent per year thereafter.[38]

Enactment of these proposals in 1953 guaranteed a significant tax savings to the Company, left the tax position of most of its fellow domestics virtually unchanged, and provided a base of taxation which the management and the legislature considered logical, equitable, and nondiscriminatory.

In addition to changes in the investment code which broadly governed portfolio policy, and which are discussed in the following chapter, Northwestern representatives succeeded in gaining legislative approval of several measures beneficial to life insurance generally or for the Company particularly. In 1949, for example, the National Association of Life Underwriters' "Model Agents' Qualification Law" was introduced and passed by the Wisconsin Legislature. This measure imposed higher standards for licensing insurance agents. In 1953 the legislative representative succeeded in facilitating passage for bills to exempt from the state corporate income tax the proceeds from life insurance carried on the lives of officers, partners, and employees. During the same legislative session, largely at the request of the Company, permission was granted life insurance companies to accept premiums discounted in advance.

The Company's successful relationships with the Wisconsin Legislature, insurance department, and state administration had been built on two firm foundations: honesty and mutual respect. Northwestern legislative representatives promised nothing the Company was incapable of honoring, and provided detailed information on any aspect of life insurance which was desired or needed by the legislators and public administrators. In the years following 1950 the Company's legislative counsel represented the major trade associations and the interests of life insurance in the state as he had the individual interests of the Company—honestly and ably. The efforts of Northwestern, and those who represented it in Madison, made important contributions to Wisconsin's reputation among the American states as having an intelligent, enlightened legal framework and public control of life insurance.

CHAPTER NINETEEN

Meeting the Investment Challenge: 1947 – 1956

THE postwar decade posed two major problems for Northwestern's investment managers: the first was the need to increase the yield on assets; the second concerned planning and action necessary to improve asset distribution and diversification. The difficulty facing management had been intensified by the extensive refunding operations of American corporations at lower interest rates which occurred during the years 1944–1946. These operations had driven down the earning rate on a substantial portion of the securities held by the Company. The extent of corporate security refunding made painfully clear to the management the necessity of providing greater protection for its earning position in the future by revising Northwestern's investment policy. The rise of interest rates, caused by the heavy demand for capital by private business and the reversal of federal monetary policy in 1951, provided opportunities to improve the yield on new investments; but investment personnel faced a formidable task in "turning over" a huge portfolio of low-yield assets and replacing them with better-producing securities.

To obtain greater protection for the Company's earning position required the acquisition of assets which would not be as subject to refunding as those which Northwestern had possessed in 1944. Logically this meant that real estate mortgages should have a more important place in the portfolio and that the Company would seek, by indenture provi-

sions, greater protection against refunding. It also implied that to a greater extent than ever before the Company would have to explore new outlets for its funds, including conversion rights or warrants to purchase common stock of the corporations to which money was lent. While this concept was not altogether new in corporate financing, this marked Northwestern's first experience with it. If these objectives were to be attained, Northwestern's mortgage lending apparatus would have to be reorganized and expanded, and the personnel of the Home Office investment departments strengthened both in number and ability. Furthermore, if investment strategy were to be bold and imaginative rather than merely reckless, the management had to base its decisions upon accurate and pertinent information; this in turn required improved research and accounting systems. Lastly, the objectives had to be won without incurring excessive costs.

During the postwar decade the life insurance companies did not lack investment opportunities such as characterized much of the previous fifteen years. Indeed, no period in United States history was comparable in the variety and intensity of demand for capital. Gross private domestic investment exceeded $420 billion for the nine years ending January 1, 1956. Of this amount new construction accounted for about $205 billion, of which over $100 billion was for nonfarm residential construction. Total life insurance company assets over the

CHART XIX-1

Income, Expenditure, and Net Available for
Investment: Northwestern, 1947–1955

(Millions of Dollars)

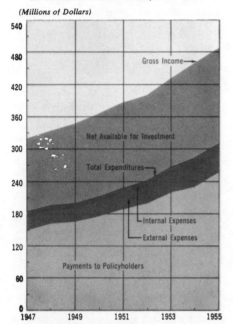

SOURCE: *Annual Statement,* Northwestern Mutual Life Insurance Company, 1947-1955.

CHART XIX-2

Distribution of Admitted Assets: Northwestern,
1947–1955

(Millions of Dollars)

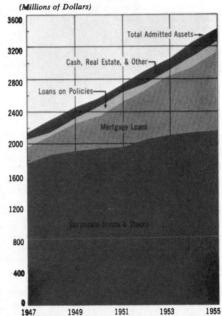

SOURCE: *Annual Statement,* Northwestern Mutual Life Insurance Company, 1947-1955.

same years increased from $48.2 billion to $90.4 billion, and the mortgage investment alone increased nearly four-fold amounting to $29.4 billion by 1956.

Northwestern's investment activity was greater in this period than for any comparable period in its history. Net income available for investment, as shown in Chart XIX-1, rose steadily from year to year and aggregated almost $1.37 billion. As a result the Company's admitted assets rose from $2.16 billion at the end of 1946 to $3.42 billion at the close of 1955. In addition, the investment managers had to re-invest $2.11 billion which was forthcoming from the repayment of loans and the sale and exchange of assets. Measured by this criterion Northwestern continued to be the sixth largest life insurance company in America.

The distribution of Northwestern's assets in the

years following 1946 clearly reflected the changes which occurred in the Company's investment policies. (See Chart XIX-2.) After a hiatus of nearly twenty years, mortgage lending again became the area of greatest investment emphasis. The Company's mortgage holdings rose more than six-fold, and at the end of 1955 amounted to $992 million. The net increase in mortgage investment was almost double that which occurred in the Company's bond and stock holdings. The real estate accounts rose from $13 million to $64 million as a result of the purchase of investment properties, and policy loans grew by almost 50 per cent to reach $122 million during 1955. The Company's cash accounts, and the remaining types of admitted assets, experienced an increase of about 64 per cent over the 1946 levels, and totaled $92.4 million by 1956.

The result of the shift in emphasis on the Company's portfolio was dramatic. Mortgage loans, which had comprised only 7.8 per cent of admitted assets in 1946, amounted to almost 29 per cent at the end of 1955. Bond and stock investments, however, while increasing in dollar value, fell from 84.8 per cent to 62.9 per cent of admitted assets. Real estate holdings rose from 0.6 per cent of assets in 1946 to 1.9 per cent in 1955, while loans on policies declined slightly from 4 per cent to 3.6 per cent. There was no perceptible change in the Company's other admitted assets relative to the total portfolio.

A Revision of Investment Policy

Until the 1930's Northwestern's investment policy had been clearly one of giving priority to mortgage loans. Funds which could not be lent on mortgage security at satisfactory rates of interest and within the quality standards imposed by the management were available for investment in railroad and, to a limited extent, public utility bonds. Due to the economic conditions of the years 1930–1945 new construction and mortgage lending opportunities contracted sharply. As a result the Company could put less money into mortgage investment, and as existing loans were repaid or foreclosed real estate liquidated, the mortgage accounts were greatly reduced. With investment opportunities restricted by depression and war conditions, like most life companies Northwestern put most of its investable funds into bonds of government units and those of public utility, industrial, and commercial enterprises.

The problems of these fifteen years had important effects upon Company investment policy and upon the attitudes and orientation of the various investment divisions. The bond department was compelled to find outlets for more than 80 per cent of Northwestern's investable income once the great demand for policy loans had subsided, and under the economic and competitive conditions of the times could do so only at lower rates of return. The waves of foreclosure of real estate mortgages placed new burdens upon Company mortgage officers, and there was a steady shift in the orientation of Home Office and branch office loan personnel away from the development of new loan outlets and toward real estate management and liquidation. As a result of the limited amount of mortgage lending in these years and the structural changes in the mortgage markets, the apparatus for originating new loans declined in size and effectiveness. In

short, although the Company's net earnings rate on total investments during the period was favorable in comparison to leading rivals, some portion of it was purchased at the cost of important going business values in the mortgage loan portfolio and the mortgage investment organization.

Protection of Northwestern's earning position required a considerable expansion of mortgage investment. This was partly because the gross rates of interest borne by mortgages were generally higher than those available on corporate and municipal bonds, but also because of the shorter period for which mortgage loans were made. During periods of rising interest rates the funds from repayment of loans could be reinvested at higher earning rates; in periods of falling interest rates there was less danger of mortgage refunding than there was of bond refunding. Northwestern committed itself to rebuilding the mortgage portfolio, but the question remained of whether to continue or to abandon the branch office lending system. The system was becoming relatively more costly, and its reorganization and relocation would become even more expensive before a sufficient volume of new business was produced to reduce unit costs to competitive levels. On the other hand, neither the mortgage investment vice president, Howard J. Tobin, nor President Fitzgerald was inclined to abandon the obvious merits of the system or to discharge the Company's loan agents, many of whom had served Northwestern for decades. The decision was reached in late 1946 to retain the branch office system and regard the cost of expanding its personnel and relocating its offices as a necessary investment expense.

Once the decision was made aggressively to rebuild the mortgage investment, the management had to consider the effects of this action upon other aspects of its investment organization and program. With the bond department no longer required to find outlets for the overwhelming proportion of the funds available for investment, more attention could be given to developing unconventional opportunities and fresh approaches. Vice President Frederick W. Walker, and Donald C. Slichter, who succeeded him in August 1949, believed that Northwestern could do as well as the industry with respect to yield and safety by following other companies and using the customary methods and markets. In their judgment, the critical test for effective investment management lay in obtaining better yields without incurring greater risks than those inherent in securities paying less interest. This test would be a significant one, for the Company desired to dispose of the low-yield corporate securities obtained in the refunding operations of previous years without incurring losses which could not be more than recouped from the higher earning power of the securities acquired in replacement. In brief, the essential tasks for bond investment management were to develop the personnel and methods of data collection and evaluation which would make Northwestern superior to its competitors.

Simply stated, the investment policy of Northwestern for the postwar years was very close to that of the years preceding 1930. The elements of the investment situation were different, of course, as was the nature of the legal framework, the tools of analysis, and the quantity of information available to investors. In 1950 investment managers were more aware of certain types of problems than were their predecessors in the Company, but to provide higher yields and a protection of earning position

it was deemed necessary to approximately recapture the portfolio distribution of the 1920's.

Achieving the Mortgage Investment Goal

The situation which confronted Vice President Tobin when he became chief mortgage officer at Northwestern in 1946 has already been explained. Whereas the life insurance industry had approximately 15 per cent of total assets in mortgages, the Company's proportion was less than 10 per cent. Many of the Company's thirty-eight branch loan offices were located in areas which bore no close relationship to the volume of lending opportunities that developed during the following five years. In the mortgage loan department itself three of the six officers were farm specialists, although the farm loan account was under $40 million and steadily diminishing. City and institutional loans of $96.3

million and residence loans of $23.7 million completed the mortgage investment, but the Company also had acquired certain properties as investments which were valued at $3.8 million. These were administered by the city loan division.

The system of farm loan finders, correspondents, and service personnel was unable to produce the needed volume of new loans because of the sharp decline in demand for farm mortgages. While a small and useful organization still existed for the origination of commercial and residential mortgages, it was too limited for any rapid expansion in lending activity on a broad geographic front.

The process of rebuilding occupied most of the decade of 1946–1955. The personnel of the city and residence mortgage divisions was increased gradually, while the accounting and clerical staff increased substantially during the first half of the decade, then declined as office procedures were refined and mechanized. In 1952 a service and research branch was created which subsequently provided effective cost accounting and statistical information; this in turn resulted in more effective administration in the Home Office and the branch agencies.

In addition to recruiting and training new Home Office mortgage personnel between 1946 and 1951, the Company was active in improving the branch office organization. During these four years seven branch offices were closed; over the next five years the number of agencies was reduced to twenty-nine, and several of the offices were relocated in communities where the amount of new construction was particularly heavy. New men, experienced in the residence and commercial realty fields, were hired and younger men were brought in as trainees. The residence loan division officers, frequently working at a disadvantage because of the Company's rather late entry into many communities, developed contracts with real estate firms to provide new loans and to service the residence business in their communities.

The struggle to increase the mortgage accounts and to build an effective network of finders and servicers was complicated by specific limitations in the Wisconsin investment code for life companies. Prior to 1953 Wisconsin companies were prohibited from lending more than 50 per cent of the "fair market value" of properties, except where the loan was amortized within a period of fifteen years; in such cases 60 per cent loans were permitted. In addition, Wisconsin companies could not lend on leaseholds or properties in Canada. These restrictions placed Northwestern at a marked disadvantage when competing with companies who could loan up to two-thirds of the appraised value of property. The Wisconsin legislature was persuaded to modify these restrictions in 1953 and restore an important degree of competitive flexibility to the Company.[1]

The effort to rebuild the Company's mortgage investment moved into high gear in 1947, was accelerated in 1950, and except for a slight decline in 1952 continued to increase through the end of 1955. Total mortgage and investment real estate acquisitions and disposals are shown in the following tabulation:

YEAR	ACQUISITIONS	REPAYMENTS	TOTAL AS OF DEC. 31
	(In millions)		
1946			$161.9
1947	$104.7	$47.1	218.8
1948	106.2	30.9	294.2
1949	106.6	31.9	368.9
1950	162.0	37.0	493.9
1951	152.2	44.0	602.0
1952	119.9	52.3	669.6
1953	157.5	62.6	764.5
1954	196.9	72.9	888.5
1955	255.9	92.9	1,051.5
Total	$1,361.9	$471.6	

By far the greatest proportion of this activity was centered in the Company's residence lending field, of which total acquisitions were $843.7 million over these years; total repayments and other disposition of residence mortgages amounted to $247.2 million. The Company also acquired $369.8 million of commercial and institutional mortgages and disposed of $157 million; investment real estate acquisitions and disposals were $71 million and $14.5 million, respectively. In the farm field the Company acquired $78.9 million of new mortgages, and repayments amounted to $55.3 million.

As a result of this activity the mortgage accounts of the Company increased sharply over the whole period, as is shown in Chart XIX-3. This increase took place at a somewhat faster rate than experienced by the life insurance industry as a whole. At the end of 1950 Northwestern's mortgage loans amounted to 17.5 per cent of the Company's admitted assets; for the industry the proportion was 25.1 per cent. Five years later mortgage loans constituted 28.9 per cent of Northwestern's admitted assets as compared to 32.6 per cent for the industry.[2] While Northwestern had not completely closed the gap, there was every indication that such would take place should no radical change occur in national economic conditions.

In addition to rebuilding the mortgage portfolio, of course, the management sought to improve the investment yields on mortgages. This objective was generally attained, although not until the last two years of the period did the net yield on the Company's mortgage investment approximate that earned by the life insurance industry.

Until 1951 the improvement in gross yield on the mortgage and investment real estate accounts was barely perceptible, moving from about 3.8 per cent in 1947 to 4.0 per cent in 1951. This was principally due to the damping effect which federal fiscal and monetary policy had upon the national structure of interest rates. Yields on new acquisitions for these four years rose from about 3.9 per cent in 1947 to 4.1 per cent during 1949–1951. Yields on mortgages liquidated through repayment were only slightly lower, ranging from about 4 per cent in 1947–1948 to around 3.95 per cent for the next three years. In April 1951 the Federal Reserve Board withdrew its support of government bond prices, and the entire structure of interest rates began to rise. The gross yield rate on Northwestern's new mortgage and investment real estate acquisitions increased correspondingly. In 1952 the rate was almost 4.5 per cent, and during 1954–1955 it was about 4.7 per cent. As a result, the gross yield on the entire portfolio climbed from 4 per cent in 1951 to 4.4 per cent during 1955.[3]

The cost of rebuilding the mortgage accounts from the low level of 1946 was substantial, however, and prevented Northwestern from realizing net yields on its mortgage and investment real estate comparable to the improvement in gross yields until after 1954. Mortgage lending expenses for the nine years ending December 31, 1955, were $31.8 million. Of this amount $214,000 was chargeable to the administration and disposal of foreclosed real estate (most of which was carried over from previous years). Home Office expenses, direct and indirect, cost the Company about $10 million. The loan agency operating expenses totalled about $7 million, and the fees and expenses of the loan finders, correspondents, and servicing organizations amounted to about $13 million. Total mortgage loan investment expenses rose from $2 million in 1947 to $5.4 million in 1955.

The most expensive years for the Company's mortgage investment campaign were 1947–1950. This was because of the limited mortgage invest-

CHART XIX-3

Mortgage Loans and Investment Real Estate: Northwestern, 1947–1955

(Millions of Dollars)

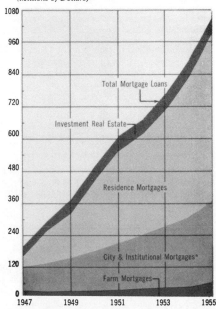

NOTES: ᵃIncludes collateral loans for years 1949-1951. Amounts for 1953-1955 do not reflect discounts written down in these years.

SOURCE: *Annual Statement,* Northwestern Mutual Life Insurance Company, 1947-1955.

ment base over which the costs of a sharply increased volume of new acquisitions could be spread. The rate of growth of the mortgage loan account was higher during this period than either before or after. As shown on the tabulation on page 304, Northwestern's mortgage investment costs rose sharply as a percentage of the dollar value of mortgages owned from 1945 to 1947–1948, then declined. For the entire industry the general variation was the same, except that the relative increase between 1945 and 1948 was less; the same held true for the general decrease from 1948 through 1955.

There was a steady improvement after 1948 in Northwestern's yield and mortgage cost position as compared to the industry. In 1948 the Company's

| | NORTHWESTERN | | INDUSTRY | |
YEAR	MORTGAGE EXPENSE	INCREASE IN MORTGAGES OWNED	MORTGAGE EXPENSE	INCREASE IN MORTGAGES OWNED
1945	0.39%	−19.7%	0.61%	−0.4%
1946	.63	−7.6	.78	8.5
1947	1.13	32.2	.88	22.3
1948	1.12	45.8	.87	26.5
1949	.80	27.7	.81	19.6
1950	.82	39.2	.77	25.6
1951	.63	25.2	.64	20.4
1952	.57	11.0	.58	9.9
1953	.59	14.9	.58	9.7
1954	.56	17.3	.57	11.8
1955	.55	18.7	,56	13.4

SOURCE: Mortgage Loan Monograph: Mortgage Loan Research and Service Division. Northwestern Mutual Life Insurance Company, 1953, extended through 1955.

net yield on mortages was only 82 per cent of the industry's; in 1952 it was over 94 per cent; and by 1956 the gap had in all probability been completely closed.

Federal guaranteed mortgages formed an important part of the portfolios of United States life insurance companies throughout the postwar decade, and between 1948 and 1954 Northwestern's mortgage portfolio contained a higher proportion of Veteran's Administration and Federal Housing Authority loans than was true of the industry as a whole. This condition was determined by the loan limits imposed by Wisconsin statute prior to 1953, which made it virtually impossible to penetrate several of the important urban conventional loan markets. Beginning in 1953 there was a sharp increase in acquisitions of conventional residential loans. The higher acquisition expense of these loans was one of the costs the Company had to pay in the latter part of the postwar decade in order to obtain a balanced mortgage loan portfolio.

From 1946 through 1950 Federal Housing Authority mortgages were more important in the Company's portfolio than were Veteran's Administration guaranteed loans; thereafter the reverse was true. The composition of Northwestern's mortgage account and the proportion which guaranteed mortgages formed of the entire portfolio, are shown below, together with the corresponding industry proportions:[4]

| | | FEDERAL | | PROPORTION OF INSURED MORTGAGES TO TOTAL MORTGAGES OWNED: | |
YEAR	VETERAN'S ADMINISTRATION	HOUSING AUTHORITY	TOTAL MORTGAGES	NORTHWESTERN	INDUSTRY
		(In millions of dollars)			
1946	$0.9	$4.7	$158.1	3.5%	—
1947	17.5	23.1	191.7	21.2	26.1%
1948	25.9	62.9	263.6	33.6	32.4
1949	27.7	100.4	331.1	38.7	36.5
1950	87.4	138.0	454.1	49.6	41.2
1951	157.7	144.4	560.4	53.9	43.6
1952	164.2	132.2	623.5	47.5	42.2
1953	192.4	120.3	715.2	43.7	41.1
1954	232.5	120.5	834.8	42.3	41.5
1955	276.7	124.0	991.1	40.4	42.9

Northwestern's guaranteed mortgage portfolio was composed exclusively of residence loans; the farm account, unlike that of certain competitors who acquired Veteran's Administration insured mortgages, was comprised only of conventional loans. Like all lenders during this period, the Company purchased insured loans at discount when the interest rates on such mortgages lagged substantially behind the improvement in interest occurring in other sectors of the economy. The yields on new loans and purchases in the residential portfolio are shown on the right.

In relation to the quality of its loans, both insured and conventional, Northwestern enjoyed good experience but probably no better than that of its competitors. Conventional loans tended to be repaid more rapidly than the insured types, particularly Veteran's Administration mortages; this was a factor of decided importance in the struggle to improve investment yields and protect the earning rate. While a few loans were defaulted during the period, the amounts involved were an infinitesimal fraction

YEAR	FHA	VA	CONVENTIONAL	TOTAL RESIDENTIAL
1947	NA	NA	NA	NA
1948	4.2%[a]	4.0%[a]	4.2%[a]	4.2%[a]
1949	4.3	4.0	4.3	4.3
1950	4.3	4.0	4.3	4.2
1951	4.3	4.0	4.6	4.1
1952	4.3	4.0	4.9	4.7
1953	4.3	4.1	4.9	4.8
1954	4.5	4.4	5.0	4.8
1955	4.5	4.5	4.9	4.8

[a] Ten month average. Yield is adjusted for loans purchased at a discount.
NA   Not available.

of the portfolio and were quickly liquidated. The experience with guaranteed loans was generally excellent. The residence loan managers, however, remained somewhat concerned about the longer ma-

turities involved, for in the event of a business depression of major proportions the relatively slow increase in the borrower's equity could cause them to more readily surrender the property than appeared likely among conventional mortgages. The possibility of wholesale foreclosures, even with the protection of federal insurance, was discomforting and had a leavening effect upon the attitudes of the residence loan division officers.

The strong demand for mortgage money in the economy permitted the management to obtain more favorable general loan terms than had been the case for over two decades. The prepayment privilege was tightened, with management insisting upon the payment of heavier premiums for the utilization of such privilege. In addition, the Company required the payment of a stand-by fee from borrowers who desired to have funds made available to them in the future. These payments for the commitment of funds were significant, amounting to almost $2 million during 1947–1955, and provided the Company with a hedge against a borrower changing his plans or delaying his commitment date.

The mortgage lending patterns developed by Northwestern during these years were unlike those which had characterized the great construction boom of the 1920's. Although some sizable loans were negotiated, there was no development comparable to the "jumbo" city loans of the earlier epoch. Instead the Company's commercial loans were distributed among such progressive chain retailers as J. C. Penney and Company, and such enterprises as suburban and regional shopping centers, independent medical centers, and certain classes of manufacturers and distributors. Such loans provided the portfolio with a balance of heterogeneity which the city mortgage accounts of the 1920's had noticeably lacked. In the residence loan field Northwestern customarily preferred one to four family units, although it did participate with other institutional lenders in financing such large-scale housing developments as Park Forest, Illinois.

In the farm field Northwestern hewed more closely to its early traditions. Whereas the Company acquired commercial, institutional, and residential mortgages over an area that embraced most of the United States, the overwhelming bulk of farm loans was concentrated in the North Central states. In this eleven-state region Northwestern had almost 90 per cent of its total farm loans as compared to slightly under 50 per cent for other large-scale institutional lenders. Since it was in this area that farm values were highest and interest rates correspondingly lower, it was improbable that the Company could greatly improve its net yield on farm loans without attaining a much broader geographic diversification. Efforts to move into the agricultural belts of central California indicated that this was among the objectives of the farm loan manager; and the great strides made to diversify southern agriculture were also attracting management's attention.

The success of rebuilding the mortgage investment at Northwestern can be seen by comparing the Company to the other huge life insurers. As shown in Table XIX–1, in 1947 Northwestern ranked seventh in size by dollar amount in both farm and urban loans among the largest ten life companies. At the end of 1955 Northwestern ranked fifth in urban loans, while it had fallen back to eighth in farm loans. When compared to the other firms in terms of mortgages as a proportion of total admitted assets, the Company rose from ninth position in 1947 to fourth in 1955 when its 28.9 per cent was exceeded only by Prudential with 41.9 per cent, Mutual Benefit with 36.4 per cent, and Mutual Life of New York with 30.9 per cent.

New Approaches in Securities Investment

The problems facing Northwestern's bond investment managers were similar to those confronting the mortgage loan officers, with the exception that it was not necessary to reorient a field organization. The major tasks were to improve yields, develop a program to dispose of low-yield securities with minimum loss, and acquire new investment outlets of the kind which would not only produce more income for policyholders, but would also make funds available to those borrowers capable of contributing the most to maintaining employment and increasing the gross national product.[5] In the estimation of Vice President Slichter this program could be successfully carried out

only by an alert, aggressive, and able investment staff composed of men interested in discovering new and safe areas of investment rather than in following old, traditional patterns. We do not wish to be inordinate risk takers, but as professional investors, we should possess sufficient skill and judgment to be able to produce superior results.[6]

The search for the type of professional investment personnel capable of attaining the Company's stated goals began almost immediately after the war.

TABLE XIX-1

Ten Largest United States Life Insurance Companies: Urban and Farm Mortgage Loan Accounts, 1947–1955

COMPANY	1947	1949	1952	1955
		(In millions of dollars)		
		Urban Loans		
Aetna	$157.7	$256.8	$470.7	$699.9
Equitable	462.8	658.3	1,153.6	1,793.0
John Hancock	151.8	241.9	498.8	890.9
Metropolitan	878.6	1,164.2	1,914.7	2,940.1
Mutual Benefit	122.0	210.3	353.4	465.8
Mutual Life	229.9	358.4	593.6	689.0
New York Life	384.7	540.7	1,360.3	1,674.1
NORTHWESTERN	159.5	298.1	578.7	926.3
Prudential	1,095.8	2,161.0	3,650.1	4,816.3
Travelers	167.4	256.9	397.3	533.5
		Farm Loans		
Aetna	$19.3	$16.0	$11.5	$8.0
Equitable	75.6	122.6	226.1	318.6
John Hancock	44.8	67.3	126.4	185.9
Metropolitan	86.2	106.9	161.6	229.9
Mutual Benefit	44.3	64.5	100.3	127.2
Mutual Life	2.5	12.6	44.9	76.8
New York Life	0.8	0.5	0.2	0.1
NORTHWESTERN	32.2	32.7	44.4	61.6
Prudential	185.6	252.2	336.1	429.1
Travelers	41.2	66.5	110.2	147.5

SOURCES: *Annual Statement* (Convention Form), 1947, 1949, 1952, and 1955, of: The Aetna Life Insurance Company, The Equitable Life Assurance Society (New York), The John Hancock Mutual Life Insurance Company, The Metropolitan Life Insurance Company, The Mutual Benefit Life Insurance Company, The Mutual Life Insurance Company of New York, The New York Life Insurance Company, The Northwestern Mutual Life Insurance Company, The Prudential Life Insurance Company, and The Travelers Life Insurance Company.

To fill gaps left by the promotion of Philip K. Robinson and the imminent retirement of Frederick W. Walker, three experienced investment men were employed in 1946–1947. Additional personnel, particularly in the areas of investment research, accounting, and law, were added throughout the period. Several of these new men were long-service Northwestern personnel; the rest were specialists with training and experience in other corporations and investment organizations.

Convinced that superior results depended upon pertinent and effective data, the research activities of the bond department were greatly expanded. Included in these activities was the development of a study of cash flow which provided accurate estimates of the quantity of cash available for investment on a week-to-week basis. Such estimates could be projected forward over several years and per-

mitted the management to make heavy advance commitments to borrowers with only minimum risks of embarrassment. The research activities of the department were coordinated with those in the mortgage field and permitted the monthly planning sessions of the president and the chief investment officers to be based on better operating data than that available throughout most of the life insurance industry.[7]

The most important general characteristics of Northwestern's bond investment activity during this period were the great increase in the securities of industrial and commercial enterprises; the equally great reduction in federal government bonds, particularly during 1947–1951; and a reluctance to purchase common stock. In comparison with United States life insurance companies as a whole, Northwestern's bond and stock portfolio was characterized

	1947		1955	
	Northwestern	The Industry	Northwestern	The Industry
United States Government	26.2%	38.7%	5.6%	9.5%
Municipal (U. S. A.)	9.2	1.2	5.9	2.3
Canadian and other foreign	2.3	2.6	1.0	1.1
Total Government:	[37.7]	[42.5]	[12.5]	[12.9]
Railroad	9.3	5.5	4.7	4.3
Public Utility	24.9	13.4	21.5	15.5
Industrial and Miscellaneous	8.5	9.6	23.0	20.1
Corporate Stocks	2.3	2.7	1.2	4.0
Total Business and Industry:	[45.0]	[31.2]	[50.4]	[43.9]
Total Bonds and Stocks:	82.6%	73.7%	62.9%	56.8%

by a greater than average holding of the securities of business and industry, particularly in the public utility and industrial-commercial fields, and of municipalities; holdings of United States bonds were correspondingly smaller. The distributions for the Company and the life insurance industry, as a percentage of total admitted assets, are indicated by the tabulation above for 1947 and 1955.

For the nine years ending December 31, 1955, the aggregate bond and stock investment grew from $1.7 billion to over $2.1 billion, an increase of about 26 per cent. As can be seen in Chart XIX–4, however, the Company's government portfolio diminished by almost 50 per cent between 1946 and 1956, while the holdings of the securites of business and industry rose by more than 98 per cent. As is shown below, the greatest gains over the period were experienced in industrial, commercial, and public utility bonds. Municipal securities increased by only $2.3 million, and all other accounts were reduced in dollar amount.

During these nine years the Company acquired bonds and stocks at a cost of $2.06 billion and disposed of securities with a book value of about $1.64 billion. Of the total value of disposals, sales accounted for $926 million with maturities, calls, and sinking fund retirements comprising the other $717 million. On the dispositions Northwestern realized a net profit of $15.9 million, of which $9.9 million resulted from sales. In addition, the Company collected about $3.8 million in commitment fees.

The bond department was most successful during these years in improving the yield on the total amount invested. This was made possible by selling bonds with low yields and replacing them with securities carrying higher rates of interest, and by a shrewd selection of investment outlets for the funds allocated to the bond department each year. The extent of this improvement in yield and the total acquisitions and disposals on an annual basis is shown on page 309. (Dollar amounts in millions.)

Although bond investment costs rose both ab-

			Net Change	
Category	1946	1955	Dollars	Per Cent
		(Millions of Dollars)		
United States Govt.	$595.1	$190.7	$—404.4	—68.0%
Municipal (U. S. A.)	199.2	201.5	+2.3	+1.2
Canadian	47.0	35.5	—11.5	—24.5
All Government	$841.3	$427.7	$—413.6	—49.2%
Railroad	$192.4	$166.9	$—25.5	—13.3%
Public Utility	494.7	735.5	+240.8	+48.7
Industrial	141.5	784.9	+643.4	+454.7
Stocks	41.8	40.6	—1.2	—2.9
All Business	$870.4	$1,727.9	$+857.5	+98.5%

Year	Securities Acquired [a]	Yield	Securities Sold [b]	Yield	Securities Matured, Called, or Retired by Sinking Fund	Yield
1947	$183.4	2.12%	$46.2	2.55%	$63.3	3.59%
1948	242.6	3.28	152.8	2.64	32.9	2.64
1949	200.7	3.23	58.8	2.61	75.0	3.27
1950	237.3	3.25	122.0	2.76	92.7	3.25
1951	223.2	3.49	90.4	2.82	109.9	3.17
1952	273.5	3.96	137.3	3.08	55.3	3.39
1953	184.4	4.23 [c]	64.0	3.01	68.1	3.54
1954	297.8	4.21 [c]	138.3	2.91	108.1	3.75
1955	212.2	4.08 [c]	116.4	2.97	111.4	4.03

[a] Cost of acquisition value.   [b] Book value.   [c] Tax yield equivalent.

solutely and relatively during the period, largely as a result of the greater amount of travel and personal

CHART XIX-4

Bond Investments: Northwestern, 1947–1955

(Millions of Dollars)

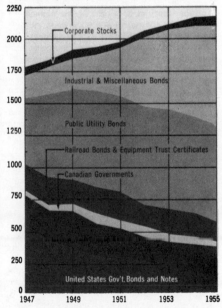

SOURCE: *Annual Statement,* Northwestern Mutual Life Insurance Company, 1947-1955.

investigation necessary in developing indenture agreements on directly placed investments, bond investment costs were materially below those incurred in the mortgage field. As a result so long as a less than 0.5 per cent difference in interest rates on bonds and mortgage loans existed, bonds produced a net yield at least equal to that produced by mortgages.

To obtain the superior results which President Fitzgerald and the investment executives desired required planning of a high degree. Each month these officials met to explore the nature of investment possibilities and the funds which Northwestern had available. The recommendations of this group were then presented to the Finance Committee for approval. The members of this committe were men of business experience and acumen, and whose judgment was respected. Leadership in the formulation of policy, however, appeared to the president to be the function of himself and his operating lieutenants. The burden of proof concerning the advisability of entering particular areas or industries rested with the professional staff. This system was generally effective, for it compelled the professionals to test their convictions internally before offering them to the trials of the market.

One example of this procedure was the decision to advance money to oil companies to be secured by proven oil deposits. The Company's industrial bond specialist had developed broad and valuable professional contacts with petroleum experts in the Southwest, largely as a result of investigating investment possibilities in the chemical and petroleum industries of Texas and Louisiana. Such contacts, including oil geologists, convinced him and Vice President Slichter that the presence of oil in the ground could be determined with reasonable accuracy, and that loans to producers could be made without undue risk and with favorable interest rates. The problem was to convince the Finance Committee. The bond department consulted able geologists from several major universities and made its reports available to the Finance Committee. After due consideration the members of the committee authorized a few such loans; the results were all that the professionals had predicted and paved the way for more extensive investment. It was the Company's experience that these investments were secured by values superior to those offered in more conventional business loans. So long as the prospective fields were independently examined by reputable consulting geologists, these loans were both safe and lucrative.

In addition to oil loans the Company's bond officers carefully analyzed opportunities in various industrial fields which were not customarily offered by the investment bankers. Northwestern's investment portfolio was expanded to include the securities of firms engaged in lumbering, paper-making, chemical development, and metallurgy. Money flowed out from Milwaukee to finance the construction of new plants and natural gas pipelines, oil tankers, and river tow boats and barges. Northwestern money contributed to the construction of new college dormitories, toll bridges and turnpikes, and toward providing new equipment for airlines and transportation companies. In 1947 the Wisconsin Legislature liberalized the investment code to permit investment in certain preferred and guaranteed stocks in amounts equal to 5 per cent of admitted assets, and also to permit the investment in bonds, notes, and debentures of industrial companies organized in Canada.[8] As a result Northwestern invest-

ment officers moved into the Canadian industrial field with alacrity. Not only did the Company invest substantially in the newly explored iron ore fields in the upper reaches of Quebec Province and Labrador, but made money available for expanding the production of aluminum, nickel, water power and chemicals in other parts of Canada.

To a very great degree the Company's corporate investments in the postwar era were made on a direct basis between lender and borrower. Although the Company did participate with other life companies and mutual savings banks in the direct placement of huge blocks of new securities, particularly in the chemical and petroleum industries, most of the direct acquisitions were undertaken by the Company alone or with the cooperation of only one or two other institutional lenders. Frequently investment bankers represented the borrower in such negotiations. This policy permitted Northwestern to obtain the best results from the efforts of its investment staff and to tailor the indenture terms more closely to the needs of the borrower. Furthermore, it enabled the management to keep more closely in touch with the operations of the borrower and provided greater flexibility for actions either to divest the securities or to offer further financial assistance. The alternative depended upon the skills and attitudes of the borrower's management.

The extent of direct placement financing grew rapidly in the postwar years.[9] At Northwestern, by the end of 1946 over 38 per cent of all nongovernment bonds and stocks had been acquired through this means; by the close of 1955 the ratio had been increased to around 70 per cent. In the public utility field the proportion of new securities acquired on a direct placement basis varied from 44 per cent per year to more than 72 per cent from 1947 through 1955. In the industrial and commerical securities field the proportion ranged from 70 per cent to 100 per cent.[10] In the field of transportation securities the Company did relatively little direct placement; other than in the area of equipment financing, railroad securities could be acquired only through open public bidding, and the Company generally abstained from financing the equipment needs of other transportation industries.

Direct placement was also a means of protecting the lender against disadvantageous refunding. Careful tailoring of the indenture in directly placed corporate issues generally limited the prerogatives of the borrower to refund. Not only did the Company specify the amount of the premium which would have to be paid for the privilege, but it placed a limit on the number of years within which refunding could occur. Furthermore, beginning in 1952–1953, in a number of bond and debenture purchase agreements, the Company sought conversion rights or warrants which provided for the right to purchase the common stock of the borrowing corporation.[11] By this means Northwestern could implement its indenture or purchase rights to acquire an equity interest and the opportunity to participate in the earnings of companies whose expansion had been financed by Northwestern funds beyond the levels possible from the yields on debt securities. In explaining this policy to a group of the Company's agents President Fitzgerald observed,

> I think it cannot be denied that the portfolios of the life companies contain more risk than has been true historically. This risk has, to some degree, been compensated for by a higher interest rate. We at Northwestern have believed that the interest return is not fully compensatory and we have been in the vanguard of investment thinking as to possible protection. We have insisted upon high premiums for prepayment of debt and no privilege of call or prepayment for a considerable period. We believe, too, that where the policyholders' funds have for sound reasons furnished a very substantial part of the money to be devoted to an enterprise, that the policyholder is entitled to some participation in the earnings over and above the payment of interest and repayment of principal.[12]

Although the Company assiduously cultivated stock conversion and warrant rights in making money available to business and industry, the extent of its activity in the field of corporate stocks was limited. Preferred and guaranteed stocks were acquired immediately after the permissive legislation of 1945; they rose to $49 million by the close of 1947. During the following years, however, these holdings were moderately reduced. Management made no attempt to acquire common stocks until 1955 when some 2,500 shares of the Phillips' Petroleum Company were obtained through conversion; and at the end of 1955 the portfolio contained only $2 million of common stock. The Company naturally would have enjoyed the capital gains earned on a more extensive holding of common stock during a period of advancing prices but believed that its policy of "complete emphasis upon the larger areas of investment activity" was justified.[13]

The distribution of Northwestern's government and corporate securities during these years was more similar to the other great life companies than it was to the industry as a whole. As can be seen in Table XIX–2, seven of the largest ten companies owned bonds and stocks in a proportion that was greater than for all United States companies. This characteristic was also true of such classifications as public utility, rail, and industrial and commercial bonds. The major differences in the distributions of Northwestern's holdings, as compared with the other large firms, were in United States government bonds and corporate stocks, where the Company's holdings were smaller than the others; and in municipal and public utility bonds, where it was among the leaders in percentage of assets involved. The investment trends of these companies is clearly apparent: bonds and stocks steadily diminished in relative importance after 1947; and within the bond and stock portfolios industrial and commercial bonds and stocks steadily replaced public utility bonds in popularity. The greater interest earnings and capital gains opportunities in such investments were among the principal reasons for the shift in emphasis. There were greater risks involved in these classes of investments, but the rewards were apparently worth the extra hazard.

The Investment Record

The other assets owned by the Company also increased during these years. Real estate, with the exception of investment properties, consisted principally of the Home Office building which was valued at over $3 million. Special real estate, which had been such a serious problem during the previous decade, was of little importance after 1946. Total foreclosed property owned by the Company consisted entirely of a few farms, most of them inherited from the previous period, and an occasional parcel of residential property. This account varied in amount from $400,000 in 1947 to $98,000 at the end of 1955. The amount held under land contracts was more substantial, but this too declined steadily from $3.2 million in 1947 to $257,000 in 1955.

Policy loans, which had absorbed nearly a quarter of Northwestern's admitted assets in the mid-'thirties, amounted to no more than 3.6 per cent of assets during 1947–1955; in volume they increased from about $80 million in 1946–1947 to $122 million during 1955. Year-end cash balances were also stable, ranging from a low of $23 million in 1949 to a high of $31 million in 1948. The remaining assets, principally composed of accrued premiums, rents, and interest, also increased in absolute amount but never exceeded 1.9 per cent of admitted assets.

TABLE XIX-2

Ten Largest United States Life Insurance Companies: Distribution of Bond and Stock Investments, 1947–1955
(As a Percentage of Total Admitted Assets)

COMPANY	U.S. FEDERAL	U.S.A. MUNICIPAL	CANADIAN	RAIL-ROAD	PUBLIC UTILITY	INDUSTRIAL & MISC.	CORPORATE STOCKS	ALL OTHER	TOTAL
				(1947)					(In millions)
Aetna	41.5	0.4	2.0	3.3	15.9	5.6	3.6	0.0	$987
Equitable	28.9	0.0	4.4	9.0	8.9	28.5	0.6	0.0	3,613
John Hancock	31.9	2.7	3.0	6.0	29.1	7.4	4.4	-0-	1,886
Metropolitan	42.5	0.3	3.4	5.8	11.4	13.5	1.2	-0-	6,676
Mutual Benefit	42.8	0.5	0.4	7.0	19.9	5.3	1.4	-0-	851
Mutual Life	40.8	0.3	3.3	0.2	17.6	15.8	1.9	0.0	1,540
New York Life	55.1	0.8	1.6	4.9	13.2	5.7	2.5	0.0	3,548
NORTHWESTERN	26.2	9.2	2.3	9.3	24.9	8.5	2.3	-0-	1,781
Prudential	49.6	0.2	2.4	3.5	7.7	8.5	1.6	-0-	5,374
Travelers	49.2	-0-	4.8	4.1	4.1	1.1	2.2	0.0	1,095
				(1949)					
Aetna	24.3	1.5	2.1	3.0	27.0	8.5	2.9	0.0	$1,138
Equitable	14.8	0.0	5.3	9.1	12.8	34.2	1.1	0.0	4,063
John Hancock	22.3	2.6	2.3	6.2	30.6	13.4	4.1	-0-	2,160
Metropolitan	29.7	0.0	3.2	4.9	13.6	23.6	1.3	-0-	7,417
Mutual Benefit	27.0	1.7	0.9	7.1	20.7	10.1	1.5	-0-	853
Mutual Life	23.8	1.5	1.3	0.2	23.3	21.7	2.3	0.0	1,536
New York Life	33.8	1.5	1.8	4.3	21.6	13.1	3.1	0.0	3,712
NORTHWESTERN	15.4	11.5	2.6	8.3	28.6	10.0	2.0	-0-	1,914
Prudential	33.0	0.4	2.4	3.0	7.9	14.8	2.1	-0-	5,286
Travelers	37.7	0.0	4.1	3.9	8.6	2.7	2.1	0.0	1,118
				(1952)					
Aetna	12.3	0.6	2.7	5.1[a]	27.4	11.0	5.1	0.1	$1,392
Equitable	8.8	0.4	2.8	10.5[a]	12.5	34.0	1.8	0.0	4,655
John Hancock	11.6	1.7	2.0	6.3	28.5	18.8	5.2	-0-	2,626
Metropolitan	15.9	-0-	1.8	5.7	13.1	32.5	1.5	-0-	8,174
Mutual Benefit	16.9	2.0	0.9	6.5	18.7	12.1	1.7	-0-	840
Mutual Life	10.1	1.3	0.7	0.9	21.6	24.6	2.9	0.0	1,410
New York Life	12.9	1.6	1.5	3.5	22.9	18.8	3.9	0.0	3,464
NORTHWESTERN	9.5	6.3	2.3	6.3	26.5	18.3	1.4	-0-	2,051
Prudential	13.9	0.9	1.6	2.1	8.8	20.3	3.0	-0-	5,173
Travelers	26.8	0.0	3.6	3.2	10.9	5.9	2.2	0.2	1,187
				(1955)					
Aetna	8.8	1.2	2.6	4.4	30.2	13.3	6.9	0.1	$1,925
Equitable	5.6	1.7	0.2	10.7[a]	12.0	33.6	2.4	0.0	5,333
John Hancock	7.9	2.2	1.1	6.0	24.1	20.6	6.9	-0-	3,154
Metropolitan	11.0	-0-	1.7	5.1	13.8	33.5	1.1	-0-	9,220
Mutual Benefit	7.8	2.3	0.6	5.9	17.6	13.8	5.1	-0-	865
Mutual Life	8.2	1.3	0.5	0.5	19.6	23.2	5.5	0.0	1,454
New York Life	6.8	2.3	0.7	4.2	21.1	19.7	7.6	0.0	3,767
NORTHWESTERN	5.6	5.9	1.0	4.7	21.5	23.0	1.2	-0-	2,148
Prudential	9.8	0.2	0.6	1.7	7.7	24.8	2.7	-0-	5,956
Travelers	20.0	0.1	2.7	2.7	13.3	6.2	2.2	0.2	1,280

SOURCES: *Annual Statement* (Convention Form), 1947, 1949, 1952 and 1955 of: The Aetna Life Insurance Company, Equitable Life Assurance Society (New York), The John Hancock Mutual Life Insurance Company, The Metropolitan Life Insurance Company, The Mutual Benefit Life Insurance Company, The Mutual Life Insurance Company of New York, The New York Life Insurance Company, The Northwestern Mutual Life Insurance Company, The Prudential Life Insurance Company, and The Travelers Life Insurance Company.

NOTES: a Includes transportation equipment.
-0- Indicates zero holding.
0.0 Indicates holding amounting to less than 0.05 per cent. "All other" bonds and stocks indicates holdings of other foreign securities.

Although Northwestern's investment managers knew that their tasks were never completed, they had reason for pride in the degree to which their basic objectives had been accomplished. The mortgage loan investment had been increased strongly and the difficult and costly reconstruction of the lending apparatus largely achieved. Diversification of the mortgage portfolio, by type and geographic location, had been attained. The acquisition costs of new mortgage investment had been heavy during the early years of rapid expansion, but by the end of the period had declined to normal levels. Finally, yields had been steadily improved and the prospect for even better earnings was excellent.

Similar organizational and portfolio improvement had been gained in the securities investment field, and the Company had explored new areas and situations to the mutual advantage of policyholders and American industry. Here also yields had been increased, and broad diversification of investment achieved by type of industry, by location, and by economic need. The management, seeking to raise yields, could easily have given way to the temptation of hastening the rate of improvement. In resisting, however, the full possibilities of benefiting from the higher interest rates after 1951 had been preserved.

Among the most important results of Northwestern's investment policies during the postwar decade was the improvement in the Company's earning position among its competitors. Among the largest fifteen companies in the industry in 1952 Northwestern ranked seventh; by the close of 1955 the Company had moved up to third place and had closed more than one-half the gap which separated it from the industry leader.[14] Among the largest ten companies, however, Northwestern had done even better. As shown in Table XIX–3, the net earning rate for the Company for the nine years 1947–1955 was 3.26 per cent—a level slightly higher than for Prudential, its closest rival in this respect. It is clear that between 1946 and 1952 Northwestern did not improve its net earning rate as rapidly as did some of its principal rivals; during 1952 the Company's 3.27 per cent ranked behind the rates earned by Prudential and Travelers, and was no better than that of Mutual Benefit. During the last three years of the period, however, Northwestern's rate rose swiftly as a consequence of the policies previously explained.

TABLE XIX-3

Ten Largest United States Life Insurance Companies: Net Investment Earnings Rates, 1947–1955
(Before Federal Income Taxes)

YEAR	AETNA	EQUITABLE	JOHN HANCOCK	METRO- POLITAN	MUTUAL BENEFIT	MUTUAL LIFE	NEW YORK LIFE	PRUDENTIAL	TRAVELERS	NORTH- WESTERN
1947	2.95	2.76	2.91	2.94	2.84	2.70	2.68	2.70	2.95	3.01
1948	2.98	2.95	2.92	3.03	2.92	2.74	2.77	2.75	3.00	3.03
1949	3.09	3.03	2.96	3.07	3.08	2.90	2.83	2.94	3.07	3.13
1950	3.10	3.07	3.00	3.07	3.09	2.95	2.95	3.15	3.10	3.15
1951	3.10	3.07	3.08	3.07	3.16	3.08	3.00	3.28	3.21	3.21
1952	3.13	3.18	3.17	3.21	3.27	3.23	3.14	3.42	3.35	3.27
1953	3.18	3.24	3.27	3.31	3.30	3.36	3.25	3.50	3.37	3.39
1954	3.21	3.36	3.34	3.41	3.44	3.46	3.36	3.58	3.38	3.52
1955	3.23	3.40	3,37	3.48	3.58	3.55	3.46	3.62	3.44	3.62
Average:	3.11	3.12	3.11	3.18	3.19	3.11	3.05	3.22	3.21	3.26

SOURCE: *Annual Reports of the Superintendent of Insurance of the State of New York*, Eighty-Ninth (1948) through Ninety-Seventh (1956), inclusive.
Insurance Year Book, The Spectator Company: New York, 1948-1956, inclusive.

Investment earnings rate formula:

$$i = \frac{y_i}{\frac{(L_0 + L_1) - y_i}{2}}$$

Where: i = earnings rate
y_i = investment earnings, current year
L_0 = Ledger assets beginning of current year
L_1 = Ledger assets end of current year

The results of Company determination to rebuild its mortgage investment are indicated by a comparison of the portfolio shifts which occurred among the largest United States life companies during these years. As shown in Table XIX 4, Northwestern substantially improved its relative mortgage loan position among the leaders between 1947 and 1955. This improvement was accompanied by a relative reduction in the bond and stock field. The aggregate rate of asset growth of the other nine companies shown here was about 66 per cent for these nine years, for Northwestern it was about 58 per cent. The Company, however, grew faster than did three of its traditional rivals—New York Life, Mutual Life, and Mutual Benefit, companies which were among its normal competitors in the marketing of insurance. Measured by its assets, Northwestern remained the sixth largest life insurance company in the United States.

Completing a Century of Trusteeship

There are many difficulties inherent in forming an evaluation of Northwestern's progress during the decade 1947 through 1956. Most of these arise simply because of the recency of events, the nature of the life insurance business being such that the results of many of the decisions made during the past ten years will not become known until much more time has elapsed. While it is impossible to draw many conclusions regarding the effects of the current management upon the development of the Company, it is clear that these officials have left an imprint upon Northwestern, and that in general their effect compares favorably with that of previous managements.

There were many things President Fitzgerald and his associates had to accomplish if Northwestern was to continue as a leader among the nation's life insurance companies. These included both long-term and limited goals. The management succeeded in preserving and strengthening the adherence to those basic philosophies and principles of operation which had given Northwestern its character and achieved for it a position of authority in life underwriting. Within the framework of this philosophy of selective underwriting and simplicity of operation Northwestern succeeded in strengthening its agency force, unrivaled among competitors, providing extensive services for insureds at low cost, and bolstering its investment position. In general, Northwestern continued to be a select-risk, specialty insurer, and measured by insurance coverage and assets re-

mained one of the strongest organizations in American life insurance.

During these years also certain characteristics were imparted to the Company which were partially or altogether new. For the first time in decades Northwestern began to evidence some of the traits of a pioneer and an innovator, both in underwriting and investment. Certain of the actions which reflected this changing character were forced upon management by competition, by economic circumstance, by the results of policies formed in the Company's own past, and by the efforts of its agents. Other decisions came about because of the personalities and energies of the management personnel themselves. There was an obviously new spirit at work in the Home Office, a spirit of inquiry and curiosity, and a willingness to test old conceptions in the light of current circumstances that frequently had been absent in the past. Certainly Northwestern had become a more interesting place in which to make a career for men of intelligence and ambition.

In addition to overcoming the structural and organizational problems which it had inherited, the management succeeded in substantially improving the yields on the Company's investment, it rebuilt the mortgage loan portfolio, and by imaginative and aggressive effort had constructed a series of protective devices which it believed would provide greater security to the Company's earning position in the future. In the area of underwriting Northwestern's field organization remained unexcelled, and a greater variety and flexibility had been provided for its insurance plans and features. If any element of doubt plagued management regarding their efforts in this area, it was that the efficiency of its marketing organization had not been fully exploited; that creditable though the selling record had been, it could have been improved without detriment to the interests of old and new policyholders alike.

How well Northwestern policyholders fared while the management was moving to accomplish their objectives is clear from the record. During the nine years of Edmund Fitzgerald's stewardship policyholders paid to Northwestern almost $2.2 billion of premiums. In return they received $1.76 billion in benefits, including dividends, and the value of policy reserves and retained surplus increased by an additional $1.4 billion. Death claims paid by the Company totaled almost $597 million; payments of matured endowments and annuities amounted to $178 million; and surrenders, payments of funds left with the Company by policy owners and beneficiaries, and disability waiver of premiums were

TABLE XIX-4   315

Ten Largest United States Life Insurance Companies: Distribution of Investments, 1947–1955
(As a Percentage of Total Admitted Assets)

COMPANY	MORTGAGE LOANS	BONDS AND STOCKS	LOANS ON POLICIES	REAL ESTATE	CASH	ALL OTHER	ADMITTED ASSETS
			(1947)				(In millions)
Aetna	13.0	72.4	2.9	1.9	1.5	8.3	$1,363
Equitable	12.0	80.3	2.6	1.2	3.1	0.8	4,499
John Hancock	8.8	84.6	2.8	1.2	1.4	1.2	2,229
Metropolitan	11.3	78.1	4.0	2.4	1.8	2.3	8,548
Mutual Benefit	15.1	77.3	3.8	1.4	1.4	1.0	1,101
Mutual Life	12.1	80.0	3.8	2.2	0.4	1.5	1,925
New York Life	9.1	83.8	3.7	0.9	1.0	1.5	4,234
NORTHWESTERN	8.9	82.6	3.7	1.6	1.4	1.8	2,156
Prudential	17.5	73.4	3.4	1.2	1.7	2.8	7,321
Travelers	12.4	65.6	3.8	0.9	0.4	18.7	1,679
			(1949)				
Aetna	16.6	69.4	2.7	1.5	1.4	8.4	$1,640
Equitable	14.9	77.3	2.5	2.5	1.8	1.0	5,256
John Hancock	11.5	80.1	2.8	2.1	1.7	1.9	2,697
Metropolitan	13.1	76.4	4.1	2.6	1.5	2.4	9,708
Mutual Benefit	22.2	68.9	3.7	1.7	1.4	2.0	1,238
Mutual Life	17.9	74.0	4.4	2.5	0.5	0.7	2,075
New York Life	11.6	79.4	3.8	2.7	1.1	1.5	4,675
NORTHWESTERN	13.6	78.3	3.6	1.8	0.9	1.8	2,443
Prudential	27.8	63.5	3.5	1.5	0.7	3.0	8,325
Travelers	17.2	59.3	3.6	0.9	0.5	18.6	1,885
			(1952)				
Aetna	22.2	64.2	1.2	2.3	1.7	8.2	$2,168
Equitable	21.0	70.8	2.8	2.4	1.3	1.6	6,572
John Hancock	17.7	74.2	1.9	2.7	1.0	2.5	3,541
Metropolitan	17.9	70.5	3.8	4.0	1.5	2.3	11,593
Mutual Benefit	31.8	58.9	2.3	3.6	1.6	1.9	1,427
Mutual Life	27.7	62.2	2.9	5.0	0.5	1.7	2,268
New York Life	25.5	65.0	3.1	4.0	0.7	1.7	5,326
NORTHWESTERN	21.4	70.5	1.8	3.6	0.9	1.8	2,910
Prudential	39.0	50.6	2.1	3.5	1.6	3.1	10,219
Travelers	22.6	52.8	0.7	3.2	0.0	20.8	2,250
			(1955)				
Aetna	24.8	67.5	1.1	1.9	2.1	2.6	$2,851
Equitable	26.2	66.3	2.6	2.3	0.9	1.7	8,048
John Hancock	23.4	68.7	1.7	2.6	1.4	2.2	4,593
Metropolitan	22.7	66.2	3.7	3.9	1.2	2.3	13,936
Mutual Benefit	36.4	53.2	3.8	3.5	1.3	1.9	1,628
Mutual Life	30.9	58.7	2.2	0.0	5.1	3.1	2,475
New York Life	26.7	62.3	3.4	4.2	0.6	1.9	6,031
NORTHWESTERN	28.9	62.9	1.9	3.6	0.8	1.9	3,415
Prudential	41.9	47.6	2.5	3.3	1.3	3.4	12,522
Travelers	25.2	47.4	0.8	2.7	0.5	23.4	2,699

SOURCES: *Annual Statement* (Convention Form), 1947, 1949, 1952, and 1955 of: The Aetna Life Insurance Company, The Equitable Life Assurance Society (New York), The John Hancock Mutual Life Insurance Company, The Metropolitan Life Insurance Company, The Mutual Benefit Life Insurance Company, The Mutual Life Insurance Company of New York, The New York Life Insurance Company, The Northwestern Mutual Life Insurance Company, The Prudential Life Insurance Company, and The Travelers Life Insurance Company.

$221 million, $369 million, and $6 million, respectively. Dividends to policyholders amounted to an additional $390 million.

For the eight years ending December 31, 1954, Northwestern policyholders, as a group, received benefits in the form of the payments described above, and the augmentation of their policy reserves and surplus equal to more than 129 per cent of the amount of their premiums.

During the ninety-six years, 1859–1954, the Company had received in premiums almost $6.4 billion; had returned to policyholders over $5 billion in dividends, and living and death benefits; and added over $3.2 billion to the policy reserves of its insureds. As shown in Table XIX–5, these benefits totaled more than $8.2 billion, equal to almost 130 per cent of premiums received. In this respect Northwestern surpassed the record of five of its major competitors over the same period of time, although its margin over the second-ranked Mutual Benefit was razor thin. The comparison with ten of the industry's largest companies for the forty-seven years, 1908–1954, indicates the same differential in Northwestern's favor, and the edge held by the Company over the giant combination companies was clearly apparent.

Furthermore, impressive as this record was, every probability suggested that future benefits would be even greater. This was because a powerful source of Northwestern's earnings had always been the per-

Present home office

TABLE XIX-5

Northwestern Mutual and Selected Life Companies: Aggregate Benefits to
Policyholders, 1859–1954

COMPANY	(1) GROSS PREMIUMS	(2) TOTAL PAYMENTS TO POLICYHOLDERS	(3) NET INCREASE IN ASSETS	(4) COL. (2) + COL. (3)	(5) COL. (4) + COL. (1)
		(Dollar amounts in billions)			
1859-1954					
NORTHWESTERN	$6.37	$5.03	$3.24	$8.27	129.8%
Mutual Benefit	3.36	2.80	1.56	4.36	129.7
New York Life	11.91	8.72	5.80	14.52	121.9
Penn Mutual	3.03	2.16	1.52	3.68	121.1
Mutual Life (N.Y.)	6.87	5.74	2.39	8.13	118.3
Equitable (N.Y.)	14.43	9.46	7.56	17.02	117.9
1908-1954					
NORTHWESTERN	$5.95	$4.79	$3.01	$7.80	131.1%
Mutual Benefit	3.06	2.55	1.45	4.00	130.7
New York Life	10.82	8.13	5.31	13.44	124.2
Penn Mutual	2.60	1.89	1.32	3.21	123.5
Travelers	4.28	2.72	2.51	5.23	122.0
Mutual Life (N.Y.)	5.69	4.96	1.91	6.87	120.7
Equitable (N.Y.)	13.40	8.85	7.13	15.98	119.3
Aetna	4.73	2.84	2.53	5.37	113.5
John Hancock	7.84	4.20	4.18	8.38	107.0
Metropolitan	30.31	19.22	12.89	32.11	105.9
Prudential	25.29	15.00	11.59	26.59	105.2

SOURCE: *Insurance Year Book* (Financial history section), 1912, 1923, 1927, 1934, 1941, 1951, 1955.

sistency of its premium-paying business beyond the commission period. During this decade the level of incoming business had been about double that issued in the previous decade and had resulted in a distortion of the ratio of business in force less than ten years to that in force for longer periods. By 1955 Northwestern had reached the point where the yearly volume passing out of the commission period was more closely related to the volume of new business, and the restoration of the older ratio would contribute substantially to the Company's earnings and hence to the benefit of policyholders.[15]

Whatever their pride of accomplishment, Fitzgerald and his associates were not content to quietly accept the splendid record of the past. The challenges confronting American life insurance were great and continually changing in such fields as underwriting, cost, distribution, and investment. Northwestern, combining sound practice and imagination, was moving more boldly ahead in all these fields. The men of Northwestern were convinced that the future would be built on the achievements and principles of a century of trusteeship, and this belief was given voice by President Fitzgerald in 1954 when he declared:

over the years the Northwestern has been the beneficiary of the very deep belief that thousands have had in it. Our principles will always be far in advance of personal and Company achievement at any one time, but the principles are right regardless of the degree of achievement. It is here that our challenge lies.[16]

Bibliography

This study is largely based on the records of the Northwestern Mutual which were not only voluminous, but with the exception of the correspondence of a number of former chief executives unusually complete. In the bibliography listed below only the most important items in the Company's files are indicated along with the principal sources of primary information about the industry and other life companies. The list of secondary works has been limited to articles, books, and other publications that have been most useful as background material for the preparation of the manuscript.

PRIMARY SOURCES

Company Materials

MANUSCRIPTS.

Kellogg, A. W., *A History of the Company,* Milwaukee: (circa 1870).

Tyrrell, Henry F., *The Testimony of Time: Diamond Anniversary History of the Northwestern Mutual Life Insurance Company,* Milwaukee: 1933.

Wilman, Frank E., *A Sketch on the Development of the Bond Department during the Last Fifty Years,* Milwaukee: 1948.

BOUND VOLUMES: complete sets.

Annual Statement (both convention-form reports to states and the less comprehensive copies issued to policyholders).

Correspondence of President George C. Markham, 1908–1918 (four volumes).

Correspondence and Memoranda of Percy H. Evans, actuary (three volumes).

Correspondence of the Agency Department.

Minutes of the Board of Trustees.

Minutes of the Executive Committee.

Minutes of the Finance Committee.

Minutes of the Insurance and Agency Committee.

Register of Mortgage Loans.

Unnumbered Circular Letters: Agency Department, 1870–1930.

CORRESPONDENCE: W. D. Van Dyke, 1909–1914.

MISCELLANEOUS.

Department reports, regular and special; pamphlets; speeches; memoranda and correspondence of various Company officers and loan agents; statistical materials prepared by various departments; and occasional minutes of agents' meetings.

Other Materials

Annual Statement (1936, 1939, 1941, 1944, 1946, 1947, 1951, 1955) for the following companies: Aetna, Equitable Life Assurance Society, John Hancock, Metropolitan Life, Mutual Benefit, Mutual Life of New York, Prudential, and Travelers.

Annual Report of the Superintendent of Insurance of New York: (1863–1951).

Legislative Acts: Wisconsin Legislation: (1857–1950).

Laws of the State of New York: (enactments and amendments to the insurance code).

New York Legislature: *Report of the Joint Committee of the Senate and Assembly of the State of New York to Investigate the Affairs of Life Insurance Companies:* (The Armstrong Report): 1906.

New York Legislature: *Exhibits in Connection with the Official Testimony taken Before the Legislative Insurance Investigating Committee of the State of New York:* 1906.

Temporary National Economic Committee: Investigation of Concentration of Economic Power, 76th Congress, 3rd Session:

Hearings, (1939–1940); *Proceedings,* (1939); *Final Report and Recommendations,* (1941).

Monograph No. 28, *Study of Legal Reserve Life Insurance Companies. Answers of the Northwestern Mutual Life Insurance Company to Investment Questionnaire from the Security and Exchange Commission through 1938.*

Wisconsin Department of Insurance: *Report of the Examination of the Northwestern Mutual Life Insurance Company:* (1918).

Supplementary Report of the Examination of the Northwestern Mutual Life Insurance Company: (1918).

Wisconsin Legislature: *Report of the Joint Committee of Senate and Assembly on the Affairs of Life Insurance Companies:* 1907.

Wisconsin Legislature: *Testimony and Exhibits Taken before the Legislative Insurance Investigating Committee of Wisconsin:* 1906.

SECONDARY SOURCES

BOOKS.

Abbott, Lawrence, *The Story of Nylic: A History of the Origin and Development of the New York Life Insurance Company from 1845 to 1929,* New York: The New York Life Insurance Co. 1930.

Buley, R. Carlyle, *The American Life Convention, 1906–1952; A Study in the History of Life Insurance.* (Two Volumes). New York: Appleton-Century-Crofts, Inc., 1953.

Clough, Shepard B., *A Century of American Life Insurance,* New York: Columbia University Press, 1946.

Corey, E. Raymond, *Direct Placement of Corporate Securities,* Boston: Harvard University Graduate School of Business Administration, 1951.

Dimock, Marshall, *The Executive in Action,* New York: Harper and Brothers, 1945.

Hendricks, Burton J., *The Story of Life Insurance,* New York: McClure, Phillips and Co., 1907.

Holmes, F. L., editor, *Wisconsin* (Vol. I), Chicago: Lewis Publishing Co., 1946.

Huebner, S. S., *Life Insurance,* (4th edition), New York: Appleton-Century-Crofts, Inc., 1950.

Insurance Year Book, The Spectator Company, New York: 1910–1956.

James, Marquis, *The Metropolitan Life,* New York: Viking Press, 1947.

Maclean, Joseph B., *Introduction to Life Insurance* (Vol. I), New York: Life Office Management Association, 1948.

May, Earl C. and Will Oursler, *The Prudential,* New York: Doubleday and Co., 1950.

Merk, Frederick, *Economic History of Wisconsin* (Vol. I), Madison: Wisconsin State Historical Society, 1916.

O'Donnell, Terence, *History of Life Insurance in its Forma-* tive Years, Chicago: American Conservation Co., 1936.

Patterson, Edwin W., *The Insurance Commissioner in the United States,* Cambridge: Harvard University Press, 1927.

Saulnier, R. J., *Urban Mortgage Lending by Life Insurance Companies,* New York: National Bureau of Economic Research, 1950.

Stalson, J. Owen, *Marketing Life Insurance,* Cambridge: Harvard University Press, 1942.

Sub-committee on Investment, Congressional Joint Committee on the Economic Report: *Factors Affecting Volume and Stability of Private Investment,* (81st Congress, 1st Session), Washington: United States Government Printing Office, 1949.

Tyrrell, Henry F., *Semi-Centennial History of the Northwestern Mutual Life Insurance Company,* Milwaukee: Northwestern Mutual Life Insurance Co., 1908.

United States Department of Commerce, Bureau of the Census: *Historical Statistics of the United States, 1789–1945,* Washington: United States Government Printing Office, 1949.

United States Department of Commerce, Bureau of the Census: *Statistical Abstract of the United States* (72nd edition), Washington: United States Government Printing Office, 1951.

Zartman, Lester W., *The Invesments of Life Insurance Companies,* New York: Henry Holt and Co., 1906.

ARTICLES, PAPERS, PERIODICALS AND NEWSPAPERS.

Beardsley, Henry Shedd, "The Despotism of Combined Millions," *The Era Magazine:* Vol. XIV, Numbers 5–6; Vol. XV, Numbers 1–10.

Bell, Haughton and Harold G. Fraine, "Legal Framework, Trends, and Development in Investment Practices of

Life Insurance Companies," *Law and Contemporary Problems* (Institutional Investments), Vol. XVII, No. 1.

The Catskill Examiner, Catskill, N. Y., April 5, 1907.

Conklin, George T., "Institutional Size—Life Insurance," *Law and Contemporary Problems* (Institutional Investments), Vol. XVII, No. 1.

Cox, Robert Lynn, "Report of Sub-committee on Life Insurance Companies," Coolidge Conference on Northwestern Agriculture, May 12, 1924.

The Eastern Underwriter, July 4, 1907; March 12, 1915; various other issues.

Guthmann, Harry G., "Institutional Investment and the Problem of Equity Financing," *Law and Contemporary Problems* (Institutional Investments), Vol. XVII, No. 1.

Hickman, W. Braddock, *Trends and Cycles in Corporate Bond Financing,* Occasional Paper 37, New York: National Bureau of Economic Research, 1952.

The Independent Weekly Review (New York), Vol. CXVI, No. 3969.

The Investment Bulletin: American Life Convention and the Life Insurance Association of America, Chicago and New York:

"City Mortgage Lending Income and Costs of Life Insurance Companies, 1950," No. 125.

"Farm Mortgage Lending Income and Costs of Life Insurance Companies, 1950," No. 127.

"The Investment Experience of the Eighteen Largest United States Life Insurance Companies in Bonds and Stocks," No. 129.

The Life Insurance Fact Book, The Institute of Life Insurance, New York, 1946–1956.

Madden, J. L., "Survey of Agricultural Industry," (unpublished draft), New York: Metropolitan Life Insurance Company, Dec. 16, 1929.

The Milwaukee Journal, various issues, 1862–1865; May-September, 1906.

The Milwaukee Sentinel, various issues, May-September, 1906.

North, Douglass, "Capital Accumulation in Life Insurance between the Civil War and the Investigation of 1905," *Men in Business,* William Miller, editor, Cambridge: Harvard University Press, 1952.

North, Douglass, "Entrepreneurial Policy and Internal Organization in the Large Life Insurance Companies at the Time of the Armstrong Investigation of Life Insurance," *Explorations in Entrepreneurial History,* Research Center in Entrepreneurial History, Harvard University, Vol. V, No. 3.

Schmidt, Charles H. and Eleanor Stockwell, "The Changing Importance of Institutional Investors in the American Capital Market," *Law and Contemporary Problems* (Institutional Investments), Vol. XVII, No. 1.

References

CHAPTER I

1. Fred L. Holmes, Wisconsin (Chicago: Lewis Publishing Co., 1946), I, 316.
2. Holmes, 412.
3. Henry F. Tyrrell, *Semi-Centennial History of the Northwestern Mutual Life Insurance Company* (Milwaukee: Privately printed, 1908), 39–40. [Hereafter cited as *Semi-Centennial History.*]
4. Shepard B. Clough, *A Century of American Life Insurance* (New York: Columbia University Press, 1946), 92.
5. J. Owen Stalson, *Marketing Life Insurance* (Cambridge: Harvard University Press, 1942), 260.
6. Clough, 93.
7. Clough, 93.
8. Orrin G. Guernsey and Josiah F. Willard, *The History of Rock County* (Rock County Agricultural Society and Technical Institute, 1856), 88–89.
9. Stalson, 104 ff.
10. A. W. Kellogg (unpublished MS, archives of the Northwestern Mutual Life Insurance Co., *circa* 1870), 33. [Hereafter cited as Kellogg, MS.]
11. Kellogg, MS, 39.
12. Kellogg, MS, 39 ff.

CHAPTER II

1. Stalson, *Marketing Life Insurance,* 110–111.
2. Kellogg, MS, 126.
3. Kellogg, MS, 47.
4. Clough, *A Century of American Life Insurance,* 58.
5. Marquis James, *The Metropolitan Life* (New York: The Viking Press, Inc., 1947), 197.
6. Henry F. Tyrrell, *The Testimony of Time: The Diamond Anniversary History of the Northwestern Mutual Life Insurance Company* (unpublished MS, archives of the Northwestern Mutual Life Insurance Co., 1933), 35. [Hereafter cited as Tyrrell, MS.]
7. Stalson, 510.
8. Kellogg, MS, 66.
9. Clough, 96–97.
10. *Wisconsin Legislation: Acts of 1863,* Chap. 323.
11. Kellogg, MS, 76.
12. Kellogg, MS, 81.
13. Kellogg, MS, 161.
14. Tyrrell, MS, 107.

CHAPTER III

1. Wesley C. Mitchell, *Business Cycles: the Problem and its Setting* (New York: National Bureau of Economic Research, 1927), 427.
2. *Wisconsin Legislation: Acts of 1851,* Chap. 172, 169.
3. *Wisconsin Legislation: Acts of 1856,* Chap. 55, 56.
4. *Wisconsin Legislation: Acts of 1866,* Chap. 120, 168.
5. Kellogg, MS, 192.
6. Kellogg, MS, 192.
7. *The Milwaukee Journal,* July 1, 1863.
8. *The Milwaukee Journal,* June 30, 1864.
9. *The Milwaukee Journal,* April 24, 1865.
10. *The Milwaukee Journal,* September 21, 1865.
11. *Wisconsin Legislation: Acts of 1866,* Chap. 100.
12. Holmes, *Wisconsin,* II, 76–77.

CHAPTER IV

1. Kellogg, MS, 174.
2. Tyrrell, MS, 45.
3. Kellogg, MS, 208–209.

CHAPTER V

1. Wisconsin Legislature: *Testimony and Exhibits Taken Before the Legislative Insurance Investigating Committee of Wisconsin* (Madison, Wis., 1906), 3. [Hereafter cited as *Wisconsin Committee Testimony.*]
2. *Proceedings of the Fifth Annual Meeting of the Association of Agents, Northwestern Mutual Life Insurance Company* (Milwaukee, Wis., 1881). [Hereafter cited as *Proceedings of the Fifth* (or other number) *Annual Meeting of the Association of Agents.*]
3. Letter to J. F. Martin, January 13, 1877.
4. Stalson, *Marketing Life Insurance,* 519.
5. Stalson, 521.
6. Letter to A. B. Alden, October 6, 1876.
7. *Proceedings of the Eleventh Annual Meeting of the Association of Agents,* January 24–26, 1887.
8. Letter to Messrs. Henderson and Wise, Leesburg, Va., January 17, 1876.
9. *Proceedings of the Fourth Annual Meeting of the Association of Agents,* January 27–28, 1880, 11.
10. See George L. Arnheim, *The Liberalization of the Life Insurance Contract* (Philadelphia: The John C. Winston Company, 1933), 228–229.
11. *Proceedings of the Fifth Annual Meeting of the Association of Agents,* January 25–27, 1881, 17.
12. Report of Willard Merrill, *Minutes of the Executive Commitee of the Northwestern Mutual Life Insurance Company,* January 1882 (in the archives of the Company). [Hereafter cited as *Exec. Comm. Minutes.*]
13. See memorandum: Percy Evans to W. D. Van Dyke, January 31, 1921.
14. *Exec. Comm. Minutes,* January 20, 1881.
15. *Exec. Comm. Minutes,* January 20, 1881.
16. Circular to policyholders of the Minnesota Mutual Life Insurance Company, July 23, 1875.
17. *Minutes of the Board of Trustees of the Northwestern Mutual Life Insurance Company,* January 27, 1880. [Hereafter cited as *Trustees Minutes.*]
18. *Trustees Minutes,* January 28, 1880.
19. *Trustees Minutes,* January 26, 1875.
20. *Trustees Minutes,* January 26, 1875.
21. *Trustees Minutes,* January 26, 1875.
22. *Trustees Minutes,* January 25, 1876.
23. *Trustees Minutes,* January 29, 1879.
24. *Exec. Comm. Minutes,* June 11, 1879.
25. Report of C. D. Nash, George Burnham, and William McLaren. *Exec. Comm. Minutes,* November 19, 1879.
26. *Trustees Minutes,* January 27, 1880.
27. Stalson, 305.
28. Tyrrell, *Semi-Centennial History,* 130.
29. Emory McClintock (notebook, in archives of Northwestern Mutual Life Insurance Company, *circa* 1887–1888).
30. State of Wisconsin: *Assembly Bill 106 A,* January 27, 1876.
31. Stalson, 820.
32. Lester W. Zartman, *The Investments of Life Insurance Companies,* (New York: Henry Holt and Co., 1906), 134–135.
33. Zartman, 136–137.
34. Zartman, 137–138, 139–142.
35. Stalson, 425–426.
36. James, *The Metropolitan Life,* 67.
37. *Insurance Year Book* (New York: The Spectator Co., 1911), 224, 216, 168. [Hereafter cited as *Spectator Year Book.*]

CHAPTER VI

1. *Historical Statistics of the United States 1789–1945* (Washington, D.C.: 1949), 26, 14. [Hereafter cited as *Historical Statistics.*]
2. See Robert F. Martin, *National Income in the United States, 1799–1938* (New York: National Industrial Conference Board, 1939), 6–7.
3. Stalson, *Marketing Life Insurance,* 820.
4. Stalson, 820–821.
5. Stalson, 534.
6. Letter from H. F. Norris to G. F. Freeman, Springfield, New York, September 30, 1895.
7. Letter to F. A. Early, Detroit, Mich., March 23, 1885.
8. Norris to Franklin Webster, New York City, October 16, 1905.
9. Norris to Henry D. Enos, Albany, N.Y., September 25, 1905.
10. Merrill to Rev. Donald Ross, Lake Forest, Ill., March 13, 1882.
11. Kimball to L. Miller, Baltimore, Md., October 7, 1889.
12. Kimball to Miller, October 29, 1889.
13. Tyrrell, MS, 348.
14. Stalson, 534. Citing testimony of David Parks Fackler before the New Jersey legislative committee investigating life insurance in 1907.
15. Merrill to Percival, February 8, 1882.
16. Quoted in Stalson, 511.

CHAPTER VII

1. Merrill to John J. Dillon, general agent, Manchester, N.H., April 10, 1882.
2. See Burton J. Hendrick, *The Story of Life Insurance* (New York: McClure, Phillips & Co., 1907), 129–133.
3. Stalson, *Marketing Life Insurance,* 488.
4. Stalson, 487–495.
5. *Exec. Comm. Minutes,* January 20, 1881.
6. *Proceedings of the Fifth Annual Meeting of the Association of Agents,* January 25–27, 1881, 15.
7. Stalson, 420–421, 490.
8. New York Legislature: *Exhibits in Connection with the Official Testimony taken Before the Legislative Insurance Investigating Committee of the State of New York:* 1906, III, 2899–2400. [Hereafter cited as *Armstrong Committee Testimony.*]
9. *Exec. Com. Minutes,* June 24, 1905.
10. *Wisconsin Committee Testimony,* 211.
11. Stalson, 501.
12. E. Carlyle Buley, *The American Life Convention,* (New York: Appleton-Century-Crofts, Inc., 1953), I, 54, 80–81.
13. Tyrrell, *Semi-Centennial History,* 265.
14. Kimball to Early W. Poindexter, Topeka, Kans., March 21, 1885.
15. Merrill to E. M. Turner, Wheeling, W. Va., September 6, 1895.
16. From personal interviews held with retired Company personnel, including Percy H. Evans, Col. Howard Greene, and Frank Wilman.
17. Merrill to Bristol, March 7, 1885.
18. Tyrrell, 187.
19. *Field Notes,* Vol. XLVIII, No. 2 (October, 1948), 8.
20. Stalson, 439.
21. Merrill to Walter P. Weedon, Honolulu, September 25, 1895.
22. Merrill to C. R. G. Johnson, Montreal, Canada, September 30, 1895.
23. Merrill to C. T. Brockway, Syracuse, N.Y., March 20, 1882.
24. Kimball to Hiram E. Stevens, St. Paul, Minn., October 2, 1889.
25. *Minutes of the Insurance and Agency Committee Northwestern Mutual Life Insurance Company,* I, 258; II, 81. [Hereafter cited as *Insurance and Agency Comm. Minutes.*]
26. Merrill to W. S. Wilson, Altoona, Pa., February 16, 1885.
27. *Wisconsin Legislation: Acts of 1891,* Chap. 267.
28. Merrill to William P. Dewey, Yankton, Del., March 22, 1882.
29. Tyrrell, 224.
30. *Circular to Agents,* December 9, 1886 (in Company archives).
31. *Exec. Comm. Minutes,* July 24, 1893.
32. Willard Merrill to George S. Merrill, Commissioner of Insurance, State of Massachusetts, Boston, September 27, 1895.
33. *Wisconsin Committee Testimony,* 610.
34. Merrill to L. M. McClellan, Valparaiso, Ind., February 4, 1882.
35. Merrill to Robert Shiells; Neenah, Wis., February 25, 1885.
36. Source of basic data: *Spectator Year Book* and Stalson, 820–821.
37. Stalson, 798–799.

CHAPTER VIII

1. *Trustees Minutes,* July 20, 1894.
2. *Historical Statistics,* 15.
3. *Exec. Comm. Minutes,* January 28, 1886 and May 3, 1886.
4. *Exec. Comm. Minutes,* July 15, 1886; October 10, 1883; and July 10, 1885. (Keenan, Quarterly Reports.)
5. *Exec. Comm. Minutes,* August 18, 1887.
6. *Exec. Comm. Minutes,* January 17, 1895.
7. Zartman, *Investments of Life Insurance Companies,* 84.
8. *Exec. Comm. Minutes,* January 30, 1903.
9. *Wisconsin Legislation: Acts of 1903,* Chap. 237.
10. Stalson, *Marketing Life Insurance,* 554. See also, *Forty-Ninth Annual Report of the Superintendent of Insurance of the State of New York* (Part 2) October, 1908, xii. [Hereafter cited as *Forty-Ninth* (or other number) *Annual Report.*]
11. *Exec. Comm. Minutes,* January 23, 1902.
12. Albert O. Barton, *LaFollette's Winning of Wisconsin,* 1894–1904 (Des Moines, Iowa: Homestead Company, 1922).
13. Charles E. Dyer, *Taxation of Life Insurance Companies;* Argument before the Wisconsin Tax Commission at Madison, October 23, 1900. (Milwaukee: Wetzel Printing Company, 1900.)
14. *Wisconsin Committee Testimony,* 1347–1348.
15. *Wisconsin Committee Testimony,* 1351–1365. See also *Wisconsin Legislation: Acts of 1901,* Ch. 21, and Tyrrell, *Semi-Centennial History,* 271.
16. Buley, *The American Life Convention,* I, 242 n.
17. Basic data from *Spectator Year Book* and *Annual Statement,* Northwestern Mutual Life, 1882–1907.

CHAPTER IX

1. Douglass C. North "Life Insurance and Investment Banking at the Time of the Armstrong Investigation of 1905–1906," *The Journal of Economic History* (Summer, 1954), 212.
2. James, *The Metropolitan Life,* 139.
3. New York Legislature, *Armstrong Committee Report,* 1906, X, 9–10, 45–46. [Hereafter cited as *Armstrong Report.*]
4. See Stalson, *Marketing Life Insurance,* 549.
5. Douglass C. North, "Entrepreneurial Policy and Internal Organization in the Large Life Insurance Companies at the Time of the Armstrong Investigation of Life Insurance," *Explorations in Entrepreneurial History* (Harvard University, Research Center in Entrepreneurial History), Vol. V, No. 3, 12–13.
6. *Armstrong Report,* X, 392–393.
7. Stalson, 484–485.
8. North, "Life Insurance and Investment Banking," The Journal of Economic History, 212.
9. See *Armstrong Report,* X, Assembly No. 996, Sec. 83, 87 for the annual dividend and surplus limitation. For other provisions see Assembly No. 996, Sec. 92, 102, 96, 17 and 198. These sections were amendments or additions to the state insurance code.
10. *Armstrong Report,* Assembly No. 996, Sec. 98.
11. *Armstrong Report,* Assembly No. 968, Sec. 98.
12. *Armstrong Report,* Assembly No. 996, Sec. 95, 39, 40, 45, 104.
13. *Laws of New York, 1906,* Chaps. 123, 231, 228, 238, 239, 286, 321, 326, 354.
14. *Armstrong Report,* X, 404, 410, 490.
15. Wisconsin Legislature: *Report of the Joint Committee of Senate and Assembly on the Affairs of Life Insurance Companies,* 1907, 1–2. [Hereafter cited as *Wisconsin Committee Report.*]
16. Tyrrell, MS, 129.
17. *Wisconsin Committee Testimony,* 134–139, 724–728.
18. *Wisconsin Committee Testimony,* 572, ff.
19. *Wisconsin Committee Report* (Minority Report on the Practicability of Government and State Insurance), 5.
20. *Wisconsin Committee Testimony,* 599.
21. *Wisconsin Committee Testimony,* 595–597.
22. *Wisconsin Committee Report,* 4.
23. *Wisconsin Committee Report,* 57, 58, 61.
24. *Wisconsin Committee Testimony,* 402–403, 424, 460.
25. *Wisconsin Committee Report,* 29.
26. *Wisconsin Committee Report,* 29.
27. *Wisconsin Committee Testimony,* 345.
28. *Wisconsin Committee Report,* 39.
29. *Wisconsin Committee Report,* 40.
30. *Wisconsin Committee Report,* 4–5.
31. *Wisconsin Committee Report,* 20.
32. *Wisconsin Committee Report,* 20–21.
33. *Wisconsin Committee Testimony,* 681, 683, 684.
34. All data on salaries and commissions of relatives of officers from *Wisconsin Committee Report,* 14–15, 47.
35. *Wisconsin Committee Report,* 13–14.
36. *Wisconsin Committee Report,* 65.
37. *The Milwaukee Sentinel,* April 17, 1906, 1.
38. *Wisconsin Committee Report,* 270–272, 279–283; 274, 275–276; 267; 264–267; 246–247.
39. *Wisconsin Committee Report,* 238–242, 243–244, 263–264.
40. *Wisconsin Committee Report,* 253–259.
41. *Wisconsin Committee Report,* 259–260 and 260–263.
42. Buley, *The American Life Convention,* I, 307.
43. Buley, 308. See also Tyrrell, MS, 131.
44. Henry Norris to all Wisconsin agents, December 17, 1907.
45. Tyrrell, MS, 131.
46. *Annual Statement,* Northwestern Mutual Life Insurance Company, 1906–1910.

CHAPTER X

1. *Trustees Minutes,* July 14–15, 1908.
2. Tyrrell, MS, 205–206.
3. *Proceedings of the Thirty-second Annual Meeting of the Association of Agents,* July 16, 1908, 79.
4. *Historical Statistics* (Data based on Kuznet's study of national income and wealth.), 26, 15.
5. Harold F. Williamson (ed.), *The Growth of the American Economy* (2d ed., New York: Prentice-Hall, Inc., 1951), 658–659.
6. Stalson, 752–753.
7. *Exec. Comm. Minutes,* August 26, 1909.
8. *Exec. Comm. Minutes,* December 30, 1911.
9. *Exec. Comm. Minutes,* January 2, 1917.
10. George E. Copeland to F. E. Saffold, November 11, 1910.

CHAPTER XI

1. *Exec. Comm. Minutes,* November 23, 1915 and December 14, 1915.
2. *Exec. Comm. Minutes,* August 15, 1916. Strictly speaking, the ten-year term policy had been introduced early in 1908, but had not been a wholly satisfactory substitute.
3. *Circular to Agents,* No. 96, May 15, 1914.
4. Buley, *The American Life Convention,* I, 493. See also, *Insurance Field,* XXXV, May 4, 1917.
5. *Instructions to Agents,* September 4, 1917.
6. *Circular to Agents,* January 25, 1918.
7. *Exec. Comm. Minutes,* December 2, 1918.
8. Percy H. Evans, "Report to the Board of Trustees" (in Company archives), October 28, 1942, 9.
9. "Insurance Medicine," *Medical Record,* September 4, 1915.
10. *Spectator Year Book,* 1910, 1920.
11. Percy H. Evans to T. A. Cary, general agent, Richmond, Virginia, October 6, 1910.
12. R. O. Becker, Aurora, Ill. as quoted in *Proceedings of the Thirty-Fourth Annual Meeting of the Association of Agents,* July 1910, 70–73.
13. Norris to C. W. Bell, commissioner of insurance of the State of Kentucky, Frankfort, October 20, 1910.
14. M. H. O. Williams to H. N. Cockerline, Albany, Oregon, January 25, 1910.
15. Speech of Judge George H. Noyes, as reported in *Proceedings of the Thirty-Fifth Annual Meeting of the Association of Agents,* July 1911, 34–35.
16. Franklin Mann to Marue A. Carroll, included in a report given by the president of the General Agents' Association; Miami, Fla., March 1940.
17. *Field Notes,* Vol. XVIII, No. 10 (June 1919).
18. Report of M. H. O. Williams to George E. Copeland, December 8, 1917.
19. *Exec. Comm. Minutes,* December 28, 1909.
20. Letter to A. H. Wiggin, June 21, 1911.
21. Joseph L. Downes and Laurence M. Miller, Baltimore, Md., to W. D. Van Dyke, May 21, 1912.
22. W. D. Van Dyke to George C. Markham, August 21, 1913.
23. *Circular to Agents,* No. 93. Also, *Exec. Comm. Minutes,* November 24, 1914.
24. Bernard R. Rose, *The Northwestern Unmasked* (New York: privately printed, 1923), 36–37.
25. Information of individual companies from *Spectator Year Book.* For total ordinary and total insurance, Stalson, *Marketing Life Insurance,* 814, 821–822.
26. Tyrrell, MS, 357.
27. *Wisconsin Legislation: Acts of 1915,* Ch. 434.
28. William H. Kingsley, president of Penn Mutual to George C. Markham, March 5, 1917.
29. 248 Fed 568, *Northwestern Mutual Life Insurance Company vs. Henry Fink, Collector of Internal Revenue.*
30. 267 Fed 968, *United States vs. Northwestern Mutual Life Insurance Company* (Seventh Circuit No. 2675, June 28, 1920). See also *The Milwaukee Journal,* June 30, 1920.
31. John Barnes, "Federal Taxation of Life Insurance Companies," a paper presented to the Association of Life Insurance Counsel, Atlantic City, N. J., May 24, 1917.

CHAPTER XII

1. George C. Markham to H. D. Rodman, June 23, 1913.
2. W. D. Van Dyke to Charles Weinfeld; Wausau, Wis., August 14, 1913.
3. George C. Markham to John R. Hegeman, president of Metropolitan Life Insurance Company, November 1, 1913; to General Agent M. W. Mack, Cincinnati, Ohio, February 18, 1914, requesting Mack to see President Marshall of Union Central Life on this matter.
4. Stalson, *Marketing Life Insurance,* 556.
5. Markham to E. B. Stephenson, Lincoln, Neb., December 27, 1910.
6. Markham to Maurice Prindiville, Chicago, Ill., June 14, 1911.
7. Markham to Van Dyke, November 25, 1912.

8. Markham to Van Dyke, November 25, 1912.
9. Markham to H. A. Miller, Des Moines, Iowa, June 23, 1913.
10. Markham to Henry Rothschild, St. Paul, Minn., November 13, 1913.
11. Markham to L. H. Bush, Des Moines, Iowa, October 6, 1917.
12. Van Dyke to all loan agents, December 12, 1917.
13. Markham to H. A. Miller, February 23, 1909.
14. *Wisconsin Legislation: Acts of 1917,* Ch. 502 (Sec. 1951 1(e)).
15. *Life Insurance Fact Book* (New York: Institute of Life Insurance, 1951), 52.
16. *Report of the Examination of the Northwestern Mutual Life Insurance Company,* February 18, 1918, 49.
17. *Supplement to the Report of the Examination of the Northwestern Mutual Life Insurance Company,* 51.
18. *Supplement to the Report of the Examination of the Northwestern Mutual Life Insurance Company,* 53.
19. *Supplement to the Report of the Examination of the Northwestern Mutual Life Insurance Company,* 54–57.

CHAPTER XIII

1. Stalson, *Marketing Life Insurance,* 753.
2. Stalson, 814–815, 822.
3. Stalson, 753.
4. Tyrrell, MS, 224.
5. Tyrrell, MS, 222.
6. Tyrrell, MS, 219.
7. *Field Notes,* Vol. XXXII, No. 10 (June 1933), 3.
8. *New York Insurance Law,* Sections 216, 42. See also Robert E. Dineen, *Cheaper By the Dozen: The Buyers' Market Hits the Ordinary Life Insurance Business* (New York: American Management Association, Insurance Series, No. 104, 1954).
9. Percy H. Evans to Robert L. Dillon, district agent, Lansing, Mich., November 12, 1928.
10. *Actuary* V. E. Henningsen to authors, April 17, 1956.
11. *Circular to Agents,* No. 152, August 18, 1925.
12. C. H. Parsons to G. P. Stickney, Milwaukee, November 20, 1926.
13. W. H. Dallas to G. E. Copeland, December 19, 1919.
14. J. J. Hughes to C. H. Parsons, May 12, 1926.
15. *Exec. Comm. Minutes,* August 9, 12, 1922, September 28, 1927.
16. Harold W. Gardiner, director of education and field training, to the authors, February 16, 1956.
17. Stalson, 608.
18. Stalson, 601–602.
19. W. H. Dallas to G. E. Copeland, January 24, 1922.
20. M. H. O. Williams to G. E. Copeland, November 2, 1923.
21. W. H. Dallas to G. E. Copeland, December 16, 1921; M. H. O. Williams to Copeland, October 24, 1923.
22. Gardiner letter to the authors.
23. Stalson, 590.
24. M. H. O. Williams to G. E. Copeland, January 30, 1920.
25. W. H. Dallas to G. E. Copeland, October 13, 1920.
26. Dallas to Copeland, December 23, 1920.
27. *Exec. Comm. Minutes,* October 24, 1923.
28. Gardiner letter to the authors.
29. Gardiner to the authors, also *Exec. Comm. Minutes,* June 15, 1934.
30. Stalson, 595.
31. Memorandum of Laflin Jones to the authors, October 21, 1956.
32. Unsigned report to C. H. Parsons, Peoria, Ill., general agency, January 14, 1926.
33. Stalson, 639.
34. Stalson, 639–640.
35. *Field Notes,* Vol. XVIII, No. 7 (March 1919).
36. *Exec. Comm. Minutes,* July 12, 1921.
37. *Exec. Comm. Minutes,* July 13, 1920.
38. Tyrrell, MS, 340. Interview with John J. Hughes, former assistant superintendent of agencies, July 19, 1955.
39. Presidential address of Marue A. Carroll to the General Agents' Assn., March 4–7, 1940, Palm Beach, Fla.
40. *Proceedings of the Annual Meeting of the Special and Soliciting Agents' Association,* July 20, 1931, 23.
41. Tyrrell, MS, 338.
42. *Report of the Policyholders Examining Committee* (in archives of the Company), 1926.
43. *Life Insurance Fact Book,* 1956, 21. *Spectator Year Book,* 1940–1947, Financial History Section.

CHAPTER XIV

1. *Exec. Comm. Minutes,* April 11, 1932 (survey year was 1931).
2. From interviews with Edmund Fitzgerald, Nelson Phelps, William W. Cary and Frank Wilman.
3. *Exec. Comm. Minutes,* August 24, 1921; March 25, 1925.
4. *Field Notes,* Vol. XIX, No. 7 (March 1920), 2.
5. *Exec. Comm. Minutes,* June 11, September 9, 1924, for example.
6. *Annual Statement,* Northwestern Mutual Life Insurance Company, 1919, 9.
7. W. D. Van Dyke memorandum (in President's File), November 3, 1925.
8. Bond Department memorandum, "Retention of U. S. Government Treasury Bonds to Meet Future Contingencies" (in archives of the Company), August 19, 1949.
9. William J. Schultz and C. Lowell Harriss, *American*

Public Finance (New York: Prentice-Hall, Inc., 1949), 680.

10. *Historical Statistics,* 95.

11. James, *The Metropolitan Life,* 239. The Federal Land Banks were rendered impotent during the height of the crisis by an injunction.

12. *Minutes of the Finance Committee* of the Northwestern Mutual Life Insurance Company, March 26, 1920. [Hereafter cited as *Finance Committee Minutes.*]

13. *Finance Committee Minutes,* June 20, 1922.

14. A. S. Ambler to F. C. Lewis, supt. of loan agents, August 6, 1923.

15. *Finance Committee Minutes,* September 19, 1923.

16. Interview with H. D. Thomas, retired vice president and manager of farm loans, Milwaukee, January 16, 1952.

17. Robert L. Cox, "Report of Sub-committee on Life Insurance Companies," May 12, 1924. Cox was a vice president of Metropolitan Life and in charge of that company's farm loans.

18. P. R. Sanborn to H. D. Thomas, March 4, 1924.

19. Sanborn to all loan agents, January 20, 1927.

20. Sanborn to all loan agents, December 8, 1928.

21. Interview with H. D. Thomas, Milwaukee, January 16, 1952.

22. H. D. Thomas to I. C. Pooley, Nashville, Tenn., April 22, 1932.

23. Van Dyke to W. E. Griswold, May 1, 1925.

24. Report of the City Loan Department, "Summary of City Loans and Special Real Estate, 1926–1932," prepared by A. H. Alexander, manager of city loans (in Company archives), January 1, 1949.

25. Raymond J. Saulnier, *Urban Mortgage Lending by Life Insurance Companies* (New York: National Bureau of Economic Research, 1950), 39–43.

26. Interview with A. H. Alexander, city loan manager, February 8, 1952.

27. "Summary of City Loan and Special Real Estate, 1926–1932."

28. "Summary of City Loan and Special Real Estate, 1926–1932."

29. Interview with Percy H. Evans, August 16, 1951.

30. Interview with Sutherland Dows, member of the Board of Trustees, April 18, 1956.

31. *Trustees Minutes,* October 19, 1932.

CHAPTER XV

1. National income data from Simon Kuznets, *National Income and Its Composition, 1919–1938* (New York: National Bureau of Economic Research, 1941). *Statistical Abstract of the United States* (72nd ed.; Washington: United States Department of Commerce, Bureau of the Budget, 1951), 263.

2. Stalson, *Marketing Life Insurance,* 752. *Life Insurance Fact Book* (1946).

3. Buley, *The American Life Convention,* II, 745–747.

4. *Exec. Comm. Minutes,* December 28, 1932. *Trustees Minutes,* January 24, 1933.

5. Conclusions based upon information supplied in interviews with Nelson D. Phelps, John J. Hughes, and Laflin C. Jones.

6. Interview with Nelson D. Phelps, substantiated by John J. Hughes.

7. Data furnished by John P. McDonald, Treasurer's Department (in Company archives).

8. For example, arrangements made with newly appointed general agents in Cleveland, Boston, and Chicago. See *Exec. Comm. Minutes,* October 15, 1943, August 15, 1947. Also interview with Nelson D. Phelps, February 9, 1956.

9. *Proceedings of the Fifty-ninth Annual Meeting of the Association of Agents,* July 1935, 184.

10. *Exec. Comm. Minutes,* January 22, 1943.

11. *Exec. Comm. Minutes,* March 15, 1946.

12. *Proceedings of the Sixty-second Annual Meeting of the Association of Agents,* July 1938.

13. *Exec. Comm. Minutes,* September 20, 1940, January 25, 1946.

14. *Exec. Comm. Minutes,* October 20, 1944.

15. Harold W. Gardiner to the authors, February 16, 1956.

16. Gardiner to the authors, February 16, 1956.

17. *Field Notes,* Vol. XXXII, No. 6 (February 1933).

18. *Field Notes,* Vol. XXXIII, No. 6 (February 1934).

19. *Field Notes* (Supplement), Vol. XXXIII, No. 3 (November 1933), 3.

20. For example, *Field Notes* reported that Equitable Life Assurance Society issued 20 per cent of its 1931 policies on women, that "in short, it is common for companies to report that business on women has doubled in recent years," November 1933, 10.

21. *Exec. Comm. Minutes,* June 15, 1934.

22. *Exec. Comm. Minutes,* December 13, 1935.

23. *Exec. Comm. Minutes,* September 17, 1937.

24. *Exec. Comm. Minutes,* October 15, 1937.

25. *Exec. Comm. Minutes,* June 17, 1938.

26. *Exec. Comm. Minutes,* September 19, 1941.

27. *Exec. Comm. Minutes,* June 21, 1940.

28. *Exec. Comm. Minutes,* May 21, 1943.

29. *Exec. Comm. Minutes,* April 21, 1944.

30. *Exec. Comm. Minutes,* December 20, 1940.

31. *Exec. Comm. Minutes,* October 18, 1940.

32. *Exec. Comm. Minutes,* December 19, 1941.

33. *Exec. Comm. Minutes,* October 19, 1945.

34. *Actuarial Comments,* September 21, 1945 (in archives of Actuary's Department), Northwestern Mutual Life Insurance Company.

35. *Actuarial Comments,* February 15, 1946.

36. *Spectator Year Book,* 1934, 1941, 1947.

37. Letter cited in *Exec. Comm. Minutes,* November 21, 1941.

38. Elgin G. Fassel, "Reserve Basis," *Transactions of the*

Actuarial Society of America, Vol. XLV, Part II, No. 112 (October 1944), 294–295.

39. Fassel, "Reserve Basis," 283.
40. Interview with Percy H. Evans, August 1951. See also Fassel, "Reserve Basis," 284, 288.
41. Interview with William W. Cary, April 18, 1956.
42. *Exec. Comm. Minutes,* April 12, 1946.
43. Alfred N. Guertin, "The Standard Non-Forfeiture and Valuation Laws," *Journal of the American Association of University Teachers of Insurance,* Vol. XI (1944), 46–60. See also Buley, 870–871, 892–894 for a description of the development of the Guertin bills.
44. Buley, 894.
45. Buley, 977.
46. Buley, 994.
47. *Field Notes,* Vol. XXXIII, No. 9 (May 1934), 11.
48. *Field Notes,* Vol. XXXIV, No. 1 (September 1934), 5.
49. *Proceedings of the Sixty-second Annual Meeting of the Association of Agents,* July 1938.
50. "Employee Trust Business and the Northwestern," memorandum (in the files of the Insurance Services and Planning Division, President's Department), 1952, 1–2, 12, 74.
51. "Employee Trust Business and the Northwestern," 1–2, 12, 74.
52. Bulletin to general agents, No. 294, July 20, 1945.
53. "Employee Trust Business and the Northwestern," 6.
54. Proposed contract forms submitted by Grant L. Hill and Sam T. Swansen for consideration by the Executive Committee. *Exec. Comm. Minutes,* December 17, 1937.
55. L. C. Jones and J. P. McDonald, "Extra Five Per Cent First Renewal Commission Question" (memorandum in the files of the Insurance Service and Planning Division, March 24, 1952.
56. Jones and McDonald, "Extra Five Per Cent First Renewal Commission Question," 2, 3.
57. *Exec. Comm. Minutes,* July 16, 1937.
58. *Exec. Comm. Minutes,* July 18, 1941.
59. *Proceedings of the Special and Soliciting Agents' Association,* July 22, 1935, 14.
60. *Life Insurance Fact Book* (1956), 13, 21, 23. Stalson, 816–817.

CHAPTER XVI

1. M. J. Cleary to E. A. Crane, general agent, Indianapolis, Ind., May 6, 1932.
2. Buley, *The American Life Convention,* II, 715–716 n. Also Cleary to Crane.
3. Telegram, Clarence C. Klocksin to Sam T. Swansen, April 7, 1932. Telegram, Robert M. LaFollette, Jr. to Sam T. Swansen, April 8, 1932. Sam T. Swansen to M. J. Cleary, Washington, D.C., April 29, 1932.
4. *Revenue Act of 1932,* Section 202, 203 (Seventy-second Congress, First Session).
5. Buley, 896–897.
6. Buley, 902.
7. Buley, 764.
8. Closing address to the Association of Agents, Annual Meeting, July 25, 1934, reported in *Field Notes,* Vol. XXXIII, No. 12 (August 1934), 4.
9. *Field Notes,* August 1934, 4.
10. *Louisville Joint Stock Land Bank vs. Radford,* 295 U.S. 555.
11. As quoted by the *National Underwriter,* Vol. XXXIX (November 22, 1935).
12. Buley, 813.
13. Stalson, *Marketing Life Insurance,* 643–644.
14. Joseph B. Maclean, *Introduction to Life Insurance* (New York: Life Office Management Association, 1948), I, 230–231.
15. Morrison Shaproth, chief counsel, Bureau of Internal Revenue to Sam T. Swansen, June 15, 1937.
16. *Tax Bulletin,* January 8, 1938, American Life Convention, cited in Buley, 818 n.
17. *National Labor Relations Board vs. Hearst Publications,* 322 U. S. 111; 64 Supreme Court 851.
18. *United States vs. Silk,* 331 U. S. 704; 67 Supreme Court 1463.
19. *Congressional Record,* 76th Congress, 3rd Session, April 14, 20, 29, 1938.
20. For example see comments of Raymond Moley, "The Great Monopoly Mystery," *The Saturday Evening Post,* March 30, 1940.
21. February 28, 1941. Cited originally in James, *The Metropolitan Life,* 348.
22. Temporary National Economic Committee, *Hearings,* Part 4, 1496. [Hereafter cited as TNEC.]
23. TNEC, Monograph No. 28, *Study of Legal Reserve Life Insurance Companies* (Washington: U.S.G.P.O., 1940), 89 n. "No instance of the removal of a director when defaulted securities of a corporation in which he was interested appeared in the portfolio was found in the case of the five largest companies."
24. TNEC, Monograph No. 28, 92–93.
25. TNEC, Monograph No. 28, 93.
26. TNEC, *Hearings,* Part 10, Exhibit No. 689.
27. TNEC, *Hearings,* Part 10, Exhibit No. 689.
28. TNEC, Monograph No. 28, 235 n.
29. TNEC, Monograph No. 28, 195 n.
30. TNEC, Monograph No. 28, 196.
31. William Montgomery, president of Acacia Life Insurance Company, *National Underwriter,* March 22, 1940, as cited in Stalson, 704–705.
32. *The Insurance Index,* December 1940, 8.
33. *Exec. Comm. Minutes,* March 29, 1933.
34. *Exec. Comm. Minutes,* December 16, 1938.
35. Interview with David Behling, June 12, 1956.
36. *The Economic Almanac* (New York: Thomas Y. Crowell & Co. [The Conference Board], 1956), 75.

CHAPTER XVII

1. *Exec. Comm. Minutes,* March 3, 1933.
2. Securities and Exchange Commission Questionnaire, II, 33.
3. Interview with H. D. Thomas, January 15, 1952.
4. *Finance Committee Minutes,* October 3, 1939; January 24, 1939; October 18, 1937; July 1, 1937; October 1, 1936; November 20, 1935; October 13, 1933; January 27, 1933. Also interview with Albert C. Fiedler.
5. Interview with H. D. Thomas.
6. Interview with H. D. Thomas.
7. *Historical Statistics,* 99.
8. Interview with H. D. Thomas.
9. Interview with H. D. Thomas.
10. *Finance Committee Minutes,* February 23; March 29, 1938.
11. *Finance Committee Minutes,* June 26, 1945.
12. Interview with Frederick W. Walker, May 7, 1952.

CHAPTER XVIII

1. *Life Insurance Fact Book* (1956), 48.
2. *Proceedings of the Sixty-seventh Annual Meeting of the Association of Agents,* July 1947.
3. *Exec. Comm. Minutes,* January 24, 1947.
4. *Trustees Minutes,* July 27, 1955.
5. *Life Insurance Fact Book* (1956), 8, 49.
6. *Exec. Comm. Minutes,* August 15, 1947.
7. *Life Insurance Fact Book,* 1956, 56. [Expenses include commissions and agency expense.]
8. Address to General Agents' Association, February 17, 1954.
9. *Exec. Comm. Minutes,* December 16, 1949.
10. *Exec. Comm. Minutes,* June 20, 1952.
11. *Exec. Comm. Minutes,* March 16, 1955.
12. *Exec. Comm. Minutes,* March 18, 1949; June 17, 1949.
13. *Exec. Comm. Minutes,* March 17, 1954.
14. From typescript copy given to authors on September 24, 1956.
15. *Exec. Comm. Minutes,* March 16, 1955.
16. *Exec. Comm. Minutes,* October 18, 1946; December 21, 1951. [L. C. Jones contributed much to an understanding of this plan.]
17. *Exec. Comm. Minutes,* January 26, 1951.
18. *Exec. Comm. Minutes,* March 16, 1951.
19. *Exec. Comm. Minutes,* March 16, 1951.
20. Agency Department Records.
21. Agency Department Records.
22. *Exec. Comm. Minutes,* December 16, 1949; September 17, 1954; June 17, 1953.
23. *Field Notes,* Vol. LIV, No. 5 (January 1955), 22.
24. *Circular to Agents,* No. 353, December 6, 1956, 1.
25. *Circular to Agents,* No. 353, December 6, 1956, 3.
26. *Exec. Comm. Minutes,* October 19, 1955; December 21, 1955.
27. *Exec. Comm. Minutes,* October 19, 1955; December 21, 1955.
28. *Exec. Comm. Minutes,* January 28, 1952; November 21, 1952.
29. *Insurance and Agency Committee Minutes,* October 17, 1946. Also *Circular to Agents,* March 4, 1947.
30. *Exec. Comm. Minutes,* July 11, 1952; July 23, 1952.
31. *Exec. Comm. Minutes,* September 19, 1952.
32. *Life Insurance Fact Book* (1956), 21.
33. *Life Insurance Fact Book* (1956), 23.
34. Buley, *The American Life Convention,* II, 1088 n. 116.
35. Gerald M. Swanstrom to authors, October 9, 1956.
36. Buley, *The American Life Convention,* II, 1035–1042.
37. Buley, *The American Life Convention,* II, 1041–1942; Gerald M. Swanstrom to authors, October 9, 1956; Orville Ware to authors, July 16, 1956.
38. Orville Ware to authors, July 16, 1956.

CHAPTER XIX

1. *Wisconsin Legislation: Laws of 1953,* Ch. 64, Sec. 4.
2. *Life Insurance Fact Book* (1956), 60, 74.
3. Data furnished authors by Mortgage Loan Research and Service Division.
4. *Life Insurance Fact Book* (1956), 75–76; Mortgage Loan Research and Service Division data.
5. Presidential address to the Pacific Coast agents' meeting, October 4, 1956.
6. D. C. Slichter letter to the authors, August 15, 1956.
7. D. C. Slichter letter to the authors, August 15, 1956.
8. *Wisconsin Legislation: Laws of 1947,* Ch. 11, Secs. 1, 2, and 3.
9. Haughton Bell and Harold G. Fraine, "Legal Framework, Trends and Development in Investment Practices of Life Insurance Companies," *Law and Contemporary Problems,* Vol. XVII, No. 1. Charles H. Schmidt and Eleanor J. Stockwell, "The Changing Importance of Institutional Investors in the American Capital Market," *idem.*
10. Report of the Bond Department, Northwestern Mutual Life Insurance Company, for the year ending December 31, 1950. Also for the year ending December 31, 1955.
11. D. C. Slichter letter to the authors.
12. Presidential address to the Pacific Coast agents' meeting, October 4, 1956.
13. Presidential address to the Pacific Coast agents' meeting, October 4, 1956.
14. Presidential address to the Pacific Coast agents' meeting, October 4, 1956.
15. Presidential address to the General Agents' Association, February 17, 1954.
16. Presidential address to the General Agents' Association, February 17, 1954.

Appendices

CHAPTER 129.

PRIVATE AND LOCAL LAWS, 1857.

AN ACT TO INCORPORATE THE MUTUAL LIFE INSURANCE COMPANY OF THE STATE OF WISCONSIN.

The People of the State of Wisconsin represented in Senate and Assembly, do enact as follows:

SECTION 1. Thomas Lappin, M. C. Smith, W. W. Holden, David Noggle, Edward McKey, Solomon Hutson, James H. Knowlton, John P. Dickson, Joseph A. Sleeper, Edward L. Dimock, B. F. Pixley, John Hackett, John M. Keep, Matt. H. Carpenter, Charles Kuehn, Simeon Mills, James Niel, J. F. Willard, John Mitchell, James R. Doolittle, George C. Northrop, H. J. Ullman, Anson Eldred, H. H. Camp, J. B. Martin, Luke Stoughton, L. J. Farwell, H. L. Dousman, J. Allen Barber, John H. Rountree, George W. Lee, James H. Earnest, A. Ludlow, James Bintliff, Peter Myers and Lucius G. Fisher, and all other persons who may hereafter associate with them in the manner hereinafter prescribed, shall be and are declared a body politic and corporate by the name of "Mutual Life Insurance Company of the State of Wisconsin," and by that name may contract and be contracted with, sue and be sued, defend and be defended against in any and all courts.

SECTION 2. This corporation shall have no powers or privileges, except such as are expressly granted by this charter.

SECTION 3. The corporation hereby created, shall have the power to insure the lives of its respective members, and to make all and every insurance appertaining to, or connected with life risks, and to grant and purchase annuities. The real estate which it shall be lawful for this corporation to purchase, hold, possess and convey shall be:

1st. Such as shall be requisite for its immediate accommodation in the convenient transaction of its business.

2d. Such as shall have been mortgaged to it in good faith, by way of security, for loans previously contracted, or for money due.

3d. Such as shall have been conveyed to it, in satisfaction of debts previously contracted in the course of its dealings.

4th. Such as shall have been purchased at sales upon judgments, decrees or mortgages obtained or made for such debts.

The said corporation shall not purchase, hold or convey real estate in any other case, or for any other purpose, and all such real estate as shall not be necessary for the accommodation of said Company, and the convenient transaction of its business, shall be sold and disposed of within six years after the said Company shall have acquired title to the same.

SECTION 4. Persons who shall hereafter insure with the said corporation, and also their heirs, executors, administrators and assigns, continuing to be insured in said corporation as hereinafter provided, shall thereby become members thereof during the period they shall remain insured by such corporation, and no longer.

SECTION 5. All the corporate powers of the said Board of Trustees, and such officers and agents as they may appoint. The Board of Trustees shall consist of thirty-six persons, all of whom must be citizens of this State. They shall elect a President annually, who shall be a member of the corporation, and they shall have power to declare by By-Laws, what number of Trustees less than a majority of the whole, but not less than nine shall be a quorum for the transaction of business, and nine shall be such quorum, until otherwise provided by By-Laws. The Trustees shall also have power to make all such By-Laws as shall be needful or proper to the due exercise of the powers hereby granted.

SECTION 6. The persons named in this act shall constitute the first Board of Trustees, and they shall at their first meeting divide themselves by lot into four classes of nine each. The term of the first class shall expire at the end of one year; the term of the second class expire at the end of two years; the term of the third class shall expire at the end of three years; the term of the fourth class shall expire at the end of the fourth year, and so on successively each and every year. The seats of these classes shall be supplied by the members of this corporation, a plurality of the votes cast constituting a choice—but an insurance of at least One Thousand Dollars in amount shall be necessary to entitle any member to a vote. This section shall not be construed to prevent a Trustee going out from being eligible to a re-election. The Board of Trustees may fill any vacancies in their number occasioned by death, resignation or by removal from the State. The election of Trustees shall be held on the first Monday of June, in each and every year, at such place in the city of Janesville, as the Board of Trustees shall designate, of which they shall give at least four weeks previous notice in two of the public newspapers printed in Milwaukee, Madison and Janesville, and the Board of Trustees at the same time shall appoint three of the members of the said corporation, Inspectors to preside at such election, and if any of said Inspectors decline or fail to attend, the Trustees shall appoint others to fill such vacancies.

SECTION 7. Every person who shall become a member of this corporation, by effecting insurance therein, shall the first time he effects insurance, and before he receives his policy, pay the rates that shall be fixed upon and determined by the Trustees, and no premium so paid shall ever be withdrawn from said Company, except as hereinafter provided, but shall be liable to all the losses and expenses incurred by this Company during the continuance of its charter.

SECTION 8. The Trustees shall determine the rates of Insurance and the sums to be insured.

SECTION 9. It shall be lawful for said corporation to invest the said premiums in the securities designated in the two following sections, and to sell, transfer and change the same, and re-invest the funds of said corporation when the Trustees shall deem expedient.

SECTION 10. The whole of the premiums received for insurance by said corporation, except as provided for in the following section, shall be invested in bonds secured by mortgages, or unincumbered real estate within this State. The real estate or other property to secure such investment of capital, shall in every case, be worth twice the amount loaned thereon.

SECTION 11. The Trustees shall have power to invest a certain portion of the premiums received not to exceed one-half thereof in public stocks of the United States, or of this State, or of any incorporated city of this State.

SECTION 12. Suits at law may be maintained by said corporation against any of its members for any cause relating to the business of said corporation. Suits at law may also be prosecuted and maintained by any member against said corporation, for loss by death if payment is withheld more than three months after the Company is duly notified of such losses, and no member of the corporation shall be debarred his testimony as a witness in any such cause on account of interest in such suit, or of his being a member of said Company, and no member of the corporation not being in his individual capacity, a party to such suit, shall be incompetent as a witness in any such suit on account of his being a member of said Company.

SECTION 13. The officers of said Company at the expiration of five years from the time that the first policy shall have been issued and bear date, and within sixty days thereafter, and during the first sixty days of every subsequent period of five years, shall cause a balance to be struck of the affairs of the Company, and shall credit each member with an equitable share of the profits of said Company, and in case of the death of the party whose life is insured, the amount standing to his credit at the last preceding striking of balance as aforesaid, shall be paid over to the person entitled to receive the same; any member who would be entitled to share in the profits, who shall have omitted to pay any premium or any periodical payment due from him to the Company, may be prohibited by the Trustees from sharing in the profits of the Company. No member except officers of the Company, and agents thereof, shall be personally liable for the losses of the Company, and such officers and agents, severally, shall be liable but only for the losses arising by reason of their own respective neglect or misconduct.

SECTION 14. On some day in the first thirty days after the expiration of the first five years, from the time when the said Company shall issue its first policy, and within the first thirty days of every subsequent five years, the officers of said Company shall cause to be made a general balance statement of the affairs of said Company, which shall be entered in a book prepared for that purpose, which shall be subject to the examination of every member of the Company, during the usual hours of business, for the term of thirty days thereafter. Such statement shall contain:

1st. The amount of premiums received during said period.

2d. The amount of expenses of said Company during the same period.

3d. The amount of losses incurred during said period.

4th. The balance remaining with the said Company.

5th. The nature of the security on which the same is invested or loaned, and the amount of cash on hand.

The said Company shall also make and transmit to the Secretary of State, on the first Monday of January, in each year, a full statement of its affairs, in the same or like manner as moneyed corporations are required to do.

SECTION 15. The operations and business of this corporation shall be carried on in the city of Janesville, at such place as the Trustees shall direct, so far as the same can be done at a principal office.

SECTION 16. No policy shall be issued by said Company until application shall be made for insurance in the aggregate for two hundred thousand dollars at least. The Trustees shall have the right to purchase for the benefit of the Company, all policies of insurance or other obligations issued by the said Company.

SECTION 17. It shall be lawful for any married woman, by herself, and in her name, or in the name of any third person, with his assent as her Trustee, to cause to be insured for her sole use the life of her husband for any definite period, or for the term of his natural life, and in case of her surviving her husband, the sum or net amount of the insurance becoming due and payable by the terms of the insurance, shall be payable to her, to and for her own use, free from the claims of the representatives of her husband, or of any of his creditors, but such exemption shall not apply where the amount of premium annually paid shall exceed three hundred dollars. In case of the death of the wife before the decease of her husband, the amount of the insurance may be made payable after death to her children, for their use, and to their guardian if under age.

SECTION 18. This act shall be perpetual, but the Legislature may at any time alter or amend the same.

SECTION 19. This act is hereby declared a public act, and shall be printed by the State printer immediately, and when so printed, the same shall take effect and be in full force.

WYMAN SPOONER,
Speaker of the Assembly.

ARTHUR McARTHUR,
Lieut. Gov. and President of Senate.

Approved March 2, 1857.

COLES BASHFORD.

APPENDIX B

General Johnston's Proposed Contract

John C. Johnston shall act as the General Agent of the company and shall be governed by the by-laws of the company, and be directed by the President and Secretary of said company when and where to establish agencies for said company and to perform all such needful services for the said company as he may be required to do; provided always that he shall not be required to perform services which his age and ability will not allow of his performing. John Henry Johnston shall devote all his time and attendance to the business of said company and in case of his neglect or refusal to perform said duties the said John C. Johnston shall have the right to substitute some other member of his family to perform the duties assigned to or intended to be performed by John Henry Johnston. The compensation to be allowed to John C. Johnson for his services shall be a salary of two thousand dollars per annum payable in monthly installments, his time of service to commence on the 1st Nov. 1858 and to continue during his natural life. The payments to be made in all cases on the Saturday preceding the last day of each month. The Trustees are to pay John Henry Johnston for his services such sum as they may deem his services to be worth, and the same allowance shall be made to the person substituted by John C. Johnston for his grandson John Henry Johnston.

It is further agreed, that upon the decease of John C. Johnston, John Henry Johnston or his substitute appointed as herein above mentioned shall receive five per cent upon the cash received upon the premiums upon the policies issued by said company up to the time of the death of John C. Johnston so long as such policies shall continue to be paid and the said John H. Johnston or his said substitute shall continue in the service of the said company, which five per cent shall be full payment for the service of the said John H. Johnston or his substitute, except insofar as said company shall deem more should be paid, and in case the payment of any greater sum should be deemed just, the said company shall have the right and power to fix the amount of said excess.

And whereas the said John C. Johnston has got up this company at his own risk and charge and he has obtained for it a large subscription, now know ye all whom it may concern, that on the 1st day when this company shall issue its first policy they shall issue to John C. Johnston a paid-up policy of $5000, which policy shall be made payable in two years from the day when the first policies shall be issued provided said John C. Johnston dies within that time but in case said John C. Johnston survives the time named then the policy to be paid at his decease as other policies are made payable.

This contract can only be abrogated for malfeasance, nonfeasance, or misfeasance as the agents of this company. The travelling expenses of John C. Johnston to be paid by the company in addition to the $2000 per annum as before stated, not exceeding $3 per day when travelling on the business of the said company.

APPENDIX C, TABLE 1

Founders—The Northwestern Mutual Life Insurance Company

NAME	ON	OFF	CITY	STATE	OCCUPATION
George W. Lee	1857	1858	Shullsburg	Wis.	Physician
Josiah F. Willard	1857	1859	Janesville	Wis.	†Farmer
Charles Kuehn	1857	1858	Manitowoc	Wis.	State Treasurer
John P. Dickson	1857	1859	Janesville	Wis.	Farmer & real estate
George C. Northrop	1857	1859	Racine	Wis.	Banker
Morris C. Smith	1857	1859	Janesville	Wis.	Merchant
Matthew H. Carpenter	1857	1858	Beloit	Wis.	Attorney
Solomon Hutson	1857	1859	Janesville	Wis.	Hotel proprietor
James H. Knowlton	1857	1859	Janesville	Wis.	Attorney
James Bintliff	1857	1858	Monroe	Wis.	Editor
Hercules L. Dousman	1857	1860	Prairie du Chien	Wis.	Fur trader
H. J. Ullman	1857	1860	Racine	Wis.	Banker
Thomas Lappin	1857	1858	Janesville	Wis.	Merchant
Edward McKey	1857	1858	Janesville	Wis.	Merchant
Leonard J. Farwell	1857	1858	Madison	Wis.	Real estate
Lucius G. Fisher	1857	1860	Beloit	Wis.	Capitalist
J. Allen Barber	1857	1860	Lancaster	Wis.	Attorney
William W. Holden	1857	1858	Janesville	Wis.	Druggist
John Hackett	1857	1861	Beloit	Wis.	Capitalist
David Noggle	1857	1858	Janesville	Wis.	Attorney
John Mitchell	1857	1858	Milwaukee	Wis.	Capitalist
James R. Doolittle	1857	1858	Racine	Wis.	U. S. Senator
Simeon Mills	1857*	1872	Madison	Wis.	Banker
Joseph A. Sleeper	1857	1859	Janesville	Wis.	†Attorney
Edward L. Dimock	1857	1859	Janesville	Wis.	†Insurance
Anson Eldred	1857	1861	Milwaukee	Wis.	Lumberman
Hoel Hinman Camp	1857	1859	Milwaukee	Wis.	Banker
Benjamin F. Pixley	1857	1862	Janesville	Wis.	Produce merchant
Arabut Ludlow	1857	1858	Monroe	Wis.	Banker
J. B. Martin	1857	1862	Milwaukee	Wis.	Miller
John M. Keep	1857	1858	Beloit	Wis.	Judge
Peter Myers	1857	1858	Janesville	Wis.	Capitalist
John H. Rountree	1857	1890	Platteville	Wis.	Real estate
Luke Stoughton	1857	1858	Stoughton	Wis.	Real estate
James H. Earnest	1857	1862	Shullsburg	Wis.	Farmer & miner
James Niel	1857	1860	Janesville	Wis.	Attorney

* Indicates broken period of service.   † Company officer.

APPENDIX C, TABLE 2

Trustees—The Northwestern Mutual Life Insurance Company

Name	On	Off	City	State	Occupation
John C. Johnston	1858	1860	Janesville	Wis.	†Insurance
Charles Norton	1858	1859	Janesville	Wis.	Attorney
John J. R. Pease	1858*	1896	Janesville	Wis.	Attorney & capitalist
Henry W. Collins	1858	1859	Janesville	Wis.	†Druggist
A. H. Scoville	1858	1860	Whitewater	Wis.	†Banker
S. C. Hall	1858	1862	Whitewater	Wis.	Speculator
M. S. Prichard	1858	1859	Janesville	Wis.	Attorney
W. A. Lawrence	1858	1858	Janesville	Wis.	Merchant
S. S. Daggett	1858	1868	Milwaukee	Wis.	†Insurance
M. S. Scott	1858	1863	Milwaukee	Wis.	Banker
E. B. Wolcott	1858	1880	Milwaukee	Wis.	†Physician
H. L. Palmer	1858	1909	Milwaukee	Wis.	†Attorney, President
Daniel Newhall	1858	1864	Milwaukee	Wis.	Grain shipper
Ezra Miller	1858	1861	Janesville	Wis.	Postmaster
S. C. Spaulding	1858	1862	Janesville	Wis.	Jeweler
William J. Whaling	1858	1859			
Lester Sexton	1859	1869	Milwaukee	Wis.	†Merchant
George B. Miner	1859	1871	Milwaukee	Wis.	Dentist
C. D. Nash	1859	1897	Milwaukee	Wis.	†Banker
Henry A. Nichols	1859	1866	Milwaukee	Wis.	Produce merchant
James Bonnell	1859	1864	Milwaukee	Wis.	†Merchant
M. Steever	1859	1861	Milwaukee	Wis.	Postmaster
A. C. Wilmanns	1859	1871	Milwaukee	Wis.	Insurance agent
J. A. Dutcher	1859	1871	Milwaukee	Wis.	Wholesale grocer
C. F. Ilsley	1859	1871	Milwaukee	Wis.	Banker
O. Alexander	1859	1863	Milwaukee	Wis.	Insurance
Mason C. Darling	1859	1865	Fond du Lac	Wis.	Banker
D. B. Whitacre	1859	1862	Berlin	Wis.	Banker
Samuel Marshall	1859*	1871	Madison	Wis.	Banker
Carl Schurz	1859	1861	Watertown	Wis.	Editor
Andrew Proudfit	1859	1861	Madison	Wis.	Merchant
Jerome I. Case	1860	1891	Racine	Wis.	Manufacturer
H. S. Baird	1860	1868	Green Bay	Wis.	Attorney
James Cody	1860	1864	Watertown	Wis.	Physician
Amasa Cobb	1860	1864	Mineral Point	Wis.	Attorney
John S. Rockwell	1860	1863	Oconomowoc	Wis.	Merchant & banker
Louis Scheffer	1860	1862	Milwaukee	Wis.	Cashier
Samuel D. Hastings	1861	1869	Madison	Wis.	State Treasurer
A. P. Waterman	1861	1902	Beloit	Wis.	Hardware merchant
John T. Hemphill	1861	1865	Sparta	Wis.	Banker
George Bremer	1861	1865	Milwaukee	Wis.	Wholesale grocer
John Rice	1861	1868	Milwaukee	Wis.	Wholesale druggist
A. B. Alden	1862	1864	Portage	Wis.	Real estate & abstracter
J. A. Bingham	1862	1865	Monroe	Wis.	Banker
J. H. Van Dyke	1862*	1904	Milwaukee	Wis.	†Attorney (President)
John Lawler	1862*	1901	Prairie du Chien	Wis.	Capitalist
Seth Doan	1862	1863	Kenosha	Wis.	Merchant
I. M. Bennett	1862	1866	Evansville	Wis.	Merchant
J. G. Thorp	1862	1863	Eau Claire	Wis.	Merchant & manufacturer
George W. Mitchell	1862*	1896	Milwaukee	Wis.	Lumberman

* Indicates broken period of service.   † Company officer.

APPENDIX C, TABLE 2, Continued

NAME	ON	OFF	CITY	STATE	OCCUPATION
W. M. Sinclair	1863*	1891	Milw.-Philadelphia	Penna.	†Merchant
Charles Scheffer	1863	1875		Minn.	Ex-State Treasurer
Harvey Durkee	1863	1870	Kenosha	Wis.	Farmer
Guido Pfister	1864	1889	Milwaukee	Wis.	Tanner
William J. Lloyd	1864	1868	Philadelphia	Penna.	Merchant
David Ferguson	1864	1894	Milwaukee	Wis.	Banker
John V. Farwell	1864	1872	Chicago	Ill.	Merchant
Henry W. Hinsdale	1864	1872	Chicago	Ill.	H. W. Hinsdale & Co.
J. W. Cattell	1864	1887	Des Moines	Iowa	Ex-State Auditor
Chauncey T. Bowen	1865	1873	Chicago	Ill.	Bowen Bros.
John Nazro	1865	1869	Milwaukee	Wis.	Wholesale hardware
Nelson Ludington	1865*	1883	Chicago	Ill.	Banker
John F. Dillon	1865	1881	Davenport	Iowa	Judge
A. W. Kellogg	1866	1866	Milwaukee	Wis.	†Secretary of Co.
Thomas Simpson	1866	1870	Winona	Minn.	Attorney
George F. Davis	1866	1881	Cincinnati	Ohio	Packer
Edward P. Allis	1866	1877	Milwaukee	Wis.	Manufacturer
John Coburn	1867	1871	Indianapolis	Ind.	Attorney
David Preston	1868	1872	Detroit	Mich.	Banker
B. R. Cowen	1868	1884	Bellaire	Ohio	Banker & Asst. Secy. Interior
Mons Anderson	1868	1872	La Crosse	Wis.	Merchant
James C. Spencer	1868	1872	Milwaukee	Wis.	Civil engineer
John Plankinton	1868*	1891	Milwaukee	Wis.	Packer
Heber Smith	1869	1875	Milwaukee	Wis.	†Vice President
S. S. Merrill	1869	1885	Milwaukee	Wis.	Railroad official
A. C. May	1869	1872	Milwaukee	Wis.	Attorney
J. E. Thompson	1870	1871			
George Burnham	1870	1889	Milwaukee	Wis.	Manufacturer
Charles G. Davison	1870	1878	St. Louis	Mo.	Railroad official
Emil Schandein	1871	1875	Milwaukee	Wis.	Brewer
Edwin Hyde	1871	1909	Milwaukee	Wis.	Contractor
O. E. Britt	1871	1879	Milwaukee	Wis.	†Railroad official (V. P. Co.)
Edward King	1871	1875	Indianapolis	Ind.	Railroad official
Dwight Durkee	1871	1893	St. Louis	Mo.	Banker & capitalist
Matthew Keenan	1871*	1895	Milwaukee	Wis.	†Miller (V. P. of Co.)
David J. Brewer	1872	1910	Leavenworth ⎫ Washington ⎭	Kans. ⎫ D.C. ⎭	Judge
Joseph Doniphan	1872	1874	Augusta	Ky.	Judge
James M. Gillett	1872	1879	Fond du Lac	Wis.	Attorney
Calvin B. Skinner	1872	1893	Watertown	Wis.	Attorney
Chauncey L. Williams	1872	1878	Madison	Wis.	Farm implement dealer
Nathaniel M. Jones	1873	1874	Memphis	Tenn.	Merchant
William E. Smith	1873	1883	Milwaukee	Wis.	Ex-Governor of Wis.
Anton Klaus	1873	1877	Green Bay	Wis.	Merchant
Frank H. Terry	1873	1874	Milwaukee	Wis.	Merchant
Angus Smith	1874	1898	Milwaukee	Wis.	Capitalist
Henry B. Sherman	1874	1878	Milwaukee	Wis.	Merchant
Peter Van Vechten	1874	1878	Milwaukee	Wis.	Deputy Collector
Willard Merrill	1874	1905	Milwaukee	Wis.	†Vice President
Luther S. Dixon	1875	1885	Milwaukee	Wis.	Judge
H. H. Sibley	1875	1891	St. Paul	Minn.	Ex-Governor of Minn.
William P. McLaren	1877	1904	Milwaukee	Wis.	†Merchant (V. P. of Co.)

* Indicates broken period of service.　　　　　　† Company officer.

APPENDIX C, TABLE 2, Continued

NAME	ON	OFF	CITY	STATE	OCCUPATION
William Orton	1878	1878	New York	N.Y.	Pres., Western Union Tel. Co.
Peyton S. Davidson	1878	1882	La Crosse	Wis.	
Albert Conro	1878	1890	Milwaukee	Wis.	Banker
David G. Hooker	1878	1888	Milwaukee	Wis.	†Counsel
Morris E. Fuller	1878	1884	Madison	Wis.	Farm implement dealer
George I. Seney	1878	1885	New York	N.Y.	Banker
Samuel C. Lawrence	1879	1911	Boston	Mass.	Manufacturer
C. J. L. Meyer	1880	1890	Fond du Lac	Wis.	Manufacturer
Alexander Mitchell	1881	1887	Milwaukee	Wis.	Railroad official
William C. Allison	1882	1890	Philadelphia	Penna.	Manufacturer
B. K. Miller	1883	1899	Milwaukee	Wis.	Attorney
Jesse Spalding	1883	1904	Chicago	Ill.	Collector of Customs
J. B. Merriam	1884	1884	Cleveland	Ohio	Oil dealer
George H. Baer	1884	1884	Baltimore	Md.	Grain merchant
Adolf J. Seasongood	1885	1888	Cincinnati	Ohio	Banker
Charles D. Fisher	1885	1888	Baltimore	Md.	Grain merchant
W. G. Fitch	1885	1891	Milwaukee	Wis.	Banker
Charles Ray	1885	1916	Milwaukee	Wis.	†Capitalist
Harry L. Horton	1885	1888	New York	N.Y.	Banker
John L. Mitchell	1887	1894	Milwaukee	Wis.	Banker
Emory McClintock	1888	1889	Milwaukee	Wis.	†Actuary
Charles E. Dyer	1888	1905	Milwaukee	Wis.	†Counsel
Jacob E. Telfair	1888	1894	New York	N.Y.	Insurance adjuster
Hubbard Cooke	1888	1893	Cleveland	Ohio	Real estate
H. K. Ellyson	1888	1890	Richmond	Va.	College president
Alfred K. Hamilton	1889	1918	Milwaukee	Wis.	Manufacturer
F. C. Winkler	1889	1921	Milwaukee	Wis.	Attorney
George F. Wheeler	1889	1903	Waupun	Wis.	Banker
Edgar P. Sawyer	1890	1890	Oshkosh	Wis.	Banker
Francis F. Adams	1890	1910	Milwaukee	Wis.	Manufacturer
James B. Grant	1890	1894	Denver	Colo.	Smelting co. official
John S. Ellett	1891	1912	Richmond	Va.	Banker
Fred Vogel, Jr.	1891*	1935	Milwaukee	Wis.	Manufacturer
Thomas C. Lawler	1891	1908	Dubuque	Iowa	Capitalist
William Dawson	1891	1897	St. Paul	Minn.	Banker
John Johnston	1891*	1904	Milwaukee	Wis.	Banker
Frank G. Bigelow	1891	1905	Milwaukee	Wis.	Banker
John Field	1892	1904	Philadelphia	Penna.	Wholesale merchant
Charles Allis	1892	1918	Milwaukee	Wis.	Manufacturer
C. A. Loveland	1893	1916	Milwaukee	Wis.	†Actuary
Henry C. Urner	1893	1908	Cincinnati	Ohio	Railroad official
Eugene S. Pike	1893	1905	Chicago	Ill.	Capitalist
C. D. Sinclair	1894	1899	Racine	Wis.	Manufacturer
E. P. Matthews	1894	1912	Milwaukee	Wis.	Manufacturer
C. G. Stark	1894	1908	Milwaukee	Wis.	Merchant
John D. Crimmins	1894	1896	New York	N.Y.	Capitalist
Joseph H. Millard	1894	1908	Omaha	Neb.	Banker
George C. Markham	1895	1919	Milwaukee	Wis.	†President
G. Stanley Mitchell	1896	1907	Milwaukee	Wis.	Manufacturer
H. F. Whitcomb	1896	1932	Milwaukee	Wis.	Capitalist
Titus Sheard	— 1896	1904	Little Falls	N.Y.	Manufacturer
C. M. Cottrill	1897	1899	Milwaukee	Wis.	Transportation

* Indicates broken period of service.   † Company officer.

APPENDIX C, TABLE 2, Continued

NAME	ON	OFF	CITY	STATE	OCCUPATION
E. J. Lindsay	1898*	1924	Milwaukee	Wis.	Merchant
B. K. Miller, Jr.	1898	1928	Milwaukee	Wis.	Attorney
Robert Hill	1899	1903	Milwaukee	Wis.	Capitalist
Ira B. Smith	1899	1907	Milwaukee	Wis.	Wholesale grocer
Otis W. Johnson	1902	1909	Racine	Wis.	Manufacturer
J. W. Skinner	1903	1912	Milwaukee	Wis.	†Secretary of Co.
Albert H. Wiggin	1903*	1914	New York	N.Y.	Banker
W. D. Van Dyke	1904	1932	Milwaukee	Wis.	†President
Mitchell Joannes	1904	1923	Green Bay	Wis.	Wholesale merchant
E. B. Butler	1904	1910	Chicago	Ill.	Wholesale merchant
Wm. H. Hotchkiss	1904	1909	Buffalo	N.Y.	Merchant
F. W. Sivyer	1904	1910	Milwaukee	Wis.	Manufacturer
George H. Benzenberg	1904	1925	Milwaukee	Wis.	Consulting engineer
Fred C. Pritzlaff	1905	1915	Milwaukee	Wis.	Hardware wholesaler
Charles H. Wacker	1905	1909	Chicago	Ill.	Pres., land assn.
George H. Noyes	1906	1916	Milwaukee	Wis.	†Counsel
J. M. Olin	1906	1920	Madison	Wis.	Attorney
Hovey C. Clark	1906	1914	Minneapolis	Minn.	Lumber manufacturer
L. J. Petit	1907	1932	Milwaukee	Wis.	Banker
E. D. Adler	1907	1936	Milwaukee	Wis.	Merchant
A. J. Frame	1908	1932	Waukesha	Wis.	Banker
Homer A. Miller	1908	1932	Des Moines	Iowa	Banker
W. N. Fitzgerald	1908	1927	Milwaukee	Wis.	Manufacturer
Murray Carleton	1909	1910	St. Louis	Mo.	Dry goods merchant
P. R. Sanborn	1909	1936	Milwaukee	Wis.	†Vice President
Joel F. Vaile	1909	1915	Denver	Colo.	Railroad official
Jacob E. Friend	1910	1912	Milwaukee	Wis.	Attorney
Henry Schoellkopf	1910	1913	Milwaukee	Wis.	Attorney
Anson W. Mayhew	1910	1918	Milwaukee	Wis.	Manufacturer
Percy C. Madeira	1910	1939	Philadelphia	Penna.	Coal mining
William C. Proctor	1910	1911	Cincinnati	Ohio	Manufacturer
William Irvine	1911	1927	Chippewa Falls	Wis.	Banker
John E. Wilder	1911	1932	Chicago	Ill.	Manufacturer
F. F. Prentiss	1911	1920	Cleveland	Ohio	Manufacturer
Henry D. Harlan	1912	1943	Baltimore	Md.	Attorney
Stuart H. Markham	1912	1918	Milwaukee	Wis.	Attorney
J. H. Gibbs	1912	1916	Boston	Mass.	Merchant
W. S. Paddock	1912	1915	Milwaukee	Wis.	Manufacturer
H. F. Norris	1912	1916	Milwaukee	Wis.	†Supt. of Agencies
Z. G. Simmons	1913*	1923	Kenosha	Wis.	Manufacturer
Charles Nagel	1914*	1932	St. Louis	Mo.	Attorney
Fred L. Sivyer	1915	1929	Milwaukee	Wis.	Manufacturer
John Barnes	1916	1919	Milwaukee	Wis.	†Counsel
Percy H. Evans	1916	1919	Milwaukee	Wis.	†Actuary
Edward R. Tinker	1916	1928	New York	N.Y.	Securities
Erskine Clement	1917	1928	Boston	Mass.	Banker
Francis G. Echols	1917	1942	Hartford	Conn.	Manufacturer
Arthur C. Smith	1917	1923	Omaha	Neb.	Merchant
Shackelford Miller	1917	1924	Louisville	Ky.	Attorney
Platt Whitman	1918	1919	Highland	Wis.	Banker
H. A. J. Upham	1919	1919	Milwaukee	Wis.	Attorney
William C. Quarles	1919	1935	Milwaukee	Wis.	Attorney

* Indicates broken period of service.   † Company officer.

APPENDIX C, TABLE 2, Continued

NAME	ON	OFF	CITY	STATE	OCCUPATION
F. L. Pierce	1919	1935	Milwaukee	Wis.	Manufacturer
F. J. Sensenbrenner	1919	1952	Neenah	Wis.	Manufacturer
Howard Greene	1919	1956	Milwaukee	Wis.	Manufacturer
Edward A. Uhrig	1919	1922	Milwaukee	Wis.	Fuel dealer
Oliver C. Fuller	1919	1927	Milwaukee	Wis.	Banker
Peter Reiss	1919	1926	Sheboygan	Wis.	Fuel dealer
W. E. Black	1919	1932	Milwaukee	Wis.	Attorney
S. O. Richardson, Jr.	1920	1927	Toledo	Ohio	Manufacturer
H. L. Butler	1920	1936	Madison	Wis.	Attorney
Albert C. Elser	1921	1942	Milwaukee	Wis.	Banker
Frank R. Bacon	1923	1949	Milwaukee	Wis.	Manufacturer
Joseph Chapman	1923	1938	Minneapolis	Minn.	Merchant
Herbert F. Johnson	1923	1928	Racine	Wis.	Manufacturer
C. B. Bird	1923	1924	Wausau	Wis.	Attorney
Thomas H. Gill	1924	1933	Milwaukee	Wis.	Attorney
William Heyburn	1925	1926	Louisville	Ky.	Hardware wholesaler
James S. Holden	1926	1932	Detroit	Mich.	Real estate
Robert E. Hunter	1925*	1928	Los Angeles	Calif.	Securities
Max W. Babb	1927	1943	Milwaukee	Wis.	Manufacturer
Louis Schriber	1927	1952	Oshkosh	Wis.	Banker
Joesph W. Simpson	1927	1947	Milwaukee	Wis.	Coal dealer
Embry L. Swearingen	1927	1928	Louisville	Ky.	Banker
Charles T. Bundy	1928	1945	Eau Claire	Wis.	Attorney
Cleaveland R. Cross	1928	1948	Cleveland	Ohio	Attorney
Charles Q. Chandler	1928	1943	Wichita	Kansas	Banker
Walter Kasten	1928	1950	Milwaukee	Wis.	Banker
Halstead G. Freeman	1928	1934	New York	N.Y.	Securities
John F. Perkins	1929	1944	Boston	Mass.	Judge
Hugh L. Rose	1929	1930	Louisville	Ky.	Banker
Louis Quarles	1929		Milwaukee	Wis.	Attorney
Robert A. Uihlein	1929*		Milwaukee	Wis.	Banker
Sutherland C. Dows	1931		Cedar Rapids	Iowa	Electric utility
W. D. Van Dyke, Jr.	1932		Milwaukee	Wis.	Mining
Fred W. Sargent	1932	1935	Chicago	Ill.	Railroad
Ethan A. H. Shepley	1932		St. Louis	Mo.	Attorney
Michael J. Cleary	1932	1947	Milwaukee	Wis.	†President
Walter R. Frame	1933	1946	Waukesha	Wis.	Banker
Mitchell Mackie	1933	1945	Milwaukee	Wis.	Manufacturer
Harold S. Falk	1933		Milwaukee	Wis.	Manufacturer
Edmund Fitzgerald	1933	1933**	Milwaukee	Wis.	Banker
Fred C. Best	1933	1945	Milwaukee	Wis.	Mortgages
C. F. Messinger	1933	1933	Milwaukee	Wis.	Manufacturer
Frank W. Smith	1934	1945	New York	N.Y.	Utility offiicial
Walter J. Kohler	1934	1940	Kohler	Wis.	Manufacturer
William W. Coleman	1934	1956	Milwaukee	Wis.	Manufacturer
Walter Davidson	1935	1942	Milwaukee	Wis.	Manufacturer
Irving Seaman	1936		Milwaukee	Wis.	Manufacturer
Robert F. Carr	1936	1945	Chicago	Ill.	Manufacturer
Rock Sleyster, M.D.	1936	1942	Milwaukee	Wis.	Doctor
Henry R. Trumbower	1936		Madison	Wis.	Professor
Benjamin Poss	1936	1952	Milwaukee	Wis.	Attorney
Merle Thorpe	1936	1955	Washington	D.C.	Magazine editor

* Indicates broken period of service.   ** On again 1943.   † Company officer.

APPENDIX C, TABLE 2, Continued

NAME	ON	OFF	CITY	STATE	OCCUPATION
Cyrus L. Philipp	1939		Milwaukee	Wis.	Transportation
Clark M. Robertson	1940		Milwaukee	Wis.	Attorney
Harry J. Harwick	1941		Rochester	Minn.	Sec.-Treas. Mayo Clinic
Henry M. Wriston	1942		Providence	R.I.	Educator
Harold M. Stratton	1942		Milwaukee	Wis.	Grain dealer
Edmund Fitzgerald	1943		Milwaukee	Wis.	†President
William P. Witherow	1943		Pittsburgh	Penna.	Manufacturer
William C. Frye	1943	1954	Milwaukee	Wis.	Manufacturer
John O'Melveny	1944		Los Angeles	Cal.	Attorney
Charles P. Vogel	1944		Milwaukee	Wis.	Manufacturer
Harry Lynn Pierson	1945		Detroit	Mich.	Manufacturer
Theodore G. Montague	1945		New York	N.Y.	Manufacturer
Charles J. Whipple	1945		Chicago	Ill.	Wholesale hardware
Charles F. Ilsley	1946		Milwaukee	Wis.	Banker
Walter S. Lindsay	1946		Milwaukee	Wis.	Manufacturer
Carl N. Jacobs	1946		Stevens Point	Wis.	Casualty insurance
Kenneth Parker	1946		Janesville	Wis.	Manufacturer
Frank A. Kemp	1947		Denver	Colo.	Manufacturer
Frazier D. MacIver	1947		Milwaukee	Wis.	Manufacturer
Stanley C. Allyn	1949		Dayton	Ohio	Manufacturer
Herman Merker	1950		Milwaukee	Wis.	Manufacturer
William E. Buchanan	1951		Appleton	Wis.	Manufacturer
Leroy J. Burlingame	1952		Milwaukee	Wis.	Attorney
Donald C. Slichter	1952		Milwaukee	Wis.	†Vice President
Edward C. Sammons	1953		Portland	Ore.	Banker
Catherine B. Cleary	1955		Milwaukee	Wis.	Banker
Lynn B. McKnight	1956		Milwaukee	Wis.	Manufacturer
James B. Morrison	1956		Washington	D.C.	Utility official

† Company officer.

APPENDIX C, TABLE 3

Executive Officers—The Northwestern Mutual Life Insurance Company

PRESIDENT	FROM	TO		ACTUARY	FROM	TO
Joseph A. Sleeper	1858	1858		Edward Ilsley	1867	1872
H. W. Collins	1858	1859		Emory McClintock	1872	1889
S. S. Daggett	1859	1868		C. A. Loveland	1889	1914
Lester Sexton	1869	1869		P. H. Evans	1915	1946
J. H. Van Dyke	1869	1874		E. G. Fassel	1946	1953
H. L. Palmer	1874	1908		V. E. Henningsen	1953	
G. C. Markham	1908	1919				
W. D. Van Dyke	1919	1932		SENIOR ACTUARY		
M. J. Cleary	1932	1947		E. G. Fassel	1953	
E. Fitzgerald	1947					
				SECRETARY		
VICE PRESIDENTS				H. W. Collins	1858	1858
Alexander Graham	1858	1858		E. L. Dimock	1858	1859
Augustus Scoville	1858	1860		H. G. Wilson	1859	1859
E. B. Wolcott	1858	1863		A. W. Kellogg	1859	1870
J. H. Van Dyke	1863	1863		Augustus Gaylord	1870	1872
James Bonnell	1863	1864		Willard Merrill	1873	1882
W. M. Sinclair	1864	1866		J. W. Skinner	1882	1905
Lester Sexton	1866	1869		C. H. Watson	1905	1906
Heber Smith	1869	1874		A. S. Hathaway	1906	1923
O. E. Britt	1874	1876		E. D. Jones	1923	1935
Matthew Keenan	1876	1894		G. L. Anderson	1935	1942
Willard Merrill	1885	1905		R. E. Perry	1943	1951
W. P. McLaren	1893	1904		R. E. Dineen	1951	1952
G. C. Markham	1901	1908		W. B. Minehan	1952	
P. R. Sanborn	1904	1932				
J. W. Skinner	1905	1912		MEDICAL DIRECTORS		
W. D. Van Dyke	1909	1919		Lewis McKnight	1875	1896
M. J. Cleary	1919	1932		J. W. Fisher	1896	1936
F. W. Walker	1926	1949		D. E. W. Wenstrand	1936	1950
P. H. Evans	1929	1946		G. F. Tegtmeyer	1950	
H. D. Thomas	1932	1945				
Edmund Fitzgerald	1933	1947		TREASURER		
Howard Tobin	1945			J. W. Willard	1858	1859
Grant L. Hill	1946			C. D. Nash	1859	1892
P. K. Robinson	1947			Charles Ray	1892	1916
D. C. Slichter	1949			C. W. Adamson	1951	
R. E. Dineen	1950					
				COMPTROLLER		
GENERAL COUNSEL				S. E. Barry	1932	1947
C. E. Dyer	1888	1905		V. E. Henningsen	1947	1953
G. H. Noyes	1906	1916		C. G. Groeschell	1953	
John Barnes	1916	1919				
George Lines	1919	1929		DIRECTOR OF UNDERWRITING		
S. T. Swansen	1930	1943		J. N. Lochemes	1945	1956
G. M. Swanstrom	1943			Paul K. Frazer	1956	

Appendices

APPENDIX D, TABLE 1

Northwestern Mutual: Regional Sources and Applications of Premium Income, 1881–1897

YEAR	(1) TOTAL PREMIUMS	(2) AMOUNT REMAINING IN REGION	(3) NET TO COMPANY	(4) NET INVESTMENT MADE IN REGION	(5) FLOW OF FUNDS FROM OTHER REGIONS
Region I: New England, Middle Atlantic, and South Atlantic States.					
			(In thousands)		
1881	$707	$837	$—130	$—19	$111
1882	829	789	40	—2	—42
1883	987	890	97	—5	—102
1884	1,167	1,000	167	—15	—182
1885	1,313	1,147	166	—18	—184
1886	1,535	1,103	432	4	—428
1887	1,856	1,427	429	—6	—435
1888	2,138	1,356	782	—4	—786
1889	2,549	1,758	791	—5	—796
1890	2,972	1,909	1,063	—2	—1,065
1891	3,339	1,977	1,362	6	—1,356
1892	3,863	2,421	1,442	—12	—1,454
1893	3,961	2,657	1,304	0	—1,304
1894	4,195	2,487	1,708	21	—1,687
1895	4,521	2,643	1,878	637	—1,241
1896	4,808	2,964	1,844	610	—1,234
1897	5,288	3,479	1,809	2,942	1,133
Total:	$46,028	$30,843	$15,185	$4,132	$—11,053
Region II: East North Central States.					
1881	$1,003	$1,254	$—251	$817	$1,068
1882	1,163	1,209	—46	2,379	2,425
1883	1,212	1,148	64	817	753
1884	1,236	1,251	—15	902	917
1885	1,296	1,247	49	1,032	983
1886	1,447	1,221	226	1,010	784
1887	1,637	1,610	27	1,130	1,103
1888	1,942	1,411	531	1,779	1,248
1889	2,107	1,652	455	1,688	1,233
1890	2,494	1,773	721	3,148	2,427
1891	2,721	1,959	762	1,813	1,051
1892	3,088	2,209	879	3,039	2,160
1893	3,125	2,177	948	4,212	3,264
1894	3,361	2,152	1,209	4,097	2,888
1895	3,810	2,605	1,205	3,364	2,159
1896	4,083	2,779	1,304	7,930	6,626
1897	4,497	2,957	1,540	1,886	346
Total:	$40,222	$30,614	$9,608	$41,043	$31,435

APPENDIX D, TABLE 1, Continued

YEAR	(1) TOTAL PREMIUMS	(2) AMOUNT REMAINING IN REGION	(3) NET TO COMPANY	(4) NET INVESTMENT MADE IN REGION	(5) FLOW OF FUNDS FROM OTHER REGIONS
Region III: West North Central States plus Colorado, Kentucky, Tennessee and Alabama.					
1881	$334	$432	$—98	$336	$434
1882	405	490	—85	998	1,083
1883	441	490	—49	566	615
1884	494	508	—14	591	605
1885	607	596	11	649	638
1886	809	636	173	955	782
1887	1,107	945	162	2,014	1,852
1888	1,417	940	477	1,863	1,386
1889	1,849	1,247	602	1,878	1,276
1890	2,348	1,560	788	3,159	2,371
1891	2,654	1,641	1,013	3,304	2,291
1892	3,076	1,780	1,296	1,950	654
1893	2,812	1,636	1,176	2,845	1,669
1894	2,804	1,585	1,219	1,593	374
1895	2,619	1,567	1,052	2,865	1,813
1896	2,676	1,697	979	1,948	969
1897	2,740	1,633	1,107	131	—976
Total:	$29,192	$19,383	$9,809	$27,645	$17,836
Grand Total:	$115,442	$80,840	$34,602	$72,820	$—38,218

The $38.2 million difference between net premium income and net investment was forthcoming from the Company's income from investments and from net income from the other states in which it did business.

Methodological Note

Total premiums by regions were obtained in the following way: First year premiums by states were given in the Company's *Annual Statement* for the years 1881-1897, as was total premium income received from all territories. An estimate of renewal premiums was then made for all states based upon the varying proportions of insurance in force for these states as shown by Company records extending back to the early 1870's. These estimates were then added to the known first-year premiums to obtain total premium estimates by states. A five-year moving average of first-year premiums was used to take more accurate account of the growth of new business in estimating the renewal premiums for the respective states. In addition, the relation of total premium income to the face value of insurance in force by states was utilized in making the estimates. While the method is subject to certain error it is believed that it permits rather accurate inference for determining the geographic sources of premium income.

Company records of all expenses incurred were used to estimate the amounts paid into each state by North-western during these years. These included the money paid to policyholders for the settlement of death claims, matured endowments, annuities, surrenders, and dividends; amounts paid agents in sales commissions, fees paid for medical examinations, and state and local taxes. These expenses and policyholder payments were estimated by the same method used in determining renewal premiums.

Investment data was also obtainable from Company records. Purchases and disposals of county and municipal securities were completely recorded during each quarter in the *Executive Committee Minutes*, as were the mortgage investments on a state basis. Only loans to policyholders required estimation and the amounts involved until 1895 were quite small. The method used in estimating renewal premiums and expenses was also employed to estimate loans to policyholders.

Explanatory Note

A minus sign (—) before amounts appearing in Columns (3), (4), and (5) indicates the following: For Column (3), that payments made by the Company in the region exceeded the premiums collected; Column (4), that the Company's existing investment in the region was reduced; and Column (5), that premium collections net of Company payments in the region exceeded net investment.

APPENDIX E, TABLE 1

Northwestern Mutual and All United States Life Insurance Companies: New Business and Insurance in Force, 1859–1956

	NORTHWESTERN MUTUAL		ORDINARY INSURANCE ALL COMPANIES		TOTAL INSURANCE ALL COMPANIES	
	(1)	(2)	(3)	(4)	(5)	(6)
YEAR[a]	NEW BUSINESS	IN FORCE	NEW BUSINESS	IN FORCE	NEW BUSINESS	IN FORCE
			(In millions of dollars)			
1859[b]	$0.41	$0.4	$30.1	$141.5	$30.1	$141.5
1860[b]	0.86	1.0	35.6	163.7	35.6	163.7
1861[b]	0.75	1.5	25.0	164.3	25.0	164.3
1862[b]	1.26	2.4	43.5	184.0	43.5	184.0
1863[b]	1.21	3.1	89.8	267.7	89.8	267.7
1864[b]	3.99	5.9	155.8	395.7	155.8	395.7
1865[c]	10.88	15.0	245.4	580.9	245.4	580.9
1866	10.57	22.5	404.5	865.1	404.5	865.1
1867	25.28	36.5	471.6	1,161.7	471.6	1,161.7
1868	24.33	50.0	579.7	1,529.0	579.7	1,529.0
1869	22.37	59.6	614.8	1,836.6	614.8	1,836.6
1870	16.59	65.2	587.9	2,023.9	587.9	2,023.9
1871	12.69	62.4	488.7	2,101.5	488.7	2,101.5
1872	13.20	64.2	489.9	2,114.7	489.9	2,114.7
1873	11.06	64.7	465.6	2,086.0	465.6	2,086.0
1874	11.07	65.3	351.8	1,997.2	351.8	1,997.2
1875	12.76	67.1	299.3	1,922.0	299.3	1,922.0
1876	11.40	67.5	232.7	1,736.0	233.4	1,736.4
1877	7.86	64.4	178.3	1,556.1	179.3	1,557.1
1878	6.58	61.4	156.5	1,480.9	158.3	1,482.9
1879	7.64	61.9	173.3	1,510.2	178.3	1,515.6
1880	8.68	65.0	208.9	1,559.3	243.7	1,578.9
1881	15.04	74.5	246.1	1,644.3	283.2	1,676.9
1882	15.92	83.4	279.4	1,742.6	331.5	1,798.1
1883	16.78	92.1	329.7	1,873.2	406.7	1,959.6
1884	17.57	98.8	339.6	1,985.0	428.7	2,093.5
1885	22.58	110.7	355.2	2,156.0	448.9	2,300.1
1886	28.08	127.6	488.1	2,230.9	620.8	2,427.6
1887	32.13	147.6	548.0	2,588.0	706.8	2,842.1
1888	40.26	172.5	544.8	2,828.8	724.2	3,134.1
1889	48.06	202.4	669.0	3,217.3	871.0	3,583.2
1890	58.76	238.9	742.1	3,620.8	984.0	4,049.6
1891	64.61	275.7	779.2	3,966.3	1,006.4	4,446.5
1892	66.58	312.5	818.8	4,314.2	1,095.7	4,897.7
1893	48.68	325.2	865.4	4,628.9	1,209.9	5,291.6
1894	46.84	340.7	785.0	4,763.1	1,358.7	5,566.2
1895	53.48	364.3	793.9	4,917.7	1,175.9	5,738.4
1896	50.40	384.2	734.3	5,055.9	1,095.2	5,943.1
1897	57.40	413.1	845.3	5,330.5	1,260.1	6,326.1
1898	72.50	457.7	931.3	5,715.0	1,353.4	6,825.0
1899	69.62	497.6	1,177.5	6,481.5	1,696.9	7,774.3
1900	61.28	529.6	1,280.3	7,093	1,846.3	8,562
1901	65.39	574.7	1,421.5	7,953	2,020.0	9,594

APPENDIX E, TABLE 1, Continued

	NORTHWESTERN MUTUAL		ORDINARY INSURANCE ALL COMPANIES		TOTAL INSURANCE ALL COMPANIES	
YEAR[a]	(1) NEW BUSINESS	(2) IN FORCE	(3) NEW BUSINESS	(4) IN FORCE	(5) NEW BUSINESS	(6) IN FORCE
			(In millions of dollars)			
1902	68.42	620.7	1,564.1	8,698	2,176.1	10,505
1903	68.30	662.9	1,726.9	9,569	2,323.4	11,547
1904	73.88	708.6	1,796.3	10,412	2,409.7	12,548
1905	90.33	764.3	1,725.7	11,054	2,386.6	13,364
1906	93.89	819.3	1,450.8	11,253	2,081.9	13,707
1907	102.24	881.6	1,345.1	11,486	1,921.4	14,063
1908	109.77	944.6	1,468.9	11,850	2,063.1	14,519
1909	113.72	1,012.9	1,655.9	12,452	2,449.0	15,420
1910	118.79	1,080.1	1,822.3	13,227	2,557.1	16,404
1911	120.99	1,147.3	2,097.2	14,579	2,870.3	18,003
1912	138.70	1,229.4	2,240.4	15,543	3,082.5	19,265
1913	133.19	1,304.4	2,549.8	16,556	3,399.9	20,564
1914	126.29	1,365.3	2,456.5	17,360	3,314.7	21,589
1915	127.40	1,420.0	2,599,7	18,249	3,601.0	22,777
1916	153.27	1,505.5	3,171.4	19,713	4,212.0	24,679
1917	160.65	1,604.4	3,727.6	21,617	4,891.0	27,189
1918	145.77	1,680.9	3,847.2	23,535	5,130.8	29,870
1919	297.10	1,916.2	6,476.2	28,167	8,314.9	35,880
1920	354.32	2,196.7	7,916.8	33,451	10,105.4	42,281
1921	259.76	2,350.5	6,635.8	36,371	8,730.2	45,983
1922	265.78	2,499.6	7,160.3	39,549	9,774.3	50,291
1923	305.48	2,689.2	8,611.8	44,219	11,936.0	56,804
1924	317.47	2,879.0	9,301.5	49,229	13,194.7	63,780
1925	348.72	3,100.8	10,563.1	54,549	15,473.0	71,690
1926	336.66	3,303.8	11,014.7	60,007	16,430.5	79,644
1927	342.54	3,499.0	11,404.9	65,015	17,135.5	87,022
1928	352.11	3,700.6	12,257.5	70,453	18,673.6	95,206
1929	379.94	3,913.2	12,957.5	76,082	19,267.3	103,146
1930	337.85	4,055.5	12,604.0	79,729	19,019.8	107,948
1931	296.26	4,096.1	11,321.4	80,619	17,226.2	108,886
1932	254.47	3,998.5	8,911.1	76,755	14,514.3	103,154
1933	191.00	3,813.8	6,786	71,899	10,866	97,985
1934	233.52	3,704.5	7,363	71,277	11,956	98,542
1935	255.45	3,705.0	7,550	71,937	12,333	100,730
1936	266.72	3,778.1	7,315	73,708	12,206	104,667
1937	262.20	3,859.2	7,593	76,034	12,621	109,572
1938	233.90	3,893.6	6,745	77,221	11,104	111,055
1939	195.18	3,911.2	6,886	78,762	11,006	113,977
1940	199.47	3,948.7	7,023	81,006	11,172	117,794
1941	236.01	4,044.7	7,937	84,290	.12,661	124,673
1942	204.95	4,126.4	7,042	87,059	11,972	130,333
1943	227.37	. 4,257.4	8,024	91,719	13,351	140,309
1944	265.15	4,437.5	9,185	97,510	14,192	149,071
1945	319.41	4,670.8	10,578	104,355	15,468	155,723
1946	470.58	5,045.8	16,246	115,929	22,903	174,553
1947	466.20	5,406.8	16,133	125,913	23,785	191,264

APPENDIX E, TABLE 1, Continued

YEAR[a]	NORTHWESTERN MUTUAL		ORDINARY INSURANCE ALL COMPANIES		TOTAL INSURANCE ALL COMPANIES	
	(1) NEW BUSINESS	(2) IN FORCE	(3) NEW BUSINESS	(4) IN FORCE	(5) NEW BUSINESS	(6) IN FORCE
	(In millions of dollars)					
1948	439.65	5,730.3	15,789	135,296	23,566	206,715
1949	410.28	6,001.5	15,850	143,974	24,416	220,515
1950	454.80	6,304.5	18,263	154,349	30,288	242,018
1951	422.70	6,560.7	19,002	164,984	29,234	262,315
1952	490.48	6,886.8	21,588	177,419	33,476	287,080
1953	519.76	7,219.1	24,908	192,038	38,134	316,722
1954	535.29	7,550.9	26,824	206,197	47,453	348,141
1955	596.05	7,933.9	32,207	225,342	50,243	389,081
1956	696.03	8,402.2				

NOTES: [a] Ending December 31 for all companies for years 1859-1956, for Northwestern for years 1866-1956.
[b] For year ending May 31.
[c] For nineteen months ending December 31, 1865.

SOURCES: Northwestern Mutual, New Business and In Force: *Annual Statement*, Northwestern Mutual Life Insurance Company, 1859-1956, inclusive; *Year Book* (New York: The Spectator Company, 1911, 1927, 1933, 1941, 1947, 1951).
New Business: 1859-1932,
Ordinary: J. Owen Stalson, *Marketing Life Insurance* (Cambridge: Harvard University Press, 1942), 813-815.

1933-1955, *Life Insurance Fact Book* (New York: Institute of Life Insurance, 1956), 21. (Exclusive of revivals, increases, and dividend additions).
In Force: 1859-1899, Stalson, 820-821.
1900-1955, *Life Insurance Fact Book* (1956), 23.
Total Insurance:
New Business: 1859-1932, Stalson, 813-815.
1933-1955, *Life Insurance Fact Book* (1956), 21. (Exclusive of revivals, increases, and dividend additions).
In Force: 1859-1899, Stalson, 820-821.
1900-1955, *Life Insurance Fact Book* (1956), 13.

APPENDIX F, TABLE 1

Northwestern Mutual: Sources of Income, 1859–1956

YEAR	(1) FROM PREMIUMS	(2) FROM[a] INVESTMENT	(3) OTHER	(4) TOTAL
		(In thousands)		
1859[b]	$13	$	$ c	$13
1860[b]	26	d		26
1861[b]	45	1		46
1862[b]	69	3		72
1863[b]	98	6		104
1864[b]	200	11		212
1865[e]	805	34		838
1866[f]	1,003	71		1,073
1867	1,573	121		1,694
1868	2,222	195		2,417
1869	3,028	310		3,339
1870	3,210	461		3,670
1871	3,114	659		3,773
1872	2,940	755		3,695
1873	2,953	954		3,906
1874	2,839	1,153		3,993
		(In millions)		
1875	2.68	1.32	0.06	4.05
1876	2.57	1.36		3.93
1877	2.29	1.42		3.71
1878	1.98	1.33		3.32
1879	1.86	1.32		3.18
1880	1.87	1.27		3.14
1881	2.18	1.19		3.37
1882	2.62	1.18		3.80
1883	3.01	1.20		4.21
1884	3.38	1.27		4.65
1885	3.78	1.32		5.10
1886	4.42	1.45		5.87
1887	5.22	1.64		6.86
1888	6.23	1.77		8.00
1889	7.35	2.03		9.38
1890	8.92	2.20		11.12
1891	10.12	2.43		12.55
1892	11.80	2.75		14.55
1893	11.92	3.04		14.96
1894	12.76	3.49		16.25
1895	13.58	3.94		17.52
1896	14.26	4.27		18.53
1897	15.12	4.86		19.98
1898	16.63	5.49		22.12
1899	18.99	5.56		24.55

Appendices

APPENDIX F, TABLE 1, Continued

YEAR	(1) FROM PREMIUMS	(2) FROM[a] INVESTMENT	(3) OTHER	(4) TOTAL
		(In millions)		
1900	20.95	6.16	0.04	27.15
1901	22.62	6.81	0.04	29.47
1902	24.58	7.01	0.05	31.64
1903	26.15	7.44	0.06	33.65
1904	28.04	8.33	0.08	36.45
1905	30.05	8.98	0.03	39.06
1906	31.84	9.86	0.23	41.93
1907	33.44	10.00	0.15	43.59
1908	35.29	11.05	0.20	46.54
1909	37.09	11.99	0.23	49.31
1910	38.86	12.53	0.46	51.85
1911	40.06	13.38	0.61	54.05
1912	43.60	13.92	0.80	58.32
1913	45.56	14.50	1.00	61.06
1914	47.54	15.28	0.76	63.58
1915	49.55	16.44	0.85	66.84
1916	51.90	17.32	1.45	70.67
1917	55.16	18.53	1.44	75.13
1918	57.36	19.34	1.22	77.92
1919	64.81	20.52	2.09	87.42
1920	73.23	21.75	1.76	96.74
1921	77.69	23.68	1.80	103.17
1922	81.91	26.49	2.25	110.65
1923	88.15	28.82	2.81	119.78
1924	94.21	30.33	3.82	128.3ᴏ
1925	100.93	32.46	4.68	138.07
1926	107.18	34.46	6.00	147.64
1927	113.02	36.88	7.79	157.69
1928	118.67	40.03	12.47	171.17
1929	124.53	41.95	9.45	175.93
1930	128.41	44.48	11.56	184.45
1931	130.46	45.18	15.41	191.05
1932	126.80	44.69	17.92	189.41
1933	119.92	44.77	19.67	183.36
1934	121.87	47.90	21.18	190.95
1935	140.45	48.04	24.95	213.44
1936	130.92	49.40	26.97	207.29
1937	128.86	50.14	25.32	204.32
1938	130.67	51.23	28.41	210.31
1939	128.61	53.91	28.55	211.07
1940	129.85	55.81	31.25	216.91
1941	138.71	58.03	30.89	227.63
1942	141.51	61.14	29.67	232.32
1943	150.94	62.48	30.45	243.87
1944	159.86	61.99	33.55	255.40

APPENDIX F, TABLE 1, Continued

YEAR	(1) FROM PREMIUMS	(2) FROM[a] INVESTMENT	(3) OTHER	(4) TOTAL
		(In millions)		
1945	175.49	63.24	48.11	286.84
1946	190.29	63.55	47.56	301.40
1947	207.95	66.37	47.27	321.60
1948	217.06	70.69	44.53	332.28
1949	222.18	77.29	49.14	348.61
1950	228.20	83.31	54.08	365.59
1951	238.94	90.09	60.48	389.51
1952	252.47	98.50	58.63	409.60
1953	261.61	106.13	64.48	432.22
1954	271.36	116.54	71.11	459.01
1955	282.13	125.49	81.89	489.51

NOTES: General: Items in column do not necessarily add to total due to rounding.

[a] Interest, rent, and dividends. Profits from sale of assets and increases in book and amortization values of assets included under "Other" income.

[b] For years ending May 31.

[c] Actually less than $500.

[d] Amounted to $300.

[e] For nineteen months ending December 31, 1865.

[f] For this and all subsequent years, year ending December 31.

SOURCE: *Annual Statement* (Convention Form and predecessors), Northwestern Mutual Life Insurance Company, 1859-1956. Comptroller's Department Records.

Appendices

APPENDIX F, TABLE 2

Northwestern Mutual: Payments to Policyholders, 1859–1956

	(1)	(2)	(3)	(4)	(5)	(6) From[a] Funds Left With Company	(7) Disability Waiver of Premium	(8)
Year	Death Claims	Matured Endowments	Surrenders	Annuities	Dividends			Total
			(In thousands of dollars)					
1859[b]								
1860[b]	$4							
1861[b]	7							$4
1862[b]	7		*e*					7
1863[b]	19		$5					7
1864[b]	26		6		$17			24
								49
1865[c]	96		14		22			133
1866[d]	108		21		*e*			129
1867	181		56		99			336
1868	326		89		215			630
1869	433		155		321			910
1870	477		298		16			791
1871	606	$1	478		497			1,582
1872	582	*e*	434		449			1,466
1873	701	1	540		560			1,802
1874	636	18	551		694			1,899
1875	646	57	548		755			2,005
1876	873	92	622		825			2,412
1877	764	419	829		880			2,892
1878	704	863	603		920			3,089
1879	820	741	311		792			2,664
1880	699	552	142		788			2,181
1881	816	575	111		769			2,271
1882	860	406	191		687			2,143
1883	985	309	258		676			2,227
1884	860	614	284		727			2,486
			(In millions of dollars)					
1885	1.05	0.49	0.32		0.78			2.64
1886	1.00	0.34	0.25		0.82			2.41
1887	1.42	0.30	0.17		1.46			3.35
1888	1.35	0.23	0.26		0.96			2.80
1889	1.89	0.46	0.27		0.93			3.55
1890	2.12	0.47	0.34		0.99			3.92
1891	2.29	0.50	0.35		1.03			4.17
1892	2.85	0.47	0.39	*e*	1.14			4.85
1893	3.18	0.36	0.61	*e*	1.14			5.30
1894	2.68	0.41	0.79	*e*	1.26			5.15
1895	3.00	0.51	0.87	*e*	1.30			5.68
1896	3.26	0.80	0.89	*e*	1.37			6.32
1897	3.73	0.83	0.65	*e*	1.51			6.73
1898	3.87	0.77	0.79	*e*	1.85			7.29
1899	4.71	0.87	0.92	*e*	2.52			9.03

APPENDIX F, TABLE 2, Continued

Year	(1) Death Claims	(2) Matured Endowments	(3) Surrenders	(4) Annuities	(5) Dividends	(6) From[a] Funds Left with Company	(7) Disability Waiver of Premium	(8) Total
				(In millions of dollars)				
1900	4.49	0.96	1.16	$0.01	3.23			9.85
1901	5.35	1.63	1.77	0.02	3.58			12.35
1902	5.18	1.84	1.86	0.04	4.18			13.10
1903	6.06	1.98	2.47	0.05	4.46			15.02
1904	6.83	1.29	3.02	0.05	5.34			16.53
1905	7.56	1.60	4.39	0.05	6.49			20.09
1906	7.49	1.66	5.21	0.06	7.37	$0.11		21.90
1907	7.91	2.02	5.54	0.07	7.91	0.12		23.57
1908	8.67	1.97	6.81	0.07	9.43	0.16		27.11
1909	8.48	2.31	7.62	0.08	10.34	0.14		28.97
1910	9.88	2.63	8.43	0.08	11.85	0.27		33.14
1911	10.83	2.84	9.28	0.07	12.60	0.23		35.85
1912	11.80	3.34	9.11	0.10	12.91	0.38		37.64
1913	11.32	3.54	8.94	0.13	12.72	0.38		37.03
1914	12.42	4.04	9.29	0.20	12.51	0.46		38.92
1915	13.85	4.50	10.60	0.24	13.27	0.57		43.03
1916	15.52	4.84	8.69	0.25	13.15	0.56		43.01
1917	14.41	6.57	7.57	0.25	13.03	0.72		42.55
1918	18.15	8.03	6.83	0.26	13.74	0.81		47.82
1919	19.17	8.16	6.53	0.25	14.73	0.83	e	49.67
1920	18.76	8.28	7.19	0.25	16.18	1.10	e	51.76
1921	18.25	7.93	9.58	0.25	17.89	0.92	e	54.82
1922	21.06	7.34	11.04	0.23	19.05	1.10	0.01	59.83
1923	22.42	7.17	11.43	0.23	20.31	1.14	0.01	62.71
1924	23.53	6.81	12.40	0.21	25.16	1.42	0.01	69.54
1925	24.82	6.56	12.97	0.20	27.27	1.92	0.02	73.76
1926	26.89	5.15	13.88	0.19	31.13	2.44	0.03	79.71
1927	29.46	4.66	16.47	0.18	33.55	3.01	0.03	87.36
1928	34.65	3.97	16.90	0.17	35.71	4.14	0.04	95.58
1929	37.75	4.54	19.48	0.16	39.73	5.67	0.05	107.38
1930	39.58	3.61	23.25	0.15	42.21	5.37	0.07	114.24
1931	44.38	3.40	32.78	0.14	44.01	6.09	0.11	130.91
1932	43.53	3.56	49.95	0.13	44.83	8.23	0.12	150.35
1933	45.07	2.98	54.65	0.13	41.95	9.22	0.18	154.18
1934	40.50	2.72	51.86	0.27	31.57	8.39	0.19	135.50
1935	43.23	2.79	36.41	1.06	34.79	9.37	0.20	127.75
1936	43.17	2.66	27.13	2.24	35.79	10.93	0.21	122.13
1937	43.46	2.70	24.67	2.86	30.38	14.74	0.24	119.05
1938	44.54	2.69	27.39	3.17	31.26	15.04	0.25	124.34
1939	43.88	3.63	24.96	3.49	31.85	15.20	0.28	123.29
1940	45.68	3.58	22.68	3.76	32.14	16.24	0.30	124.38
1941	43.62	3.24	19.72	3.93	33.23	18.17	0.34	122.25
1942	44.93	3.75	16.29	4.12	34.29	18.27	0.34	121.99
1943	46.34	3.66	11.25	4.36	35.07	17.84	0.35	118.87
1944	49.46	4.79	9.09	4.47	34.95	19.85	0.36	122.97

Appendices

APPENDIX F, TABLE 2, Continued

YEAR	(1) DEATH CLAIMS	(2) MATURED ENDOWMENTS	(3) SURRENDERS	(4) ANNUITIES	(5) DIVIDENDS	(6) FROM [a] FUNDS LEFT WITH COMPANY	(7) DISABILITY WAIVER OF PREMIUM	(8) TOTAL
			(In millions of dollars)					
1945	51.98	7.99	9.50	4.54	36.47	21.43	0.39	132.30
1946	54.85	5.82	11.22	4.67	38.14	24.58	0.41	139.69
1947	57.60	6.99	12.21	4.76	41.13	27.69	0.46	150.84
1948	60.59	7.66	14.62	4.91	43.15	31.08	0.49	162.48
1949	60.38	10.24	18.21	4.98	37.55	34.06	0.57	166.00
1950	65.16	11.39	22.08	4.94	37.96	37.28	0.62	179.43
1951	66.29	13.28	23.84	4.85	39.75	42.24	0.69	190.94
1952	68.11	15.56	24.67	4.80	41.32	43.81	0.76	199.04
1953	71.20	18.37	33.89	4.77	44.60	48.06	0.78	221.67
1954	71.50	22.91	35.29	4.69	48.03	49.41	0.87	232.77
1955 1956	75.84	28.33	36.17	4.61	56.34	55.35	0.88	257.51

NOTES:
  [a] Consists of dividends accruing at interest and policy proceeds belonging to policyholders and beneficiaries.
  [b] For years ending May 31.
  [c] For nineteen months ending December 31, 1865.
  [d] For this and all subsequent years ending December 31.
  [e] Amounts of less than $10,000.
  Amounts in individual columns do not necessarily add to equal Total column due to rounding.

SOURCE: *Annual Statement*, Northwestern Mutual Life Insurance Company, 1859-1956. Records of the Comptroller's Department.

APPENDIX F, TABLE 3

Northwestern Mutual: Acquisition, Marketing, and Certain Externally Incurred Expenses, 1859–1956

YEAR	(1) AGENTS'[a] COMPENSATION	(2) MEDICAL EXAMINATION	(3) ADVERTISING	(4) LEGAL & LEGISLATIVE	(5) HOTEL & TRAVEL	(6) TAXES	(7) OTHER[b]	(8) TOTAL
			(In thousands of dollars)					
1859[c]	$1							$1
1860[c]	2		$1[d]					3
1861[c]	3	$1	1[d]					4
1862[c]	6		1[d]					8
1863[c]		No distribution of these expenses given in Company records for 1863-1864						N.A.
1864[c]								N.A.
1865[c]	111	12	15[f]			$5		143
1866[g]	124	10	12[f]			6		151
1867	196	19	22[f]			13		249
1868	368	31	24			19		442
1869	379	26	17			33		455
1870	359	17	14			42		432
1871	320	19	18			37		395
1872	300	19	11			38		367
1873	269	18	8	$8		41		344
1874	352	18	8	17		39		433
1875	273	18	2	18		28		339
1876	264	19	3	16		32		334
1877	216	16	13	19		41		305
1878	213	14	6	19		28		279
1879	203	14	6	17		30		269
1880	245	16	11	18		35		325
1881	337	22	6	19		32		416
1882	392	26	6	16		39		479
1883	398	26	7	13		59		502
1884	420	26	8	11		60		525
1885	490	35	8	17		65		614
1886	633	46	7	16		79		782
1887	754	54	7	19		82		916
1888	950	73	7	17		91		1,137
1889	1,122	87	7	22		100		1,337
1890	1,396	104	6	28		115		1,649
1891	1,540	117	6	25		133		1,821
1892	1,709	127	7	31		152		2,026
1893	1,472	92	6	41		163		1,775
1894	1,411	104	6	58		164		1,743
1895	1,545	120	15	48	$2	194		1,923
1896	1,620	119	6	40	—	231		2,016
1897	1,689	122	6	74	6	269		2,167
1898	2,028	142	3	59	7	329		2,568
1899	2,476	160	4	71	9	563		3,283
1900	2,548	148	6	33	8	676		3,419
1901	2,689	158	5	19	9	606		3,485
1902	2,871	171	6	21	11	634		3,714

APPENDIX F, TABLE 3, Continued

Year	(1) Agents'[a] Compensation	(2) Medical Examination	(3) Advertising	(4) Legal & Legislative	(5) Hotal & Travel	(6) Taxes	(7) Other[b]	(8) Total
			(In thousands of dollars)					
1903	2,928	184	6	20	11	671		3,820
1904	3,094	187	7	24	13	701		4,026
1905	3,393	203	8	23	12	720		4,359
1906	3,535	199	8	29	17	781		4,569
1907	3,708	208	7	28	5	803		4,759
1908	3,538	196	8	7	3	861		4,613
1909	3,711	209	8	13	6	872		4,819
1910	3,998	220	9	8	5	974		5,214
1911	4,268	231	8	13	6	994		5,520
1912	4,736	295	7	18	7	1,206	$4	6,273
1913	4,805	267	7	11	6	1,130	1	6,227
1914	4,772	269	9	10	15	1,165	—	6,240
1915	4,977	260	10	21	8	1,236	—	6,512
1916	5,456	293	10	28	7	1,181	—	6,975
1917	5,769	310	10	14	7	1,346	—	7,456
1918	5,668	213	10	25	11	1,472	—	7,399
1919	7,936	414	7	22	16	1,767	—	10,162
1920	9,480	485	8	15	17	1,958	—	11,963
1921	8,576	375	9	9	22	2,084	—	11,075
1922	8,685	359	15	17	21	2,262	5	11,364
1923	9,659	399	10	19	27	2,638	6	12,758
1924	10,275	405	17	31	23	3,347	12	14,110
1925	11,044	419	14	53	32	3,184	8	14,754
1926	11,408	406	21	39	43	3,386	11	15,314
1927	11,716	402	21	43	35	3,398	18	15,633
1928	12,191	417	22	9	41	3,325	15	16,020
1929	12,751	434	21	15	53	3,550	9	16,833
1930	12,323	426	53	25	59	3,353	12	16,251
1931	11,512	375	61	16	47	3,632	13	15,656
1032	10,298	357	40	18	46	3,573	33	14,365
1933	8,880	307	49	34	50	3,877	22	13,219
1934	8,941	388	207	16	67	3,716	25	13,360
1935	9,991	416	246	22	79	3,934	22	14,710
1936	10,043	437	245	34	91	3,271	42	14,163
1937	10,032	436	237	29	92	3,262	19	14,107
1938	9,600	379	245	11	97	3,425	31	13,788
1939	8,978	387	249	50	95	3,441	35	13,235
1940	8,805	366	242	30	96	4,423	18	13,980
1941	9,685	384	216	27	88	3,681	21	14,102
1942	9,845[h]	361	186	24	71	3,694	29	14,210
1943	10,748	317	298	20	65	5,121	30	16,599
1944	11,861	413	305	8	65	4,632	24	17,308
1945	13,287	410	305	21	68	4,456	27	18,574
1946	15,516	575	372	15	176	4,086	67	20,807
1947	17,423	590	385	68	77	4,324	63	22,930
1948	17,201	573	400	12	77	3,414	85	21,761
1949	17,232	551	450	13	94	3,583	108	22,030

APPENDIX F, TABLE 3, Continued

Year	(1) Agents'[a] Compensation	(2) Medical Examination	(3) Advertising	(4) Legal & Legislative	(5) Hotal & Travel	(6) Taxes	(7) Other[b]	(8) Total
			(In thousands of dollars)					
1950	18,079	582	444	25	101	5,487	82	24,800
1951	19,065	600	399	26	108	6,764	63	27,025
1952	20,749	682	406	50	141	9,266	68	31,361
1953	22,026	792	390	28	248	10,278	67	33,829
1954	22,976	812	479	41	304	10,792	88	35,491
1955	24,061	802	471	39	292	11,994	77	37,737
1956								

Notes:

[a] Includes salaries and expenses during years until 1890 as well as commissions and collection fees.

[b] Includes expenses for settlement of contested claims, fees and contributions to trade associations, and expenses of meetings and conventions.

[c] For year ending May 31.

[d] Includes postage of Home Office correspondence.

[e] For nineteen months ending December 31, 1865.

[f] Includes printing costs.

[g] For this and all succeeding years, the year ending December 31.

[h] Beginning this year compensation includes Company contributions to retirement fund.

[i] Beginning this year compensation includes Company social security tax contribution.

APPENDIX F, TABLE 4

Northwestern Mutual: Home Office and Other Expenses, 1859–1956

	(1)	(2)	(3)	(4)	(5)	(6)	(7)
		HOME OFFICE	SUPPLIES,		ASSET LOSSES [b]		
	SALARIES &	RENT AND	EQUIPMENT &	COSTS OF	AND BOOK VALUE	ALL	
YEAR	WAGES [a]	MAINTENANCE	COMMUNICATION	INVESTMENT	REDUCTIONS	OTHER	TOTAL
			(In thousands of dollars)				
1859 [c]						$3 [d]	$3
1860 [c]	$2	$1					3
1861 [c]	3					4 [d]	7
1862 [c]	4					4 [d]	8
1863 [c]						25 [e]	25
1864 [c]						50 [e]	50
1865 [f]	18		$4			3 [g]	25
1866 [h]	18		4			2	24
1867	29		7			7	43
1868	47 [i]		27			8	82
1869	62		32			8	102
1870	68		24			20	112
1871	72		28			20	120
1872	77		32		$27	24	160
1873	78		26		11	22 [j]	138
1874	90	3	36	$2	16	3	151
1875	96	3	48	8	7	5	166
1876	105	4	30	7	78	3	226
1877	113	3	31	12	15	16 [k]	189
1878	109	5	26	16	18	3	176
1879	110	2	29	25	23	6	196
1880	113	6	28	25	2	5	178
1881	117	4	32	33	17	1	204
1882	124	4	33	33	8	4	206
1883	130	4	39	35	12	9	230
1884	126	3	41	43	4	11	227
1885	150	3	44	3	*m*	6	207
1886	157	7	72	43	94	8	380
1887	158	15	64	42	219	25	523
1888	168	17	67	54	29	8	342
1889	177	17	80	62		5	340
1890	191	16	102	73		3	383
1891	212	13	115	69		5	413
1892	236	16	125	69	5	3	453
1893	260	20	116	74	5	8	483
1894	262	17	131	94	17	3	523
1895	334	17	121	119		22 [n]	613
1896	358	24	125	153	5	5	669
1897	382	22	133	221	5	7	770
1898	433	56	144	235	143	7	1,017
1899	445	56	261	303	15	13	1,092
1900	449	59	131	331	50	8	1,027
1901	475	56	132	299	33	19	1,014
1902	482	72	132	311		5	1,003

APPENDIX F, TABLE 4, Continued

Year	(1) Salaries & Wages[a]	(2) Home Office Rent and Maintenance	(3) Supplies, Equipment & Communication	(4) Costs of Investment	(5) Asset Losses[b] and Book Value Reductions	(6) All Other	(7) Total
			(In thousands of dollars)				
1903	514	74	152	327	969	9	2,044
1904	545	66	160	305		12	1,089
1905	577	67	200	283	19	8	1,154
1906	590	76	184	286	21	3	1,159
1907	636	84	211	251	232	11	1,425
1908	690	84	237	229	27	10	1,277
1909	765	85	201	245	17	9	1,322
1910	836	88	226	245	92	17	1,504
1911	842	86	222	202	15	10	1,377
1912	867	105	226	200	2	30	1,430
1913	888	104	232	161	2	12	1,399
1914	908	190	373	144	28	17	1,660
1915	946	353	232	154	1,074	34	2,793
1916	977	331	241	161	998	28	2,736
1917	1,041	355	257	172	722	40	2,587
1918	1,071	375	281	160	555	47	2,489
1919	1,203	399	269	175	130	208[p]	2,384
1920	1,415	432	373	194	183	178	2,775
1921	1,532	532	349	222	594	280	3,509
1922	1,501	541	395	238		110	2,785
1923	1,601	486	395	247		100	2,829
1924	1,760	499	423	286		100	3,068
1925	1,881	492	457	318		59	3,207
1926	2,025	509	454	347	18	263	3,616
1927	2,171	504	438	375	197	376	4,061
1928	2,308	511	466	390	1,070	235	4,980
1929	2,415	525	515	543	93	214	4,305
1930	2,468	546	521	654	391	129	4,709
1931	2,557	537	498	834	952	225	5,603
1932	2,546	571	555	1,044	1,010	481	6,207
1933	2,464	723	390	1,621	1,402	522	7,122
1934	2,726	916	646	1,750	10,344	409	16,791
1935	2,868	917	593	2,543	1,808	516	9,245
1936	2,846	943	577	2,517	1,916	1,293	10,092
1937	3,135	983	583	2,673	3,366	976	11,716
1938	3,186	1,001	561	2,659	4,153	467	12,027
1939	3,200	1,061	536	2,785	5,680	274	13,636
1940	3,154	1,027	499	2,503	5,787	800	13,774
1941	3,221	1,062	589	2,616	4,185	410	12,083
1942	3,475	1,099	503	2,394	3,773	604	11,848
1943	3,382	1,060	409	1,881	7,877	478	15,087
1944	3,535	1,050	462	1,392	9,595	594	16,628
1945	3,524	1,058	480	939	1,842	439	8,282
1946	4,071	1,119	564	898	1,697	484	8,833
1947	4,849	1,273	799	1,450	1,902	675	10,948

APPENDIX F, TABLE 4, Continued

Year	(1) Salaries & Wages[a]	(2) Home Office Rent and Maintenance	(3) Supplies, Equipment & Communication	(4) Costs of Investment	(5) Asset Losses[b] and Book Value Reductions	(6) All Other	(7) Total
			(In thousands of dollars)				
1948	5,098	1,015	828	1,864	2,521	283	11,609
1949	5,338	996	753	1,806	2,637	291	11,821
1950	5,797	1,176	903	2,271	2,877	363	13,386
1951	6,482	1,245	969	2,218	3,255	462	14,631
1952	7,039	1,223	840	2,292	5,187	525	17,106
1953	7,186	1,395	1,371	2,449	4,185	411	16,997
1954	7,731	1,454	1,469	2,689	3,481	350	17,174
1955 1956	8,056	1,522	1,427	3,337	4,703	385	19,430

Notes:

[a] Includes per diem and other Trustee compensation, Company contributions to employees retirement fund, and contributions to Social Security, medical and surgical insurance.

[b] On real estate and securities. From 1859 through 1946 the sums represented are net differences between profits and losses on sales and in adjustments of book values and amortization of securities. Most of the sums shown represent book adjustments and amortization; the Company suffered sales losses during the years 1942-1944 of over $13 million.

[c] For years ending May 31.

[d] Individual items not indicated in *Annual Statements* for these years.

[e] Represents all Company expenses except payments made to policyholders for these years.

[f] For nineteen months ending December 31, 1865.

[g] For rent, travel, fuel and light.

[h] For year ending December 31 (all subsequent years treated the same).

[i] Includes payment to consulting surgeon and abstract company.

[j] Includes $4,200 payment toward new headquarters building.

[k] Includes $12,100 for meeting costs of state insurance examination.

[m] Amount of less than $500.

[n] Includes $13,900 for meeting costs of state insurance examination.

[p] Includes War Service Premium Refund of $49,000.

General note: Data for income and expenditure charts used in body of this work do not include book and amortization adjustments in values of real estate and securities. Changes in value are included in values given for assets owned by the Company (See Appendix D, Table 5).

Source: *Annual Statement* (Convention Form and predecessor forms), Northwestern Mutual Life Insurance Company, 1859-1956, incl. Also Comptroller's Department Records.

APPENDIX F, TABLE 5

Northwestern Mutual: Distribution of Admitted Assets, 1859–1956

	(1)	(2) STOCKS AND	(3) LOANS ON	(4)	(5)	(6)	(7)
YEAR	MORTGAGES	BONDS	POLICIES	REAL ESTATE	CASH	OTHER	TOTAL
			(In thousands of dollars)				
1859[a]			$5		$4	$1	$9
1860[a]			17		8	1	26
1861[a]	$3		35		16	3	57
1862[a]	21	$4	55		22	5	107
1863[a]	50	9	72		28	3	162
1864[a]	96	25	113	$7	27	8	276
1865[b]	235	85	395	15	62	114	906
1866[c]	505	135	787	45	107	170	1,749
1867	942	130	1,334	45	194	481	3,126
1868	1,584	125	1,989	129	71	857	4,755
1869	2,523	125	2,784	250	45	1,031	6,758
			(In millions of dollars)				
1870	3.80	0.12	3.77	0.32	0.03	0.95	8.99
1871	5.06	0.14	4.06	0.32	0.17	0.91	10.66
1872	6.49	0.17	4.31	0.32	0.15	1.00	12.44
1873	7.99	0.18	4.40	0.32	0.19	1.01	14.09
1874	9.50	0.35	4.31	0.35	0.12	0.88	15.51
1875	10.60	0.38	4.16	0.50	0.55	0.93	17.12
1876	11.61	0.38	3.85	0.58	0.77	0.87	18.06
1877	12.19	0.75	3.28	0.79	0.28	0.88	18.17
1878	11.47	1.20	2.61	1.26	0.59	0.82	17.95
1879	10.40	1.91	2.16	1.67	1.11	0.85	18.00
1880	10.00	2.47	1.88	1.82	1.58	0.60	18.35
1881	11.04	2.49	1.62	1.76	1.38	0.57	18.86
1882	14.33	1.25	1.49	1.53	0.63	0.57	19.80
1883	15.71	1.20	1.40	1.27	0.92	0.62	21.12
1884	17.38	0.86	1.27	1.06	1.20	0.76	22.53
1885	19.24	0.65	1.16	1.32	1.09	0.81	24.27
1886	21.12	0.61	1.06	1.57	1.41	0.90	26.67
1887	24.21	0.61	0.86	1.32	0.85	1.01	28.86
1888	27.35	1.12	0.79	1.24	1.07	1.10	32.67
1889	30.03	2.08	0.70	1.19	1.79	1.33	37.12
1890	35.46	2.96	0.60	1.00	0.91	1.42	42.35
1891	40.72	2.97	0.55	1.03	1.82	1.74	48.83
1892	45.08	4.63	0.49	1.00	3.17	1.87	56.24
1893	51.41	5.29	0.48	1.05	3.16	2.68	64.07
1894	55.85	7.17	0.55	1.18	5.47	3.13	73.35
1895	59.04	11.77	2.37	1.41	4.61	3.70	82.90
1896	66.07	13.77	4.20	1.82	1.92	4.05	92.63
1897	66.79	19.00	5.52	2.99	4.13	4.95	103.38
1898	72.01	22.53	6.32	3.82	5.31	5.46	115.45
1899	70.56	35.47	6.87	4.31	4.09	5.35	126.65
1900	72.48	45.70	7.46	4.61	3.89	5.37	139.51
1901	73.61	57.08	8.91	4.58	3.63	4.34	151.95
1902	76.54	65.83	11.04	4.26	2.93	4.44	165.04

APPENDIX F, TABLE 5, Continued

	(1)	(2) STOCKS AND BONDS	(3) LOANS ON POLICIES	(4)	(5)	(6)	(7)
YEAR	MORTGAGES			REAL ESTATE	CASH	OTHER	TOTAL
			(In millions of dollars)				
1903	85.72	67.45	14.06	3.61	2.47	4.89	178.20
1904	93.39	70.95	16.87	3.38	3.59	6.60	194.78
1905	99.07	78.87	18.98	3.24	1.45	6.81	208.42
1906	110.92	77.30	22.11	2.73	2.79	5.25	221.10
1907	121.74	73.44	30.58	2.29	1.68	3.09	232.82
1908	129.2	74.8	34.0	2.1	3.2	4.7	248.0
1909	138.8	78.2	36.3	1.9	2.2	5.0	262.4
1910	150.7	74.2	40.6	2.2	1.8	4.3	273.8
1911	153.6	80.7	42.7	2.1	3.2	3.3	285.6
1912	159.3	85.0	44.6	2.9	3.5	2.5	297.8
1913	169.4	84.4	49.4	3.8	3.5	0.1	310.6
1914	178.7	85.7	55.1	4.6	3.3	0.8	328.2
1915	181.9	93.9	56.8	5.0	4.4	1.6	343.6
1916	194.1	101.4	57.0	4.1	3.2	3.3	363.1
1917	207.1	110.4	49.0	4.1	1.7	11.2	393.5
1918	210.5	125.8	59.8	4.5	2.1	12.1	414.8
1919	199.5	163.2	59.1	4.1	2.0	13.0	440.9
1920	212.5	172.1	66.2	3.9	3.3	15.6	472.7
1921	224.5	182.1	78.6	2.9	3.8	15.2	507.1
1922	232.7	204.6	84.5	2.8	3.9	17.8	546.3
1923	248.5	223.8	90.5	2.2	4.1	19.9	589.0
1924	273.0	235.5	96.9	2.4	3.9	20.3	632.0
1925	290.1	257.7	103.6	2.6	4.0	20.2	678.2
1926	318.6	270.4	111.7	3.1	3.2	21.8	728.8
1927	343.7	285.7	120.6	3.5	4.0	24.1	781.6
1928	371.2	301.5	130.6	4.2	4.6	27.1	839.2
1929	396.4	297.9	155.6	5.4	4.2	29.0	888.5
1930	411.4	305.5	179.7	7.5	4.7	30.9	937.7
1931	408.7	306.6	215.0	12.7	4.7	29.6	977.3
1932	394.5	297.4	247.9	21.1	5.3	29.8	996.0
1933	376.9	287.1	249.5	33.2	10.3	41.3	998.3
1934	321.9	369.6	233.9	40.7	10.9	41.4	1,018.4
1935	296.5	471.1	216.8	43.4	10.0	34.2	1,072.0
1936	303.1	535.9	199.5	46.9	10.9	33.6	1,129.9
1937	306.1	586.6	192.5	48.7	10.9	33.6	1,178.4
1938	308.6	644.0	185.5	48.4	12.4	34.2	1,233.1
1939	303.6	715.9	170.3	54.2	14.0	34.4	1,292.4
1940	305.2	796.3	154.4	49.9	14.3	38.9	1,359.0
1941	291.9	904.9	139.5	50.0	17.2	36.4	1,439.9
1942	269.1	1,035.0	124.6	45.5	17.2	34.3	1,525.7
1943	242.4	1,194.8	108.0	29.2	29.7	33.3	1,637.4
1944	213.7	1,359.5	94.8	22.3	32.7	34.7	1,757.7
1945	172.5	1,554.3	85.4	14.5	26.2	34.8	1,887.7
1946	158.1	1,711.7	79.8	13.0	20.7	35.8	2,019.1
1947	191.7	1,781.2	79.8	34.4	29.2	39.8	2,156.1
1948	263.6	1,833.9	83.5	37.0	31.1	42.1	2,291.2
1949	331.1	1,913.7	87.9	43.7	23.0	43.3	2,442.7

APPENDIX F, TABLE 5, Continued

Year	(1) Mortgages	(2) Stocks and Bonds	(3) Loans on Policies	(4) Real Estate	(5) Cash	(6) Other	(7) Total
			(In millions of dollars)				
1950	454.1	1,923.7	93.4	45.4	30.5	46.7	2,593.8
1951	560.4	1,963.2	99.2	46.8	28.9	49.4	2,747.9
1952	623.5	2,051.4	103.5	51.2	27.5	52.9	2,910.0
1953	712.6	2,106.3	110.4	53.2	30.1	57.2	3,069.7
1954	831.8	2,146.2	116.5	57.4	30.8	60.1	3,242.8
1955	987.9	2,148.3	122.1	64.1	28.0	64.4	3,414.8
1956	1,119.6	2,154.6	133.7	74.1	27.9	66.8	3,576.8

Individual amounts do not always add to equal totals because of rounding.

NOTES:
 [a] For year ending May 31.
 [b] For nineteen months ending December 31, 1865.
 [c] For this and all subsequent years, year ending December 31.

SOURCE: *Annual Statement*, Northwestern Mutual Life Insurance Company, 1859-1956. Records of Comptroller's Department.

APPENDIX G, TABLE 1

Northwestern Mutual: Net Interest Rate Earned and Dividend Rate Paid, 1860–1956
(Company Data)

Year	Rate Earned	Dividend Rate Next Year	Year	Rate Earned	Dividend Rate Next Year
1860	3.64		1905	4.48	4.5
1861	4.06		1906	4.50	4.5
1862	4.43		1907	4.57	4.5
1863	4.80		1908	4.67	4.5
1864	4.54		1909	4.65	4.5
1865	4.83		1910	4.67	4.5
1866	6.53		1911	4.82	4.6
1867	5.87		1912	4.74	4.6
1868	6.81		1913	4.78	4.6
1869	6.60		1914	4.85	4.6
1870	6.84		1915	4.82	4.6
1871	7.53	7.0	1916	4.90	4.6
1872	7.57	7.927	1917	4.94	4.6
1873	8.11	7.927	1918	4.90	4.6
1874	7.99	7.927	1919	4.88	4.6
1875	8.54	7.927	1920	4.92	4.6
1876	7.89	7.927	1921	5.14	4.6
1877	7.24	7.927	1922	5.34	4.6
1878	7.24	7.0	1923	5.32	4.8
1879	6.82	7.0	1924	5.21	4.8
1880	5.51	6.833	1925	5.12	5.0
1881	5.48	6.0	1926	5.08	5.0
1882	5.50	5.625	1927	5.09	5.0
1883	5.62	5.6	1928	5.09	5.0
1884	5.68	5.6	1929	5.02	5.0
1885	5.58	5.6	1930	4.99	5.0
1886	5.51	5.6	1931	4.93	5.0
1887	5.75	5.6	1932	4.83	4.8
1888	5.52	5.6	1933	4.51	4.6
1889	5.65	5.6	1934	4.39	4.5
1890	5.39	5.6	1935	3.97	4.5
1891	5.52	5.6	1936	3.70	4.175
1892	5.30	5.6	1937	3.87	4.0
1893	5.16	5.5	1938	2.77	4.0
1894	5.14	5.4	1939	3.73	4.0
1895	5.38	5.3	1940	3.70	3.75
1896	5.07	5.2	1941	3.70	3.75
1897	4.92	5.1	1942	3.70	3.75
1898	4.78	5.0	1943	3.60	3.65
1899	4.50	5.0	1944	3.44	3.65
1900	4.33	4.8	1945	3.33	3.4
1901	4.62	4.8	1946	3.10	3.4
1902	4.31	4.5	1947	3.01	3.4
1903	4.30	4.5	1948	3.03	3.1
1904	4.50	4.5	1949	3.13	3.1

APPENDIX G, TABLE 1, Continued

Year	Rate Earned	Dividend Rate Next Year	Year	Rate Earned	Dividend Rate Next Year
1950	3.15	3.1	1954	3.52	3.25
1951	3.21	3.1	1955	3.62	3.3
1952	3.27	3.2	1956	3.77	3.35
1953	3.39	3.2			

SOURCE: Actuarial Department Records, Northwestern Mutual Life Insurance Company.

APPENDIX G, TABLE 2

Investment Interest Rate Earned by Northwestern, 1860–1918 (From Non-Company Sources)

Year	Rate	Year	Rate	Year	Rate
1860	N.A.	1880	5.7	1900	5.0
1861	N.A.	1881	5.9	1901	4.5
1862	5.1	1882	5.8	1902	4.0
1863	7.0	1883	6.1	1903	4.0
1864	8.1	1884	5.5	1904	5.7
1865	8.6	1885	5.9	1905	4.7
1866	6.7	1886	5.6	1906	4.7
1867	4.6	1887	5.4	1907	4.8
1868	5.5	1888	5.9	1908	4.9
1869	6.4	1889	6.3	1909	4.9
1870	8.1	1890	5.8	1910	4.9
1871	7.8	1891	5.1	1911	5.0
1872	7.9	1892	5.7	1912	4.9
1873	8.3	1893	5.7	1913	4.9
1874	8.4	1894	5.4	1914	5.0
1875	8.7	1895	5.7	1915	4.9
1876	7.8	1896	5.3	1916	5.0
1877	7.6	1897	5.3	1917	5.1
1878	6.8	1898	5.6	1918	5.0
1879	7.1	1899	4.6		

SOURCES: 1860-1904: Lester W. Zartman, *The Investments of Life Insurance Companies* (New York: Henry Holt and Co., 1906), 74-75. 1905-1907: *Insurance Year Book*, 1910 (Spectator Co.) 295. 1908-1918: *Insurance Year Book*, 1919 (Spectator Co.), 292.

Index

COMPANIES AND MEN

Business Enterprise in America

An Arno Press Collection

Allen, Hugh. **The House of Goodyear:** A Story of Rubber and of Modern Business. 1943

Bennett, Howard F. **Precision Power:** The First Half Century of Bodine Electric Company. 1959

Broehl, Wayne G., Jr. **Precision Valley:** The Machine Tool Companies of Springfield, Vermont. 1959

Broehl, Wayne G., Jr. **Trucks, Trouble and Triumph:** The Norwalk Truck Line Company. 1954

Bruchey, Eleanor S. **The Business Elite in Baltimore, 1880-1914.** 1976

Burgess, George H. and Miles C. Kennedy. **Centennial History of the Pennsylvania Railroad Company, 1846-1946.** 1949

Cleland, David Ira. **The Origin and Development of a Philosophy of Long-Range Planning in American Business.** 1976

Darr, Richard K. **A History of the Nashua and Lowell Rail-Road Corporation, 1835-1880.** 1976

Engelbourg, Saul. **International Business Machines:** A Business History. 1976

Gibb, George Sweet. **The Whitesmiths of Taunton:** A History of Reed & Barton, 1824-1943. 1943

Gibb, George Sweet and Evelyn H. Knowlton. **History of Standard Oil Company (New Jersey): The Resurgent Years, 1911-1927.** 1956

Giddens, Paul H. **Standard Oil Company (Indiana): Oil Pioneer of the Middle West.** 1955

Gloster, Jesse Edward. **North Carolina Mutual Life Insurance Company.** 1976

Gras, N[orman] S. B. **The Massachusetts First National Bank of Boston, 1784-1934.** 1937

Hidy, Ralph W. and Muriel E. Hidy. **History of Standard Oil Company (New Jersey): Pioneering in Big Business, 1882-1911.** 1955

Holbert, Hayward Janes. **A History of Professional Management in American Industry.** 1976

Hungerford, Edward. **Men and Iron:** The History of New York Central. 1938

James, Marquis. **Biography of a Business, 1792-1942:** Insurance Company of North America. 1942

James, Marquis. **The Metropolitan Life:** A Study in Business Growth. 1947

Kaufman, Charles N. **The History of the Keller Manufacturing Company.** 1976

Kuniansky, Harry Richard. **A Business History of Atlantic Steel Company, 1901-1968.** 1976

Larson, Henrietta M. and Kenneth Wiggins Porter. **History of Humble Oil & Refining Company:** A Study in Industrial Growth. 1959

Loth, David. **Swope of G.E.:** The Story of Gerard Swope and General Electric in American Business. 1958

Marcosson, Isaac F. **Anaconda.** 1957

Morison, Samuel Eliot. **The Ropemakers of Plymouth:** A History of the Plymouth Cordage Company, 1824-1949. 1950

Myers, Kenneth Holston. **Marketing Policy Determination by a Major Firm in a Capital Goods Industry:** A Case Study of Bucyrus-Erie Company, 1880-1954. 1976

Nevins, Allan. **History of the Bank of New York and Trust Company, 1784-1934.** 1934

Nevins, Allan and Frank Ernest Hill. **FORD:** Volume I, The Times, the Man, the Company; Volume II, Expansion and Challenge, 1915-1933; Volume III, Decline and Rebirth, 1933-1962. Three vols. 1954/1957/1963

Payne, Peter Lester and Lance Edwin Davis. **The Savings Bank of Baltimore, 1818-1866:** A Historical and Analytical Study. 1956

Plavchan, Ronald J. **A History of Anheuser-Busch, 1852-1933.** 1976

Puth, Robert C[hristian]. **Supreme Life:** The History of a Negro Life Insurance Company. 1976

Sanderlin, Walter S. **The Great National Project:** A History of the Chesapeake and Ohio Canal. 1946

Schwarzman, Richard C. **The Pinal Dome Oil Company:** An Adventure in Business, 1901-1917. 1976

Thomas, Norman F. **Minneapolis-Moline:** A History of Its Formation and Operations. 1976

Twyman, Robert W. **History of Marshall Field & Co., 1852-1906.** 1954

Wainwright, Nicholas B. **History of the Philadelphia National Bank:** A Century and a Half of Philadelphia Banking, 1803-1953. 1953

White, Gerald T. **Formative Years in the Far West:** A History of Standard Oil Company of California and Predecessors Through 1919. 1962

Williamson, Harold F. and Orange A. Smalley. **Northwestern Mutual Life:** A Century of Trusteeship. 1957